International Law and Organization

International Law and Organization

An Introduction

Thomas R. Van Dervort

SAGE Publications
International Educational and Professional Publisher
Thousand Oaks London New Delhi

For information:

SAGE Publications, Inc.
2455 Teller Road
Thousand Oaks, California 91320
E-mail: order@sagepub.com

SAGE Publications Ltd.
6 Bonhill Street
London EC2A 4PU
United Kingdom

SAGE Publications India Pvt. Ltd.
M-32 Market
Greater Kailash I
New Delhi 110 048 India

Printed in the United States of America

Library of Congress Cataloging-in-Publication Data

Van Dervort, Thomas R.
    International law and organization: An introduction / author,
  Thomas R. Van Dervort.
        p.   cm.
    Includes bibliographical references and index.
    ISBN 0-7619-0189-2 (pbk.). — ISBN 0-7619-0188-4 (cloth)
    1. International organization.   2. International law.   I. Title.
  JX3091.V36   1997
  341—dc21   97-4656

This book is printed on acid-free paper.

98 99 00 01 02 03 10 9 8 7 6 5 4 3 2 1

Acquiring Editor:	Peter Labella
Editorial Assistant:	Frances Borghi
Production Editor:	Sanford Robinson
Production Assistant:	Denise Santoyo
Book Designer/Typesetter:	Janelle LeMaster
Cover Designer:	Ravi Balasuriya
Print Buyer:	Anna Chin

This book is dedicated to my grandchildren,
Olivia, Benjamin, and *Joshua.*

Brief Outline

Contents

Preface

This book is designed for anyone who wishes to understand the basic concepts of international law. International law has been regarded by many as a dry and boring subject that is unrealistically normative and without much relevance to world politics; this book attempts to challenge these assumptions.

The end of the Cold War, the breakup of the Soviet Union, and the demonstration of areas of major-power cooperation in the United Nation's Security Council have sparked a new interest in the ancient subject of international law. Educators are emphasizing the importance of awaking an international consciousness and concern about the global community. The United Nation's General Assembly has declared the 1990s the "Decade of International Law." All these developments indicate the need for an introductory textbook that can promote an understanding of the basic principles and functions of international law.

Why This Book Is Needed

Traditional international law has been presented as *public international law* in most introductory texts. This orientation artificially confines the scope of inquiry to that narrow field of "law among nations," where states, not people, are the major focus. Students and readers of such publications become frustrated by this level of abstraction, which alienates them from any realistic link to the more familiar concepts of domestic law.

This book endeavors to introduce the subject of international law as a dynamic process involving the development of normative principles of human behavior that affect both individuals and governments in their daily lives. *Private international law* refers to those concepts of normative behavior of an international character affecting individuals, corporations, and governments as administered by the domestic courts in individual nation-states. It is this aspect of the field of international law that has displayed the greatest expansion in modern times, and it demonstrates the link with concepts of domestic law. Treaties and international agreements that have become a part of the law adjudicated in domestic courts are the real evidence of the existence of international law.

Part I of the text consists of a historical overview of the development of international law from the Roman concept of *jus gentium* to the post-World War II developments of modern international law. This background is essential for the proper understanding of modern concepts of international law and how it differs from domestic law. An overview of the most significant developments in contemporary international legal practice is provided in Chapter 3. This historical development discusses the roots of modern human rights and business law as well as the significant developments in regard to collective security.

In Part II, the text moves to discuss the basic principles of international law in more specific fields. Human rights law, business law, intellectual property and consumer protection, labor and environmental law, international crimes and extradition, and diplomatic and sovereign immunity are given separate chapters of development. The focus in these chapters is on the application of international legal principles in domestic courts. Illustrative case opinions will be used sparingly to provide concrete examples that emphasize court application and individual or group access to the courts. Private party access to the courts for settlement of disputes based on international legal principles is one of the most important areas of expansion of international law.

The principles of sovereign immunity and the modern restrictive nature (as opposed to absolute sovereign immunity) will be stressed,

explaining the division between those disputes that are subject to court adjudication and those in which an act of state is involved. This line divides private from public international law, and here, the text will make a transition to the discussion of disputes between sovereign nation-states. This more traditional area of public international law will become the major focus for the remainder of the text included in Part III.

Chapters devoted to the legal status of states and intergovernmental organizations, the law of treaties, adjudication, and enforcement will be included. Again, specific case opinions will be used to illustrate specific concepts. International tribunals, rather than domestic courts, will be the source of these opinions. Arbitration tribunals, regional courts, and the International Court of Justice will be drawn on for these authoritative judgments, which will provide more specific illustrations of application of legal principles in practice.

The text will include a concluding chapter and a set of appendixes containing some of the most important documents in international law for illustrative and reference purposes. Those who want a quick overview and do not want to get bogged down in the details of the substantive chapters on individual areas of legal development, should read Parts I and III first. Part II includes the more detailed areas of law and more extensive case material. These chapters may be selected depending on the reader's interests.

Modern Internet sources have been included along with traditional sources to encourage students to use this new technology to go beyond the text material. Individualized projects for term papers enable students to gain in-depth knowledge in areas of their greatest interest.

The text includes significant study aids in the form of marginal definitions of key terms, chapter summaries, and discussion questions at the end of each chapter. As mentioned earlier, the appendixes include basic documents that will be referred to in the text development. They provide extensive reference to the exact words and context of major treaties and legal documents.

The Audience for This Book

This introduction is designed to meet the needs of the general public, college-level students, and those who aspire to achieve professional careers in law and international relations.

The approach used in this book addresses the needs of the general public in that it does not assume prior knowledge of the technical terms used in traditional international law texts. These terms will be defined briefly in the margins of the text and explained as they appear in the discussion of the subject matter. Fundamental concepts will be stressed rather than discussion of the details of emerging concepts.

The major focus of this introduction to international law text addresses the general education needs of undergraduate students interested in international relations, history, economics, political science, philosophy, and communication studies. Only about half of the undergraduate schools in the United States offer such a course, and it is hoped that better teaching materials will encourage more schools to offer such an elective.

An international law course is an essential component of undergraduate international relations programs and should be required of students preparing for careers in this field. International Business Law is a course that introduces students to some of the same material included in this text. Indeed, one of the major purposes for including "private international law" is to accommodate this need in undergraduate programs.

A recent survey sponsored by the American Society of International Law (ASIL) indicates growing interest in international law among undergraduates but less than adequate resources in the form of teachers with the interest and professional background to teach the subject. Consolidating international business law and political science courses in international law is one way to deal with this problem. Using a more generalized approach, the undergraduate professor can meet the needs of students not only from the fields of business, economics, and history but also potential teachers, journalists, and those preparing for communication fields, philosophy, and law.

The ASIL survey, conducted in 1990, revealed a prospering climate in law schools for expansion of international law courses. Growing interest, particularly among law school deans, indicates the expanding practice of law in areas of international dispute settlement. Law professors complain, however, about the lack of undergraduate background of their students.

Most of the textbooks in the field of international law are huge tomes using the case study approach typical of law school texts. This text is designed to provide an undergraduate introduction to the field that will lay a foundation for related courses at more advanced levels.

Illustrating Legal Process

Most undergraduate students who are likely to take an introductory course in international law are unfamiliar with the basic concepts of legal process. Therefore, it is important to explain how a cause of legal action is identified and filed in a court of proper jurisdiction. This text will provide illustrations of basic principles of court jurisdiction and process involving actions in national courts as well as in international tribunals.

The importance of world trade and commercial transactions will be given considerable attention in order to serve the needs of students who are thinking about going into international business career fields. The settlement of disputes involving private contracts and transactions will be illustrated through procedures involving enforcement of foreign judgments and protection of property rights in foreign courts. International regulation of business practices will also be given attention as well as labor-management dispute settlement procedures. Environmental restrictions further regulate business practices and are an important part of the emerging international law affecting commerce and trade.

The processes of fact-finding and adjudication will be emphasized throughout this text by discussion of selected illustrative court opinions from both domestic courts and international tribunals. At the undergraduate level of education, a few in-depth examples are more effective than the confusion generated by the typical law school approach of extensive reproduction of case law opinions. The object of this text is to stimulate student interest in, and basic understanding of, the field of international law. A student who elects to pursue a legal career or go on to graduate school in business will find opportunity for more extensive study of the detailed fields of international law.

Acknowledgments

I am indebted to many individuals who contributed to the development of this textbook. I must first of all thank my students who have taught me over the years about the kind of educational materials that would best meet their needs and assist them in achieving their goals. I am especially indebted to Dr. John R. Vile, chair of the Department of Political Science at Middle Tennessee State University, who encouraged me to undertake this project. He graciously read and commented on all the chapters and provided helpful suggestions and corrections. Middle Tennessee State University also has provided additional assistance in the form of travel support to attend international conferences abroad, enabling me to extend my knowledge in the field of international law and organization.

Professor Jonathan Charney of Vanderbilt University Law School, Charlotte Ku, Executive Director of the American Society of International Law, and Professor John King Gamble at Pennsylvania State University have been very helpful in their encouragement of this effort. Their advice and council have been greatly appreciated. Professors Moses Tesi, George Vernardakis, and Anne Sloan of Middle Tennessee State University have read portions of this text and assisted me greatly with their advice and comments. My friend Harry Horne, retired Canadian diplomat with over twenty years of practical experience in foreign service all over the world, has read some of the chapters, and his comments and encouragement have been appreciated.

My editor, Peter Labella, and his assistant, Frances Borghi, at Sage Publications were extremely helpful in their support and guidance throughout this project. They were instrumental in finding an excellent group of reviewers, including Veronica Ward and James Larry Saulbee, who offered extensive comments on the original manuscript. These comments greatly enhanced the final version of the text, and I am deeply indebted to them for their helpful suggestions.

Finally, I must take responsibility for the remaining errors in this text. I wish to invite any reader to communicate with me about errors or suggestions for future revisions of this introduction to international law and organization. My e-mail address is 103366.3665@compuserve.com.

Thomas R. Van Dervort
Middle Tennessee State University

List of Acronyms

AAA	American Arbitration Association
ADA	Americans With Disabilities Act
ADR	alternative dispute resolution
ASEAN	Association of Southeast Asian Nations
ASIL	American Society of International Law
ATA	Anti-Terrorism Act
BIRPI	United International Bureaus for the Protection of Intellectual Property
BLA	Base Labor Agreement
CAV	Compania Azucarera Vertientes
CENTO	Central Treaty Organization
CFCs	chlorofluorocarbons
CFE	Conventional Forces in Europe Treaty
CFI	Court of First Instance
CIS	Community of Independent States
CISG	Convention on the International Sale of Goods
CITES	Convention on Trade in Endangered Species
CPR Covenant	Covenant on Civil and Political Rights
CSCE	Conference on Security and Cooperation in Europe (now OSCE)
CZ	contiguous zone
DBCP	dibromochlorpropane
DEA	Drug Enforcement Administration
DNI	National Office of Investigation
DSB	Dispute Settlement Board
EC	European Community
ECHR	European Court of Human Rights

ECJ	European Court of Justice	ICJ	International Court of Justice
ECSC	European Coal and Steel Community	IEEPA	International Emergency Economic Powers Act
EEA	European Economic Area	IGO	intergovernmental organization
EEC	European Economic Community	IJC	International Joint Commission
EEOC	Equal Employment Opportunity Commission	ILC	International Law Commission
EEZ	exclusive economic zone	ILO	International Labor Organization
EPA	Environmental Protection Agency	IMF	International Montary Fund
EU	European Union	IMO	International Marine Organization
EURATOM	European Atomic Energy Community	INA	Immigration and Nationality Act
FNC	Treaty of Friendship, Navigation and Commerce	INGO	International nongovernmental organization
FSIA	Foreign Sovereign Immunities Act	INTERPOL	International Criminal Police Organization
FTCA	Federal Tort Claims Act	ISO	International Standards Organization
GATT	General Agreement on Tariffs and Trade	ITC	International Trade Commission
GESAMP	Group of Experts on the Scientific Aspects of Marine Pollution	ILST	International Law of the Sea Tribunal
GNP	gross national product	ITO	International Trade Organization
IACHR	Inter-American Court of Human Rights	ITU	International Telecommunications Union
IAEA	International Atomic Energy Agency	MARPOL	International Convention for the Prevention of Pollution From Ships
IATA	International Air Transport Association	MFN	most-favored nation
ICAO	International Civil Aviation Organization		
ICC	International Chamber of Commerce		
ICCPR	International Covenant on Civil and Political Rights		

MINURSO	U.N. Mission for the Referendum in Western Sahara
MNE	multinational enterprise
NAFTA	North American Free Trade Agreement
NATO	North Atlantic Treaty Organization
NGO	nongovernmental organizations
NPT	Nuclear Proliferation Treaty
NUSS	Nuclear Safety Standards Program
OAS	Organization of American States
OAU	Organization of African Unity
OECD	Organization for Economic Cooperation and Development
OPIC	Overseas Private Investment Cooperation
PCT	Patent Cooperation Treaty
PCIJ	Permanent Court of International Justice
PLO	Palestine Liberation Organization
SEATO	Southeast Asia Treaty Organization
SWAPO	South-West African People's Organization
TRIPS	trade-related intellectual property rights
UCC	Universal Copyright Convention

UNEF II	U. N. Emergency Force II
UNEP	U.N. Environment Program
UNESCO	U.N. Educational, Scientific and Cultural Organization
UNCHE	U.N. Conference on the Human Environment
UNCIO	U.N. Conference on International Organization
UCIL	Union Carbide India Limited
UNCLOS I, II, III	United Nations Conference on the Law of the Sea
UNCTAD	U.N. Conference on Trade and Development
UNHCR	United Nations High Comissioner for Refugees
UNIDROIT	International Institute for the Unification of Private Law
INIFIL	U.N. Interim Force in Lebanon
UNO	United Nations Organization
UNTAG	U.N. Transistion Assistance Group
UOIJ	Union of India
WIPO	World Intellectual Property Organization
WTO	World Trade Organization
VCLT	Vienna Convention on the Law of Treaties

I An Introduction

This book is divided into three parts, the first of which provides a historical overview of the major ideas and developments that have produced the modern principles of international law.

The Origins and Development of International Law

1

International law as we know it today is largely a product of Western civilization. However, rules that may be described by the modern term *international law* had their origin in the history of both the ancient and medieval world. Human beings have felt the need to develop some system of rules to regulate intercommunity relations ever since they came in contact with other political cultures.

The origin of law in general predates recorded history, and international law in particular is simply an extension of the need for the establishment of normative rules in the conduct of relations with other political entities. Such rules governing the conduct of separate political entities have emerged much more slowly and have been much more difficult to enforce. However, their roots can be found in the origin of the concepts of Western political thought that extend to the distant past. Evidence of rules and procedures found in modern international law date back over 5,000 years to the dawn of recorded history.

Nussbaum reports such evidence in a treaty between the rulers of Lagash and Umma, two ancient Mesopotamian communities, which provided for the settlement of a boundary dispute through arbitration, with solemn oaths for the observance of the agreement that is dated at about 3100 B.C. (cited in von Glahn, 1992, p. 25). However, these ancient communities were not organized into modern nation-states. The modern concept of international law is a product of the evolution of the modern nation-state system that originated in Europe only three to five hundred years ago and has become worldwide in scope only in the twentieth century.

The Western Origins of Law Development

International law grew out of the traditions and general principles of law that developed in Western Europe. The emergence of this particular body of law had to await the specific organizational developments of the widespread concept of the nation-state in historical perspective. Contrary to popular belief, the territorial nation-state system known today is of fairly recent origin. Most of the civilized areas of the world were organized originally as city-states (urban communities) able to control relatively small rural areas surrounding them. Empires developed through conquest and alliances. These larger organizational structures were loose federations maintained by treaty arrangements and rules of conduct among city-states.

In Western Europe, the most influential of these ancient empires was the extraordinary development of the Ancient Roman Empire. The rise and fall of the Roman Empire extended over a period of one thousand years and produced concepts of intercommunity relationships that form the antecedents to the development of modern international law.

Rome began as a city-state and gradually extended its authority first throughout the Italian peninsula (509-265 B.C.), then to the areas bordering the Mediterranean (264-133 B.C.). These developments resulted in the destruction of the north African city-state of Carthage and the conquest of Macedonia, including the Greek city-states (196 B.C.). At its height in 150 A.D., the Roman Empire controlled the allegiance of peoples of a vast area stretching from the British Isles to the Nile Valley and from the Iberian peninsula (Spain) to the area now known as Turkey.

The success of the Roman Empire in developing such a vast system and maintaining it for such an extraordinarily long period of time was due not only to its superior military forces but also to the political achievements of an early republican form of government and the development of superior legal institutions. The network of trea-

ties and alliances combined superior force with legal rules and principles of conduct that became recognized as superior to the tribal customs of more primitive organizational structures. The early conquest of the Greek city-states ultimately resulted in the merger of Roman and Greek ideas of law and reason. The Greek city-state of Athens in particular was accepted as a place of superior intellectual developments, and many of the ideas of the Greek academy founded by Plato and Aristotle were incorporated into Roman thought.

The legal concepts of natural law and *jus gentium* were particularly important in the evolution of the idea of international law. The ancient world did not think of law as man-made and merely imposed by superior force. They viewed law as the product of right reason emanating from assumptions about the nature of man and society. Those norms and principles derived from the rational nature of human beings (the law of reason) represent a particular school of thought about law in general and international law in particular. **Natural law,** or *jus naturale,* can be traced back to Greek Stoic thought of the third century B.C. Natural law was adopted by the Romans and blended with *jus gentium* to govern the relations of non-Romans in the Roman Empire.

> **Natural law:** Rules of conduct supposedly inherent in the relations between human beings and discoverable by reason.
>
> **Jus gentium:** The law of tribes—common principles of law derived from the practice of various groups throughout the Roman Empire and applied to govern the empire.

The Roman Concept of Jus Gentium

That body of Roman law that applied to all non-Romans in the empire as well as to relationships between Romans and non-

Romans was called *jus gentium*, or the law of tribes. It was based on the norms and concepts common to the various groups throughout the Roman Empire. This body of law came to be viewed by early writers and jurists as universal in applicability because it consisted of norms common to divergent groups who may not have had contact with one another. Since it governed the relations among the widely disparate peoples within the empire, *jus gentium* provided international law with many concepts that most of the classical writers depended on when they discussed international law.

In the later stages of the empire, this body of law was augmented with ideas derived from natural law and accepted as a method of discovery of universal law. The Stoic philosopher and Roman Emperor Marcus Aurelius (121-180 A.D.) formulated ideas of universal law and a world community:

> If the intellectual capacity is common to us all, common too is the reason, which makes us rational creatures. If so, that reason also is common which tells us to do or not to do. If so, law also is common. If so, we are citizens. If so, the universe is as it were a state—for of what other single polity can the whole race of mankind be said to be fellow members?—and from it, this common state, we get the intellectual, the rational, and the legal instinct, or whence do we get them? (*Meditations*, chap. IV, sec. 4)

This merging of Greek Stoic thought and the practical institutions of *jus gentium* influenced the early modern European political theorists to fashion utopian schemes involving international law and organization. These philosophers included Erasmus, Thomas More, the Duc de Sully, Hugo Grotius, William Penn, Jean-Jacques Rousseau, and Immanuel Kant.

The Statute of the International Court of Justice includes as a source of applicable law "general principles recognized by civilized nations." There is considerable controversy about the meaning and significance of such "general principles." At least one author asserts that "it is often maintained that this principle derives from the old Roman idea of *jus gentium*, or law of peoples, which the Romans used throughout their Empire" (Coplin, 1966, p. 11).

The Fundamental Postulate of Law

The first principle of international law is the customary practice that underlies the whole system of legal relations among peoples—namely, that contractual relationships are legally binding. This principle is older than recorded history and is accepted as self-evident because of its ancient origin and continued acceptance.

The Latin phrase, meaning that treaties shall be observed, is *pacta sunt servanda.* The duty to observe treaties in good faith has been recognized by State[1] practice from the beginning of recorded

> **Pacta sunt servanda:**
> *The duty to observe treaties in good faith.*

history. Explanation of its existence has eluded many writers; some consider it to be a principle of natural law, others a general principle of law, and yet others a principle of customary law. In fact, it may have all three of these attributes.

Professor J. L. Brierly (1963), a noted British authority, does not rely on consent to explain the existence of law, international or domestic; it exists, not because it has been consented to but because it is believed to be binding:

> If we are to explain why any kind of law is binding, we cannot avoid some such assumption as that which the middle ages made, and

which Greece and Rome made before them, when they spoke of natural law. The ultimate explanation of the binding force of all law is that man, whether he is a single individual or whether he is associated with other men in a state, is constrained, in so far as he is a reasonable being, to believe that order and not chaos is the governing principle of the world in which he has to live. (pp. 55-56)

Law itself is not an expression of fact or an assertion that a rule stated as law is inevitably followed without exception. The law is frequently violated in domestic as well as in international relations. The function of every social order, including that of the law in general, is to bring about certain reciprocal behavior of human beings to induce them to refrain from certain acts deemed detrimental to society and to perform others that are regarded as useful to society.

Professor Hans Kelsen (1967), a U.S. authority, defines law as a "normative order, and since legal norms provide for coercive acts as sanctions, the law is a coercive order" (pp. 4-5). In legal terms, a violation of the law is a *delict*, or an illegal act. Such acts of violation of law are not necessarily crimes; they also include civil wrongs, breach of contract, torts (or personal injury wrongs), and other forms of wrongful conduct. The law is a system of norms asserting that under certain conditions when a wrongful act occurs in violation of a legal norm, a *sanction* (or certain negative consequences) ought to take place.

Religion, Diplomacy, and War in the Middle Ages

The legal contributions of the Greek and Roman civilizations have left an important legacy of thought and ideas about law and intercommunity relationships that form the basic concepts of Western jurisprudence. The Dark Ages, Middle Ages, and the Renaissance in Western Europe ultimately revived many of these ideas, but the feudal society that emerged from the breakup of the Roman Empire was a distinctively different form of organization that lasted for a period of time rivaling that of the Roman Empire itself.

Feudalism refers to the peculiar association of landholding involving the personal relationship of lord and vassal that developed in Western Europe during the Middle Ages (roughly between the fifth and fifteenth centuries). Its central feature, in the agrarian economies of that age, was territorial, in which rights in land became the basis of wealth and power. During the period, the personal connection between lord and vassal became more and more associated with rights in land, termed the *fief*. Feudal society began as a band of free fighting men associated with a prominent leader. These companions followed their chieftain into battle and swore to fight to the death to support him. In return, the chieftain provided food, shelter, and entertainment in times of peace. During the economic and political decay of the later stages of the Roman Empire, this sort of clientage became linked with landholding. Small farmers found it impossible to compete with the great estates, and many commended themselves to powerful landlords, giving up their lands and receiving back the right to their use under the lords' protection.

The feudal system spread throughout Europe during the Middle Ages, became hereditary, and ultimately produced a chain of nobility. Through a process known as *subinfeudation*, the system of allegiances became very confused as vassals granted part of their fiefs to others who then owed allegiance to them rather than to the original lord of the land, and the feudal hierarchy was lost, resulting in what might be called "organized anarchy." The Catholic Church became the major integrating factor in these feudal societies, but despite the efforts of the church to restrict feudal warfare, little was accomplished until the royal power had grown strong enough to become a national sovereign able to enforce justice rather than being merely the apex of a contractual system of fiefdoms.

Similar relationships developed at various times in other parts of the world, such as the Muslim Empire, Japan, and China. However, these feudal societies differed widely concerning their organizational structure and development. Feudalism declined in Western Europe with the rise of towns and money economy as land ceased to be the only important form of wealth. The city-states of Italy led the way toward the development of commercialism and new wealth derived from trade. The feudal system became outdated by early technology in the form of new weapons, the use of gunpowder, navigation, development of navies to engage in war and commerce, and the emergence of capitalism.

The rise of the modern **nation-state** can be dated from only about the sixteenth century, first in England and then in France and Spain. Other parts of Europe consolidated into modern nation-states somewhat later, but the process of nationalism has had its most dramatic expansion in modern times. The consolidation of national territories into more clearly defined boundaries and the acceptance of a national identity and allegiance to one sovereign, or source

> *Nation-state:* The consolidation of national territories into more clearly defined boundaries and the acceptance of a national identity and allegiance to one source of authority. This sense of nationalism has become the representative unit of political organization in modern times.

of authority, marked the development of the nation-state.

Imperialism on the part of the powerful nation-states of Western Europe is also associated with the rise of nationalism, which ultimately produced two world wars of devastating proportions, introducing warfare on a global scale. However, the nation-state system has emerged as the dominant concept of social organization, and the relationships between independently sovereign national entities characterizes modern international law.

Feudalism, chivalry, and the guild system developed during the Middle Ages. The Roman Catholic Church was the major unifying force in Western Europe, but its power and influence developed slowly. Its narrowly limited authority in religious matters and belief in the supremacy of the papacy reached their height during the Middle Ages. The empire founded by Charlemagne in 800 ultimately disintegrated, and with the church's support, the Holy Roman Empire was founded. This effort had little effect on the forces of feudalism and disintegration that characterized the period. Nevertheless, the period had elements of unity and a distinct medieval culture existed, which reached its peak during the twelfth and thirteenth centuries. It was then that the diverse strains of Greco-Roman culture, Christianity, and the Germanic peoples were finally synthesized.

The **Renaissance period** (roughly the fourteenth through the sixteenth centuries) was the complex transition to the modern society in Western Europe. The term *renaissance* means "rebirth" and aptly describes a process that began in the trading centers of

> *Renaissance period:* The great revival of art, literature, and learning in Europe during the fourteenth, fifteenth, and sixteenth centuries, based on classical sources. It began in Italy and spread gradually to other countries, marking the transition of the medieval world to the modern.

Europe, particularly the city-states of Italy—Venice, Genoa, Milan, and Florence. The strategic location of these cities, given the stimulus of the Crusades and situation between the Holy Land and Western Europe, accounts for their leadership. Capital accumulated through trade was eventually available for other enterprises—banking, and to a lesser degree, industry. The wealthy merchants were patrons of the arts and literature, which stimulated the rediscovery of the human spirit of inquiry, paving the way for modern political attitudes.

These commercial developments eventually spread to other parts of Western Europe. However, the transformation of the medieval to the modern period produced profound political, social, and economic changes. Inequalities in wealth and power generated tensions resulting in the establishment of ambitious despots as rulers. These changes may be described as the steady articulation of Europe into self-consciously independent units recognizing no law but the necessities of their own self-preservation. Colonial expansion and rivalries for the riches of conquest, trade, and commercial exploitation increased the tensions, and warfare among these political units was common.

The Renaissance also ushered in a new era of diplomacy. The emerging trading centers and city-states of Europe behaved as independent and sovereign powers rather than as members of the larger unity of Christendom. They developed techniques such as the institution of resident ambassadors to carry on the diplomacy required by this new conception of the State. Niccolò Machiavelli (1469-1527), one of the most famous of these diplomats and advisers to princes, sought to reduce Statecraft to a science based on the analysis of past political practice and directed to the preservation of the State by any effective means.

Prolonged civil wars characterized the period in many parts of Europe; the Hundred Years War in France, the Wars of the Roses in England, and factional struggles between the nobles of Spain were caused mainly by the feudal nobility whose interests lay in the perpetuation of royal weakness. These power struggles were later manifest in the ferment of changes that affected all aspects of life; religion, education, science, and the arts were profoundly altered.

The **Reformation** was the great movement for reform of both doctrines and institutions of the Christian Church that started in Germany at the beginning of the sixteenth century. The bitter religious struggles of the period produced the Thirty Years War, which devastated European society and demonstrated lawlessness on a grand scale. However, it ultimately produced the emergence of the principles of State sovereignty that ushered in the new nation-state system.

> **Reformation:** The great movement for reform of Christian church doctrine and institutions that resulted in bitter division between Protestants and Catholics during the sixteenth and seventeenth centuries.

The Role of the Church and Ecclesiastical Law

The most important integrative element of the medieval period was the Catholic Church, a single religion, which increasingly centralized its institutional administration and developed a set of common legal standards that affected religious matters irrespective of race, nationality, or location. This ecclesiastical law, often referred to as **canon law,** influenced many areas regarded today as lying

> **Canon law:** The law used in church courts, which was based in part on elements of Roman law.

within the sphere of international law. It included the conclusion of treaties and their observance, authority over territory, the right of conquest with the sanction of the Church, papal activity in arbitration, and the general emphasis in canon law on arbitration as a desirable method for settling disputes. Above all, the Church exerted an influence on and attempted to regulate many facets of warfare.

Most early Christians believed all wars to be immoral. However, by at least the fifth century, the Church recognized the concept of "just" and "unjust" wars. St. Augustine (354-430) greatly influenced the formulation of Church doctrine against heresies and schisms of his time. His greatness lies in the synthesis he achieved of Christianity and classical thought, and his ideas have greatly influenced the development of Christian theology down to the present day. In St. Augustine's formulation, "just wars" were "those which avenge injuries when the nation or city against which warlike action is to be directed has neglected either to punish wrongs committed by its own citizens or to restore what has been unjustly taken by it" (Brownlie, 1963, p. 5).

Throughout the Middle Ages, the Church attempted to eliminate private wars and to mitigate the evils of legitimate intercommunity conflict. That the Church had a role to play in regulating these conflicts was generally accepted throughout Europe. Peace settlements and truce agreements were mediated by the Church, and Church sanctions were imposed against violators. The most important classical writers of modern international law first emerged from this tradition toward the end of the medieval period, which accompanied the rise of the nation-state.

Francisco de Vitoria (1480-1546) was a well-known Dominican professor of theology at the Spanish University of Salamanca.

His works emphasized the question of just wars, and he examined the basis of Spanish authority in the Americas, particularly with regard to relations between the Indians and Spaniards. He took the position that the Indians were the true owners of their lands and goods before the arrival of the Spaniards. He argued that imperial claims to world domination were invalid. Just war could not be waged against the Indians simply because they refused to acknowledge papal claims since the pope was neither the civil nor the spiritual overlord of the world, according to Vitoria. He also invoked the principle of *res nullius* (that only unoccupied lands could be legally claimed by discovery) to refute the Spanish claims that they had obtained valid title to Indian lands by discovery.

Vitoria upheld certain claims by the Spaniards based on rights under natural law and *jus gentium*, which included the right to travel and to carry on trade with natives, provided that they did not injure such peoples. If these rights were denied to visitors, then they had been injured, and a resulting war waged against the Indian populations in question represented a just war (see von Glahn, 1992, p. 28).

Francisco Suarez (1548-1617) was another Spanish professor of theology who focused on the subject of international law in his writings. Suarez made a distinction between natural law and *jus gentium*, asserting that the latter was in fact a body of law applying between independent States rather than one common to all States and that it represented a body of rules voluntarily instituted among humankind. He therefore represents the modern conception of a society or community of sovereign States, tied together by a body of law applying to their mutual relations.

International law is not to be confused with *world law*. The early characterization of international law was that of *jus gentium*, or the law of peoples, and later was referred to as "law among nations," as opposed to "law above nations." The modern term *international law* dates from the nineteenth century. There is considerable criticism as to whether or not its features can be clearly established as law in the sense of that familiar concept in domestic relations.

The Law Merchant and Commercial Development

Meanwhile, the forces of commerce, navigation, and trade produced a purely secular (nonreligious) body of law that became recognized throughout Europe. The original stimulus came from the Crusades, which called for massive transportation from Western Europe to the Holy Land. These expeditions in turn stimulated the demand for Eastern products, which were brought overland from China, India, and other parts of the eastern Mediterranean, where the Italians bought them, carried them home, and sold them for transport by sea or by land to other parts of Europe.

This new commercial activity gave rise to markets, fairs, and banks. The rapid development of maritime and overland trade eventually led to large commercial centers, in Italy and elsewhere, that had need for laws to govern their business transactions. Neither the secular Germanic law, the Roman law, nor that of the Church provided legal concepts suited to the needs of the commercial community. The guilds and merchants' associations began to follow their own practices, and with the assistance of ambassadors to the various courts of Europe, they were successful in setting up a system of specialized commercial courts. These courts worked out rules and procedures based on the customs of merchants that were considered practical and fair. Soon these same rules were being applied both in governmental and church courts, and eventually the **Law Merchant** became an international body of generally accepted commercial rules that transcended political boundaries.

> **Law Merchant:**
> Common commercial rules and procedures used throughout Europe in the Renaissance period.

Even in England, where there was resistance to the revival of the Roman civil law tradition, such commercial courts were established and the principles of this commercial code recognized. Codes of maritime law (admiralty law) developed along with many innovations in commercial and financial procedures. A direct line of development can be traced from these early codes to modern commercial codes.

The Thirty Years War

During the sixteenth century, a new secular and critical attitude toward the Roman Catholic Church brought about the disintegration of the whole medieval world of ideas and beliefs. On October 31, 1517, a youthful Augustinian monk, Martin Luther (1483-1546), posted his Ninety-Five Theses on the door of the All Saints Church in Wittenberg, Germany. He was protesting the practices of the Church in selling indulgences (absolution) in exchange for contributions to a massive project of building the basilica of St. Peters in Rome. Luther's theses not only denounced the abuses attributed to the vendors of indulgences but denied also the principles on which these grants of absolution were given.

This defiant act in Germany touched off a series of developments that challenged the core religious authority of the Roman Catholic Church. Even as late as 1910, the traditional Catholic views on the Protestant Reformation were expressed by Pope Pius

X in his encyclical when he exclaimed that the founders of Protestantism were

> men puffed up by pride and rebellious spirit: enemies of the Cross of Christ, seeking after earthly things . . . and whose god was their belly. They have in mind not the correction of morals, but the negation of the fundamental tenets of faith, caused a great confusion and opened to themselves and to others a path of licentious living. (cited in La Piana, 1969)

The Protestants, of course, had another point of view, contending that it was Church bureaucracy that corrupted the faith and usurped the powers of the spirit to the benefit of a clerical caste. This most powerful of all church schisms (or divisions) had much broader implications than just for theology. Extremist cults as well as a great variety of sectarian movements began to emerge all over Europe. The Anabaptists, Calvinists, Huguenots, and many others followed Luther in breaking with the doctrine of the Catholic Church. The ambitious monarchs and prime ministers of the emerging nation-states of Europe seized on this opportunity to turn the religious issues into political and national issues that could secure their secular control over religious matters.

The Thirty Years War began within the territory of the Holy Roman Empire (of the German Nations) in 1618 and eventually involved almost all of the Continental European powers before it ended in 1648. The war perpetuated the disunity and chaos characteristic of the Reformation and made permanent the split between Protestant and Catholic Europe. France emerged as the leading Continental power, whereas Spain relinquished the military supremacy she had enjoyed for over a century.

Bohemia was a part of the Holy Roman Empire that had been ruled by the Hapsburgs since the sixteenth century but that was in the midst of a national and religious revival under the leadership of the strongly Protestant and fiercely patriotic local nobility. One of the most respected principles of diplomatic immunity was grossly violated when the Bohemians (today's Czechs) "threw the despised agents of a despised Holy Roman Emperor from a window onto a dung heap" (Janis, 1993, pp. 153-154). This incident became known as the "defenstration of Prague" and signaled the onset of the great religious and nationalistic war of Europe.

Catholic Germany, in conjunction with the armies of Hapsburg Spain, succeeded in defeating the Bohemians, but at this point, the first of the foreign interventions began. Denmark invaded Germany in 1625 as the protector of Protestant interests; then Sweden, and later France, entered the war on the Protestant side. Cardinal Richelieu, the famous French prime minister, was not motivated by any affection for Protestantism but saw an opportunity to defeat the Spanish and Austrian Hapsburgs, the traditional enemies of France. For the next fifteen years, French, Spanish, Swedish, and German troops fought in Germany, Italy, Flanders (Belgium and Holland), and the Pyrenees (on the French border with Spain).

The traditional role of the Church as mediator in European disputes was no longer a possibility for settlement since the Church was an indirect party in this conflict. The Bohemian claim, and that of many principalities and monarchies of northern Europe, was that people of a certain language, society, and tradition had a right to choose their own religion and to govern themselves, free from the competing universalistic claims of the emperor and Pope. For three awful decades, the dispute raged. Some have estimated that half the German population died as a result of war, siege, starvation, pillage, and disease.

The peace settlement had to be negotiated in the separate cities of Munster and Osnabruck because the parties refused to sit down together. In 1648, the **Peace of Westphalia** legitimated the right of sovereigns to govern their peoples free of outside interference based on political, legal, or religious principles. The two peace treaties elaborated in great detail which sovereign ruled what territory. This property settlement stilled much of the conflict over land and loyalty that had devastated most of Europe.

> **Peace of Westphalia:**
> Treaties ratified in 1648 that brought an end to the Thirty Years War in Europe and established the principles of internal sovereignty.

The Emergence of the Nation-State System

The restraining forces of the moral and ethical doctrines of the Roman Catholic Church and its canon law sanctions were severely weakened by the Reformation. The practices of States, treaties, and general principles of secular law had to be strengthened to replace this loss. This transition in Western Europe accepted the abandonment of the medieval idea of a world-state and took instead as its fundamental postulate the existence of a number of States—secular, national, and territorial. However, it denied their absolute separateness and irresponsibility, proclaiming that these States were bound together by the supremacy of law. This reassertion of a community of nations would have to take into account the new political structure of Europe.

The Concept of Sovereignty

To many, the concepts of sovereignty and international law are incompatible. This is due in part to the rise of a self-conscious nationalism that has characterized the modern era. The doctrine of **sovereignty** was developed to define the new kind of State that emerged from the Reformation and the Peace of Westphalia. This concept has become the central problem in the study both of the nature of the modern State and of the theory of international law. For this reason, it is important to examine its origins and later development with particular care.

> **Sovereignty:**
> Supreme and independent political authority of the nation-state within its own territory.

Professor J. L. Brierly, who taught public international law at Oxford University until his death in 1955, asserts that the first explicitly formulated theory of sovereignty was published in 1576 as the *De Republica*, authored by Jean Bodin, a French theorist. Bodin was deeply influenced by the political and social developments of his day. France had been torn by faction and civil war, and Bodin was convinced that the cause of her miseries was the lack of a government strong enough to curb the subversive influences of feudal rivalries and religious intolerance. He asserted that the best way to combat these evils was to strengthen the French monarchy.

Bodin's thinking reflected a process that was actually taking place in his own day throughout Western Europe; unified States were emerging from the feudal societies of medieval times, and the central authority was everywhere taking the form of a strong personal monarchy supreme over all rival claimants to power, secular or ecclesiastical. He concluded, therefore, that the essence of Statehood is the unity of its government. A State could have only one ultimate dispute-settling authority, which he referred to by the Latin phrase *summa potestas*, or supreme power. This term was later translated into the French vernacular as *souveraineté* and hence the English *sovereignty*. Bodin defined a State "as a multitude of families and the possessions that they have in common, ruled by a supreme power and by reason" (as quoted in Brierly, 1963, p. 8). Bodin was convinced that a confusion of uncoordinated independent authorities must be fatal to a State; therefore, there must be one final source, and not more than one, from which its laws proceed.

Bodin understood the essential manifestation of sovereignty as the power to make laws, and since the sovereign makes the laws, clearly, the sovereign cannot be bound by those laws. However, even Bodin conceded that there are some laws that bind the sovereign: the divine law, the law of nature or reason, the law common to all nations, and also certain laws that he called the *leges imperii*, the laws of government, or what we would call *constitutional law* today.

The concept of law in the Middle Ages was viewed as something not wholly manmade. The medieval mind throughout Europe accepted the idea that behind the merely positive laws of any human society there stood a fundamental law of higher binding force embodying the wisdom of the past and that to have validity, positive law must conform to the higher law.

Bodin's formulation of the new essence of the nation-state was not accepted by everyone. Many have thought and acted as if sovereignty is absolute and that there is no higher law or constraining force above the nation-state. Others have been guided by the ideas expressed by Machiavelli to construct their own version of sovereignty. Machiavelli formulated no theory of politics or law in his conception of the art of government based on the notion of the State as an entity entirely self-sufficient and nonmoral.

Hugo Grotius and the Natural Law School

Huigh Cornets de Groot (1583-1645), better known as **Hugo Grotius**, is the classical writer who has been used as a reference for the transition from medieval to modern concepts of international law. He is generally accepted as the father of modern international law. This appellation does not refer to the idea that he created it but that he expounded the emerging practices of the new nation-states in a modern conceptualization that was both farsighted and practical.

According to Brierly, Alberico Gentili was the first writer to make a definite separation of international law from theology and ethics and to treat it as a branch of jurisprudence. Gentili was an Italian Protestant who fled to England to avoid persecution and became professor of civil law in Oxford. His first important work was the *De jure belli* published in 1598. Grotius acknowledged that he was greatly indebted to Gentili, from whom he first learned the concept of *rebus sic stantibus* (nullification of treaties when there has been a fundamental change in circumstances).

Grotius was born in Holland in 1583, where even as a boy, he acquired a reputation for learning. He became a master of every subject to which he turned his interest; he was a lawyer, historian, and poet whose great desire was to see the reunion of the Christian Church. He lived the life of a man of affairs, practicing the law and serving in official positions. His practice involved him in disputes over political questions, which landed him in prison for over two years, but he escaped through the devotion of his wife who smuggled him out in a box that supposedly contained books. He eventually became ambassador of Sweden at the French Court.

Grotius became involved in questions of international law by accepting a very challenging assignment from his client, the Dutch East India Company. In 1601, during the war against Spain, a fleet of the Dutch East India Company captured a Portuguese vessel. The ship was brought to Holland and sold as a prize of war since Portugal was under Spanish domination. Surprisingly, some of the stockholders objected to this action, claiming that Christians should not wage war against each other. Grotius was retained to provide a legal opinion on the objections raised by some of the stockholders. He fulfilled his assignment by writing an essay in 1604-1605 under the title *Commentary on the Law of Prize and Booty*. Most of this work remained in manuscript form and was discovered only in 1864. The twelfth chapter, however, was revised and published in 1609 under the title *Mare liberum (The Freedom of the Seas)*.

His greatest work was *Three Books on the Law of War and Peace, De jure belli ac pacis*, published in 1625. It was the first systematic treatment of positive international law. Grotius's reputation and the circumstances of the times converged to make this practical work a great success in attracting readers and users of these volumes. He was already so eminent that anything from his pen would have attracted attention. He also had the advantage of belonging to a country that had secured its independence from Spanish control in the sixteenth century and become the example for others to follow in developing the modern nation-state system. In many ways, Holland was the leading country of Europe at the beginning of the seventeenth century. Dutch independence from Spain had been the first great triumph of the idea of nationalism. They had successfully asserted the right of revolt against universal monarchy. New methods of trade and commerce produced wealth and prosperity, but there were also new conceptions of government based on freer institutions and on some measure of religious tolerance.

Grotius emphasized the laws of warfare rather than those of peace. He had a practical purpose in this as he explained from his observations involving the Thirty Years War:

> I saw prevailing throughout the Christian world a license in making war of which even barbarous nations should be ashamed; men resorting to arms for trivial or for no reasons at all, and when arms were once taken up no reverence left for divine or human law, exactly as if a single edict had released a madness driving men to all kinds of crime. (cited in Brierly, 1963, p. 29)

Three schools of international law developed after Grotius, but all of them acknowledge the contributions of this most important writer at the beginning of the nation-state system. These three schools of jurisprudence have been called the Naturalists, the Positivists, and the Grotians. The Naturalists were led by Samuel Pufendorf who denied that any positive law of nations originated from custom or treaties; his followers maintained that international law was merely a part of the law of nature.

The Positivists opposed the followers of Pufendorf, believing that a positive law of nations had its true origin in the consent of States. Some of the writers of this school denied the very existence of a law of nature. A Dutch jurist, Cornelius van Bynkershock, became the leading Positivist of this school.

Grotius occupied a middle ground between these schools of jurisprudence, maintaining that both of these sources of law were equally important. The Grotians therefore continued to accept both reason and consent as fundamental sources of law.

In his three books on the law of war and peace, Grotius provided supporting evidence for the concepts of just and unjust wars as had other writers before him. However, his contribution was in opening up debate on the subject of the conduct of warfare. He urged moderation in warfare and discussed the status and fate of hostages, the destruction of property, the problem of the defeated people's religious beliefs, and many other questions ignored by his predecessors. The topics of neutrality, freedom of the seas, treaties, and diplomatic practice were treated with much new and original material and thought.

Grotius was the first writer to proclaim the concept of freedom of the world's oceans. Subjects that remain controversial today, such as *rebus sic stantibus*, nullification of treaty obligations when the conditions prevailing at the time are substantially changed, were discussed. He considered war a punitive measure of self-help. Sovereign equals could inflict penalties or sanctions for retribution to enforce the law. He regarded war as a punitive action aimed against State crimes, analogous to the domestic punishment of crimes committed by individuals (see von Glahn, 1992, pp. 29-31).

The Assent of the Positivists

The three schools of international jurisprudence mark the evolution of more recent concepts concerning the essential nature of international law. The **Naturalists** represent the older thinking, basing the law of nations on moral principles to be deduced from a more basic natural order. This approach has lost ground in the evolution of modern thought, which today sees law as a positive action of governmental authority. The steady growth of the **Positivists**, who base their concept of

> **Naturalists:** *School of jurisprudence that bases law on moral principles deduced from basic human values and sense of community order.*
>
> **Positivists:** *School of jurisprudence based on historical evidence of practices involving expressed or implied consent.*

international law on the historical evidence of actual practices and the reasons behind them, has shown itself to be a more productive tool. The eclectic **Grotians** have also had to give ground to the Positivists in subordinating a postulated law of nature to a more pragmatic examination of the actual practices of nations.

> **Grotians:** *School of jurisprudence that recognizes both the law of reason and consent as equally important sources or causes of law development.*

L. F. L. Oppenheim, the noted modern authority on international law, made a distinction between *source* and *cause* in this debate and pointed out that the basis of international law was the common consent of the States composing the world community. As Oppenheim (1955; usually referred to as "Lauterpacht's Oppenheim") pointed out, three factors proved to be of particular importance in the development of contemporary international law: (a) the willingness of most States, after the Congress of Vienna (1814-1815), to submit to the rules of law; (b) the conclusion of numerous law-making treaties during the past 150 years; and (c) the rise of the positivist school to a position of prominence in legal thought (pp. 106-107).

By the end of the nineteenth century, the only source of international law was conceded to be by the expressed or implied consent of the States involved. This view was typical of the age of nationalism and absolute sovereignty that prevailed on the part of virtually every statesman and publicist during the nineteenth century.

The Rise of Nationalism and Colonialism

The Peace of Westphalia, in 1648, brought a period of relative stability in Europe. However, the age of colonialism was only getting started. Spanish, French, and English colonies emerged in the New World. Although the early Spanish conquests in America had been condemned by Vitoria, the emerging European law of nations offered little protection for the rights of more primitive peoples who were considered "uncivilized nations." The North American colonies, developed under British authority, displayed some respect for the principles of international law in dealing with indigenous natives, but the acceptance of the unilateral use of force and threat of force in negotiating treaties definitely favored the stronger party in any negotiations concerning settlement of disputes that arose.

The American Revolution had its seeds in the French and Indian War (in the New World), called the Seven Years War in Europe (1754-1763). This war was a struggle for world power between France and England. The major-power struggle began in the late seventeenth century, and at first, the colonies were not considered of much importance; however, by the middle of the eighteenth century, the chief issue between the two nations was the colonies in America and in India. The English colonies in America formed a narrow band along the Atlantic coast. The French settlements stretched through Canada in a great arc behind the English colonies all the way from the mouth of the St. Lawrence River, via the Great Lakes, to the Mississippi Delta.

Fighting began in America over the French encroachments claimed by the British in the Ohio Valley. George Washington was sent on an expedition to warn the French to stop these encroachments and returned with word that it was their "absolute Design to take possession of the Ohio." Fighting began in America in 1754, a year before war was declared in Europe. The war was a bloody and uncontrolled affair by

European standards, involving the use of rival Indian tribes on both sides where the taking of scalps was introduced.

The Treaty of Paris, in 1763, formally ended the war and awarded all of Canada to Great Britain, and Louisiana to Spain. France was left a beaten and bitter enemy. The British debt accumulated because of the war and led to increased taxes on the colonies. Washington's experiences with British military commanders earned his disrespect, which was shared by many colonials. An economic depression also set in at the war's end in the colonies, and these conditions ultimately led to the Declaration of Independence in 1776.

The American war of liberation from British colonial rule followed the Dutch example earlier, and by means of the Declaration of Independence, Americans proclaimed a new philosophy of self-determination of peoples. Self-determination and "popular sovereignty" became one of the major concepts of the new world order of the twentieth century. The U.S. Constitution, ratified in 1789, also established a federal system of shared sovereignty within a community of states called the United States of America.

Modern nationalism, however, was still evolving, and the French Revolution produced one of its most significant characteristics—direct citizen loyalty to the nation and obligation to fight for it. Prior to the French Revolution in 1789, European armies had been recruited from the nobility or paid for as mercenaries and professional soldiers. The French Revolution introduced conscription and a citizen army during Napoleon's time. The principles of the French Revolution—*Liberté, Egalité, Fraternité*—produced the logical conclusion that if the State belonged to the people, then the people must fight for it.

The French Revolution was a series of upheavals in France between 1789 and 1799 that overthrew not only the country's traditional institutions of monarchy, aristocracy, and church but also its whole social structure. The idea of "popular sovereignty" did not produce such a beneficent result in France as it had in the United States. In France, the bloody execution of much of the nobility, the institution of Jacobin dictatorship and terror, and the rise of Napoleon Bonaparte to the position of "popular dictatorship" upset the European order.

Bonaparte asked his foreign minister, Talleyrand, about this concept of law of nations, and Talleyrand replied that it meant "that nations ought to do to one another in peace, the most good, and in war, the least evil possible" (cited in Janis, 1993, p. 2). Napoleon did not take this advice and waged war throughout Europe, even invading Russia and capturing Moscow. This expansive and irresponsible nationalism was finally subdued by a concert of allied powers of Europe. The Congress of Vienna (1814-1815) established a balance of political forces in Europe that accepted the classical principles of international law, but it also established the so-called **Concert of Europe**, which became the instrument of the extension of colonialism by exercising what it believed to be the power to deny the legal existence of certain nations without regard to their previous existence.

> **Concert of Europe:**
> The system of great power hegemony that developed out of the Congress of Vienna (1814-1815) ending the Napoleonic Wars. An informal system of consultation and balance of powers that included Russia, England, France, Austria, and Prussia.

The Concert of Europe did provide an informal organization that preserved peace in Europe for almost a century until it dis-integrated into two opposing and rigid alliance systems leading directly to World War I. However, the expansion of European colonialism reached its height in the nineteenth century, and the Berlin Conference (1884-1885) declared all of Africa south of the Sahara subject to European colonialism. The fourteen European powers who met in Berlin did agree to end slavery and its trade, protect Africans and foreigners, and further Western culture.

The most important critic of international law in the nineteenth century was John Austin (1790-1859), a British legal scholar and professor of jurisprudence at London University. He acknowledged in 1832 that international legal rules were effective in many respects but that the legal system lacked the development of an international sovereign to enforce it. For Austin, international law could not be the same sort of positive law as that enacted by sovereign States for internal application:

> The law obtaining between nations is not positive law: for every positive law is set by a given sovereign to a person or persons in a state of subjection to its author. As I have already intimated, the law obtaining between nations is law (improperly so called) set by general opinion. The duties which it imposes are enforced by moral sanctions: by fear on the part of nations, or by fear on the part of sovereigns, of provoking general hostility, and incurring its probable evils, in case they shall violate maxims generally received and respected. (Austin, 1832, quoted in Janis, 1993, p. 3)

Early Twentieth-Century Developments

The Concert of Europe was an exclusive club of great European powers during the nineteenth century. It met sporadically on some thirty occasions, mainly to deal with pressing political issues, but it also began the process of considering issues that were concerned with the maintenance of existing peaceful conditions, the substitution of pacific for violent methods of manipulating the distribution of power, defining the ground rules, and formulating general international legislation applicable to the ordinary relations of States. Professor Inis Claude (1984) concludes that

> the Concert system gave Europe, for the first time since the rise of national states, something imperfectly resembling an international parliament, which undertook to deal by collective action with problems ranging from the regulation of international traffic on the great rivers of the Continent to the adjustment of relations between belligerent and neutral states, and from the redivision of Balkan territories to the carving up of Africa. (p. 27)

Law Development in the Abstract

Around the turn of the century, a new system for consideration of international problems having a broader base of representative States emerged. The Hague system was a conscious effort to construct a regular conference for the consideration of issues of international relations in times of peace. In 1893, a number of European nations wanted to promote international trade through coordination of domestic legislation to regulate questions concerning the rules governing international commercial transactions. Since then, the Hague, in the Netherlands, has become the site for the location of approximately one dozen such conferences.

The more famous **Hague Peace Conferences** initiated in 1899, and meeting again in 1907, undertook to resolve a variety of issues that were more controversial than facilitating trade and commerce. The first of these conferences, in 1899, was attended by only twenty-six States and was predominantly European in composition. This conference completed three conventions and three declarations. The most important of these was the creation of a **Permanent Court of Arbitration**, which consisted of a panel of leading experts nominated by the signatories. Arbitration of disputes was purely voluntary, each party choosing two from the panel and the arbitrators selecting a fifth member. The use of international commissions of inquiry to provide for impartial fact-finding was recommended.

The 1899 conference also established a single code of land warfare that complemented the 1864 Geneva Convention applying to war at sea. Although other proposals were defeated, the success of finding areas of agreement in the abstract led to a second conference in 1907. The 1907 conference was attended by forty-four States, including the bulk of the Latin American Republics. It was the first time that representatives of nearly all constituted States of that day met to discuss issues of major international concern. The inclusion of non-European States signaled the acceptance of major diplomatic assemblies of small States on equal terms with the great powers. The U.S. representatives attended both of these

> **Hague Peace Conferences:** Held in 1899 and in 1907 to resolve a variety of issues of international law in the abstract. They concluded a number of treaties that served to codify international law among most of the world's nations.
>
> **Permanent Court of Arbitration:** Established in 1900 under the 1899 Hague Convention for Pacific Settlement of International Disputes and revised in 1907. It provided a panel of arbitrators that have been useful in peaceful settlement of disputes.

conferences and were active participants. President Theodore Roosevelt was even instrumental in initiating the second Hague Peace Conference.

The results of the second conference, however, were not uniformly good. The three conventions of 1899 were revised and ten new treaties signed. The following subjects were covered:

* The pacific settlement of disputes
* Limitation of the employment of force for recovery of contractual debts
* The opening of hostilities
* The law and customs of war on land
* The rights and duties of neutral powers and persons
* The status of enemy merchant ships at the outbreak of hostilities
* The conversion of merchant ships into warships
* The laying of automatic contact mines, bombardment of naval forces in time of war
* A convention of maritime war using the principles of the Geneva Convention
* The right of capture in naval war
* The creation of an International Prize Court (which was never ratified)
* The rights and duties of neutral powers in naval war

British and German interests clashed over issues of naval arms limitations. Germany rejected any disarmament proposals and led the way in rejecting compulsory arbitration of international disputes. However, these conferences indicated an initial willingness to search for areas of agreement among the assembled States of the world.

Public International Unions

During the late nineteenth and early twentieth centuries, progress was made in the area of creating public international unions that became the first permanently functioning **intergovernmental organizations** (IGOs). These unions occurred in essentially nonpolitical fields and reflected the need for practical solutions to the problems created by the unprecedented flow of commerce in goods,

> *Intergovernmental organizations (IGOs):* Public international unions formed by sovereign States and given certain attributes of sovereignty.

services, people, ideas, germs, and social evils. The first of these was the German *Zollverein*, which was initially created in 1834 but was renegotiated and strengthened under the dominant influence of Prussia in 1867. This was a German customs union among the thirty-eight German States—kingdoms, duchies, and free cities—of this period.

The International Telegraphic Union (1865) and the Universal Postal Union (1874) were successfully initiated prior to the twentieth century and were later merged into the important International Telecommunications Union of today. The International Union of Railway Freight Transportation was created in 1890, and many other early IGOs were established in diverse fields such as agriculture, health, standards of weights and measures, patents and copyrights, and narcotics and drugs.

World War I: Causes and Effects

It is generally conceded today that World War I (1914-1918) was caused by mistakes and miscalculations in an atmosphere involving the explosive mixture of rigid alliance systems, nationalism, mechanistic militarism, and irresponsible leadership. This was the first great conflict to involve most of the civilized world. Some 65 million men were mobilized, of whom more than 8.5 million died and 21 million were wounded. The League of Nations was established as a part of the peace settlement that concluded the war.

The Underlying Causes of World War I

The fundamental causes of the war go back to the emergence of modern German nationalism and the forceful leadership of Otto von Bismarck, chancellor of Prussia during the latter part of the nineteenth century. British, French, and Spanish national unification had occurred earlier, but Germany and Italy remained divided into kingdoms, principalities, duchies, and free cities even into the twentieth century. Austria-Hungary was the more powerful central European Empire before the rise of the Prussian Empire in the nineteenth century. The Russian Empire was the colossus to the east that had also achieved enough unity and strength to be considered a major European power by the early twentieth century.

The rise of German unity and military power during the nineteenth century upset the delicate balance of power that had held the Concert of Europe together for nearly a century. Bismarck is credited with having manipulated France into declaring war against Prussia in 1870 by altering the famous "Ems Dispatch," an insulting communication between the monarchs of the two nations, which he edited. The Franco-Prussian War (1870-1871) resulted in a disastrous defeat for France and the loss of the major French territory of Alsace-Lorraine (between France and Germany). The Prussian victory, aided by the unification of the German States, led to the creation of the German Empire, which was announced at the end of the war in the palace of Louis XIV at Versailles. Wilhelm I was proclaimed emperor.

Russia and Austria-Hungary were tied to Germany by the uncertain threads of diplomacy and family. In 1882, Bismarck strengthened his position by negotiating the Triple Alliance, joining together Austria-Hungary, Italy, and Germany. By 1890, Germany's dominant diplomatic position on the continent of Europe was unquestioned. In 1894, France began to emerge from her diplomatic isolation to enter into the Dual Alliance with Russia, which had in the meantime cooled toward Germany. Russian need for capital from France made it easier to conclude this treaty, which acted as a counterbalance to the Triple Alliance. Great Britain, meanwhile, stood outside these continental rivalries, but political and economic pressures were gradually forcing her to make a choice.

Germany's nationalism, her threatening imperialism, her fast-growing industrial competition, and above all her large-scale naval program jarred British complacency. In a series of comparatively rapid maneuvers, the differences between Great Britain and France were reconciled, and, in 1904, the *Entente Cordiale* was arranged. The more difficult obstacles to Anglo-Russian agreement were also overcome, and in 1907, Great Britain, France, and Russia formed the Triple Entente. The division of Europe into two armed camps was now complete.

The Immediate Causes of World War I

The existence of the Triple Alliance and the Triple Entente increased the tension in Europe. Long-held grudges, fears, and suspicions exacerbated the tension. The French brooded over their lost territory of Alsace-

Lorraine. The Italians, although allied with Austria-Hungary, grieved over the unredeemed areas of Trentino, Trieste, and Fiume. Polish nationalists saw in war an opportunity for the re-creation of a unified State broken by the partitions of the eighteenth century. Austria-Hungary seethed with dissident national groups, of which the Czechs were especially vocal. In the Balkans (the area known today as Yugoslavia before its disintegration), the various national rivalries were in a situation of permanent crisis (not much different from today). Outside intervention threatened to absorb the Balkan States into either the Austro-Hungarian Empire or the Russian Empire. The suspicions of the rival powers were heightened by the growth of conscript armies (in all the major powers except Britain) and expanding navies. In this atmosphere of fear and recrimination, there were no strong forces to moderate the growing "international anarchy." The Hague Peace Conferences of 1899 and 1907 did not produce any effective restrictions on the war-making activities of nations.

In the Balkans, Serbian nationalist propaganda against the Austro-Hungarian monarchy grew more unrestrained after the Balkan wars. A Serbian group of conspirators planned and carried out the assassination of the heir to the Austro-Hungarian throne, Archduke Francis Ferdinand. The opportunity came when the archduke and his wife visited Sarajevo, in Bosnia, on June 28, 1914. The Serbian government was long aware of the plot and had done nothing to suppress it. This incident set into motion a chain reaction that moved the two alliances into war.

The autocratic leaders of the nations making up both the Triple Alliance and the Triple Entente were hereditary monarchs. Considerable democratic influence in areas of domestic policy had developed, but in foreign policy, the monarch had complete authority. Kaiser Wilhelm of Germany (the successor to the first Emperor Wilhelm I) had dismissed Bismarck in 1890, and succeeding chancellors were weaker leaders. Many of these monarchs were interrelated through previous diplomatic marriages; Kaiser Wilhelm and Czar Nicholas II of Russia were cousins. But even these ties could not stop the almost immediate escalation of forces once set into motion.

Kaiser Wilhelm was a personal friend of the assassinated archduke and his wife, Sophie. He had just visited them at their castle and was deeply moved by the report that the archduke's last words to his wife were, "Sophie, Sophie, do not die, live for our children," before death claimed them both. The Kaiser's fury, aimed at the Serbs, led to an impetuous and fateful step of assuring Austria that she could count on Germany's "faithful support" even if the punitive action that she was planning to take against Serbia would bring her into conflict with Russia (Stoessinger, 1974, p. 4).

The Kaiser's July 5 promise of support was received while the aging and frail emperor of Austria-Hungary, Francis Joseph, was considering a course of action in response to the assassinations. Count Leopold von Berchtold, the foreign minister, and Conrad von Hoetzendorff, the military chief of staff, were the major advisers to the emperor. Both urged military mobilization measures, and after some reluctance on the emperor's part, the orders were given. An ultimatum was prepared that the Austrian foreign minister was certain Serbia would reject. Although Serbia agreed to comply with most of the demands in the ultimatum, the Austrian foreign minister, Berchtold, broke diplomatic relations with Serbia and convinced the ailing Francis Joseph to order partial mobilization. On July 28, 1914, war was declared by Austria-Hungary on Serbia.

The German Kaiser, after reviewing the wording of the ultimatum and the Serbian reply, had second thoughts about his rash July 5 "blank check" promise of support. The Serbs appealed to Russia for support, and French President Poincare gave assurances of support to the Russian leaders. The major advisers to Czar Nicholas II were his foreign minister, Sazonov, and the minister of war, Sukhomlinov. Sazonov was especially influential in convincing the czar to mobilize the Russian troops, and he was strengthened by the French assurances. His reaction to the situation was highly emotional and explosive, viewing the ultimatum as a pretext for Austrian aggression against Serbia and imperial expansion into the Balkans.

Austria's partial mobilization was, however, more than enough to defeat the Serbs in order to deter the Russians. Russia therefore ordered partial mobilization of their troops in hopes that the quick Russian response would deter Austria from attacking Serbia in the first place. "Thus, both the Austrian and Russian decisions to mobilize a part of their armies were in essence, bluffs designed to deter the other side" (Stoessinger, 1974, p. 14).

An exchange of telegrams between the cousins, Czar Nicholas II and Kaiser Wilhelm, with a German offer to mediate did not stop the escalation. The Kaiser believed that the czar had used the German mediation effort as a way to get five days' head start in his own military preparations behind Wilhelm's back. The British foreign secretary, Sir Edward Grey, had encouraged the German mediation effort, but this action was now seen by the Kaiser as an English trick combining threat with bluff and an attempt to prevent Germany from mobilizing. On July 31, the Kaiser proclaimed a "state of threatening danger of war" and

issued a twelve-hour ultimatum to Russia, demanding demobilization. When the Russians refused to comply, Wilhelm ordered full mobilization. German Chancellor Theobold von Bethmann-Hollweg is reported to have said on August 1, "If the iron dice must roll, may God help us." The Austrian emperor exclaimed, "We cannot go back now."

The well-oiled German military machine now began to roll. Germany declared war on Russia on August 1 and on France on August 3. The German generals were committed to the von Schlieffen Plan of conducting a two-front war in the event of a general European conflict. This plan required an attack on France through Belgium, if the Russians started to mobilize. The slow-moving Russian military could be expected to take some time before sufficient forces could be focused for attack, and the superior speed of the German forces could expect to gain the advantage of a first strike against France before having to divert its strength to the eastern front.

Barbara Tuchman (1962), in her much acclaimed book, *The Guns of August*, paints a vivid picture of the German war machine:

> Once the mobilization button was pushed, the whole vast machinery for calling up, equipping, and transporting two million men began turning automatically. . . . From the moment the order was given, everything was to move at fixed times according to a schedule precise down to the number of train axles that would pass over a given bridge within a given time. (pp. 74-75)

Even the Kaiser seemed powerless to stop the machine once put into motion. The British had treaty obligations to defend Belgian neutrality. The German ambassador in London reported that England would observe neutrality toward Germany if Germany refrained from attacking France. But the trains had already begun to roll, and the German chief of staff, von Moltke, informed the Kaiser that the plan could not be reversed. He explained:

> The deployment of millions cannot be improvised. If your Majesty insists on leading the whole army to the East it will not be an army ready for battle but a disorganized mob of armed men with no arrangements for supply. Those arrangements took a whole year of intricate labor to complete and once settled, it cannot be altered. (Tuchman, 1962, p. 79)

Germany's invasion of Belgium on August 3 forced Parliament's hand, and Great Britain declared war on Germany the next day. All the great European powers were now at war.

Major Events During the War

Italy refused to enter the war with Austria and Germany on the grounds that the Central Powers were the aggressors. Since it had not been attacked, Italy claimed that it was therefore absolved from fulfilling its treaty obligations. The two sides became the **Allies**—Russia, France, Great Britain, and Serbia—and the **Central Powers**—Austria-Hungary and Germany. The relative strength of these two sides at the beginning of the war was uneven. The Allies were superior over the Central Powers at

> **Allies:** Principally, Russia, France, Great Britain, and Serbia, which declared war against the Central Powers after being attacked in World War I. Later joined by Italy and the United States.
>
> **Central Powers:** Principally, Austria-Hungary and Germany, which were considered the aggressors in World War I. Later joined by the Ottoman Empire (Turkey).

sea, but the formidable submarine weapons of Germany threatened to even the sides. On land, there was an overall manpower advantage of potential resources on the part of the Allies, but the Russian army was badly equipped and poorly organized.

The Allies were able to stop the German attack short of Paris and eventually pushed them back on the western front. On the eastern front, the Russian armies were overrun by the German forces. The Austrian arm of the eastern attack was considerably less successful. In the west of Germany, the attack became bogged down in trench warfare in northern France. This stalemate caused the Allies to begin negotiating secret treaties with Italy to bring her into the war. They felt that their ultimate manpower advantage would finally bring victory if they could hold out against the German superior equipment. These secret agreements anticipated an opportunity to divide up the spoils of victory. Italy was encouraged to enter the war on the Allies' side by being promised Trieste, the Tirol in Austria, and certain portions of the Turkish Empire.

Turkey entered the war on the side of the Central Powers in October of 1914. This ultimately brought Italy into the war on the side of the Allies after being promised a share in the dividing up of the Ottoman Empire if the Allies were victorious. The war was not going well for the Allies on land during this early phase of the conflict; however, British command of the seas was sufficient to keep the supply lines open, effect a successful blockade of Germany, and conquer German overseas colonies with the help of the Japanese in the Far East.

Violations of the rules of war occurred on both sides. The British passenger ship, the *Lusitania* was torpedoed without warning by a German submarine on May 7, 1915, off the southern coast of Ireland. The ship sank in less than 20 minutes with the loss of 1,198 persons, including 128 U.S. citizens. The Germans asserted that the ship was carrying arms for the Allies (which later proved to be true) and that U.S. citizens had been warned against taking passage on British vessels. Popular feeling in the United States rose to a high pitch after the *Lusitania* disaster, producing strong sentiment for declaring war on Germany.

President Woodrow Wilson protested, and stern diplomatic notes were exchanged between the United States and Germany. The Germans responded at length (one year later) by deciding to forego "unrestricted" submarine warfare but reserved the right to resume it at any time. This action temporarily conciliated the United States, and on December 12, 1916, the Central Powers asked the United States to forward a note to the Allies proposing that peace talks be initiated. Although the offer was rejected by the Allies, Wilson became involved as a mediator. However, Wilson was unaware of the extensive secret agreements between the Allies to carve up the German, Austro-Hungarian, and Ottoman Empires. These agreements would have complicated a negotiated settlement at this point. U.S. sympathy for the Allied side in the conflict increased, and in early 1917, the war sentiment mounted in the United States.

President Wilson laid down the conditions of peace that he said the United States would support. These included "peace without victory," "self-determination of peoples," "freedom of the seas," and creation of an organization to keep the peace after the war was over. A plot to involve Mexico in the war on the side of Germany if the United States joined the Allies was uncovered. But only after Germany resumed unrestricted submarine warfare and news of the Russian Revolution, did the U.S. Congress vote to declare war on April 6, 1917.

Czar Nicholas II was forced to abdicate when faced with revolution in the streets and an external war with the Central Powers. A provisional government was set up, but Russia could not carry on the war effort because the people and the soldiers demanded peace. Indeed, the revolt started in the military. The Bolsheviks (a faction of the Communist Party) took over in November, signed a truce in December, and concluded a peace treaty with the Central Powers, known as the **Brest-Litovsk Treaty**. This agreement abandoned all Russian claims to Poland, Lithuania, Estonia, the Ukraine, Latvia, Transcaucasia, and Finland. It also ceded Kars and Batum to Turkey. The Central Powers had won the war on the eastern front and could devote their entire resources to the western front.

> **Brest-Litovsk Treaty:** *Concluded between Bolshevik Russia and the Central Powers ending World War I on Germany's eastern front. Germany was forced to renounce this treaty by the armistice agreement at the end of the war.*

U.S. forces were late in arriving, but they substantially strengthened the Allies, who were ultimately successful in fending off the initial German attack with concentrated forces. The Allies then staged their own counteroffensive. An intensive campaign to undermine the morale of the German soldier proved even more effective. President Wilson's speeches, promising a just peace, sapped the German will to fight. Wilson's famous **Fourteen Points** were enumerated in a speech to Congress, January 8, 1918, and were quickly taken by the peoples of Central Europe as the basis for an honorable peace. They could be summarized as follows:

> **Fourteen Points:** *President Wilson's promise for peace with honor that influenced the Germans to conclude an armistice agreement ending hostilities in World War I.*

1. Open covenants of peace, openly arrived at
2. Freedom of the seas
3. The removal, so far as possible, of economic barriers, such as tariffs, and so on
4. Reduction of armaments
5. Impartial adjustment of colonial claims
6. The evacuation of Russian territory and the encouragement of its people to follow their own political development
7. The evacuation and restoration of Belgium
8. The liberation of French territory, including Alsace-Lorraine
9. Readjustment of Italian frontiers along national lines
10. The autonomous development of the peoples of Austria-Hungary
11. The evacuation of Romania, Serbia, and Montenegro, and the provision of free access to the sea for Serbia
12. The autonomous development of nationalities under Turkish rule
13. The establishment of an independent Poland with free access to the sea
14. The formation of an association of nations

The Peace Settlement

A moderate government in Germany was installed after these announcements. The new chancellor, Prince Max von Baden, was installed to seek a negotiated peace, and an offer was made to President Wilson to start discussions. Five weeks of intensive fighting continued, and Wilson demanded to meet only with the "veritable representatives" of the people of Germany. The German leaders hesitated, but the realization that the abdication of the Kaiser would bring peace was evident to many Germans. Wilson's refusal to negotiate with the imperial autocrats, and mutiny in the German fleet at Kiel, produced a somewhat staged revolution in Germany.

After being told that the army would no longer obey him, the Kaiser abdicated on November 9, 1918, and the German Republic was proclaimed. The armistice agreement ending hostilities was signed on November 11. It provided for evacuation to the east bank of the Rhine River, immediate return of all allied prisoners, the continuation of the blockade during the peace negotiations, renunciation of the treaties of Brest-Litovsk and Bucharest, and reparations to be paid for damages. The Germans sought an armistice based on Wilson's Fourteen Points, which they thought would be preliminary to a "peace with honor," as Wilson had promised. The terms of the armistice required virtually unconditional surrender, and the powerless Germans were faced with a dictated peace.

At the peace conference, held in Paris in 1919, five treaties were negotiated among the allied powers. Separate treaties with Germany, Austria, Bulgaria, Hungary, and Turkey took a year to complete. The principal actors at the conference were the major allied powers, led by Woodrow Wilson, Georges Clemenceau of France, and Lloyd George of Great Britain. These were the "Big Three" who dominated the conference. Vittorio Orlando of Italy became dissatisfied with the proposed settlements of the Adriatic questions and withdrew from the inner council.

Wilson's Fourteen Points proved too idealistic. He was forced to compromise on several important points to get his major objective, the League of Nations. Clemenceau, Lloyd George, and Orlando had to work around the secret agreements they had made to prosecute the war. In the end, this enormous peace settlement carved up the map of Europe and much of the rest of the world.

Italy got Trentino from Austria, Trieste, and a large part of Istria (along the northern Adriatic). Wilson insisted that Fiume, on the Adriatic, be withheld. Italian adventurers, led by Gabriele d'Annunzio, took it anyway, and the conference left Italy and the newly created State of Yugoslavia to settle the disputed territory themselves. Great Britain acquired German East Africa and part of the German Cameroons, and the British self-governing colonies of South Africa, Australia, and New Zealand were given South-West Africa and the German areas in New Guinea and Samoa. France was given most of German Togoland and the Cameroons. Japan got the German islands in the Pacific north of the equator and Shantung, which Germany had once taken from China.

The important areas of the now vanquished Ottoman Empire were even more complicated to deal with. Secret treaties to carve up these lands and an uprising in Turkey resulted in the need for two treaties that were not completed until 1923 with the Treaty of Lausanne. Syria was given to France; Palestine was offered to the United States, but Wilson refused. Great Britain received Mesopotamia, Transjordan, and Palestine; the Dodecanese Islands in the Aegean were given to Italy; the Hejaz and Arabian territory along the Red Sea were to be independent.

Wilson was unhappy with these developments because they violated his principle of self-determination of peoples. He was particularly angered by the Japanese acquisition of Shantung. Japan agreed to turn it back to China in the future and did so. Wilson's advisers proposed that instead of permitting an actual transfer of these colonies to new owners, they would administer them as trustees of the League of Nations. The trustees were required to report to the league on their administration and to make progress toward eventual self-governance.

Self-determination did guide many of the territorial settlements in Europe, and a number of new States were created whose nationalistic aspirations were finally realized. Poland, which had been partitioned in the eighteenth century, was now restored. However, drawing the boundaries was difficult, resulting in the famous "Polish Corridor," which gave Poland access to the Baltic. This corridor cut off East Prussia from the rest of Germany. The settlement also created the new States of Latvia, Lithuania, Estonia, and Finland.

What had once been Austria-Hungary was dissolved to create Austria, Czechoslovakia, Hungary, Yugoslavia, and an enlarged Romania. The difficult problem of following the "self-determination of peoples" principle was extremely complex because of the intermixture of peoples and their bitter rivalries. However, despite the extensive compromising, the map of Europe after the war conformed more to the desires of the various nationalities than did the map of 1914.

Such vast changes would inevitably accentuate old hatreds and give birth to new fears that could not be foreseen at the time. Wilson placed his faith in the League of Nations, which he insisted be a part of the Treaty of Versailles settling the German issues. The German delegation refused to sign the Treaty on grounds that it was not in accord with the Fourteen Points, but they had little alternative at that point, and finally, the German National Assembly accepted the treaty under protest on June 23, 1919. The French could not resist their ultimate revenge for the Franco-Prussian War and staged an elaborate ceremony for the signing of the Treaty of Versailles in the Hall of Mirrors where Bismarck had insisted on proclaiming the new German Empire in 1871.

The Covenant of the League of Nations

The international legal instrument, known as the Treaty of Versailles, included the

Covenant of the League of Nations. President Wilson chaired the nineteen-member commission that drafted the covenant. The basic outlines of the organization produced by this document drew on familiar developments illustrated in the Concert of Europe,

> ***Covenant of the League of Nations:*** *That part of the treaty of Versailles providing for creation of institutions for the general maintenance of international peace and security after World War I.*

the Hague conferences, and the experience of the earlier public international unions. It did not seek fundamental change in the traditional concepts of international law. Its main purpose was to organize these existing elements into a permanently functioning organizational structure.

Membership in the league was open to all States, provided they gave "effective guarantees" of their willingness to accept the necessary international obligations and gained the approval of a two-thirds majority of the Assembly, composed of all the member States. Forty-five original signatories named in the annex to the covenant became original members by early 1920. The United States was the only major power that refused to ratify the covenant. Ironically, the nation that had done the most to initiate the league refused to ratify it in the Senate by the needed two-thirds majority. Wilson, although he had not kept the Senate well-informed during the peace conference, now made an extensive effort to convince the people of the United States. On a whistle-stop train campaign throughout the country, he fell victim to a severe stroke and became paralyzed for the remainder of his term as president. The Senate's rejection of the Covenant of the League of Nations and the refusal to ratify the statute of the "World Court"[2] signified a return to U.S. isolationism.

The league was created and did approximate universal membership at the time, reaching sixty-three States who participated; the maximum at any given point in time was sixty States. Germany was admitted in 1926 and the Soviet Union in 1934. Both of these major powers were given permanent seats on the Council, recognizing their importance.

War was not legally prohibited by the covenant, but the basic principles of the covenant stressed peaceful settlement of disputes, that war should be prevented, and that any aggressor who violated the covenant should be dealt with promptly and effectively by the collective action of all its members. The covenant included a three-month cooling-off period, following a decision by the dispute settlement body hearing the case.

Article 14 provided for the creation of an international court. The **Permanent Court of International Justice** was established by a separate treaty. The statute of the World Court was drafted by an advisory commission of jurists and adopted by the Assembly in 1920, effective in 1921. It was individually ratified by a majority of the league members. The "World Court," as it has come

> ***Permanent Court of International Justice:*** *The first permanent court brought into being by the League of Nations to settle disputes and give advisory opinions. Basically continued after World War II as the International Court of Justice.*

to be known informally, was a major addition to the Hague creation of the Permanent Court of Arbitration. The statute of the court did contain the principle of compulsory jurisdiction. However, the fear of undermining sovereignty led to the development of an optional clause that enabled States to include exceptions that applied reciprocally in disputes with other States. This has severely weakened the concept and is a major source of controversy today.

In Article 16, the covenant provided enforcement action against a State that broke its agreements to keep the peace. A violation of the covenant obligations was to be interpreted as an act of war against all other members. The offending State was to be subjected to immediate total economic and political isolation and the cost shared by all members. The Council, composed of the major powers, was empowered to recommend military sanctions.

The Assembly, composed of all members, was given the following basic functions:

1. Admission of members to the league
2. Control of the budget
3. Selection of nonpermanent members of the Council
4. Formulation of rules concerning the selection and terms of the Council members
5. Consideration of matters referred to it by the Council
6. Instigation of plans for the revision of treaties

The Council, which initially included five permanent members and a minimum of four nonpermanent members, was to include the following basic responsibilities:

7. Conciliation of disputes
8. Expulsion of members who violated the covenant
9. Supervision of the mandates
10. Approval of staff appointments to the Secretariat
11. Authority to move the league headquarters
12. Formulation of plans for disarmament
13. Recommendation of methods for peaceful settlement of disputes and application of sanctions
14. The obligation to meet at the request of any league member to consider any threat to international peace

The United States, Great Britain, France, Italy, and Japan were originally designated permanent members of the Council. Although the U.S. seat was held open, the absence of this important world power left a gap in the practice of the league. Both Germany and the Soviet Union were given permanent member status on the Council. The elected members varied from eight to fifteen during the league's brief twenty-year history.

The Secretariat, like the Assembly, had to establish its own procedures since there was almost a total lack of guidelines in the covenant. Sir Eric Drummond became the first secretary-general of the league and served the initial development of the administrative machinery of the league from 1919 to 1933. The staff persons who became involved in these activities began the process of developing an international corps of civil servants with dedication to principles of service to the purposes of the organization.

The league accomplished much more than its critics have given it credit for. The fact that it could not stop the ultimate development of World War II was not the fault of the organizational structure but of its lack of important members (such as the United States) and the lack of will to enforce its provisions until it was too late to stop World War II. The league machinery was used to hear at least thirty disputes during its first decade, and most of these were resolved satisfactorily.

In the next chapter, we will explore the developments of the twentieth century that ultimately produced a new world order that is struggling to develop the institutions and principles that might satisfy the requirements of a positive law among nations.

Chapter Summary

1. The modern concept of international law is a product of the evolution of the modern nation-state system that originated in Europe only some three to five hundred years ago.

2. International law is not world law but assumes the sovereign equality of States. It was first called *jus gentium* by the Ancient Romans and later became known as the law *among* nations, as opposed to *above* nations.

3. The fundamental postulate of international law, and perhaps all law, is that contractual relationships are legally binding—*pacta sunt servanda*. The duty to observe treaties in good faith has been recognized by State practice from the beginning of recorded history.

4. The concept of natural law can be traced back to Greek Stoic philosophy of the third century B.C. It asserts that natural rules of conduct are inherent in the relations between human beings and discoverable by reason.

5. The concept of *jus gentium* was based on the norms and concepts common to the various groups that composed the Roman Empire. This "law of tribes" was blended with the Greek idea of natural law to govern the relations between Romans and non-Romans during the period of the Roman Empire.

6. *Jus gentium* provided international law with many concepts that most classical writers depended on in developing the theory behind modern international law.

7. The medieval period in Europe was characterized by feudalism and loosely bound together by the Catholic Church and its canon law, which attempted to regulate disputes among the disparate political communities of the era. Church doctrine recognized the concept of "just" and "unjust" war and attempted to mitigate the evils of warfare.

8. Commercial development and intercommunity trade was stimulated by the Crusades and ultimately produced a generally accepted body of commercial law known as the Law Merchant that became a part of the domestic law of most European communities. Codes of domestic admiralty law (maritime regulation) were developed along with many innovations in commercial and financial procedures.

9. Late in the Middle Ages, the Reformation involved the great schism of the Christian Church, splitting the communities of Europe into Protestant and Catholic areas of loyalty that ultimately produced the Thirty Years War.

10. The Peace of Westphalia legitimated the right of sovereigns to govern their peoples free of outside interference based on political, legal, or religious principles. With this fundamental European treaty, the new nation-state system took as its basic postulate the existence of a number of States—secular, national, and territorial.

11. The concept of sovereignty was first formulated in a scholarly sense by Jean Bodin who referred to it as *summa potestas*, or supreme power, which he asserted must be vested in one ultimate dispute-settling authority. To him, sovereignty was the essential element of a nation-state, but it was not considered absolute. It was limited by morality, international law, and constitutional law.

12. Hugo Grotius is generally accepted as the father of modern international law because he explained the emerging principles and practices of the new nation-state in a modern conceptualization that was both farsighted and practical. Grotius was the first writer

to proclaim the concept of freedom of the world's oceans, and he accepted the idea that sovereign equals could inflict penalties, or sanctions, to enforce the law.

13. The modern positivist school of jurisprudence won broad acceptance during the classical period of international law in the nineteenth century, and the concept of nationalism and absolute sovereignty prevailed.

14. The American and French Revolutions proclaimed a new philosophy of self-determination of peoples and "popular sovereignty." In America, it produced a new freedom, but in France and Europe it was associated with the rise of a dangerous form of nationalistic imperialism that resulted in the Napoleonic Wars.

15. The Concert of Europe emerged to subdue Napoleon and institute a balance-of-power system that preserved European peace for nearly a century, but it also accepted, and even promoted, European colonialism throughout the world.

16. The Hague Peace Conferences around the turn of the twentieth century brought nations together in efforts to develop treaty obligations that would promote law development in the abstract. The Permanent Court of Arbitration was created in 1899 to provide a means of peaceful settlement of disputes and impartial fact-finding.

17. In the early part of the twentieth century, public international unions were the first intergovernmental organizations (IGOs) set up on a permanent basis to provide functional services in nonpolitical areas of international concern.

18. These developments did little to prevent the forces of nationalism and German-French rivalry for territory and power in Europe. German ambitions and the development of a rigid alliance system involving the Triple Alliance between Germany, Austria-Hungary, and Italy and an opposing alliance of Britain, France, and Russia increased European tensions.

19. World War I (1914-1918) was caused by mistakes and miscalculations in an atmosphere involving the explosive mixture of rigid alliances, nationalism, mechanistic militarism, and irresponsible leadership.

20. The major parties in the conflict became known as the Central Powers (Germany, Austria-Hungary, and Turkey) and the Allies (Russia, France, Great Britain, Serbia, and later Italy and the United States). The Allies negotiated secret treaties to induce Italy to enter the war against the Central Powers. U.S. neutrality during the first part of the war was ended after Germany resumed unrestricted submarine warfare, after Germany plotted to involve Mexico in the war if the United States joined the Allies, and after news of the Russian Revolution.

21. The Russian Bolsheviks quickly concluded a treaty to end the war on the German eastern front that gave major concessions to the Central Powers.

22. Woodrow Wilson's Fourteen Points were instrumental in bringing about an armistice agreement in 1918. The demoralized German troops and Wilson's refusal to negotiate with imperial autocrats influenced the abdication of the German Kaiser. The Germans agreed to the armistice on the basis of Wilson's promise of "peace with honor" but were saddled with punitive reparations payments and stripped of their colonial possessions in the world and many parts of Europe.

23. The peace settlement carved up the map of Europe and much of the rest of the world. Wilson's principle of "self-determination of peoples" was only partially implemented and was complicated by the secret agreements made during the war.

24. The Covenant of the League of Nations was included as a part of the Treaty of Versailles that concluded the peace settlement with Germany. However, the U.S. Senate refused to ratify the league covenant portion of the treaty, and the separate World Court statute, reverting to a policy of isolation.

25. Most of the world's nations did ratify the Covenant of the League of Nations, which provided a reasonably adequate institutional structure and important new principles of collective security, peaceful settlement of disputes, and a Permanent Court of International Justice. The league system was used to hear at least thirty disputes during its first decade, most of which were resolved satisfactorily. However, the major powers lacked the will to impose the available sanctions against Japanese, Italian, and German aggression before it was too late to prevent World War II.

Key Terms

natural law
jus gentium
pacta sunt servanda
nation-state
Renaissance period
Reformation
canon law
Law Merchant
Peace of Westphalia
sovereignty

Naturalists
Positivists
Grotians
Concert of Europe
Hague Peace Confer-
    ences
Permanent Court of
    Arbitration
intergovernmental
    organizations (IGOs)

Allies
Central Powers
Brest-Litovsk Treaty
Fourteen Points
Covenant of the
    League of Nations
Permanent Court of
    International Justice

▮   ▮   ▮

Discussion Questions

1. How do the concepts of "natural law" and *jus gentium* relate to the development of international law?

2. Are contracts the most fundamental source of law?

3. What developments contributed to the rise of the nation-state out of the feudalism of the Middle Ages?

4. How did the Law Merchant and admiralty law develop and become integrated into the national legal systems of Europe?

5. What is the importance of the Peace of Westphalia (1648) in the development of classical international law? What basic agreement was reached and how did this agreement form the basis of the modern nation-state system?

6. How did the French Revolution alter the international order of Europe and ultimately give rise to the Concert of Europe?

7. What innovations in international law characterized the Hague Peace Conferences around the turn of the century?

8. What functional intergovernmental organizations developed around the turn of the twentieth century? Why were they needed?

9. What were the underlying causes of World War I?

10. How did secret agreements during the war contribute to failure to establish a lasting peace settlement? What major changes in national boundaries in Europe were produced by the peace settlement?

11. What was the basic organizational structure and importance of the League of Nations?

Notes

1. Except in quoted material, the word *State* will be capitalized when it refers to a country or to government of a country and lowercased (*state*) when it refers to a state or government of a state within the United States.

2. "World Court" is an informal usage referring to the combined experience of the Permanent Court of International Justice (under the League of Nations) and the International Court of Justice (under the U.N. Charter).

Suggested Readings

Brierly, J. L. (1963). *The law of nations* (6th ed., H. Waldock, Ed.). New York: Oxford University Press.

Claude, I. L. (1984). *Swords into plowshares* (4th ed.). New York: Random House.

Henkin, L. (1979). *How nations behave: Law and foreign policy* (2nd ed.). New York: Columbia University Press.

Janis, M. W. (1993). *An introduction to international law* (2nd ed.). Boston: Little, Brown.

Stoessinger, J. G. (1974). *Why nations go to war.* New York: St. Martin's.

Tuchman, B. (1962). *The guns of August.* New York: Macmillan.

2 *World War II*

Causes and Effects

The most important underlying causes of World War II were the results of the peace settlement in World War I and the rise of militaristic imperialism among the leaders of Germany, Italy, and Japan. The great test of the League of Nation's ability to settle disputes involving the major powers began in 1931.

Causes of World War II

The Japanese involvement in World War I is often forgotten because she did not take part in the European theater of operations. The Far East had long been the scene of European colonial adventures. The treatment of Asians and other races and nations by Europeans was one of general inequality. Japan was the first Asian nation to gain

their respect as having the social, economic, and organizational potential for status in the European club of nations. Unequal treaties reflecting this European colonialism had been concluded with most nations of the Far East. Reform of the Meiji government in Japan brought diplomatic efforts to secure revision of these unequal treaties. In 1894, Britain agreed to abolish its treaty rights, and others quickly followed.

By the turn of the century, Japan already showed signs of imperialistic designs of its own. She became involved in Korean affairs, where China was a principal rival. In 1894, Japan insisted on pressing its claims to the point of war. In the Treaty of Shimononeki (1895) China was forced to recognize Korean independence and ceded Taiwan to Japan. Only the intercession of Russia, France, and Germany prevented Japan from securing also the Liaodung (Kwantung) Peninsula in southern Manchuria. Rivalry between Russia and Japan became more acute as Japan increased its production of modern armaments and industry. In 1902, an alliance was signed with Britain, marking a new advance in Japan's international standing. The Russo-Japanese War over Korea and Manchuria resulted in a decisive victory for Japan against Czarist Russia. Japan had defeated a European power, which further increased her prestige.

The United States brokered the peace settlement of this conflict, which was signed in Portsmouth, New Hampshire, in 1905. Russia recognized Japan's supremacy in Korea, transferred to Japan Liaodung and Russian rights in south Manchuria, and ceded the southern half of the island of Sakhalin to Japan. These gains gave Japan a paramount position in East Asia that would be extended in the next twenty years. With the outbreak of World War I in 1914, Japan declared war on Germany and seized the German islands in the North Pacific.

Japan also launched an attack on German bases in China's Shantung Province, paving the way for an ultimatum to China in 1915 that sought not only to transfer all former German rights but additional privileges throughout the country. At the Versailles Peace Conference, Japan was a victorious ally but in very precarious company as the only Asian State represented. Although Japan secured for itself all of Germany's Pacific islands and a permanent seat on the League of Nations Council, she was refused formal recognition of wartime gains on the China mainland. She therefore became one of the dissatisfied nations at the peace conference.

Japanese Aggression

The pressure on China continued after the establishment of the League of Nations, and at the Washington Conference of 1921-1922, China recognized Japan's economic interests in Shantung. However, in 1931 Japan launched a series of attacks in Manchuria on the initial pretext of protecting the rights involved in its lease of railway property. With the capture of Mukden, Japan's purpose to take over Manchuria became apparent. Great Britain and France were unwilling to take economic or military action against Japan. The United States was outside the league membership, but she attempted to intervene informally. Secretary of State Simpson did condemn the Japanese for aggression in violation of their treaty obligations, but the response was not effective in deterring the Japanese aggression.

Appeasement and fear of another escalation into world war seemed to reflect the great-power attitudes during this period of reflection on the causes of World War I. The league-sponsored Lytton Commission investigated but arrived nearly seven months after the Mukden incident. By this time, the Japanese had completed their conquest of Manchuria and established their own puppet government, which they promptly named Manchukwo. The Lytton report castigated the Japanese for their military aggression, but no further action was taken to bring about compliance with the Covenant of the League of Nations.

Italian Aggression

Italy had been even more dissatisfied with the peace settlement at Versailles in 1919 and acted aggressively even before the peace talks had finished. The Italians were "latecomers" to European colonialism and development of overseas territories. Fascism was a nationalist movement that sought to create a modern Roman Empire. By early 1934, Mussolini was building up military forces in Eritrea and Italian Somaliland. A serious armed clash occurred at Wal-Wal in Ethiopian territory. Emperor Haile Selassie of Ethiopia requested that the matter be submitted to arbitration under the terms of an earlier treaty with Italy, but Italy responded with demands for an apology and reparations. Ethiopia then appealed to the League of Nations Council, and Italy backed off, agreeing to the proposed arbitral procedure as a delaying tactic.

British and French **appeasement** reflected their fear of Hitler, who was courting the support of Mussolini on the continent. They gave the Italian dictator tacit assurance that they would not unduly interfere with his African ambitions. The League Council delayed while the British and French tried to negotiate an African territorial settlement. Finally, on October 3, 1935, a full-scale invasion of Ethiopia was launched by the Italian forces in Eritrea.

> **Appeasement:**
> Attempt to placate aggression associated with British Prime Minister Chamberlain's agreement with Hitler, known as the Munich Pact, ceding the Sudetenland in Czechoslovakia to Germany before World War II.

The league's response to this invasion was prompt and unprecedented. Within four days, the Council voted unanimously to impose economic sanctions, and possibly military sanctions, branding Italy as the aggressor in violation of the covenant. This was the first collective security decision invoking the provisions of the covenant, and surprisingly, they were to be applied against a major power. Under the voting provisions of the Council, a permanent member of that body could not use its veto in a dispute involving itself as a party. However, the league provisions also required Assembly action to bring Article 16 into effect. The members had interpreted the covenant to allow each State to reserve the right to determine if it would participate in economic sanctions. On October 11, fifty of the fifty-four league members endorsed cooperative economic sanctions against Italian aggression.

These measures nearly worked. Italy was severely affected by the sanctions, which could have been more complete, but again the British and French governments agreed not to push sanctions to the point of risking war. In December of 1935, the British Hoare-Laval proposal shocked public opinion in most of the world by offering to give Italy control of most of Ethiopia. Both Haile Selassie and Mussolini refused the offer. By July 1936, sanctions against Italy were abandoned, and Mussolini assumed the title of emperor of Ethiopia.

German Aggression

Germany was the most dissatisfied of all the participants in World War I. The Germans had signed the Versailles Treaty under protest and felt betrayed by the promised "peace with honor" during the war. The Allies imposed punitive reparations payments, first set in the amount of $33 billion, an astronomical sum, which were later reduced and then canceled. Adolf Hitler gained popular support from the people of Germany by his tirades against the unjust settlement. The economic disasters of rampant inflation and then massive unemployment destroyed the German economy. The lack of experience with democratic institutions and economic ruin contributed to the Nazi rise to power in 1933. Hitler began to restore employment through massive public works programs and an effort to restore German industrial and military power.

By 1936, he was ready to challenge the Allies. He ordered his troops to march into the Rhineland in violation of the Versailles Treaty. His orders were "if met with any resistance, pull back." Not only was there no resistance, the British Hoare-Laval proposal was offered partly out of fear of a German-Italian alliance and was an attempt to keep them apart. In the end, both aggressors were appeased rather than punished.

After the Ethiopian and Rhineland failures of will, the league process of collective control of political conflict disintegrated. Germany met no opposition in taking over Austria and Czechoslovakia. Each State had to find its own way to avoid conflict in the escalation of events that led directly to World War II. Japan invaded China in 1937, and China's pleas before the league were virtually rejected. Ultimately, when Germany invaded Poland in 1939, World War II began.

There was no uncertainty as to the immediate causes of World War II. Germany, Italy, and Japan were deliberate and intentional aggressors bent on imperial territorial conquest by military force. The world's nations finally organized to effect a military defeat of these Axis Powers, as they were now called. The league had reflected a mind-set among the major powers that sought to prevent the causes of World War I, and it had failed to prevent World War II.

World War II began in 1939 with the German invasion of Poland. It was, by far, the most destructive and extensive military conflict in the history of the world. As the war progressed, it involved all the major world powers, and all the smaller States, who enlisted on one side or the other. The major **Axis Powers** were Germany, Italy, and Japan, which formed an aggressive alliance. The Allies became known as the **United Nations**, which were formed to oppose the Axis aggression and violations of international law.

The major theaters of the war were Europe as a whole, eastern and southeastern Asia, Indonesia, the coastal areas of North Africa, the islands of Japan, the North Atlantic, and the island areas of the Central and Southwest Pacific. Some 60 million people perished as a result of this awesome struggle against lawless tyranny. The United States became the recognized leader of the coalition of States, who finally came together to preserve their survival as independent nations and to enforce the basic principles of international law.

Although the United States did not formally enter the war until after the Pearl Harbor attack in 1941, the events during the early stages of the war in Europe made it inevitable that the United States would become involved. After Congress declared war on Japan, the Germans and Italians declared war against the United States. Ultimately, the majority of the Latin American States joined with the Allies and declared war against the three Axis nations. Most of the European nations were already involved. Like the Kaiser and Bismarck before him, Adolf Hitler invaded the low countries, Holland and Belgium, to attack France and bring it to its knees. The British army was forced to evacuate the continent through the tiny port of Dunkirk. Japan had attacked China in 1937 and already occupied major portions of that nation.

By 1941, the major allied nations were the United States, Great Britain and its commonwealth of nations, the USSR, France,

> *Axis Powers:* Principally, Germany, Italy, and Japan, which formed an aggressive alliance before World War II.
>
> *United Nations:* The alliance formed to oppose the Axis Powers, which eventually included forty-six countries committed to disarming the aggressors and enforcing the law.

and China. Even before the war began, the U.S. Department of State, headed by Secretary Cordell Hull, initiated the most concentrated and elaborate study of international organization ever conducted by a government. President Franklin D. Roosevelt and Cordell Hull understood that there would not be a successful conclusion to this war without a clear understanding of its purposes and objectives. The mistakes of World War I must not be repeated.

U.S. foreign policy objectives in the period between the wars had been hampered by the spirit of isolationism that had set in after Woodrow Wilson's presidency. The Great Depression of the 1930s was Roosevelt's principal concern, but he understood that neglect of foreign policy along with the Smoot-Hawley Tariffs, the highest in the nation's history imposed in 1930, had been major factors in the economic problems of the country.

President Roosevelt's progress in persuading Congress to adopt his foreign policy was much more difficult than with his domestic programs. His policies toward Latin America, however, were an exception. The "Good Neighbor Policy" to improve relations with Latin American countries was enthusiastically supported, whereas his belief that the United States should support the collective security efforts of Great Britain and France was generally resisted. The temper of the people at that time favored isolation from the troubles of the world.

The **Monroe Doctrine**, which declared U.S. opposition to any further attempts at European colonization in the Americas after 1823, became the mainstay of U.S. foreign policy and conservative isolationist sentiment. This much-elaborated de-

Monroe Doctrine:
Originally announced by President Monroe in 1823 to oppose any further European colonization in the Americas. It became the cornerstone of American Foreign Policy and isolationist sentiment.

fensive doctrine became an instrument for expanding U.S. influence in the Americas. In 1889-1890, the Union of American Republics was created in Washington before the Spanish-American War. After the war, the United States attempted a brief experiment with colonialism through President Theodore Roosevelt's interpretation of the concept known as the "Roosevelt Corollary to the Monroe Doctrine," announced in 1904. The corollary attempted to convert an essentially defensive doctrine into a unilateral police power to intervene in the internal affairs of Latin American countries. This development had been sharply attacked by the Latin American States, and in the 1930s, the U.S. Department of State worked to reverse this animosity. The Roosevelt Corollary was abandoned in 1936, and the Buenos Aires Treaty was signed, pledging the American States to consultation in the event of a threat to the peace.

Wartime Planning for Peace

World attention was now focused on postwar planning through a series of meetings of the heads of the major allied States or their foreign ministers. Each of these meetings resulted in the signing and proclamation of a document declaring postwar goals. The first of these was the Inter-Allied Declaration, signed in London in June of 1941. Representatives of the British Commonwealth governments (Canada, South Africa, India, Australia, and New Zealand) and the European governments-in-exile pledged their cooperation in working for the elimination of the threat of aggression and in striving for economic and social security for all free peoples.

Two months later, President Roosevelt and Prime Minister Churchill met aboard ship, off Newfoundland, and agreed on the

Atlantic Charter:
Declaration by President
Roosevelt and Prime Minister Churchill on August
14, 1941, summarizing
the common principle underlying the policies of
the two countries concerning the world crisis,
ruling out secret agreements, and defining war
aims.

terms of a document known as the **Atlantic Charter**. Roosevelt was assured that there would be no secret agreements, and a set of common principles, including commitment to disarm the aggressor nations pending a "permanent system of general security," was agreed on. Churchill pushed for wording that involved the establishment of an "effective international organization." During the period from 1940 to 1943, the U.S. State Department's plan for peace took the definite direction of advocating a system of regional organizations until Secretary of State Hull personally intervened in 1943 with his own global preferences (see Bennett, 1988, p. 43).

After the Pearl Harbor attack on the United States, the representatives of twenty-six nations allied against the Axis Powers signed the **Declaration by the United Nations** in Washington D.C. in January of 1942. The use of the term *United Nations* to apply to the combined efforts of these nations began at this point. The signatories subscribed to the principles of the Atlantic Charter as their war-and-peace aims in addition to a pledge of full cooperation and effort in defeating the Axis States. As the war progressed, twenty additional States adhered to the declaration.

Declaration by the United Nations:
Commitment to oppose
Axis aggression, originally signed by twenty-six
countries, joined by another twenty States before the war was over.

Russian Involvement in the War

One of the most perplexing aspects of World War II is the relationship between Adolf Hitler and Joseph Stalin. Before Hitler attacked Poland in 1939, he negotiated a secret agreement with Stalin to divide up Poland and assigned Finland, Estonia, Latvia, Lithuania, and part of Romania to the Soviet sphere of influence. This was a secret protocol added to the nonaggression pact concluded between the two dictators. Nine days later, Hitler invaded Poland, and Great Britain and France declared war on Germany, initiating World War II.

One can only speculate about Stalin's reasons for doing this. He knew Hitler would eventually attack Russia, but perhaps he hoped that his capitalist enemies in Western Europe would exhaust each other in a long and bloody war. He would have more time to prepare for the German invasion, and a weakened Germany would be an easier enemy to deal with later. Hitler wanted to complete his conquest of Western Europe without fear of a two-front war. The **German-Soviet Non-Aggression Pact** placed Russia among the Axis Powers during this first phase of the war.

German-Soviet Non-Aggression Pact: Agreement between Hitler and Stalin, which included a secret protocol to divide up Poland just before World War II began.

What is even more perplexing is why Adolf Hitler attacked Russia on June 22, 1941. German troops had marched through Holland, Belgium, and France in short order. By June 22, 1940, France fell to the German army, signing a compact that left three-fifths of France in German control. The "Battle of Britain" was an intensive air attack in preparation for an invasion of the British Isles called Operation Sea Lion. The objective of the air attack had been to knock out the British air defenses and demoralize the British will to resist. Hitler could have dealt Britain a fatal blow with an invasion, but in a totally unexpected and sudden change of plans, Hitler launched the attack on Russia, code named "Barbarossa."

Professor John G. Stoessinger (1974) offers fascinating insight into the mentality of Adolf Hitler. Among the causes of war, one may find the irrational, as Stoessinger explains: "The key to an understanding of Hitler's invasion of Russia is more likely found in the realm of psychology than in the fields of political science or strategic thought" (p. 33). Hitler's mindless hatred for the Slavic people, and the Jews whom he thought controlled them, is Stoessinger's explanation.

On March 30, 1941, the German dictator assembled his generals in the new Reich chancellery in Berlin and gave them a long speech on the subject of the coming massacre of the Soviet Union. The purpose of the invasion was the total annihilation of Russia. He told his generals that they were to conduct the campaign with merciless harshness, and no quarter would be given. Breaches of international law would be excused since Russia had not participated in the Hague Conference and thus had no rights under it. Soviet commissars who surrendered were to be executed. In conclusion, Hitler stated, "I do not expect my generals to understand me, but I shall expect them to obey my orders" (Payne, 1973, p. 419). Five years later at the Nuremberg trials, several generals confessed that they had been horrified by the "Commissar Order" but had lacked the courage to object.

During the final weeks before Barbarossa was to go into effect, Hitler indulged in fantasies of what he would do to the hated Russians:

In a few weeks we shall be in Moscow, there is absolutely no doubt about it. I will raze this damned city to the ground and I will make an artificial lake to provide energy for an electric power station. The name of Moscow will vanish forever. (Payne, 1973, p. 431)

The irony of this irrational decision to annihilate Russia was that this campaign failed to heed the lessons of Napoleon and others who had met their doom in the snows of Russia. So certain of victory were the German soldiers that they came in light uniforms with no provisions to cope with the Russian winter. Hitler had named his attack Barbarossa after the crusader of the Holy Roman Empire who had failed in his mission to the East and drowned. To compound the irony, he had launched the campaign on the exact anniversary of Napoleon's invasion of Russia in 1812.

Including Russia in the Peace Plans

Russia now became allied with the United Nations, and, on October 30, 1943, the foreign ministers of the USSR, Great Britain, the United States, and the Chinese ambassador to the Soviet Union met in Moscow. At the **Moscow Conference** these States pledged their efforts to establish a general international organization "based on the principle of sovereign equality of all peace-loving states, and open to membership by all such states, large and small, for the maintenance of international peace and security."

> *Moscow Conference:* Secured commitment of Great Britain, the USSR, China, and the United States to establish a general organization to maintain peace and security (1943.)

One month later, President Roosevelt, Premier Stalin, and Prime Minister Churchill met in Teheran. They issued in their final communiqué the results of the **Teheran Conference**, which included the following statement:

> *Teheran Conference:* Personal commitment of Stalin, Churchill, and Roosevelt to the establishment of a United Nations Organization (1943).

We recognize fully the supreme responsibility resting upon us and all the United Nations to make a peace which will command the goodwill of the overwhelming masses of the peoples of the world and banish the scourge and terror of war for many generations. . . . We shall seek the cooperation and active participation of all nations large and small . . . [for] the elimination of tyranny and slavery, oppression and intolerance. We will welcome them, as they choose to come, into a family of Democratic Nations.

The United Nations Charter

Clearly, the cornerstone of the new **United Nations Charter** was to establish the change in a fundamental norm of international law that had been building an international consensus since World War I and the Covenant of the League of Nations. The United States became a party accepting, and promoting, this change with the **Kellogg-Briand Pact** of 1928. The Kellogg-Briand Pact outlawed war as an instrument of national policy. It was ratified by all the major powers, including the United States, Germany, and Japan, and was used as the basis for the trial of German and Japanese individuals accused of war crimes (see Chapter 14 for more elaboration.) Now it became the keystone of the new organization. Article 2(4) of the charter provides the following specific wording, which is a more refined formulation of this basic new norm of international law:

> **United Nations Charter:** *Basic constitutional document creating the United Nations Organization and defining the powers of its major organs.*

> **Kellogg-Briand Pact:** *A multilateral treaty renouncing war as an instrument of national policy. Also known as the Pact of Paris, this treaty included sixty-three parties prior to the outbreak of World War II.*

All members shall refrain in their international relations from the threat or use of force against the territorial integrity or political independence of any state, or in any other manner inconsistent with the purposes of the United Nations.

The only exception was expressed in Article 51:

Nothing in the present Charter shall impair the inherent right of individual or collective self-defense if an armed attack occurs against a member of the Organization, until the Security Council has taken the measures necessary to maintain international peace and security.

Unlike the limited restraints of the Covenant of the League of Nations and the provisions of the Kellogg-Briand Pact, the U.N. Charter's prohibition against unilateral force was to apply universally. Members were bound by it, and they were to see to it that nonmembers also complied as expressed in Article 2(6).

The legal term **norm** refers to a fundamental concept issued by competent legal authority that forms the objects described by rules of law. The customary acceptance of the use of force unilaterally had now been replaced with a nearly universal treaty that prohibited such use, or threat, of force. This provision of the charter contains its truly lawmaking character.

> **Norm:** *Fundamental standard established by competent legal authority defining legal duty and responsibility.*

Hans Kelsen (1967, pp. 8-9) makes the distinction between a norm and **rules of law**. A norm is the fundamental concept

> **Rules of law:** *As opposed to a norm, rules of law are sets of logical consequences involved in the practical application of the fundamental norm.*

around which rules of law are developed to implement or grant exceptions in practice. Courts have always had to contend with questions of application of fundamental norms in practice. This distinction between law and the science of law, between legal norms and rules of law, is fundamental according to Kelsen. The norms issued by the lawmaking authority are subject to application through rules of law applied in practice to a situation involving a given set of facts. The U.N. Charter makes the Security Council, not the World Court, the essential fact-finding and rule application body, but the prohibition against unilateral force establishes the legal norm that if aggression occurs, sanctions "ought" to take place.

This fundamental norm change in international law was agreed to by the major powers before the actual work of the San Francisco Conference (discussed later) began. It was the "ought" concept around which all subsequent debate would revolve, and it became self-evident that this new norm, and building the functional capacity to enforce it, was the purpose of the efforts of the United Nations Organization.

Major-Power Planning

At an extensive estate in the Georgetown section of Washington D.C. called **Dumbarton Oaks**, the major powers conducted high-level negotiations to coordinate their positions concerning the calling of a general conference to draft the actual wording of the charter. From August to October of 1944, these delicate negotiations involving the United States, the USSR, Great Britain, France, and China were conducted. It was agreed that

> **Dumbarton Oaks:**
> Conference held in 1944 to coordinate major-power agreement on issues involving the United Nations Organization.

these "Big Five" would be permanent members of the Security Council with veto power similar to that of the Council of the League of Nations. Three other organs were agreed to in this preliminary draft, which included the General Assembly, the Secretariat, and a court. A commission of international jurists would be created to make recommendations concerning the issues involving the court. However, at this point there was no provision for a Trusteeship Council, and the Economic and Social Council was to be subordinate to the General Assembly.

At Dumbarton Oaks, the areas of disagreement involved the important voting formula in the Security Council and issues of membership of constituent republics of the Soviet Union. The Soviet Union insisted on an unlimited veto privilege for the permanent members of the council and requested individual membership for all her sixteen union republics on the basis of their constitutional autonomy. Other unsettled issues included the nature of the International Court, whether a new court should be constructed or a continuation of the Permanent Court of Justice authorized, and arrangements for transition from the League of Nations to the new organization.

In February of 1945, Roosevelt, Churchill, and Stalin met at Yalta, in the Crimea, to discuss a wide range of subjects relating to the war and postwar plans. The **Yalta Conference** has been the subject of much debate. Winston Churchill was not pleased with the results on many issues. He felt that Roosevelt had been too willing to support some of Stalin's demands concerning postwar Europe and what to do with Germany after the war. Roosevelt clearly appeared to side with Stalin on these issues in

> **Yalta Conference:**
> Personal commitment and agreement reached by Stalin, Churchill, and Roosevelt in 1945 concerning postwar planning.

a deliberate effort to keep the Russians committed to cooperation after the war.

On the issues involving the United Nations Organization, the Security Council voting formula that was agreed on excluded the use of the permanent members' veto on procedural matters. It was clearly agreed that a permanent member must abstain from voting in that body when it was asked to consider a dispute involving that member as a party. This would exclude a major power from being able to veto action against itself. Stalin accepted this position on the voting formula partly in exchange for a concession on multiple membership for the Soviet Union republics of the Ukraine and Belorussia along with the USSR as members of the General Assembly. Roosevelt anticipated difficulty in gaining acceptance of such a concession at home and held out the possibility of asking for similar multiple membership for the United States. The Big Three (the United States, the USSR, and Great Britain) did agree to issue invitations to a conference to be held at San Francisco beginning on April 25, 1945, and that the United States would issue the invitations.

This was another departure from the League of Nations experience in that the charter conference would be held during the final stages of the war, before any armistice was declared, while the peak of cooperative sentiment was strongest, and it would be divorced from the specific issues of what to do with Germany, Italy, and Japan after the war. Germany surrendered during the San Francisco Conference, and Japan did not surrender until two months after the drafting conference had completed its work.

The Big Three also reached agreement on the essential principles of the trusteeship concept in the U.N. Charter. No territories were to be specifically designated as trust territories until after the San Francisco Con-

ference, but the three categories to which trusteeship would apply were (a) existing mandates under the League of Nations, (b) territories detached from the enemy as a result of the present war, and (c) any other territory voluntarily placed under trusteeship. There was to be further consultation with the sponsoring States prior to the San Francisco Conference.

The smaller Latin American States expressed their concern about these major-power agreements even before the official drafting conference. The Latin American States were meeting in Mexico City during the time period of the Yalta Conference, and Secretary of State Stettinius traveled directly from Yalta to Mexico City to chair the U.S. delegation. The Inter-American Conference on Problems of Peace and War issued a list of several suggestions for change, including (a) stress on universality of membership, (b) amplification of the powers and role of the General Assembly, (c) expansion of the jurisdiction and competence of the International Court, (d) an expanded role for regional organizations within the general framework and (e) adequate representation of Latin America on the Security Council. They were, as yet, unaware of the voting formula agreements at Yalta, but their attitudes gave notice of battles to come at San Francisco (see Bennett, 1988, pp. 46-47).

The San Francisco Conference

This historic gathering of all forty-six States that had declared war on one or more of the Axis Powers convened at the **San Francisco Conference** at the end of April, 1945. At the U.N. Conference on International Organization (UNCIO), delegates hammered out detailed wording of the original U.N. Charter,

> **San Francisco Conference:** *Formally, the U.N. Conference on International Organization (UNCIO), which actually drafted the U.N. Charter in 1945.*

which was subsequently amended in 1965 to expand the Security Council from its original eleven members to fifteen.

The issue of multiple representation for the two Soviet constituent republics was decided by agreement of the original participants at the conference. In this manner, Argentina, Belorussia, the Ukraine, and Denmark were added to the roster of participants. The Soviet Union's request to include the provisional government of Poland at the conference was refused, but Poland was allowed to adhere to the U.N. Charter as an original member.

This enormous conference of fifty States, represented by 282 official delegates and more than 1,400 delegation advisers and staff members, was confronted with problems of size, organization, communications, and national pride and prestige as well as the main task of reconciling conflicting positions among States. A secretariat of more than 1,000 professional staff and 4,000 secretaries, translators, and other assisting personnel was provided by the host country, the United States. English and French were adopted as the working languages of the conference, but Russian, Chinese, and Spanish were accepted as official languages.

At San Francisco, the small States, led by H. V. Evatt of Australia, made their most concerted attack on the voting formula in the Security Council. The small and medium States objected to the deviation from the principle of sovereign equality in the privileged position of the five permanent members of the Security Council and the lack of clarity concerning the application of the veto in specific situations. The major powers, led by the U.S. delegation, vigorously defended the veto concept and the purposes of the five permanent members. It is reported that Senator Connally (D-Texas) who was a U.S. delegate, at a dramatic moment, tore up a copy of the proposed charter, announcing that "without the veto there would be no charter." The smaller States had to accept this prior agreement of the Big Five powers, but other areas of compromise gave important concessions to the smaller States.

At the small States' insistence, four of the major powers issued a statement clarifying their interpretation of the voting formula, which listed several matters that would be regarded as procedural issues, not subject to the veto. However, "procedural issues" were not completely defined, and they admitted that there would be a possibility for a "double veto" in situations not covered in which dispute existed as to whether or not the issue was substantive or procedural. These unspecified issues would be settled by a substantive vote. Clearly, procedural matters could be decided by any seven of the original eleven Security Council members. Thus, the major powers agreed to limit their authority and substantially reduce the potential use of the double veto. In general, the major powers have regarded their published statement in San Francisco to be as binding as the U.N. Charter (see Bennett, 1988, p. 48).

Although the small States were unsuccessful in removing the veto power from the process for amending the charter, there were some concessions concerning the method of calling for a conference to propose amendments. Ratification of all proposed **charter amendments** still require the potential veto of all permanent members of the Security Council and a two-thirds majority of all members in the General Assembly.

> *Charter amendments:* Require Security Council approval to which the major-power veto applies, and a two-thirds vote of the General Assembly is required.

Article 51 (self-defense) reflected the small States' insistence that regional organizations must be given a role in cases in which

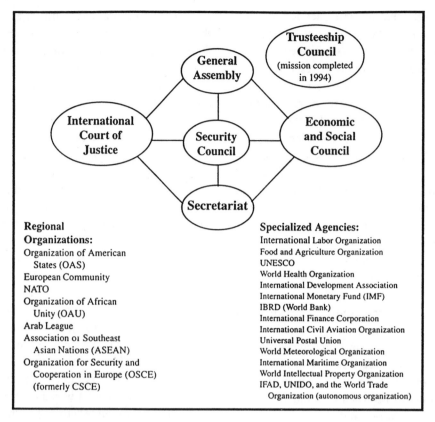

Figure 2.1. The United Nations System

the Security Council was immobilized. The small States also won important concessions in regard to the **Trusteeship Council**. The charter added two lengthy chapters on the trusteeship system, including creation of an independent council that was given major-organ status. The **Economic and Social Council** was also given a similar rank, increasing the number of major organs from the four suggested by the great powers at Dumbarton Oaks, to the six included in the charter. These six organs have coordinating functions under the charter umbrella, but they are also given a certain degree of independence and autonomy in their spheres of authority.

The following diagram (Figure 2.1) provides an overview of the basic institutions of the United Nations system.

The entire Chapter XI, dealing with non-self-governing territories, was the most important achievement of the small States at San Francisco. Wilson's concept of "self-determination of peoples" was given its most specific expression in this section of the U.N. Charter. Chapter XI has been regarded as the "Bill of Rights" for all politically dependent peoples. The charter requires that all "Members of the United Nations which have assumed responsibili-

Trusteeship Council: Major organ of the United Nations created to ensure self-determination of dependent peoples under the former League of Nations mandates.

Economic and Social Council: Major organ of the United Nations created to coordinate social, cultural, economic, educational, health, and human rights programs.

ties for the administration of territories whose peoples have not yet attained a full measure of self-government recognize the principle that the interests of the inhabitants of these territories are paramount." It recognizes the "sacred trust" of the colonial powers to advance the inhabitants' political, social, and educational welfare and to submit regular reports to the secretary-general on these conditions in the territories under their authority.

This concept of self-determination is still vague and not clearly defined, but issues of self-determination of peoples assumed the highest priority among the smaller and medium States. In 1960, the General Assembly declared that all dependent peoples have a right to independence and self-determination.

The charter made special reference to the concept of promoting respect for and observance of human rights and fundamental freedoms. The powers and functions of the Economic and Social Council included the drafting of conventions and calling for international conferences within its own area of competence. These developments also reflect the influence of the smaller States at the drafting conference. They succeeded in strengthening the General Assembly, the Secretariat, and the **International Court of Justice.**

> *International Court of Justice:*
> New name given to the World Court in the U.N. Charter. The court was strengthened by making it one of the six major organs of the U.N. system.

The new Statute of the International Court of Justice was nearly identical to that of the Permanent Court of International Justice and represented more continuity than change. The major change from the League of Nations developments was that the U.N. Charter specifically incorporated the court into the United Nations, giving it the status of one of the six functional organs. The members of the organization are automatically parties to the court's statute. However, nonmembers may adhere to the statute separately.

Article 94 of the U.N. Charter requires compliance with the decisions of the court by parties in dispute before it, and parties are given recourse to the Security Council, "which may, if it deems necessary, make recommendations or decide upon measures to be taken to give effect to the judgment." The General Assembly or the Security Council may request advisory opinions of the court on any legal question, and other organs may do likewise through the General Assembly. The "optional clause," permitting reservations concerning compulsory jurisdiction of the court, however, remains an impediment.

The new structure of the international organization that replaced the League of Nations was in essence an elaborated version of the old organization. Increased clarity of significant norm changes was added, and a new emphasis placed on self-determination of peoples established. The extensive planning and involvement in the process of drafting the charter gave consideration to the diverse interests of existing nations, large and small. This process took advantage of the wartime cooperation of most of the nations of the world and was separated from the peace settlements ending the war. In contrast with the experience of the League of Nations, the United States was the first nation to ratify the new document. The Senate vote was 82 to 2, reflecting a clear consensus in the United States that U.S. citizens would accept their international leadership obligations in the new world order. Ratification by all five of the permanent members of the Security Council and a majority of the other signatories, the charter requirements to make the change, were ac-

TABLE 2.1   Original Members of the United Nations Organization, 1945

Americas	Europe	Asia/Oceana	Africa
Argentina	Belgium	Australia	Egypt
Bolivia	Belorussia (Belarus)	China (Taiwan until 1971;	Ethiopia
Brazil	Czechoslovakia (split in 1993)	People's Republic of China	Liberia
Canada	Denmark	now seated)	South Africa
Chile	France	India	
Colombia	Greece	Iran	
Costa Rica	Luxembourg	Iraq	
Cuba	Netherlands	Lebanon	
Dominican Republic	Norway	New Zealand	
Ecuador	Poland	Philippines	
El Salvador	Turkey	Saudi Arabia	
Guatemala	Ukraine	Syria	
Haiti	USSR (until 1991; now the		
Honduras	Russian Federation)		
Mexico	United Kingdom		
Nicaragua	Yugoslavia (split in 1992)		
Panama			
Paraguay			
Peru			
United States			
Uruguay			
Venezuela			

complished by October 24, 1945 (see Table 2.1).

The 50th anniversary of the United Nations Organization was celebrated in 1995. Many important developments have taken place in the half century of the organization's existence. These developments reflect both the failures and the promising potential for the development of a more effective international legal order. Although public opinion seems to expect far more than the current international structure, and the willingness of independent States, can deliver, it is generally conceded that such an organization is indispensable in the modern world.

The U.N. Charter represents the basic constitutional structure of the international legal community. It creates a framework for consideration of problems that affect the community of nations; it does not solve these problems. Only the interaction of nation-states, influenced by considerations of their own interests and values, can produce solutions to these problems. The charter provisions make it possible to pursue these goals through peaceful means and establish procedures for reacting to aggression.

The rest of this book will draw on the half century of legal development that has taken place within the framework of the U.N. Charter and the underlying principles of the historical development of the nation-state system. Later chapters will discuss the current norms and rules of law in various areas of concern, and the application of these principles will be illustrated. However, the rest of this chapter will be devoted to an attempt to analyze the effects of the historical development of the United Nations Organization. The broader concept of the United Nations system illustrates the dynamic process of change in international law that is taking place.

One of the basic conceptual problems involved in any analysis of the international community is that we have developed a mind-set that assumes a goal of movement toward a governmental entity analogous to that of the nation-state itself. Hence, sovereignty and authority to create law by majority rule, at least in representative assemblies, appear as unconscious goals, and we are disappointed when we find that these principles do not apply in regard to the world community. Therefore, it is difficult to understand how law can be developed and changed in a society characterized by separate and sovereign nation-states.

Since there is no universal international legislative authority intended in the U.N. Charter, the system must depend on the traditional mechanisms of international law development by treaty consent or implied consent in the historical practices of States regarded as legally binding. The General Assembly is therefore not a legislative body but serves a similar purpose in that it is authorized to encourage the "progressive development of international law and its codification" (Chapter IV, Article 13).

The basic norms of international law are relatively few and have been developed over many years of experience that demonstrate the mutually advantageous qualities of these basic norms. Through the collective efforts of many of the established international agencies, and particularly the U.N. General Assembly, these general norms have been codified through multilateral treaties that seek to clarify these principles. This is a slow and cumbersome process, but it can lead to significant change in the content of the legal norms over time.

In a rapidly changing world, new problems require the establishment of international standards for acceptable response on the part of the individual State. Agreement does not have to be universal; individual States may negotiate bilateral or multilateral treaty obligations concerning the regulation of these situations. The individual State is also affected by emerging international standards of expected behavior, and most States have changed their internal laws to approach these international standards. Regional organizations have further increased the influence of other nations on individual States, and this has led to significant innovation in regional characteristics of international law.

The underlying social, economic, and political problems that nations face in the modern world are the primary stimulus to international legal cooperation. Creating legal obligations and better methods of dispute settlement is the result of diplomacy and the desire to solve conflict situations through mutually satisfactory agreements.

The purposes of the U.N. system, as stated in the charter, are really quite modest. They are listed in Article 1 of the charter and include the following: (a) to maintain international peace and security, (b) to develop friendly relations among nations, (c) to achieve international cooperation, and (d) to be a center for harmonizing the actions of nations. These are the minimal conditions within which mature nations with responsible leadership can conduct their affairs without resorting to military intimidation or aggressive use of force.

The Practical Effects of the U.N. System

The U.N. system, and the nations that compose it, has not only accomplished its stated purposes, it has moved far beyond these original purposes in dealing with problems not envisioned by the charter framers. Indeed, the U.N. system has undergone a metamorphic change that in many ways reflects the vast social, economic, and technological changes in the world community of nations. The norms established by the charter have resulted in placing substantial restrictions on the use of force in international politics. This is true, not because of any paper provisions of the charter but because nations have acted to enforce these rules through the development of innovative collective security measures.

Collective Security

The U.N. Charter does not promise an end to warfare and human suffering; it promises an effective collective security system. This promise has been in doubt for the past half century. The advent of the Cold War shortly after the end of World War II led to a much diminished set of expectations concerning the system envisioned by the charter framers, which required the cooperation of the major powers. Extensive use of the Security Council veto by the Soviet Union frustrated efforts to build an effective U.N. military force that could guarantee this type of collective security. However, the Cold War balance-of-power system involving a bipolarity of alliance systems did function to prevent World War III in a precarious "balance of terror." Nuclear weapons and fear of escalation to nuclear war averted major catastrophe, but the U.N. system also continued to function as a moderating force. The ideological tension between capitalist and communist countries contributed to many armed conflicts that were also moderated by the forces of law, reason, diplomacy, and prudence.

In contrast to the end of World War I, no peace treaty was concluded with Germany after World War II. The Cold War prevented agreement among the Allies concerning the postwar status of Germany. That country was divided into Soviet, British, French, and U.S. occupation zones, and Berlin was given a special status of joint occupation by these allied powers immediately after the war. Berlin was in the middle of the Soviet occupation zone, 100 miles from the occupation zones of the Western Powers. Soviet violations of agreements made at Yalta and Potsdam in 1945 were the first indications of Cold War tensions. It became evident that freely elected governments in the Eastern European countries would be denied by Soviet communist dictatorship. Communist governments were created in Hungary and Czechoslovakia in violation of Allied agreements. Shortly thereafter, the Soviets declared a blockade of access through their occupation zone in Germany to supply Berlin. The United States reacted with the Berlin Airlift to maintain vital supplies to the people of that important city.

As early as 1946, Winston Churchill had warned that an "iron curtain" was descending "from Stettin in the Baltic to Trieste in the Adriatic." President Harry Truman reacted to the threatened communist takeover of Greece and Turkey by announcing the Truman Doctrine of aid and assistance to these countries. The Marshall Plan for reconstruction of Europe included aid to West Germany. George F. Kennan's recommended **containment policy** began to formulate a general response to these developments by creation of a series of military alliance systems, including the North Atlantic Treaty Organization (NATO), the Southeast Asia Treaty Organization (SEATO), and the Central Treaty Organiza-

> *Containment policy:* Major Cold War strategy of U.S. foreign policy. It involved a series of military alliances to contain communist aggression.

tion (CENTO). The Soviets countered with the Warsaw Pact, a similar military alliance in Eastern Europe.

In the Far East, Soviet expansion into Manchuria and the northern half of Korea took place just before the surrender of Japan. Attempts to come to some agreement concerning Korea were unsuccessful. In 1947, the United States first submitted the question to the General Assembly. The assembly adopted a resolution providing for election of a Korean National Assembly to be conducted under the surveillance of the U.N. Temporary Commission on Korea. This resolution required prompt withdrawal of the Soviet and U.S. forces from Korea when such a unified government was established. The U.N. commission was refused access to North Korea, and the government of South Korea, south of the 38th parallel, was recognized by the General Assembly as the only legitimate government in Korea. A second commission, created in 1948, reported in 1949 that U.S. forces had been withdrawn from South Korea but could not verify the claims of Soviet withdrawal from the North. On June 25, 1950, North Korean forces launched a large-scale invasion across the 38th parallel into South Korea.

The Security Council was promptly convened to respond to this attack. A Soviet boycott of the Security Council existed at the time, in protest against the refusal of that body to seat the Chinese communist government at the United Nations, but the council was nonetheless determined to act. The de facto takeover of mainland China in 1949 created a dispute over which Chinese government was entitled to the permanent seat for China in the Security Council. With the Soviet Union absent and the Nationalist Chinese representative still seated in the Security Council, that body adopted three crucial resolutions. Absence from the council was interpreted as an abstention, and therefore no veto was cast. The first resolution declared the armed attack by North Korean forces a breach of the peace and called for the cessation of hostilities and withdrawal of North Korean forces. The second resolution recommended that member States assist the Republic of Korea in repelling the attack and in restoring international peace and security in the area. A final resolution authorized a unified command using the U.N. flag and requested the United States to designate a commander and organize the combined forces.

The Soviet Union then returned to take its seat in the Security Council and began exercising its veto in that body. The General Assembly reacted to this situation by adopting the **Uniting for Peace Resolution** in November of 1950. This resolution provides a means of calling an emergency special session of the General Assembly within twenty-four hours whenever the Security Council is deadlocked and "fails to exercise its primary responsibility for maintenance of international peace and security in any case where there appears to be a threat to the peace, breach of the peace, or act of aggression." Emergency sessions of the assembly can be called by any nine (at that time seven) members of the Security Council or by a majority of the U.N. members.

> *Uniting for Peace Resolution:* General Assembly resolution that assumes a role in recommending actions to maintain international peace and security. It provides a means for calling special sessions of the General Assembly within twenty-four hours.

The General Assembly's actions, however, are in the nature of recommendations that member States act. This body does not have the authority to order action as is possessed by the Security Council in the U.N. Charter. Nonetheless, the General Assembly has been involved in many other actions in the field of peace and security. It authorized peacekeeping forces and effectively brought about a withdrawal of French and British forces from the Suez Canal in 1956, and it branded the People's Republic of China as an aggressor in Korea. The Korean War resulted in the restoration of the *status quo ante;* that is, the North Korean invasion was repulsed, leaving a divided Korea with hostile forces poised on each side of a demilitarized zone along the 38th parallel.

Cold War tensions mounted as first West and then East Germany and a divided Korea became frozen in place. Austria, however, was granted independence in 1955 through an agreement among the Allies, including the Soviet Union. Yugoslavia, under the leadership of Marshall Tito, was able to break away from the dictates of the Soviet Union in 1948 and pursued its own brand of communism. In Indochina, the French attempted to restore their colonial domination of the area after the war but were confronted with a determined Vietminh communist insurgency. A humiliating defeat at Dien Bien Phu, in Vietnam, brought the French to a peace conference at Geneva in 1954. The Geneva Conference of mid-1954 and the formulation, a few weeks later, of the Southeast Asia Treaty Organization (SEATO) marked the end of French military and the beginning of a U.S. military presence in Indochina.

The **Geneva Conference** resulted in several agreements to cease hostilities in Indochina and to establish three independent sovereign States: Laos, Cambodia, and Vietnam. The accords on Vietnam provided for a "provisional military demarcation line" at the 17th parallel. Vietminh forces were to regroup

> **Geneva Conference:**
> Or Geneva Accords of 1954, which relinquished French domain in Indochina, creating Laos, Cambodia, and Vietnam. It provided for general elections in Vietnam and a "provisional military demarcation line" at the 17th parallel.

north of the line, and the forces of the French Union were to regroup to the south. The line was to have military significance only, and the political unification of Vietnam was to be brought about by a general election two years later under the supervision of a neutral three-power International Control Commission consisting of Canada, India, and Poland.

The United States was not a party to the Geneva Accords but pledged to abide by them and to view any violation of them with great concern. The U.S. **SEATO** alliance system, including Australia, France, New Zealand, Pakistan, the Philippine Republic, Thailand, the United Kingdom, and the United States, was concluded in 1955. The agreement included an additional protocol in which these eight members designated the States of Cambodia, Laos, and "the free territory under the jurisdiction of the State of Vietnam" to be under SEATO protection.

> **SEATO:** A military alliance that included Australia, France, New Zealand, Pakistan, the Philippines, Thailand, the United Kingdom, and the United States. It involved a U.S. protocol that included South Vietnam under its protection.

The Vietminh, in the North under the leadership of Ho Chi Minh, regarded SEATO as a clear violation of the Geneva Accords, and South Vietnam, with U.S. encouragement, refused to allow the elections promised at Geneva. President Diem, in South Vietnam, declared in July of 1955 that since South Vietnam had not signed the Geneva Accords, he was not prepared to permit elections under the conditions specified by them. The situation gradually worsened as the fighting in South Vietnam escalated. Both sides contended that the Geneva agreements were violated. President Eisenhower sent in military advisers, and by 1960, almost 1,000 U.S. citizens were serving in South Vietnam in that capacity. During John F. Kennedy's brief 1,000 days in office, U.S. involvement deepened.

President Lyndon Johnson had already become personally committed to the war in Vietnam before he became president. In March of 1965, Johnson authorized massive combat troops to the war in Vietnam. After the famous Gulf of Tonkin incident, which presumably involved an attack on U.S. vessels in international waters, the United States authorized a large-scale operation ultimately involving more than half a million U.S. troops. This series of developments placed the United States on the side of what the rest of the world regarded as neocolonialism. There was little attempt to seek U.N. approval for this action, and its members were deeply divided on the issue. Lacking moral support for its actions in the international community, and facing growing dissent within the United States, Johnson refused even to be nominated by his party for a second term. The war dragged on into the Nixon presidency and ultimately ended with U.S. withdrawal. Vietnam became unified under communist Vietminh control.

In the 1980s, the Soviet Union had a similar experience in Afghanistan, where the opposing major power was also forced to admit its mistake and withdrew. Most of the conflicts of the Cold War were internal civil war situations with outside involvement that threatened to escalate the conflict. The United Nations was forced to take a backseat.

However, U.N. developments that would provide important changes were taking place. One of the most persistent problems affecting the stalemate in the Security Council was refusal to recognize the de facto change of governments in China. Refusal to recognize the People's Republic of China persisted for twenty years. In 1971, President Richard Nixon's new China policy led to a dramatic shift at the United Nations. The U.S. position favored a "two-China policy," but this was defeated at the United Nations, and the major organs agreed to treat this issue as merely one of credentials. The People's Republic of China replaced the nationalist government on Taiwan in 1971 at the United Nations.

This development has led progressively to a more open China that is able to cooperate with the other permanent members in the Security Council on a number of issues. More recently, in the post-Cold War era, China's abstention on crucial votes has demonstrated a willingness to cooperate in actions to maintain international peace and security.

During the Cold War, the United Nations remained active in building the conditions for a more effective collective security system. On the periphery of strategic Cold War confrontations, Secretary-General Dag Hammarskjöld and the international community began to fashion a response in the form of limited **peacekeeping operations.** Peacekeeping missions came to be defined as the use of observer teams or military units composed mainly of forces from medium-sized neutral nations, such as the Netherlands, Canada, Norway, and Sweden, acting as a buffer between opposing military forces to police cease-fire agreements and to reduce escalation of the conflict. Peacekeeping forces, as opposed to observer teams, were used in the Egyptian-Israeli conflict, the Congo, Cyprus, and Lebanon, before the end of the Cold War.

> *Peacekeeping operations:* Innovative U.N. missions involving observer teams and military units to act as a buffer between opposing military forces to maintain cease-fire agreements and encourage negotiated settlements.

At the height of the Cold War tensions, however, there was indication that both the

Soviet Union and the United States accepted "spheres of influence" where each was relatively free to take military action. Examples of these situations included the suppression of independence movements in Hungary and Czechoslovakia in the 1960s by the Soviet Union and the invasion of the Dominican Republic (1960s), the Cuban Missile crisis in 1962, and the use of force in Grenada and Panama in the 1980s by the United States. A similar sphere of influence seemed to be operative with regard to China's extension of control over Tibet in the 1970s and India's absorption of the tiny Portuguese colony of Goa.

This period of accepted "spheres of influence" was the period of greatest weakness of the U.N. system, and some observers even declared Article 2(4) dead (Franck, 1970). Louis Henkin (1971) ably defended the potential for revival of the system to restore the basic norm of the charter. During the Cold War, few conflicts clearly fit the specific definition of Article 2(4) of the U.N. Charter, as aggressive wars of territorial aggrandizement. Only the conflict over Kashmir, between India and Pakistan (1947, 1965, and 1971), and the war between Iran and Iraq in the 1980s would meet this strict definition. In 1990, a new opportunity for collective security action through the Security Council developed. The astounding events involving the breakup of the Soviet Union in 1989 and the massive revolts in Eastern European countries led finally to a peace settlement in Europe. East and West Germany were unified, and a comprehensive peace settlement to World War II fixed the borders of Germany and Poland. Restructuring in the former Soviet Empire led to the composition of a Security Council that now might function as it was originally intended.

Iraq's invasion of Kuwait offered the clearest example of territorial aggression since the events at the beginning of World War II. A member nation of the United Nations had been attacked and occupied by the forces of Iraq, led by Saddam Hussein. The Security Council acted in an unprecedented employment of all the sanctions included in the charter, except ousting Iraq from the United Nations, to affect implementation of the provisions of Chapter VII. The Iraqi action was condemned, and a strict military blockade soon escalated to full authorization of military action to remove Iraqi forces from Kuwait. The lightening speed with which this was accomplished astounded the world and demonstrated that major-power cooperation could be effective in the post-Cold War era.

In February of 1991, President George Bush declared that a "new world order" had begun—in which the United Nations would fulfill the vision of its founders and "respect for human rights [would] find a home among all nations" ("Address to Joint Session of Congress," 1991, p. 162). The Cold War could now be considered finally over. The most important result of the Cold War is that it remained "cold," and World War III has been averted. There are still very dangerous situations in the world today, but the potential for worldwide military conflict has been greatly diminished. Perhaps nuclear weapons and advanced technology have contributed to this successful outcome. The nuclear age, the emergence of nuclear parity between the East and West during the Cold War, and the awesome destructive capability of modern warfare have worked to keep conflicts contained and to promote restraint.

Expansion of Self-Determination

The concept of self-determination of peoples included in the U.N. Charter has had, perhaps, an equally far-reaching effect on the emerging character of the international community. Winston Churchill is reported to have refused to preside over the liquidation of the British Empire, but his successors have, however reluctantly, done so. There are no colonial empires today, including the former Soviet Empire. The fifty-one States (including Poland) that became original members of the United Nations Organization in 1945 no longer characterize the world community of nations. By 1965, the constituent membership of the organization had doubled, and by 1985 it had tripled (see Tables 2.2 and 2.3). By the end of the century, the number of members may approach four times the original membership. The Trusteeship Council has now discharged its basic responsibilities under the charter. However, it may find a new function in the post-Cold War era in administering failed States.

These developments have profound implications for the future, and already they have changed the original European character of the content of international law. The U.N. Charter provides that new States admitted to **membership in the United Nations** require the approval of the General Assembly after recommendation by the Security Council, where the major-power veto counts.

> *Membership in the United Nations:*
> Requires General Assembly approval after recommendation by the Security Council, where major-power veto may be exercised.

The Rise of the Trading State

The expansion of economic interdependence in the last half century has led to the realization that the premier trading States of the post-World War II era—Germany and Japan—had benefited from their relative isolation from involvement in the military conflicts of the Cold War. This has led to a realization that modern nations, in a political environment that makes aggressive war extremely costly, can advance their interests more effectively through world trade and economic competition than by force. Commercial development and trade relationships among nations are now considered effective means of enhancing the welfare of the people of a given nation. War and the use of force, even the extensive production of armaments, do not enhance the economic well-being of nations; trade does (Rosecrance, 1986).

Increased Knowledge and Experience

International organizations, such as the United Nations, have greatly enhanced our knowledge and the store of information with which to make more effective decisions in international relations. Observer teams and peacekeeping operations have provided innovations and experience. The registration of treaties, the extensive variety and increased experience of investigative and fact-finding techniques, and greater knowledge of international conflict situations improve the capacity of the system to respond with decisions tailored to the circumstances of the case at hand. Improved clarity of international norms and alternative dispute settlement techniques, including mediation, arbitration, and adjudication are alternative methods that have been made available. All of these developments have increased the reliance of the world's nations on law and legal institutions to settle disputes by peaceful means.

Beyond the Cold War

The two areas of unfinished business left over from the Cold War era are the Arab-

TABLE 2.2 United Nations Members Admitted From 1945 to 1965

Americas	Europe	Asia/Oceana	Africa
Jamaica	Albania	Afghanistan	Algeria
Trinidad and Tobago	Austria	Burma	Benin
	Bulgaria	Cambodia	Burkina
	Finland	Cyprus	Burundi
	Hungary	Indonesia	Cameroon
	Iceland	Israel	Central African Republic
	Ireland	Japan	Chad
	Italy	Jordan	Congo
	Malta	Kuwait	Gabon
	Portugal	Laos	Gambia
	Romania	Malaysia	Ghana
	Spain	Maldives	Guinea
	Sweden	Mongolia	Ivory Coast
		Nepal	Kenya
		Pakistan	Libya
		Singapore	Madagascar
		Sri Lanka	Malawi
		Thailand	Mali
		Yemen	Mauritania
			Morocco
			Niger
			Nigeria
			Rwanda
			Senegal
			Sierra Leone
			Somalia
			Sudan
			Tanganyika (until 1961)
			Tanzania
			Togo
			Tunisia
			Uganda
			Zaire
			Zambia
			Zanzibar (until 1963)

Israeli conflict and the division of Korea. These situations remain dangerous, although there are signs of some progress. The two States of North and South Korea were admitted as separate members of the United Nations in 1991. The breakup of the Soviet Union resulted in a rush of new applications to the United Nations. Belorussia and the Ukraine were already members, but many of the other constituent republics applied for, and were granted, membership. Latvia, Lithunania, and Estonia were granted membership, ending a long-protested absorption into the Soviet Union in violation of international law. By September 1993, there were 184 members of the United Nations Organization and a new phase of the new world order had begun. (Table 2.4 lists nations admitted to the United Nations from 1985 to 1995.)

TABLE 2.3 United Nations Members Admitted from 1965 to 1985

Americas	Europe	Asia/Oceana	Africa
Antigua and Barbuda	Federal Republic of Germany	Bahrain	Angola
The Bahamas	(until 1990; now Germany)	Bangladesh	Botswana
Barbados	German Democratic Republic	Bhutan	Cape Verde
Belize	(until 1990; now Germany)	Brunei	Camoros
Dominica		Fiji	Djibouti
Grenada		Oman	Equatorial Guinea
Guyana		Papua New Guinea	Guinea Bissau
Saint Vincent and		Qatar	Lesotho
the Grenadines		Solomon Islands	Mauritius
Suriname		United Arab Emirates	Mozambique
		Vanuatu	São Tomé and Principe
		Vietnam	Seychelles
		Western Samoa	Swaziland
		Yemen	Zimbabwe

TABLE 2.4 United Nations Members Admitted From 1985 to 1995

Americas	Europe	Asia/Oceana	Africa
	Andorra	Kazakhstan	Eritrea
	Armenia	Kyrgystan	Namibia
	Azerbaijan	Marshall Islands	
	Bosnia/Herzegovina	Micronesia	
	Croatia	North Korea	
	Czech Republic	Palau	
	Estonia	South Korea	
	Germany (including East and	Tazikistan	
	West Berlin)	Turkmenistan	
	Georgia	Uzbekistan	
	Latvia		
	Liechtenstein		
	Lithuania		
	Macedonia		
	Moldova		
	Monaco		
	San Marino		
	Slovakia		
	Slovenia		

The Arab-Israeli conflict involves a situation of instability that does not fit any established norms of international law. The United Nations itself was involved in the creation of the State of Israel, and for over forty years, the United Nations has attempted to resolve the conflict through repeated resolutions and peacekeeping efforts. The series of Arab-Israeli wars (1948, 1956, 1963, and 1973) has frustrated the efforts of all parties.

The Arab States and Israel are now beginning to move toward a mutual recognition of their rights to exist and to be entitled to secure borders. Israel has recognized a tentative Palestinian right to exist and has begun turning over limited control of Gaza and Jericho to the Palestine Liberation Organization. These matters are still a long way from being settled, and the situation remains on the critical list.

The end of the Cold War, and the new cooperation within the Security Council after the Gulf War, reflected profound changes that at first brought euphoria, optimism, and confidence in the West. But civil war erupted in many areas of the former Soviet Union and in Eastern Europe. The former Yugoslav Federal Republic disintegrated, and fighting broke out among ethnic groups within the area, which seemed to turn the clock back to 1914.

Tito (born Josip Broz) was the wartime leader who put together a constitutional federation dividing up the Serbian plurality to maintain balance in six multi-ethnic republics. This artificial union apparently could not survive without his leadership. After Tito's death in 1980, the republics agreed to rotate the presidency, with each republic taking turns in executive authority. Serbia refused to relinquish its executive position, according to the agreement, and the republics began to break away from the federation. The breakaway republics of Slovenia, Croatia, Bosnia-Herzegovina, and Macedonia sought recognition as independent States and admission to the United Nations. Germany encouraged the European Community to recognize Slovenia and Croatia in a premature move that was brought to the Security Council by the remnant government of Yugoslavia, which now represented only Serbia and Montenegro. The General Assembly and the Security Council approved the admission of the breakaway republics in 1992. They became separate members, and the major organs refused to recognize claims of the Serbs and Montinegroans to act as the successor to the Yugoslavian seat.

A major test of the new post-Cold War world order involves issues of "self-determination of peoples" on a scale that no one could have expected from the wording of the U.N. Charter. It seems to encourage dissident elements to become new States and threatens to become a cause of new types of violence and disorder throughout the world. There are some 6,000 identifiable ethnic, cultural, and linguistic groups throughout the world that may now aspire to become nation-states. Daniel Patrick Moynihan (1993) has referred to this development as "pandemonium," and it threatens to bring disintegration on a scale reminiscent of the old feudal order before the Peace of Westphalia.

At the same time, the forces of integration in Northern and Western Europe have been steadily advancing toward a united European Community since the Rome Treaty in 1950. The European Community has created a new regional set of institutions that promote economic integration and protection of human rights. However, it discovered that the diverse variety of military institutions that had been created to allay fears among ancient rivals was not equipped to deal with the Yugoslav crisis.

The new Balkan crisis now produced evidence of significant violations of basic human rights under international law. International respect for human rights had been gaining ground during the final phases of the Cold War. Soviet Premier Gorbachev had negotiated significant commitments to human rights that led to the clear indication that basic democratic freedoms would be respected. The exercise of these rights had brought the movements in the former communist countries to overthrow communist regimes and restructure their societies. Now the situation in Yugoslavia demonstrated the worst atrocities and disrespect for basic human rights experienced in Europe since the Nazi period. Indiscriminate killing of civilians, "ethnic cleansing," brutal mistreatment of prisoners, and mass rapes of civilian prisoners were reported.

Security Council actions created a humanitarian relief organization, sending in a peacekeeping operation to protect civilians not involved in combat. In a series of actions, the Security Council imposed an arms embargo affecting all sides and attempted to isolate the conflict, preventing its spread to other neighboring countries. Ultimately, the continued senseless killing of innocent civilians brought the authority to conduct limited air strikes to protect civilians in Sarajevo and other cities designated as "safe zones."

The General Assembly and the Security Council have acted to create a special War Crimes Tribunal, which has been constituted at the Hague in the Netherlands, to punish violators of human rights. It has authority to conduct investigations, bring indictments, and try those accused of violations of international human rights law.

Iraq remains under extensive imposition of U.N. sanctions after the Gulf War. There is a continuing U.N. attempt to protect the Kurdish minorities in the north of Iraq and the Shi'ite Moslems in the south of the country. The Security Council actions resulted in reprisals taken by Saddam Hussein against these dissident elements in that country, and the Council could not refuse to come to their assistance. No-fly zones have been established in northern and southern Iraq, policed by allied aircraft to protect the basic human rights of these minorities to continue to exist.

Similar unprecedented implementation of international human rights law and humanitarian relief efforts of the United Nations Organization demonstrate the initial direction that is being pursued by the world community. U.N. involvement in the civil wars in Liberia and Cambodia to protect fundamental human rights have now been supplemented with unprecedented actions in Somalia and Haiti. Somalia is a case of intervention based on the humanitarian sentiment of the world community, which refused to allow civil war and anarchy within a particular country to result in the starvation of most of the population. The action was based on the idea that since Somalia had no government, there was no international intervention against the sovereignty of a government that no longer existed.

In Haiti, the U.N. Security Council has acted to impose a blockade against a military dictatorship that ousted the democratically elected president of that country, Aristide. This, too, is an unprecedented intervention into the domestic affairs of a nation-state. The refusal to honor agreements, violations of human rights, and the massive exodus of refugees are among the causes for Security Council action. However, these problems exist in many parts of the world, and such precedents may bring far-reaching consequences. One of the more respected international observers, Max M. Kempelman, comments in a recent publication of the Council on Foreign Affairs:

The U.N. Security Council has been a focal point for many of the efforts to respond constructively to internal conflicts. It has power under the Charter to respond not only to acts of aggression and breaches of peace, but also to threats to peace. The U.N. Security

Council has been increasingly willing to treat internal conflicts as presenting such threats. In so doing, it is making new law and creating new precedents. (cited in Damrosch, 1993b, p. x)

A case is pending before the World Court concerning the limits of Security Council authority under the U.N. Charter. It is not certain that the court will accept jurisdiction. But these issues indicate a need for significant restructuring of U.N. institutions. Although the collective security system in some respects has not fulfilled the expectations of the framers of the charter—for example, in the creation of a U.N. military command—it has gone beyond the charter in other respects.

The first two chapters of this text have provided the necessary background of historical experience concerning the development of the concept of international law, allowing us to describe the general characteristics of contemporary legal development. In subsequent chapters, the general norms and specific content of international law will be discussed. International law, like all law, is a dynamic process that is constantly in development. It has fundamental norms that are time honored, and perhaps even self-evident, that provide stability in the regulation of human affairs. But it also has the opportunity to provide innovation to deal with change in a dynamic society by the creation of new norms and rules of law.

■   ■   ■

Chapter Summary

1. The causes of World War II involved repeated acts of territorial aggression on the part of Germany, Italy, and Japan. The worldwide conflict began with the invasion of Poland in 1939 and ultimately involved almost all of the world's nations.

2. The "United Nations" was the official name assumed by the States that allied themselves to oppose the Axis Powers and their flagrant violations of international law.

3. Wartime planning for peace began in the United States even before this country entered the war. The Declaration by the United Nations in 1942 committed the signatories to disarm the aggressor nations and to establish a permanent system of international security.

4. The Soviet Union at first appeared to side with the Axis Powers, agreeing, in a secret protocol, to a nonaggression pact with Germany to divide up Poland. Germany later attacked Russia in 1941, and Stalin then joined the United Nations effort.

5. At the Moscow Conference, in 1943, the USSR, Great Britain, the United States, and China pledged their efforts to establish a general organization of nations for the maintenance of international peace and security. Roosevelt, Stalin, and Churchill personally committed themselves to these goals at the Teheran Conference one month later.

6. The U.N. Charter established the fundamental change in international law that prohibited the use of force against the territorial integrity or political independence of any

State. Such use of force had been accepted in traditional international law, and the charter therefore makes a fundamental change in international norms.

7. A norm is a fundamental legal objective established by competent lawmaking authority. The U.N. Charter seeks universal membership and intends for the fundamental norm that it establishes to apply to all States. This makes it a lawmaking treaty.

8. The five major powers—the United States, the USSR, Great Britain, France, and China—became the five permanent members of the Security Council. They engaged in extensive wartime planning to unify their positions on key provisions of the U.N. Charter beginning at Dumbarton Oaks in 1944.

9. At Yalta, in 1945, the Big Five powers agreed to call a general conference, to be held in San Francisco in April of 1945, to draft the U.N. Charter. All forty-six States who signed the Declaration by the United Nations to oppose Axis aggression were invited.

10. The original States invited to San Francisco agreed to extend invitations to Argentina, Belorussia, the Ukraine, and Denmark. Poland was not invited but was allowed to adhere to the U.N. Charter as an original member. These fifty States hammered out the specific wording of the charter. Differences between the major powers and the smaller States were evident.

11. There was no compromising on the major-power veto in the Security Council, but the small States won major concessions in strengthening the General Assembly, the Secretariat, and the International Court of Justice. The most important small-State concession was the strong emphasis on self-determination of peoples and protection for non-self-governing territories.

12. The U.N. Charter created six major organs that would be coordinated but that would leave considerable autonomy of action to each organ. The Security Council would have the primary responsibility for maintenance of international peace and security with authority to impose sanctions ranging from specific performance orders to the imposition of military force.

13. The Security Council was originally composed of eleven members—the five permanent members and six members elected by the General Assembly for two-year terms. Only the permanent members have a veto privilege on substantive matters, and the veto must be exercised to block action. Originally, seven members were required to take action. In 1965, a charter amendment expanded the council to fifteen members requiring nine votes to decide issues.

14. The General Assembly was given authority to encourage the progressive development of international law and its codification. It has many other responsibilities in the selection of other officials and States to serve in the various organs of the organization and to deal with budget issues. A charter amendment requires Security Council approval and a two-thirds majority of the General Assembly.

15. The purposes of the United Nations Organization are to maintain international peace and security, develop friendly relations and international cooperation, and be a center for harmonizing the actions of nations. Collective security is its most important aim.

16. Failure of major-power cooperation in the Security Council during the Cold War diminished expectations concerning the system as intended by the U.N. Charter framers. However, the General Assembly has assumed a secondary role in maintenance of peace and security when the Security Council is blocked. Actions were taken against North Korean aggression, and a major military command was established in 1950.

17. Cold War tensions forced the United Nations to take a backseat during the height of the Cold War when the major powers established spheres of influence and engaged in interventions in civil wars in many parts of the world. A U.S.-led alliance system could be considered to have succeeded in containing communist aggression and contributing to the demise of communism as a threat to world security.

18. The United Nations Organization ultimately recognized the People's Republic of China and developed innovative peacekeeping techniques on the periphery of Cold War strategic confrontations. Limited peacekeeping operations, involving U.N. observer teams and military units whose mission was to act as a buffer between opposing military forces, were established.

19. Expansion of the U.N. membership has transformed the organization, tripling the original member States by 1985. New members are admitted by approval of both the General Assembly and the Security Council. The majority of the membership is now definitely non-European in character.

20. The breakup of the Soviet Union, the restructuring of former communist nations in Eastern Europe, and the reunification of Germany marked the end of the Cold War by 1989. A comprehensive peace treaty was concluded with Germany, establishing firm borders between Germany and Poland.

21. The swift U.N. Security Council authorization of military sanctions against Iraq, reversing its aggressive invasion of Kuwait in 1990, demonstrated the ability of the council to function as intended. The council's responsibility for maintenance of international peace and security is being pursued, and more recent actions indicate a willingness to go beyond the U.N. Charter in enforcing international human rights law.

Key Terms

appeasement	rules of law
Axis Powers	Dumbarton Oaks (1944)
United Nations	Yalta Conference (1945)
Monroe Doctrine (1823)	San Francisco Conference (1945)
Atlantic Charter (1941)	Charter amendments
Declaration by the United Nations (1942)	Trusteeship Council
	Economic and Social Council
German-Soviet Non-Aggression Pact (1939)	International Court of Justice
	containment policy
Moscow Conference (1943)	Uniting for Peace Resolution
Teheran Conference (1943)	Geneva Conference (1954)
United Nations Charter	SEATO (1955)
Kellogg-Briand Pact (1928)	peacekeeping operations
norm	membership in the United Nations

Discussion Questions

1. How did the causes of World War II differ from the causes of World War I?

2. What efforts were made to prosecute the war against the Axis Powers as a collective security action to enforce international law?

3. How was Russia brought into the war effort on the side of the United Nations?

4. Why was wartime planning for peace after the war considered important to secure a lasting peace?

5. What fundamental norm change in international law was the basis of the U.N. Charter?

6. Is the concept of major-power veto in the Security Council a practical necessity?

7. What happened at the San Francisco Conference to indicate that the smaller States could influence the outcome of the final U.N. Charter document?

8. Has the Cold War really ended? What current disputes are a result of the Cold War era?

9. Have the basic purposes of the United Nations Organization been achieved in the post-Cold War period?

10. Are the concepts of self-determination and human rights adequately defined in the U.N. Charter? Where do you draw the line between the internal affairs of a State and legitimate international concerns?

Suggested Readings

Appendix A: The United Nations Charter.

Damrosch, L. F. (Ed.). (1993). *Enforcing restraint: Collective intervention in internal conflicts*. New York: Council on Foreign Relations Press. (Excellent articles on Yugoslavia, Iraq, Haiti, Liberia, Somalia, Cambodia, and civilian impact on economic sanctions.)

Field, W. J., & Jordan, R. S. (1988). *International organizations: A comparative approach* (2nd ed.). New York: Praeger.

Gotlieb, G. (1993). *Nation against state*. New York: Council on Foreign Relations Press.

Klare, M. T., & Thomas, D. C. (1991). *World security: Trends and challenges at century's end*. New York: St. Martin's Press. (Excellent articles on a wide range of security issues, including theory, use of force issues, nuclear proliferation, arms trade, terrorism, international regimes, human rights, global debt, world hunger, and environmental issues.)

Moynihan, D. P. (1993). *Pandaemonium: Ethnicity in international politics*. New York: Oxford University Press.

Payne, R. (1973). *The life and death of Adolf Hitler*. New York: Praeger.

Rosecrance, R. (1986). *The rise of the trading state*. New York: Basic Books.

3 Contemporary International Law

The magnitude of the social, economic, political, and environmental changes witnessed in the twentieth century has dwarfed that of all previous centuries in world history. In many ways we are too close to these changes to realize their significance, but we live in a world of profound changes.

Since the beginning of the twentieth century, the world's population has quadrupled; major inventions such as the airplane, resulting in worldwide air transportation, now link the planet; supersonic aircraft and nuclear missiles make all nations vulnerable to attack by other nations; technological inventions such as radio and television provide instant communication through satellite transmissions; the astounding growth of industry, commerce, and world trade makes all nations increasingly dependent on each other; and the modern nation-state system has spread from its original European base to encompass a world characterized by over 200 sovereign entities. Growth is one measure of success of the human species, and in the twentieth century, human communities have grown by such a magnitude that they now produce a threat to the very environment that supports life on the planet.

These developments have required the emergence of a new world order that is reflected in the contemporary principles of international law. Law development in any society is produced by the realistic forces of politics and interaction of interests and values within that society. The emergence of a worldwide community of nations with a functioning set of differentiated political decision-making institutions, and a set of legal principles that define its functions, is the most important development of the twentieth century. This system is not *world government*, if that term is defined to mean a sovereign lawmaking authority that imposes its will on the world's peoples. However, the United Nations Organization has demonstrated a capacity to function as a coordinating international problem identification and problem-solving set of institutions.

The twentieth-century world community encompasses much more than the United Nations Organization. Over 200 sovereign nations have the recognized capacity to negotiate treaties and create legal obligations of a bilateral, multilateral, or universal "lawmaking" character. The U.N. Charter is a treaty of lawmaking character that creates legal obligations for members and nonmembers alike and is specifically intended to create dispute settlement institutions with authority to enforce their decisions. Since 1946, the United Nations has registered over 30,000 formal treaties that form the great body of specific international law. Most of the general principles of international law have been codified in hundreds of lawmaking treaties intended to establish rules of universal application in areas such as treaties, diplomacy, law of the sea, airspace, outer space, and warfare. Some 380 intergovernmental organizations (IGOs) have been formed by sovereign nations to conduct functional operations of mutual interest to their members. Some of these functional organizations are overarching regional sets of institutions that deal with social, economic, and political issues. Others are military alliances and organizations that facilitate cooperation in controlling international criminal activity. Still others function to facilitate trade and deal with issues of international commerce.

The astounding growth of private international organizations in this century illustrates the depth of the emerging international community. The Union of International Associations reports that by 1986 there were nearly 5,000 such organizations with members from three or more countries that promote the international interests of their members. These include the International Red Cross, the International Chamber of Commerce, Greenpeace, and Amnesty International. These figures do not include the thousands of major corporations involved in international commerce and trade. There is also a growing community of average citizens who see themselves as "citizens of the world," participate actively in expressing their concerns about international problems, and recognize a common interest in preserving the humanitarian values of life on this planet.

These developments were not accomplished without an enormous sacrifice of blood, treasure, sweat, and tears. The twentieth century also witnessed human destruction on a scale never before realized in the history of mankind. Two world wars and countless smaller armed conflicts distinguish this century as the bloodiest in human history. The image of international conflict is so powerful that it nearly obscures the more important periods of peace in this century.

War is not the normal state of affairs among nations but, rather, the rare exception when the constraints of morality and law have proven inadequate. Each peace settlement is usually an attempt to reorder the legal structure to provide more adequate rules that will bring stability and mutual accommodation concerning similar and future conflicts. Most treaties before the twentieth century were peace settlements that concluded wars. However, in the late nineteenth and early twentieth centuries, nations began to discover new uses for the instruments of contractual obligations, in the form of treaties, to regulate their affairs in peacetime and to attempt to find alternative means of dispute settlement.

Part I of this text has provided the necessary background of historical experience concerning the development of the concept of international law to allow us to describe the general characteristics of contemporary legal developments. Modern international law represents the accumulation of these historical experiences that have resulted in customary practices regarded as legally binding by modern nation-states. Increasingly, these practices have become formalized in modern lawmaking treaties intended to codify, advance, and clarify the general norms of State conduct in international relations.

The development of a vast array of functioning institutions that deal with international issues and make decisions on the basis of established principles of law are now characteristic features of the international legal system. The United Nations system is the most important organizational structure representing the world community of nations. But important regional communities of nations are a part of that system as are the overwhelming majority of the world's nation-states. International law is still in a primitive stage of development in comparison with most municipal legal systems. Although many problems contribute to ineffective enforcement, this chapter will attempt to explain the characteristic features of the contemporary international legal system.

The Scope of Modern International Law

What then is international law? The world community has undergone such profound change in the twentieth century that even the terminology used to define familiar concepts must change to fit modern reality. In Chapter 1, we said that international law is not world law but that it had its origins in the Roman concept of *jus gentium*, or the law of peoples, and was later referred to as law *among* nations, as opposed to law *above* nations.

At the time of the American Declaration of Independence and the founding of the federal republic, English law had developed from the accumulated principles of justice derived from the decisions of the early courts. The common law of England was thought to be an expression of natural law obtained through practical experience. Several prominent legal scholars had engaged in systematic studies of the enormous volume of case law opinions of the courts to provide secondary commentary of the law in the form of restatements or simplifications of the general principles of common law. William Blackstone's influential four-volume work published in 1765-1769 was titled *Commentaries on the Laws of England*. This restatement of the law was highly regarded in the United States and provided much of the theoretical basis for the American Revolution.

> **Common law:** Refers to the English legal heritage that accepts judicial decisions as a source of law.

> **Restatements (of the law):** General principles of the law derived from practice and restated in simplified form.

As Professor Mark W. Janis explains, it is sometimes forgotten that the law of nations, as it was conceived and formulated in the seventeenth and eighteenth centuries, was a law that "was generally applicable to individuals as well as to states" (Janis, 1993, pp. 227-228). As Janis reminds us, Blackstone's definition of the "law of nations" in 1765 was the following:

> The Law of nations is a system of rules, deducible by natural reason, and established by universal consent among the civilized inhabitants of the world; in order to decide all disputes, to regulate all ceremonies and civilities, and to ensure the observance of justice and good faith, in that intercourse which must frequently occur between two or more independent states, and the individuals belonging to each. (Blackstone, 1765-1769/1969, p. 66)

Blackstone also wrote that the law of nations was "adopted in [its] full extent by the common law, and is held to be a part of the law of the land" (p. 67), a notion long familiar to U.S. lawyers.

During the nineteenth century, the ascendance of the positivist school of jurisprudence in Western Europe took a slightly different view of international law that has had profound implications in defining the scope of the body of law that is the subject matter of this text. According to Janis (1993), the term *international law* was first used by Jeremy Bentham in 1789. Bentham's influential term was not merely the substitution of international law for the previous term *law of nations* to apply to the same body of law, but he went much further to place the subject matter of international law in a narrow scope that involved only the transactions between sovereigns. "More or less inadvertently, Bentham changed the boundaries of the field he sought to define" (p. 405).

Bentham's restrictive definition, excluding individuals and private parties from the field of international law, was generally adopted by the nineteenth-century legal Positivists who went further than Bentham in elaborating the ramifications of the definition. John Austin, a leading nineteenth-century Positivist, extended Bentham's narrow definition when he wrote that because international law claimed to regulate matters between sovereign States and because sovereigns by his definition could not be regulated by any outside authority, international law was only a form of "positive morality" and not really "law" at all (see Janis, 1993, p. 3).

It became obvious to practitioners of the law that disputes between individuals and corporations (private parties), in which the parties were citizens of two different States, could be adjudicated in the domestic courts under certain conditions. That body of the common law that Blackstone had referenced in his definition as regulation of "that intercourse which must frequently occur between two or more independent states, and the individuals belonging to each," was no longer included in the term international law. On the continent of Europe, this area of the domestic law, or **municipal law**, became known as **private international law.**

> **Municipal law:** Used by international lawyers to refer to the domestic law of individual nations.
>
> **Private international law:** International law as interpreted by municipal courts and applied to disputes between private parties.

In the United States, U.S. Supreme Court justice Joseph Story became the author of an influential treatise on the principles of common law in application to private disputes involving international matters that he called **conflict of laws.** Story's *Commentaries on the Conflict of Laws, Foreign and Domestic* was published in 1834 and led to the unique terminology used only in the United States for the principles of private international law.

> **Conflict of laws:** The area of common law in the United States that includes general principles of private international law.

Following Bentham's artificial division of international law thus led to a bright line's being drawn between *public* and *private* international law. Professor Janis's research has led him to the following conclusion about the nineteenth-century use of these two branches of law—public and private:

> The former was deemed to apply to states, the latter to individuals. Positivists could scorn both sides of the subject: public international law was "international" but not really "law"; private international law was "law" but not really "international." For most of the nine-

teenth and early twentieth centuries, the positivist definition of public international law as a law for states alone dominated the theory of international law. (Janis, 1993, p. 234)

In France, the field that had originally been considered parts of the same subject in the seventeenth and eighteenth centuries became subdivided even further into not only public and private international law but also into a third juridical field—the law of international commerce. These artificial divisions persist even today in the United States where political science departments often teach courses in public international law. Private international law has been traditionally left to the exclusive domain of law schools or taught as part of international business law in business law departments.

Much has happened in all three of these artificially divided areas of important international concern. Practitioners and scholars alike have had difficulty seeing the entire field as a whole. This excessive compartmentalization in modern university and academic circles has been frequently criticized, and efforts are underway to bring about greater coordination and understanding of the linkages between disciplines. This need in the field of international law is particularly acute because of the major changes that characterize the international community and State practice in many areas of private law.

Law schools in the United States have taken the lead in redefining modern international law in a more holistic manner, often using the term **transnational law** to describe it. Judge Philip Jessup, who served as the first U.S. justice on the International

> **Transnational law:** Modern term used to describe the broader field of law regulating actions and events that transcend national frontiers, including both private and public international law.

Court of Justice (ICJ), delivered an imaginative and influential series of lectures at Harvard University titled "Transnational Law" in 1956. He defined the term "to include all law which regulates actions or events that transcend national frontiers. Both public and private international law are included, as are other rules which do not wholly fit into such standard categories" (Jessup, 1956, p. 2).

The ferment created by these lectures has begun to spread throughout the legal community as an important contribution to our thinking about the significance of international law in all aspects of the law. Many law schools now have transnational law programs in which courses in both public and private international law (or conflict of laws), constitutional law, economic regulation, comparative law, political theory, and jurisprudence are integrated into one program. Most law schools are involved in efforts to infuse awareness of the internationalization of the law into all their courses.

This movement has barely touched the traditional undergraduate curriculum; only half of four-year institutions even teach a course in international law. Most of these courses combine international organization and **public international law** subject matter; private international law is barely mentioned. Business schools often teach courses in international business law, but none of these courses are generally part of the exposure for students at the undergraduate level. This text is designed to provide undergraduates with at least an introductory exposure to the entire system of modern international law. Individual nation-state implementation of many aspects of international law is an important feature of the new world order.

> **Public international law:** The field of law limited to the body of law regulating sovereign nation-states and their transactions.

The New World Legal Order

The new world order, which this text is intended to describe, is as much related to a new perception of international law as it is to the astounding developments of the post-Cold War era in international relations. This text adopts the broader view of international law expressed by Blackstone and Jessup. It is intended to expose undergraduate students to the broad range of domestic, or municipal, practices of States in the application of legal principles of an international character as well as to the significant developments in public international law.

However, an introductory course for undergraduates must of necessity limit this exposure in significant ways. Part II of this text, beginning with Chapter 4, provides illustrations of the application of principles of international law as used in the U.S. courts. These courts, both state and federal, provide access to individuals in specific areas of jurisdiction that involve disputes between private parties. The Foreign Sovereign Immunities Act of 1976 represents an important departure from previous concepts of absolute sovereign immunity and allows states to be sued by private parties in areas of commercial activity not involving acts of State. Government assets of foreign countries can be seized to ensure responsible behavior on the part of governments as well. Individuals have a broad range of rights and duties involving international disputes that can be directly adjudicated in national courts.

This text is designed for U.S. students and therefore focuses on U.S. court practices in the area of transnational law (private international law or conflict of laws areas). Similar developments in other countries will be briefly discussed, but necessity prevents any attempt to expand the discussion to all national legal systems. Anyone who has attempted to discuss U.S. law is forced into the same dilemma. All of the fifty United States have their own laws that are united only by the limitations of the U.S. Constitution. Modern international law is beginning to assume similar characteristics of a federal structure that require some means of simplification for purposes of understanding.

Part III of this text will extend this federal analogy to the traditional international plane of disputes involving acts of State, or public international law. The process of adjudication through international tribunals will be the principal focus of this discussion, and the distinctions between municipal and international tribunals will be illustrated. Finally, we will examine the extensive array of enforcement mechanisms available to individual States, multinational organizations, and the United Nations Organization to enforce the norms and rules of international law.

This approach to the vast subject matter of modern international law is designed to expose the beginning student to the potential for the international legal system eventually to achieve a more effective world order. The outlines of this system of law development can be seen through three selected statements from the highest decision-making authorities in their respective realms of dispute settlement.

Private International Law

First is the realm of individual nation-states in which aspects of international law have become part of the law of the land and are being adjudicated by clearly defined judicial authority. The U.S. Supreme Court, in deciding the *Paquete Habana and the Lola* case in 1900, provides a familiar illustration of the initial avenue available to private parties to seek redress of grievances in international legal disputes. The case concerned two private Cuban fishing vessels and their contention that the U.S. government had seized their property illegally during the Spanish-American War. The Court found in favor of the private plaintiffs in this case by applying the principles of customary international law. Justice Gray, speaking for a majority of the Court, defined one aspect of international law in the following words:

> International law is part of our law, and must be ascertained and administered by the courts of justice of appropriate jurisdiction as often as questions of right depending upon it are duly presented for their determination. (*Paquete Habana*, 175 U.S. 677 [1900])

Public International Law

At the level of international tribunals, another statement provides evidence of another definition of international law appropriate to the public law jurisdiction of the World Court. The Permanent Court of International Justice, in the famous *Case of the S.S. "Lotus,"* involving a dispute between France and Turkey, had occasion to define its jurisdiction. The case also concerned private parties, but the specific issue before the court concerned the authority of the Turkish courts to try a French citizen for a criminal offense committed on the high seas where a French vessel collided with a Turkish ship. Here the court defines international law in a more traditional manner:

> International law governs relations between independent states. The rules of law binding upon States therefore emanate from their own free will as expressed in conventions or by usages generally accepted as expressing principles of law and established in order to regulate the relations between these co-existing independent communities or with a view to the achievement of common aims. (*The Lotus* case [1927] P.C.I.J., ser. A. No. 10, at 18)

The Court found in favor of Turkey because France was unsuccessful in convincing the court that there was sufficient evidence that Turkey had limited its jurisdiction by any previous agreement or customary practice regarded as legally binding.

U.N. Security Council Enforcement

A third level of dispute settlement and enforcement authority is given to the U.N. Security Council in Chapter VII, Articles 39, 41, and 42 of the U.N. Charter.

> The Security Council shall determine the existence of any threat to the peace, breach of the peace, or act of aggression and shall make recommendations, or decide what measures shall be taken in accordance with Articles 41 and 42, to maintain or restore international peace and security. (Article 39)

Articles 41 and 42 prescribe the mandatory sanctions that may be imposed by the Security Council, beginning with those measures not involving the use of armed force, and then, if these measures prove to be inadequate, "it may take such action by air, sea, or land forces as may be necessary to maintain or restore international peace and security" (Article 42).

These three statements, when taken together, provide a sketch of the international legal system that has emerged in the twentieth century. This entire text will attempt more adequately to fill in the details of the linkages that are beginning to knit the fabric of international law into a coherent whole. The whole of international law is not clearly defined, and its development is still in a primitive state. However, the basic outline is there for all who seek an understanding of modern international law.

The Sources of International Law

The first two chapters of this text provide a broad historical perspective concerning the question of the sources of law in general and international law in particular. Our broader interpretation of the scope of international law includes both private and public international aspects of law as well as aspects of international business law. This scope requires a broader interpretation of the sources of law than the traditional concepts of pubic international law alone.

A leading international business law text authored by Ray August (1993) defines international law as simply "the body of rules and norms that regulates activities carried on outside the legal boundaries of nations. In particular, it regulates three international relationships: (1) those between states, (2) those between states and persons, and (3) those between persons and persons." He further asserts that "Business today is truly international. Worldwide, approximately half of all business transactions are done across national borders. A firm, therefore, that chooses to ignore all but the laws and legal procedures of its own country is choosing to work half-blind" (p. 1).

Indeed, the development of the Law Merchant as a body of commercial law became incorporated into the municipal laws of most European countries during the Renaissance. Its practical effect was to harmonize the rules of trading nations to facilitate trade and commerce. These rules were incorporated into the national legal structure, and special commercial courts were developed to settle disputes. The legislative enactments of rules governing international transactions today may be considered a part of private international law, as are common law developments.

On the international plane, involving transactions between sovereign nation-states, there is no formal machinery for the making of law, such as a well-defined court system and a legislative authority to make law. However, the treaty instrument for establishing binding obligations between nations has undergone extensive development in the twentieth century, as will be explained more fully later in this chapter. Private international law is subject to the limitation that it may not violate the rules of public international law to which it has previously given its consent either through formal agreements or customary practice regarded as legally binding.

The sources of public international law are generally considered to be adequately described by the Statute of the International Court of Justice in Article 38(1), which lists the sources that the court is permitted to use and which most other courts use as well:

The Court, whose function is to decide in accordance with international law such disputes as are submitted to it, shall apply:

(a) international conventions, whether general or particular, establishing rules expressly recognized by the contesting states;

(b) international custom, as evidence of a general practice accepted as law;

(c) the general principles of law recognized by civilized nations;

(d) subject to the provisions of Article 59, judicial decisions and teachings of the most highly qualified publicists of various nations, as subsidiary means for the determination of rules of law.

The positive law of the Statute of the International Court of Justice thus recognizes three principal and traditional sources of international law. These sources are treaties, custom, and general principles of law. The theory behind this formulation is often referred to as the doctrine of sources. Treaties are perhaps the most obvious method of documenting State consent to an international obligation. However, customary practice regarded as legally binding and the general principles of law recognized by civilized nations are vague and difficult to define. These sources leave much to the imagination when compared with the relatively clear lawmaking processes used in most domestic legal systems. However, British and U.S. common law have considerable similarity.

Treaties

The Statute implies that treaties should be given preference, and in practice, the ICJ and other international tribunals turn first to treaty provisions for the applicable law when they are relevant to the issue in controversy. However, treaties themselves are subject to rules of validity, and if they are considered in conflict with fundamental principles of law (*jus cogens*), they are not enforceable. Thus, the secret protocol to the German-Russian Non-Aggression Pact to divide up Poland before World War II is not only nonenforceable but a violation of international law itself. This means that there is no clear hierarchy intended by the order of these sources of international law.

Customary Practice as a Source of Law

Customary international law is the product of State practice and *opinio juris,* or the opinion of judicial authority that these practices are regarded as legally binding. A norm of international law is established if States act in conformity with it and the international community accepts that norm as obligatory under law. This is difficult to document and subject to varying interpretation. International tribunals have been conservative in their acceptance of such principles and have demanded evidence of acceptance by the international community. When such tribunals examine the evidence necessary to establish customary law, they consider actions of a limited number of States, often only the largest, most prominent, or most interested among them. Thus, it is clear that not all States must accept these norms, but they must be regarded as obligatory by the international community (see the *Paquete Habana* case in Chapter 4 for illustration).

General Principles of Law

This concept was derived from the ancient Roman idea of *jus gentium,* but it reflects the idea of that body of law, not its precise content during the Roman period. This idea is associated with natural law as perceived by evidence that it is essential to the rule of law in all societies. Thus, if all the principal domestic legal systems employ the same rule of law, that rule is a general principle of law. Some modern jurists have proposed such a search designed to identify rules of natural law. International tribunals have been reluctant to apply such rules; however, when they have, they tend to treat them as axiomatic, without showing which domestic legal systems, if any, use them (see Charney, 1993, p. 536).

The use of these sources of international law will be illustrated by the opinions of international tribunals in the substantive chapters that follow in this text. However, it is clear that even though the ICJ is restricted to these sources, there is considerable flexibility and opportunity for the Court to apply the spirit of the law and not merely the letter of the law in its adjudicatory function. In areas of uncertainty, there is even room for deciding issues on the basis of fairness (*ex equo et bono*) if the parties agree.

The U.N. System of Law Development

The dynamic system of international law development, which will be discussed more fully throughout this text, has many dimensions that are a source of great confusion, particularly for the beginning student. The most fundamental distinction is that the basic instrument of formal creation of legally binding obligations—the treaty instrument—may be used to create norms and rules at three different levels of complexity. The treaty instrument may be used to create *particular, general,* or *universal* rules of law.

The form often referred to as creating particular international law is the **bilateral treaty**, intended to bind two States in their relations with each other. The typical bilateral treaty is known as the "foundation treaty" or treaty of friendship and commerce. The United States has negotiated some 130 of these treaties with

> **Bilateral treaty:** *Source of law binding two States in their relations with each other.*

individual States around the globe. They create particular obligations between the parties (see the French-U.S. example in Appendix E).

Multilateral treaties, on the other hand, are negotiated between more than two States and create general obligations among the parties involved. Such treaties have been used to create regional organizations that may transfer functional aspects of individual State sovereignty to a prescribed decision-making structure. These regional entities, or IGOs, may thus take on a legal identity that gives them limited characteristics as sovereign entities.

> **Multilateral treaty:** *Source of law binding several States in their relations with each other.*

A third type of multilateral treaty, intended to clarify and develop universal norms and rules of conduct binding all States, is commonly referred to as a **lawmaking treaty.** These treaties may be used to codify the customary practices of States regarded as legally binding and restate these principles in modern terms that clarify the customary law. The U.N. Charter is perhaps the most universal of these documents. However, the charter itself charges the General Assembly with "promoting international cooperation in the political field and encouraging the progressive development of international law and its codification" (Chapter IV, Article 13, 1a).

> **Lawmaking treaty:** *Source of law intended to codify existing rules of universal international law or to create new rules of customary law.*

For the past fifty years, the General Assembly has taken this task seriously and has achieved a great degree of success in devising a process of law development that has surpassed even the expectations of the framers of the U.N. Charter at the San Francisco Conference in 1945. Although the

General Assembly does not have formal legislative authority under the charter, it does have limited authority to impose mandatory rules (with some exceptions) to the internal functioning of the U.N. administrative organization.

One of the leading experts on U.N. lawmaking is Professor Oscar Schachter of Columbia University, whose detailed analysis of U.N.-sponsored law development draws the conclusion that the total product of the past fifty years reveals a distinctive, multilayered legal order. Not only have these efforts of the U.N. political bodies succeeded in codifying most of the major areas of traditional international law, the demands of its members have initiated new law and created legal regimes that seek systematic solutions to world problems. The U.N. political bodies, although denied legislative power, have discovered that they can act like legislatures by adopting lawmaking treaties and declarations of law (see Schachter, 1994, p. 1; see also Charney, 1993, for an important discussion of universal international law).

Codification of Customary Law

The Legal Committee of the General Assembly (6th Committee) deals with a wide range of legal problems assigned to it by the assembly. It regularly reviews the recommendations and reports of the International Law Commission, composed of a panel of experts who have done much of the work of drafting the modern codes. Even before the International Law Commission could begin its technical work of **codification**, two important general conventions of a lawmaking character

> **Codification:** To restate the rules of a particular field of customary law into treaty form intended to clarify and express the rules of universal law.

were drafted and opened for ratification in 1946. The Convention on Genocide was drafted by the Legal Committee and the General Convention on Privileges and Immunities of the United Nations was drafted by a subcommittee of the Legal Committee.

The major work of codification of customary practice of States underwent a slow and meticulous process initiated by the International Law Commission after it was constituted in 1949. Its thirty-four members are chosen as experts in law representing the major legal systems of the world, and no two may be of the same nationality. The initial membership on this body included some of the most prominent and respected legal experts in the world.

The procedures of the **International Law Commission** are extensive, involving fourteen steps in a process designed to produce a draft product that has a reasonable chance of achieving universal, or near universal, success in ratification by individual States. The most successful of these efforts by the commission in laying the groundwork for the adoption of important lawmaking conventions include the Vienna Convention series, opened for ratification in the 1960s. These include the Vienna Convention on Diplomatic Relations (1961) and the Vienna Convention on Consular Relations (1963). These conventions modified and clarified diplomatic and consular practices throughout the world.

> **International Law Commission:** The U.N. special commission of legal experts representing the world's major legal systems that are charged with drafting codes of customary practice.

According to many legal experts, the commission's most fundamental accomplishment has been in its preparatory work concerning the law of treaties. Treaties are especially important because they constitute the major source of international law. Careful work by the commission resulted in the adoption of the Vienna Convention on the Law of Treaties in 1969. Through the work of the commission, many of the uncertainties in the customary law of treaties have been removed.

The most extensive and innovative lawmaking treaties to emerge from this process are the International Law of the Sea Conventions. The commission was instrumental in providing the groundwork for a series of three conventions in this broad area of major international concerns. The United Nations Conference on the Law of the Sea (UNCLOS I) in 1958 adopted four separate conventions on the territorial sea, the high seas, fisheries, and the continental shelf. This codification of existing law was extensive. However, the 1958 conference left unanswered many important questions, including those having to do with the breadth of the territorial sea and conflicting limits on fishing rights.

A second U.N. Conference on the Law of the Sea (UNCLOS II) was initiated in 1960. The issues raised at this conference were extensive and could not be resolved. A host of new issues became evident, including the potential for mining the deep seabed and exploitation of resources beyond the national jurisdiction of individual States. The oceans cover 70% of the earth's surface and are the most important resources of the world. In 1967, Ambassador Arvid Pardo of Malta introduced an imaginative proposal to link the desirability of restoring order and uniformity in the realm of the oceans to the needs of developing States for substantial and growing resources. He urged that the resources of the seabed and ocean floor beyond national jurisdiction be declared "the common heritage of mankind" to be shared by all States both coastal and landlocked. Ambassador Pardo suggested the establishment of an international authority

with jurisdiction to regulate, promote, and protect that common heritage for the benefit of all but with special attention to the needs of developing States.

From Codification to Political Lawmaking

The General Assembly responded to this proposal by setting up an ad hoc committee of at first forty-two members, which it later expanded to eighty-six and then to ninety-one members, to do the preparatory work for a third law of the sea conference (UNCLOS III) planned initially for 1973. At this stage in the process, the U.N. General Assembly moved from the technical concerns of codification, which had characterized the work of the International Law Commission, into a much more ambitious and political phase of law development. The Seabed Committee, as it became known, involved a conference agenda that was "awesomely ambitious" in the words of one observer. This committee of ninety-one members could not meet its 1973 deadline, and debate within the committee extended through annual meetings until 1982.

The 1982 United Nations Conference on the Law of the Sea (UNCLOS III) treaty was signed by 117 nations of the world and represents one of the most ambitious attempts at international lawmaking ever undertaken. The United States, Japan, and eight European nations, however, did not sign this treaty in 1982. It was scheduled to go into effect one year after receiving the necessary ratifications by sixty-one individual nation-states. This point was reached in 1994, and the treaty went into effect in 1995. However, the effects of the treaty were already manifest during the more than ten years of availability for ratification.

This achievement illustrates the process of lawmaking that characterizes all of these general treaties. They are technically not binding on a particular State unless ratified by the nation's internal ratification processes. However, they are the best evidence of the content of international law when ratified by a majority of the world's nations and intended to have universal effect. Although the United States did not initially sign the 1982 Convention on the Law of the Sea nor has it ratified it at the time of this writing, the U.S. Congress has extended its jurisdiction in accordance with the treaty's provisions. U.S. disagreements concerning the Deep Seabed Authority led to compromises in 1994 that make it more likely that the major industrial nations who refused to sign the agreement in 1982 will eventually ratify this significant treaty and cooperate in the legal regime that it initiates (Oxman, 1994, p. 687).

The **1982 Convention on Law of the Sea** is a truly astounding achievement covering all aspects of ocean access and usage. It is composed of 320 articles covering issues of the limits of the territorial seas (twelve-mile limit) with the right of "transit passage" through and over straits used for international navigation. It defines a contiguous zone of regulation (twenty-four-mile limit) and an exclusive economic zone of up to two hundred miles from the State's baseline. Contiguous States have rights and responsibilities for regulation of natural resources, scientific research, and fishing in this area. Issues concerning exploitation of the resources of the continental shelf are regulated, and a **Deep Seabed Authority** will regulate the pollution and exploitation of resources un-

> **1982 Convention on Law of the Sea:** *The most extensive example of the lawmaking process developed by the U.N. efforts to encourage the progressive development of international law.*

der the high seas beyond the two-hundred-mile limit. Provisions are made for compulsory submission of disputes not settled by negotiation to a variety of arbitral or judicial procedures, including a newly created International Tribunal for the Law of the Sea and a Seabed Disputes Chamber. Figure 3.1 provides a convenient overview of these new maximum limitations in the 1982 Convention on Law of the Sea.

> **Deep Seabed Authority:** *The international regime set up to regulate the exploration and exploitation of the resources under the high seas.*

Although this particular convention went far beyond the initial confines of the preparatory work of the International Law Commission, its technical work has succeeded in codifying the major traditional subjects of customary law with the exception of the general area of State responsibility. In part because of the substantial accomplishment of the codification of existing customary law, the commission has begun to move on to more politically controversial subjects. The membership has also changed to include more individuals with diplomatic and government service backgrounds. However, even in the field of State responsibility, the reports of the commission and the draft articles it has produced have become widely invoked by practitioners as evidence of general international law (Spinedi & Sunma, 1987).

Other influential studies and products of the International Law Commission include (a) model rules of arbitration procedure, (b) the principles of the Nuremberg trials, (c) a declaration of rights and duties of States, (d) a code of offenses against peace and security of humankind, (e) the question of defining aggression, and (f) the effect of reservations to multilateral conventions. Its most important work at the present time concerns the groundwork for a draft con-

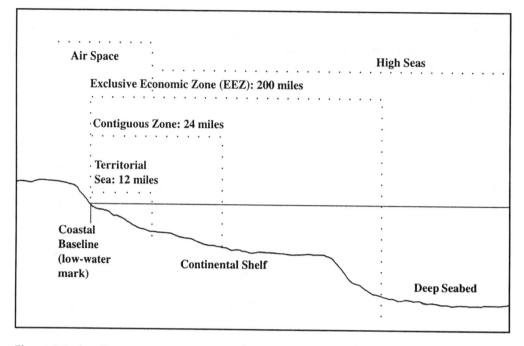

Figure 3.1. Sea Zones
NOTE: In 1987, the U.S. Congress extended its jurisdiction to conform with these limits of the sea zones as defined in the 1982 convention, despite its failure to ratify the formal convention.

vention concerning the establishment of a permanent U.N. criminal court. The ad hoc U.N. Criminal Tribunal established to try persons accused of crimes against humanity in the former Yugoslavia and Rwanda is perhaps the test for a more permanent body that will have jurisdiction over certain aspects of international crime.

Other Major Lawmaking Conventions

The General Assembly occasionally declares and even creates law by resolution. In 1961 and 1963, it adopted unanimous resolutions declaring principles for space law that were later incorporated into the 1967 Treaty on Outer Space declaring outer space *res communis,* or not subject to claim as the territory of any State. As a result of a proclamation by the Assembly concerning the

International Geophysical Year (1957-58), the Antarctic Treaty was made possible among the States having claims in that area. The treaty provides for continued cooperation in scientific research among the parties and prohibits all military activity in Antarctica. It also creates an international legal regime to administer the treaty obligations.

> ***Res communis:*** *Concept of territory belonging to the entire community and not subject to claim by any particular State.*

The specialized agencies of the United Nations have also initiated important legal developments in human rights, labor welfare, and international trade. The U.N. Commission on Human Rights within the Economic and Social Council has devoted its major energies to the development and encouragement of multilateral treaties within its area of competence. The extensive list of resulting documents constitute what is sometimes referred to as the **International Bill of Rights**. It consists of the following documents, the titles of which generally describe some of the fundamental human rights:

> **International Bill of Rights:** *The body of universal international law relating to fundamental human rights.*

* The 1945 U.N. Charter
* The 1948 Universal Declaration of Human Rights
* The 1966 International Covenant on Civil and Political Rights
* The 1966 International Covenant on Economic, Social and Cultural Rights
* The 1948 Convention on the Punishment of the Crime of Genocide
* The 1965 International Convention on the Elimination of All Forms of Racial Discrimination
* The 1973 International Convention on the Suppression and Punishment of the Crime of Apartheid
* The 1979 Convention on the Elimination of All Forms of Discrimination of Women
* The 1982 Declaration on Elimination of All Forms of Discrimination Based on Religion or Belief
* The 1984 Convention Against Torture and Other Cruel, Inhuman or Degrading Treatment or Punishment

Since 1919, the International Labor Organization (ILO) has opened for ratification more than 170 conventions dealing with every aspect of labor welfare. By setting standards and incorporating these standards through ratification into the domestic law of individual States, the organization has served as a model for the process that is emerging throughout the field of U.N. lawmaking.

A notable development in the area of international trade is the 1966 Convention on the Settlement of Investment Disputes Between States and Nationals of Other States. Progress continues to be made through the efforts of the International Bank for Reconstruction and Development. The convention provides for binding arbitration of disputes in which private investors as well as States are involved.

In addition to the extensive development of lawmaking treaties, there is an emerging body of **administrative law** that many analysts overlook. Many of these treaties create specialized agencies or organizational structures that set up administrative bodies engaged in the day-to-day decision making of these agencies. The international civil service has its own body of law, developed in part by the quasi-judicial administrative tribunals. Rules have been adopted by the U.N. organs to govern the activities of various subsidiary bodies, including armed peacekeeping forces, humanitarian missions, and regulatory bodies. These areas of internal law may have significant impact on the relations between U.N. organs and governmental agencies or private persons.

> **Administrative law:** *That body of rules and regulations established by administrative agencies of governmental entities.*

International Legal Regimes

The term **international legal regimes** is of fairly recent origin, becoming a widely used concept only since the early 1970s. According to a comparative study done by Warner J. Field and Robert S. Jordan (1988), it applies to arrangements involving mostly States but affecting also the nongovernmental actors in a wide variety of

> **International legal regimes:** *Administrative legal communities within a functional area that have developed extensive rules of procedure and expectations.*

activity areas, including fisheries conservation, international food production and distribution, international trade issues, telecommunications policy, and meteorological coordination across national boundaries. Regimes may be formal or informal as well as global or regional. The concept applies to goal-oriented activities in specific functional areas regulating these activities.

Oran Young (1980) defines regimes as "recognized patterns of practice around which expectations converge." The core of every regime is "a collection of rights and rules." He also asserts that in formal terms "the members of international regimes are always sovereign States, though the parties carrying out the actions governed by international regimes are often private entities (for example, fishing companies, banks or private airlines)" (p. 333).

Essentially, this is a concept derived from public administration and is being widely used for analytical purposes in that field. International legal regimes provide a conceptualization of what is beginning to happen within a broad range of functional areas of international law, and these developments are a major part of the new world order. The U.N. agencies and regional organizations have provided the legal setting for international regimes in many of the areas of law development described in this chapter. The Antarctica Treaty of 1959, the Deep Seabed Authority created by the 1982 International Law of the Sea Convention, the inspection system created as a result of the Nuclear Non-Proliferation Treaty (NPT), and the International Monetary Fund are good examples of international legal regimes.

Resolutions of the General Assembly, particularly when adopted without dissent, are extensively used as established rules. An important example is the Declaration on Principles of International Law concerning Friendly Relations and Co-operation among States in Accordance With the Charter of the United Nations, which was adopted by consent in 1970. It elaborates the major principles of international law in the U.N. Charter, particularly on use of force, dispute settlement, nonintervention in domestic affairs, self-determination, duties of cooperation and observance of obligations, and "sovereign equality." This document is generally referred to as the "Friendly Relations Declaration," and it has become the international lawyer's favorite example of an authoritative U.N. resolution (Schachter, 1994, p. 3).

Applying and interpreting law takes place constantly throughout the U.N. system. However, there is a significant distinction between arguments that are political in nature and those that are legal in nature. A **political question** seeks a change in the established law. A **legal question** is one that seeks an authoritative determination of what the law is on a particular subject. The ICJ has authority to decide legal questions and is the ultimate institution to which to refer those questions of a legal character. The U.N. Charter provides for a procedure to submit such questions to the Court for its determination, and increasingly more important questions are being submitted to it, both in its advisory capacity and in contested cases. Many of these cases will be examined and discussed throughout this text.

> *Political question:* An issue that requires a change in the existing law.
>
> *Legal question:* An issue that seeks the authoritative determination of existing law on a particular subject.

The Major Regional Organizations

The U.N. Charter recognizes the utility of independent regional organizations and specifies that membership in the United Nations does not preclude the "existence of regional arrangements or agencies for dealing with such matters relating to the maintenance of international peace and security as are appropriate for regional action provided that such arrangements or agencies are consistent with the Purposes and Principles of the United Nations" (Article 52[1]). The charter even directs the Security Council to "encourage settlement of local disputes through regional organizations" (Article 52[3]).

The Organization of American States

The oldest regional association is the **Organization of American States** (OAS). The association has gone through many changes since its inception as the Pan American Union in 1890. This initial agency was incorporated into the OAS in 1948 and has now developed an elaborate structure similar to that of the United Nations. However, the organization is neither controlled by, nor directly responsible to, the United Nations. The OAS Charter establishes its essential purposes as follows:

> *Organization of American States (OAS):* The oldest regional international organization, including nearly all of the nations of the Western Hemisphere.

a. To strengthen the peace and security of the continent;

b. To prevent possible causes of difficulties and to ensure the pacific settlement of disputes that may arise among the Member States;

c. To provide for common action on the part of those States in the event of aggression;

d. To seek the solution of political, juridical and economic problems that may arise among them; and

e. To promote, by cooperative action, their economic, social and cultural development. (Article 4)

These aims make the OAS a very comprehensive intergovernmental organization that includes all of the countries of the Western Hemisphere except Canada and Cuba. The supreme organ, in which each member State has one vote, is the OAS General Assembly. It decides general policy, determines the structure and functions of OAS organs, and has the authority to consider any matter relating to friendly relations among the member States.

The OAS Council has the executive functions and meets frequently. It operates at the ambassadorial level through permanent representatives. The council oversees the Secretariat and has the main tasks of coordinating the specialized agencies, coordinating the activities to promote collaboration with the United Nations and other IGOs, and preparing the budget. In addition, it formulates the statutes of its subsidiary organs that are themselves plenary bodies. They include the Inter-American Economic and Social Council, the Inter-American Juridical Committee, and the Inter-American Council for Education, Science, and Culture.

To carry out the peacekeeping functions of the OAS, the Meeting of Consultation of Ministers of Foreign Affairs plays a prominent role as a consulting organ. Its task is to consider problems of an urgent nature (Article 39) and to serve as the organ of consultation under the OAS Treaty. This body is also a plenary unit on which all member States are represented. It can be convened by a majority of the OAS Council at the request of any member government. However, a meeting is obligatory and must be convened without delay in the event of an armed attack against a member State or against the region as defined in the Rio Treaty of 1947—that is, the Western Hemisphere. If the Meeting of Consultation of Ministers of Foreign Affairs is not obligatory, the council may constitute itself as the provisional organ of consultation. This gives the council considerable power, and in fact, it has been able to settle some disputes without summoning a meeting of foreign ministers. The OAS does not have the authority to impose the kind of mandatory sanctions given to the U.N. Security Council alone in Chapter VII of the U.N. Charter.

Human rights norms are expressed in the Charter of the OAS, the American Declaration of the Rights and Duties of Man, and the American Convention on Human Rights. These norms are monitored by the Inter-American Commission on Human Rights. The OAS reaction to the harsh measures imposed by Cuba's revolutionary government beginning in 1959 led to an investigation by the Inter-American Commission on Human Rights. The commission found that there was widespread suspension of the human rights implicit in the OAS Charter and the other Latin American human rights declarations. When Cuba ignored OAS pressure to curtail this mistreatment of its citizens, the OAS barred Cuba from further participation in the OAS in 1962. The American Convention on Human Rights, which became effective in 1978, is a greatly strengthened set of legal standards. The Human Rights Commission is given power to hear and determine human rights violations and make recommendations to the Inter-American Court of Human Rights. This court is beginning to develop a history of case decisions that will be discussed further in the body of this text.

The European Communities

European economic and political integration since World War II has become the most extensive and multifaceted of all the attempts at regionalism. It is not really one community but consists of a series of gradual steps involving numerous treaties and institutional developments among a variety of functional communities. Today, this system is characterized by two generally describable European communities—the European Union and the organizations of a broader community of European States.

The European Union. The core European community grew out of initial attempts to pursue an ultimate goal of European federation through a piecemeal process, beginning with economic integration and then proceeding toward political integration. The European Coal and Steel Community (ECSC) was first created by multilateral treaty in 1950. This initial integration regulating the major basis of industrial production was a successful beginning and led to the creation of the European Economic Community (EEC) by the Treaty of Rome in 1956. This second major agreement developed a process of economic integration beginning with a "common market" and reduction of tariff barriers among the original six members. A third important treaty further integrated the regulation of atomic energy. The treaty for the European Atomic Energy Community (EURATOM) went into effect in January of 1958. These three treaties formed the basis for the institutions that have become an integrated system of regional international organization known today as the **European Union.**[1]

The European Union (EU) now includes France, Germany, Italy, the United Kingdom, the Netherlands, Luxembourg, Bel-

> **European Union:** The core European community of fifteen nations that have developed the most integrated and comprehensive regional organization.

gium, Spain, Portugal, Ireland, Denmark, Greece, Austria, Finland, and Sweden. These fifteen countries must all adhere to the ECSC treaty, the Treaty of Rome, and the EURATOM treaty. The EU thus creates a reformed set of governing institutions with an integrated structure. The four major organs of the EEC are the European Parliament, the Commission of the European Union, the Council of Ministers, and the European Court of Justice.

The **European Parliament** is an evolving institution that has the potential for assuming a much stronger role in the future. This body was transformed from the Assembly under the original three treaties into an elected parliament in 1979, and its name was later changed to the European Parliament. Members are elected by political parties in their own countries through direct popular elections. They debate issues of significance in the development of progress toward European union. The adoption of the Single European Act in 1987 introduced several amendments into the EEC Treaty that strengthened the participation of the European Parliament in the EU institutional decision-making process. However, the Council of Ministers continued to retain the last word (Field & Jordan, 1988, p. 136). The process of concluding the Maastricht Treaty of 1992 significantly strengthened the European Parliament, produced a commitment to a common currency, and anticipates major changes in the direction of greater security and political integration (see Treaty on European Union in Appendix B). The Parliament now has what is called a "codecision" procedure that amounts to a legislative veto in the significant areas of the EU

European Parliament: The representative body of the European Union that is composed of elected representatives from each country in direct elections by each country's voters.

TABLE 3.1 Number of Elected Representatives in the European Parliament

Austria	21
Belgium	25
Denmark	16
Germany	99
Greece	25
Spain	64
Finland	16
France	87
Ireland	15
Italy	87
Luxembourg	6
Netherlands	31
Portugal	25
Sweden	22
United Kingdom	87
Total representatives	626

single market, education, culture, health, consumer protection, environmental protection, transportation, and research affairs. Thus, the Parliament now has consultative, cooperative, and codecisional roles in the legislative process of the European Union (Folsom, 1995, p. 45). The list in Table 3.1 indicates the number of seats allocated (which varies with population) to each of the fifteen countries in the European Parliament. The range of representatives is from sixteen to ninety-nine, and the entire body is composed of 626 seats.

The Commission of the European Union proposes and later implements European legislation in line with the treaties. It has 20 members—two each from Germany, France, Italy, the United Kingdom, and Spain—and one from each of the other ten member States. They are appointed by unanimous agreement between the governments, but they then act independently of the governments in the community interest.

The Council of Ministers is the dominant institution at present, with the authority to override the Parliament and direct the commission. It is responsible for taking major decisions on the basis of commission proposals. The council is made up of ministers representing the fifteen governments. It is composed of ministers from each member State, selected according to topics scheduled for discussion at the next session, with meetings taking place once a month. On certain subjects, a system of weighted voting exists under which the larger States enjoy more votes than each of the rest. Much of the voting in the Council of Ministers now takes place on a "qualified majority" basis. A total of 76 votes are distributed roughly according to population size of the member State. To adopt legislation or otherwise proceed by qualified majority vote, at least 54 votes must be cast in favor (Folsom, 1995, p. 55). The fifteen heads of the executive departments of their respective governments hold European Council meetings called "summits" three times a year.

The Court of Justice of the EU consists of fifteen judges, one from each member State of the union, appointed for six-year terms. This court has supranational authority to interpret the trade obligations contained in the treaties and regulations of the three segments of the European Union: the EEC, ECSC, and EURATOM. In 1989, the Court of First Instance was created to relieve the Court of Justice of some of its caseload. The Court of First Instance has fifteen judges who usually sit in panels of five. This court's jurisdiction is limited to direct actions or proceedings by individuals or legal persons except those regarding antidumping complaints. There is a right of appeal from the Court of First Instance to the Court of Justice. This is the only international tribunal with compulsory jurisdiction, including the right of individuals to bring legal actions in limited areas. The rulings of the Court of Justice set legal precedents that become part of the legal framework of each member State.

The astounding progress made toward a politically integrated Europe is still a dynamic process that may produce something more closely resembling the federal structures of other countries such as the United States. That point has not yet been reached. The EU development is a unique regional system with a lawmaking process that contributes to the body of international law. It has already produced an economic integration involving some 367.7 million people in the fifteen European nations that produced a combined gross national product (GNP) of $6,593.5 billion in 1993 (Folsom, 1995, pp. 32-33). See Table 3.2 for a timeline of the development of the European Union.

The Broader European Community. The larger European community associated with the European Human Rights Convention includes all of the EU members but also includes many nonmembers of the European Union. The 1950 European Convention for the Protection of Human Rights and Fundamental Freedoms created the **European Court of Human Rights (ECHR)**, which became operational in 1958 and began hearing cases in Strasbourg, France, in 1959. This special human rights court hears cases referred to it by the European Commission on Human Rights, the investigative body of the more comprehensive group of twenty-three States that now adhere to the European Human Rights system. This court has the broadest compulsory jurisdiction of any court in the area of human rights and has achieved a reputa-

> ***European Court of Human Rights (ECHR):*** *International human rights tribunal associated with the broader European community of twenty-three States that have created a process of supranational authority in this functional area.*

TABLE 3.2   A Timeline of European Union

1951	European Coal and Steel Community
1957	Treaty of Rome, European Economic Community, European Atomic Energy Community Treaty
1968	EEC Customs Union fully operative
1973	The United Kingdom, Ireland, and Denmark join the EC
1979	Direct elections to European Parliament
1981	Greece joins EC
1986	Spain and Portugal join EC
1987	Single European Act amends Treaty of Rome to initiate campaign for a community without internal frontiers
1990	East Germany merged into community via reunification process
1991	COMECON defunct; trade relations with Eastern Europe develop rapidly
December 31, 1992	Target date for implementation of community without internal frontiers and expanded trade relations with EFTA nations creating a European Economic Area (EEA)
January 1, 1993	Target date for amendment of Treaty of Rome to provide for greater economic, monetary and political union per Maastricht accords (Treaty on European Union)
November 1, 1993	Maastricht accords ratified and operational, EEC officially becomes EC
January 1, 1994	EEA (minus Switzerland) ratified and operational, European Monetary Institute established
January 1, 1995	Austria, Finland, and Sweden join EU, Norway votes no again
January 1, 1997	Earliest target date for a common currency (ECU or European Currency Union) managed by European Central Bank
January 1, 1999	Latest date for a common currency (ECU) managed by European Central Bank

tion for the exercise of supranational power. Its judgments are directly enforceable in the national courts of the member States.

The Commission of the European Union has proposed that the European Union accede to the European Human Rights Convention. This would mean that the union itself would be bound by the convention and the specific rights enumerated in it. These rights include property, privacy, fair trial, equal treatment, and religious, associational, and trade or professional rights. Article F of the Maastricht Treaty on European Union requires the union to respect fundamental rights as guaranteed by the European Human Rights Convention but stops short of actual accession to it.

According to Professor Ralph H. Folsom (1995), "If the Union acceded to the Con-

vention's 'right of individual petition,' EU citizens would be able to file complaints with the European Commission on Human Rights in Strasbourg, France against acts of the Union's institutions" (p. 73). Neither the Human Rights Commission nor the Court of Human Rights are European Union institutions. They operate in the broader European sphere of nations beyond the inner fifteen Union States.

The North Atlantic Treaty Organization (NATO)

After the breakup of the Soviet Union and the demise of the Warsaw Pact defense alliance in 1990, the future of **NATO** has been uncertain. This Cold War alliance system, instigated by the United States in 1949, was seen as the primary protection against the extension of Soviet control in West and Central Europe. It originally included the United States, the United Kingdom, Canada, France, West Germany, Italy, Portugal, Denmark, Norway, Iceland, Belgium, Holland, Luxembourg, Greece, and Turkey. These nations were committed to the principle that an attack on any one of them would be treated as an attack on all.

NATO has become the world's most organized and integrated military force, especially since the breakup of the Warsaw Pact. During the Cold War, it was relied on for Europe's fundamental security needs and it allowed for the progressive development of economic integration. However, France became concerned that this regional international organization was effectively subject to U.S. domination and withdrew from NATO in 1966. The end of the Cold War after 1990 left the organization's solidarity in doubt. Without a Cold War opponent, the organization has been in search of a new role in the post-Cold War era.

In 1990, Germany's Manfred Worner, then NATO's Secretary General, proposed an association with the former Warsaw Pact countries just before that organization was dissolved. In June of 1994, Russia became the twenty-first State to sign the Partnership for Peace Program involving cooperation with NATO in joint military exercises, peacekeeping, and the exchange of military doctrine and weaponry. A week later, Russian President Boris Yeltsin signed an agreement with the EU Commission president on economic matters removing quotas on Russian exports into EU countries.

Membership in the Partnership for Peace Program does not constitute full NATO membership, and Germany and the United States are at odds on whether Russia should ultimately become a full-fledged member of NATO. The war in Bosnia that has contin-

ued for three and a half years was finally ended by a peace treaty negotiated between the independent States of Croatia, Bosnia-Herzegovina, and Serbia in December of 1995. The peace treaty, signed in Paris and agreed to by the U.N. Security Council, involves the use of NATO as a multinational peace implementation force (IFOR) to police the agreement. France and Russia have agreed to cooperate in this effort to end the Bosnia crisis and will participate in the peacekeeping mission. This unique turn of events will involve French, Russian, and NATO troops in a military security operation for the first time since World War II. It is the largest military mission undertaken by NATO in its entire history and will involve over sixty thousand troops—twenty thousand from the United States and the rest coming from more than thirty other countries—placed under NATO command. The recognized weakness of the security forces of the EC independent of the United States has been demonstrated in

> ### North Atlantic Treaty Organization (NATO): *The military alliance of European countries, including the United States and Canada, that is the most organized and integrated military force in the world. It has recently assumed a new peacekeeping role in Bosnia.*

the Bosnia crisis, and the **North Atlantic Treaty Organization** has been given a new role in post-Cold War Europe.

The Conference on Security and Cooperation in Europe (CSCE)[2]

The CSCE is another major regional international organization of Europe. It consists of fifty-three, mostly European, States, including Russia, Canada, and the United States. This organization unites East and West European countries in promoting European security and even extends official "observer" status to Japan. The CSCE was born in 1972 just after conclusion of the first Strategic Arms Limitations Treaty between the United States and the Soviet Union.

The two major defining moments in the evolving CSCE institutional process include the Helsinki Final Act of 1975 and negotiation of the 1989 Concluding Document of Vienna, which contains a mandate for the Negotiation on Conventional Armed Forces in Europe. These contributions toward the knitting of East and West European security interests and humanitarian concerns have had far-reaching implications. The Helsinki Final Act led to a commitment to human rights on the part of the Soviet Union that ultimately led to the breakup of the Soviet Union itself and the independence of the Eastern bloc countries. The preparation at Vienna led to the successful conclusion of the 1990 Conventional Forces in Europe Treaty (CFE) or Treaty of Paris supported by France, which perceived the CFE as a genuine "European" alternative to resolving regional security problems outside the U.S.-dominated NATO.

Since the ending of the Cold War, the **Conference on Security and Cooperation in Europe (CSCE)** has adopted a new stance in relationship with the former Warsaw Pact nations. Instead of a confrontational approach between East and West, it has begun to take on a new cooperational approach to development of more permanent institutions. The 1991 CSCE Madrid Conference produced the framework of the CSCE Parliament, and the 1992 meeting of the CSCE Council of Ministers produced the Prague Document on the non-proliferation of nuclear weapons and limitations on arms transfers within Europe.

The CSCE places priority emphasis on human rights issues. The CSCE's Conference on the Human Dimension meets annually to exchange information about questionable State practices and unresolved human rights problems. In 1995, Russia agreed to receive a permanent human rights mission from the CSCE to monitor events in Chechnya, the rebellious Muslim region of Russia that seeks independence. In March of 1995, CSCE efforts led to conclusion of a Pact of Stability that requires the former Soviet bloc countries wishing to join either the European Union or NATO to first settle any border disputes and ethnic conflicts. The pact includes agreement to permit the CSCE to be the watchdog agency for ensuring compliance. This may prevent any future Yugoslavia-like conflicts (see Slomanson, 1995, pp. 144-146).

The Organization of African Unity (OAU)

The OAU is a regional organization created in 1963, consisting of most of the independent African States except South Africa. It was established to promote unity; to coordinate political, economic, cultural, medical, scientific, and defense policies; to defend the independence and territorial integrity of the member States; and to eliminate colonialism on the continent. Toward these ends, the **Organization of African Unity (OAU)** has established a commission to mediate all disputes among African nations.

Conference on Security and Cooperation in Europe (CSCE):
The evolving institutions uniting East and West European nations in co-operative efforts to promote human rights and independent national security interests. This organization includes Russia, the United States, and Canada along with fifty other European nations.

Organization of African Unity (OAU): Consists of most of the African States that have established a regional international organization of general importance in the area.

This regional organization has become more prominent in response to conflicts in the region and assisting the United Nations in peacekeeping missions on the African continent.

The policy-making body of the organization is the Assembly of Heads of State and Government, consisting of the leaders of the fifty-two member nations or their representatives. At its annual meetings, the assembly approves decisions made at periodic conferences by the Council of Ministers, which consists of the foreign ministers of the member countries. Efforts at conflict resolution are made through a central organ of the conflict prevention, resolution, and management system now in place within the organization. A peace fund was created within the OAU to finance the system's operations. Technical research, mainly in agriculture, is conducted through a scientific and research commission. The organization, although maintaining its political nature, has become involved with economic integration and cooperation as part of the effort to establish an African Economic Community whose treaty was signed by African leaders in 1991. After receiving the required ratifications, the treaty entered into force in April of 1994.

The end of major issues of colonialism by the mid 1990s may have profound effects on the character of the OAU in the future. After many years of effort to secure the ending of apartheid in South Africa and Statehood for Namibia (the former South West African mandate governed by South Africa), these objectives have finally been achieved. Namibia gained its independence in 1990. With the election of Nelson Mandela to the presidency of South Africa, the emphasis of the OAU has begun to shift away from its primary political strategy of supporting black nationalist anticolonial movements.

The Arab League

The League of Arab States is another regional organization composed of twenty-one Middle Eastern States and the Palestine Liberation Organization (PLO). The Arab league was established in 1945 to promote comprehensive cooperation among countries of Arabic language and culture. It established the Council of Arab Economic Unity in 1964 to promote an Arab Common Market and various other economic programs. Since 1968, the league has developed institutions that include the Arab Fund for Economic and Social Development, the Arab Bank for Economic Development in Africa, and the Arab Monetary Fund.

The primary goal of the League of Arab States is political collaboration for preserving the independence and the State sovereignty of its members. The Council of the League of Arab States deployed interleague peacekeeping forces in Kuwait in 1961 and Lebanon in 1976. However, these efforts have been hampered by the bitter rivalries that exist between the Arab States. The effort in Lebanon ended in failure in 1989 when Syria refused league demands to withdraw its troops from Lebanon and Iraq (Syria's archenemy). The league has been divided over many recent developments. Egypt was suspended from the league in 1979 because of the Camp David Agreements in 1978 to make peace with Israel. The 1991 Persian Gulf War further disintegrated Arab unity. However, the PLO has negotiated an autonomy agreement with Israel for control of Gaza and the West Bank area. Egypt and Jordan have reached peace settlements with Israel, and although Syria and Lebanon are, as of this writing, still at war with Israel, a comprehensive peace settlement securing the boarders of Israel may at long last be accomplished.

Other Regional Organizations

The United Nations Organization has made significant efforts to create, and strengthen, regional institutions for permanent consultation and resolution of regional issues in all major areas of the world. These efforts have recently resulted in the formation of the Association of South East Asian Nations (ASEAN), which provides a new regional forum launched in 1994 in Bangkok, Thailand.

Most of the other regional organizations in the world today are economic in character. They include the Organization for Economic Cooperation and Development (OECD), the so-called Group of 77, the Organization of Petroleum Exporting Countries (OPEC), and the Latin American Economic Association of States. The Community of Independent States (CIS) was created in 1991 and includes seven of the fifteen States that became independent with the breakup of the Soviet Union. They have declared their intention to pursue a policy of strengthening international peace and security and to undertake to discharge the international obligations under the treaties and agreements entered into by the former Union of Soviet Socialist Republics. They are making provisions for joint control over nuclear weapons and for their nonproliferation.

All of these multilateral organizations display varying degrees of law development potential. They create varying degrees of institutional and administrative processes that must be considered part of the dynamic system of international law development in the twentieth century. The most important of these economic and political organizations that does not clearly fit into the regional pattern is the astounding development of the General Agreement on Tariffs and Trade.

The World Trade Organization

The **General Agreement on Tariffs and Trade (GATT)** emerged outside the originally anticipated United Nations Organization initially named the International Trade Organization (ITO). The ITO never materialized because of Cold War pressures. However, the United States, as the world's largest trading State, has succeeded in creating a multilateral legal regime in the area of world trade. The GATT treaties have been negotiated for ten-year periods, which have progressed through three decades of law development. The Kennedy Round, the Tokyo Round, and the Uruguay Round, as these decade treaties have become known, have substantially reduced tariffs worldwide. The most recent, the Uruguay Round, has produced significant innovations, including the creation of a new **World Trade Organization** with significant authority to settle disputes among the more than 130 nations that will be involved. The U.S. Congress passed this new treaty through the normal process of legislative enactment involving both houses of Congress in 1994.

> *General Agreement on Tariffs and Trade (GATT):* The most extensive treaty regulating issues of tariffs and trade among more than 130 States.

> *World Trade Organization (WTO):* The new set of institutional arrangements set up to administer and settle disputes among the members of the GATT.

Enforcement and International Legal Regimes

The international community has now turned its attention toward developing more adequate enforcement mechanisms. Many of these treaties created organizational structures for the monitoring of relevant developments and processing complaints of violations. Even before the demise of the Soviet Union, public attitudes concerning respect for human rights, fears of terrorism, and arms buildup demanded responses that were more than appeals to behave. The end of the Cold War and dissoluion of the Communist bloc accelerated these tendencies. It became possible to achieve agreement on a variety of procedures to induce and even compel States to carry out their legal obligations. The enforcement powers of the Security Council were reinvigorated, virtually overnight, and a new perspective on compliance became evident. Schachter (1994) reports figures obtained from the U.N. Secretariat revealing the remarkable increase in Chapter VII sanctions: "In the 45 years prior to 1990, the Council adopted only 14 resolutions under Chapter VII. From 1990 through 1993, it adopted 58 Chapter VII resolutions, 25 of them in 1993" (p. 12).

However, the long-range effectiveness of any system of law cannot really be measured by how many times **sanctions** have been applied. All those who violate the law are never punished, even in the most well ordered national legal systems. No legal system is perfect, and the international legal system is far from achieving the level of success of most national legal systems. Most people, as well as most States, obey the law because they believe it is the right thing to do—because they prefer to live in an ordered society. The international community has discovered innovative techniques for promoting this most significant aspect of general law enforcement.

> *Sanctions:* Measures taken to induce compliance with the rules of international law.

Public international law cannot be enforced by the same methods used in municipal law because of the nature of the parties involved. Enforcement is essentially an executive and administrative function in municipal law as well as in international law. Courts are frequently misunderstood as enforcement agents when in fact their basic function is to decide what the law is as applied to a given set of facts. Courts must also decide questions of fact in dispute, and they have developed elaborate procedures for this purpose. Their main function, however, is to apply the law to the established facts in discretely defined cases. The lack of a clearly defined court system with compulsory jurisdiction to hear cases submitted to them and decide on the basis of established principles of law is considered one of the chief weaknesses of the international legal system.

However, even in cases in which States have submitted to having their disputes settled by international tribunals or arbitral bodies, the problem of enforcement of their judgments remains. Nation-states cannot be treated like individuals in municipal courts. Individuals can be arrested and punished through fines and deprivation of liberties. Public international law faces the dilemma involved in peacekeeping and enforcement actions that to punish an entire society for violations of the law would be unfair. The concept of war crimes and crimes against humanity has been developed to meet this dilemma. Individuals may be punished for these crimes by any State through their municipal court system when personal jurisdiction is obtained. The difficulty of apprehending and punishing individuals who have committed such crimes when they are protected by their own national governments is another weakness of the international legal system.

The concept of criminal liability in international law is a new concept. Traditional public international law has been considered more analogous to civil liability in municipal law. Most disputes between States are not breaches of the peace, threats to the peace, or acts of aggression. They involve disputes over violations of treaty obligations or in areas where legal principles have not been clearly established. Where these issues threaten the vital interests of nation-states or emerging groups that aspire to become nation-states, a threat to the peace may develop. By encouraging peaceful resolution of these disputes through negotiation and the development of legal principles that will stabilize the situation, the international community follows a preventive strategy of law enforcement.

Many of the lawmaking treaties developed through the U.N. legal process are not merely statements of rules. They include significant procedures of enforcement through establishing agencies to monitor complaints and prepare fact-finding reports that are submitted to U.N. agencies for action. The early functional international unions in the areas of communications and transportation have now evolved into elaborate systems that are widely relied on to regulate vital services such as those provided by the International Telecommunications Union (ITU) and the International Civil Aviation Organization (ICAO). However, in more recent developments, these techniques have gained greater significance in more controversial areas, such as human rights. The International Convenant on Civil and Political Rights and the International Convention on the Elimination of All Forms of Racial Discrimination incorporate similar techniques. They have also been used by the ILO and the treaty organizations dealing with narcotic drugs.

The fact-finding process institutionalized by these bodies often uses the complaints of individuals and private organizations in their investigation by the appropriate committee. These investigative committees consult with the accused State and seek authority to conduct independent investigations within the State where alleged violations are reported. Their conclusions are openly discussed with the accused State, and efforts are made to devise methods of prevention of future violations. Ultimately, these reports are transmitted to a parent body and made public. The Security Council and other organs of the United Nations use these reports as part of the fact-finding process available to them when considering sanctions.

For example, a working group of the Human Rights Commission has investigated some fifteen thousand cases of "enforced or involuntary disappearances" each year for several years. In-depth inquiries on specific problems such as torture and investigation of countries accused of systematic abuses have been conducted and reported to the political organs. In some cases, these country *rapporteurs* within the commissions have acted more like prosecutors before U.N. bodies, and even when official action is not taken, they have the effect of mobilizing shame. In other cases, fact-finding results have brought about conciliation and negotiated solutions in which internal reforms have affected behavior.

U.N. action may be facilitative, such as the use of armed peacekeeping forces to assist governments in complying with transborder truce and cease-fire agreements or, in some cases, in maintaining internal law and order. Again fact-finding plays a significant role in this process. Expulsion from the benefits of an international organization is another form of sanction that may be imposed as well as suspension from voting privileges, which can be used as an inducement to comply with international legal obligations. The range of options available to the U.N. Security Council to enforce compliance is substantial and must be tailored to the particular situation at hand. The more experience that accumulates through the use of these sanctions, the more effective the international community can become in its enforcement functions. However, the function is inherently problematical, and the ultimate solution lies in greater respect for the rule of law and peaceful procedures for dispute resolution.

Much of international law has been incorporated into the municipal law of individual States and is applied in the same manner as all law. Private disputes can be initiated by private parties and adjudicated in national courts in a broad range of circumstances. Commercial international transactions and dispute resolution techniques have been broadly facilitated by international agreements concerning the enforcement of foreign judgments and judgments of arbitral tribunals. Control of international terrorism involves implementation of international agreements concerning extradition of persons who are alleged to have committed crimes for which there is sufficient probable cause. Individual nation-states still possess the right of self-defense (Article 51 of the U.N. Charter). They may also employ a broad range of economic and political self-help measurers to induce compliance with international norms, as long as they do not involve the use of force.

This text attempts to provide more detailed understanding of the basic principles of law that have been developed in substantive areas. Part II explores the traditional areas of international law that have been incorporated into the domestic law of States. In these areas, individuals have limited but expanding access to direct action through the courts of individual States to effect legal remedies. Both public and private remedies are available in the areas of human rights, business transactions, intellectual property rights, labor, and environmental protection. International crimes and extradition are substantive areas in which public law prevails, but there is increasing protection of individual rights in these affairs. Diplomatic and sovereign immunity are substantive areas of international law that are of major concern to domestic courts, but they mark the dividing line between substantive areas that are purely public.

In Part III, the areas of international law that have only public law remedies will be discussed. These areas include the legal status of States and IGOs, the law of treaties, adjudication of disputes, and international compliance measures.

■   ■   ■

Chapter Summary

1. Contemporary international law represents the accumulation of historical experiences regarded as legally binding by modern nation-states. It includes the rules governing the vast array of functioning institutions that deal with international issues and make decisions on the basis of established principles of law.

2. The scope of modern international law includes both public and private aspects of international law and concepts of international business law. It could be defined simply as the entire body of norms, rules, and procedures that govern relationships that transcend national boundaries and are regarded by governmental authority as legally binding.

3. Evidence of the legally binding nature of such rules can be found in the legislative enactments of national governments and their customary practices. These municipal sources may be limited by explicit international agreements in conformity with fundamental principles of international law regarded as legally binding.

4. The sources of public international law are primarily treaties and customary practices of States regarded as legally binding. They also include the general principles of law recognized by civilized nations.

5. The lawmaking functions of the international legal community are different from those of individual States. Public international law may be created or altered through the processes of bilateral, multilateral, or lawmaking treaties. Therefore, sources of international law may be particular, general, or universal in character.

6. Codification of customary international law has produced lawmaking treaties covering most of the areas of customary international law. These treaties are intended to specify and clarify existing international law. They provide authoritative rules that may limit State sovereignty even when that State has not ratified the convention.

7. Lawmaking treaties that go beyond clarification of existing customary practice of States are those multilateral treaties ratified by a sufficiently large number of States and intended to create new universal norms and rules of State limitation. These treaties may create new customary rules of State practice.

8. Hundreds of these multilateral treaties, codifying and extending the general principles of international law, have been concluded through the efforts of the U.N. system, which is designed to encourage the progressive development of international law.

9. A large body of international administrative law is being developed by the specialized agencies of intergovernmental organizations and the major organs of the U.N. system.

10. International legal regimes are being created through the development of procedures for enforcement being built into the lawmaking treaties in many significant areas of international law. These procedures involve investigations and fact-finding reports by intergovernmental agencies that are beginning to be used in enforcement procedures by the political agencies of the United Nations.

11. The major regional IGOs have significant functions within the international legal order and have developed important institutions for the progressive development of international law among their member States. The most important of these organizations are the Organization of American States, the European Union, and the European Court of Human Rights.

12. The General Agreement on Tariffs and Trade creating a new World Trade Organization is one of the most important developments of modern international law binding member States to limitations in trade practices and providing for new institutions of dispute settlement.

13. International enforcement mechanisms and procedures have been improved since the end of the Cold War. The Security Council has become much more active in its enforcement responsibilities. However, enforcement of the law against nation-states is substantially different from law enforcement within independent sovereign nation-states.

14. Concepts of criminal liability of individuals for war crimes and crimes against humanity have been developed, and procedures are being established for prosecution of some of these individuals. However, traditional international law generally involves concepts more clearly associated with civil liability.

15. Much of international law has been incorporated into the municipal law of individual nation-states. Many of these treaties and laws give individuals access to the ordinary courts to resolve their disputes. National courts thus provide increasing means of adjudication and enforcement of international law.

16. Individual nation-states still possess a considerable range of self-help measures in applying economic and political sanctions short of the use of force to induce States to observe international commitments.

Key Terms

common law
restatements
municipal law
private international law
conflict of laws
transnational law
public international law
bilateral treaty
multilateral treaty
lawmaking treaty
codification
International Law Commission
1982 Convention on Law of the Sea
Deep Seabed Authority
res communis
International Bill of Rights
administrative law

international legal regimes
political question
legal question
Organization of American States (OAS)
European Union
European Parliament
European Court of Human Rights (ECHR)
North Atlantic Treaty Organization (NATO)
Conference on Security and Cooperation in Europe (CSCE)
Organization of African Unity (OAU)
General Agreement on Tariffs and Trade (GATT)
World Trade Organization (WTO)
sanctions

Discussion Questions

1. What is international law?
2. How does public international law differ from municipal law?
3. What is meant by private international law? Why is it an important part of modern international law?
4. Why is international business law an important part of modern international law?
5. Would *transnational law* be a more appropriate term for the understanding of the broader considerations of modern international law? Why or why not?
6. How do the sources of public international law differ from the sources of municipal law?
7. What are the major distinctions between bilateral, multilateral, and lawmaking treaties?
8. How has customary international law been codified through U.N.-sponsored procedures?
9. Why does the 1982 Convention on Law of the Sea represent a major milestone in the development of universal international law?
10. What is administrative law, and how have intergovernmental agencies contributed to the development of international law?
11. What is the importance of the major regional organizations in the development of international law?
12. How can international law be enforced?

Notes

1. To further explain the difference between the EC and the EU: The European Economic Community (EEC) officially became the European Community (EC) when the Maastricht accords were ratified and operationalized November 1, 1993. The excerpts from the Maastricht Treaty (see Appendix B) state specifically that "by this Treaty, the High Contracting Parties establish among themselves a European Union, hereinafter called 'the Union.' " It goes on to say that "the Union shall be founded on the European Communities." This refers to the Rome Treaty (which created the EEC and hence refers to the EC today), the European Coal and Steel Community (ECSC), and the European Atomic Energy Community (EURATOM). This group of communities is known as the European Union (EU), which dates from 1993.

2. The CSCE changed its name to the Organization for Security and Cooperation in Europe (OSCE) in 1994 as a result of the Budapest Summit. As of 1997 it includes 55 participating states.

Suggested Readings

Appendix B: Treaty on European Union

Charney, J. I. (1993). Universal international law. *American Journal of International Law, 87*, 529-551.

Folsom, R. H. (1995). *European union law in a nutshell* (2nd ed.). St. Paul, MN: West.

Schachter, O. (1994). United Nations law. *American Journal of International Law, 88*, 1-23.

Internet Sources

Browse: Use the terms *international law* and *international organization* to discover a world of information on the World Wide Web. It provides access to private and public sources of current importance. However, the problem is more related to reliability and validity of the material obtained in this manner. More reliable specific sites are listed below:

Internet Gate (http://www.libraries.psu.edu/crsweb/docs/forgate.htm) will get you started by providing search strategies and hypertext addresses of interest in international law. Use *international law* to narrow your search.

U.N. Home Page (http://www.un.org/) will get you to U.N. agencies around the world.

For access to specific treaties and updates on which States have ratified major conventions and what reservations they have made, use (http://www.un.org/Depts/Treaty). You must now register to access this site.

Information sources on the European Union (EUROPA) (http://www.europa.en.int/en/index.html)

Organization of American States (http://www.oas.org/homepag.htm)

World Trade Organization (http://www.unicc.org/wto/)

Get questions

II The Individual and International Law

The next seven chapters of this text are devoted to areas of international law that provide remedies that may be initiated by individuals or corporations as well as remedies for violations of international law that may be pursued by governments. Private parties may bring legal actions in civil litigation in the areas of human rights, both individual and property rights, in the domestic courts of individual states. In modern times, the international community has promoted the development of a multifaceted series of treaties that confer on individuals and corporate entities access to domestic courts in order to secure certain fundamental rights and allow them to obtain protection through court orders or awards for damages sustained. These private rights are limited by the exercise of sovereignty by modern nation-states, but even the capacity of private parties to sue governmental entities has expanded in modern times.

Legal process involves both civil and criminal actions in domestic courts of individual States. The area of private law is confined to civil legal actions in tort, or personal injury wrongs, and contract. Private individuals, corporations, and even governmental agencies may bring legal actions in these areas to obtain either court orders requiring specific performance or to obtain restoration for injuries sustained. Criminal actions are considered part of public law of individual states and require charges to be brought officially by a state prosecutor. However, even in the United States, the individual has fundamental rights to due pro-cess of law that have been recognized in international law.

The foundation of all law is based on a fundamental sense of justice and the historical assertion that universal standards are applicable to all human societies. The seventeenth century brought a shift in emphasis away from natural law toward a theory of natural rights. The rights of people, or human rights, were given much greater emphasis in international law after the development of the U.N. Charter. Traditional international law had placed more emphasis on the State's right to protect its own nationals abroad. The doctrine of natural rights led to the development of customary international law pertaining to the protection of aliens. It became customary practice of states that aliens were entitled to minimal standards of descent treatment because each state had a fundamental obligation to protect its citizens. It followed that whoever gives a citizen ill treatment indirectly injures the State of his or her nationality and that the State concerned has a right to protect its citizen.

The traditional concept of protection of aliens provided some degree of protection for the individual, but the result was that in many cases, individuals in their capacity as aliens enjoyed a larger measure of protection by international law than in their capacity as citizens of their own State. The major goal of the modern human rights movement is to remove this distinction and promote a common set of minimal standards for all human beings, nationals as well as aliens.

The international community's concern for individual human rights can be traced back to the treaty of Westphalia in 1648, which established the principle of equality of rights for those of the Catholic and Protestant faiths. Both the Congress of Vienna in 1815 and the Congress of Berlin in 1878 provided for individuals' rights to exercise their religion freely. Various antislavery movements culminated in the League of Nations Anti-Slavery Convention of 1926. The Hague Peace Conferences of 1899 and 1907 established principles that have led to the modern protocols concerning the conduct of warfare and treatment of prisoners. The Treaty of Versailles and the "minorities treaties" required some States to respect the rights of members of minorities living within their boundaries. The concept of self-determination had its international beginnings in the mandates developed out of the peace settlement ending World War I.

World War II demonstrated "man's inhumanity to man" on a global scale and led to concerted efforts to promote human rights on the global level. The United States and several other countries proposed that a Bill of Human Rights be included in the U.N. Charter. This effort did not succeed, but the preamble and Articles 55 and 56 of the U.N. Charter make it clear that international protection of human rights is one of the organization's highest priorities. Article 68 of the charter did require establishment of a Commission on Human Rights, and in 1948, the organization adopted the Universal Declaration of Human Rights without a dissenting vote. It includes civil, political, economic, social, and cultural rights that are universally considered to be minimal standards. However, this resolution has little direct effect in domestic courts and is considered nonenforceable in national courts. That is, it was not intended to confer rights and responsibilities that are actionable in the domestic law of states; however, international and domestic courts may take judicial notice of such evidence in determining the existence of customary principles of international law. (See Separate Opinion of Vice-President Ammoun in Advisory Opinion on the Continued Presence of South Africa in Namibia, 1971 I.C.J. Reports 16, 76.)

The next phase of development of the modern human rights conventions intended to make enforceable those rights laid down in the Universal Declaration of Human Rights. The Human Rights "Covenants" are the result of this effort to bring about directly enforceable rights in domestic courts. Originally, there was to be only one treaty of implementation; however, the complexity of undertaking the task of multilateral negotiations in the mists of the Cold War and at a time when U.N. membership more than doubled required the drafting of two treaties. After more than twelve years of debate, the Covenant on Civil and Political Rights (CPR Covenant) and the Covenant on Economic, Social, and Cultural Rights were adopted by the General Assembly in 1966 and opened for ratification by individual States. Ten years later, in 1976, they both entered into force, making them universally applicable.

These documents, along with the Genocide Convention and the Apartheid Convention, have been included as appendixes to this text. They should be consulted for a more detailed understanding of their contents. The two covenants establish international regimes for systematic review and development of progressive improvement in human rights compliance. Another of these major documents is the Convention Against Torture and Other Cruel, Inhuman or Degrading Treatment or Punishment (the Torture Convention). This prohibition has been used in U.S. federal court as support-

ing a fundamental principle of international law (*jus cogens*) and is directly applicable in individual cases.

In the chapters that follow, a few cases of particular utility in explaining concepts of law and innovative developments will be used, and it is therefore important that the student become familiar with the basic method of case analysis. A case in law represents *opinio juris* and is evidence of the specific meaning and application of law in a particular set of circumstances. Therefore, case opinions have a narrow meaning in law and answer particular questions of law in dispute. These case opinions will provide some of the basic evidence of changes in international law and how it is beginning to be applied even in the domestic courts of the United States.

The first of these substantive chapters will illustrate a range of human rights decisions that demonstrate aspects of state responsibility to individuals. The vast area of human rights implications cannot be covered in an introductory text in any comprehensive manner. This introductory substantive chapter is intended to demonstrate some of the ways that the universal concepts of human rights are beginning to affect the application of the law in individual States as well as in international tribunals. The range of legal actions extending to international humanitarian intervention authorized by the U.N. Security Council will be illustrated.

This text is designed to be an introduction to international legal implications for a wide range of students who may be interested in international trade and business law. Individual and corporate rights in conducting business activities are therefore dealt with in the chapters that follow. Enforcement of foreign court judgments is a subject that broadly affects civil litigation and the implementation of private rights.

Protection of real and intellectual property rights in the areas of patents and copyrights is of increasing importance to individuals, corporations, and nations in international relations. Labor and environmental regulation are also major topics of interest to the international community. Environmental concerns are perhaps the most pervasive issues that will determine our future capacity to enjoy human rights on this planet. These areas of international legal development will be discussed in Chapters 5 through 8 of this text.

International crimes and extradition are areas of law that are of increasing concern to the international community. Principles of State jurisdiction in the criminal area and the concept of universal crimes will be explained in Chapter 9. Increasingly, the individual State and the international community are finding ways to hold individuals accountable for criminal activity. The extent of State jurisdiction in criminal matters, extradition, and international crimes will be defined and illustrated in this chapter.

The more traditional areas of international law concerning diplomatic and sovereign immunity will be discussed in the final substantive chapter in this section. In these areas also the major law enforcement agency is the individual state, but international law holds states accountable for their violations of diplomatic and sovereign immunity. This chapter is intended to make the transition to topics of more purely public international law issues.

Diplomatic immunity and sovereign immunity are major principles of international law that have their effects within individual States and limit the domestic jurisdiction of individual nation-states. The limits of national court jurisdiction are illustrated in these areas and lead us to the plane of public international law that involves disputes between sovereign states concerning acts of State. The "act of State doctrine" will be illustrated through significant court decisions in this section. This concept ultimately defines the limits of national court jurisdiction.

4 An Introduction to Individual State Practice

International law is deeply rooted in the U.S. experience. It is part of our constitutional law and common-law heritage. It is inscribed in Article 1, Section 8, Clause 10 of the Constitution where Congress is given the power "to define and punish Piracies and Felonies committed on the high seas, and offenses against the Law of Nations." It is embodied in the area of common law known as Foreign Relations Law of the United States, and it is recognized in congressional acts that seek to implement our treaty obligations.

This broad potential for implementation of international law through the domestic courts of the United States must be tempered by the realization that the courts have incorporated the law of nations quite sparingly. The principal reason for this sparse application is due to the constitutional division of authority between the legislative, executive, and judicial branches of government. The judiciary has been reluctant to become embroiled in foreign policy ques-

tions, which it recognizes are primarily political in nature and properly within the authority given to the president and Congress—the political branches. Another concern of the courts relates to the largely imprecise nature of the traditional rules of international law. As the specificity of the body of public international law increases, the courts of the United States are more likely to accept court jurisdiction in areas previously considered nonjusticiable, or not subject to adjudication.

Even though the Constitution gives Congress the power to define offenses against the law of nations, this has not been held to preclude the courts from applying international legal principles that have not been defined by Congress but that are derived from our common-law English heritage.

The general norm of the application of international law in U.S. courts is expressed in the first of our illustrative cases, the *Paquete Habana* case, delivered by the U.S. Supreme Court in 1900. This case also illustrates the practical use of the concept of customary international law. Both international tribunals and national courts may apply customary practice of nation-states regarded as legally binding to resolve disputes.

Reading Case Law Opinions

Before reading this case, it may be useful to discuss the general properties of case law and the educational methods associated with the approach of **case law analysis.** Modern law schools in the United States use case law analysis extensively as an educational tool. Even undergraduates find this method appealing because it allows them to focus on the application of principles of law to a particular set of facts. However, one must be aware that most case law opinions are statements by authoritative courts relevant to issues of law in dispute. The courts draft their opinions for purposes of explaining what the law is on a given subject. Since the facts of disputes may be substantially different, these court decisions in common law or statutory law interpretation are very precise formulations of court practice. They are the most specific examples of the law because they illustrate actual practice and may be cited in future cases in which the facts are essentially the same. Different facts may require the application of another rule because the situation is different.

To read and understand case law properly, it is necessary to have some familiarity with the typical elements of a case law opinion. The *title and citation* of the case is important because it tells you what court

> **Case law analysis:** The educational method of reading and analyzing selected cases that illustrate the application of law in particular fact situations.

decided the case and when it was decided. The Supreme Court of the United States is the most authoritative court in the land. The opinion will generally explain any *previous actions by lower courts* involved in the case at hand and provide a short description of the previously ascertained facts in the case. The purpose of this section of the opinion is to inform the reader of the specific *fact situation* that raises an issue of law in dispute. Identification of the specific *issue of law in dispute* is usually made explicit by the Court because it is the issues of law that are decided in a case law opinion. There may be several legal issues involved in a single case. The answers to these issues of law that are raised by the case are the **holdings** of the Court and represent practical rules of law known as *precedents*.

> **Holding:** The specific kernel of law expressed as a legal rule in terms that will identify the particular fact situation and the application of that rule.

The larger body of the case law opinion is usually an explanation of why the Court "held" the way it did. This is known as the court's reasoning and provides the valuable process of reasoning used to arrive at the precedent or holding. **Legal reasoning** is more precise than merely the expression of one's opinion or preference on a particular topic. Learning to follow the thought processes of the courts

> **Legal reasoning:** Logical deduction or analogistic reasoning that proceeds from generally accepted norms to logical application in specific fact situations.

through reading court opinions provides valuable insight into the particular properties of legal reasoning and how it differs from political reasoning. It is not necessary to follow a formal case briefing procedure in reading these cases at the undergraduate level. However, your instructor may provide specific instructions for you to follow in preparing for class discussion of the cases used in this text. The following case provides a good opportunity for the beginning student to learn about these basic elements of case law. Many cases will be used in this section of the text, and they may become more complex as we progress. These cases have been edited to conserve space. Where you see three asterisks (* * *), the original text has been cut and there may be a shortened summary of the discussion in the original text included within brackets.

Common Law and Customary Practice Illustrated

The *Paquete Habana* case is the classic example of the limited opportunities of private parties to gain access to the courts of the United States to enforce international law. As you read this first case, keep in mind several basic points of analysis. Look for the following points of the case as you read and then come back to these questions to prepare for class discussion on these points.

1. What were the basic facts revealed in this case that brought it to the Supreme Court of the United States?
2. What was the legal question before the court?
3. How did the Court answer this legal question?
4. What evidence of customary practice of States was used by the Court to establish the rule of law that was applied?
5. What remedy did the Court provide to settle this dispute?

This case also illustrates the difficult-to-understand concept of customary international law and how courts determine the existence of customary practice of States regarded as legally binding. Note that the facts of this case narrow the issue to a precise question that the Court proceeds to answer by reference to historical practice of the most significant nations. From the beginning of the United States, the federal courts have acted as prize courts (described later) and have that exclusive jurisdiction.

Congress declared war against Spain in 1898, and the president ordered the U.S. Navy to patrol Cuban waters to prevent activities that might aid Spain in its war efforts. The Navy thus seized two coastal fishing vessels near the coast of Cuba. One was the *Paquete Habana* and the other was the *Lola*.

The "prize courts" of nations at war have traditionally determined the lawfulness of military seizures of foreign vessels. A "prize" is a captured enemy or neutral vessel suspected of carrying materials to aid the enemy. The federal district court at the trial level of the federal court hierarchy examined U.S. domestic law to determine the validity of the seizure based on presidential executive decrees regarding the Law of Prize. The lower court's decision upheld the seizure of these coastal fishing vessels. The case was then appealed to the U.S. Supreme Court, where the majority of the Court overruled the lower court's decision based on considerations of customary international law.

The *Paquete Habana* Case

Supreme Court of the United States, 1900.
175 U.S. 077, 20 S.Ct. 290, 14 L.Ed. 320.

Supreme Ct vol. 20 page 290

Mr. Justice GRAY delivered the opinion of the court:

These are two appeals from decrees of the district court of the United States for the southern district of Florida condemning two fishing vessels and their cargoes as prize of war.

Each vessel was a fishing smack, running in and out of Havana, and regularly engaged in fishing on the coast of Cuba; sailed under the Spanish flag; was owned by a Spanish subject of Cuban birth, living in the city of Havana; was commanded by a subject of Spain, also residing in Havana. . . . Her cargo consisted of fresh fish, caught by her crew from the sea, put on board as they were caught, and kept and sold alive. Until stopped by the blockading squadron she had no knowledge of the existence of the war or of any blockade. She had no arms or ammunition on board, and made no attempt to run the blockade after she knew of its existence, nor any resistance at the time of the capture.

* * *

We are then brought to the consideration of the question whether, upon the facts appearing in these records, the fishing smacks were subject to capture by the armed vessels of the United States during the recent war with Spain.

Customary Int. Law

By an ancient usage among civilized nations, beginning centuries ago, and gradually ripening into a rule of international law, coast fishing vessels, pursuing their vocation of catching and bringing in fresh fish, have been recognized as exempt, with their cargoes and crews, from capture as prize of war.

[The Court then describes the earliest known acts protecting foreign fishermen in time of war. In 1403 and 1406, Henry IV of England issued orders protecting fishermen of foreign states. The order of 1406 placed all fishermen of France, Flanders, and Brittany, with their fishing vessels and boats and equipment, everywhere on the sea, under his special protection. As long as they were coming or going from fishing activities in good conduct, they were not to be hindered by His Majesty's officers. This practice, based on prior agreement with the French king for reciprocal treatment, was followed in a treaty made October 2, 1521, between Emperor Charles V and Francis I of France. In 1536, Dutch edicts permitted herring fishing in time of war. Early French practice even permitted admirals to accord fishing truces in time of war. In ordinances passed in 1681 and 1692, France curtailed this practice, apparently because of the failure of her enemies to accord reciprocal treatment.]

The doctrine which exempts coast fishermen, with their vessels and cargoes, from capture as prize of war, has been familiar to the United States from the time of the War of Independence.

On June 5, 1779, Louis XVI, our ally in that war, addressed a letter to his admiral, informing him that the wish he had always had of alleviating, as far as he could, the hardships of war, had directed his attention to that class of his subjects which devoted itself to the trade of fishing, and had no other means of livelihood; that he had thought that the example which he should give to his enemies . . . would determine them to allow to fishermen the same facilities which he should consent to grant; and that he had therefore given orders to the commanders of all his ships not to disturb English fishermen, nor to arrest their vessels laden with fresh fish . . . ; provided they had no offensive arms, and were not proved to have made any signals creating a suspicion of intelligence with the enemy; and the admiral was directed to communicate the King's intentions to all officers under his control. By a royal order in council of November 6, 1780, the former orders were confirmed; and the capture and ransom, by a French cruiser, of *The John and Sarah*, an English vessel, coming from Holland, laden with fresh fish, were pronounced to be illegal. 2 *Code des Prises* (ed. 1784) 721, 901, 903.

Among the standing orders made by Sir James Marriott, Judge of the English High Court of Admiralty, was one of April 11, 1780, by which it was "ordered that all causes of prize of fishing boats or vessels taken from the enemy may be consolidated in one monition, and one sentence or interlocutory, if under 50 tons burthen, and not more than 6 in number." *Marriott's Formulary*, 4. But by the statements of his successor, and of both French and English writers, it appears that England, as well as France, during the American Revolutionary War, abstained from interfering with the coast fisheries. *The Young Jacob and Johanna*, 1 C.Rob. 20; 2 Ortolan, 53; Hall, § 148.

In the treaty of 1785 between the United States and Prussia, article 23 (which was proposed by the American Commissioners, John Adams, Benjamin Franklin, and Thomas Jefferson, and is said to have been drawn up by Franklin), provided that, if war should arise between the contracting parties, "all women and children scholars of every faculty, cultivators of the earth, artisans, manufacturers, and fishermen, unarmed and inhabiting unfortified towns, villages, or places, and in general all others whose occupations are for the common subsistence and benefit of mankind, shall be allowed to continue their respective employments, and shall not be molested in their persons, nor shall their houses or goods be burnt or otherwise destroyed, nor their fields waisted by the armed force of the enemy, into whose power, by the events of war, they may happen to fall; but if anything is necessary to be taken from them for the use of such armed force, the same shall be paid for at a reasonable price." 8 Stat. at L. 96; 1 Kent, Com. 91, note; Wheaton, *History of the Law of Nations*, 306, 308. Here was the dearest exemption from hostile molestation or seizure of the persons, occupations, houses, and goods of unarmed fishermen inhabiting unfortified places. The article was repeated in the later treaties between the United States and Prussia of 1799 and 1828. 8 Stat. at L. 174, 384. And Dana, in a note to his edition of Wheaton's International Laws, says: "In many treaties and decrees, fishermen catching fish as an article of food are added to the class of persons whose occupation is not to be disturbed in war." Wheaton, *International Law* (8th ed.) § 345, note 168.

Since the United States became a nation, the only serious interruptions, so far as we are informed, of the general recognition of the exemption of coast fishing vessels from hostile capture, arose out of the mutual suspicions and recriminations of England and France during the wars of the French Revolution.

[The Court then surveys the measures and countermeasures taken by both governments. In referring to Lord Stowell's judgment in *The Young Jacob and Johanna*, 1 C.Rob. 20, which was relied on by counsel for the United States, the Court points out that the decision condemning a Dutch fishing vessel was based on the strong evidence of fraud and on an order of the English government of January 24, 1798, instructing the commanders of its ships to seize French and Dutch fishing vessels. Lord Stowell's opinion recognized the custom observed in former wars not to capture such vessels. The Court suggests that what had been custom, in a period of 100 years may have grown, "by the general assent of civilized nations, into a settled rule of international law."]

[Furthermore, French prize tribunals both before and after Lord Stowell's decision recognized the existence of such a rule of international law. In 1780, an order in council of Louis XVI declared illegal the capture by a French cruiser of *The John and Sarah*, an English vessel laden with fresh fish. In 1801, the Council of Prizes held that the capture of a Portuguese fishing vessel by a French cruiser was contrary to "the principles of humanity, and the maxims of international law."]

[On May 23, 1806 the British government "ordered in council, that all fishing vessels under Prussian and other colors, and engaged for the purpose of catching fish . . . shall not be molested . . ." An order in council of May 2, 1810, directing the capture of certain vessels, specifically excepted "vessels employed in catching and conveying fish fresh to market. . . ."]

In the war with Mexico, in 1846, the United States recognized the exemption of coast fishing boats from capture. . . .

[I]t appears that Commodore Conner, commanding the Home Squadron blockading the east coast of Mexico, on May 14, 1846, wrote a letter . . . to Mr. Bancroft, the Secretary of the Navy, enclosing a copy of the commodore's "instructions to the commanders of the vessels of the Home Squadron, showing the principles to be observed in the blockade of the Mexican ports," one of which was that "Mexican boats engaged in fishing on any part of the coast will be allowed to pursue their labors unmolested"; and that on June 10, 1846, those instructions were approved by the Navy Department. . . .

In the treaty of peace between the United States and Mexico, in 1848, were inserted the very words of the earlier treaties with Prussia, already quoted, forbidding the hostile molestation or seizure in time of war of the persons, occupations, houses, or goods of fishermen. 9 Stat. at L. 939, 940.

[The Court then notes that France had forbidden the molestation of enemy coastal fisheries during the Crimean, Italian, and Prussian wars and that England had justified destruction by her cruisers of fisheries on the Sea of Azof during the Crimean War on the ground that these were on a large scale and intended directly for the support of the Russian army.]

Since the English orders in council of 1806 and 1810, before quoted, in favor of fishing vessels employed in catching and bringing to market fresh fish, no instance has been found in which the exemption from capture of private coast fishing vessels honestly pursuing their peaceful industry has been denied by England or by any other nation. And the Empire of Japan (the last state admitted into the rank of civilized nations), by an ordinance promulgated at the beginning of its war with China in August, 1894, established prize courts, and ordained that "the following enemy's vessels are exempt from detention," including in the exemption "boats engaged in coast fisheries," as well as "ships engaged exclusively on a voyage of scientific discovery, philanthropy, or religious mission." Takahashi, *International Law*, 11, 178.

International law is part of our law, and must be ascertained and administered by the courts of justice of appropriate jurisdiction as often as questions of right depending upon it are duly presented for their determination. For this purpose, where there is no treaty and no controlling executive or legislative act or judicial decision, resort must be had to the customs and usages of civilized nations, and, as evidence of these, to the works of jurists and commentators who by years of labor, research, and experience have made themselves peculiarly well acquainted with the subjects of which they treat. Such works are resorted to by judicial tribunals, not for the speculations of their authors concerning what the law ought to be, but for trustworthy evidence of what the law really is. *Hilton v. Guyot*, 159 U.S. 113, 163, 164, 214, 215, 16 S.Ct. 139, 40 L.Ed. 95, 108, 125, 126.

Wheaton places among the principal sources of international law "text-writers of authority, showing what is the approved usage of nations, or the general opinion respecting their mutual conduct, with the definitions and modifications introduced by general consent." As to these he forcibly observes: "Without wishing to exaggerate the importance of these writers, or to substitute, in any case, their authority for the principles of reason, it may be affirmed that they are generally impartial in their judgment. They are witnesses of the sentiments and usages of civilized nations, and the weight of their testimony increases every time that their authority is invoked by statesmen, and every year that passes without the rules laid down in their works being impugned by the avowal of contrary principles." Wheaton, *International Law* (8th ed.), § 15.

Chancellor Kent says: "In the absence of higher and more authoritative sanctions, the ordinances of foreign states, the opinions of eminent statesmen, and the writings of distinguished jurists, are regarded as of great consideration on questions not settled by conventional law. In cases where the principal jurists agree, the presumption will be very great in favor of the solidity of their maxims; and no civilized nation that does not arrogantly set all ordinary law and justice at defiance will venture to disregard the uniform sense of the established writers on international law." 1 Kent, Com. 18.

[The Court then discusses the views of French, Argentine, German, Dutch, English, Austrian, Spanish, Portuguese and Italian writers, on international law, and concludes this way:]

This review of the precedents and authorities on the subject appears to us abundantly to demonstrate that at the present day, by the general consent of the civilized nations of the world, and independently of any express treaty or other public act, it is an established rule of international law, founded on considerations of humanity to a poor and industrious order of men, and of the mutual convenience of belligerent states, that coast fishing vessels, with their implements and supplies, cargoes and crews, unarmed and honestly pursuing their peaceful calling of catching and bringing in fresh fish, are exempt from capture as prize of war. . . .

This rule of international law is one which prize courts administering the law of nations are bound to take judicial notice of, and to give effect to, in the absence of any treaty or other public act of their own government in relation to the matter. . . .

[Finding no express intention on the part of the United States to enforce the 1898 blockade of Cuba against coastal fishermen peacefully pursuing their calling, the Court ordered the reversal of the District Court decree and the payment to the claimants of the proceeds of the sale of the vessels and cargo, together with damages and costs.]

Modern Court Applications of Human Rights Law

The U.S. Constitution also makes treaties the "supreme law of the land." The "supremacy clause" in Article IV, Paragraph 2 states specifically:

> This Constitution, and the Laws of the United States which shall be made in Pursuance thereof; and all Treaties made, or which shall be made, under the authority of the United States, shall be the supreme law of the land; and the judges of every state shall be bound thereby, any Thing in the Constitution or Laws of any State to the Contrary notwithstanding.

Not only does the U.S. Constitution make treaties the supreme law of the land, it also gives Congress the authority to enact legislation pursuant to treaties to enforce their provisions. To implement the constitutional mandate for national control over foreign relations, the First Congress established original district court jurisdiction over "all causes where an alien sues for a tort only [committed] in violation of the law of nations" (Judiciary Act of 1789, ch. 20, § 9[b], 1 Stat. 73, 77, 1789, codified at 28 U.S.C. § 1350).

This legislation, often referred to as the **Alien Tort Claims Act,** has been relatively obscure until it was recently revived under very unusual conditions in the case of *Filartiga v. Pena-Irala,* decided by the Second Circuit Court of Appeals in 1980 (630 F.2d 876). This case involved a torture and wrongful death action brought by citizens of Paraguay living in the United States who had applied for

> **Alien Tort Claims Act:** *Grants the federal courts jurisdiction over "any civil action by an alien for a tort only, committed in violation of the law of the nations or a treaty of the United States." (28 U.S.C. § 1350.)*

permanent political asylum in this country. The defendant in this case was also a citizen of Paraguay who was inspector general of police in Asunción, Paraguay, when the alleged acts of kidnapping, torture and wrongful death occurred in Paraguay.

The defendant, Pena-Irala, had subsequently entered the United States under a visitor's visa, and after the plaintiffs learned of his presence in this country, they contacted the U.S. Immigration and Naturalization Service, who arrested Pena-Irala for being in the country illegally since he had resided in the United States for more than nine months. While under arrest and before his deportation to Paraguay, the plaintiffs, Dr. Filartiga and his daughter Dolly, caused Pena-Irala to be served with a summons and civil complaint. The complaint alleged that Pena-Irala had wrongfully caused the death of Dr. Filartiga's son by torture and sought compensatory and punitive damages in the amount of $10 million. The plaintiffs cited the U.N. Charter, the Universal Declaration on Human Rights, the U.N. Declaration Against Torture, the American Declaration of the Rights and Duties of Man, and other pertinent declarations, documents, and practices constituting the customary international law of human rights and the law of nations, as well as the Alien Tort Claims Act and the Supremacy Clause of the U.S. Constitution.

The district court of appeals dismissed the action on jurisdictional grounds, and the Filartigas appealed to the Second Circuit Court of Appeals where the majority reversed the lower court judgment. The court's holding on the legal question involved was this:

> Construing this rarely-invoked provision, we hold that deliberate torture perpetrated under color of official authority violates universally accepted norms of the interna-

tional law of human rights, regardless of the nationality of the parties. Thus, whenever an alleged torturer is found and served with process by an alien within our borders, § 1350 provides federal jurisdiction.

The Convention Against Torture and Other Cruel, Inhuman or Degrading Treatment or Punishment was drafted in 1984 and entered into force on June 26, 1987. The United States ratified this treaty on October 29, 1990. This convention codifies, in a specific and comprehensive manner, an internationally recognized human right. Article 1 of the treaty defines torture as any act by which severe physical or mental pain or suffering is intentionally inflicted for purposes of punishment, intimidation, coercion, or discrimination, by or at the instigation of or with the consent or acquiescence of a public official or agent of an official, acting in an official capacity. This definition exempts lawful sanctions.

Article 14 of the Torture Convention calls for each party to accord the victim of torture both a legal right to redress and an enforceable right to fair and adequate compensation. The U.S. Congress promulgated further legislation pursuant to this treaty obligation in the form of the Torture Victim Protection Act of 1991. This legislation provides "an Act to carry out the obligation of the United States under the United Nations Charter and other international agreements pertaining to the protection of human rights by establishing a civil action for recovery of damages from an individual who engages in torture or extrajudicial killing."

In 1992, the Ninth Circuit Court of Appeals delivered the following decision in a case involving the "brutal excesses of an anti-Semitic military junta" that ruled Argentina in 1976.

■   ■   ■

Siderman v. the Republic of Argentina
United States Court of Appeals, 965 F.2d 699, Ninth Circuit, 1992.
Cert. denied 113 S.Ct. 1812 (1993).

Before: FLETCHER, CANBY and BOOCHEVER, Circuit Judges. FLETCHER, Circuit Judge:

* * *

FACTS

The factual record, which consists only of the Sidermans' complaint and numerous declarations they submitted in support of their claims, tells a horrifying tale of the violent and brutal excesses of an anti-Semitic military junta that ruled Argentina. On March 24, 1976, the Argentine military overthrew the government of President Maria Estela Peron and seized the reins of power for itself, installing military leaders of the central government and the provincial governments of Argentina. That night, ten masked men carrying machine guns forcibly entered the home of Jose and Lea Siderman, husband and wife, in Tucuman Province, Argentina. The men, who were acting under the direction of the military governor of Tucuman, ransacked the home and locked Lea in the bathroom. They then blindfolded and shackled 65-year old Jose, dragged him out of his home, tossed him into a waiting car, and drove off to an unknown building. For seven days the men beat and tortured Jose. Among their tools of torture was an electric cattle prod, which they used to shock Jose until he fainted. As they tortured him, the men repeatedly shouted anti-Semitic epithets, calling him a "Jew Bastard" and a "Shitty Jew." They inflicted all of these cruelties upon Jose Siderman because of his Jewish faith.

At the end of this nightmarish week, his body badly bruised and his ribs broken, Jose was taken out of the building and driven to an isolated area, where the masked men tossed him out of the car. The men told Jose that if he and his family did not leave Tucuman and Argentina immediately, they would be killed. On the day of Jose's release, he and Lea fled to Buenos Aires in fear for their lives. Their son Carlos followed shortly thereafter, and the night Carlos left Tucuman, military authorities ransacked his home. In June 1976, Jose, Lea, and Carlos left Argentina for the United States, where they joined Susana Siderman de Blake. She is the daughter of Jose and Lea and is a United States citizen.

Before the hasty flight from Tucuman to Buenos Aires, Jose was forced to raise cash by selling at a steep discount part of his interest in 127,000 acres of land. Prior to their departure for the United States, the Sidermans also made arrangements for someone to oversee their family business, Inmobiliaria del Nor-Oeste, S.A. ("INOSA"), an Argentine corporation. Susana Siderman de Blake, Carlos Siderman and Lea Siderman each owned 33% of INOSA and Jose owned the remaining one percent. Its assets comprised numerous real estate holdings including a large hotel in Tucuman, the Hotel Gran Corona. The Sidermans granted management powers over INOSA to a certified public accountant in Argentina.

After the Sidermans left Argentina for the United States, Argentine military officers renewed their persecution of Jose. They altered real property records in Tucuman to show that he had owned not 127,000, but 127, acres of land in the province. They then initiated a criminal action against him in Argentina, claiming that since he owned only 127 acres he had sold land that did not belong to him. Argentina sought the assistance of our courts in obtaining jurisdiction over his person, requesting via a letter rogatory that the Los Angeles Superior Court serve him with documents relating to the action. The court, unaware of Argentina's motives, complied with the request.

Soon thereafter, while he was travelling in Italy, Jose was arrested pursuant to an extradition request from Argentina to the Italian government. Argentina charged that Jose had fraudulently obtained the travel documents enabling him to leave Argentina in 1976. Jose was not permitted to leave Cremora, Italy, for seven months, and actually was imprisoned for 27 days, before an Italian Appeals Court finally held that Argentina's extradition request would not be honored, as it was politically motivated and founded on pretextual charges.

The Argentine military also pursued INOSA with vigor. In April 1977, INOSA was seized through a sham "judicial intervention," a proceeding in which property is put into receivership. The purported reasons for the intervention were that INOSA lacked a representative in Argentina and that INOSA had obtained excessive funds from a Tucuman provincial bank. Though these reasons were pretexts for persecuting the Sidermans because of their religion and profiting from their economic success, the Sidermans were unable to oppose the intervention because Argentine officials had imprisoned and killed the accountant to whom they had granted management powers over INOSA. In 1978, the Sidermans retained an attorney in Argentina and brought a derivative action in a Tucuman court in an effort to end the intervention. The Court ordered that the intervention cease, and the order was upheld by the Supreme Court of Tucuman, but the order remains unenforced and the intervention has continued. Argentine military officials and INOSA's appointed receivers have extracted funds from INOSA, purchased various assets owned by INOSA at sharply discounted prices, and diverted INOSA's profits and revenues to themselves.

In 1982, Jose, Lea, and Carlos, who by then had become permanent residents of the United States, and Susana, a United States citizen since 1967, turned to federal court for relief. They filed a complaint asserting eighteen causes of action based on the torture and harassment of Jose by Argentine officials and the expropriation of their property in Argentina. Named defendants included the Republic of Argentina, the Province of Tucuman, INOSA, and numerous individual defendants who participated in the wrongdoing. In December 1982, the Sidermans properly served Argentina and Tucuman with the Summons and Complaint. The Argentine Embassy subsequently sought assistance from the U.S. State Department, which informed Argentina that it would have to appear and present any defenses it wished to assert to the district court, including the defense of sovereign immunity, or risk a default judgment. The State Department also provided a directory of lawyer referral services. Despite receiving this information, Argentina did not enter an appearance, and the Sidermans filed a motion for default judgment.

On March 12, 1984, the district court dismissed the Sidermans' expropriation claims *sua sponte* on the basis of the act of state doctrine and ordered a hearing for the Sidermans to prove up their damages on the torture claims. The Sidermans moved for reconsideration of the court's dismissal of the expropriation claims. On September 28,

1984, the Court denied the motion for reconsideration and entered a default judgment on the torture claims, awarding Jose damages and expenses totalling $2.6 million for his torture claims and awarding Lea $100,000 for her loss of consortium claim.

The damages award finally elicited a response from Argentina, which filed a motion for relief from judgment on the ground that it was immune from suit under the FSIA [Foreign Sovereign Immunities Act of 1976] and that the district court therefore lacked both subject matter and personal jurisdiction. The United States filed a suggestion of interest, asking the Court to consider the issue of foreign sovereign immunity but indicating no view of the merits. On March 7, 1985, the district court vacated the default judgment and dismissed the Sidermans' action on the ground of Argentina's immunity under the FSIA. The Sidermans filed a timely notice of appeal. We have jurisdiction over the appeal pursuant to 28 U.S.C. § 1291.

* * *

II. TORTURE CLAIMS

The question of Argentina's immunity from the Sidermans' torture claims is squarely presented, without the procedural complications surrounding the district court's treatment of the expropriation claims. The district court dismissed the torture claims on the ground that they fell within no exception to immunity under the FSIA. In defending the district court's decision on appeal, Argentina argues that the Sidermans' claims are foreclosed by the Supreme Court's opinion in *Argentine Republic v. Amerada Hess* 488 U.S. 428 (1989). Since *Amerada Hess* represents the Court's most extensive treatment of the FSIA and its exceptions to immunity, we begin with a discussion of the case before turning to the Siderman's arguments about why the case does not preclude their torture claims.

* * *

A. *JUS COGENS*

The Sidermans contend that Argentina does not enjoy sovereign immunity with respect to its violation of the *jus cogens* norm of international law condemning official torture. While we agree with the Sidermans that official acts of torture of the sort they allege Argentina to have committed constitute a *jus cogens* violation, we conclude that *Amerada Hess* forecloses their attempt to posit a basis for jurisdiction not expressly countenanced by the FSIA.

As defined in the Vienna Convention on the Law of Treaties, a *jus cogens* norm, also known as a "peremptory norm" of international law, "is a norm accepted and recognized by the international community of states as a whole as a norm from which no derogation is permitted and which can be modified only by a subsequent norm of general international law having the same character." Vienna Convention on the Law of Treaties, art. 53, May 23, 1969, 1155 U.N.T.S. 332, 8 I.L.M. 679 [hereinafter "Vienna Convention"]; *see also Restatement* § 102 Reporter's Note 6. *Jus cogens* is related to customary international law (the direct descendant of the law of nations), which the *Restatement* defines as the "general and consistent practice of states followed by them from a sense of legal obligation." *Restatement* § 102(2). Courts ascertain customary international law "by consulting the works of jurists, writing professedly on public law; or by the general usage and practice of nations; or by judicial decisions recognizing and enforcing that law." *United States v. Smith*, . . . (Story, J.); see also *The Paquete Habana* . . . (in ascertaining and administering customary international law, courts should resort "to the customs and usages of civilized nations, and, as evidence of these, to the works of jurists and commentators"); *Filartiga v. Pena-Irala* . . . Courts seeking to determine whether a norm of customary international law has attained the status of *jus cogens* look to the same sources, but must also determine whether the international community recognizes the norm as one "from which no derogation is permitted." *Committee of U.S. Citizens Living in Nicaragua v. Reagan* 859 F.2d 929 (D.C.Cir.1988) [hereinafter "CUSCLIN"] (quoting Vienna Convention, art. 53). In CUSCLIN, the only reported federal decision to give extended treatment to *jus cogens*, the Court described *jus cogens* as an elite subset of the norms recognized as customary international law. Id.

While *jus cogens* and customary international law are related, they differ in one important respect. Customary international law, like international law defined by treaties and other international agreements, rests on the consent of states. A state that persistently objects to a norm of customary international law that other states accept is not bound by that norm, see *Restatement* § 102 Comment d, just as a state that is not party to an international agreement is not bound by the terms of that agreement. International agreements and customary international law create norms known as *jus dispositivum*, the category of international law that "consists of norms derived from the consent of states" and that is founded "on the self-interest of the participating states. . . ." *Jus dispositivum* binds only "those states consenting to be governed by it."

In contrast, *jus cogens* "embraces customary laws considered binding on all nations," . . . and "is derived from values taken to be fundamental by the international community, rather than from the fortuitous or self-interested choices of nations. . . ." Whereas customary international law derives solely from the consent of states, the fundamental and universal norms constituting *jus cogens* transcend such consent, as exemplified by the theories underlying the judgments of the Nuremberg tribunals following World War II. . . . The legitimacy of the Nuremberg prosecutions rested not on the consent of the Axis Powers and individual defendants, but on the nature of the acts they committed: acts that the laws of all civilized nations define as criminal. . . . The universal and fundamental rights of human beings identified by Nuremberg—rights against genocide, enslavement, and other inhumane acts . . . are the direct ancestors of the universal and fundamental norms recognized as *jus cogens*. In the words of the International Court of Justice, these norms, which include "principles and rules concerning the basic rights of the human person," are the concern of all states; "they are obligations *erga omnes*." *The Barcelona Traction (Belgium v. Spain)*, 1970 I.C.J. 3, 32.

Because *jus cogens* norms do not depend solely on the consent of states for their binding force, they "enjoy the highest status within international law." CUSCLIN, 859 F.2d at 940. For example, a treaty that contravenes *jus cogens* is considered under international law to be void *ab initio*. See Vienna Convention, art. 53; *Restatement* § 102 Comment k. Indeed, the supremacy of *jus cogens* extends over all rules of international law; norms that have attained the status of *jus cogens* "prevail over and invalidate international agreements and other rules of international law in conflict with them." *Restatement* § 102 Comment k. A *jus cogens* norm is subject to modification or derogation only by a subsequent *jus cogens* norm. Id.

The Sidermans claim that the prohibition against official torture has attained the status of a *jus cogens* norm. There is no doubt that the prohibition against official torture is a norm of customary international law, as the Second Circuit recognized more than ten years ago in the landmark case of *Filartiga v. Pena-Irala*. . . . Dr. Filartiga and his daughter, citizens of Paraguay, [sued] Paraguayan officials who had tortured Dr. Filartiga's son to death. They alleged jurisdiction under the Alien Tort Statute, which grants the district courts "original jurisdiction of any civil action by an alien for a tort only, committed in violation of the law of nations or a treaty of the United States." 28 U.S.C. § 1350. Dr. Filartiga claimed that the defendants' torture of his son, perpetrated under color of official authority, violated a norm of customary international law prohibiting official torture, and the Court agreed. Judge Kaufman, writing for the court, explained that "there are few, if any, issues in international law today on which opinion seems to be so united as the limitations on a state's power to torture persons held in its custody." . . . Judge Kaufman catalogued the evidence in support of this view, citing several declarations of the United Nations General Assembly and human rights conventions prohibiting torture, modern municipal law to the same effect, and the works of jurists, and finally concluded "that official torture is now prohibited by the law of nations."

Other authorities have also recognized that official torture is prohibited by customary international law. In *Forti v. Suarez-Mason* [*supra*], a suit predicated on atrocities committed by the same Argentine military government alleged to be responsible for the torture of Jose Siderman, the district court held that "official torture constitutes a cognizable violation of the law of nations," and described the prohibition against official torture as "universal, obligatory, and definable." Similarly, in *Tel-Oren v. Libyan Arab Republic*, [*supra*] (opinion of Edwards, J.), which involved an action against the Palestine Liberation Organization for its acts of terrorism, Judge Edwards identified torture as a violation of customary international law. Judge Bork, although raising considerable opposition to the application of customary international law in U.S. courts, see Id. (opinion of Bork, J.), at the same time conceded that the international law prohibition against torture is not disputed. Id. The *Restatement of Foreign Relations* also holds to the view that customary international law prohibits official torture. *Restatement* § 702(d). Finally, the world now has an international agreement focused specifically on the prohibition against torture: The Convention Against Torture and Other Cruel, Inhuman or Degrading Treatment or Punishment, 39 U.N.GAOR Supp. (No. 51), 23 I.L.M. 1027 (1984) [hereinafter "Torture Convention"], which entered into force on June 26, 1987. The United States signed the Torture Convention in April 1988, the United States Senate gave its advice and consent in October 1988, *see* 136 Cong.Rec.

S17486-92 (daily ed. October 27, 1990), and it now awaits the President's filing of the instrument of ratification with the Secretary-General of the United Nations.

In light of the unanimous view of these authoritative voices, it would be unthinkable to conclude other than that acts of official torture violate customary international law. And while not all customary international law carries with it the force of a *jus cogens* norm, the prohibition against official torture has attained that status. In CUSCLIN, 859 F.2d at 94142, the D.C. Circuit announced that torture is one of a handful of acts that constitute violations of *jus cogens*. In *Filartiga*, though the Court was not explicitly considering *jus cogens*, Judge Kaufman's survey of the universal condemnation of torture provides much support for the view that torture violates *jus cogens*. In Judge Kaufman's words, "[a]mong the rights universally proclaimed by all nations, as we have noted, is the right to be free of physical torture." Supporting this case law is the *Restatement*, which recognizes the prohibition against official torture as one of only a few *jus cogens* norms. *Restatement* § 702 Comment n (also identifying *jus cogens* norms prohibiting genocide, slavery, murder or causing disappearance of individuals, prolonged arbitrary detention, and systematic racial discrimination). Finally, there is widespread agreement among scholars that the prohibition against official torture has achieved the status of a *jus cogens* norm. . . .

Given this extraordinary consensus, we conclude that the right to be free from official torture is fundamental and universal, a right deserving of the highest status under international law, a norm of *jus cogens*. The crack of the whip, the clamp of the thumb screw, the crush of the iron maiden, and, in these more efficient modern times, the shock of the electric cattle prod are forms of torture that the international order will not tolerate. To subject a person to such horrors is to commit one of the most egregious violations of the personal security and dignity. . . . That states engage in official torture cannot be doubted, but all states believe it is wrong, all that engage in torture deny it, and no state claims a sovereign right to torture its own citizens. *See Filartiga*, . . . (noting that no contemporary state asserts "a right to torture its own or another nation's citizens"); at n. 15 ("The fact that the prohibition against torture is often honored in the breach does not diminish its binding effect as a norm of international law."). Under international law, any state that engages in official torture violates *jus cogens*.

The question in the present case is what flows from the allegation that Argentina tortured Jose Siderman and thereby violated a *jus cogens* norm. The Sidermans contend that when a foreign state's act violates *jus cogens*, the state is not entitled to sovereign immunity with respect to that act. This argument begins from the principle that *jus cogens* norms "enjoy the highest status within international law," CUSCLIN, [*supra*] and thus "prevail over and invalidate . . . other rules of international law in conflict with them," *Restatement* § 102 Comment k. The Sidermans argue that since sovereign immunity itself is a principle of international law, it is trumped by *jus cogens*. In short, they argue that when a state violates *jus cogens*, the cloak of immunity provided by international law falls away, leaving the state amenable to suit.

* * *

Unfortunately, we do not write on a clean slate. We deal not only with customary international law, but with an affirmative Act of Congress, the FSIA. We must interpret the FSIA through the prism of *Amerada Hess*. Nothing in the text or legislative history of the FSIA explicitly addresses the effect violation of *jus cogens* might have on the FSIA's cloak of immunity. Argentina contends that the Supreme Court's statement *in Amerada Hess* that the FSIA grants immunity "in those cases involving alleged violations of international law that do not come within one of the FSIA's exceptions," 488 U.S. at 436, 109 S.Ct. at 688, precludes the Sidermans' reliance on *jus cogens* in this case. Clearly, the FSIA does not specifically provide for an exception to sovereign immunity based on *jus cogens*. In *Amerada Hess*, the Court had no occasion to consider acts of torture or other violations of the peremptory norms of international law, and such violations admittedly differ in kind from transgressions of *jus dispositivum*, the norms derived from international agreements or customary international law with which the Amerada Hess Court dealt. However, the Court was so emphatic in this pronouncement "that immunity is granted in those cases involving alleged violations of international law that do not come within one of the FSIA's exceptions," *Amerada Hess*, 488 U.S. at 436, 109 S.Ct. at 688, and so specific in its formulation and method of approach, Id. At 439, 109 S.Ct. at 690 ("Having determined that the FSIA provides the sole basis for obtaining jurisdiction over a foreign state in federal court, we turn to whether any of the exceptions enumerated in the Act apply here"), that we conclude that if violations of *jus cogens* committed outside the United States are to be exceptions to immunity, Congress must make them so. The fact that there has been a violation of *jus cogens* does not confer jurisdiction under the FSIA.

* * *

C. Implied Waiver Exception

The FSIA provides that "[a] foreign state shall not be immune from the jurisdiction of courts of the United States or of the States in any case . . . in which the foreign state has waived its immunity either explicitly or by implication, notwithstanding any withdrawal of the waiver which the foreign state may purport to effect except in accordance with the terms of the waiver." 28 U.S.C § 1605(a)(1).

* * *

We conclude that the Sidermans have presented evidence sufficient to support a finding that Argentina has implicitly waived its sovereign immunity with respect to their claims for torture. The evidence indicates that Argentina deliberately involved United States courts in its efforts to persecute Jose Siderman. If Argentina has engaged our courts in the very course of activity for which the Sidermans seek redress, it has waived its immunity as to that redress.

* * *

The district court erred in dismissing the Sidermans' torture claims.

CONCLUSION

The Sidermans' complaint and the evidence they have presented in support of their allegations paint a horrifying portrait of anti-Semitic, government-sponsored tyranny. The record that so far has been developed in this case reveals no ground for shielding Argentina from the Sidermans' claims that their family business was stolen from them by the military junta that took over the Argentine government in 1976. It further suggests that Argentina has implicitly waived its sovereign immunity with respect to the Sidermans' claims for torture.

We REVERSE and REMAND for further proceedings consistent with this opinion.

Discussion Questions

1. Compare the sources of international law used by the Court in the *Paquete Habana* case with the sources used in the *Siderman* case. How has customary international law been codified and extended in this century?
2. What remedy is illustrated in the *Siderman* case? What are the consequences for Argentina if it refuses to enforce a foreign court judgment?
3. What is meant by *jus cogens* and how is it used in this case? Is *jus cogens* an exception to sovereign immunity provided for in the Foreign Sovereign Immunities Act of 1976?
4. How did Argentina waive sovereign immunity according to the Court in this decision?

> *Comment:* Since the landmark decision in the *Filartiga* case (1980 to 1996), some two dozen similar cases have resulted in successful court decisions for the plaintiffs in U.S. federal courts. The development of a significant body of case law surrounding the Alien Tort Claims Act and the Torture Victim Protection Act is proceeding to strengthen international enforcement of human rights law, giving individuals access to U.S. courts on a limited basis. This is not the only basis for enforcing human rights law, but it is an additional avenue of enforcement that "has proven to be an important tool in the struggle to protect human rights," according to the authors of a recent book titled *International Human Rights Litigation in U.S. Courts* (Stephens & Ratner, 1996, p. 233). After a careful review of this evolving body of case law in the U.S. courts, the authors conclude the following:
>
> > The cases have had a significant impact on the individual plaintiffs and on the human rights movements in their home countries, in the United States, and internationally. The lawsuits have forced gross human rights abusers to answer for their crimes—abusers who had escaped responsibility for their actions because of the weakness of other enforcement

mechanisms. The cases have also enabled human rights activists to pressure governments—particularly the U.S. government—to take stronger positions on humans rights issues. In addition, human rights litigation contributes to the development of international human rights law. (p. 233)

The multimillion-dollar judgments that have been awarded to the victims in these cases have been difficult to collect. As of 1996, there had been no successful payments of the entire award; however, many collection actions are pending. In a class action suit against the estate of Ferdinand Marcos, former president of the Philippines, the jury awarded $1.2 billion in punitive damages (Stephens & Ratner, 1996, p. 241), which may result in a large payment to human rights victims and their families. Most of these cases have been awarded by default judgments, as in the *Siderman* case, illustrated in this text. Some countries will not honor default judgments, but although collection is difficult, it is not impossible. Some judgments may become enforceable in a defendant's home country due to a change in the political climate. The victims in many of these cases take consolation from knowing that they have forced those responsible for serious human rights violations to flee from the United States.

Radovan Karadzic, the leader of the Bosnian-Serb forces, has two civil actions against him in U.S. federal courts as well as international criminal indictments issued by the new International Tribunal for Violations of International Humanitarian Law in the former Yugoslavia. (Criminal actions will be discussed in Chapters 9 and 13.) In these civil actions, the Second Circuit held that (a) genocide and war crimes do not require State action and (b) Karadzic acted under color of law of a de facto State and therefore met the State action requirement of the torture and summary execution claim (70 F.ed 232 [2d Cir. 1995]). A summary of the key cases brought under the Alien Tort Claims Act and the Torture Victim Protection Act is available in Stephens and Ratner (1996, pp. 239-244).

Professor Richard B. Lillich has proposed an International Convention on the Redress of Human Rights Violations and the encouragement of other States to enact legislation similar to that in the United States (cited in Stephens & Ratner, 1996, p. xxi).

The General Principles of Human Rights Law

The two previously illustrated cases are only examples of a broad set of general rules of law that have evolved through court practice. The basic method of common-law development is through the accumulation of court precedents that have extended the law through logical interpretation of fundamental concepts. This is a cumulative process, and each time the courts confront a new set of facts, they may refer to it as a **case of first impression**. In such cases, the law may be extended by incremental application. Over time, the body of the law grows and develops. In the Anglo-American legal tradition, the courts have retained an accepted

> **Case of first impression:** A fact situation that presents itself to the Court for adjudication for the first time.

area of lawmaking that continues to be recognized as an authoritative source of law. In the civil law countries on the continent of Europe and most other legal systems throughout the world, court decisions are considered merely evidence of what the law is. This distinction is relatively unimportant today, and both of these major legal traditions draft court opinions for future reference that operate to maintain consistency in court practices.

The general principles of law that evolve in this manner have been restated by prestigious judicial authorities over the years. Blackstone's *Commentaries* was only one of these authoritative restatements of the law of England that influenced early American court practice. In modern times, the prestig-

> **American Law Institute:** An authoritative body of highly respected lawyers, judges, and law professors who have clarified and restated the body of case law into general principles of law.

ious **American Law Institute,** composed of prominent legal scholars, has produced an authoritative reference available in most libraries. Because of the extensive developments in U.S. court practice, the current *Restatement (Third) of the Foreign Relations Law of the United States* (American Law Institute, 1987; hereinafter *Restatement [Third]*) was updated in 1987 and provides an important source of general reference. A practicing international lawyer would want more specific reference to current case law in preparing a legal action. However, for introductory purposes, the general principles that have emerged are more useful.

In the specific area of human rights, the American Law Institute includes a definition of human rights to involve "freedoms, immunities, and benefits which, according to widely accepted contemporary values, every human being should enjoy in the society in which he or she lives." States have recognized many specific human rights and assumed the obligation to respect them. The general obligation to respect these rights is clearly stated in Section 701:

§ 701. Obligation to Respect Human Rights

A state is obligated to respect the human rights of persons subject to its jurisdiction

(a) that it has undertaken to respect by international agreement;

(b) that states generally are bound to respect as a matter of customary international law (§ 702); and

(c) that it is required to respect under general principles of law common to the major legal systems of the world.

The American Law Institute also provides an authoritative listing of the generally accepted customary violations of human rights, as of 1987, in Section 702, and the general remedies provided in international law, in Section 703 as follows:

§ 702. Customary International Law of Human Rights

A state violates international law if, as a matter of state policy, it practices, encourages, or condones

(a) genocide,

(b) slavery or slave trade,

(c) the murder or causing the disappearance of individuals,

(d) torture or other cruel, inhuman, or degrading treatment or punishment,

(e) prolonged arbitrary detention,

(f) systematic racial discrimination, or

(g) a consistent pattern of gross violations of internationally recognized human rights.

§ 703. Remedies for Violation of Human Rights Obligations

(1) A state party to an international human rights agreement has, as against any other state party violating the agreement, the remedies generally available for violation of an international agreement, as well as any special remedies provided by the agreement.

(2) Any state may pursue international remedies against any other state for a violation of customary international law of human rights ·(§ 702).

(3) An individual victim of a violation of human rights agreement may pursue any remedy provided by that agreement or by other applicable international agreements.

These general statements are vague and difficult to enforce. However, precedents are accumulating for successful developments indicating that these rules are beginning to have some effect on the actual practices of States. There are multiple jurisdictional issues to overcome and lack of general compulsory jurisdiction of international tribunals to hear and decide all types of legal questions. States generally must submit to adjudication by an international tribunal. This can be done by prior acceptance of compulsory jurisdiction by treaty obligation, or it may by done on the agreement of the parties. One of the most important precedents in the human rights field occurred in 1988 when the Inter-American Court of Human Rights, an agency of the Organization of American States (OAS), decided the *Velásquez Rodriguez* case.

This case arose out of a period of political turbulence, violence, and repression in Honduras. It originated in a petition against Honduras received by an agency of the OAS, the Inter-American Commission on Human Rights, in 1981. The thrust of the petition was that Angel Manfredo Velásquez Rodriguez (Velásquez) was arrested without warrant in 1981 by members of the National Office of Investigations (DNI) and the G-2 of the Armed Forces. The "arrest" was a seizure by seven armed men dressed in civilian clothes who abducted him in an unlicensed car. The petition referred to eyewitnesses reporting his later detention, "harsh interrogation and cruel torture." Police and security forces continued to deny the arrest and detention. Velásquez had disappeared. The petition alleged that through this conduct, Honduras violated several articles of the American Convention on Human Rights.

In 1986, Velásquez was still missing, and the commission concluded that the government of Honduras "had not offered convincing proof that would allow the Commission to determine that the allegations are not true." Honduras had recognized the contentious jurisdiction of the Court, to

which the commission referred the matter. The Court made its own investigation, holding closed and open hearings, calling witnesses, and requesting the production of evidence and documents. The statement of facts that follows is taken from the Court's opinion and consists both of its independent findings and its affirmation of some findings of the commission.

The commission presented a number of witnesses before the Court to testify whether "between the years 1981 and 1984 (the period in which Velásquez disappeared) there were numerous cases of persons who were kidnapped and who then disappeared, these actions being imputable to the Armed Forces of Honduras and enjoying the acquiescence of the Government of Honduras" and whether in those years there were effective domestic remedies to protect such kidnapped persons. A number of witnesses testified that they were kidnapped, imprisoned in clandestine jails, and tortured by members of the Armed Forces. Explicit testimony described the severity of the torture (including beatings, electric shocks, hanging, burning, drugging, and sexual abuse) to which witnesses had been subjected. Several witnesses indicated how they knew that their captors and torturers were connected with the military. The Court received testimony indicating that "somewhere between 112 and 130 individuals were disappeared from 1981 to 1984."

According to testimony, the kidnappings followed a pattern, such as disguised kidnappers using automobiles with tinted glass and false license plates. A witness who was president of the Committee for the Defense of Human Rights in Honduras testified about the existence of a unit in the Armed Forces that carried out the disappearance, giving details about its organization and commanding personnel. A former member of the Armed Forces testified that he had belonged to the battalion carrying out the kidnappings. He confirmed parts of the testimony of witnesses, claiming that he had been told of the kidnapping and later torture and killing of Velásquez, whose body was dismembered and buried in different places. The Court rejected the government's challenge to this testimony on grounds that the witness "had deserted from the Armed Forces and had violated his military oath." All such testimony was denied by military officers and the director of Honduran Intelligence.

The commission also presented evidence showing that from 1981 to 1984 domestic judicial remedies in Honduras were inadequate to protect human rights. Courts were slow to deal with writs of habeas corpus, and judges were often ignored by police. Authorities denied detentions even in cases where the persons sought were later released. Judges named to execute the writs were themselves threatened and on several occasions were imprisoned. Law professors and lawyers defending political prisoners were pressured not to act; one of the two lawyers to bring a writ of habeas corpus was arrested. In no case was the writ effective in relation to a disappeared person.

The Court ordered Honduran security and military officials to testify and to produce certain evidence. A number of nongovernmental human rights organizations submitted briefs as *amici curiae*.

In view of threats against witnesses it had called, the commission asked the Court to take provisional measures contemplated by the American Convention on Human Rights. Soon thereafter, the commission re-ported the death of a Honduran summoned by the Court to appear as a witness, killed "on a public thoroughfare [in the capital city] by a group of armed men who . . . fled in a vehicle." Four days later, the Court was informed of two more assassinations, one victim being a man who had testified before the Court as a witness hostile to the Honduran government. After a public hearing, the Court decided on "additional provisional measures" requiring Honduras to report within two weeks (a) on measures that it adopted to protect persons connected with the case, such as past or potential witnesses; (b) on its judicial investigations of threats against such persons; and (c) on its investigations of the assassinations, including action it intended to take to punish those responsible.

The excerpts from the Court's opinion to follow refer to several articles of the American Convention on Human Rights. This convention, creating the Inter-American Court of Human Rights and the commission referred to throughout the opinion, has now been ratified by the great majority of OAS member States. However, the United States has not ratified it. Article 4 gives every person "the right to have his [or her] life respected. . . . No one shall be arbitrarily deprived of his [or her] life." Article 5 provides that no one "shall be subjected to torture or to cruel, inhuman, or degrading punishment or treatment." Article 7 gives every person "the right to personal liberty and security," prohibits "arbitrary arrest or imprisonment," and provides for such procedural rights as notification of charges, recourse of the detained person to a competent court, and trial within a reasonable time or release pending trial.

Velásquez Rodriquez Case

Inter-American Court of Human Rights, 1988.
Ser. C No. 4, 9 Hum. Rts. L.J. 212 (1988).

[Parts I through VI omitted. Numbered paragraphs are included to show omissions]

VII

123. Because the Commission is accusing the Government of the disappearance of Manfredo Velásquez, it, in principle, should bear the burden of proving the facts underlying its petition.

124. The Commission's argument relies upon the proposition that the policy of disappearances, supported or tolerated by the Government, is designed to conceal and destroy evidence of disappearances. When the existence of such a policy or practice has been shown, the disappearance of a particular individual may be proved through circumstantial or indirect evidence or by logical inference. Otherwise, it would be impossible to prove that an individual has been disappeared.

126. The Court finds no reason to consider the Commission's argument inadmissible. If it can be shown that there was an official practice of disappearances in Honduras, carried out by the Government or at least tolerated by it, and if the disappearance of Manfredo Velásquez can be linked to that practice, the Commission's allegations will have been proven to the Court's satisfaction, so long as the evidence presented on both points meets the standard of proof required in cases such as this.

127. The Court must determine what the standards of proof should be in the instant case. Neither the Convention, the Statute of the Court nor its Rules of Procedure speak to this matter. Nevertheless, international jurisprudence has recognized the power of the courts to weigh the evidence freely, although it has always avoided a rigid rule regarding the amount of proof necessary to support the judgment (Cfr. Corfu Channel, Merits, Judgment I.C.J. Reports 1949; Military and Paramilitary Activities in and against Nicaragua *(Nicaragua v. United States of America)*, Merits, Judgment, I.C.J. Reports 1986, paras. 29-30 and 59-60).

129. The Court cannot ignore the special seriousness of finding that a State Party to the Convention has carried out or has tolerated a practice of disappearances in its territory. This requires the Court to apply a standard of proof which considers the seriousness of the charge and which, notwithstanding what has already been said, is capable of establishing the truth of the allegations in a convincing manner.

130. The practice of international and domestic courts shows that direct evidence, whether testimonial or documentary, is not the only type of evidence that may be legitimately considered in reaching a decision. Circumstantial evidence, indicia, and presumptions may be considered, so long as they lead to conclusions consistent with the facts.

131. Circumstantial or presumptive evidence is especially important in allegations of disappearances, because this type of repression is characterized by an attempt to suppress any information about the kidnapping or the whereabouts and fate of the victim.

* * *

134. The international protection of human rights should not be confused with criminal justice. States do not appear before the Court as defendants in a criminal action. The objective of international human rights law is not to punish those individuals who are guilty of violations, but rather to protect the victims and to provide for the reparation of damages resulting from the acts of the States responsible.

135. In contrast to domestic criminal law, in proceedings to determine human rights violations the State cannot rely on the defense that the complainant has failed to present evidence when it cannot be obtained without the State's cooperation.

136. The State controls the means to verify acts occurring within its territory. Although the Commission has investigatory powers, it cannot exercise them within a State's jurisdiction unless it has the cooperation of that State.

137. Since the Government only offered some documentary evidence in support of its preliminary objections, but none on the merits, the Court must reach its decision without the valuable assistance of a more active participation by Honduras, which might otherwise have resulted in a more adequate presentation of its case.

138. The manner in which the Government conducted its defense would have sufficed to prove many of the Commission's allegations by virtue of the principle that the silence of the accused or elusive or ambiguous answers on its part may be interpreted as an acknowledgment of the truth of the allegations, so long as the contrary is not indicated by the record or is not compelled as a matter of law. This result would not hold under criminal law, which does not apply in the instant case. . . .

* * *

VIII

142. During cross-examination, the Government's attorneys attempted to show that some witnesses were not impartial because of ideological reasons, origin or nationality, family relations, or a desire to discredit Honduras. They even insinuated that testifying against the State in these proceedings was disloyal to the nation. Likewise, they cited criminal records or pending charges to show that some witnesses were not competent to testify.

143. It is true, of course, that certain factors may clearly influence a witness' truthfulness. However, the Government did not present any concrete evidence to show that the witnesses had not told the truth, but rather limited itself to making general observations regarding their alleged incompetency or lack of impartiality. This is insufficient to rebut testimony which is fundamentally consistent with that of other witnesses. The Court cannot ignore such testimony.

144. Moreover, some of the Government's arguments are unfounded within the context of human rights law. The insinuation that persons who, for any reason, resort to the inter-American system for the protection of human rights are disloyal to their country is unacceptable and cannot constitute a basis for any penalty or negative consequence. Human rights are higher values that "are not derived from the fact that (an individual) is a national of a certain state, but are based upon attributes of his human personality" (American Declaration of the Rights and Duties of Man, Whereas clauses and American Convention, Preamble).

* * *

IX

147. The Court now turns to the relevant facts that it finds to have been proven. They are as follows:

    a. During the period 1981 to 1984, 100 to 150 persons disappeared in the Republic of Honduras, and many were never heard from again (testimony of Miguel Angel Pavón Salazar, Ramón Custodio López, Efrain Diaz Arrivillaga, Florencio Caballero and press clippings).

    b. Those disappearances followed a similar pattern. . . .

    c. It was public and notorious knowledge in Honduras that the kidnappings were carried out by military personnel, police or persons acting under their orders. . . .

    d. The disappearances were carried out in a systematic manner, regarding which the Court considers the following circumstances particularly relevant:

        i. The victims were usually persons whom Honduran officials considered dangerous to State security. . . .

        ii. The arms employed were reserved for the official use of the military and police, and the vehicles used had tinted glass, which requires special official authorization. . . .

        iii. The kidnappers blindfolded the victims, took them to secret, unofficial detention centers and moved them from one center to another. They interrogated the victims and subjected them to cruel and humiliating treatment and torture. Some were ultimately murdered and their bodies were buried in clandestine cemeteries. . . .

        iv. When queried by relatives, lawyers and persons or entities interested in the protection of human rights, or by judges charged with executing writs of habeas corpus, the authorities systematically denied any knowledge of the detention, the whereabouts or the fate of the victims. That attitude was seen even in the cases of persons who later reappeared in the hands of the same authorities who had systematically denied holding them or knowing their fate. . . .

v. Military and police officials as well as those from the Executive and Judicial Branches either denied the disappearances or were incapable of preventing or investigating them, punishing those responsible, or helping those interested discover the whereabouts and fate of the victims or locate their remains. The investigative committees created by the Government and the Armed Forces did not produce any results. The judicial proceedings brought were processed slowly with a clear lack of interest and some were ultimately dismissed. . . .

e. On September 12, 1981, between 4:30 and 5:00 p.m., several heavily armed men in civilian clothes driving a white Ford without license plates kidnapped Manfredo Velásquez from a parking lot in downtown Tegucigalpa. Today, nearly seven years later, he remains disappeared, which creates a reasonable presumption that he is dead. . . .

f. Persons connected with the Armed Forces or under its direction carried out that kidnapping. . . .

g. The kidnapping and disappearance of Manfredo Velásquez falls within the systematic practice of disappearances referred to by the facts deemed proved in paragraphs a-d.

* * *

h. There is no evidence in the record that Manfredo Velásquez had disappeared in order to join subversive groups, other than a letter from the Mayor of Langue, which contained rumors to that effect. The letter itself shows that the Government associated him with activities it considered a threat to national security. . . .

* * *

X

149. Disappearances are not new in the history of human rights violations. However, their systematic and repeated nature and their use, not only for causing certain individuals to disappear, either briefly or permanently, but also as a means of creating a general state of anguish, insecurity and fear, is a recent phenomenon. Although this practice exists virtually worldwide, it has occurred with exceptional intensity in Latin America in the last few years.

150. The phenomenon of disappearances is a complex form of human rights violation that must be understood and confronted in an integral fashion.

151. The establishment of a Working Group on Enforced or Involuntary Disappearances of the United Nations Commission on Human Rights by Resolution 20(XXXVI) of February 29, 1980, is a clear demonstration of general censure and repudiation of the practice of disappearances, which had already received world attention at the UN General Assembly (Resolution 33/173 of December 20, 1978), the Economic and Social Council (Resolution 1979/38 of May 10, 1979) and the Subcommission for the Prevention of Discrimination and Protection of Minorities (Resolution 5B[XXXII]) of September 5, 1979. The reports of the rapporteurs or special envoys of the Commission on Human Rights show concern that the practice of disappearances be stopped, the victims reappear and that those responsible be punished.

152. Within the inter-American system, the General Assembly of the Organization of American States (OAS) and the Commission have repeatedly referred to the practice of disappearances and have urged that disappearances be investigated and that the practice be stopped. . . .

153. International practice and doctrine have often categorized disappearances as a crime against humanity, although there is no treaty in force which is applicable to the States Parties to the Convention and which uses this terminology (Inter-American Yearbook on Human Rights, 1985, pp. 369, 687 and 1103). The General Assembly of the OAS has resolved that it "is an affront to the conscience of the hemisphere and constitutes a crime against humanity" (AG/RES. 666, supra) and that "this practice is cruel and inhuman, mocks the rule of law, and undermines those norms which guarantee protection against arbitrary detention and the right to personal security and safety" (AG/RES. 742, supra).

* * *

155. The forced disappearance of human beings is a multiple and continuous violation of many rights under the Convention that the States Parties are obligated to respect and guarantee. The kidnapping of a person is an arbitrary deprivation of liberty, an infringement of a detainee's right to be taken without delay before a judge and to invoke the appropriate procedures to review the legality of the arrest, all in violation of Article 7 of the Convention. . . .

156. Moreover, prolonged isolation and deprivation of communication are in themselves cruel and inhuman treatment, harmful to the psychological and moral integrity of the person and a violation of the right of any detainee to respect for his inherent dignity as a human being. Such treatment, therefore, violates Article 5 of the Convention. . . .

157. The practice of disappearances often involves secret execution without trial, followed by concealment of the body to eliminate any material evidence of the crime and to ensure the impunity of those responsible. This is a flagrant violation of the right to life, recognized in Article 4 of the Convention. . . .

158. The practice of disappearances, in addition to directly violating many provisions of the Convention, such as those noted above, constitutes a radical breach of that treaty in that it implies a crass abandonment of the values which emanate from the concept of human dignity and of the most basic principles of the inter-American system and the Convention. . . .

* * *

161. Article 1(1) of the Convention provides:

1. The States Parties to this Convention undertake to respect the rights and freedoms recognized herein and to ensure to all persons subject to their jurisdiction the free and full exercise of those rights and freedoms. . . .

162. This article specifies the obligation assumed by the States Parties in relation of each of the rights protected. Each claim alleging that one of those rights has been infringed necessarily implies that Article 1(1) of the Convention has also been violated.

* * *

164. Article 1(1) is essential in determining whether a violation of the human rights recognized by the Convention can be imputed to a State Party. In effect, that article charges the States Parties with the fundamental duty to respect and guarantee the rights recognized in the Convention. Any impairment of those rights which can be attributed under the rules of international law to the action or omission of any public authority constitutes an act imputable to the State, which assumes responsibility in the terms provided by the Convention itself.

165. The first obligation assumed by the States Parties under Article 1(1) is "to respect the rights and freedoms" recognized by the Convention. The exercise of public authority has certain limits which derive from the fact that human rights are inherent attributes of human dignity and are, therefore, superior to the power of the State.

* * *

166. The second obligation of the States Parties is to [guarantee] the free and full exercise of the rights recognized by the Convention to every person subject to its jurisdiction. This obligation implies the duty of the States Parties to organize the governmental apparatus and, in general, all the structures through which public power is exercised, so that they are capable of juridically ensuring the free and full enjoyment of human rights. As a consequence of this obligation, the States must prevent, investigate and punish any violation of the rights recognized by the Convention and, moreover, if possible attempt to restore the right violated and provide compensation as warranted for damages resulting from the violation.

167. The obligation to guarantee the free and full exercise of human rights is not fulfilled by the existence of a legal system designed to make it possible to comply with this obligation [but rather] requires the government to conduct itself so as to effectively ensure the free and full exercise of human rights.

168. The obligation of the States is, thus, much more direct than that contained in Article 2, according to which:

Where the exercise of any of the rights or freedoms referred to in Article 1 is not already ensured by legislative or other provisions, the States Parties undertake to adopt, in accordance with their constitutional processes and the provisions of this Convention, such legislative or other measures as may be necessary to give effect to those rights or freedoms.

169. According to Article 1(1), any exercise of public power that violates the rights recognized by the Convention is illegal. . . .

170. This conclusion is independent of whether the organ or official has contravened provisions of internal law or overstepped the limits of his authority. Under international law a State is responsible for the acts of its agents undertaken in their official capacity and for their omissions, even when those agents act outside the sphere of their authority or violate internal law.

171. This principle suits perfectly the nature of the Convention, which is violated whenever public power is used to infringe the rights recognized therein. If acts of public power that exceed the State's authority or are illegal under its own laws were not considered to compromise that State's obligations under the treaty, the system of protection provided for in the Convention would be illusory.

172. Thus, in principle, any violation of rights recognized by the Convention carried out by an act of public authority or by persons who use their position of authority is imputable to the State. However, this does not define all the circumstances in which a State is obligated to prevent, investigate and punish human rights violations, nor all the cases in which the State might be found responsible for an infringement of those rights. An illegal act which violates human rights and which is initially not directly imputable to a State (for example, because it is the act of a private person or because the person responsible has not been identified) can lead to international responsibility of the State, not because of the act itself, but because of the lack of due diligence to prevent the violation or to respond to it as required by the Convention.

* * *

174. The State has a legal duty to take reasonable steps to prevent human rights violations and to use the means at its disposal to carry out a serious investigation of violations committed within its jurisdiction, to identify those responsible, impose the appropriate punishment and ensure the victim adequate compensation.

175. This duty to prevent includes all those means of a legal, political, administrative and cultural nature that promote the safeguard of human rights and ensure that any violations are considered and treated as illegal acts, which, as such, may lead to the punishment of those responsible and the obligation to indemnify the victims for damages. It is not possible to make a detailed list of all such measures, as they vary with the law and the conditions of each State Party. Of course, while the State is obligated to prevent human rights abuses, the existence of a particular violation does not, in itself, prove the failure to take preventive measures. . . .

* * *

178. In the instant case, the evidence shows a complete inability of the procedures of the State of Honduras, which were theoretically adequate, to ensure the investigation of the disappearance of Manfredo Velásquez and the fulfillment of its duties to pay compensation and punish those responsible, as set out in Article 1(1) of the Convention.

179. As the Court has verified above, the failure of the judicial system to act upon the writs brought before various tribunals in the instant case has been proven. Not one writ of habeas corpus was processed. No judge had access to the places where Manfredo Velásquez might have been detained. The criminal complaint was dismissed.

180. Nor did the organs of the Executive Branch carry out a serious investigation to establish the fate of Manfredo Velásquez. There was no investigation of public allegations of a practice of disappearances nor a determination of whether Manfredo Velásquez had been a victim of that practice. The Commission's requests for information were ignored to the point that the Commission had to presume, under Article 42 of its Regulations, that the allegations were true. . . .

* * *

182. The Court is convinced, and has so found, that the disappearance of Manfredo Velásquez was carried out by agents who acted under cover of public authority. However, even had that fact not been proven, the failure of the State apparatus to act, which is clearly proven, is a failure on the part of Honduras to fulfill the duties it assumed under Article 1(1) of the Convention, which obligated it to guarantee Manfredo Velásquez the free and full exercise of his human rights.

* * *

XII

189. Article 63(1) of the Convention provides:

If the Court finds that there has been a violation of a right or freedom protected by this Convention, the Court shall rule that the injured party be ensured the enjoyment of his right or freedom that was violated. It shall also rule, if appropriate, that the consequences of the measure or situation that constituted the breach of such rights or freedom be remedied and that fair compensation be paid to the injured party.

Clearly, in the instant case the Court cannot order that the victim be guaranteed the enjoyment of the right or liberty violated. The Court, however, can rule that the consequences of the breach of the rights be remedied and rule that just compensation be paid.

190. During this proceeding, the Commission requested the payment of compensation, but did not offer evidence regarding the amount of damages or the manner of payment. Nor did the parties discuss these matters.

191. The Court believes that the parties can agree on the damages. If an agreement cannot be reached, the Court shall award an amount. The case shall, therefore, remain open for that purpose. The Court reserves the right to approve the agreement and, in the event no agreement is reached, to set the amount and order the manner of payment.

[In the concluding paragraphs, the Court unanimously declared that Honduras violated Articles 4, 5, and 7 of the Convention, all three read in conjunction with Article 1(1); and unanimously decided that Honduras was required to pay fair compensation to the victim's next-of-kin.]

Discussion Questions

1. How does the legal process in criminal and civil procedures differ from this example illustrated by the Inter-American Court procedure? Does the Commission function somewhat like a prosecutor in domestic criminal cases? Was this a criminal process? Discuss.

2. Was there an adequate fact-finding process involved in this decision?

3. What effect is this decision likely to have?

Comment: The Inter-American Court of Justice delivered two additional opinions against Honduras for similar disappearances, and in a third case, in 1989, the Court found lack of evidence to hold Honduras responsible. The damage awards in the cases where Honduras was held responsible were quite modest ($80,000 for each family) and Honduras paid the families only after several years of delay and without taking into consideration the vast inflation since the time of the Court's order.

The United States has not been the most persistent and unwavering supporter of the human rights conventions. It has not ratified the American Convention on Human Rights although the United States is the most powerful member of the OAS. It has, however, ratified five of the more important human rights treaties in the past two decades. Its long delay in ratifying the Genocide Convention (1989), the CPR covenant (1992), and the Convention on the Elimination of All Forms of Racial Discrimination (1994) have been sources of criticism. Also, the extensive use of reservations and declarations by the

United States in ratifying these covenants has been the subject of much criticism. These issues will be discussed in Chapter 12 in connection with treaties. The United States has not ratified the Covenant on Economic, Social and Cultural Rights or the Apartheid Convention.

The Legal Concepts of Nationality, Refuge, and Asylum

Fundamental to the enforcement of international human rights is the concept of nationality. Under customary international law, a State is responsible for the protection of its citizens. Traditionally, this concept was less emphasized than the reciprocal concept that the citizens of each State are the subjects of the sovereign. In 1923, the Permanent Court of International Justice decided that in the absence of treaty obligations, each State has the right to decide who its nationals are. In an advisory opinion concerning the Nationality Decrees in Tunis and Morocco, the Court exercised its general obligation to presume that the sovereign nation-state is not limited unless there is specific evidence of its express or implied consent. Major twentieth-century problems of Statelessness, dual nationality, and refugees developed because of this principle.

Statelessness results from the refusal of a State to provide its protection to individuals. This may result (a) from dislocations caused by war, revolution, or other political reasons (de facto) or (b) from a conflict of nationality laws, by some act of denationalization undertaken by a government against some of its citizens, or by an individual act of expatriation which is not followed by the acquisition of a new allegiance (de jure). The international and human problems of Statelessness and of refugees have been of particular concern to the U.N. General Assembly, the Economic and Social Council, the International Law Com-

> *Statelessness:* A condition of being without a country to turn to for protection.

mission, and the Office of High Commissioner for Refugees. In 1961, the United Nations General Assembly opened for signature a Convention on the Reduction of Statelessness that establishes circumstances under which a country could be required to grant nationality to Stateless individuals.

The convention seeks to reduce Statelessness by enumerating those conditions (such as marriage, divorce, adoption, naturalization, or expatriation) under which an individual will not lose his or her nationality. Conditions under which an individual could lose nationality include the swearing of allegiance to another State, renunciation of nationality, serving in a public capacity in another State, or acts of treason or other actions endangering the security of the State. States are prohibited from depriving their nationals of their identity as punishment or as a discriminatory instrument for political, racial, religious, or ethnic reasons. This convention came into force in 1975.

Dual nationality is a situation in which an individual holds citizenship in more than one country. This can occur because each State, in the absence of treaty obligations, determines who its nationals are. Some States have traditionally determined nationality by place of birth *(jus soli)* and others by blood relationship of the parents *(jus sanguinis)*. Most States use a combination of both of these methods today. Dual nationality can

> ***Dual nationality:*** A condition of owing allegiance to two or more countries because of the conflict of nationality laws of each State.

also result when a person is naturalized whose country of origin does not allow nationals to expatriate themselves, or in instances of marriage and adoption. Dual nationality can become a problem for individuals who may be liable for compulsory military service in both or several States, be subject to double taxation, or might lose the diplomatic protection of a State. To alleviate such dilemmas, some States have agreements covering such issues. In the absence of specific agreements, claims are frequently resolved in favor of the State possessing de facto jurisdiction over the individual—namely, the State in which the individual habitually resides and over whom the State exerts primary jurisdiction. A person with dual or multiple nationality is well-advised to investigate his or her status thoroughly before moving between different jurisdictions claiming that person's allegiance.

The problems of Statelessness, refugees, and **asylum** are a major source of controversy and uncertainty in modern international law. The basic human rights documents, such as the Universal Declaration of Human Rights, provide for the "right to leave any country, including [one's] own." Professor David Martin (1982) observes that "a significant piece" is missing from this proclaimed right. "That right means little unless one has somewhere else to go, yet the Declaration announces no corresponding right to enter anyone else's country. The right to seek and enjoy asylum therefore amounts to a right against the country of origin, not a claim against another state that the refugee might hope to enter" (pp. 601-602, note).

Individual **nationality** is a bond between an individual and a State establishing mutual rights and duties between them. The

> **Asylum:** *The granting of entry and protection by a country that is not that of the individual's nationality.*

State has a right, for example, to require its nationals to serve in the military and pay taxes on earnings accrued

> **Nationality:** *A bond between an individual and a State establishing mutual rights and duties.*

anywhere in the world. The primary right that the individual can expect from the State in return is to be protected by the State. Modern travel requires passport documents identifying the nationality of the individual and providing some assurance that the State will provide assistance while such persons are abroad. Under international law, an individual must obey the laws of the host State while in its territory. However, the parent State has a responsibility to provide protection in the form of diplomatic inquiries and protests on behalf of individuals harmed by State conduct that violates international law.

In 1955, the International Court of Justice (ICJ) was confronted with an issue that required it to determine the meaning of nationality for purposes of determining the jurisdiction of the Court to hear a case between the State of Liechtenstein against Guatemala. In the *Nottebohm* case the ICJ established an important principle of international law concerning which State can represent an individual as its national before an international tribunal. Although the Court acknowledged that each State has the right to determine who its nationals are, there is a different rule that must be applied when a sovereign State brings a legal action against another sovereign State.

Nottebohm was born a German national in 1881. He went to Guatemala in 1905 to take up residence and establish headquarters for his business activities in commerce and plantations. In 1939, shortly after Germany's attack on Poland, he applied for naturalization as a Liechtenstein citizen. The naturalization procedure in that country required his acceptance into the "Home

Corporation" of a Liechtenstein commune in order to acquire nationality, prove loss of former nationality upon naturalization, and establish residence in Liechtenstein for at least three years. These requirements were subject to waiver and were waived after appropriate fees, taxes, and documents were received. In October of 1939, he took the oath of allegiance and obtained a Liechtenstein passport, had it visaed by the Guatemalan Consul General in Zurich in December of 1939, and returned to Guatemala in early 1940 to resume his business activities.

In 1943, after Guatemala entered World War II against Germany, Guatemalan authorities took Nottebohm into custody and arranged for his removal to the United States for internment during the war as a dangerous enemy alien. Internment continued until 1946, and after his release, Nottebohm went to Liechtenstein. Guatemalan decrees and legislation during the war relating to enemy aliens, and final legislative measures in the late 1940s, transferred ownership of most of Nottebohm's property in that country to the government.

In 1951, Liechtenstein brought proceedings, on behalf of Nottebohm, against Guatemala before the International Court of Justice. Both countries had ratified the optional clause of the Court's statute providing for compulsory jurisdiction. Liechtenstein filed a memorial (charges) in which it alleged that the government of Guatemala, by arresting and expelling Nottebohm and seizing his property without compensation, violated international law and thus was obliged to pay damages to Liechtenstein. In its replies, Guatemala contended that the Liechtenstein claim was inadmissible since Nottebohm's naturalization as a Liechtenstein citizen was not in accordance with generally recognized principles. It was fraudulently obtained by Nottebohm to acquire the status of a neutral, without any intention of establishing a "durable link" between himself and Liechtenstein. Guatemala further alleged, in the alternative, that Nottebohm had not pursued local remedies and that, in any event, the Guatemalan action against Nottebohm and his property was not in violation of international law.

The Court did not reach the merits of these further contentions but disposed of the case on the basis of Guatemala's first defense. It rejected Liechtenstein's argument that Guatemala was precluded from challenging Nottebohm's Liechtenstein nationality since it had admitted Nottebohm on a Liechtenstein passport. After examining the facts in this case, the Court expressed its opinion in the following passage from the decision.

Nottebohm Case (Liechtenstein v. Guatemala)
International Court of Justice, 1955.
[1955] I.C.J.Rep. 4.

* * *

According to the practice of States, to arbitral and judicial decisions and to the opinions of writers, nationality is a legal bond having as its basis a social fact of attachment, a genuine connection of existence, interests and sentiments, together with the existence of reciprocal rights and duties. It may be said to constitute the juridical expression of the fact that the individual upon whom it is conferred, either directly by the law or as the result of an act of the authorities, is in fact more closely connected with the population of the State conferring nationality than with that of any other State. . . .

Diplomatic protection and protection by means of international judicial proceedings constitute measures for the defence of the rights of the State. . . .

Since this is the character which nationality must present when it is invoked to furnish the State which has granted it with a title to the exercise of protection and to the institution of international judicial proceedings, the Court must ascertain whether the nationality granted to Nottebohm by means of naturalization is of this character or, in other words, whether the factual connection between Nottebohm and Liechtenstein in the period preceding, contemporaneously with and following his naturalization appears to be sufficiently close, so preponderant in relation to any connection which may have existed between him and any other State, that it is possible to regard the nationality conferred upon him as real and effective, as the exact juridical expression of a social fact of a connection which existed previously or came into existence thereafter. . . .

At the time of his naturalization does Nottebohm appear to have been more closely attached by his tradition, his establishment, his interests, his activities, his family ties, his intentions for the near future to Liechtenstein than to any other State? . . .

[The Court then summarized Nottebohm's activities, stressing his relationships with Guatemala and indicating how minimal his connections with Liechtenstein were.]

These facts clearly establish, on the one hand, the absence of any bond of attachment between Nottebohm and Liechtenstein and, on the other hand, the existence of a long-standing and close connection between him and Guatemala, a link which his naturalization in no way weakened. That naturalization was not based on any real prior connection with Liechtenstein, nor did it in any way alter the manner of life of the person upon whom it was conferred in exceptional circumstances of speed and accommodation. In both respects. It was lacking in the genuineness requisite to an act of such importance, if it is to be entitled to be respected by a State in the position of Guatemala. It was granted without regard to the concept of nationality adopted in international relations.

Naturalization was asked for not so much for the purpose of obtaining a legal recognition of Nottebohm's membership in fact in the population of Liechtenstein, as it was to enable him to substitute for his status as a national of a belligerent State that of a national of a neutral State, with the sole aim of thus coming within the protection of Liechtenstein but not of becoming wedded to its traditions, its interests, its way of life or of assuming the obligations—other than fiscal obligations—and exercising the rights pertaining to the status thus acquired.

Guatemala is under no obligation to recognize a nationality granted in such circumstances. Liechtenstein consequently is not entitled to extend its protection to Nottebohm vis-à-vis Guatemala and its claim must, for this reason, be held to be inadmissible. . . .

[The opinion of the Court, holding the claim by Liechtenstein to be inadmissible, was supported by eleven votes. There were three dissenting opinions. Each dissenting judge opposed final disposition of the case on the record then before the Court and would have joined the claim of Guatemala concerning nationality to a full hearing on the merits.]

Discussion Questions

1. How does the majority define nationality for purposes of determining the jurisdiction of the Court to hear the case? Discuss.
2. Can an individual State define nationality differently for its own purposes? Explain.
3. If the Court had accepted the case and decided this question on its merits, what effect would this alternative present for the Court?

> *Comment:* International courts and arbitration tribunals have frequently applied this principle to exclude situations involving persons who could be considered nationals of the State against whom the legal action is brought. To allow such actions would subvert the principle of sovereign immunity. States would be very reluctant to allow another State to become a haven for individuals to launch actions against their

own countries. Liechtenstein might have become a major attraction for the sale of naturalization for the purposes of gaining access to the Court's jurisdiction. This would undermine the credibility of the Court, which must depend on the willingness of States to voluntarily submit to the Court's jurisdiction.

Refugee Status and Treaty Obligations

Mass migrations of undocumented aliens have become an ever increasing source of tensions between modern nations and are perhaps one of the most important sources of potential conflict. This problem has become particularly acute since the end of the Cold War. The dislocations resulting from situations in Bosnia, Rwanda, Iraq, Somalia, Chechnya, Haiti, Cuba, Cambodia, and many other places in the world have produced an estimated fifty million people uprooted by war and persecution.

The extent of universal international law on this subject is extremely weak if not totally uncertain. Since 1948, when the Declaration of Human Rights was adopted, a series of ad hoc resettlement efforts has succeeded, in general, in finding new homes for those who have chosen to leave or to seek asylum. However, the conditions of the individuals in the most dire situations is a source of major controversy. The United Nations High Commissioner for Refugees (UNHCR) has repeatedly called on States to respect an emerging norm of temporary refuge that asserts that persons fleeing "serious danger resulting from unsettled conditions of civil strife" are protected from forced repatriation.

The United States has accepted a specific treaty obligation concerning the status of refugees known as the 1967 Protocol Relating to the Status of Refugees. It was ratified in 1968, and Congress added a definition of **refugee** to its immigration laws in

> **Refugee:** A person who has left his or her country of nationality because of persecution or fear of persecution.

1980. The Refugee Act of 1980 defines a refugee as a person fleeing "because of persecution or a well-founded fear of persecution on account of race, religion, nationality, membership in a particular social group, or political opinion." Individuals seeking asylum in the United States thus have several distinct but interrelated options available to them. They may (a) seek asylum under the Immigration and Nationality Act (INA), 8 U.S.C. § 208, (b) seek statutory withholding of deportation under INA § 243(h), or (c) appeal to the treaty obligations the United States has assumed under the 1967 Protocol Relating to the Status of Refugees.

Situations involving the application of international law have multiple dimensions that are interrelated. In 1968, when the Refugee Convention was ratified by Congress or even in 1980, when the United States immigration laws were amended to provide for asylum, there was little understanding of how it could be abused by individual and state actions. Immediately after the passage of the 1980 Act, the Cuban government released 120,000 Cuban asylum seekers in the *Mariel boatlift*. Among the refugees included in this massive invasion were Cubans believed to have been serving prison terms for nonpolitical crimes and hence ineligible for admission to the United States. The result was prolonged detention for many, since Cuba refused to receive them back.

The situation in Haiti in 1991 following a military coup d'état that ousted Jean-Bertrand Aristide, the first democratically elected president in Haitian history, produced another massive migration of refugees to the United States. The situation in Haiti involved reports of hundreds of Haitians killed, tortured, detained without a warrant, or subjected to violence and the destruction of their property because of their political beliefs. Thousands had been forced into hiding or to flee. The OAS imposed sanctions that will be discussed later in this chapter in a more thorough account of the events that ultimately led to U.N. Security Council action to impose sanctions and authorize humanitarian intervention.

The OAS-imposed economic sanctions contributed further to the mass exodus of Haitians. During the six months after October 1991, the Coast Guard stopped 34,000 Haitians fleeing in all kinds of boats, many of them unsafe, makeshift crafts. Because so many of these interdicted Haitians could not be safely processed on Coast Guard cutters, the Department of Defense established temporary facilities at the U.S. Naval Base in Guantanamo, Cuba, to accommodate them during the screening process. In May of 1992, the Navy determined that no additional migrants could safely be accommodated at Guantanamo.

That same month, President Bush issued a new executive order authorizing the Coast Guard to return all fleeing Haitians, forcibly and summarily, to Haiti without any process whatsoever. Haitian refugee groups amended an ongoing lawsuit to challenge the practice of summarily returning Haitians as violations of both Article 33 of the U.N. Protocol Relating to the Status of Refugees and Section 243(h) of the Immigration and Nationality Act. Article 33 of the Protocol mandates that "no Contracting State shall expel or return (*refouler*) a refugee in any manner whatsoever to the frontiers of territories where his life or freedom would be threatened on account of his . . . political opinion." Article 33's domestic statutory analogue, Section 243(h) of the INA, directs that "the Attorney General shall not deport or return any alien . . . to a country if the Attorney General determines that such alien's life or freedom would be threatened on account of his . . . political opinion." Although candidate Bill Clinton criticized the Bush policy during his presidential campaign, he retained it after taking office.

In one of the most controversial opinions of the U.S. Supreme Court, *Sale v. Haitian Centers Council, Inc.* (509 U.S. 155 [1993]), the Court upheld the actions of both Presidents Bush and Clinton in declaring that Article 33 was not intended to have such extraterritorial effect and applied only when the refugee was within U.S. territory. Interdictions on the high seas and return to the country of origin that might result in their death or continued oppression without screening for validity of their claims were thus accepted. This decision, written by Justice Stevens for the eight-member majority, admits that the decision may go against the moral intent of the treaty and statute, but they decided in favor of the president out of deference to executive authority.

Justice Blackmun, in dissent, disagreed point by point with the majority's views and included the following statement:

> I believe that the duty of nonreturn expressed in both the Protocol and the statute is clear. The majority finds it "extraordinary" . . . that Congress would have intended the ban on returning "any alien" to apply to aliens at sea. That Congress should have meant what it said is not remarkable. What is extraordinary in this case is that the Executive, in disregard of the law, would take to the seas to intercept fleeing refugees and force them back to their persecutors—and that the Court would strain to sanction that conduct.

A companion piece to the Haitian Centers Council case concerned the legality of the U.S. government's detention, for nearly two years in a barbed wired internment camp at Guantanamo Bay, Cuba, of some 310 Haitians who had established credible fears of political persecution. The issues raised by the *Sale* case, representing the plaintiffs, concerned denial of **due process rights** of the detainees. The U.S. government's position was that the Haitians lacked due process rights because they were being held outside the territory of the United States. Shortly before the decision of the Supreme Court in *Sale v. Haitian Centers Council Inc.*, the Brooklyn federal district court ordered the Guantanamo Haitians immediately released. "If the Due Process Clause does not apply to the detainees at Guantanamo," the judge noted, the government "would have discretion deliberately to starve or beat them, to deprive them of medical attention, to return them without process to their persecutors, or to discriminate among them based on the color of their skin" (*Sale v. Haitian Centers*, 823 F.Supp. 1028, 1042 E.D.N.Y. [1993]).

> **Due process rights:** Procedural rights granted under the U.S. Constitution to individuals protecting them from arbitrary denial of life, liberty, or property.

Protection of Aliens

The equality of treatment of aliens and the State's own nationals is the most widely held view in modern State practice. It is derived from concepts of State equality and territorial sovereignty and is often referred to as the **equal treatment doctrine**. Citizenship is usually used to describe special privileges given to nationals, such as voting rights and holding public office, which are still broadly restricted to nationals. However, many of the distinctions between nationals and aliens have been removed through the broad adoption of the principle of equal treatment. Colonial practices of securing privileged status through what have been termed "unequal treaties" with less developed societies have been broadly rejected in modern State practice. These treaties often provided that foreigners were exempted from local laws and jurisdiction, and these special privileges were referred to as "extraterritoriality."

> **Equal treatment doctrine:** The general principle that aliens are to be treated equally with regard to basic human rights with those afforded the State's own citizens.

Western nations have found favor with the notable precedent established in the *Roberts* case (United States-Mexican General Claims Commission, 1927), which held that equality of treatment of aliens and nationals is important, but not the ultimate test of the acts of authorities. This international tribunal decided that the ultimate test is whether aliens are treated according to **minimal standards of civilized nations.** Mexico claimed that the conditions under which Roberts (a national of the United States) was detained were the same as those for its own nationals. However, the Court found that this was not good enough. Roberts had been detained for "assaulting a house," involving an exchange of small-weapons fire. He was held in a Mexican jail for nineteen months, denied a trial within the twelve months required by the Mexican Constitution, and held under conditions deemed by the Court to be cruel and inhumane imprisonment.

> **Minimal standards of civilized nations:** A vague standard that has been asserted and applied in some extreme cases in which a State has been held responsible for treatment beneath the minimum standard, even though it may be equal to that afforded its own citizens.

Treatment of aliens is often governed by bilateral treaties, particularly with regard to investments, inheritance, and ownership of property. **Legal remedies** for private persons in domestic courts for violations of international law are becoming increasingly available. The *Restatement (Third)* includes the principle that "A private person, whether natural or juridical, injured by a violation of international law by a state, may bring a claim against that state or assert that violation as a defense" (American Law Institute, 1987, § 906). This may occur in a court or other tribunal of that State pursuant to its law or in a court or other tribunal of the injured person's State, except when prohibited by international agreement.

> **Legal remedies:** A right to access to a legal procedure to adjudicate particular disputes.

Treaties concerned with rights of property by descent or inheritance have long been treated in the United States as conferring rights on aliens. Similarly, treaties according nationals of the contracting States equal treatment have been construed to give aliens judicial remedies. However, treaties concerning the use of force such as the U.N. Charter have been interpreted as not conferring enforceable rights on individuals injured by violations. The courts in the United States have tended to deny relief either because the treaty was deemed not to confer individual rights or remedies, or on the ground that the issues raised were "political questions" that should be left to the political branches of government. A treaty provision of the International Covenant on Civil and Political Rights requires each State party to ensure "an effective remedy" to any person whose rights have been violated. It also requires that the right to such remedy be determined by "competent authority provided for by the legal system of the state" and that the remedies granted be enforced by the State.

A number of limitations on individual remedies in domestic courts will be more fully discussed later, but they include sovereign immunity particularly in regard to questions involving "acts of State" or where immunity has not been waived. However, even where sovereign immunity applies, suits may ordinarily be brought against a responsible official (see *Restatement [Third]*, § 131, Reporters' Note 4).

The overwhelming majority of the world's nation-states have accepted these general principles of international human rights law today because it is in their economic and political interest to do so. The issues relating to refugees and massive migrations of oppressed people are perhaps the most serious immediate human rights concerns of the international community at the end of the twentieth century.

The United Nations Organization has recently strengthened its coordination of efforts to enforce human rights by creating the new post of U.N. High Commissioner for Human Rights. The landmark vote of the General Assembly on December 20, 1993, creating this new post was considered by many to be significant in strengthening coordination in this area. The commissioner is expected "to play an active role in removing the current obstacles and meeting the challenges to the full realization of all human rights" ("Vienna Declaration," 1994, p. 84).

However, the ultimate solution to the refugee problem is to confront the source of these problems in promoting solutions to the violations of basic human rights that drive people to leave their own countries. Massive migrations of individuals fleeing oppression in their own countries have been cited as justification for intervention in what would normally be the internal affairs of that country. India intervened in the civil war in Bangladesh because of the massive migration of millions of refugees fleeing from the conditions in East Pakistan before the creation of Bangladesh. There have been numerous other examples, including the unprecedented conditions in Rwanda of massive genocide driving nearly half the population out of the country. To conclude this introductory chapter on human rights, the following example of developments that led to U.N. Security Council humanitarian intervention in Haiti will demonstrate the multiple factors involved in the political action taken by the agency authorized to confront threats to the peace, breaches of the peace, and acts of aggression.

Humanitarian Intervention: The Case of Haiti

Humanitarian intervention has been supported as part of customary international law by writers such as Grotius, Vattel, and Westlake to be legally valid when a State treated its people "in such a way as to deny their fundamental human rights and to shock the conscience of mankind" (Oppenheim, 1955, p. 312). Almost all writers as well as governments believed that the coming of the League of Nations did not affect this type of intervention. However, Article 2(4) of the Charter of the United Nations appears, to some, to prohibit humanitarian intervention, particularly if it involves the threat or use of force (von Glahn, 1996, p. 582). The precise wording of the text of the charter, nonetheless, uses the phrase "against the territorial integrity or political independence of any state," and Chapter VII gives the Security Council authority to take enforcement measures to maintain international peace and security.

Claims of **humanitarian intervention** in the past have been the subject of major controversy among international legal experts. However, the actions in Somalia, Haiti, Bosnia, and Rwanda have been authorized by the United Nations Security Council as evidence of a moral consensus that the "conscience of mankind" is outraged by a repetition of repulsive practices within a State. The action in Haiti in September of 1994 is perhaps the most successful example of modern intervention under United Nations auspices.

> **Humanitarian intervention:** May be legally justified under customary international law when a State treats its people in such a way as to deny their fundamental human rights and shock the conscience of mankind. Such intervention in modern times can be legally supported when actions are authorized by the U.N. Security Council.

The Haitian intervention involved many issues of international law, but the principle concern of the international community was humanitarian intervention. The background of this issue involved a number of preliminary actions by the OAS before the issue was taken to the Security Council seeking its authority. The background to these events is extensively described by Domingo E. Acevedo (1993) in an edited book published by the Council on Foreign Relations titled *Enforcing Restraint* (Damrosch, 1993b).

Haiti has been a member State of the OAS from its post-World War II beginnings in 1948, and the countries of the Western hemisphere have repeatedly expressed their allegiance to democracy and to the "democratic ideal." The U.N. Charter does not require any one form of government, but the OAS Charter includes a statement that "The solidarity of the American States and the high aims which are sought through it require the political organization of those States on the basis of the effective exercise of representative democracy" (Article 3[d]).

However, the OAS Charter does not authorize military intervention in matters that are within the internal jurisdiction of the member States. Nonetheless, the Haitian crisis of the early 1990s would see the authority of the OAS stretched to its legal limits, and then the issue was referred to the Security Council of the United Nations, which does have this power under Chapter VII of the charter when the situation represents a "threat to the peace, a breach of the peace or an act of aggression."

Haiti is the most backward country in the Western hemisphere. It had never developed a democratic tradition and was notorious for the denial of basic human rights. "Papa Doc" Duvalier had become ruler of Haiti for life in 1964. His regime was enforced by violence and terror maintained by the infamous "tonton Macoutes" who harassed, kidnapped, or killed aspiring political leaders, journalists, labor organizers, youth organizers, lawyers, and human rights activists who were considered a threat to the regime. In 1971, Jean-Claude Duvalier was designated successor to the aging leader and the "constitution" was changed to allow the son of the dictator to become president for life.

In 1986, Jean-Claude was overthrown, and a National Council of Government, headed by Lieutenant General Henry Namphy, replaced the son of "Papa Doc." Although elections were scheduled for November 29, 1987, a massacre of voters took place on election day. Another election took place on January 17, 1988, and Leslie Manigat was elected president. He took office in February. In less than four months, on June 20, 1988, he was overthrown by a military coup and forced to leave the country. By the end of the year, an Inter-American Commission on Human Rights had concluded that the military had consolidated its power and

recommended that a timetable be established so that free and fair elections could be held in Haiti under international supervision.

By 1990, the OAS had secured agreement with the government of Haiti to allow monitoring of free elections by outside observer groups. The 1990 elections were monitored by an extensive number of independent groups. The OAS sent monitors from twenty-six member countries with over two hundred persons on the OAS team. A U.N. observer group was composed of thirty-nine international staff and 154 observers. Other nongovernmental groups conducted independent monitoring of the elections, including one headed by former President Jimmy Carter. All of these groups verified that the election was reasonably free and fair. In 1990, Reverend Jean-Bertrand Aristide was elected by 67% of the popular vote in the first verified free election in Haiti's history.

However, even before Aristide could assume office, there was a failed coup only three weeks after the election. Aristide was able to secure the cooperation of loyal members of the military and stormed into the presidential palace to arrest the leader of the coup. Aristide was then sworn in as president in February of 1991.

The OAS had done little during the Cold War era to apply sanctions against Latin American dictatorships. A former minister of foreign affairs of Costa Rica, Gonzalo Facio, has noted that "the OAS' traditional failure to act in defense of democracy, which became characteristic of the decades of the seventies and the eighties, was not the result of an absence of legal authority to act" (cited in Acevedo, 1993, p. 121). This restraint was lifted in 1991 when, according to Domingo Acevedo (1993), "The Organization's concern for the effective exercise of representative democracy took a quantum leap with approval . . . of the Santiago Commitment to Democracy and the Renewal of the Inter-American System" (p. 123). A resolution on representative democracy calls for an automatic meeting of the OAS Permanent Council:

> In the event of any occurrences giving rise to the sudden or irregular interruption of the democratic political institutional process or of the legitimate exercise of power by the democratically elected government in any of the Organization's member states, in order, within the framework of the Charter, to examine the situation, decide on and convene an ad hoc meeting of the Ministers of Foreign Affairs, or a special session of the General Assembly, all of which must take place within a ten-day period.

The Council further states that the purpose of any such meeting should be "to look into the events collectively and adopt any decisions deemed appropriate, in accordance with the Charter and international law."

President Aristide began a number of reforms in Haiti after taking office. These reforms included a campaign to investigate and prosecute persons for human rights violations. These investigations involved several leaders of the tonton Macoutes who had not fled the country. International human rights groups expressed concern over a number of issues related to detainees, political opponents of Aristide, and certain methods of interrogation and incarceration. Perhaps Aristide's biggest mistake was to appoint General Raoul Cédras to replace the general who had supported him in putting down the failed coup before he took office. On September 30, 1991, just eight months after Aristide had taken office, General Cédras led the Haitian military in a coup d'état that displaced the constitutionally elected government.

The OAS reacted immediately by action of the Permanent Council, demanding adherence to the Haitian Constitution and convening the Consultation of Ministers of Foreign Affairs. This more powerful decision-making body condemned the coup as a denial of self-determination of the Haitian people and took the strongest actions ever adopted by the organization. These actions involved diplomatic isolation—suspension of all economic, financial, and commercial relations with Haiti, except for humanitarian aid. The U.N. General Assembly condemned the coup and recommended measures to support the OAS actions. The OAS further requested member States to "deny access to port facilities to any vessel that violates the embargo, actions to monitor the embargo, and to deny visas to perpetrators or supporters of the coup and to freeze their assets" (OAS Resolution MRE/RES, 3/92, May 17, 1992).

The U.N. Secretary General appointed Dante Caputo as special representative for Haiti on December 11, 1992, to engage in negotiations. As the embargo began to have its effect, the refugee problem became more acute with thousands daily fleeing the island, many attempting to go to the United States. This crisis had begun to directly affect the United States and other countries in the region.

By July 3, 1993, Ambassador Dante Caputo was successful in securing the Governor's Island Agreement to restore Aristide to authority in Haiti. Both Aristide and Cédras signed these agreements to return Aristide by October 30, 1993. A team of U.S. and Canadian military advisers were scheduled to land in Haiti and help train the Haitian police to observe human rights. When these advisers arrived by ship off Port au Prince, the U.S. vessel carrying them was recalled because of the threat from armed civilians at the harbor; their safety could not be ensured. This failure to secure the port was a violation of the Governor's Island agreement, and the Security Council took prompt action to impose sanctions. This action resulted in the Security Council authorization of an OAS multinational force to take military action to impose the agreement. Security Council Resolution 867 of 1993 and Resolution 940 of 1994 authorized operation "Uphold Democracy" involving a multinational Force from 27 countries to invade Haiti. This action took place peacefully for the most part after a delegation headed by former President Jimmy Carter persuaded General Cédras to allow the intervention without resistance. The invasion took place in September of 1994, and in March of 1995, the troops of the multinational invasion force were replaced by U.N. administration. President Aristide has served out his term in office and was not eligible for a second term. New elections were held on December 17, 1995, producing a victory for Aristide's party. Rene Preval was elected as the new President. He is an agronomist who was Aristide's first prime minister in 1991 and belongs to Aristide's Lavalas Platform coalition. The police forces of Haiti have been reformed through U.N. advisory teams. Haiti still suffers from immense poverty, the refugee count has increased, and the election turnout was quite low. In contrast to the nearly 100% turnout of voters in the 1990 election, the 1995 election turnout was estimated to be somewhere between 25% and 30% of the voters. These developments indicate that the situation in Haiti will not be easily changed. However, democracy has been restored and there is considerable improvement in the protection of human rights.

The OAS Charter has been amended to authorize suspension of any member State whose democratically elected government has been overthrown. These developments represent substantial changes in international law, at least for States that have formally committed themselves to democratic institutions. It is also another precedent in favor of international enforcement action and intervention for humanitarian purposes when there are gross violations of human rights.

President Clinton cited ten reasons in justification of the humanitarian intervention in which the United States took a prominent part:

1. To end human rights violations
2. To secure U.S. borders by ending the threat of a refugee exodus
3. To defend democracy
4. To uphold the reliability of U.S. commitments
5. To achieve an objective using force only as a last resort, in accordance with U.N. policies
6. To end spending millions of dollars to take care of Haitian refugees
7. To increase stability and prosperity by restoring a democracy
8. To ensure that dictators would not be allowed to break their commitments to the United States and the United Nations
9. Haiti's proximity to the United States
10. Because the mission should be concluded relatively easily in view of the military weakness of Haiti

These actions of the Security Council, the OAS, the United States, and other participating countries represent major innovations in application of principles of international law in dangerous and humanitarian situations. Similar actions have been taken in Somalia, Rwanda, and

Bosnia. These developments are evidence of a new world order that may not be able to control every situation, but precedents are mounting that the international community will not tolerate gross violations of humanitarian law.

The next chapters will select particular areas of major interest to explain some of the more significant developments in the less dramatic areas of business law, property rights and consumer protection, labor and environmental regulation, and criminal jurisdiction. These substantive chapters will start with the more mundane problems of enforcement of foreign court judgments and build to areas of international cooperation and regulation. Criminal jurisdiction is still jealously protected as an area of national sovereignty. Diplomatic and sovereign immunity will end the substantive chapters in Part II, and in the final chapters of Part III of this text the areas of international law that do not afford remedies to individuals but that are confined to the actions of nation-states alone will be discussed. In these final chapters, the text will return to vital concepts concerning nation-states, such as what constitutes international personality, treaty formulation and validity, and international tribunals that operate on the international plane. Finally, the range of methods of enforcement or compliance measures will be developed.

■ ■ ■

Chapter Summary

1. International law is deeply rooted in the U.S. Constitution and the common-law heritage of our courts. The general constitutional norm is that international law is part of our law and must be ascertained and administered by our courts.

2. However, there are many exceptions to this general norm, involving appropriate court jurisdiction, "political question" exceptions, vagueness of customary rules, and discretion in treaty interpretation.

3. The *Paquete Habana* case illustrates that U.S. courts have followed the common-law tradition of our English heritage and assert a right to ascertain and apply customary international law as a remedy for individuals against violations of that law.

4. Case law analysis is an important educational tool that makes students aware of the difficulties of application of legal rules to particular fact situations. It involves specific identification of the basic elements of a case law opinion and understanding of the legal reasoning involved in the case.

5. The holding of the court is the specific kernel of law that can be used as precedent for future cases. Following precedent in fact situations that are essentially alike is required for the Court to remain consistent. Different fact situations may require the application of different rules.

6. Identification of the legal issues in the case is essential for an understanding of the opinion because the essential purpose of Court opinions is to answer questions of law in dispute. The specific answer to the legal question is the Court's holding.

7. The Alien Tort Claims Act and the Torture Victim Protection Act are specific acts of Congress giving individuals access to the federal courts to effect remedies in civil litigation for injuries sustained from violations of international law. A tort is a civil wrong of a personal injury or property damage nature as opposed to contract violation.

8. The *Filartiga* case illustrates one application of the Alien Tort Claims Act in which the defendant can be served within the territorial jurisdiction of the United States. This statute makes it possible for even an alien to sue another alien in our courts for violations of international law.

9. The *Siderman* case represents a historic precedent in U.S. courts of applying international humanitarian law in civil litigation against the government of another country in its own domestic courts. The *Filartiga* and *Siderman* cases are narrow rulings with broad implications. They demonstrate that there is an evolving common law of mankind that can be enforced through civil litigation.

10. Modern courts have much more specific international legal standards to apply because of the progressive development of international law through the lawmaking process of the United Nations over the last fifty years.

11. The general principles of applicable human rights law may be found in the *Restatement (Third) of the Foreign Relations Law of the United States*, published by the authoritative American Law Institute.

12. States are obligated to respect human rights in a broad range of areas, including prohibitions against genocide, slavery, murder, torture, prolonged arbitrary detention, and racial discrimination.

13. Remedies for the violation of these rights include a potential for the individual to bring legal actions in civil litigation as well as the right of his or her State to pursue legal remedies in public international law.

14. In the *Velásquez Rodriguez* case, an international tribunal, the Inter-American Court of Human Rights, found Honduras responsible for basic violations of international humanitarian law in the disappearances of individuals and failure to afford fundamental due process. These actions have been rare, but there is emerging determination on the part of the international community to enforce human rights standards.

15. In the absence of treaty obligations, each State is able to determine who its nationals are by virtue of its sovereign legal authority. This basic principle has produced serious problems of Statelessness, dual nationality, and refugee status that are of major concern to the international community.

16. The International Covenant on Reduction of Statelessness and other U.N. efforts to construct a right of temporary asylum for persons who find themselves in conditions of being without national protection is having some positive effect.

17. However, the right to freedom of movement and expatriation from one's own country does not yet confer a corresponding right to enter another country and become its national.

18. In the *Nottebohm* case, the ICJ defined nationality for purposes of asserting international legal protection for that individual as having a genuine link with that society. States are free to decide who their nationals are, but the Court will apply an international standard when a State brings a legal action against another State on behalf of its subjects.

19. U.N. agencies assert that there is an emerging norm of temporary refuge for persons fleeing from serious danger resulting from unsettled conditions of civil strife and that they are protected against forced repatriation.

20. Each State still reserves the right to determine who its nationals are through its internal immigration and naturalization laws. International agreements have been reached by a relatively small group of countries to provide asylum to refugees fleeing persecution.

21. The United States has ratified the 1967 Protocol Relating to the Status of Refugees, and Congress has enacted the Refugee Act of 1980, which defines a refugee as a person fleeing because of persecution or a well-founded fear of persecution on account of race, religion, nationality, membership in a particular social group, or political opinion.

22. *Sale v. Haitian Centers Council* illustrates the problems of interpretation and enforcement of these obligations in international practice. The Supreme Court has upheld the right of the president to order interdiction of aliens on the high seas and their return to their country of origin as within the discretionary authority given to that office by the Congress and not limited by our treaty obligations.

23. However, other Court decisions have released refugees detained in Guantanamo, Cuba, by the U.S. government because of failure to provide them with their constitutional right not to be deprived of their liberty without due process of law.

24. The equal treatment doctrine is the most broadly held standard of alien treatment by other countries. It means that aliens are given the same basic human rights as those afforded their own nationals. However, aliens may be denied entry, voting rights, and the right to hold public office.

25. Universal human rights standards define a "minimal standard of civilized nations." The development of modern human rights treaties must not fall below a minimum that may constitute cruel and unusual punishment.

26. Legal remedies for private persons in domestic courts for violations of international law are becoming increasingly available. Many treaties protect access to the courts in regard to disputes involving investments, inheritance, and ownership of property.

27. However, treaties concerning the use of force and other political treaties have been interpreted as not conferring enforceable rights in national courts on individuals injured by violations. Relief may be denied because the Court decides that the treaty was not intended to confer such a right or that the issue raised significant political questions that should be left to the political branches of government.

28. Humanitarian intervention may be justified under international law when a State denies fundamental human rights. This must involve gross violations of human rights. The authority and practice of the U.N. Security Council provides clear evidence of precedents for humanitarian intervention. The findings of the General Assembly also support intervention when the condition shocks the conscience of mankind.

Key Terms

case law analysis
holding
legal reasoning
Alien Tort Claims Act
case of first impression
American Law Institute
Statelessness

dual nationality
asylum
nationality
refugee
due process rights
equal treatment
doctrine

minimal standards of
civilized nations
legal remedies
humanitarian
intervention

∎ ∎ ∎

Discussion Questions

1. How does the Constitution of the United States provide authority for the courts to apply principles of international law?

2. What are the major exceptions to the domestic application of principles of international law in State and federal courts?

3. What are the basic elements of case law analysis? What was the legal holding in the *Paquete Habana* case? How did the Court document customary international law on this subject?

4. Compare the sources of international law used in *Paquete Habana* and the *Siderman* case. What are the major differences and how do they illustrate the development of international law in the twentieth century?

5. What is meant by *jus cogens*, and how did the Court apply that principle in the *Siderman* case?

6. What is the basic purpose and function of the *Restatement (Third) of the Foreign Relations Law of the United States?*

7. How have international tribunals acted to increase compliance with fundamental human rights standards as illustrated in the *Velásquez Rodriguez* case? How do these actions differ from criminal proceedings?

8. Why have problems of Statelessness, dual nationality, and refugee status caused humanitarian concern in the twentieth century?

9. How does *Sale v. Haitian Centers Council* demonstrate the difficulties of national court interpretation of treaty obligations?

10. What are the basic standards of treatment of aliens in foreign countries?

11. Does systematic abuse of fundamental human rights standards justify military intervention into the internal affairs of that country? Under what conditions and who decides?

Suggested Readings

Appendix C: Universal Declaration of Human Rights

Appendix D: International Covenant on Civil and Political Rights

Lillich, R. B. (1993). Damages for gross violations of international human rights awarded by U.S. courts. *Human Rights Quarterly, 15*, 207.

Martin, D. (1982). Large scale migrations of asylum seekers. *American Journal of International Law, 76*, 598-609.

Steiner, H. J., Vagts, D. F., & Koh, H. H. (1994). *Transnational legal problems* (4th ed.). New York: Foundation Press.

Stephens, B., & Ratner, M. (1996). *International human rights litigation in U.S. courts*. Irvington-on-Hudson, NY: Transnational.

Internet Sources

Browse: Use *human rights law* or *international organizations* for general searches. The World Wide Web Virtual Library (http://www.undcp.org/unlinks.html) is also a good starting point.

The Human Rights Web (http://www.hrweb.org)

5 *International Business Law*

This chapter will discuss aspects of international law that both promote international commerce and regulate international business practices. There are at least four basic perspectives from which the reader may wish to view development of international law in the economic area of concerns: (a) the interests of the average consumer toward products of value to the individual, (b) the interests of business entities in maximizing profits, (c) the interests of individual nations in maximizing benefits for their societies, and (d) the global interests of those concerned about preservation of resources on this planet. Finding agreement among these diverse interests has not been easy, but the international community has identified some significant areas where these interests converge and provide a basis for development of international obligations that seek to balance these important objectives.

International Monetary Cooperation

The United States emerged from World War II as the most productive and economically powerful country in the world. This nation took a leadership role in developing the **International Monetary Fund (IMF)** even before the United Nations was established. The Bretton Woods Conference of 1944 resulted in the development of two major intergovernmental organizations (IGOs) designed to promote economic development, reconstruct war-damaged economies, and promote world trade and commerce. The purpose of the IMF, according to its charter, is "to promote international monetary cooperation, to facilitate the expansion and balanced growth of international trade and to promote stability in foreign exchange." The **World Bank** is the second organization created at the Bretton Woods Conference in 1944. It is a separate organization

> **International Monetary Fund (IMF):** An institution set up to promote international monetary cooperation and balanced growth of international trade by promoting stability in foreign exchange.

> **World Bank:** An institution designed to provide financial assistance to countries by financing specific development projects and programs. Its activities are coordinated with the IMF by annual joint meetings, but they are separate (IGOs).

from the IMF, but these two IGOs work together in close cooperation and hold joint annual meetings. The World Bank's mission is to promote reconstruction and economic development by assisting countries through the financing of specific development projects and programs.

The IMF can only influence monetary stability; it does not have the authority to control exchange rates. Fluctuating exchange problems remain a substantial risk for those engaged in international trade. The fund lends money to developing countries to assist them with fundamental problems blocking development, such as high interest rates and inflated oil prices. It also works closely with commercial banks in this process. It has a board of governors, twenty-two executive directors, and a managing director. The board meets annually with the World Bank. The executive directors exercise managerial authority over the fund's operations. Six directors are appointed by the United States, the United Kingdom, France, Germany, Japan, and China, and the remaining sixteen are elected by the other IMF participants. However, there are some exceptions under the Articles of Organization, which allow for the appointment of additional directors.

Voting in the IMF is weighted in proportion to each nation's special drawing rights or quotas. The fund helps members deal with any balance-of-payment problems. The IMF was originally set up on the gold standard, but this was amended in 1973 to reflect the reality of floating exchange rates. Membership in the IMF commits a nation to adhere to the initial goals of the organization. Members must act in a way that promotes stable exchange rates and must pursue economic and fiscal policies that foster growth in an orderly way. Members must also be careful not to pursue policies with another member that may discriminate

against a third member. These commitments are based on an understanding that if major nations do not cooperate, they will all suffer from a recurrence of the chaotic conditions of the 1930s.

The IMF has its headquarters in Washington, D.C., with a staff of approximately 1,700. Recently, Russia and several of the republics of the former Soviet Union have been accepted as members. Quota subscriptions (dues) constitute the basic resource of the fund, and as of July 1989, the IMF had at its disposal more than $120 billion. Each member's quota is related to its national income, monetary reserves, trade balance, and other economic criteria. A country's subscription will influence its voting power and allotment of special drawing rights.

Trade Considerations

After World War II, the Germans and Japanese realized that their economic futures depended on international trade, and they restructured their internal policies to reflect this dependence. The miraculous recovery of these industrial economies and their emerging strengths as world economic powers is broadly recognized today. Although the United States remains the most important world trading nation, it has begun to recognize important deficiencies in its ability to compete with these rising world trading powers. Traditionally, the vast market potential in the domestic markets of the United States was thought sufficient by most businesses. Many U.S. companies never viewed themselves as a part of a world marketplace and did not structure their market objectives or economic goals to this emerging reality. Up to the late 1970s, only about 12% of U.S. gross national product was involved in international trade. However, in the 1980s, the country began to feel

Billions of dollars

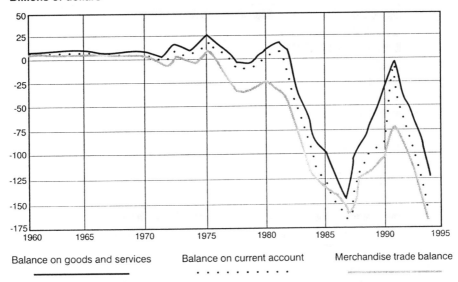

Figure 5.1. U.S. International Transaction Balances: 1960 to 1994
SOURCE: Chart prepared by the U.S. Bureau of the Census.

the effect of mounting deficits in its balance of payments.

Since the 1970s, the country's imports have increased dramatically and its share of export markets has dropped. In the early 1980s, this adverse performance was attributed to the high value of the U.S. dollar, which made U.S. goods very expensive for export to foreign buyers who had to exchange their currencies for dollars to buy U.S. goods. The decade of the 1980s saw intense international efforts to shore up the dollar value. However, the floating exchange rate policies of the IMF must ultimately allow realistic changes to occur. By 1992, the dollar's value had declined by over 50% from 1985.

Massive efforts in the United States have been undertaken to provide large-scale incentives and public awareness to encourage small and medium-sized manufacturers and service companies to enter foreign markets. During the 1980s, only about 250 of the largest U.S. multinational corporations accounted for 85% of U.S. exports. The U.S.

Department of Commerce has undertaken to introduce small firms to the methods of engaging in international trade. These efforts are beginning to pay off, and by the end of the 1980s, these "new-to-export" companies were contributing substantially to the U.S. export base. Today, more than a quarter of the U.S. gross national product (GNP) is involved in international trade. This represents a doubling in the extent of U.S. involvement over a period of only about a decade.

Balance-of-Payment Problems

An assessment of the international trade position of the United States over the period from 1960 to 1994 indicates a precipitous decline in U.S. balance of payments. This decline fell sharply in the 1980s, recovered considerably in the early 1990s, and has dropped sharply since 1991 (see Figure 5.1).

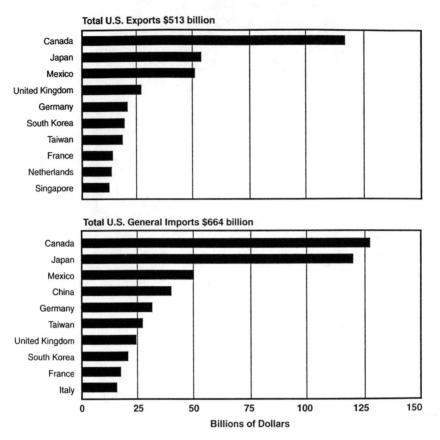

Figure 5.2. Top Purchasers of U.S. Exports and Suppliers of U.S. General Imports: 1994
SOURCE: Chart prepared by U.S. Bureau of the Census.

This general deficit was, however, not uniform in regard to all sectors. The United States actually had a trade surplus in the areas of trade in advanced-technology products in 1994 of over $22 billion. In general, the U.S. surpluses are led by aerospace industries, information technology, and communication products. Capital goods, industrial supplies, and food and beverages are also strong competitors in the world market; however, we continue to import more consumer goods and automotive products than we export. Some of the most important U.S. export products are airplanes, electronics, computers, and semiconductors. Import of petroleum products also accounted for a large part of the total trade deficit.

The largest U.S. foreign trading partners are indicated in Figure 5.2. Canada, Japan, Mexico, the United Kingdom, Germany, South Korea, Taiwan, France, the Netherlands, and Singapore were the largest buyers of our exports in 1994. And Canada, Japan, Mexico, China, Germany, Taiwan, the United Kingdom, South Korea, France, and Italy were the countries from whom we imported the largest value of goods and services in 1994.

Over the last ten years, the U.S. share of world merchandise exports remained fairly constant at about 12%, with Germany at more than 11% and Japan at almost 9%. These figures are only for merchandise exchanges and do not tell the entire trade story. The United States has continued to maintain strength in business services, including banking, transportation, insurance, and tourism. Moreover, these trade statistics fail to take into account sales and purchases of merchandise and services by foreign affiliates of U.S. companies.

International Economic Law

The *Restatement (Third) of the Foreign Relations Law of the United States* (American Law Institute, 1987) defines international economic law as "all the international law and international agreements governing economic transactions that cross state boundaries or otherwise have implications for more than one state, such as those involving movement of goods, funds, persons, intangibles, technology, vessels or aircraft" (Part VIII, Introductory Notes). This area is dominated by specific agreements, and very little customary international law is involved. In the absence of specific agreements, each State retains the authority to regulate these matters in its own national interest. However, the United States has engaged in some 130 bilateral agreements similar to the "foundation treaty" with France found in Appendix E. These treaties of commerce and friendship have long served as the basic instruments of regulation of trade between individual States.

The New Multilateral Trading System

The World Trade Organization (WTO) was established on January 1, 1995. It is the legal and institutional foundation of the multilateral trading system throughout the world and provides the principal contractual obligations determining how governments frame and implement domestic trade legislation and regulations. The preamble of the agreement states that members should conduct their trade and economic relations with a view to

raising standards of living ensuring full employment and a large and steadily growing volume of real income and effective demand, and expanding the production of and trade in goods and services, while allowing for the optimal use of the world's resources in accordance with the objective of sustainable development, seeking both to protect and preserve the environment and to enhance the means for doing so in a manner consistent with their [members of the WTO] respective needs and concerns at different levels of development.

The fundamental principles of the multilateral trading system are (a) trade without discrimination, (b) predictable and growing access to markets, (c) promoting fair competition, and (d) encouraging development and economic reform. Under the "most-favored nation" (MFN) clause, members are bound to grant to the products of other members no less favorable treatment than that accorded to the products of any other country. Once such products have entered a market, they must be treated no less favorably than the equivalent domestically produced goods.

The new tariff reductions made by over 120 countries in the Uruguay Round are contained in some 22,500 pages of national tariff schedules that are considered an integral part of the WTO. Tariff reductions, phased in over the course of five years, will result in a 40% cut in industrial countries' tariffs in industrial products from an average of 6.3% to 3.8%.

The new agreement extends and clarifies previous GATT rules that laid down the basis on which governments could impose compensating duties on two forms of "unfair" competition: **dumping** and **subsidies**. The WTO agreement is designed to provide increased fairness in farm products, intellectual property, and trade in services. The previous GATT provisions intended to favor developing countries are maintained in the WTO and therefore encourage industrial countries to assist trade with developing nations. Developing countries are given transition periods to adjust to the more difficult WTO provisions. Least-developed countries are given even more flexibility and benefit from accelerated implementation of market access concessions for their goods.

> **Dumping:** *Selling exported goods at prices below their normal value.*
>
> **Subsidy:** *Financial assistance granted by a government to a private person or company.*

The main functions of the WTO are (a) administering and implementing the multilateral and plurilateral trade agreements that together make up the WTO, (b) acting as a forum for multilateral trade negotiations, (c) seeking to resolve trade disputes, (d) overseeing national trade policies, and (e) cooperating with other international institutions involved in global economic policy making.

The highest WTO authority is the Ministerial Conference, which meets every two years. The day-to-day work of the WTO falls to a number of subsidiary bodies, principally the General Council, which also convenes as the Dispute Settlement Board and as the Trade Policy Review Body. The General Council delegates responsibility to three other major bodies—namely, the Councils for Trade in Goods, Trade in Services, and Trade-Related Aspects of Intellectual Property Rights.

Three other bodies are established by the Ministerial Conference and report to the General Council. They are the Committee on Trade and Development; the Committee on Balance of Payments; and the Committee on Budget, Finance and Administration. The General Council has also established a Committee on Trade and Environment that presented its first report in December of 1996.

Each of the plurilateral agreements that constitute the WTO has its own management body that reports to the General Council. They include those on civil aircraft, government procurement, dairy products, and bovine meat.

The new WTO Secretariat is located in Geneva, Switzerland, and will have a staff of about 450, headed by the director-general and four deputy directors. Their functions include servicing the WTO delegate bodies with respect to negotiations and the implementation of agreements. The Secretariat has a particular responsibility to provide technical support to developing countries, especially the least-developed countries. WTO economists and statisticians provide trade performance and trade policy analyses, and the legal staff assists in the resolution of trade disputes involving the interpretation of WTO rules and precedents.

Enforcement of Foreign Court Judgments

For the individual or firm seeking to do business in international trade, a multitude of issues are added risks of doing business over great distances and engaging in transactions that cross national boundaries and involve multiple national legal jurisdictions. There are risks of language and cultural barriers, miscommunications, currency fluctuations, international hostilities, and political interference, as well as risks of trade controls or restrictions on investment. Some of the most serious of these concerns of international risk management to business interests involve how to engage in contractual negotiations that stipulate the ground rules for settlement of disputes between contracting parties. A major course in modern law schools that every potential lawyer is encouraged to take is one on international transactions. In this introductory text, we can only initiate one's thought processes to create an awareness of the legal issues involved.

The first of the illustrative case opinions in this section introducing business law is *Hilton v. Guyot*, decided by the U.S. Supreme Court in 1895. Justice Gray's opinion in this case involves observations about international law that confirm much of the previous discussion in this text about the interrelated nature of public and private international law and is an appropriate introduction to court practice in the settlement of private matters of a transnational character in national courts. The issue involved is whether there is an obligation of the federal courts in the United States to honor foreign court judgments in the absence of specific treaty obligations. Note that subsequent congressional action and treaties between France and the United States have provided more adequate specificity to the current legal obligations of the courts in these matters. However, the basic principles explained in this decision are still relevant today.

▌   ▌   ▌

Hilton v. Guyot
Supreme Court of the United States.
1895. 159 U.S. 113, 16 S.Ct. 139, 40 L.Ed. 95.

[An action was brought in the Circuit Court for the Southern District of New York by the liquidator and the surviving members of a French firm against two U.S. citizens who had been trading as partners. The plaintiffs had recovered a judgment in the French courts, of which nearly $200,000 remained unpaid. The defendants' answer denied that they were indebted to the plaintiffs and asserted that the French judgment was procured by fraud. The defendants also filed a bill in equity to enjoin the prosecution of the action. The plaintiffs prevailed in both cases, and the defendants, by writ of error and appeal, brought the cases to the Supreme Court.]

* * *

Mr. Justice GRAY, after stating the case, delivered the opinion of the court.

International law, in its widest and most comprehensive sense—including not only questions of right between nations, governed by what has been appropriately called the "law of nations," but also questions arising under what is usually called "private international law," or the "conflict of laws," and concerning the rights of persons within the territory and dominion of one nation, by reason of acts, private or public, done within the dominions of another nation—is part of our law, and must be ascertained and administered by the courts of justice as often as such questions are presented in litigation between man and man, duly submitted to their determination.

The most certain guide, no doubt, for the decision of such questions is a treaty or a statute of this country. But when, as is the case here, there is no written law upon the subject, the duty still rests upon the judicial tribunals of ascertaining and declaring what the law is, whenever it becomes necessary to do so, in order to determine the rights of parties to suits regularly brought before them. In doing this, the courts must obtain such aid as they can from judicial decisions, from the works of jurists and commentators, and from the acts and usages of civilized nations. . . .

No law has any effect, of its own force, beyond the limits of the sovereignty from which its authority is derived. The extent to which the law of one nation, as put in force within its territory, whether by executive order, by legislative act, or by judicial decree, shall be allowed to operate within the dominion of another nation, depends upon what our greatest jurists have been content to call "the comity of nations." Although the phrase has been often criticised, no satisfactory substitute has been suggested.

"Comity," in the legal sense, is neither a matter of absolute obligation, on the one hand, nor of mere courtesy and good will, upon the other. But it is the recognition which one nation allows within its territory to the legislative, executive, or judicial acts of another nation, having due regard both to international duty and convenience, and to the rights of its own citizens, or of other persons who are under the protection of its laws. . . .

Chief Justice Taney, . . . speaking for this court, while Mr. Justice Story was a member of it, and largely adopting his words, said: "The comity thus extended to other nations is no impeachment of sovereignty. It is the voluntary act of the nation by which it is offered, and is inadmissible when contrary to its policy, or prejudicial to its interests. But it contributes so largely to promote justice between individuals, and to produce a friendly intercourse between the sovereignties to which they belong, that courts of justice have continually acted upon it as a part of the voluntary law of nations." "It is not the comity of the courts, but the comity of the nation, which is administered and ascertained in the same way, and guided by the same reasoning, by which all other principles of municipal law are ascertained and guided." *Bank v. Earle* (1839) 13 Pet. 519, 589; Story, Confl.Laws, § 38. . . .

In order to appreciate the weight of the various authorities cited at the bar, it is important to distinguish different kinds of judgments. Every foreign judgment, of whatever nature, in order to be entitled to any effect, must have been rendered by a court having jurisdiction of the cause, and upon regular proceedings, and due notice. In alluding to different kinds of judgments, therefore, such jurisdiction, proceedings, and notice will be assumed. It will also be assumed that they are untainted by fraud, the effect of which will be considered later.

A judgment in rem, adjudicating the title to a ship or other movable property within the custody of the court, is treated as valid everywhere. . . .

Other judgments, not strictly in rem, under which a person has been compelled to pay money, are so far conclusive that the justice of the payment cannot be impeached in another country, so as to compel him to pay it again. For instance, a judgment in foreign attachment is conclusive, as between the parties, of the right to the property or money attached. Story, Confl.Laws (2d Ed.) § 592a. . . .

Other foreign judgments which have been held conclusive of the matter adjudged were judgments discharging obligations contracted in the foreign country between citizens or residents thereof. Story, Confl. Laws, §§ 330-341. . . .

The extraterritorial effect of judgments *in personam*, at law, or in equity may differ, according to the parties to the cause. A judgment of that kind between two citizens or residents of the country, and thereby subject to the jurisdiction in which it is rendered, may be held conclusive as between them everywhere. So, if a foreigner invokes the jurisdiction by bringing an action against a citizen, both may be held bound by a judgment in favor of either; and if a citizen sues a foreigner, and judgment is rendered in favor of the latter, both may be held equally bound. . . .

The effect to which a judgment, purely executory, rendered in favor of a citizen or resident of the country, in a suit there brought by him against a foreigner, may be entitled in an action thereon against the latter in his own country, as is the case now before us, presents a more difficult question, upon which there has been some diversity of opinion.

* * *

The English cases [discussed in the omitted portion] have been stated with the more particularity and detail, because they directly bear upon the question, what was the English law, being then our own law, before the Declaration of Independence? They demonstrate that by that law, as generally understood, and as declared by Hardwicke, Mansfield, Buller, Camden, Eyre, and Ellenborough, and doubted by Kenyon only, a judgment recovered in a foreign country for a sum of money, when sued upon in England, was only prima facie evidence of the demand, and subject to be examined and impeached. . . .

The law upon this subject as understood in the United States at the time of their separation from the mother country was clearly set forth by Chief Justice Parsons, speaking for the supreme judicial court of Massachusetts, in 1813, and by Mr. Justice Story in his Commentaries on the Constitution of the United States, published in 1833. Both those eminent jurists declared that by the law of England the general rule was that foreign judgments were only prima facie evidence of the matter which they purported to decide; and that by the common law, before the American Revolution, all the courts of the several colonies and states were deemed foreign to each other, and consequently judgments rendered by any one of them were considered as foreign judgments, and their merits re-examinable in another colony, not only as to the jurisdiction of the court which pronounced them, but also as to the merits of the controversy, to the extent to which they were understood to be re-examinable in England. . . .

It was because of that condition of the law, as between the American colonies and states, that the United States, at the very beginning of their existence as a nation, ordained that full faith and credit should be given to the judgments of one of the states of the Union in the courts of another of those states. . . .

From this review of the authorities, it clearly appears that, at the time of the separation of this country from England, the general rule was fully established that foreign judgments *in personam* were prima facie evidence only, and not conclusive of the merits of the controversy between the parties. But the extent and limits of the application of that rule do not appear to have been much discussed, or defined with any approach to exactness, in England or America, until the matter was taken up by Chancellor Kent and by Mr. Justice Story. . . .

Mr. Justice Story, in his Commentaries on the Conflict of Laws, first published in 1834, after reviewing many English authorities, said: "The present inclination of the English courts seems to be to sustain the conclusiveness of foreign judgments,"—to which, in the second edition, in 1841, he added: "Although, certainly, there yet remains no inconsiderable diversity of opinion among the learned judges of the different tribunals." Section 606.

He then proceeded to state his own view of the subject, on principle, saying: "It is, indeed, very difficult to perceive what could be done if a different doctrine were maintainable to the full extent of opening all the evidence and merits of the cause anew on a suit upon the foreign judgment. Some of the witnesses may be since dead; some of the vouchers may be lost or destroyed. The merits of the cause, as formerly before the court upon the whole evidence, may have been decidedly in favor of the judgment; upon a partial possession of the original evidence, they may now appear otherwise. Suppose a case purely sounding in damages, such as an action for an assault, for slander, for conversion of property, for a malicious prosecution, or for a criminal conversation; is the defendant to be at liberty to retry the whole merits, and to make out, if he can, a new case upon new evidence? Or is the court to review the former decision, like a court of appeal, upon the old evidence? In a case of covenant, or of debt, or of a breach of contract, are all the circumstances to be reexamined anew? If they are, by what laws and rules of evidence and principles of justice is the validity of the original judgment to be tried? Is the court to open the judgment, and to proceed *ex aequo et bono?* Or is it to administer strict law, and stand to the doctrines of the local administration of justice? Is it to act upon the rules of evidence acknowledged in its own jurisprudence, or upon those of the foreign jurisprudence? These and many more questions might be put to show the intrinsic difficulties of the subject. Indeed, the rule that the judgment is to be prima facie evidence for the plaintiff would be a mere delusion if the defendant might still question it by opening all or any of the original merits on his side; for, under such circumstances, it would be equivalent to granting a new trial. It is easy to understand that the defendant may be at liberty to impeach the original justice of the judgment by showing that the court had no jurisdiction, or that he never had any notice of the suit, or that it was procured by fraud, or that upon its face it is founded in mistake, or that it is irregular and bad by the local law, *fori rei judicatae*. To such an extent the doctrine is intelligible and practicable. Beyond this, the right to impugn the judgment is in legal effect the right to retry the merits of the original cause at large, and to put the defendant upon proving those merits." Section 607. . . .

In view of all the authorities upon the subject, and of the trend of judicial opinion in this country and in England, following the lead of Kent and Story, we are satisfied that where there has been opportunity for a full and fair trial abroad before a court of competent jurisdiction, conducting the trial upon regular proceedings, after due citation or voluntary appearance of the defendant, and under a system of jurisprudence likely to secure an impartial administration of justice between the citizens of its own country and those of other countries, and there is nothing to show either prejudice in the court, or in the system of laws under which it was sitting, or fraud in procuring the judgment, or any other special reason why the comity of this nation should not allow it full effect, the merits of the case should not, in an action brought in this country upon the judgment, be tried afresh, as on a new trial or an appeal, upon the mere assertion of the party that the judgment was erroneous in law or in fact. The defendants, therefore, cannot be permitted, upon that general ground, to contest the validity or the effect of the judgment sued on.

But they have sought to impeach that judgment upon several other grounds, which require separate consideration.

It is objected that the appearance and litigation of the defendants in the French tribunals were not voluntary, but by legal compulsion, and, therefore, that the French courts never acquired such jurisdiction over the defendants that they should be held bound by the judgment. . . .

The present case is not one of a person traveling through or casually found in a foreign country. The defendants, although they were not citizens or residents of France, but were citizens and residents of the state of New York, and their principal place of business was in the city of New York, yet had a storehouse and an agent in Paris, and were accustomed to purchase large quantities of goods there, although they did not make sales in France. Under such circumstances, evidence that their sole object in appearing and carrying on the litigation in the French courts was to prevent property in their storehouse at Paris, belonging to them, and within the jurisdiction, but not in the custody, of those courts, from being taken in satisfaction of any judgment that might be recovered against them, would not, according to our law, show that those courts did not acquire jurisdiction of the persons of the defendants.

It is next objected that in those courts one of the plaintiffs was permitted to testify not under oath, and was not subjected to cross-examination by the opposite party, and that the defendants were therefore deprived of safeguards which are by our law considered essential to secure honesty and to detect fraud in a witness; and also that documents and papers were admitted in evidence, with which the defendants had no connection, and which would not be admissible under our own system of jurisprudence. But it having been shown by the plaintiffs, and hardly denied by the defendants, that the practice followed and the method of examining witnesses were according to the laws of France, we are not prepared to hold that the fact that the procedure in these respects differed from that of our own courts is, of itself, a sufficient ground for impeaching the foreign judgment. . . .

There is no doubt that both in this country, as appears by the authorities already cited, and in England, a foreign judgment may be impeached for fraud. . . .

It has often, indeed, been declared by this court that the fraud which entitles a party to impeach the judgment of one of our own tribunals must be fraud extrinsic to the matter tried in the cause, and not merely consist in false and fraudulent documents or testimony submitted to that tribunal, and the truth of which was contested before it and passed upon by it. . . .

But it is now established in England, by well-considered, and strongly-reasoned decisions of the court of appeal, that foreign judgments may be impeached, if procured by false and fraudulent representations and testimony of the plaintiff, even if the same question of fraud was presented to and decided by the foreign court. . . .

But whether those decisions can be followed in regard to foreign judgments, consistently with our own decisions as to impeaching domestic judgments for fraud, it is unnecessary in this case to determine, because there is a distinct and independent ground upon which we are satisfied that the comity of our nation does not require us to give conclusive effect to the judgments of the courts of France; and that ground is the want of reciprocity, on the part of France, as to the effect to be given to the judgments of this and other foreign countries. . . .

[References to various French statutes, discussed at p. 707, infra, omitted.]

The defendants, in their answer, cited the above provisions of the statutes of France, and alleged, and at the trial offered to prove, that by the construction given to these statutes by the judicial tribunals of France, when the judgments of tribunals of foreign countries against the citizens of France are sued upon in the courts of France, the merits of the controversies upon which those judgments are based are examined anew, unless a treaty to the contrary effect exists between the republic of France and the country in which such judgment is obtained (which is not the case between the republic of France and the United States), and that the tribunals of the republic of France give no force and effect, within the jurisdiction of that country, to the judgments duly rendered by courts of competent jurisdiction of the United States against citizens of France after proper personal service of the process of those courts has been made thereon in this country. We are of opinion that this evidence should have been admitted. . . .

By the law of France, settled by a series of uniform decisions of the court of cessation, the highest judicial tribunal, for more than half a century, no foreign judgment can be rendered executory in France without a review of the judgment au fond (to the bottom), including the whole merits of the cause of action on which the judgment rests. . . .

[An extensive discussion of *Holker v. Parker*, noted at p. 733, infra, and of other French authorities and authorities of other civil law countries omitted.]

It appears, therefore, that there is hardly a civilized nation on either continent which, by its general law, allows conclusive effect to an executory foreign judgment for the recovery of money. In France and in a few smaller states—Norway, Portugal, Greece, Monaco, and Hayti—the merits of the controversy are reviewed, as of course, allowing to the foreign judgment, at the most, no more effect than of being prima facie evidence of the justice of the claim. In the great majority of the countries on the continent of Europe—in Belgium, Holland, Denmark, Sweden, Germany, in many cantons of Switzerland, in Russia and Poland, in Roumania, in Austria and Hungary (perhaps in Italy), and in Spain—as well as in Egypt, in Mexico, and in a great part of South America, the judgment rendered in a foreign country is allowed the same effect only as the courts of that country allow to the judgments of the country in which the judgment in question is sought to be executed.

The prediction of Mr. Justice Story in Section 618 of his Commentaries on the Conflict of Laws, already cited, has thus been fulfilled, and the rule of reciprocity has worked itself firmly into the structure of international jurisprudence.

The reasonable, if not the necessary, conclusion appears to us to be that judgments rendered in France, or in any other foreign country, by the laws of which our own judgments are reviewable upon the merits, are not entitled to full credit and conclusive effect when sued upon in this country, but are *prima facie* evidence only of the justice of the plaintiffs' claim.

In holding such a judgment, for want of reciprocity, not to be conclusive evidence of the merits of the claim, we do not proceed upon any theory of retaliation upon one person by reason of injustice done to another, but upon the broad ground that international law is founded upon mutuality and reciprocity, and that by the principles of international law recognized in most civilized nations, and by the comity of our own country, which it is our judicial duty to know and to declare, the judgment is not entitled to be considered conclusive.

By our law, at the time of the adoption of the constitution, a foreign judgment was considered as prima facie evidence, and not conclusive. There is no statute of the United States, and no treaty of the United States with France, or with any other nation, which has changed that law, or has made any provision upon the subject. It is not to be supposed that, if any statute or treaty had been or should be made, it would recognize as conclusive the judgments of any country, which did not give like effect to our own judgments. In the absence of statute or treaty, it appears to us equally unwarrantable to assume that the comity of the United States requires anything more.

If we should hold this judgment to be conclusive, we should allow it an effect to which, supposing the defendants' offers to be sustained by actual proof, it would, in the absence of a special treaty, be entitled in hardly any other country in Christendom, except the country in which it was rendered. . . .

[Both cases were reversed and the cause remanded for a new trial.]

Mr. Chief Justice FULLER, dissenting.

Plaintiffs brought their action on a judgment recovered by them against the defendants in the courts of France, which courts had jurisdiction over person and subject-matter, and in respect of which judgment no fraud was alleged, except in particulars contested in and considered by the French courts. The question is whether under these circumstances, and in the absence of a treaty or act of congress, the judgment is re-examinable upon the merits. This question I regard as one to be determined by the ordinary and settled rule in respect of allowing a party who has had an opportunity to prove his case in a competent court to retry it on the merits; and it seems to me that the doctrine of *res judicata* applicable to domestic judgments should be applied to foreign judgments as well, and rests on the same general ground of public policy, that there should be an end of litigation.

This application of the doctrine is in accordance with our own jurisprudence, and it is not necessary that we should hold it to be required by some rule of international law. The fundamental principle concerning judgments is that disputes are finally determined by them, and I am unable to perceive why a judgment *in personam*, which is not open to question on the ground of want of jurisdiction, either intrinsically or over the parties, or of fraud, or on any other recognized ground of impeachment, should not be held, *inter partes*, though recovered abroad, conclusive on the merits. . . .

The subjects of the suit were commercial transactions, having their origin, and partly performed, in France, under a contract there made, and alleged to be modified by the dealings of the parties there, and one of the claims against them was for goods sold to them there. They appeared generally in the case, without protest, and by counterclaims relating to the same general course of business, a part of them only connected with the claims against them, became actors in the suit, and submitted to the courts their own claims for affirmative relief, as well as the claims against them. The courts were competent, and they took the chances of a decision in their favor. As traders in France they were under the protection of its laws, and were bound by its laws, its commercial usages, and its rules of procedure. The fact that they were Americans and the opposite parties were citizens of France is immaterial, and there is no suggestion on the record that those courts proceeded on any other ground than that all litigants, whatever their nationality, were entitled to equal justice therein. . . . We are dealing with the judgment of a court of a civilized country, whose laws and system of justice recognize the general rules in respect to property and rights between man and man prevailing among all civilized peoples. Obviously, the last persons who should be heard to complain are those who identified themselves with the business of that country, knowing that all their transactions there would be subject to the local laws and modes of doing business. The French courts appear to have acted "judicially, honestly, and with the intention to arrive at the right conclusion," and a result thus reached ought not to be disturbed. . . .

I cannot yield my assent to the proposition that, because by legislation and judicial decision in France that effect is not there given to judgments recovered in this country which, according to our jurisprudence, we think should be given to judgments wherever recovered (subject, of course, to the recognized exceptions), therefore we should pursue the same line of conduct as respects the judgments of French tribunals. The application of the doctrine of *res judicata* does not rest in discretion; and it is for the government, and not for its courts, to adopt the principle of *retorsion*, if deemed under any circumstances desirable or necessary.

As the court expressly abstains from deciding whether the judgment is impeachable on the ground of fraud, I refrain from any observations on that branch of the case.

Mr. Justice HARLAN, Mr. Justice BREWER, and Mr. Justice JACKSON concur in this dissent.

Discussion Questions

1. How does Justice Gray's opinion define *comity*?
2. What are some of the valid reasons cited in the opinion for refusing to enforce another country's money judgments?
3. What is meant by the term *reciprocity*, and how important is it in questions involving international law?
4. What is the specific holding in this case?
5. How does Justice Gray use customary law to support his reasoning?
6. Do you agree with the majority opinion in this case or with the dissenters? Why?

> *Comment:* The specific precedent in *Hilton v. Guyot* has not been formally overruled; however, it is no longer followed in the great majority of state and federal courts in the United States. It has been superseded by the Foreign Money Judgments Recognition Act, which has been construed to allow enforcement unless there is another valid exception barring enforcement of the claim. Thus, ultimately, the view of the dissenters prevails today.

General Contract Practices

> **Contracts:** *That body of law governing enforcement of private agreements. Such contracts are privately negotiated and may stipulate the method of dispute settlement as long as they do not violate the law.*

The uncertainty of the law in this area of business risk has long been a major concern of the business community. Negotiating business **contracts** has become a major art form in modern practice. Since these are private transactions, the parties may stipulate methods of enforcement of the contract and the forum for dispute settlement in the contract. The most frequent practice is

> **Arbitration:** *Settlement of disputes by prior agreement to accept the decision of a third party as authoritative.*

to provide for **arbitration** at a designated place by an established arbitration procedure. The International Chamber of Commerce (ICC International Court of Arbitration), the London Court of International Arbitration, and the American Arbitration Association (AAA) have established arbitral boards and procedures that are frequently used. Many international treaty provisions relate to recognition and enforcement of awards by arbitration tribunals. The U.S.-French "establishment treaty" offers a good example of the specific treaty provisions that recognize enforcement of foreign court judgments and arbitration awards (see Appendix E). However, the issues of forum and applicable law could result in very costly litigation if proper legal advice is not sought. Some modern contracts even specify the applicable rules of law to be used in the settlement of contract disputes.

The *Restatement (Third)* clearly states that money and property judgments are entitled to recognition and "may be enforced by any party or its successors or assigns against any other party, its successors or assigns, in accordance with the procedure for enforcement of judgments applicable where enforcement is sought" (American Law Institute, 1987, § 481). However, this general rule is subject to the following exceptions as stated in § 482 as follows:

> **§ 482. *Grounds for Nonrecognition of Foreign Judgments***
>
> (1) A court in the United States may not recognize a judgment of the court of a foreign state if:
>   (a) the judgment was rendered under a judicial system that does not provide impartial tribunals or procedures compatible with due process of law; or
>   (b) the court that rendered the judgment did not have jurisdiction over the defendant in accordance with the law of the rendering state and with the rules set forth in § 421.

> (2) A court in the United States need not recognize a judgment of the court of a foreign state if:
>   (a) the court that rendered the judgment did not have jurisdiction of the subject matter of the action;
>   (b) the defendant did not receive notice of the proceedings in sufficient time to enable him to defend;
>   (c) the judgment was obtained by fraud;
>   (d) the cause of action on which the judgment was based, or the judgment itself, is repugnant to the public policy of the United States or of the State where recognition is sought;
>   (e) the judgment conflicts with another final judgment that is entitled to recognition; or
>   (f) the proceeding in the foreign court was contrary to an agreement between the parties to submit the controversy on which the judgment is based to another forum.

[Note: § 421 applies the principle of reasonableness to the question of court jurisdiction.]

Treaty Interpretation by National Courts

National courts as well as international tribunals are involved in treaty interpretation. Treaty construction from a national court's perspective may be significantly different from that of an international tribunal. In general, the type of treaty dealt with by domestic courts is more likely to affect rights of private parties and to be relatively detailed and specific. Treaties concerning taxation, tariffs, and extradition are illustrative of these types of treaties, as well as treaties of friendship, commerce, and navigation. More general treaty obligations that may be the subject of international tribunals are often intended only to bind the governmental authority and are not intended to extend specific rights to individuals in domestic courts.

A national court may be reluctant to construe a treaty in a way that is inconsistent with national interests and values as expressed by the nation's executive or legislative branches. Nonetheless, when the treaty is specifically intended to confer rights on private parties or is enacted into the domestic law, the courts have an obligation to interpret the treaty as the "law of the land."

Note that the relationship between a national court and an international tribunal has little similarity to a domestic appellate system. Even when a treaty provides for arbitration of disputes arising under it, national tribunals are often the **de facto** courts of last resort on questions of interpretation. If the issue arises in an international tribunal, the nation-states involved must initiate the dispute **de novo,** and the international court is not bound by the national court's decision. However, international tribunals may require that the parties (States) exhaust all local remedies before the case is ripe for international adjudication.

In this section of the text, we focus on the rights of private parties; we will discuss the decisions of international tribunals later in Part III. The following illustrative case involves interpretation of treaty obligations in a private dispute involving alleged treaty rights and enforcement of domestic legislation concerning prohibitions against discrimination in employment practices in the United States.

> **De facto:** *Latin phrase meaning "in fact" or as a practical matter, as opposed to the strictly legal meaning.*
>
> **De novo:** *Latin phrase meaning "anew" or as a new action before a court, as opposed to an appeal.*

Sumitomo Shoji America, Inc. v. Avagliano
Supreme Court of the United States. 1982.
457 U.S. 176, 102 S.Ct. 2374. 72 L.Ed.2d 765.

[The allegations of the complaint were described as follows:

Petitioner, Sumitomo Shoji America, Inc., is a New York corporation and a wholly-owned subsidiary of Sumitomo Shoji Kabushiki Kaisha, a Japanese general trading company or *sogo shosha*. Respondents are past and present female secretarial employees of Sumitomo. All but one of the respondents are U.S. citizens; that one exception is a Japanese citizen living in the United States. Respondents brought this suit as a class action claiming that Sumitomo's alleged practice of hiring only male Japanese citizens to fill executive, managerial, and sales positions violated both 42 U.S.C. § 1981 and Title VII of the Civil Rights Act of 1964, as amended, 42 U.S.C. § 2000e et seq. Respondents sought both injunctive relief and damages.

[Sumitomo moved to dismiss the complaint on two grounds: (a) Discrimination on the basis of Japanese citizenship did not violate the legislation, and (b) Sumitomo's practices were protected under the 1953 Treaty of Friendship, Commerce and Navigation between the United States and Japan. The district court dismissed the 1981 claim, but not the Title VII claims, finding Sumitomo not covered by Article VIII(1) of the Treaty. It certified the treaty question to the Court of Appeals, which reversed and remanded for further proceedings. The Supreme Court granted certiorari and reversed in an opinion by Chief Justice BURGER].

Interpretation of the Friendship, Commerce and Navigation Treaty between Japan and the United States must, of course, begin with the language of the Treaty itself. The clear import of treaty language controls unless "application of the words of the treaty according to their obvious meaning effects a result inconsistent with the intent or expectations of its signatories." *Maximov v. United States*, 373 U.S. 49, 54, 83 S.Ct. 1054, 1057, 10 L.Ed.2d 184 (1963). See also The Amiable Isabella, 6 Wheat. (10 U.S.) 1, 72, 5 L.Ed. 191 (1821).

Article VIII(1) of the Treaty provides in pertinent part:

> "*Companies of either Party* [italics added] shall be permitted to engage, within the territories of the other Party, accountants and other technical experts, executive personnel, attorneys, agents and other specialists of their choice."

Clearly Article VIII(1) only applies to companies of one of the Treaty countries operating in the other country. Sumitomo contends that it is a company of Japan, and that Article VIII(1) of the Treaty grants it very broad discretion to fill its executive, managerial and sales positions exclusively with male Japanese citizens.

Article VIII(1) does not define any of its terms; the definitional section of the Treaty is contained in Article XXII. Article XXII(3) provides:

> "As used in the present Treaty, the term 'companies' means corporations, partnerships, companies, and other associations, whether or not with limited liability and whether or not for pecuniary profit. Companies constituted under the applicable laws and regulations within the territories of either Party *shall be deemed companies thereof* and shall have their juridical status recognized within the territories of the other Party." [Emphasis added]

Sumitomo is "constituted under the applicable laws and regulations" of New York; based on Article XXII(3), it is a company of the United States, not a company of Japan. As a company of the United States operating in the United States, under the literal language of Article XXII(3) of the Treaty, Sumitomo cannot invoke the rights provided in Article VIII(1), which are available only to companies of Japan operating in the United States and to companies of the United States operating in Japan.

The Governments of Japan and the United States support this interpretation of the Treaty. Both the Ministry of Foreign Affairs of Japan and the United States Department of State agree that a United States corporation, even when wholly owned by a Japanese company is not a company of Japan under the Treaty and is therefore not covered by Article VIII(1). The Ministry of Foreign Affairs stated its position to the American Embassy in Tokyo with reference to this case:

> "The Ministry of Foreign Affairs, as the Office of [the Government of Japan] responsible for the interpretation of the [Friendship, Commerce and Navigation] Treaty, reiterates its view concerning the application of Article 8, Paragraph 1 of the Treaty: For the purpose of the Treaty, companies constituted under the applicable laws . . . of either Party shall be deemed companies thereof and therefore, a subsidiary of a Japanese company incorporated under the laws of New York is not covered by Article 8 Paragraph 1 when it operates in the United States."

The United States Department of State also maintains that Article VIII(1) rights do not apply to locally incorporated subsidiaries. Although not conclusive, the meaning attributed to Treaty provisions by the government agencies charged with their negotiation and enforcement is entitled to great weight. *Kolovrat v. Oregon*, 366 U.S. 187, 194, 81 S.Ct. 922, 926, 6 L.Ed.2d 218 (1961).

Our role is limited to giving effect to the intent of the Treaty parties. When the parties to a treaty both agree as to the meaning of a treaty provision, and that interpretation follows from the clear treaty language, we must, absent extraordinarily strong contrary evidence defer to that interpretation.

III

Sumitomo maintains that although the literal language of the Treaty supports the contrary interpretation, the intent of Japan and the United States was to cover subsidiaries regardless of their place of incorporation. We disagree.

Contrary to the view of the Court of Appeals and the claims of Sumitomo, adherence to the language of the Treaty would not "overlook the purpose of the Treaty." 638 F.2d, at 556. The Friendship, Commerce and Navigation Treaty between Japan and the United States is but one of a series of similar commercial agreements negotiated after World War II. The primary purpose of the corporation provisions of the Treaties was to give corporations of each signatory legal status in the territory of the other party, and to allow them to conduct business in the other country on a comparable basis with domestic firms. Although the United States negotiated commercial treaties as early as 1778, and thereafter throughout the 19th and early 20th centuries, these early commercial treaties were primarily concerned with the trade and shipping rights of individuals. Until the 20th century, international commerce was much more an individual than a corporate affair.

As corporate involvement in international trade expanded in this century, old commercial treaties became outmoded. Because "corporation[s] can have no legal existence out of the boundaries of the sovereignty by which [they are] created," *Bank of Augusta v. Earle*, 13 Peters (38 U.S.) 519, 588, 10 L.Ed. 274 (1839), it became necessary to negotiate new treaties granting corporations legal status and the right to function abroad. A series of treaties negotiated before World War II gave corporations legal status and access to foreign courts, but it was not until the postwar Friendship, Commerce and Navigation Treaties that United States corporations gained the right to conduct business in other countries. The purpose of the treaties was not to give foreign corporations greater rights than domestic companies, but instead to assure them the right to conduct business on an equal basis without suffering discrimination based on their alienage.

The treaties accomplished their purpose by granting foreign corporations "national treatment" in most respects and by allowing foreign individuals and companies to form locally-incorporated subsidiaries. These local subsidiaries are considered for purpose of the Treaty to be companies of the country in which they are incorporated; they are entitled to the rights, and subject to the responsibilities of other domestic corporations. By treating these subsidiaries as domestic companies, the purpose of the Treaty provisions—to assure that corporations of one treaty party have the right to conduct business within the territory of the other party without suffering discrimination as an alien entity—is fully met.

Nor can we agree with the Court of Appeals view that literal interpretation of the Treaty would create a "crazy-quilt pattern" in which the rights of branches of Japanese companies operating directly in the United States would be greatly superior to the right of locally incorporated subsidiaries of Japanese companies. 638 F.2d, at 556. The Court of Appeals maintained that if such subsidiaries were not considered companies of Japan under the Treaty, they, unlike branch offices of Japanese corporations, would be denied access to the legal system, would be left unprotected against unlawful entry and molestation, and would be unable to dispose of property, obtain patents, engage in importation and exportation, or make payments, remittances and transfers of funds. 638 F.2d, at 556. That this is not the case is obvious; the subsidiaries, as companies of the United States, would enjoy all of those rights and more. The only significant advantage branches may have over subsidiaries is that conferred by Article VIII(1).

IV

We are persuaded, as both signatories agree, that under the literal language of Article XXII(3) of the Treaty, Sumitomo is a company of the United States; we discern no reason to depart from the plain meaning of the Treaty language. Accordingly, we hold that Sumitomo is not a company of Japan and is thus not covered by Article VIII(1) of the Treaty. The judgment of the Court of Appeals is reversed, and the case is remanded for further proceedings consistent with this opinion.

Reversed and Remanded.

Discussion Questions

1. How did the lower courts in this case treat the question of treaty exemption from violations of Title VII of the Civil Rights Act of 1964, making it unlawful to discriminate on the basis of sex in employment practices?

2. What was the legal issue and the court's holding in this case? How would you word the holding as a precedent for future cases?

3. How does the Court use communication from the foreign ministry of Japan and the U.S. State Department to assist in ascertaining the intent of the treaty provisions?

4. Would the outcome of this case be different if the business activity involved were that of a branch office of the parent company in Japan involved in negotiating trade contracts?

Harmonizing Contract Law Among Nations

One of the more recent efforts to harmonize, or unify, international standards for sales contracts involved in international trade is the United Nations **Convention on the International Sale of Goods (CISG).** This treaty is the product of fifty years of effort by several organizations, all of which are still involved in the process of unification and harmonization of international commercial law. The differences between countries following the common law heritage of England and the civil law practices of continental Europe (and most of the rest of the world) were brought together in this formulation of general international law on the specific subject of sale of goods.

> **Convention on the International Sale of Goods (CISG):** A major international treaty that seeks to harmonize the law of contracts regarding the sale of goods in international trade and merges legal concepts of civil law and common law countries.

This area of contract law had long been a subject of unnecessary complexity even within the United States where some states had developed common law distinctions that inhibited trade and commercial practices within the area of commercial transactions among the states of the United States. Early in this century the successful efforts of the American Law Institute produced a model uniform code harmonizing these differences that is known as the **Uniform Commercial Code.** All states in the United States except Louisiana (which has a civil law tradition) adopted the UCC as positive statutory law to facilitate trade and commerce and to reduce the complexity of commercial transactions. International transactions, however, were not successfully harmonized until the CISG came into effect in January of 1988.

> **Uniform Commercial Code:** A codification of contract law within the United States in an attempt to harmonize that body of law among the states of the United States.

The United States was one of the first nations to ratify the CISG treaty in 1986. It was the first time in U.S. history that a treaty had been used to enact a private law, which is generally a power reserved to the individual states under the U.S. Constitution. Purely domestic transactions in the United States will still be governed by the UCC; however, international transactions are now governed by the international treaty law of the CISG in the absence of a specific contractual stipulation to the contrary. The harmonized rules of the CISG apply to contracts for the commercial sale of goods between parties whose places of business are in different nations and when the places of business are located in countries that have ratified the convention. It excludes consumer goods sold for personal, family, or household use; goods bought at auction; stocks, securities, negotiable instruments, or money; ships, vessels, or aircraft; electricity; assembly contracts for the supply of goods to be manufactured or produced; contracts for the supply of labor or other services; products liability; and contracts in which the parties choose to be bound by some other law.

The CISG has been ratified by all of the major trading nations of the world, and many more countries are expected to adopt it in the years to come. It is a significant element in the growing stability and predictability of the legal environment necessary to promote trade. Some lawyers fear that national courts will begin to interpret the CISG differently, according to the precepts of their own legal, economic, and political systems and that this will destroy the uniformity that was the goal of the CISG. Nonetheless, it is a major step in the direction of more clearly understood legal obligations among private trading parties throughout the world.

Risk Management Agents

Small and medium-sized firms have access to a number of reputable professional managers to help them in dealing with the multiple risks involved in entering foreign markets. The risks of exporting, licensing, and investment are substantially reduced by using an experienced management team. These consultants include not only the professional managers within the firm, but also advisers, agents, and intermediaries who specialize in assisting companies that go international. Important services are provided by the international banker, the export trading company, the export management company, the freight forwarder, the government trade specialist, the lawyer, and the political risk analyst. Many experienced international business managers will advise that the selection of an overseas agent is the single most important step in entering a foreign market. Foreign sales agents, or buying agents, are extremely helpful in dealing with local marketing issues.

Foreign distributors are independent firms that purchase goods for resale directly from the U.S. exporter. They assume the risk of buying and warehousing goods in the local market and provide additional product support services. The distributor often extends credit to its customers and assumes responsibility for local advertising and promotion.

> *Foreign distributor:* Agent in the foreign country who assumes the risk of buying and warehousing goods in the local market and provides support services abroad.

The **freight forwarder** or **customs broker** serves as a specialized agent handling the extensive documentation, or paperwork, required in an export or import shipment. When they represent U.S. importers, they are called customs brokers. Freight forwarders act as the shipper's (seller's) agent for exporting.

> *Freight forwarder:* An agent who handles the paperwork required in export shipments.
>
> *Customs broker:* An agent who handles the paperwork required in import shipments.

The **international banker** provides important services not only in financing business transactions but also in moving money and shipping documents through their services, enabling the shipper to receive assured payment for goods. They offer a range of specialized international banking services that are necessary for doing business abroad. Many international bankers possess a great wealth of expertise and foreign contacts and are therefore able to play an advisory role in international business.

> *International banker:* A financial institution that provides services not only of a financial nature but in handling shipping documents and enabling the shipper to receive assured payment for goods.

The **International Trade Administration** of the U.S. Department of Commerce maintains district offices throughout the United States. This public agency makes trade specialists available to consult with companies on a wide range of topics of interest to the firm seeking to enter the foreign trade market. The agency maintains a *Foreign Trade Index*, which is a master computer file containing information on foreign importers, agents, distributors, and potential end users of U.S. products. The *Agent/Distributor Service* helps U.S. companies locate qualified overseas representatives. This agency also maintains *service officers* located in sixty-three foreign service posts who will help locate and make recommendations on the selection of suitable representatives abroad. The *World Traders Data Report* contains detailed profiles on individual foreign firms, including trade and financial information. This report contains valuable information about the firm's employees, product lines, its general reputation in the trade, and the names of its trading partners. Further services include the department's *Trade Opportunities Program*, giving leads on specific business opportunities abroad, including the names of prospective customers. The new *Automatic International Transfer System* will provide a centralized computer bank linked by satellite to all U.S. foreign and commercial service offices in the United States and abroad, which will provide quicker access to market information.

The Multinational Enterprise (MNE)

In addition to the usual forms of business enterprises that may be engaged in international trade and business ventures, there is the **multinational enterprise (MNE)**. The most visible MNEs are the largest multinational corporations that have become involved in a wide variety of types of business activity in every sector of the globe. The activities of these global enterprises are somewhat obscured by the privacy rights of firms to protect their business secrets and the complex nature of business dealings. The global power, influence, and ability of these financial giants to manipulate market forces and avoid the restraints of competitive enterprise have aroused concern and prompted new regulatory attempts by governments.

There are over 200 MNEs that have annual sales exceeding $1 billion (U.S.) and have more currency reserves at their disposal than do most governments of the world. The top ten multinational giants have annual revenues larger than the yearly gross national product of two-thirds of the countries in the world. MNEs make up nearly 40% of a list of the 100 largest concentrations of global economic wealth; the remainder of the list consists of modern nation-states. These MNEs now challenge the basic assumption that nation-states are the world's fundamental economic and political units.

Among the concerns about MNE behavior are complaints that little is known about the organizational structure and policy formation procedures of the MNE. The cost of acquiring this information about secretive global corporations is prohibitively high, and coordinated information gathering from several countries is currently difficult. These giant enterprises are frequently insensitive to the host country's need for cultural cohesion and may interfere with developmental policies of the host. Corporate planning often fails to include adequate consideration for the host country's capacity to absorb the total consequences of MNE activity. They may waste the environment by using high-polluting means of production and rigorous resource extraction processes. Their financial practices concerning credit, retail prices, transfer pricing, industrial property, and valuation of imports and liabilities owed abroad often hurt the host country's balance-of-payments posture and taxation efforts.

At the present time, MNEs enjoy freedom from control by any single legal jurisdiction, especially that of the host country, through the use of choice-of-forum clauses in contracts, use of tax haven countries, and subjection to extraterritorial application of one country's legal rules (usually those of the enterprise's home country) at the expense of otherwise governing legal rules of the host country (Folsom, Gordon, & Spanogle, 1992).

The MNE has undue strength in labor negotiations worldwide because of easy relocation to a less expensive labor environment in another country and because of the capacity to freeze indefinitely numbers of available jobs by freezing investment levels. These practices tend to avoid upgrading the quality of local labor while total resources available to the MNE permit displacement of local entrepreneurship. They also restrict the development and dissemination of technology and intrude on the sovereignty of the host country by becoming directly involved in local political processes, paying bribes, serving as an intelligence gathering conduit for the government of another country, and cooperating with another country in the operation of certain politically inspired trade policies directed at the host country. In short, the major charges are that the MNE is uncontrolled and arrogant.

Although the supporters of multinationals deny many of these complaints, many countries have responded with laws regulating foreign investment. These regulations include areas of banking, communication, defense suppliers, natural resource extraction, and transportation where national interests seek to avoid becoming vulnerable to control or information access by foreigners. These laws are also designed to monitor foreign investment activity, to determine the conditions under which investment may be made, and to regulate the product and technology flows that such investment produces.

The international community's response has been through the **U.N. Commission on Transnational Corporations**, which has drafted a code of conduct for MNEs and is engaged in coordination of information about certain companies by providing consultants and conducting training sessions for host country representatives. The topic of **technology transfer** has become one of major concern to developing countries, and the U.N. Conference on Trade and Development (UNCTAD) has been vigorously working on a code of conduct for the transfer of technology. The U.N. General Assembly adopted a code on restrictive business practices in 1980. However, it has been given little attention by governments, many of whom view it as an obstacle to trade and irrelevant to the 1990s (Folsom et al., 1992).

The World Bank has developed a public forum for the resolution of disputes between private corporations and host coun-

> **U.N. Commission on Transnational Corporations:** A U.N. agency that has promoted a draft code of conduct for MNEs and coordinates information and advice about MNEs for potential host countries.

> **Technology transfer:** Agreements to share technology with the host country so that eventually a greater independence can be achieved.

tries involving investment disputes. The Convention on the Settlement of Investment Disputes Between States and Nationals of Other States provides an arbitration procedure that may be used by host States in negotiating important financial contracts (see Appendix G for wording.) The U.S. government also supports an investment guarantee program administered by the Overseas Private Investment Corporation (OPIC). These programs are not regulatory in character but do serve to reduce the risks involved on the part of the private investor and the host country.

International regulation of MNEs is likely to continue to increase in the future. The **Organization for Economic Cooperation and Development (OECD)** has also been active in this area, and the **International Institute for the Unification of Private Law (UNIDROIT)** is working on an international trade law code regarding the formulation and interpretation of contracts, especially leasing agreements. The United States has been active in attempting to enforce antimonopolistic practices when international activities have an effect in the United States. The European Community has also taken steps to regulate more tightly MNE activity on a sector basis, such as in areas of company law, taxation, and employment policy.

> **Organization for Economic Cooperation and Development (OECD):** *A U.N. agency that promotes economic cooperation and facilitates economic development.*
>
> **International Institute for the Unification of Private Law (UNIDROIT):** *A U.N. agency involved in activity to harmonize and unify private law practices internationally.*

In 1977, the U.S. Congress passed the **Foreign Corrupt Practices Act**, which makes it unlawful for any domestic concern to make use of the mails or any means of interstate commerce corruptly in furtherance of or the giving of anything of value to any official or foreign political party for purposes of influencing or inducing action to assist in obtaining or retaining business (for precise wording see 15 U.S.C. § 78dd-2). This language prohibits bribery of a public official in business practices abroad but has been somewhat weakened by the 1988 amendments to the act that removed the controversial basis for liability when the MNE had "reason to know" that some of its payments through intermediaries would end up in the hands of foreign officials.

> **Foreign Corrupt Practices Act:** *An act of Congress prohibiting bribery of officials as a business practice (see 15 U.S.C. § 78dd-2).*

Forms of Corporate Business Structure

The creation and regulation of business entities is essentially a matter of municipal law. In general, the kind of organizational form that a business can assume depends on its place of creation. These forms are essentially limited to sole proprietorships, partnerships, and corporations. Multinational enterprises are businesses operating in more than one State, and they take on a variety of operational structures that reflect their international character. If the home or parent organization is located within a single nation it is more accurately referred to as a **national multinational corporation.** However, the most complex form of enterprise is the **international multinational corporation,** which may have multiple parent companies located in multiple States. In States other than a firm's home State or States, the business operates through subordinate organizations. The choice of the particular form of these subordinates may be dictated by home and host

> **National multinational corporation:** *A corporation with a single parent company located within a single nation.*

> **International multinational corporation:** *A corporation having more than one parent company, with the parent corporations located in two or more States.*

State laws, but the range of choices is essentially limited to representative offices, agencies, branches, and subsidiaries. As a general rule, home States regulate the parent companies and host States regulate the subordinates. However, there are attempts of home States to regulate foreign subordinates with laws that have extraterritorial effect, and host States may attempt to regulate the parents by piercing the fictional veil that separates the subordinates from their parents.

These basic forms of business organizational structure vary considerably in their particular requirements and the rights and responsibilities that go along with them in each country. For example, in civil law countries of continental Europe every form of business organization is a "company" (*société* in French, *Gesellschaft* in German). However, some companies have limited liability and others do not. In common law countries, having an English legal heritage, associations such as partnerships are formed without formalities and are regarded as an aggregate of persons rather than a separate juridical entity. The corporate structure of businesses with limited liability is a particular status that reduces the risk of the particular investor, and each country has somewhat different rules regarding the achievement of this status according to municipal law. Thus, generally, the place of incorporation of the firm is considered to determine the nationality of the particular business entity.

Companies are juridical entities with legal identities separate from that of their owners. Several important consequences follow from this separate legal identity: (a) The liability of the owners is limited to their investment in the company; (b) the owners are neither managers nor agents nor representatives of the company; and (c) the rights and benefits accruing to the company belong to the company and not its owners.

The municipal character of this area of business regulation is underscored by the following case that came before the International Court of Justice in 1970. Belgium brought this suit against Spain concerning the actions of the Spanish government in declaring the Barcelona Traction, Light, and Power Company bankrupt. The court was asked to ignore the separate legal identity of a Canadian company owned principally by Belgian nationals so that Belgium could bring a claim on the owners' behalf.

Case Concerning the *Barcelona Traction*, Light and Power Company, Limited *(Belgium v. Spain)*, Second Phase

International Court of Justice.
[1970] I.C.J. 3.

[Rejecting the claim of Belgium, the court said in part:]

28. . . . The claim is presented on behalf of natural and juristic persons, alleged to be Belgian nationals and shareholders in the Barcelona Traction, Light and Power Company, Limited. The submissions of the Belgian

Government make it clear that the object of its Application is reparation for damage allegedly caused to these persons by the conduct, said to be contrary to international law, of various organs of the Spanish State towards that company and various other companies in the same group.

* * *

30. The States which the present case principally concerns are Belgium, the national State of the alleged shareholders, Spain, the State whose organs are alleged to have committed the unlawful acts complained of, and Canada, the State under whose laws Barcelona Traction was incorporated and in whose territory it has its registered office ("head office" in the terms of the by-laws of Barcelona Traction).

31. Thus the Court has to deal with a series of problems arising out of a triangular relationship involving the State whose nationals are shareholders in a company incorporated under the laws of another State, in whose territory it has its registered office; the State whose organs are alleged to have committed against the company unlawful acts prejudicial to both it and its shareholders; and the State under whose laws the company is incorporated, and in whose territory it has its registered office.

32. In these circumstances it is logical that the Court should first address itself to what was originally presented as the subject-matter of the third preliminary objection: namely the question of the right of Belgium to exercise diplomatic protection of Belgian shareholders in a company which is a juristic entity incorporated in Canada, the measures complained of having been taken in relation not to any Belgian national but to the company itself.

33. When a State admits into its territory foreign investments or foreign nationals, whether natural or juristic persons, it is bound to extend to them the protection of the law and assumes obligations concerning the treatment to be afforded them. . . .

35. . . . In the present case it is therefore essential to establish whether the losses allegedly suffered by Belgian shareholders in Barcelona Traction were the consequence of the violation of obligations of which they were the beneficiaries. In other words: has a right of Belgium been violated on account of its nationals' having suffered infringement of their rights as shareholders in a company not of Belgian nationality?

36. Thus it is the existence or absence of a right, belonging to Belgium and recognized as such by international law, which is decisive for the problem of Belgium's capacity.

> "This right is necessarily limited to intervention [by a State] on behalf of its own nationals because, in the absence of a special agreement, it is the bond of nationality between the State and the individual which alone confers upon the State the right of diplomatic protection, and it is as a part of the function of diplomatic protection that the right to take up a claim and to ensure respect for the rules of international law must be envisaged." (Panevezys-Saldutiskis Railway, Judgment, 1939, P.C .I.J., Series A/B, No. 76, p. 16.)

It follows that the same question is determinant in respect of Spain's responsibility towards Belgium. Responsibility is the necessary corollary of a right. In the absence of any treaty on the subject between the Parties, this essential issue has to be decided in the light of the general rules of diplomatic protection.

37. In seeking to determine the law applicable to this case, the Court has to bear in mind the continuous evolution of international law. Diplomatic protection deals with a very sensitive area of international relations, since the interest of a foreign State in the protection of its nationals confronts the rights of the territorial sovereign, a fact of which the general law on the subject has had to take cognizance in order to prevent abuses and friction. From its origins closely linked with international commerce, diplomatic protection has sustained a particular impact from the growth of international economic relations and at the same time from the profound transformations which have taken place in the economic life of nations. These latter changes have given birth to municipal institutions, which have transcended frontiers and have begun to exercise considerable influence on international relations. One of these phenomena which has a particular bearing on the present case is the corporate entity.

38. In this field international law is called upon to recognize institutions of municipal law that have an important and extensive role in the international field. This does not necessarily imply drawing any analogy between its own institutions and those of municipal law, nor does it amount to making rules of international law dependent upon categories of municipal law. All it means is that international law has had to recognize the corporate entity as an institution created by States in a domain essentially within their domestic jurisdiction. This in turn requires that,

whenever legal issues arise concerning the rights of States with regard to the treatment of companies and shareholders, as to which rights international law has not established its own rules, it has to refer to the relevant rules of municipal law. Consequently, in view of the relevance to the present case of the rights of the corporate entity and its shareholders under municipal law, the Court must devote attention to the nature and interrelation of those rights.

* * *

40. There is, however, no need to investigate the many different forms of legal entity provided for by the municipal laws of States, because the Court is concerned only with that exemplified by the company involved in the present case: Barcelona Traction—a limited liability company whose capital is represented by shares. There are, indeed, other associations, whatever the name attached to them by municipal legal systems, that do not enjoy independent corporate personality. The legal difference between the two kinds of entity is that for the limited liability company it is the overriding tie of legal personality which is determinant; for the other associations, the continuing autonomy of the several members.

41. Municipal law determines the legal situation not only of such limited liability companies but also of those persons who hold shares in them. Separated from the company by numerous barriers, the shareholder cannot be identified with it. The concept and structure of the company are founded on and determined by a firm distinction between the separate entity of the company and that of the shareholder, each with a distinct set of rights. The separation of property rights as between company and shareholder is an important manifestation of this distinction. So long as the company is in existence the shareholder has no right to the corporate assets.

* * *

44. Notwithstanding the separate corporate personality, a wrong done to the company frequently causes prejudice to its shareholders. But the mere fact that damage is sustained by both company and shareholder does not imply that both are entitled to claim compensation. Thus no legal conclusion can be drawn from the fact that the same event caused damage simultaneously affecting several natural or juristic persons. Creditors do not have any right to claim compensation from a person who, by wronging their debtor, causes them loss. In such cases, no doubt, the interests of the aggrieved are affected, but not their rights. Thus whenever a shareholder's interests are harmed by an act done to the company, it is to the latter that he must look to institute appropriate action; for although two separate entities may have suffered from the same wrong, it is only one entity whose rights have been infringed.

* * *

48. The Belgian Government claims that shareholders of Belgian nationality suffered damage in consequence of unlawful acts of the Spanish authorities and, in particular, that the Barcelona Traction shares, though they did not cease to exist, were emptied of all real economic content. It accordingly contends that the shareholders had an independent right to redress, notwithstanding the fact that the acts complained of were directed against the company as such. Thus the legal issue is reducible to the question of whether it is legitimate to identify an attack on company rights, resulting in damage to shareholders, with the violation of their direct rights.

* * *

50. In turning now to the international legal aspects of the case, the Court must, as already indicated, start from the fact that the present case essentially involves factors derived from municipal law the distinction and the community between the company and the shareholder—which the Parties, however widely their interpretations may differ, each take as the point of departure of their reasoning. If the Court were to decide the case in disregard of the relevant institutions of municipal law it would, without justification, invite serious legal difficulties. It would lose touch with reality, for there are no corresponding institutions of international law to which the Court could resort. Thus, the Court has, as indicated, not only to take cognizance of municipal law but also to refer to it. It is to rules generally accepted by municipal legal systems which recognize the limited company whose capital is represented by shares, and not to the municipal law of a particular State, that international law refers. . . ..

51. On the international plane, the Belgian Government bar advanced the proposition that it is inadmissible to deny the shareholders' national State a right of diplomatic protection merely on the ground that another State possesses a corresponding right in respect of the company itself. In strict logic and law this formulation of the Belgian claim to *jus standi* assumes the existence of the very right that requires demonstration. In fact the Belgian Government has repeatedly stressed that there exists no rule of international law which would deny the national State of the shareholders the right of diplomatic protection for the purpose of seeking redress pursuant to unlawful acts committed by another State against the company in which they hold shares. This, by emphasizing the absence of any express denial of the right, conversely implies the admission that there is no rule of international law which expressly confers such a right on the shareholders' national State.

52. International law may not, in some fields, provide specific rules in particular cases. In the concrete situation, the company against which allegedly unlawful acts were directed is expressly vested with a right, whereas no such right is specifically provided for the shareholder in respect of those acts. Thus the position of the company rests on a positive rule of both municipal and international law. As to the shareholder, while he has certain rights expressly provided for him by municipal law . . . , appeal can, in the circumstances of the present case, only be made to the silence of international law. Such silence scarcely admits of interpretation in favour of the shareholder.

* * *

70. In allocating corporate entities to States for purposes of diplomatic protection, international law is based, but only to a limited extent, on an analogy with the rules governing the nationality of individuals. The traditional rule attributes the right of diplomatic protection of a corporate entity to the State under the laws of which it is incorporated and in whose territory it has its registered office. These two criteria have been confirmed by long practice and by numerous international instruments. This notwithstanding, further or different links are at times said to be required in order that a right of diplomatic protection should exist. Indeed, it has been the practice of some States to give a company incorporated under their law diplomatic protection solely when it has its seat *(siège social)* or management or centre of control in their territory, or when a majority or a substantial proportion of the shares has been owned by nationals of the State concerned. Only then, it has been held, does there exist between the corporation and the State in question a genuine connection of the kind familiar from other branches of international law. However, in the particular field of the diplomatic protection of corporate entities, no absolute test of the "genuine connection" has found general acceptance. Such tests as have been applied are of a relative nature, and sometimes links with one State have had to be weighed against those with another. In this connection reference has been made to the *Nottebohm* case. In fact the Parties made frequent reference to it in the course of the proceedings. However, given both the legal and factual aspects of protection in the present case the Court is of the opinion that there can be no analogy with the issues raised or the decision given in that case.

71. In the present case it is not disputed that the company was incorporated in Canada and has its registered office in that country. The incorporation of the company under the law of Canada was an act of free choice. Not only did the founders of the company seek its incorporation under Canadian law but it has remained under that law for a period of over fifty years. It has maintained in Canada its registered office, its accounts and its share registers. Board meetings were held there for many years; it has been listed in the records of the Canadian tax authorities. Thus a close and permanent connection has been established, fortified by the passage of over half a century. This connection is in no way weakened by the fact that the company engaged from the very outset in commercial activities outside Canada, for that was its declared object. Barcelona Traction's links with Canada are thus manifold.

* * *

76. . . . [T]he record shows that from 1948 onwards the Canadian Government made to the Spanish Government numerous representations which cannot be viewed otherwise than as the exercise of diplomatic protection in respect of the Barcelona Traction company. Therefore this was not a case where diplomatic protection was refused or remained in the sphere of fiction. It is also clear that over the whole period of its diplomatic activity the Canadian Government proceeded in full knowledge of the Belgian attitude and activity.

77. It is true that at a certain point the Canadian Government ceased to act on behalf of Barcelona Traction, for reasons which have not been fully revealed, though a statement made in a letter of 19 July 1955 by the Canadian Secretary of State for External Affairs suggests that it felt the matter should be settled by means of private

negotiations. The Canadian Government has nonetheless retained its capacity to exercise diplomatic protection; no legal impediment has prevented it from doing so; no fact has arisen to render this protection impossible. It has discontinued its action of its own free will.

78. The Court would here observe that, within the limits prescribed by international law, a State may exercise diplomatic protection by whatever means and to whatever extent it thinks fit, for it is its own right that the State is asserting. Should the natural or legal persons on whose behalf it is acting consider that their rights are not adequately protected, they have no remedy in international law. All they can do is to resort to municipal law, if means are available, with a view to furthering their cause or obtaining redress. . . .

79. The State must be viewed as the sole judge to decide whether its protection will be granted, to what extent it is granted, and when it will cease. It retains in this respect a discretionary power the exercise of which may be determined by considerations of a political or other nature, unrelated to the particular case. Since the claim of the State is not identical with that of the individual or corporate person whose cause is espoused, the State enjoys complete freedom of action. Whatever the reasons for any change of attitude, the fact cannot in itself constitute a justification for the exercise of diplomatic protection by another government, unless there is some independent and otherwise valid ground for that.

* * *

81. The cessation by the Canadian Government of the diplomatic protection of Barcelona Traction cannot, then, be interpreted to mean that there is no remedy against the Spanish Government for the damage done by the allegedly unlawful acts of the Spanish authorities. It is not a hypothetical right which was vested in Canada, for there is no legal impediment preventing the Canadian Government from protecting Barcelona Traction. Therefore there is no substance in the argument that for the Belgian Government to bring a claim before the Court represented the only possibility of obtaining redress for the damage suffered by Barcelona Traction and, through it, by its share holders.

* * *

83. The Canadian Government's right of protection in respect of the Barcelona Traction company remains unaffected by the present proceedings. . . .

* * *

88. It follows from what has already been stated above that, where it is a question of an unlawful act committed against a company representing foreign capital, the general rule of international law authorizes the national State of the company alone to make a claim.

* * *

92. Since the general rule on the subject does not entitle the Belgian Government to put forward a claim in this case, the question remains to be considered whether nonetheless, as the Belgian Government has contended during the proceedings, considerations of equity do not require that it be held to possess a right of protection. It is quite true that it has been maintained, that, for reasons of equity, a State should be able, in certain cases, to take up the protection of its nationals, shareholders in a company which has been the victim of a violation of international law. Thus a theory has been developed to the effect that the State of the shareholders has a right of diplomatic protection when the State whose responsibility is invoked is the national State of the company. Whatever the validity of this theory may be, it is certainly not applicable to the present case, since Spain is not the national State of Barcelona Traction.

93. On the other hand, the Court considers that, in the field of diplomatic protection as in all other fields of international law, it is necessary that the law be applied reasonably. It has been suggested that if in a given case it is not possible to apply the general rule that the right of diplomatic protection of a company belongs to its national State, considerations of equity might call for the possibility of protection of the shareholders in question by their own national State. This hypothesis does not correspond to the circumstances of the present case.

94. In view, however, of the discretionary nature of diplomatic protection, considerations of equity cannot require more than the possibility for some protector State to intervene, whether it be the national State of the company, by virtue of the general rule mentioned above, or, in a secondary capacity, the national State of the shareholders who claim protection. In this connection, account should also be taken of the practical effects of deducing from considerations of equity any broader right of protection for the national State of the shareholders. It must first of all be observed that it would be difficult on an equitable basis to make distinctions according to any quantitative test: it would seem that the owner of 1 per cent. and the owner of 90 per cent. of the share-capital should have the same possibility of enjoying the benefit of diplomatic protection. The protector State may, of course, be disinclined to take up the case of the single small shareholder, but it could scarcely be denied the right to do so in the name of equitable considerations. In that field, protection by the national State of the shareholders can hardly be graduated according to the absolute or relative size of the shareholding involved.

95. The Belgian Government, it is true, has also contended that as high a proportion as 88 per cent. of the shares in Barcelona Traction belonged to natural or juristic persons of Belgian nationality, and it has used this as an argument for the purpose not only of determining the amount of the damages which it claims, but also of establishing its right of action on behalf of the Belgian shareholders. Nevertheless, this does not alter the Belgian Government's position, as expounded in the course of the proceedings, which implies, in the last analysis, that it might be sufficient for one single share to belong to a national of a given State for the latter to be entitled to exercise its diplomatic protection.

96. The Court considers that the adoption of the theory of diplomatic protection of shareholders as such, by opening the door to competing diplomatic claims, could create an atmosphere of confusion and insecurity in international economic relations. The danger would be all the greater inasmuch as the shares of companies whose activity is international are widely scattered and frequently change hands. It might perhaps be claimed that, if the right of protection belonging to the national States of the shareholders were considered as only secondary to that of the national State of the company, there would be less danger of difficulties of the kind contemplated. However, the Court must state that the essence of a secondary right is that it only comes into existence at the time when the original right ceases to exist. As the right of protection vested in the national State of the company cannot be regarded as extinguished because it is not exercised, it is not possible to accept the proposition that in case of its non-exercise the national States of the shareholders have a right of protection secondary to that of the national State of the company. Furthermore, study of factual situations in which this theory might possibly be applied gives rise to the following observations.

97. The situations in which foreign shareholders in a company wish to have recourse to diplomatic protection by their own national State may vary. It may happen that the national State of the company simply refuses to grant it its diplomatic protection, or that it begins to exercise it (as in the present case) but does not pursue its action to the end. It may also happen that the national State of the company and the State which has committed a violation of international law with regard to the company arrive at a settlement of the matter, by agreeing on compensation for the company, but that the foreign shareholder find the compensation insufficient. Now, as a matter of principle, it would be difficult to draw a distinction between these three cases so far as the protection of foreign shareholders by their national State is concerned, since in each case they may have suffered real damage. Furthermore, the national State of the company is perfectly free to decide how far it is appropriate for it to protect the company, and is not bound to make public the reasons for its decision. To reconcile this discretionary power of the company's national State with a right of protection falling to the shareholders' national State would be particularly difficult when the former State has concluded, with the State which has contravened international law with regard to the company, an agreement granting the company compensation which the foreign shareholders find inadequate. If, after such a settlement, the national State of the foreign shareholders could in its turn put forward a claim based on the same facts, this would be likely to introduce into the negotiation of this kind of agreement a lack of security which would be contrary to the stability which it is the object of international law to establish in international relations.

98. It is quite true . . . that international law recognizes parallel rights of protection in the case of a person in the service of an international organization. Nor is the possibility excluded of concurrent claims being made on behalf of persons having dual nationality, although in that case lack of a genuine link with one of the two States may be set up against the exercise by that State of the right of protection. It must be observed, however, that in these two types of situations the number of possible protectors is necessarily very small, and their identity normally not

difficult to determine. In this respect such cases of dual protection are markedly different from the claims to which recognition of a general right of protection of foreign shareholders by their various national States might give rise.

99. It should also be observed that the promoters of a company whose operations will be international must take into account the fact that States have, with regard to their nationals, a discretionary power to grant diplomatic protection or to refuse it. When establishing a company in a foreign country, its promoters are normally impelled by particular considerations; it is often a question of tax or other advantages offered by the host State. It does not seem to be in any way inequitable that the advantages thus obtained should be balanced by the risks arising from the fact that the protection of the company and hence of its shareholders is thus entrusted to a State other than the national State of the shareholders.

100. In the present case, it is clear from what has been said above that Barcelona Traction was never reduced to a position of impotence such that it could not have approached its national State, Canada, to ask for its diplomatic protection, and that, as far as appeared to the Court, there was nothing to prevent Canada from continuing to grant its diplomatic protection to Barcelona Traction if it had considered that it should do so.

101. For the above reasons, the Court is not of the opinion that, in the particular circumstances of the present case, *jus standi* is conferred on the Belgian Government by considerations of equity.

* * *

103. Accordingly,

THE COURT rejects the Belgian Government's claim by fifteen votes to one, twelve votes of the majority being based on the reasons set out in the present Judgment.

Discussion Questions

1. What is the legal issue before the International Court of Justice in the *Barcelona Traction* case?
2. How did the court decide this issue?
3. What was the essential reasoning of the court in deciding the legal question as it did?
4. Does the ICJ decision preclude legal action by the owners in the Spanish courts?
5. If Canada decided to bring the same action in the ICJ, would the decision have been different? Why?

The Limits of Private Arbitration

Arbitration clauses in modern business contracts are a common means of reducing uncertainties in dispute settlement regarding these agreements. Modern treaty practice and court decisions have increased the ability of contracting parties to rely on these agreements to settle their disputes. However, as will be illustrated in the next case, there are limits to the enforcement of arbitration settlements when public law issues arise.

Arbitration contracts are preferred in transnational arrangements because they have the advantage of neutrality over a forum clause that stipulates a particular State's courts. Even in domestic transactions, businesspeople prefer arbitration because it is usually a quicker, cheaper, and more informal process.

Treatment of international arbitration in U.S. courts will be determined largely by the multilateral U.N. Convention on the Recognition and Enforcement of Foreign Arbitral Awards. Some 90 nations, including most leading commercial countries, have ratified this convention, which imposes the obligation (a) to recognize an agreement to arbitrate and refer litigants in its courts to arbitration unless the agreement is found to be void and (b) to recognize awards under such agreements and enforce them by proceedings not substantially more burdensome than those applicable to domestic awards.

In *Mitsubishi Motors Corporation v. Soler Chrysler-Plymouth, Inc.,* the U.S. Su-

preme Court had to decide whether or not to enforce an arbitration agreement when a question of public policy was raised.

■   ■   ■

Mitsubishi Motors Corporation v. Soler Chrysler-Plymouth, Inc.
Supreme Court of the United States, 1985.
473 U.S. 614, 105 S.Ct. 3346. 87 L.Ed.2d 444.

[In 1979, Soler Chrysler-Plymouth Inc. (Soler) entered into a distributorship agreement with Chrysler International S.A. (CISA), a Swiss subsidiary of Chrysler Corporation, to sell Plymouth passenger cars in a region in Puerto Rico. Paragraph 26 of that agreement authorized Chrysler to have Soler's orders filled by any Chrysler affiliate. At the same time CISA, Soler and Mitsubishi Motors Corporation (Mitsubishi), a joint venture of CISA and Mitsubishi Heavy Industries, Inc., entered into a Sales Agreement referring to Paragraph 26. Paragraph VI of the Sales Agreement contained the following arbitration clause:

ARBITRATION OF CERTAIN MATTERS
"All disputes, controversies or differences which may arise between MMC and BUYER out of or in relation to Articles I-B through V of this Agreement or for the breach thereof, shall be finally settled by arbitration in Japan in accordance with the rules and regulations of the Japan Commercial Arbitration Association."

[After a number of years of satisfactory operation under the agreements, business slackened and disputes arose between Soler and Mitsubishi. Mitsubishi filed a request in Tokyo for arbitration under the agreement and brought an action in the U.S. District Court in Puerto Rico to compel arbitration. Soler denied the allegations and asserted causes of action under the Sherman Act, the Automobile Dealers Day in Court Act, and Puerto Rican statutes. The district court ordered arbitration on all issues except some that were not appealed. The Court of Appeals reversed that part of the order that submitted Soler's antitrust claims to arbitration. The Supreme Court granted certiorari and reversed. In an opinion by Justice Blackmun, it found the antitrust claims were intended by the parties to be arbitrable and that that result was not precluded by the statute. The opinion relied heavily on *Scherk v. Alberto-Culver Co.* Excerpted below are critical portions of the opinion rejecting the argument that the antitrust issues were not arbitrable.]

We now turn to consider whether Soler's antitrust claims are nonarbitrable even though it has agreed to arbitrate them. In holding that they are not, the Court of Appeals followed the decision of the Second Circuit in *American Safety Equipment Corp. v. J. P. Maguire & Co.*, 391 F.2d 821 (1968). Notwithstanding the absence of any explicit support for such an exception in either the Sherman Act or the federal Arbitration Act, the Second Circuit there reasoned that "the pervasive public interest in enforcement of the antitrust laws, and the nature of the claims that arise in such cases, combine to make . . . antitrust claims . . . inappropriate for arbitration." Id., at 827-828. We find it unnecessary to assess the legitimacy of the *American Safety* doctrine as applied to agreements to arbitrate arising from domestic transactions. As in *Scherk v. Alberto-Culver Co.*, 417 U.S. 506, 94 S.Ct. 2449, 41 L.Ed.2d 270 (1974), we conclude that concerns of international comity, respect for the capacities of foreign and transnational tribunals, and sensitivity to the need of the international commercial system for predictability in the resolution of disputes require that we enforce the parties' agreement, even assuming that a contrary result would be forthcoming in a domestic context. . . .

At the outset, we confess to same skepticism of certain aspects of the *American Safety* doctrine. As distilled by the First Circuit, 723 F.2d, at 162, the doctrine comprises four ingredients. First, private parties play a pivotal role in aiding governmental enforcement of the antitrust laws by means of the private action for treble damages. Second, "the strong possibility that contracts which generate antitrust disputes may be contracts of adhesion militates against automatic forum determination by contract." Third, antitrust issues, prone to complication, require sophisticated legal and economic analysis, and thus are "ill-adapted to strengths of the arbitral process, i.e., expedition, minimal requirements of written rationale, simplicity, resort to basic concepts of common sense and simple equity." Finally, just as "issues of war and peace are too important to be vested in the generals, decisions as to antitrust regulation of business are too important to be lodged in arbitrators chosen from the business community—particularly those from a foreign community that has had no experience with or exposure to our law and values." See *American Safety*, 391 F.2d, at 826-827.

Initially, we find the second concern unjustified. The mere appearance of an antitrust dispute does not alone warrant invalidation of the selected forum on the undemonstrated assumption that the arbitration clause is tainted. A party resisting arbitration of course may attack directly the validity of the agreement to arbitrate. . . .

Next, potential complexity should not suffice to ward off arbitration. We might well have some doubt that even the courts following *American Safety* subscribe fully to the view that antitrust matters are inherently insusceptible to resolution by arbitration, as these same courts have agreed that an undertaking to arbitrate antitrust claims entered into after the dispute arises is acceptable. . . .

For similar reasons, we also reject the proposition that an arbitration panel will pose too great a danger of innate hostility to the constraints on business conduct that antitrust law imposes. International arbitrators frequently are drawn from the legal as well as the business community; where the dispute has an important legal component, the parties and the arbitral body with whose assistance they have agreed to settle their dispute can be expected to select arbitrators accordingly. We decline to indulge the presumption that the parties and arbitral body conducting a proceeding will be unable or unwilling to retain competent, conscientious, and impartial arbitrators.

We are left, then, with the core of the *American Safety* doctrine—the fundamental importance to American democratic capitalism of the regime of the antitrust laws.

The importance of the private damages remedy, however, does not compel the conclusion that it may not be sought outside an American court. . . . And so long as the prospective litigant effectively may vindicate its statutory cause of action in the arbitral forum, the statute will continue to serve both its remedial and deterrent function.

There is no reason to assume at the outset of the dispute that international arbitration will not provide an adequate mechanism. To be sure, the international arbitral tribunal owes no prior allegiance to the legal norms of particular states; hence, it has no direct obligation to vindicate their statutory dictates. The tribunal, however, is bound to effectuate the intentions of the parties. Where the parties have agreed that the arbitral body is to decide a defined set of claims which includes, as in these cases, those arising from the application of American antitrust law, the tribunal therefore should be bound to decide that dispute in accord with the national law giving rise to the claim. Cf. *Wilko v. Swan*, 346 U.S., at 433-434, 74 S.Ct., at 185-186. And so long as the prospective litigant effectively may vindicate its statutory cause of action in the arbitral forum, the statute will continue to serve both its remedial and deterrent function.

Having permitted the arbitration to go forward, the national courts of the United States will have the opportunity at the award enforcement stage to ensure that the legitimate interest in the enforcement of the antitrust laws has been addressed. The Convention reserves to each signatory country the right to refuse enforcement of an award where the "recognition or enforcement of the award would be contrary to the public policy of that country." Art. V(2)(b), 21 U.S.T., at 2520; see *Scherk*, 417 U.S., at 519, n. 14, 94 S.Ct., at 2457, n. 14. While the efficacy of the arbitral process requires that substantive review at the award enforcement stage remain minimal, it would not require intrusive inquiry to ascertain that the tribunal took cognizance of the antitrust claims and actually decided them.

As international trade has expanded in recent decades, so too has the use of international arbitration to resolve disputes arising in the course of that trade. The controversies that international arbitral institutions are called upon to resolve have increased in diversity as well as in complexity. Yet the potential of these tribunals for efficient disposition of legal disagreements arising from commercial relations has not yet been tested. If they are to take a central place in the international legal order, national courts will need to "shake off the old judicial hostility to arbitration," *Kulukundis Shipping Co. v. Amtorg Trading Corp.*, 126 F.2d 978, 985 (CA2 1942), and also their customary and understandable unwillingness to cede jurisdiction of a claim arising under domestic-law to a foreign or transnational tribunal. To this extent, at least, it will be necessary for national courts to subordinate domestic notions of arbitrability to the international policy favoring commercial arbitration. See *Scherk*, supra. . . .

[A dissenting opinion by Justice Stevens, joined by Justice Brennan and, in large part, by Justice Marshall, found that there was no intention to arbitrate the antitrust claims. It pointed out that the clause applied only to two-party disputes between Soler and Mitsubishi and that this antitrust claim involved Chrysler as well. It also noted that the clause covered only a few articles of the agreement, none of which were directly involved in the antitrust allegations. Portions of the dissent addressing the public policy issue follow.]

The Court assumes for the purposes of its decision that the antitrust issues would not be arbitrable if this were a purely domestic dispute, . . . but holds that the international character of the controversy makes it arbitrable. The holding rests on vague concerns for the international implications of its decision and a misguided application of *Scherk v. Alberto-Culver*, 417 U.S. 506, 94 S.Ct. 2449, 41 L.Ed.2d 270 (1974).

Discussion Questions

1. How was the arbitration clause between Mitsubishi and Soler Chrysler-Plymouth worded?
2. Is there a means of enforcing such a contract when one party refuses to submit to arbitration? What method was used in this case?
3. How does the court decide the question involving the court's authority to force Soler to submit to arbitration?
4. After the arbitration judgment is decided, what opportunity do the U.S. courts have to ensure that public policy questions are adequately considered in their decision to enforce the arbitration judgment?

Home State regulation of its own parent corporations, to ensure that the State's regulatory rules are followed, is an important concern of the courts. U.S. courts will entertain such issues when asked to enforce foreign court judgments or arbitration awards. However, they have even been willing to apply public policy regulations extraterritorially when there is a conspiracy originating in another country and the private action has its effect in this country. (This concept will be discussed later in connection with criminal jurisdiction, in Chapter 10.) Therefore, matters of public policy enforcement provide an important limitation on enforcement of private contractual agreements. The most important forms of national regulation include (a) regulation of competition, (b) regulation of injuries caused by defective products, (c) prohibition of use of bribes and corrupt practices, (d) regulation of securities, (e) regulation of labor and employment, (f) environmental regulations, (g) establishment of accounting standards, and (h) taxation.

▮   ▮   ▮

Chapter Summary

1. International law both promotes trade and commerce and regulates international business practices. The interests of the consumer, the business entity, and the nation as

well as global interests are important considerations in the development of international legal obligations.

2. The International Monetary Fund and the World Bank were created in 1944. The IMF is an important IGO that promotes monetary stability through the decisions of the board of governors to moderate fluctuations in foreign exchange and by promoting international monetary cooperation and balanced growth of international trade.

3. The World Bank is a separate IGO but works closely with the IMF and meets with the monetary fund annually to coordinate activities. The World Bank provides financial assistance to countries by promoting specific development projects and programs.

4. Since World War II, the United States has been the world's most important economic power and remains the nation with the largest share of world merchandise exports. However, balance-of-payment deficits during the 1980s caused the value of the dollar to decline by over 50%.

5. Significant efforts are being made to encourage more firms to become engaged in international trade and to become more competitive with foreign producers. This enhanced economic competition benefits the consumer because more competition means better quality goods and services at lower prices.

6. International economic law includes all international agreements governing economic transactions that cross State boundaries or otherwise have implications for more than one State, such as those involving movement of goods, funds, persons, intangibles, technology, vessels, or aircraft.

7. There is very little customary international law in this area, and in the absence of specific agreements between nations, the individual nation retains the authority to regulate these matters in its own interest. However, the United States has negotiated some 130 bilateral agreements, often referred to as treaties of friendship and commerce or "foundation" treaties, with other countries regulating these commercial relationships. The World Trade Organization now provides the legal and institutional foundation of the multilateral trading system.

8. The individual business firm seeking to do business in international trade must concern itself with problems of risk management. International transactions involve negotiation of contracts that stipulate the means of resolving disputes over private commercial agreements. Trade and commerce are facilitated by a stable climate of legal rules that make it possible to reasonably assess these risks.

9. *Hilton v. Guyot* illustrates the uncertainty of enforcement of foreign court judgments in the national courts of one of the trading partners in the absence of specific treaty obligations. Modern trade agreements between nations have reduced this uncertainty, and today, as a general rule, national courts will enforce foreign court judgments unless they come within certain recognized exceptions.

10. The exceptions to this general rule include a finding that the procedures were incompatible with due process of law or when the tribunal did not have proper and reasonable jurisdiction, when the defendant was not given fair notice of the legal action or an opportunity to defend against it, when the judgment was obtained by fraud, when the judgment is contrary to public policy of the State being asked to honor the foreign court judgment, when the judgment is in conflict with another final judgment that is entitled

to recognition, or when the proceeding in the foreign court was contrary to private contractual agreement between the parties.

11. Today, international business contracts usually provide for arbitration of disputes and designate a neutral forum to avoid costly litigation when there is no agreement as to which nation's courts are to be used.

12. Modern treaty obligations recognize foreign court judgments and provide for the enforcement of arbitration awards. However, these treaties are subject to court interpretation and are not always intended to extend private rights. The *Sumitomo* case illustrates national court interpretation of treaty provisions and the extent to which the courts will refer to official government agencies in determining the intent of treaty provisions.

13. A company incorporated in the United States is subject to our laws the same as any U.S. corporation, even though it may be owned by citizens of another country. A branch office of a foreign parent corporation may, however, be exempt from certain public policy rules because it is a foreign corporation.

14. The U.N. Convention on the International Sale of Goods (CISG) is a major treaty law development that harmonized international standards for sales contracts involved in international trade. It has been ratified by the United States and went into force in 1988. This treaty governs contract obligations where there is no specific stipulation in the contract itself concerning dispute settlement.

15. The CISG is a major step toward more uniform practices in both common law and civil law countries in providing more clearly understood legal obligations among private international trading parties throughout the world.

16. U.S. firms wishing to engage in international trade are aided in risk management by the services of foreign distributors, freight and customs agents, international banking institutions, and the U.S. government's International Trade Administration. These agencies provide services that distribute the risk and facilitate foreign trade.

17. The multinational enterprise (MNE) is a modern development of businesses with global power and influence that has aroused concern and prompted new regulatory attempts by governments. The top ten MNEs have annual revenues larger than the yearly gross national product (GNP) of two-thirds of the countries of the world. Critics assert that they are uncontrolled and arrogant.

18. Most States have instituted extensive regulatory rules in an attempt to prevent many of the adverse effects of MNEs to offset their great potential economic power. U.N. agencies have drafted codes of conduct for MNEs and have assisted developing nations with greater access to more adequate information in dealing with these economic giants.

19. The international community is now considering new proposals that will likely result in more regulation of MNEs in the future. The United States has encouraged the use of the World Bank's arbitration institutions in dispute settlement involving investment contracts with foreign governments and enacted the Foreign Corrupt Practices Act in 1977, making it illegal to bribe foreign officials in their business dealings abroad.

20. The complexity of forms of corporate business structure has resulted in some difficulty in defining the nationality of particular business entities. In addition to the traditional sole proprietorship, partnership, and corporate forms, multinationals now include

international corporations that may have several parent corporations that are nationals of several different States.

21. In the *Barcelona Traction* case, the ICJ decided that the nationality of a corporation is determined by its place of incorporation and that a State cannot bring legal action in an international tribunal on behalf of the shareholders from a State other than that of the place of incorporation.

22. The limits of private arbitration settlements are illustrated by the court's opinion in the *Mitsubishi Case*, which agreed to enforce a private contract to arbitrate a dispute with the understanding that ultimate enforcement of that judgment would enable the U.S. courts to determine if it violates any public policy rules of this country. Enforcement of the Sherman Antitrust Act provisions is a matter reserved for the U.S. courts and cannot be entrusted to foreign courts or arbitration settlements.

23. Public policy regulation is an area of exercise of national sovereignty that is an exception to the general rule that courts will enforce foreign judgments. These areas of regulation include antitrust issues, defective products, bribes and corrupt practices, securities, labor and employment, environmental pollution, accounting standards, and taxation.

Key Terms

International Monetary Fund (IMF)
World Bank
dumping
subsidy
contracts
arbitration
de facto
de novo
Convention on the International Sale of Goods (CISG)
Uniform Commercial Code
foreign distributor
freight forwarder
customs broker

international banker
International Trade Administration
multinational enterprise (MNE)
U.N. Commission on Transnational Corporations
technology transfer
Organization for Economic Cooperation and Development (OECD)
International Institute for the Unification of Private Law (UNIDROIT)
Foreign Corrupt Practices Act
national multinational corporation
international multinational corporation

Discussion Questions

1. How does the International Monetary Fund attempt to stabilize major foreign exchange rates?

2. Why do reasonably stable monetary standards facilitate the expansion and balanced growth of international trade?

3. What basic functions are served by the World Bank? How does the World Bank cooperate with the IMF?

4. What are the major concerns of the United States in relationship to the current balance-of-payments deficit? What have been the major responses of the government to attempt to deal with this problem?

5. What are some of the characteristic features of modern bilateral treaties of friendship and commerce, or "foundation treaties?"

6. How does *Hilton v. Guyot* illustrate the difficulty of national courts in the enforcement of foreign court judgments in the absence of treaty obligations?

7. Why do modern international business contracts often stipulate arbitration as the means of settlement of private contract disputes?

8. What are the major exceptions to the general rule that national courts will enforce foreign judgments?

9. How does the *Sumitomo* case illustrate specific interpretation of treaty obligations? How important is the intent of the State parties to the treaty?

10. Why is the U.N. Convention on the International Sale of Goods an important advancement of internationally agreed-on standards in international trade?

11. What kinds of professional agencies are available to business firms to assist them in risk management in the field of international trade? What services do they provide?

12. What are the problems associated with multinational enterprises that have aroused concern and prompted new regulatory attempts by national governments?

13. Why would it be difficult to regulate an international multinational corporation? How does the ICJ determine the nationality of corporations? Why?

14. Are foreign courts and international arbitration boards capable of deciding issues of public policy for another State? Why not?

15. What are the major areas of public policy regulation that national courts regard as exercises of State sovereignty?

Suggested Readings

Appendix E: Convention of Establishment Between the United States and France

Appendix F: International Covenant on Economic, Social and Cultural Rights

Appendix G: Convention on the Settlement of Investment Disputes Between States and Nationals of Other States

August, R. (1993). *International business law*. Englewood Cliffs, NJ: Prentice Hall.

Folsom, R. H., Gordon, M. W., & Spanogle, J. A. (1992). *International business transactions* (4th ed.). St. Paul, MN: West.

Hoellering, M. F. (1994). Managing international commercial arbitration: The institution's role. In J. C. Green (Ed.), *Doing business worldwide: Executing the international transaction*. Chicago: American Bar Association and American Society of International Law.

Schaffer, R., Earle, B., & Agusti, F. (1993). *International business law and its environment* (2nd ed.). St. Paul, MN: West.

Internet Sources

Browse: Use *international trade law* to access a variety of sources relevant to this chapter.

World Trade Organization (http://www.unicc.org/wto/)

U.S. Department of Commerce (http://www.doc.gov/)

6 Intellectual Property and Consumer Protection

One of the most dynamic areas of international law development is the area of intellectual property disputes. This area includes both artistic property rights and industrial property rights. Copyrights, patents, and trademarks are the principal areas of concern. However, industrial "know-how," or technology, is also of major interest. Particularly in developing countries, technology transfers are of major importance in the development of joint venture agreements. Licensing regulations of modern nation-states are complex considerations involving the balancing of intellectual property rights and the interests of the developing State in promoting economic and social development. Consumer protection regulation to protect the safety of the consumer in the area of products liability is a traditional area of private law with many international ramifications. These subjects will be discussed in this chapter, and illustrations of the more significant aspects of how these developments affect the individual will be presented.

Forms of Intellectual Property Rights

Copyrights and neighboring rights are given at least minimal protection in most countries. They protect private parties who are authors of any work that can be fixed in a tangible medium for the purpose of communication, such as literary, dramatic, musical, or artistic works; sound recordings; films; radio and television broadcasts; and (at least in some countries) computer programs. Unlike a patent, a copyright does not give its owner the right to prevent others from using the idea or the knowledge contained in the copyrighted work. Copyrights place legal restrictions on the reproduction or alteration of the author's work without license from the author.

> **Copyrights:** *Protect authors of works that can be fixed in a tangible medium for purpose of communication. They place legal restrictions on the reproduction or alteration of the author's work without license from the author.*

A **patent** is a statutory privilege granted by the government to inventors, and to others deriving their rights from the inventor, for a fixed period of years, to exclude other persons from manufacturing, using, or selling a patented product or from using a patented method or process.

> **Patent:** Statutory privilege granted by a nation to inventors for a fixed period of years, to exclude others from manufacturing, using, or selling a patented product without license from the inventor.

Thus, there is a higher degree of direct governmental involvement in patent rights than in the more private nature of copyrights. Traditionally, both of these basic areas of intellectual property rights are areas of municipal law that have become the subject of major concern to the international community. International treaty law to harmonize the definition and protection of these rights and to make it easier for owners to acquire rights in different countries is rapidly developing. These treaty obligations tend to divide the subject matter of intellectual property rights into artistic property and industrial property.

Artistic Property Rights

Individual European nations began the practice of recognizing copyrights on a widespread basis only in the eighteenth century, and the Belgian Copyright Law of 1886 became the first of several continental comprehensive acts granting both pecuniary and moral rights to authors with minimal formality required to secure their protection. The common law countries have followed a different path of case law development that later become manifest in statutory form. Efforts to secure international recognition of these rights led to the **Berne Convention** of 1886. This major multilateral convention has evolved to become one of the two most widely adopted sets of legal standards for copyright recognition. The overwhelming majority of the modern nations of the world have achieved a substantial degree of uniformity since 1989 when the United States ratified the Berne Convention.

> **Berne Convention (1886):** A major copyright convention recognizing moral rights included in the continental European concept of copyright law.

The issue of moral rights included in the continental European concept of copyright law has been a major area of disagreement with the common law countries. The personal rights of authors to prohibit others from tampering with their works are called "moral rights." They are independent of pecuniary rights, which entitle the author to exploit a work for economic gain. In the continental European countries, which have long recognized moral rights, they continue to exist even after the pecuniary rights have been transferred. In France, for example, they are considered inalienable.

The concept of **moral rights** emerged from the nineteenth-century German legal philosophy that involved a debate between the Naturalists, who advocated theories of personal rights (*Persoenlichkeitsrecht*), and the Positivists, who ultimately conceded that

> **Moral rights:** In copyright law, they entitle authors to prohibit others from tampering with their works by distortion, mutilation, modification, or refusing to recognize the author.

such rights ought to exist even if they did not exist in nature. The 1886 Belgian Copyright Law recognized three basic moral rights: (a) the right to object to distortion, mutilation, or modification of one's work; (b) the right to be recognized as the author; and (c) the right to control public access to the work. In 1928, the Berne Convention was amended to specifically recognize these three moral rights and bind the parties to recognize national copyright laws as defined in the convention.

Moral rights are not recognized as such in the copyright laws of the United Kingdom, the United States, and countries that have a common law heritage. Most recently, the United Kingdom became a party to the Berne Convention and supports its new obligation to protect the moral rights of authors by claiming that an author can bring an action for libel to complain of distortion, mutilation, or modification of a work, and an action for passing off (fraud) to protect the creator's rights. U.S. courts and legal writers have often denied the existence of moral rights, but with the U.S. ratification of the Berne Convention in 1989, such explanations are no longer viable.

Industrial Rights

Patents, trademarks, and know-how are distinct forms of industrial intellectual property rights that must first be defined in order to discuss aspects of their international regulation. Patents are governmental grants of legal monopoly to the inventor for a given period of time to promote the development of such innovations. The owner of a patent may be prevented from exploiting the grant by other laws, such as those protecting national security or unfair competition, or by contractual agreement, but the heart of the patent concept is the right of the owner to invoke the State's powers to prevent others from using his or her discovery without the owner's consent. A patent is therefore valid only within the territory of the State granting it. A State cannot prevent the use of patented technology outside its territory. States will, however, stop the importation of goods from third countries that infringe a patent. For these reasons, protection of patents abroad has been seen in the development of treaty obligations that allow inventors to register their patents in other countries.

Trademarks are recognized property rights to use identifying marks that characterize a particular product or service. From the perspective of the owner, a trademark is the right to put a product protected by the mark into circulation for the first time. From the viewpoint of the consumer, a trademark serves to designate the origin or source of a product or service, indicate a particular standard of quality, represent the goodwill of the manufacturer, and protect the consumer from confusion. Such marks include "true trademarks" (appearing on goods), trade names (business names), service marks (used by providers of services), "collective marks" (marks used by a group or organization), and certification marks (marks that certify a certain quality, origin, or other fact) that offer various forms of protection against fraud and deception. Trademarks are acquired both by use and by registration. In most countries, a mark can be registered even if it has never been used in commerce.

> **Trademarks:** *Rights to use identifying marks that characterize a particular product or service.*

Know-how, or technology, is practical expertise acquired from study, training, and experience. Unlike other forms of intellectual property, it is not protected by specific statutory enactments. The legal protection given to technology comes about in connection with its use by an assignee, licensee, or employee. The owner of such know-how may prevent these persons from disclosing secrets to third parties and may require these same people to pay for the training or

> **Know-how:** *Technology or practical expertise acquired from study, training, and experience. Legal protection may be derived from contractual agreements that may be enforceable in court.*

assistance or use of the know-how they acquire from the owner. Thus, these rights are determined by private contractual relationships and enforceable to the extent that national courts will enforce the contract alleged.

World Intellectual Property Organizations

Efforts toward defining international intellectual property rights are increasingly focused around the **World Intellectual Property Organization (WIPO)**. WIPO was created in 1967 with the adoption of the Stockholm Convention and is the successor to the International Bureau of Paris and the International Bureau of Berne, which had previously administered the Paris Convention for the Protection of Industrial Property (the Paris Union) and the Berne Convention for the Protection of Literary and Artistic Works (the Berne Union). These two bureaus were functionally joined together as the United International Bureaus for the Protection of Intellectual Property (BIRPI) and administered by WIPO.

World Intellectual Property Organization (WIPO): A U.N. agency that coordinates and administers most of the efforts of international treaties concerning protection of intellectual property rights.

WIPO has much broader authority than its predecessors and not only administers the functions of the Paris and Berne conventions but is the administrator for several new conventions established since its existence. This organization's governing body is called the General Assembly, and it is made up of representatives of signatories of the Stockholm Convention who are members of at least one of the unions. It is a specialized agency of the United Nation's Organization, and its members include the overwhelming majority of the nations of the world.

Activities of WIPO include sponsoring and hosting conferences for the development of new intellectual property rights agreements. The Patent Cooperative Treaty of 1970 was a result of a WIPO initiative. This agency also conducts studies, through the appointment of expert committees, that promote new legal and technological developments, and it regularly reports the results both through monthly journals and occasional reports.

In 1994, WIPO announced the development of a major center for arbitration of intellectual property rights that promises to provide a more efficient means of settling disputes in this area. Contractual agreement to resolve disputes through the services of this center are now available to private parties interested in managing the risks of intellectual property rights in international trade and commerce. WIPO, based in Geneva, will offer a consultation facility to interested parties. It will also help parties draft an agreement to refer cases to one of the alternative dispute resolution procedures administered by the center. Draft rules for the center's alternative dispute resolution (ADR) procedures are being reviewed by experts in the field. A WIPO committee is also drafting a treaty for intergovernmental intellectual property disputes (Hoellering, 1994).

A major task undertaken by WIPO is to facilitate the transfer of technology to and among developing countries. Two permanent committees devoted to the two major areas of intellectual property rights—industrial property rights and copyrights—are responsible for helping countries modernize their national intellectual property laws, develop administrative agencies for supervision of those laws, and increase the creation and protection of new intellectual property by their own nationals. Although these activities are extensive, many other efforts of individual States and international organizations are also concerned with developments in this area. The principle intergovernmental Organizations (IGOs) include the U.N. Educational, Scientific and Cultural Organization (UNESCO) and the U.N. Conference on Trade and Development (UNCTAD).

UNESCO administers the **Universal Copyright Convention (UCC)**, one of the few major multilateral intellectual property treaties that is not administered by WIPO. The UCC was created in 1952 to extend inclusivity for the major areas of copyright protection to States—most notably the United States—who were unwilling to join the Berne Union because of requirements that contradicted their national laws. The UCC has become the most widely recognized basis for international copyright protection. It was revised in 1971 and offers the most liberal form of identifying a work as protected by the simple use of a symbol (©) in the publication. It therefore continues to function as a means of promoting cooperation among nations in the area of copyright.

The World Trade Organization has become another important IGO that administers and resolves disputes between nations in the area of intellectual property rights. Extensive negotiations were conducted within the GATT under the Uruguay Round on trade-related intellectual property rights (TRIPS). The major thrust of the new agreement from the U.S. perspective was to secure greater protection for intellectual property rights. However, the developed nations were unsuccessful in securing an anticounterfeiting code when met with resistance from the developing nations.

> **Universal Copyright Convention (UCC):** *The most widely recognized basis for international copyright protection. It is administered by UNESCO and offers the most liberal form of identifying a protected work by using the copyright symbol ©.*

UNCTAD was created by the U.N. General Assembly, which defined its mission as "to promote international trade . . . particularly between countries at differing stages of development, between developing countries and between countries with differing systems of economic and social organization." UNCTAD's major effort at constructing a **Code of Conduct on the Transfer of Technology** has gone through four drafting efforts and is frustrated by the intransigence of seemingly irreconcilable positions. Developing countries have been advocates of an expansive code that would apply both to the parent companies transferring technology and their foreign subsidiaries, a view generally opposed by the developed world.

> **Code of Conduct on the Transfer of Technology:** *A major effort by UNCTAD to develop an agreement that would apply to both the parent companies and their foreign subsidiaries in technology transfers.*

Technology Transfers

Issues surrounding the transfer of knowledge across national borders have become the most important feature of the North-South dialogue and controversy between these major divisions of the international community. The more industrially developed States of the world seek to protect their assumed proprietary rights to their advanced technology, and the less developed States argue that such rights inhibit development of their own economies and are remnants of colonial dependency.

At the core of this controversy is the desire of Third World countries, and often even more advanced developing countries such as Brazil, South Korea, Taiwan, and Singapore, to obtain protected information quickly and affordably irrespective of the proprietary rights and profit motives of current holders who are mainly persons from the most developed countries. The developing nations, represented by the **Group of 77,** insist that a Code of conduct in the area of transfer technology must be an "internationally legally binding Code," and the industrialized nations' position is that it consist of "guidelines for the international transfer of technology."

> **Group of 77:** A group of seventy-seven original developing nations that have formed a relatively stable coalition to promote their concept of the "new economic order."

Theft of intellectual property and use of counterfeit, or "gray market" (produced without authorization), goods are rapidly increasing in developing and developed countries. Some developing countries see illegal technology transfers as part of their economic development strategy and encourage piracy or choose not to oppose it.

In general, legal protection against intellectual property theft and counterfeit goods is not very effective. It usually depends on private contractual agreements, private detection, and civil legal action by the injured party. Unless there is an international treaty agreement, the individual nation-state is free to regulate intellectual property as it sees fit. There is no universal international law requiring respect for other countries' policies in the area of intellectual property rights. Third World countries have attempted to regulate patent and know-how licensing agreements directly through national legislation, such as the Brazilian Normative Act No. 17 (1976) and the Mexican Technology Transfer Law (1982) (repealed in 1991). The United States has sought to protect its interests through less direct methods that predominantly concern patent and antitrust law.

U.S. public opposition and congressional concern about intellectual property piracy have been fueled by reports of widespread unfair competition produced by such practices. Unlicensed low-cost reproduction of entire copyrighted books are reported to be rampant in diverse areas such as Nigeria, Saudi Arabia, and South Korea. Apple computers have been inexpensively counterfeited in Hong Kong. General Motors estimates that about 40% of its auto parts are counterfeited in the Middle East. Recordings and tapes are duplicated almost everywhere without license or fee.

Extraterritorial Effects of Intellectual Property Rights

Concerns about unfair competition involving intellectual property rights involve substantial amounts of money that could assist in achieving a more favorable balance of payments for the United States. In the early 1990s, it could be estimated that despite the massive and uncontrolled piracy of U.S. technology, our nationals received nearly ten times as much from other countries in royalty payments than other countries received from U.S. nationals. This indicates that the major advantage of this country is its intellectual innovation and development of technology. Intellectual freedom in the United States has produced creative and innovative works that are in high demand around the world. U.S. technology is not only exploited abroad without compensating creative talent, but the United States is also the target for sale of much of the piracy of counterfeit and gray market goods.

Trademark and copyright holders may register with the Customs Service and seek to blockade pirated items made abroad. This is authorized in the Lanham Trademark Act of 1946 and the Copyright Act of 1976. Patent piracy is most often challenged in proceedings against unfair import practices under Section 337 of the Tariff Act of 1930 as revised by the Omnibus Trade and Competitiveness Act of 1988. Determination of violations and the recommendation of remedies to the President under Section 337 are the exclusive province of the **International Trade Commission (ITC).** Section 337 proceedings result in general exclusion orders permitting seizure of patent counterfeits at any U.S. point of entry. However, for most seizure remedies to work, the holder must notify the customs service of an incoming shipment of offending goods.

> **International Trade Commission (ITC):** *A federal regulatory commission of the U.S. government responsible for determining violations of international trade and competitive regulations and recommending to the president appropriate actions.*

Infringement and triple damages actions (i.e., recovery for three times the damages that can be documented) may be initiated in U.S. courts against importers and distributors of counterfeit goods. However, service of process and jurisdictional barriers often preclude effective relief against foreign pirates. International solutions have been equally difficult in enforcement. Various U.S. statutes authorize the president to withhold trade benefits from or apply trade sanctions to nations inadequately protecting the intellectual property rights of U.S. citizens. These sanctions are slowly beginning to take effect, and changes in foreign State behavior are indicated by new copyright laws in many of the most abusive States. In 1986 alone, Singapore adopted a new copyright law; new patent and copyright laws were instituted in Korea; and in Taiwan, new copyright, patent, fair trade, and amended trademark laws were put into effect. Brazil has also introduced legislation intended to allow copyrights on computer programs. In 1995, the detection of major illegal producers of computer software in China by the United States resulted in the successful negotiation of a favorable agreement under threat to impose major import restrictions against China.

Patent Protection

Since patents are a matter of national law, the inventor seeking to protect a patent must apply for patents in each country where protection is sought. In the United States, patent practice is a specialized branch of the legal profession, and the complexity of the subject usually requires the services of a patent agent. Obtaining international patent protection, therefore, usually involves retaining the services of specialists in each country.

More than one hundred countries have patent laws; however, they are widely varied in their degree of protection. Many Third World nations refuse to grant patents on pharmaceuticals, and the methods of obtaining patents and their length of protection varies substantially. In some developing countries, effective forms of relief are lacking even though there is nominal patent protection. These factors cause holders to take a chance and limit their applications to those markets where they foresee demand or competition for their product. Nonetheless, U.S. nationals continue to receive tens of thousands of patents in other countries. Today, the reverse is also true, and over 50% of the patents issued under the U.S. law are issued to residents of foreign countries.

To receive the benefits of a patent, the invention must meet the legislatively defined criteria of novelty, inventiveness, industrial utility, or some combination thereof. **Novelty** means that no other inventor can have obtained a patent for the same invention; **inventiveness** is the idea that the "subject matter" of an invention cannot "have been obvious at the time the invention was made to a person having ordinary

> **Novelty:** *Patent criterion meaning that no other inventor can have obtained a patent for the same invention.*
>
> **Inventiveness:** *Patent criterion that the subject matter of an invention cannot have been obvious at the time of the invention.*

skill in the art to which said subject matter pertains" (U.S. Copyright Act of 1976, as amended § 103). **Industrial utility** means that the product or process is one that can be used in industry and commerce. Most patent laws also specify particular categories of inventions that are not patentable, such as inventions contrary to law or public morals and those injurious to health and safety.

> **Industrial utility:** Patent criterion requiring that the product or process is one that can be used in industry and commerce.

A device used in socialist countries (i.e., China, Cuba, North Korea, and Vietnam) for rewarding inventors is the **inventor's certificate**. This certificate certifies to the authorship of an invention and establishes the exclusive right of the State, and the State's agencies, to use the invention without special authorization. The inventor is given an award in the form of a royalty or limited compensation. These countries also grant patents but exclude certain areas, such as pharmaceuticals. Inventors may apply for

> **Inventor's certificate:** Used in socialist countries to provide an award in the form of royalties in areas where patents are not granted.

either a patent, an inventor's certificate, or both for most inventions, but certificates are awarded only for certain inventions, such as new medicines, medical treatments, foodstuffs, animal species, plant varieties, and basic scientific discoveries.

In Germany, Japan, and Spain, a scheme for protecting lesser inventions is generally referred to as a **petty patent** or an inventor's right in a utility model *(Gebrauchsmuster)*. These petty patents were established in Germany and Japan around the turn of the century (1891 for Germany and 1905 in Japan). The German *Gebrauchsmuster* will be granted for a period of three years following a determination by the German Patent Office that the invention is novel. In Japan, a petty patent is good for fifteen years and will be issued only after the Patent Office determines both novelty and inventiveness.

> **Petty patent:** A scheme for protecting lesser inventions as used in Germany or Japan. They are considered patents in U.S. law.

Issues of what constitutes a "patent" under U.S. patent law are discussed in the following illustrative case.

■   ■   ■

American Infra-Red Radiant Co., Inc. v. Lambert Industries, Inc.
United States Court of Appeals. Eighth Circuit, 1966.
360 F.2d 977.

GIBSON, CIRCUIT JUDGE

* * *

The patents in question were issued to plaintiff American Infra-Red Radiant Co., Inc., as assignor of the inventor, Gunther Schwank, with plaintiff Hupp Corporation serving as a nonexclusive licensee of American Infra-Red, with right to sue for patent infringement. Defendants are engaged in making and marketing devices similar to those covered in the patents and are charged by plaintiffs with infringement of both patents.

The subject matter of this litigation is an infrared gas burner. US Patent No. 2,775,294 ('294) is for the burner tile or plate, and US Patent No, 2,870,830 ('830) is for the burner housing exclusive of the burner plate. The two units when placed together constitute the operational infrared gas burner device. . . .

Having . . . disposed of patent '294 (burner plate) [by determining that it lacked "novelty" and "invention" and was therefore unpatentable], we now must determine the validity of the '830 (housing unit) patent. Defendants assert a statutory bar against the '830 patent based on title 35 § 102(d) of the *United States Code*. Apparently the inventor Gunther Schwank had the device, structure, or design of the burner housing which is the basis of the '830 patent also patented in Germany under a *Gebrauchsmuster* which is a lesser type of patent issued for petty or useful models and designs. Defendants contend that if *Gebrauchsmuster* No. 1, 660,844 issued to Schwank is a patent, United States Patent '830 is invalid under provisions of title 35, § 102(d) of the *United States Code*, which holds in its pertinent part:

> *Sec. 102* A person shall be entitled to a patent unless—(d) the invention was first patented . . . in a foreign country prior to the date of the application for patent in this country on an application filed more than twelve months before the filing of the application in the United States.

This contention is correct. It is admitted that the *Gebrauchsmuster* application was made in Germany on May 27. 1953, which is more than twelve months prior to the application in the United States on October 28, 1954. The registration was effective or granted on July 9, 1953, with the name of the inventor, title, and registration number being published in the *Patentblatt* (Official Journal) on August 6, 1953. Obviously then the *Gebrauchsmuster* was granted prior to the United States application in October 1954. Although plaintiffs make some contention that defendants have not shown that the exact type of structure as is represented in the '830 patent is the basis of the *Gebrauchsmuster*, we feel that the record clearly discloses that the structures are the same. In fact Schwank in his '830 application stated:

> That no application for patent on this invention or discovery has been filed by me . . . in any foreign country . . . except as follows: Germany May 22, 1953.

The crucial premise therefore, is whether a *Gebrauchsmuster* is a patent within the meaning of aforesaid § 102(d). If it is, § 102(d) is a statutory bar to its validity. . . .

Unlike the law in this country in which we generally only have one class of patent covering all types of patentable structures, processes, or compositions of matter, Germany has two distinct classes of invention protection. It appears that in Germany the standard as regards patentable inventions for regular patents is very high, making it difficult to secure such a patent for minor or simpler inventions. To meet this situation the *Gebrauchsmuster* law was adopted as supplementary legislation to give a measure of, though limited, protection to useful or petty models which do not possess a sufficiently high standard of invention to meet the requirements of the regular patent laws. *Gebrauchsmusters*, however, cover only structures, not processes, formulas, or compositions of materials; and there is no examination by the patent office for novelty, thus leaving the question of novelty to first arise when suit is brought.

In addition to being an important and integral part of the patent law of Germany it is apparent that the *Gebrauchsmuster* has the elements of the more conventional patent. The rights granted an inventor under the *Gebrauchsmuster* law give a monopoly for a term of three years, renewable for an equivalent period, thus giving a total of six years of protection. The *Gebrauchsmuster* gives the inventor the exclusive right of use of the article and to recover damages for infringement, with the claims made and accepted measuring the scope of the protection afforded. There is even a limited publication of the *Gebrauchsmuster*. If the application is granted, the title, inventor, date and file number are published in the official *Patentblatt*. Though specifications and drawings are not disclosed in any official publication, the application which contains the specifications, drawings and claims is registered and the entire file is open to public examination in the patent office.

There are no judicial cases indicating how a *Gebrauchsmuster* should be treated under the provisions of § 102(d) and only scant authority as to how *Gebrauchsmusters* are to be treated under other provisions of our patent law. What authority there is, however, seems to indicate that the *Gebrauchsmuster* should be treated as a foreign patent. Judge Lindley in *Permutit Co. v. Graver Corporation*, 37 F.2d 385 at p. 390, 1930, observed:

Evidently a *Gebrauchsmuster* is a patent within the meaning of the federal statute, as Judge Haight said in the case of *Safety Gas Lighter Co. v. Fischer Bros. & Corwin*, 236 F. 955 at p. 962: "The rights conferred on an inventor by a German *Gebrauchsmuster*, except as to time, seem to be quite as extensive as those guaranteed by a patent in this country. Its grant is the act of the government. Although only the title is published, in the sense that it is printed in an official publication, the specifications and drawings of the patent are open and accessible to the public, as are also the claims, which measure the scope of the protection afforded to the inventor, as soon as the title, date of application, and registration are published in the *Patentblatt*. As it is not essential that a foreign patent, to have the effect mentioned in section 4886 of the Revised Statutes, should be printed, but that the act of the officials in granting it and accessibility of its disclosures to the public are the decisive factors, I am at a loss to understand how the fact that only a title is printed, or how the scope of the invention which it protects, or that the examination made in the Patent Office before it is granted is limited, can have any effect on it under our laws."

This case was affirmed by the Seventh Circuit, 43 F.2d 898, and . . . the Supreme Court, 284 U.S. 52. Speaking for the [Supreme] Court, Mr. Justice Brandeis held the patent invalid without discussing the force and effect of a German *Gebrauchsmuster*. . . .

Of considerable interest to us is the position of the United States Patent Office in regard to *Gebrauchsmusters*. It appears that for many years the Patent Office has treated the *Gebrauchsmuster* as a patent. This policy is illustrated by a discussion in the *Official Gazette* under date of November 2, 1965. In discussing the status of the *Gebrauchsmuster* the *Gazette* reads:

1. Right of priority.—An application for a *Gebrauchsmuster* is considered to be an application for a patent in a foreign country, and consequently the right of priority of title 35, § 119 of the *United States Code* can be based upon such an application. This was decided by the Board of Examiners in Chief (now Board of Appeals) in 1908 . . . and has been the consistent practice ever since.

2. Prior patents.—The Examiners may use the *Gebrauchsmuster*, however, as a prior patent effective as of the date of registration, in the same manner as they would use the patents of countries which do issue specifications in printed form; . . .

From the entire publication we believe that it has been the past and the present practice of the Patent Office to treat the *Gebrauchsmuster* as a patent. . . .

Section 119 of title 35 establishes a right of priority for foreign filed patents. Its pertinent part states:

An application for a patent for an invention filed in this country by any person who has . . . previously regularly filed an application for a patent for the same invention in a foreign country . . . shall have the same effect as the same application would have if filed in this country on the date on which the application for patent for the same invention was first filed in such foreign country, if the application in this country is filed within twelve months from the earliest date on which such foreign application was filed; but no patent shall be granted on any application for patent for an invention which had been patented . . . more than one year before the date of the actual filing of the application in this country. . . .

As we have seen it has long been the policy of the Government, both through international convention and internal policy to treat the *Gebrauchsmuster* as a patent entitled to the priority granted under § 119. Since the *Gebrauchsmuster* is considered a patent for the purpose of § 119 in obtaining the benefit of an earlier filing date to establish its priority, the same construction should be placed on the words "patent" as used in § 102(d). It is receiving the advantage of being a patent under § 119; therefore it should be subject to the disadvantages imposed under that same section and under § 102(d).

The word "patent" has many general connotations and nuances but must be considered in the context in which it is used by Congress in implementing the constitutional grant of authority conferred by Article I, section Eight, para. 8 of the Constitution: "To promote the Progress of Science and useful Arts, be securing for limited Times to Authors and Inventors the exclusive Right to their respective Writings and Discoveries." . . . As used by Congress in the different sections dealing with the establishment of a patent system we must apply the particular connotation, which is to a certain extent a work of art, that would make effective the Congressional intent. Webster's *New World Dictionary* defines "patent" as (among other definitions) "n.1. A document open to public examination and granting a certain right or privilege; letters patent; especially, a document granting the monopoly right to produce, use, sell, or get profit from an invention, process, etc. for a certain number of years." Black's Law Dictionary generally defines a patent as "A grant of some privilege, property, or authority, made by the government or sovereign of a country to one or more individuals." The German *Gebrauchsmuster* falls within these accepted definitions of a patent.

We note that Congress made no differentiation in the type of foreign patent that would be affected by the statutes. Therefore, we may assume that Congress intended to include in the term "patents" all foreign patents that fall within the well known classical definitions. Obviously the length of the period of protection is not decisive on this issue. Each country has the right to its own view and policy on this point. In fact our policy as expressed by Congress has changed, once granting only fourteen years of protection, now granting seventeen years; and is susceptible to further variation as a matter of legislative policy. Our Constitution commands no precise length of time, only "limited times." Therefore, as a matter of policy or Congressional intent it would not seem that the brevity of the *Gebrauchsmuster* would alter its essential nature.

For the above reasons we have concluded that a *Gebrauchsmuster* is a foreign patent within the purposes of § 119 and § 102(d). It is an important part of the German patent system. It has all of the attributes normally attributed to a patent which include an application setting forth claims, protection granted by the Government for a limited time, a right of action in the inventor to protect the invention against infringement, notice to the public in an official publication, and availability to the public of the specifications and claims. Furthermore. the *Gebrauchsmuster* falls within the general definition of "patent" in that it does command a sovereign grant of right of exclusive use for limited periods. Finally, the United States Patent Office has long treated it as a patent, granting it full rights of priority, with there being no statutory or Constitutional policy which would deny a lesser form of patent the force of a regular patent. We are, therefore, of the opinion that the *Gebrauchsmuster* No. 1,660,844 obtained by Schwank prior to the United States application on an application filed more than twelve months before the United States filing is a patent within the meaning of the patent law and as such is a statutory bar to the validity of patent '830 under title 35, § 102(d) of the *United States Code*.

Discussion Questions

1. How does U.S. law recognize the international validity of patents?
2. How does this case illustrate the protection of private rights of foreigners in U.S. courts?
3. What difficulties are evident from this discussion that make the determination of patent rights problematical?

The two basic types of patent systems in the world community are by registration and by examination. The **registration** method is exemplified by France where "registration," accompanied by appropriate documents and fees, without making an inquiry about the patentability of the invention, is characteristic. Under this system, the validity of the patent grant is most difficult to gauge until a time comes to defend it against alleged infringement in an appropriate tribunal. In other countries, such as the United States and Germany, the patent grant is made following a careful **examination** of the prior art and statutory criteria on patentability or a "deferred examination" is made following public notice given to permit an "opposi-

> **Registration:**
> *Method of patent recording used in several countries, such as France. Does not involve careful examination of patentability and leaves this for litigation.*

> **Examination:**
> *Method of patent process that involves extensive and careful examination of the patentability and provides a nonbinding approval. Used in the U.S. and Germany.*

tion." The latter system provides more predictability to the process. However, both systems depend heavily on the ultimate court challenge to determine infringement.

The principal treaties regarding patents are the 1970 Patent Cooperation Treaty and the 1883 Convention of the Union of Paris, which have been frequently revised and amended. The Paris Convention has been ratified by over eighty-five countries, including the United States, and remains the basic international agreement dealing with treatment of foreigners under national patent laws. The major provisions of this treaty obligation include the following:

1. The "right of national treatment" (Article 2) prohibits discrimination against foreign holders of local patents and trademarks.
2. Important "rights of priority" are granted to patent holders, provided they file within twelve months of their home country patent applications.
3. The convention obviates the need to file simultaneously in every country where intellectual property protection is sought.

The **Patent Cooperation Treaty (PCT)** has been ratified by about forty countries, including the United States, and is designed to achieve greater uniformity and less cost in the international patent filing process and in the examination of prior art. By filing in selected countries (Japan, Sweden, Russia, and the United States or at the European Patent Office at Munich or The Hague), the international patent application is communicated to each national patent office where protection is sought. This process facilitates searches and preliminary examinations to formulate a nonbinding opinion on whether the claimed invention is novel, inventive, and industrially applicable. Nothing in the treaty, however, limits the freedom of each nation to establish substantive conditions of patentability and determine infringement remedies. This process was therefore greatly facilitated when the U.S. ratified the PCT provisions on preliminary examination reports.

> **Patent Cooperation Treaty (PCT):**
> *Provides greater uniformity and less cost in the international patent filing process by allowing regional filing in selected countries that are cross-referenced in patent offices of all member States.*

The European Patent Convention is designed to permit a single office at Munich or The Hague to issue patents of all countries party to the treaty. The EU Patent Convention is designed to create a single community patent valid throughout the European Union. These are major innovations that promise further simplification of registration and protection.

Another aspect of U.S. patent law is illustrated in the following case, which is characteristic of the fact that many domestic courts will not stop someone in their territory from using a patented technology to produce a product that is shipped abroad.

Deepsouth Packing Co. v. Laitram Corp.
United States Supreme Court, 1972.
406 U.S. 518 (1972).

Mr. Justice WHITE . . .

The United States District Court for the Eastern District of Louisiana has written:

> Shrimp, whether boiled, broiled, barbecued or fried, are a gustatory delight, but they did not evolve to satisfy man's palate. Like other crustaceans, they wear their skeletons outside their bodies in order to shield their savory pink and white flesh against predators, including man. They also carry their intestines, commonly called veins, in bags (or sand bags) that run the length of their bodies. For shrimp to be edible, it is necessary to remove their shells. In addition, if the vein is removed, shrimp become more pleasing to the fastidious as well as more palatable. *Laitram Corp. v. Deepsouth Packing Co.*, 301 F. Supp. 1037, at p. 1040 (1969).

Such "gustatory" observations are rare even in those piscatorially favored federal courts blissfully situated on the Nation's Gulf Coast, but they are properly recited in this case. Petitioner and respondent both hold patents on machines that devein shrimp more cheaply and efficiently than competing machinery or hand labor can do the job. Extensive litigation below has established that respondent, the Laitram Corp., has the superior claim and that the distribution and use of petitioner Deepsouth's machinery in this country should be enjoined to prevent infringement of Laitram's patents. . . . We granted certiorari [in this proceeding] . . . to consider the question: Is Deepsouth. barred from the American market by Laitram's patents, also foreclosed by the patent laws from exporting its deveiners, in less than fully assembled form, for use abroad? . . .

[Laitram's patents apply to a slitter and a tumbler mechanism.] Both the slitter and the tumbler are combination patents; that is "[n]one of the parts referred to are new, and none are claimed as new; nor is any portion of the combination less than the whole claimed as new, or stated to produce any given result. The end in view is proposed to be accomplished by the union of all, arranged and combined together in the manner described. And this combination, composed of all the parts mentioned in the specification, and arranged with reference to each other, and to other parts of the [machine] in the manner therein described, is stated to be the improvement, and is the thing patented." (*Proutry v. Ruggles*, 41 U.S. 336, at p. 341, 1842)

[In this case] Deepsouth seeks judicial approval, expressed through a modification of the injunction against it, for continuing its practice of shipping deveining equipment to foreign customers in three separate boxes, each containing only parts of the 1¾ ton machines. The company contends that by this means both the "making" and the "use" of the machines occur abroad and the Laitram's lawful monopoly over the making and use of the machines throughout the United States is not infringed.

Laitram counters that this course of conduct is based upon a hyper technical reading of the patent code that, if tolerated. will deprive it of its right to the fruits of the inventive genius of its assignors. . . .

The District Court, faced with this dispute, noted that three prior circuit courts had considered the meaning of "making" in this context and that all three resolved the question favorably to Deepsouth's position. . . .

The Court of Appeals for the Fifth Circuit reversed, thus departing from the established rules of the Second, Third and Seventh Circuits. In the Fifth Circuit panel's opinion those courts that previously considered the question "worked themselves into . . . a conceptual box" by adopting "an artificial, technical construction" of the patent laws, a construction, moreover, which in the opinion of the panel. "[subverted] the Constitutional scheme of promoting 'the Progress of Science and useful Arts' " by allowing an intrusion on a patentee's rights. . . .

We disagree with the Court of Appeals for the Fifth Circuit. . . .

The [U.S. Patent Code] makes it clear that it is not an infringement to make or use a patented product outside of the United States. [However, anyone who "without authority makes, uses or sells any patented invention within the United States during the term of the patent therefore infringes the patent." *United States Code*, title 35, § 271.] . . . Thus, in order to secure the injunction it seeks, Laitram must show a . . . direct infringement by Deepsouth in the United States, that is, that Deepsouth "makes," "uses," or "sells" the patented product within the bounds of this country.

Laitram does not suggest that Deepsouth "uses" the machine. Its argument that Deepsouth sells the machines— based primarily on Deepsouth's sales rhetoric and related indicia such as price—cannot carry the day unless it can be shown that Deepsouth is selling the "patented invention." The sales question thus resolves itself into the question of manufacture: did Deepsouth "make" (and then sell) something cognizable under the patent law as the patented invention or did it "make" (and then sell) something that fell short of infringement?

The Court of Appeals, believing that the word "makes" should be accorded "a construction in keeping with the ordinary meaning of that term," . . . held against Deepsouth on the theory that "makes: 'means what it ordinarily connotes—the substantial manufacture of the constituent parts of the machine.' " . . .

We cannot endorse the view that the "substantial manufacture of the constituent parts of [a] machine" constitutes direct infringement when we have so often held that a combination patent protects only against the operable assembly of the whole and not the manufacture of its parts. "For as we point out in *Mercoid v. Mid-Continent Investment Co.* 320 U.S. 661, at p. 676 (1944) a patent is on the assembled or functioning whole, not on the separate parts." *Mercoid Corp. v. Minneapolis-Honeywell Regulator Co.*, 320 U.S. 680, at 680 (1944).

. . . In sum, if anything is settled in the patent law, it is that the combination patent covers only the totality of the elements in the claim and that no element, separately viewed, is within the grant." *Aro Mfg. Co. v. Convertible Top Replacement Co.*, 365 U.S. 336, at p. 344 (1961).

It was this basic tenet of the patent system that led Judge Swan to hold in the leading case, *Radio Corp. of America v. Andrea*. 79 F.2d 626 (1935), unassembled export of the elements of an invention did not infringe the patent.

[T]he relationship is the essence of the patent.

. . . No wrong is done the patentee until the combination is formed. His monopoly does not cover the manufacture or sale of separate elements capable of being, but never actually, associated to form the invention. Only when such association is made is there a direct infringement of his monopoly, and not even then if it is done outside the territory for which the monopoly was granted. . . .

We reaffirm this conclusion today. . . .

Mr. Justice BLACKMUN, with whom the Chief Justice, Mr. Justice POWELL, and Mr. Justice REHNQUIST join, dissents.

By a process of only the most rigid construction, the Court, by its decision today, fulfills what Judge Clark in his able opinion for the Fifth Circuit, distressingly forecast:

To hold otherwise [as the Court does today] would subvert the Constitutional scheme of promoting "the Progress of Science and useful Arts by securing for limited Times to Authors and Inventors the exclusive Right to their respective Writings and Discoveries." (*United States Constitution*, Art. 1 § 8, clause 8) It would allow an infringer to set up shop next door to a patent-protected inventor whose product enjoys a substantial foreign market and deprive him of his valuable business. If this Constitutional protection is to be fully effectuated, it must extend to an infringer who manufactures in the United States and then captures the foreign markets from the patentee. The Constitutional mandate cannot be limited to just manufacturing and selling within the United States. The infringer would then be allowed to reap the fruits of the American economy—technology, labor, materials, etc.—but would not be subject to the responsibilities of the American patent laws. We cannot permit an infringer to enjoy these benefits and then be allowed to strip away a portion of the patentee's protection. . . .

I share the Fifth Circuit's concern and I therefore dissent.

Discussion Questions

1. Is there any real difference in the manufacture and shipment of the parts of a patented product separately than in shipping the entire product assembled?
2. What is the holding in this case?
3. Do you agree with the dissenters or with the majority in this case? Explain.

Trademark Protection

About fifty thousand trademark applications are filed each year by U.S. citizens with the appropriate authorities in other countries. In the United States, trademarks are protected by common law and by state and federal registrations. Federal registration is permitted by the U.S. Trademark Office for all marks capable of distinguishing the goods on which they appear from other goods. Since 1989, the U.S. law has allowed applications when there is a bona fide intent to use a trademark within twelve months and, if there is good cause for the delay in actual usage, up to twenty-four additional months. Injunctions, damages, and seizures of goods by customs officials may follow infringement. Congress created criminal offenses and private triple damages remedies for the first time in the Trademark Counterfeiting Act of 1984. Unlike patents and copyrights, trademarks may be renewed continuously and may be licensed or assigned to others by the possessor through franchise agreements. National trademark law sometimes accompanies international licensing, as the next case illustrates.

In *Scotch Whisky Association v. Barton Distilling Company* the U.S. Supreme Court demonstrates the extraterritorial application of the Lanham Act of 1946 to foreign licensees engaging in deceptive practices.

Scotch Whisky Association v. Barton Distilling Company
United States Court of Appeals, Seventh Circuit (1973).
489 F.2d 809.

FAIRCHILD, Circuit Judge.

Two of plaintiffs are producers of Scotch whisky in Scotland, marketed throughout much of the world, including Panama and the Canal Zone. Plaintiff Association was formed to promote the interests of distillers and merchants in Scotland. Defendant Barton is a Delaware corporation which produces and markets alcoholic beverages in the United States and elsewhere. One of defendant's products is Scotch whisky sold under the trademark House of Stuart. This action concerns a product distributed under the "House of Stuart Blended Scotch Whisky" label in Panama, which reached the Canal Zone as well.

In 1964, as amended in 1965, defendant made an agreement appointing a Panamanian corporation, Diers & Ullrich, its exclusive distributor in Panama. Defendant supplied Diers & Ullrich with House of Stuart labels and bottles, shipped from the United States, and vatted Scotch malts, shipped from Scotland. Diers & Ullrich mixed the Scotch malts with locally produced spirits and sold the product under the House of Stuart label. It appears without dispute that the House of Stuart label indicates that the product has its origin in Scotland, and that when applied to the Diers & Ullrich product there was a false designation of origin.

15 U.S.C. § 1125(a), part of the Lanham Trademark Act of 1946, provides in part that one who affixes or uses in connection with any goods a false designation of origin and causes the goods to enter into commerce shall be civilly liable to a person doing business in the locality falsely indicated.

Plaintiffs alleged that defendant conspired in the use of labels indicating origin in Scotland on spurious Scotch whisky, but the district court found no more than that defendant knew, or should have known, of the practice of Diers & Ullrich. The district court, 338 F.Supp. 595, concluded that the use of the label was a false designation of the place of origin in violation of 15 U.S.C. § 1125(a) and certain provisions of the International Convention of Paris for the Protection of Industrial Property; and that defendant was responsible for the use of the label. Judgment was entered enjoining defendant from using the words "Scotch whisky" or its House of Stuart trademark or otherwise indicating origin in Scotland in connection with a product similar to the one involved, and awarded plaintiffs reasonable attorneys' fees.

On appeal, defendant contends: (1) that the district court lacked jurisdiction over the subject matter, (2) that under the circumstances an injunction was unnecessary and should not have been issued; and (3) that the award of attorneys' fees was unwarranted.

(1) Jurisdiction

[1] The essence of defendant's position is that the goods bearing the challenged label were produced in Panama and caused to enter into the commerce of Panama, not the interstate or foreign commerce "which may lawfully be regulated by Congress." See 15 U.S.C. § 1127, so defining "commerce" and providing "The intent of this chapter is to regulate commerce within the control of Congress by making actionable the deceptive and misleading use of marks in such commerce."

[2, 3] It is true that it was the labels and bottles supplied by defendant which were transported from within the United States to Panama. Although defendant's agreement gave it the power to control the ingredients of the product, and thus defendant was properly charged with responsibility for the blending and labeling, this process did not happen within the United States. We think, however, that so literal a concept of entering into commerce is untenable. No principle of international law bars the United States from governing the conduct of its own citizens upon the high seas or even in foreign countries when the rights of other nations or their nationals are not infringed. Congress has the power to prevent unfair trade practices in foreign commerce by citizens of the United States, although some of the acts are done outside the territorial limits. The question is whether Congress intended the Act to apply to a situation of this type. *Steele v. Bulova Watch Co.*, 344 U.S. 280, 285-286, 73 S.Ct. 252, 97 L.Ed. 252 (1952).

In *Steele*, the Supreme Court construed another section of the act, 15 U.S.C.§ 1114(1), which creates a civil cause of action against one who uses an infringing mark "in commerce." The Court upheld a broad concept of "commerce."

Steele was a United States citizen who registered the trademark "Bulova" in Mexico. He imported parts from the United States and assembled and sold watches in Mexico. Plaintiff Bulova Watch Company manufactured, advertised, and sold watches in the United States and elsewhere, using a trademark registered in the United States. Defective spurious Bulova watches filtered back to the United States and were brought to jewelers for repair by dissatisfied owners. In deciding that the Act applied, the Court considered both the purchase of parts in the United States, and the advent of some watches in the United States, as well as the adverse reflection Steele's goods could have on plaintiff's reputation both in the United States and elsewhere.

Defendant correctly points out that there are factual differences between *Steele* and the case at bar. Steele personally sold watches in Mexico under an infringing mark while defendant sold mislabeled whisky in Panama only vicariously; Steele's Bulova trademark was ultimately nullified by Mexican decree while here it has not been demonstrated that Diers & Ullrich violated any Panamanian law; some of Steele's watches did come into the United States and damage the American owner of the trademark in this country while the Diers & Ullrich product appears to have reached only Panama and the Canal Zone, and damaged the Scotch plaintiff only in those markets. None the less, viewing the entire course of business and the responsibility found on the part of defendant, we think the "commerce" involved began with defendant's acts in the United States and continued to the ultimate distribution of the whisky.

In *Steele*, the Supreme Court emphasized the invalidation of the Mexican trademark registration because of the danger otherwise of affront to Mexican sovereignty: the extraterritorial application of the United States trademark laws would nullify the affirmative grant of trademark protection within Mexico by the Mexican government. However, in the case at bar no such conflict is present. First, although the Panamanian government has apparently not prohibited the sale of local spirits under the designation of "Scotch whisky," it has taken no affirmative action to protect either the United States licensor or the Panamanian distributor in doing so. Moreover, the injunction is directed only against the United States licensor which acts only vicariously in Panama where Diers & Ullrich is not prohibited by the injunction from continuing to manufacture and market adulterated whisky.

Although there is no evidence that the adulterated Scotch whisky filtered into the United States, defendant concedes that sales of the product (though few) were made in the Canal Zone. Title 4, section 471 of the Canal Zone Code provides that the trademark laws of the United States have the same force and effect in the Canal Zone as in the continental United States.

[4] We note that had the defendant made the same arrangements with an American licensee who packaged the mislabeled House of Stuart Scotch Whisky in the United States and shipped it to Panama, there would be no question but that the defendant caused the mislabeled goods to enter commerce. The purpose underlying the Lanham Act, to make actionable the deceptive use of false designations of origin, should not be evaded by the simple device of selecting a foreign licensee. *Steele*, p. 287, 73 S.Ct. 252.

Defendant argues that *Vanity Fair Mills, Inc. v. T. Eaten*, 234 F.2d 633 (2d Cir., 1956), cert. denied 352 U.S. 871, 77 S.Ct. 96, 1 L.Ed.2d 76 (1956), cert. denied 352 U.S. 913, 77 S.Ct. 144, 1 L.Ed. 2d 120 (1956) precludes extraterritorial application of the Lanham Act here. However, in *Vanity Fair* the defendant was a foreign national who acted in his home country under a presumably valid trademark registration in that country. *Vanity Fair, supra*, at p. 642. Defendant also cites *George W. Luft Company v. Zande Cosmetic Company*, 142 F.2d 536 (2d Cir., 1944), cert. denied 323 U. S. 756, 65 S.Ct. 90, 89 L.Ed. 606 (1944); however, in *Luft*, the defendants had obtained a registered and valid trademark from a foreign country and the decision in *Luft* preceded enactment of the Lanham Trademark Act as well as the interpretation of it in *Steele*.

We conclude that a cause of action was established under the Lanham Act and that the district court had jurisdiction. It is unnecessary to discuss plaintiffs' reliance on the Convention of Paris for the Protection of Industrial Property and its implementation by 15 U.S.C. § 1126(b).

(2) Injunctive Relief

[5,6] Defendant concedes that it is generally within the sound discretion of a court of equity to grant or deny an injunction against conduct which has ceased before the trial has taken place. It contends, however, that there was an abuse of discretion here, where, after the commencement of this action, but two years before trial, it took steps to halt the practice complained of and eventually severed relations with Diers & Ullrich.

The amended agreement with Diers & Ullrich was dated April 21, 1965 and the action was brought April 8, 1969. Defendant had not exercised its rights to inspect and control the Diers & Ullrich product at least up to the time of an apparently ineffective request in the summer of 1968. In 1966 and later there were events which should reasonably have caused defendant to inquire about the practice. The district court found that defendant knew or should have known of the spurious product, and that the spurious product was produced as late as July, 1969.

We are unable to say that there was an abuse of discretion in granting an injunction.

(3) Attorneys' Fees

[7,8] The district court awarded reasonable attorneys' fees to plaintiff, to be assessed after any right of appeal has been exhausted or expired. The general rule in American courts is that attorneys' fees are not ordinarily recoverable in the absence of a statute or enforceable contract providing therefore. *Fleischmann Corp. v. Maier Brewing*, 386 U.S.714, 717, 87 S.Ct. 1404, 18 L. Ed.2d 475 (1967). Limited exceptions are noted at p. 718-719, 87 S.Ct. 1404. See also *Mills v. Electric Auto-Lite*, 396 U.S. 375, 392, 90 S.Ct. 616, 24 L.Ed.2d 593. Exceptions were listed by this court in *Walker v. Columbia Broadcasting System, Inc.*, 443 F.2d 33, 35-37.

The present case does not fall within any of the exceptions. We do not view it as presenting "overriding considerations of justice" (see *Fleischmann* and *Mills*) nor an instance of a defense maintained in bad faith, vexatiously, wantonly, or for oppressive reasons (see *Walker*).

In so far as the judgment appealed from awarded attorneys' fees, it is reversed, and in all other respects, affirmed. Costs on appeal awarded to plaintiffs-appellees.

Discussion Questions

1. How does this case illustrate the extraterritorial application of trademark law?
2. Where and what violations of U.S. trademark law were involved in this case?
3. Was international law involved in this case? Why or why not?

The treaties of widest international application are the Paris Convention and the Arrangement of Nice, as revised in 1967, to which the United States is a party. These treaties extend the principle of national treatment and provide for a right of priority of six months for trademarks. The Nice Agreement adopts a single classification system for goods and services that has brought considerable order out of chaos in this field. Efforts are being made to improve the efficiency of the process by development of an international filing and examination scheme like that in force for patents.

Copyright Protection

To retain a U.S. copyright, the author must give formal notice of a reservation of rights when publishing the work. Protection extends for fifty years after the death of the author. The author also controls "derivative works," such as movies made from books, and only the author or assignees may make copies, display, perform, and first sell the work. Registration with the U.S. Copyright Office is not required to obtain these rights, but it is essential to federal copyright infringement remedies. Infringers are subject to criminal penalties, injunctive relief, and civil damages. Educators, critics, and news reporters are allowed **fair use** of the work, a traditional common law doctrine that has now been codified in the 1976 Copyright Act.

> **Fair use doctrine:** Privilege to use copyrighted material in reasonable manner without consent. Section 107 of the Copyright Act sets forth factors to be considered.

Without the benefit of an appropriate treaty provision, copyright registrations must be acquired in each country recognizing such rights. However, copyright holders receive national treatment, translation rights, and other benefits under the Universal Copyright Convention (UCC). The UCC excuses foreigners from registration requirements provided notice of a claim of copyright (©) is adequately given (e.g., Folsom, Gordon, & Spanogle, 1992). The UCC establishes a minimum term for copyright protection of 25 years after publication, prior registration, or death of the author. Various additional benefits can be had in many other countries through the Berne Convention (i.e., moral rights). In both conventions, the registration requirements are suspended for copyright holders from participating States. Unlike the UCC, the Berne Convention allows for local copyright protection independent of protection granted in the country of origin and does not require copyright notice. The Berne Convention establishes a more generous minimum term of the life of the author plus fifty years. U.S. ratification of the Berne Convention in 1989 created copyright relations with an additional twenty-five nations. Ratification has eliminated U.S. registration requirements for foreign copyright holders and required protection of the moral rights of authors to integrity and recognition of their creative rights. It is generally considered that unfair competition law at the federal and state levels will provide the legal basis in U.S. law for these moral rights. A limited class of visual artists explicitly receive these treaty rights under the Visual Artists Rights Act of 1990 (Folsom et al., 1992, p. 228).

Product Liability Laws

Most modern nations have some form of product liability laws that attempt to discourage manufacturers from putting defective products into the marketplace. Private legal actions can be brought by injured parties under various national causes of legal action in contract, negligence, and strict liability. Japan and most of the developing world use only the first two of these theories in providing compensation for injuries sustained. This third legal concept is a special liability that first emerged in the common law development of the United States and the British commonwealth countries. This concept of "strict liability" has recently been adopted by the European Community, which has established a common standard of special liability similar to that practiced in the United States.

Japanese product liability law is similar to that practiced in most developing countries and is less protective of consumer interests than the strict liability standards of the United States and the EU countries. Although both Japan and the United States recognize a cause of action in contract and negligence, Japan does not recognize the concept of **strict liability**, which merely requires proof that a defective product was the proximate cause of the injuries sustained.

> *Strict liability:* A concept in product liability law allowing recovery of damages when there is sufficient proof of a defective product being a proximate cause of injuries sustained regardless of care exercised.

In common law countries, the evolution of case law development has produced two major concepts that distinguish products liability actions in these nations from those of the developing countries and Japan. Although the proof requirements to show a common law breach of contract are the same as those set out in the Japanese Civil Code, breach of contract is seldom used in products liability cases because of limitations of privity, restricting those who may be considered parties to the dispute. In negligence, however, the concepts of *res ipsa loquitur* (the thing speaks for itself) and doctrine of negligence per se (in and of itself) make it easier for the claimant to prevail in common law countries. The doctrine of *res ipsa loquitur* excuses a claimant who can show that a product was defective when it left the hands of the defendant from having to prove that the defendant caused the defect. Negligence per se excuses a claimant from showing that the defendant breached a duty of care in those cases in which the defendant violated a statutory manufacturing or disclosure agreement. If the plaintiff can show that the manufacturer violated a statutory safety requirement, the failure to observe the requirements is in and of itself an automatic breach of the manufacturer's duty of reasonable care.

The common law theory of strict liability offers even more protection for the consumer. Under this theory, defendants are held liable for products that are unreasonably dangerous no matter what their intentions may have been or whether or not they exercised reasonable care. This theory is succinctly set out in the *Restatement of Torts (Second)* § 402A, as follows:

§ 402A. **Special Liability of Seller of Product for Physical Harm to User or Consumer**

(1) One who sells any product in a defective condition unreasonably dangerous to the user or consumer or to his property is subject to liability for physical harm thereby caused to the ultimate user or consumer or to his property, if
   (a) the seller is engaged in the business of selling such a product, and
   (b) it is expected to and does reach the user or consumer without substantial change in condition in which it is sold.
(2) The rule stated in Subsection (1) applies although
   (a) the seller has exercised all possible care in the preparation and sale of his product, and
   (b) the user or consumer has not bought the product from or entered into any contractual relation with the seller.

In the United States, this concept emerged through the development of the common law of individual states. However, it has become almost universal among the state practices and in many states has been recognized in statutory form and legislative enactment. Many jurisdictions require that the defective product must be "unreasonably dangerous," which means that the claimant has to show either (a) that the product was dangerous beyond the expectations of the ordinary consumer or (b) that a less dangerous alternative was economically feasible for the manufacturer to produce, and the manufacturer failed to produce it.

The European Union countries had various practices in regard to products liability laws that were unified through an EC directive from the European Community Commission requiring member States to modify their product liability laws to meet community standards. The 1985 EC directive established standards similar to the strict liability theory used in common law countries. The directive differs only in that it does not require the claimant to show that the defect was unreasonably dangerous. The directive provides the following:

(1) A product is defective when it does not provide the safety which a person is entitled to expect, taking all circumstances into account, including:
   (a) the presentation of the product;
   (b) the use to which it could reasonably be expected that the product would be put;
   (c) the time when it was put into circulation.
(2) A product does not have a defect for the sole reason that a better product is subsequently put into circulation.

Although the directive was not implemented immediately, the EC member States had all complied by 1991 (Sweden, Austria, and Finland will also have to comply). The EC directive is more similar to the strict liability rule as it is applied in British Commonwealth countries than to the rule applied in the United States. The EU member States are allowed to set a total maximum liability limit that a product producer may have to pay. It states that "any member state may provide that a producer's total liability for damage resulting from a death or personal injury and caused by identical items with the same defect shall be limited to an amount which may not be less than 70 million ECU." (ECU 70 million is approximately U.S. $80 million.) Many states in the United States have altered their products liability laws to limit liability in several ways, and the U.S. Congress is seriously considering intervention in this area that has traditionally been considered a reserved power of the states.

Extraterritorial Application of Product Liability Laws

The courts in the United States have been the most willing to apply their unfair competition laws and product liability laws extraterritorially. A product that was manufactured abroad and imported into the United States is subject to the same liability as products manufactured in this country. The U.S. courts have also held that a U.S. manufacturer or seller of defective products sold abroad can be held liable for damages sustained in other countries. U.S. courts, however, consider two important issues when determining whether they can exercise jurisdiction in a product liability case. These two issues are personal jurisdiction and *forum non conveniens*.

Although product liability is a creature of the laws of the individual states of the United States, the federal courts may exercise **diversity jurisdiction** when the oppos-

Diversity jurisdiction: Provides access to the federal courts in civil cases when the opposing parties are citizens of different states and the sum in question is greater than $50,000.

Long-arm statutes: Legislative acts that provide for personal jurisdiction by substituted service of process over persons or corporations that are not residents of that jurisdiction but have minimal contacts with that state.

ing parties are citizens of two different states (or a U.S. state and a foreign national) and the sum in question is greater than $50,000. Federal diversity rules require the federal court to apply the substantive law of the U.S. state where the case was originally filed. Thus, both state and federal courts in the United States may handle product liability suits. State and federal **long-arm statutes** enabling the defendant to be served and affecting personal jurisdiction are quite broad and cover virtually any business activity in the local forum. There is also the federal constitutional requirement of due process that is required by a showing that the defendant had **minimal contacts** with the forum. The minimal contacts test allows a court to assume jurisdiction only if (a) the defendant purposefully availed itself of doing business in the forum and (b) the defendant reasonably could have anticipated that it would have to defend itself there.

The issues of *in personam* jurisdiction are discussed in the following case involving the World-Wide Volkswagen Corporation and the manufacturers of the Audi automobile in question in this product liability suit. The issue here is narrowly drawn as to the appropriate forum for such legal action, not whether the World-Wide Volkswagen corporation is subject to suit in some other U.S. forum. This action is in the nature of an injunction brought against the court in Oklahoma to prevent the case from being tried in that state. Action in New York would still be possible.

Minimal contacts: Requirements that foreign persons or corporations have minimal voluntary contacts with a particular jurisdiction in order to be subject to a state's personal jurisdiction.

In personam *jurisdiction:* Power of a court over the person of a defendant in contrast to the court's power over the defendant's property interest (in rem).

▌   ▌   ▌

World-Wide Volkswagen Corp. v. Woodson
United States Supreme Court, 1980.
444 U.S. 286 (1980).

Mr. Justice WHITE delivered the opinion of the Court.

The issue before us is whether, consistently with the Due Process Clause of the Fourteenth Amendment of the United States Constitution, an Oklahoma court may exercise *in personam* jurisdiction over a nonresident automobile retailer and its wholesale distributor in a products liability action, when the defendants' only connection with Oklahoma is the fact that an automobile sold in New York to New York residents became involved in an accident in Oklahoma.

Respondents Harry and Kay Robinson purchased a new Audi automobile from petitioner Seaway Volkswagen Inc. (Seaway) in Massena, N.Y., in 1976. The following year the Robinson family, who resided in New York, left that state for a new home in Arizona. As they passed through the state of Oklahoma, another car struck their Audi in the rear, causing a fire which severely burned Kay Robinson and her two children.

The Robinsons subsequently brought a products-liability action in the District Court for Creek County, Okla., claiming that their injuries resulted from defective design and placement of the Audi's gas tank and fuel system. They joined as defendants the automobile's manufacturer, Audi NSU Auto Union Aktiengesellshaft (Audi); its importer Volkswagen of America, Inc. (Volkswagen): its regional distributor, petitioner World-Wide Volkswagen Corp. (World-Wide): and its retail dealer, petitioner Seaway. Seaway and World-Wide entered special appearances, claiming that Oklahoma's exercise of jurisdiction over them would offend the limitations on the state's jurisdiction imposed by the Due Process Clause of the Fourteenth Amendment.

The facts presented to the District Court showed that World-Wide is incorporated and has its business office in New York. It distributes vehicles, parts, and accessories, under contract with Volkswagen, to retail dealers in New York, New Jersey, and Connecticut. Seaway, one of these retail dealers, is incorporated and has its place of business in New York. Insofar as the record reveals, Seaway and World-Wide are fully independent corporations whose only relations with each other and with Volkswagen and Audi are contractual only. Respondents adduced no evidence that either World-Wide or Seaway does any business in Oklahoma, ships or sells any products to or in that state, has an agent to receive process there, or purchases advertisements in any media calculated to reach Oklahoma. In fact, as respondents' counsel conceded at oral argument, there was no showing that any automobile sold by World-Wide or Seaway has ever entered Oklahoma with the single exception of the vehicle involved in the present case.

Despite the apparent paucity of contacts between petitioners and Oklahoma, the District Court rejected their constitutional claim and reaffirmed that ruling in denying petitioners motion for reconsideration. Petitioners then sought a writ of prohibition in the Supreme Court of Oklahoma to restrain the District Judge, respondent Charles S. Woodson, from exercising *in personam* jurisdiction over them. They renewed their contention that, because they had no "minimal contacts" with the state of Oklahoma, the actions of the District Judge were in violation of their rights under the Due Process Clause.

The Supreme Court of Oklahoma denied the writ, holding that personal jurisdiction over petitioners was authorized by Oklahoma's "long-arm" statute. . . . The court's rationale was contained in the following paragraph:

> In the case before us, the product being sold and distributed by the petitioners is by its very design and purpose so mobile that petitioners can foresee its possible use in Oklahoma. This is especially true of the distributor, who has the exclusive right to distribute such automobile in New York, New Jersey and Connecticut. The evidence presented below demonstrated that goods sold and distributed by the petitioners are used in the state of Oklahoma, and under the facts we believe it reasonable to infer, given the retail value of the automobile, that the petitioners derive substantial income from automobiles which from time to time are used in the state of Oklahoma. . . .

As has long been settled, and as we reaffirm today, a state court may exercise personal jurisdiction over a nonresident defendant only so long as there exist "minimum contacts" between the defendant and the forum state. The concept of minimum contacts, in turn, can be seen to perform two related, but distinguishable, functions. It protects the defendant against the burdens of litigating in a distant or inconvenient forum. And it acts to ensure that the states through their courts, do not reach out beyond the limits imposed on them by their status as coequal sovereigns in a federal system.

The protection against inconvenient litigation is typically described in terms of "reasonableness" or "fairness." We have said that the defendant's contacts with the forum state must be such that maintenance of the suit "does not offend 'traditional notions of fair play and substantial justice.' " The relationship between the defendant and the forum must be such that it is "reasonable . . . to require the corporation to defend the particular suit which is brought there." Implicit in this emphasis on reasonableness is the understanding that the burden on the defendant, while always a primary concern, will in an appropriate case be considered in light of other relevant factors, including the forum state's interest in adjudicating the dispute; the plaintiff's interest in obtaining convenient and effective relief, at least when that interest is not adequately protected by the plaintiff's power to choose the forum; the interstate judicial system's interest in obtaining the most efficient resolution of controversies; and the shared interest of the several states in furthering fundamental substantive social policies.

The limits imposed on state jurisdiction by the Due Process Clause, in its role as a guarantor against inconvenient litigation, have been substantially relaxed over the years. . . . Nevertheless. we have never accepted the proposition that state lines are irrelevant for jurisdictional purposes, nor could we, and remain faithful to the principles of interstate federalism embodied in the Constitution. . . .

Thus, the Due Process Clause "does not contemplate that a state may make binding a judgment *in personam* against an individual or corporate defendant with which the state has no contacts, ties, or relations." . . . Even if the defendant would suffer minimal or no inconvenience from being forced to litigate before the tribunals of another state; even if the forum state has a strong interest in applying its law to the controversy; even if the forum state is the most convenient location for litigation, the Due Process Clause, acting as an instrument of interstate federalism, may sometimes act to divest the state of its power to render a valid judgment. . . .

Applying these principles to the case at hand, we find in the record before us a total absence of those affiliating circumstances that are a necessary predicate to any exercise of state court jurisdiction. Petitioners carry on no activity whatsoever in Oklahoma. They close no sales and perform no services there. They avail themselves of none of the privileges and benefits of Oklahoma law. They solicit no business there either through salespersons or through advertising reasonably calculated to reach the state. Nor does the record show that they regularly sell cars at wholesale or retail to Oklahoma customers or residents or that they indirectly, through others, serve or seek to serve the Oklahoma market. In short, respondents seek to base jurisdiction on one, isolated occurrence and whatever inferences can be drawn therefrom: the fortuitous circumstance that a single Audi automobile, sold in New York to New York residents, happened to suffer an accident while passing through Oklahoma.

It is argued, however, that because an automobile is mobile by its very design and purpose it was "foreseeable" that the Robinsons' Audi would cause injury in Oklahoma. Yet "foreseeability" alone has never been a sufficient benchmark for personal jurisdiction under the Due Process Clause. . . .

If foreseeability were the criterion, a local California tire dealer could be forced to defend in Pennsylvania when a blowout occurs there, a Wisconsin seller of a defective automobile jack could be haled before a distant court for damage caused in New Jersey, or a Florida soft drink concessionaire could be summoned to Alaska to account for injuries happening there. Every seller of chattels would in effect appoint the chattel his agent for service of process. His amenability to suit would travel with the chattel. We recently abandoned the outworn rule of *Harris v. Balk* (198 U.S. 215 [1905]) that the interest of a creditor in a debt could be extinguished or otherwise affected by any state having transitory jurisdiction over the debtor. Having inferred the mechanical rule that a creditor's amenability to a *quasi in rem* action travels with his debtor, we are unwilling to endorse an analogous principle in the present case.

This is not to say, of course, that foreseeability is wholly irrelevant. But the foreseeability that is critical to due process analysis is not the mere likelihood that a product will find its way into the forum state. Rather, it is that the defendant's conduct and connection with the forum state are such that he should reasonably anticipate being haled into court there. . . .

When a corporation "purposefully avails itself of the privilege of conducting activities within the forum state," it has clear notice that it is subject to suit there, and can act to alleviate the risk of burdensome litigation by procuring insurance, passing the expected costs on to customers, or, if the risks are too great, severing its connection with the state. Hence if the sale of a product of a manufacturer or distributor such as Audi or Volkswagen is not simply an isolated occurrence, but arises from the efforts of the manufacturer or distributor to serve directly or indirectly, the market for its product in other states, it is not unreasonable to subject it to suit in one of those states if its allegedly defective merchandise has there been the source of injury to its owner or to others.

But there is no such or similar basis for Oklahoma jurisdiction over World-Wide or Seaway in this case. Seaway's sales are made in Massena, N.Y. World-Wide's market, although substantially larger, is limited to dealers in New York, New Jersey, and Connecticut. . . .

. . . In our view, whatever marginal revenues petitioners may receive by virtue of the fact that their products are capable of use in Oklahoma is far too attenuated a contact to justify that state's exercise of *in personam* jurisdiction over them.

Because we find that petitioners have no "contacts, ties, or relations" with the state of Oklahoma, the judgment of the Supreme Court of Oklahoma is Reversed.

Mr. Justice MARSHALL, with whom Mr. Justice BLACKMUN joins, dissenting.

. . . The majority asserts that "respondents seek to base jurisdiction on one, isolated occurrence and whatever inferences can be drawn therefrom: the fortuitous circumstance that a single Audi automobile, sold in New York to New York residents, happened to suffer an accident while passing through Oklahoma." If that were the case, I would readily agree that the minimum contacts necessary to sustain jurisdiction are not present. But the basis for the assertion of jurisdiction is not the happenstance that an individual over whom petitioner had no control made a unilateral decision to take a chattel with him to a distant state. Rather, jurisdiction is premised on the deliberate and purposeful actions of the defendants themselves in choosing to become part of a nationwide, indeed a global, network for marketing and servicing automobiles.

Petitioners are sellers of a product whose utility derives from its mobility. . . . Petitioners know that their customers buy cars not only to make short trips, but also to travel long distances. In fact, the nationwide service network with which they are affiliated was designed to facilitate and encourage such travel. Seaway would be unlikely to sell many cars if authorized service were available only in Massena, N.Y. . . .

To be sure, petitioners could not know in advance that this particular automobile would be driven to Oklahoma. They must have anticipated, however, that a substantial portion of the cars they sold would travel out of New York. Seaway, a local dealer in the second most populous state, and World-Wide, one of only seven regional Audi distributors in the entire country . . ., would scarcely have been surprised to learn that a car sold by them had been driven in Oklahoma on Interstate 44, a heavily traveled transcontinental highway. . . .

It is misleading for the majority to characterize the argument in favor of jurisdiction as one of " 'foreseeability' alone." As economic entities petitioners reach out from New York, knowingly causing effects in other states and receiving economic advantage both from the ability to cause such effects themselves and from the activities of dealers and distributors in other states. While they did not receive revenue from making direct sales in Oklahoma, they intentionally became part of an interstate economic network, which included dealerships in Oklahoma, for pecuniary gain. In light of this purposeful conduct I do not believe it can be said that petitioners "had no reason to expect to be haled before a[n Oklahoma] court." . . .

Discussion Questions

1. Who is bringing this legal action in the U. S. Supreme Court against whom? What is the legal basis of the action?

2. Why is the Oklahoma forum considered a denial of due process of law under the U.S. Constitution?

3. What alternative court jurisdictions are available to the original claimants who filed this case in Oklahoma?

A similar concept that may result in the denial of jurisdiction in products liability cases is that of *forum non conveniens*. This device allows the court to determine if the forum State has sufficient interest in the outcome of the dispute to take jurisdiction. The factors considered are (a) the private interests of the parties (i.e., the ease and cost of access to documents and witnesses) and (b) the public interest factors (i.e., the interest of

> **Forum non conveniens:** *Discretionary power of the court to decline jurisdiction when convenience of the parties and the ends of justice would be better served in another forum.*

the forum State, the burden on the courts, and notions of judicial comity).

Use of the *forum non conveniens* test has been widely criticized in the United States when it is used by multinational companies to avoid responsibility for injuries that occur outside the United States, especially in developing countries where the remedies available to claimants are often limited to negligence and contract remedies. In response to this argument, some U.S. states have statutorily forbidden their courts from applying *forum non conveniens* in product liability cases.

In the next case, involving the Dow Chemical Company, the Texas Supreme Court discusses the extraterritorial application of U.S. product liability law after the Texas legislature had statutorily abolished the use of *forum non conveniens* in wrongful death and personal injury actions arising out of an incident in a foreign State or country.

▋ ▋ ▋

Dow Chemical Company v. Castro Alfaro
Supreme Court of Texas, 1990.
786 SW 2d 674 (1990).

[Domingo Castro Alfaro, a Costa Rican resident and employee of the Standard Fruit Company, and eighty-one other Costa Rican employees and their wives brought suit against Dow Chemical Company and Shell Oil Company in Texas. The two companies were incorporated in Delaware but carried on business in Texas. The employees claimed that they had suffered personal injuries as a result of exposure to dibromochloropropane (DBCP), a pesticide manufactured by Dow and Shell, which they allege was furnished to Standard Fruit. The employees exposed to DBCP allegedly suffered several medical problems, including sterility. The trial court dismissed the case on grounds of *forum non conveniens*. The Court of Appeals reversed. The Texas Supreme Court affirmed the Court of Appeals, noting that the Texas legislature had statutorily abolished the use of *forum non conveniens* in wrongful death and personal injury actions arising out of an incident in a foreign State or country.]

DOGGETT, Justice, concurring.

Because its analysis and reasoning are correct I join in the majority opinion without reservation. I write separately, however, to respond to the dissenters who mask their inability to agree among themselves with competing rhetoric. In their zeal to implement their own preferred social policy that Texas corporations not be held responsible at home for harm caused abroad, these dissenters refuse to be restrained by either express statutory language or the compelling precedent, previously approved by this very court, holding that *forum non conveniens* does not apply in Texas. To accomplish the desired social engineering, they must invoke yet another legal fiction with a fancy name to shield alleged wrongdoers, the so-called doctrine of *forum non conveniens*. The refusal of a Texas corporation to confront a Texas judge and jury is to be labeled "inconvenient" when what is really involved is not convenience but connivance to avoid corporate accountability. . . .

I. THE FACTS

Respondents claim that while working on a banana plantation in Costa Rica for Standard Fruit Company, an American subsidiary of Dole Fresh Fruit Company, headquartered in Boca Raton, Florida, they were required to handle dibromochloropropane [DBCP], a pesticide allegedly manufactured and furnished to Standard Fruit by Shell Oil Company [Shell] and Dow Chemical Company [Dow]. The Environmental Protection Agency [EPA] issued a notice of intent to cancel all food uses of DBCP on September 22, 1977. Before and after the EPA's ban of DBCP in the United States, Shell and Dow apparently shipped several hundred thousand gallons of the pesticide to Costa Rica for use by Standard Fruit. The Respondents, Domingo Castro Alfaro and other plantation workers, filed suit in a state district court in Houston, Texas, alleging that their handling of DBCP caused them serious personal injuries for which Shell and Dow were liable under the theories of products liability, strict liability and breach of warranty.

Rejecting an initial contest to its authority by Shell and Dow, the trial court found that it had jurisdiction under the *Texas Civil Practice and Remedies Code* § 71.031 (1986), but dismissed the cause on the grounds of *forum non conveniens*. The court of appeals reversed and remanded, holding that Section 71.031 provides a foreign plaintiff with an absolute right to maintain a death or personal injury cause of action in Texas without being subject to *forum non conveniens* dismissal," 751 S.W. 2d 208. Shell and Dow have asked this court to reverse the judgment of the court of appeals and affirm the trial court's dismissal. . . .

II. *FORUM NON CONVENIENS—*
"A COMMON LAW DOCTRINE OUT OF CONTROL"

As a reading of *Texas Civil Practice and Remedies Code* § 71.031 . . . makes clear, the doctrine of *forum non conveniens* has been statutorily abolished in Texas. The decision in *Alien v. Bass*, 47 S.W. 2d 426 (Tex. Ct. of Civil Appeals, El Paso, 1932, writ refused) approved by this court, clearly holds that, upon a showing of personal jurisdiction over a defendant, Article 4678, now section 71.031 of the Texas Civil Practice & Remedies Code, "opens the courts of this state to citizens of a neighboring state and gives them an absolute right to maintain a transitory action of the present nature and to try their cases in the courts of this state." Id. at 427.

Displeased that Alien stands in the way of immunizing multinational corporations from suits seeking redress for their torts causing injury abroad, the dissenters doggedly attempt to circumvent this precedent. Unsuccessful with arguments based upon Texas law, they criticize the court for not justifying its result on public policy grounds.

A. USING THE "DOCTRINE" TO KILL THE LITIGATION ALTOGETHER

Both as a matter of law and of public policy, the doctrine of *forum non conveniens* is without justification. The proffered foundations for it are "considerations of fundamental fairness and sensible and effective judicial administration." . . . In fact, the doctrine is favored by multinational defendants . . . because a *forum non conveniens* dismissal is often outcome-determinative, effectively defeating the claim and denying the plaintiff recovery. The contorted result of the doctrine of *forum non conveniens* is to force foreign plaintiffs "to convince the court that it is more convenient to sue in the United States, while the American defendant argues that . . . [the foreign court] is the more convenient forum."

A *forum non conveniens* dismissal is often, in reality, a complete victory for the defendant. As noted in *Irish Nat'l Ins. Co. v. Aer Lingus Teoranta* 739 F.2d 90 at p. 91 (2nd Circuit Ct. of Appeals, 1984):

> [i]n some instances, . . . invocation of the doctrine will send the case to a jurisdiction which has imposed such severe monetary limitations on recovery as to eliminate the likelihood that the case will be tried. When it is obvious that this will occur, discussion of convenience of witnesses takes on a Kafkaesque quality— everyone knows that no witnesses ever will be called to testify.

In using the term *forum non conveniens*, "the courts have taken refuge in a euphemistic vocabulary, one that grosses over the harsh fact that such dismissal is outcome-determinative in a high percentage of the *forum non conveniens* cases. . . ." Empirical data available demonstrate that less than four percent of cases dismissed under the doctrine of *forum non conveniens* ever reach trial in a foreign court. A *forum non conveniens* dismissal usually will end the litigation altogether, effectively excusing any liability of the defendant. The plaintiffs leave the courtroom without having had their case resolved on the merits.

B. THE GULF OIL FACTORS—BALANCED TOWARD THE DEFENDANT

Courts today usually apply *forum non conveniens* by use of the factors set forth at length in *Gulf Oil Corp. v. Gilbert*, 330 U.S. 501 at pp. 508-509 (1947). Briefly summarized, those factors are (i) the private interests of the litigants (ease and cost of access to documents and witnesses); and (ii) the public interest factors (the interest of the forum state, the burden on the courts, and notions of judicial comity). In the forty-three years in which the courts have grappled with the *Gulf Oil factors*, it has become increasingly apparent that their application fails to promote fairness and convenience. Instead, these factors have been used by defendants to achieve objectives violative of public policy.

1. The Obsolete Private Interest Factors

In their discussion of the private interest factors supposedly designed to promote convenience and fairness, the dissenters choose to avoid entire bodies of law concerning jurisdiction and venue. The dissenters ignore 154 years of Texas venue law designed to give defendants the privilege of being sued in their home country. See Langley, "A Suggested Revision of the Texas Venue Statute," *Texas Law Review*, vol. 30. P. 547 at p. 547 (1952) . . .

In his dissent, Justice Gonzalez correctly crystallizes the private interest factors as "those considerations that make the trial of a case relatively easy, expeditious, and inexpensive for the parties," 786 S.W. 2d 695. Advances in transportation and communications technology have rendered the private factors largely irrelevant:

> A forum is not necessarily inconvenient because of its distance from pertinent parties or places if it is readily accessible in a few hours of air travel. It will often be quicker and less expensive to transfer a witness or a document than to transfer a lawsuit. Jet travel and satellite communications have significantly altered the meaning of "*non conveniens.*"

. . . Even Justice Hecht, in his dissent, recognizes that these factors have been rendered largely obsolete: "Ease of travel and communication, availability of evidence by videotape and facsimile transmission, and other technological advances have reduced the significance of some private inconvenience factors." 786 S.W. 2nd 708. In sum, the private factors are no longer a predominant consideration—fairness and convenience to the parties have been thrust out of the *forum non conveniens* equation. As the "doctrine" is now applied, the term "*forum non conveniens*" has clearly become a misnomer.

2. The Public Interest Factors

The three public interest factors asserted by Justice Gonzalez may be summarized as (1) whether the interests of the jurisdiction are sufficient to justify entertaining the lawsuit; (2) the potential for docket backlog; and (3) judicial comity.

a. The Interest of Texas

The dissenting members of the court falsely attempt to paint a picture of Texas becoming an "irresistible forum for all mass disaster lawsuits," and for "personal injury cases from around the world." They suggest that our citizens will be forced to hear cases in which "[t]he interest of Texas in these disputes is likely to be . . . slight." Although these suppositions undoubtedly will serve to stir public debate, they have little basis in fact.

The dissenting justices each know that for a Texas jury to hear a case, Texas must obtain *in personam* jurisdiction over the defendants in question.

Due process mandates that these requirements be satisfied before a Texas court may assert jurisdiction over a defendant. The personal jurisdiction-due process analysis will ensure that Texas has a sufficient interest in each case entertained in our state's courts.

Specifically, Texas has a substantial interest in the case at bar. As stated previously, this suit has been filed against Shell, a corporation with its world headquarters in Texas, doing extensive business in Texas and manufacturing chemicals in Texas. The suit arose out of alleged acts occurring in Texas and alleged decisions made in Texas. The suit also has been filed against Dow, a corporation with its headquarters in Michigan, but apparently having substantial contacts with Texas. Dow operates the country's largest chemical plant in Texas, manufacturing chemicals within sixty miles of the largest population center in Texas, where millions of Texans reside. Shell and Dow cannot now seek to avoid the Texas civil justice system and a jury of Texans.

b. Docket Backlog

The next justification offered by the dissenters for invoking the legal fiction of "inconvenience" is that judges will be overworked. Not only will foreigners take our jobs, as we are told in the popular press; now they will have our courts. The xenophobic suggestion that foreigners will take over our courts "forcing our residents to wait in the corridors of our court houses while foreign causes of action are tried," is both misleading and false.

It is the height of deception to suggest that docket backlogs in our state's urban centers are caused by so-called "foreign litigation." This assertion is unsubstantiated empirically both in Texas and in other jurisdictions rejecting *forum non conveniens*. Ten states including Texas, have not recognized the doctrine. Within these states, there is no evidence that the docket congestion predicted by the dissenters has actually occurred. The best evidence, of course, comes from Texas itself. Although foreign citizens have enjoyed the statutory right to sue defendants living or doing business here since the 1913 enactment of the predecessor to Section 71.031 of the Texas Civil Practice and Remedies Code, reaffirmed in the 1932 decision in *Allen*, Texas has not been flooded by foreign causes of action. . . .

c. Judicial Comity

Comity—deference shown to the interests of the foreign forum—is a consideration best achieved by rejecting *forum non conveniens*. Comity is not achieved when the United States allows its multinational corporations to adhere to a double standard when operating abroad and subsequently refuses to hold them accountable for those actions. As S. Jacob Scherr, Senior Project Attorney for the Natural Resources Defense Counsel, has noted:

> There is a sense of outrage on the part of many poor countries where citizens are the most vulnerable to exports of hazardous drugs, pesticides and food products. At the 1977 meeting of the UNEP Governing Council, Dr. J. C. Kiano, the Kenyan minister for water development, warned that developing nations will no longer tolerate being used as dumping grounds for products that had not been adequately tested "and that their peoples should not be used as guinea pigs for determining the safety of chemicals."

Comity is best achieved by "avoiding the possibility of 'incurring the wrath and distrust of the Third World as it increasingly recognizes that it is being used as the industrial world's garbage can.' "

The factors announced in *Gulf Oil* fail to achieve fairness and convenience. The public interest factors are designed to favor dismissal and do little to promote the efficient administration of justice. It is clear that the application of *forum non conveniens* would produce muddled and unpredictable case law, and would be used by defendants to terminate litigation before a consideration of the merits ever occurs.

III. PUBLIC POLICY & THE TORT LIABILITY OF MULTINATIONAL CORPORATIONS IN UNITED STATES COURTS

The abolition of *forum non conveniens* will further important public policy considerations by providing a check on the conduct of multinational corporations (MNCs). The misconduct of even a few multinational corporations can affect untold millions around the world. For example, after the United States imposed a domestic ban on the sale of cancer-producing TRIS treated children's sleepwear, American companies exported approximately 2.4 million pieces to Africa, Asia and South America. A similar pattern occurred when a ban was proposed for baby pacifiers that had been linked to choking deaths in infants. These examples of indifference by some corporations toward children abroad are not unusual.

The allegations against Shell and Dow, if proven true, would not be unique, since production of many chemicals banned for domestic use has thereafter continued for foreign marketing. Professor Thomas McGarity, a respected authority in the field of environmental law, explained:

> During the mid-1970s. the United States Environmental Protection Agency (EPA) began to restrict the use of some pesticides because of their environmental effects, and the Occupational Safety and Health Administration (OSHA) established workplace exposure standards for toxic and hazardous substances in the manufacture of pesticides. . . . [I]t is clear that many pesticides that have been severely restricted in the United States are used without restriction in many Third World countries, with resulting harm to fieldworkers and the global environment.

By 1976, "29 percent, or 161 million pounds, of all the pesticides exported by the United States were either unregistered or banned for domestic use." It is estimated that these pesticides poison 750,000 people in developing countries each year, of which 22,500 die. Some estimates place the death toll from the "improper marketing of pesticides at 400,000 lives a year."

Some United States multinational corporations will undoubtedly continue to endanger human life and the environment with such activities until the economic consequences of these actions are such that it becomes unprofitable to operate in this manner. At present, the tort laws of many third world countries are not yet developed. Industrialization "is occurring faster than the development of domestic infrastructures necessary to deal with the problems associated with industry." When a court dismisses a case against a United States multinational corporation, it often removes the most effective restraint on corporate misconduct.

The doctrine of *forum non conveniens* is obsolete in a world in which markets are global and in which ecologists have documented the delicate balance of all life on this planet. The parochial perspective embodied in the doctrine of *forum non conveniens* enables corporations to evade legal control merely because they are transnational. This perspective ignores the reality that actions of our corporations affecting those abroad will also affect Texans. Although DBCP is banned from use within the United States, it and other similarly banned chemicals have been consumed by Texans eating foods imported from Costa Rica and elsewhere. In the absence of meaningful tort liability in the United States for their actions, some multinational corporations will continue to operate without adequate regard for the human and environmental costs of their actions. This result cannot be allowed to repeat itself for decades to come.

As a matter of law and of public policy, the doctrine of *forum non conveniens* should be abolished. Accordingly, I concur.

Discussion Questions

1. What is the specific legal issue in this case and how was it decided?
2. Are there valid reasons for the doctrine of *forum non conveniens*?
3. Even if the Texas legislature had not enacted legislation abolishing the concept of *forum non conveniens*, would you agree that an analogous situation would call for its rejection?

The Texas legislature, apparently reacting to fears that Texas might become an "irresistible forum for all mass disaster lawsuits and for personal injury cases around the world," subsequently repealed the prohibitory statute. However, several other states also recognize the doctrine, and even without such a prohibition, the courts may refuse to grant the petition for *forum non conveniens*.

The worst industrial disaster in world history occurred in India in 1984. Union Carbide Corporation, a U.S. parent company, had delegated considerable responsibility to its Indian subsidiary in the construction and management of the chemical plant involved. As a result of the deaths of thousands due to negligence, the U.S. parent company became responsible for the acts of its subsidiary in India.

In the following case, the U.S. Court of Appeals determined the issues involved in declaring the U.S. courts *forum non conveniens* for the settlement of this enormous host of claims against Union Carbide. The district court's dismissal of the action in the United States was sustained by the Circuit Court of Appeals on the condition that Union Carbide Corporation (the U.S. parent company) submit to the jurisdiction of the Indian courts and agree to satisfy any judgment taken against it in the courts of India.

In Re Union Carbide Corporation Gas Plant Disaster at Bhopal
United States Court of Appeals (2d. Cir.).
809 F. 2d 195 (1987).

[This case arose out of what has been considered the most devastating industrial disaster in history—the deaths of over 2,000 persons and injuries of over 200,000 caused by the release of a lethal gas known as methyl isocyanate from a chemical plant operated by Union Carbide India Limited (UCIL) in Bhopal, India, in 1984. The accident occurred on the night of December 2, 1984, when winds blew the deadly gas from the plant operated by UCIL into densely occupied parts of the city of Bhopal. UCIL is incorporated under the laws of India. Of its stock, 51% is owned by Union Carbide Corporation (UCC), a U.S. corporation, 22% is owned or controlled by the government of India, and the balance is held by approximately 23,500 Indian citizens. The stock is publicly traded on the Bombay Stock Exchange. The company is engaged in the manufacture of a variety of products, including chemicals, plastics, fertilizers, and insecticides, at fourteen plants in India and employs over nine thousand Indian citizens. Approximately 650 people are employed at the Bhopal plant. It is managed and operated entirely by Indian citizens, and all products produced at Bhopal are sold in India. The operations of the plant were regulated by more than two dozen Indian governmental agencies.

[Four days after the accident, the first of some 145 actions in federal district courts in the United States was commenced on behalf of victims. In the meantime, India enacted the Bhopal Gas Leak Disaster Act, granting to its government (the Union of India [UOI]), the exclusive right to represent the victims in India or elsewhere. In April 1985, the Indian government filed a complaint in the Southern District of New York on behalf of all of the victims. India's decision to bring suit in the United States was attributed to the fact that although nearly 6,500 lawsuits had been instituted by victims in India against UCIL, the Indian courts did not have jurisdiction over UCC, the parent company. UCC contended that the actions are properly tried in the courts of India on the doctrine of *forum non conveniens*, The district court dismissed the action on the condition that UCC submit to the jurisdiction of the Indian courts and that UCC agree to satisfy any judgment taken against it in the courts of India.]

MANSFIELD, Circuit Judge

As the district court found, the record shows that the private interests of the respective parties weigh heavily in favor of dismissal on grounds of *forum non conveniens*. The many witnesses and sources of proof are almost entirely located in India, where the accident occurred, and could not be compelled to appear for trial in the United States. The Bhopal plant at the time of the accident was operated by some 193 Indian nationals, including the managers of seven operating units employed by the Agricultural Products Division of UCIL, who reported to Indian Works Managers in Bhopal. The plant was maintained by seven functional departments employing over 200 more Indian nationals. UCIL kept at the plant daily, weekly, and monthly records of plant operations and records of maintenance, as well as records of the plant's Quality Control, Purchasing, and Stores branches, all operated by Indian employees. The great majority of documents bearing on the design, safety, start-up, and operation of the plant, as well as the safety training of the plant's employees, is located in India. Proof to be offered at trial would be derived from interviews of these witnesses in India and study of the records located there to determine whether the accident was caused by negligence on the part of the management or employees in the operation of the plant, by fault in its design, or by sabotage. In short, India has greater ease of access to the proof than does the United States.

The plaintiffs seek to prove that the accident was caused by negligence on the part of UCC in originally contributing to the design of the plant and its provision for storage of excessive amounts of the gas at the plant. As Judge Keenan found, however, UCC's participation was limited, and its involvement in plant operations terminated long before the accident. Under 1973 agreements negotiated at arm's length with UCIL, UCC did provide a summary "process design package" for construction of the plant and the services of some of its technicians to monitor the progress of UCIL in detailing the design and erecting the plant. However, the UOI controlled the terms of the agreements and precluded UCC from exercising any authority to "detail design, erect, and commission the plant," which was done independently over the period from 1972 to 1980 by UCIL process design engineers who supervised, among many others, some 55 to 60 Indian engineers employed by the Bombay engineering firm of Humphreys and Glasgow. The preliminary process design information furnished by UCC could not have been used to construct the plant. Construction required the detailed process design and engineering data prepared by hundreds of Indian engineers, process designers, and subcontractors. During the ten years spent constructing the plant, its design and configuration underwent many changes.

The vital parts of the Bhopal plant, including its storage tank, monitoring instrumentation, and vent gas scrubber, were manufactured by Indians in India. Although some 40 UCIL employees were given some safety training at UCC's plant in West Virginia, they represented a small fraction of the Bhopal plant's employees. The vast majority of plant employees were selected and trained by UCIL in Bhopal. The manual for start-up of the Bhopal plant was prepared by Indians employed by UCIL.

In short, the plant has been constructed and managed by Indians in India. No Americans were employed at the plant at the time of the accident. In the five years from 1980 to 1984, although more than 1,000 Indians were employed at the plant, only one American was employed there and he left in 1982. No Americans visited the plant for more than one year prior to the accident, and during the five-year period before the accident the communications between the plant and the United States were almost nonexistent.

The vast majority of material witnesses and documentary proof bearing on causation of and liability for the accident is located in India, not the United States, and would be more accessible to an Indian court than to a United States court. The records are almost entirely in Hindi or other Indian languages, understandable to an Indian court without translation. The witnesses for the most part do not speak English but Indian languages understood by an Indian court but not by an American court. These witnesses could be required to appear in an Indian court but not in a court of the United States. Although witnesses in the United States could not be subpoenaed to appear in India, they are comparatively few in number and most are employed by UCC, which, as a party, would produce them in India, with lower overall transportation costs than if the parties were to attempt to bring hundreds of Indian witnesses to the United States. Lastly, Judge Keenan properly concluded that an Indian court would be in a better position to direct and supervise a viewing of the Bhopal plant, which was sealed after the accident. Such a viewing could be of help to a court in determining liability issues.

After a thorough review, the district court concluded that the public interest concerns, like the private ones, also weigh heavily in favor of India as the situs for trial and disposition of the cases. The accident and all relevant events occurred in India. The victims, over 200,000 in number, are citizens of India and located there. The witnesses are almost entirely Indian citizens. The Union of India has a greater interest than does the United States in facilitating the trial and adjudication of the victims' claims. Despite the contentions of plaintiffs and amici that it would be in the public interest to avoid a "double standard" by requiring an American parent corporation (UCC) to submit to the jurisdiction of American courts, India has a stronger countervailing interest in adjudicating the claims in its courts according to its standards rather than having American values and standards of care imposed upon it.

India's interest is increased by the fact that it has for years treated UCIL as an Indian national, subjecting it to intensive regulations and governmental supervision of the construction, development, and operation of the Bhopal plant, its emissions, water and air pollution, and safety precautions. Numerous Indian government officials have regularly conducted on-site inspections of the plant and approved its machinery and equipment, including its facilities for storage of the lethal methyl isocyanate gas that escaped and caused the disaster giving rise to the claims. Thus, India has considered the plant to be an Indian one and the disaster to be an Indian problem. It therefore has a deep interest in ensuring compliance with its safety standards. Moreover, plaintiffs have conceded that in view of India's strong interest and its greater contacts with the plant, its operations, its employees, and the victims of the accident, the law of India, as the place where the tort occurred, will undoubtedly govern.

* * *

The district court's dismissal of the actions against Union Carbide Corporation is upheld. The doctrine of *forum non conveniens* is a rule of U.S. law, which states that where a case is properly heard in more than one court, it should be heard by the one that is most convenient. Given the facts of this case, the courts of India are the more convenient forum.

[When the case was heard in India, the plaintiffs did not try to argue that Union Carbide's liability was based on the traditional English law principle of *Respondeat Superior*, which says that the superior is liable for the torts of the agent. Instead, it premised the parent company's liability on a new "single-enterprise" theory: the fact that the company was a multinational corporation with a "global purpose, organization, structure, and financial resources," and that it was therefore responsible for the torts of its subsidiaries, as one entity. India contended that a parent company should maintain a multinational financial responsibility for the acts of its subsidiaries. Union Carbide claimed that it was protected by the long-standing rules relating to the limited liability of corporate enterprises. These questions were not addressed by the Indian courts here; however, later cases seem to show that Indian law is headed toward the single-enterprise theory. International lawyers fear that unlimited liability for the acts of affiliate corporations would be a strong disincentive to foreign investment in India.

[In 1989, the Supreme Court of India approved a settlement fund of $470 million to compensate the victims of the disaster.]

Discussion Questions

1. Why did the court hold in favor of the Indian forum for settlement of this dispute?
2. Was this a reasonable means of resolving the issues of *forum non conveniens* in this dispute?
3. Are these kinds of problems likely to become more frequent occurrences in the future?
4. What would happen if Union Carbide refused to submit to Indian jurisdiction?

Extraterritorial Effects of Competition Laws

As has been previously discussed, U.S. courts have been willing to recognize extraterritorial effects of the Sherman Antitrust Act, which prohibits collusion in restraint of trade or monopolistic practices. The intent of this legislation is to protect the consumer by ensuring the functioning of competition. Anticompetitive behavior abroad may well adversely affect the price of goods in the United States. The remedies provided in U.S. law include civil litigation by any adversely affected corporation, which may sue the violator for triple damages. Actions may also be instituted by the federal government against violations of the antitrust law.

The federal courts started with a limited concept of applying the antitrust law extraterritorially when the effects of the monopolistic practice are felt in the United States (effects test). The evolutionary development of federal practice of applying extraterritorial jurisdiction to U.S. antitrust law has produced heated criticism in the courts and legislatures of other countries. At one point in this development, the courts were even willing to allow a foreign corporation to sue another foreign corporation in U.S. courts for violation of the Sherman Antitrust Act even though no U.S. companies or U.S. consumers were directly affected by any of the acts in question. By the 1970s, some federal courts of appeal had become critical of the earlier effects test developed by Judge Learned Hand, and they began to modify it. The earlier test formulated by Judge Hand had failed to take into account the legitimate interests of foreign nations, and the appeals courts began to develop the "jurisdictional rule of reason" that took into account (a) whether there was some effect on U.S. commerce, (b) whether the restraint was of a type and magnitude to be considered a violation of the U.S. antitrust laws, and (c) the comity interests of the United States in antitrust enforcement.

The U.S. Congress attempted its own solution in 1982 when it enacted the Foreign Trade Antitrust Improvements Act that essentially adopted the effects test and sought to clarify the standard to be applied in determining the extraterritorial effect of

U.S. antitrust laws. The act provides that U.S. antitrust law does not apply to conduct, unless such conduct has a "direct, substantial, and reasonably foreseeable effect on United States commerce or on the business of a person engaged in exporting goods from the United States to foreign nations." These clarifications and tests have not resulted in unanimity in the practical application by the federal courts. However, it is clear that all U.S. judges are unanimous in their acceptance of some form of the effects test.

In international law, the farthest reach of accepted territorial jurisdiction is the principle of objective territoriality, which will be discussed more fully in later chapters. Under the objective principle, a State may exercise jurisdiction over conduct commenced outside its territory when the act or effect of the act is physically completed inside its territory. However, other nations have vigorously resisted extension of this effects test beyond physical effects in the host country and limited to consequences that result in that nation, such as the effects from anticompetitive conduct. This more limited European effects test has meant that companies can conspire to limit competition in exports to a nation without that nation's being able to claim jurisdiction over the conspiracy. In Germany, for example, each *exportkartell* unifies the marketing power of German corporations in a single industry for potent export activity outside the Common Market.

The controversy between U.S. antitrust policy and those of other countries has been brewing for some forty years. After an antitrust action brought by the Justice Department against the uranium production industry involving foreign producers, several countries produced **blocking legislation** to attempt to curb the extraterritorial effect of U.S. antitrust legislation. A U.S. producer alleged that uranium producers outside the United States had formed a cartel to raise the price of uranium. When the producer sought discovery against foreign producers to document its charges, foreign nations protested. They asserted that this litigation was an attempt by the United States to enforce its economic policies abroad. Canada, Australia, France, the Netherlands, New Zealand, Switzerland, Germany, and the United Kingdom enacted blocking legislation designed to prevent discovery of documents located in their countries and bar the enforcement of foreign judgments there. In addition, some of these countries included "clawback" provisions under which the foreign companies can sue in their own country to recover against local U.S. assets all or part of the amount of an antitrust judgment rendered in the United States.

> **Blocking legislation:** Statutes enacted in some countries designed to block the use of foreign courts by their nationals or to deny discovery powers and bar enforcement of foreign judgments under certain conditions.

The controversy reached its peak in the early 1980s when these blocking statutes came into play during the Laker Airways antitrust litigation. The liquidators for Laker Airways alleged that a combination and conspiracy in restraint of trade had caused Laker's bankruptcy, and they sued for a sum in excess of $1 billion (U.S. $350 million in compensatory and $700 million in punitive triple damages). This clash of national courts produced numerous legal actions and counteractions both here and in the United Kingdom.

The federal district court accepted jurisdiction, and then the Court of Appeals in the United Kingdom invoked its blocking statute, known as the British Protection of Trading Interests Act, to prohibit Laker (a national of the United Kingdom) from further participation in the U.S. legal action and prohibiting discovery in the United Kingdom. In a well-reasoned federal appeals court decision, *Laker Airways v. Sabena, Belgian World Airlines* (731 F.2d 909 [1984]), the court upheld the district court's preliminary judgment and held that (a) both the United States and the United Kingdom shared concurrent prescriptive jurisdiction over transactions giving rise to the antitrust plaintiff's claim and (b) principles of comity and concurrent jurisdiction authorized defensive preliminary injunction designed to permit the United States claim to go forward in the U.S. court free of foreign interference consisting of English proceedings designed solely to rob the U.S. court of its jurisdiction.

What occurred in the Laker Airways case was tantamount to international legal warfare. The blocking actions on the part of European countries were partially successful in the end. However, subsequent developments have produced some movement on the part of U.S. courts in the direction of becoming more careful in their application of the extraterritorial effects test in antitrust actions that may offend other nations. The EC and other nations have begun a spirited effort to beef up their own antitrust laws. There are still controversial differences between U.S. and EC policies concerning mergers and conspiracies in restraint of trade, but these two competing giants in the world economy are beginning to reconcile their differences.

∎   ∎   ∎

Chapter Summary

1. Intellectual property rights include copyrights, patents, trademarks, and know-how. Copyrights are distinguished from patents in that patents are a national grant of a monopoly for a fixed period to promote inventions. Copyrights protect authors of tangible works from the reproduction or alteration of the work without license from the author. Trademarks are identifying marks that characterize a particular product or service, and know-how is practical expertise acquired from study, training, and experience.

2. These forms of intellectual property are protected in most societies by national policies, although the form and extent of protection varies considerably from State to State. International efforts to secure protection of these rights has advanced considerably in modern times through multilateral treaty instruments and creation of IGOs with administrative responsibilities in this area of international law. These treaties tend to group intellectual property rights into artistic property rights and industrial rights and treat them separately.

3. Artistic property rights involve copyright protection that is regulated internationally by two major conventions. The earlier Berne Convention (1886) recognized not only pecuniary rights (entitling the author to exploit a work for economic gain) but also moral rights (entitling the author to protection against modification and nonrecognition of creative rights). Common law countries have had difficulty recognizing moral rights

and formed the Universal Copyright Convention in 1952. These two conventions are quite similar in many respects and the United States is a party to both.

4. Industrial rights include patents, trademarks, and know-how. Patents are governmental grants of protection and therefore must be recognized in each State to secure such rights. Several multilateral treaties have been developed to facilitate the filing for patent protection in other countries. Trademarks identify rights acquired by use and registration and protect against fraud and deception. These rights have also been recognized through international treaty obligations. However, know-how is protected through contractual agreements between private parties that may be enforced in the courts as contracts.

5. The World Intellectual Property Organization (WIPO) now administers most of the major international agreements in the field of intellectual property rights. This U.N. agency continues to promote new agreements and has just opened a new Center for Arbitration of Intellectual Property Disputes that will facilitate settlement of these disputes.

6. The U.N. Educational, Scientific and Cultural Organization (UNESCO) administers the Universal Copyright Convention (UCC), which is the most widely recognized and offers the most liberal form of identifying a protected work. The new World Trade Organization and the U.N. Conference on Trade and Development (UNCTAD) are engaged in efforts to promote new measures for the harmonization of mechanisms to promote protection of intellectual property rights.

7. The subject of technology transfers is perhaps the major issue separating developing nations and the developed nations in trade matters. The more industrially developed States seek to protect assumed proprietary rights to their advanced technology, and the less developed States argue that such rights inhibit development of their own economies and are remnants of colonial dependency.

8. Intellectual property piracy is alleged to be rampant in many countries of the developing world where these countries either view technology transfers as part of their development strategy or choose not to oppose it. However, the efforts of developed nations are slowly securing changes in these practices through systematic application of customs and trade sanctions. The U.S. Congress has authorized the International Trade Commission to recommend seizure of illegal goods entering the United States, and the president has authority to take such action under the Tariff Act as revised by the Trade and Competitiveness Act of 1988. Various U.S. statutes authorize the president to withhold trade benefits from nations inadequately protecting the intellectual property rights of U.S. citizens.

9. The criteria for gaining the benefits of a patent in the United States include novelty, inventiveness, and industrial utility. Exclusive right to production is granted for seventeen years. However, international agreements allow citizens of other countries to apply for patents in this country.

10. The Patent Cooperation Treaty now provides greater uniformity and lower cost in filing patents by setting up regional locations for filing and the international patent application, which is communicated to the member State patent offices through a coordinated system. The European Patent Convention and the EC Patent Convention create a single community patent valid throughout the countries of the new European Union.

11. The U.S. Congress has created criminal offenses and private triple damages remedies for trademark counterfeiting, and the courts have even applied injunctive remedies against U.S. citizens who violate their contractual agreements and engage in deceptive practices abroad.

12. Copyright protection extends for fifty years after the death of the author in U.S. law, and infringers may be subject to criminal penalties, injunctive relief, and civil damages. Under the UCC international agreement, foreigners do not have to register, provided they give notice of a claim by the symbol ©. The ratification of both UCC and the Berne Convention by the United States in 1989 has extended the benefits of both these treaties to U.S. copyright holders.

13. Most modern nations have some form of product liability laws that attempt to discourage manufacturers from putting defective products into the marketplace. Private legal actions in contract, negligence, and strict liability are the basic means of consumer protection. Japan and most of the developing nations of the world, however, do not accept the strict liability concept. Most other modern industrialized nations provide a special liability that does not require proof of breach of duty of care in gaining compensation for injuries sustained by defective products. Other more consumer-protective doctrines in negligence also provide benefits that go beyond those of Japan and most developing societies.

14. The courts in the United States have been the most willing to apply their unfair competition laws and product liability laws extraterritorially. A product manufactured abroad and imported into the United States is subject to the same liability as products manufactured in this country. Courts in the United States have also held that a U.S. manufacturer or seller of defective products sold abroad can be held liable for damages sustained in this country. These actions may, however, be limited by the doctrines of *in personam* jurisdiction and *forum non conveniens*.

15. A U.S. constitutional interpretation of the due process clause also prevents a defendant from being required to answer to legal action filed in a forum where the defendant does not have minimal contacts or where that party could not have anticipated legal liability.

16. U.S. state and federal courts have allowed access to foreign plaintiffs in liability suits against U.S. firms, requiring these firms to exercise responsibility for damages incurred abroad.

17. Extraterritorial enforcement of the Sherman Antitrust Act and other national legislation has been exercised by U.S. courts when the illegal action was commenced in a foreign country but the effect of this action can be found to take place in the United States. The general principle of objective territorial jurisdiction in international law allows such enforcement. However, the U.S. effects test is severely objected to by other countries.

18. Several modern nation-states—Canada, Australia, France, the Netherlands, New Zealand, Switzerland, Germany, and the United Kingdom—have enacted blocking statutes designed to prevent enforcement of extreme forms of the U.S. effects practices. These statutes have been used to prevent the nationals of these States from suing in U.S. courts under certain circumstances and to deny requests for discovery powers in their jurisdictions.

Key Terms

copyrights
patent
Berne Convention
(1886)
moral rights
trademarks
know-how
World Intellectual
Property Organiza-
tion (WIPO)
Universal Copyright
Convention (UCC)

Code of Conduct on
the Transfer of
Technology
Group of 77
International Trade
Commission (ITC)
novelty
inventiveness
industrial utility
inventor's certificate
petty patent
registration

examination
Patent Cooperation
Treaty (PCT)
fair use doctrine
strict liability
diversity jurisdiction
long-arm statutes
minimal contacts
in personam jurisdiction
forum non conveniens
blocking legislation

▮   ▮   ▮

Discussion Questions

1. What are the major intellectual property rights recognized by most nation-states today? What are their basic differences?

2. What are the major artistic property right conventions and how do they differ from each other? How does U.S. ratification of both of these conventions affect U.S. holders of copyrights?

3. What major treaties have facilitated the registration of patents and trademarks? How have they facilitated international protection of these rights?

4. What are the major issues causing disagreement between the developing societies and the industrially developed societies concerning protection of intellectual property rights?

5. How can agreements between developing countries and international corporations result in contractual agreements to share technology?

6. What measures are available in the United States to counteract intellectual property piracy regarding illegal goods coming into the United States? How about counterfeit goods sold in other countries?

7. What legal actions are possible in the United States for damages sustained from defective products produced in the United States but sold abroad? What about products produced abroad and sold in the United States?

8. What is meant by the "effects doctrine" in application of antitrust actions to conspiracies in restraint of trade? Why are other countries concerned about this form of extraterritorial application of our laws?

Suggested Readings

Folsom, R. H., Gordon, M. W., & Spanogle, J. A. (1992). *International business transactions* (4th ed.). St. Paul, MN: West.

Internet Sources

Browse: Use *International trade law* and *intellectual property law.*

For information on WIPO (http://www.wipo.org). Also available through the U.N. Homepage (http://www.un.org//).

U.S. Department of Commerce (http://www.doc.gov/).

7 International Labor Regulation

The modern international community is increasingly involved in a unique form of coordinating activities among nations that is similar to the familiar regulatory activities of individual nations. Indeed, the cooperation of national regulatory agencies is necessary to carry out these international regulatory functions. Successful cooperation in functional areas such as the International Telecommunication Union (ITU) and the International Civil Aviation Organization (ICAO) has established regulatory regimes that are essential elements linking the international community. These vital areas of international cooperation have demonstrated that domestic sovereignty can be retained while engaging in functional cooperation on the international plane.

The ITU was founded in 1865 and is the oldest intergovernmental organization (IGO). In 1947, it became a specialized agency of the United Nations and now has a membership of 164 countries. It is the international organization responsible for (a) the regulation and planning of telecommunications worldwide, (b) the estab-lishment of equipment and systems operating standards, (c) the coordination and dissemination of information required for the planning and operation of telecommunications services, and (d) the promotion of, and contribution to, the development of telecommunications and related infrastructures.

The ICAO was established in 1947 after the ratification of the Convention on International Civil Aviation, which now has been ratified by 162 countries. The regulatory activities of the ICAO are designed to ensure the safe and orderly growth of international civil aviation throughout the world.

Regulation in the areas of human rights, labor, and environmental concerns is more controversial, and nation-states have been more sensitive to the domestic political implications of any attempt to impose global standards. This chapter will focus on developments in the area of international labor law since it is the area of international regulation with the longest historical development. The next chapter will discuss a newer area of international regulation involving environmental law. Both of these subjects are quite complex and evolutionary in their development. Historical development of international norms in these areas provide an agreed normative "floor" below which national constitutional norms may not fall. These norms also have logical consequences. Prohibition of slavery and slave trade has the obvious implication, for example, that forced labor is also prohibited. It also follows logically that collective bargaining and minimum standards of working conditions are necessary to enforce these international norms.

The International Labor Organization (ILO) is generally credited with having developed the most effective review methods among the global organizations. Since its creation in 1919, this organization has pioneered in safeguarding human rights through a gradual process of institutionalizing and coordinating efforts to implement the vague provisions of the Universal Declaration of Human Rights and the covenants involving general principles of political, economic, and social rights. Norms of customary international environmental law are widely recognized, and a bewildering array of international environmental organizations and agencies have been developed in the past twenty years. The U.N. Environment Program (UNEP) was created in 1972 as a result of the important Stockholm global conference on the environment. This agency is therefore much newer than the ILO and has not yet achieved the degree of coordination exemplified by the ILO.

Individual State policies vary widely in the areas of labor and environmental protection legislation and enforcement through municipal regulatory agencies. These differences are inherent in the concept of sovereignty and self-determination of nations. International regulatory activity seeks to promote minimal standards and coopera-tion among nations to reduce international conflict and to promote compliance with universal norms. States retain their sovereignty and independence through the general principle of international law that a State is free to act unless its action infringes on the rights of other States or it has specifically agreed to a limitation on its sovereignty.

International Labor Standards

The Universal Declaration of Human Rights is a general expression of these fundamental principles adopted in 1948 by the General Assembly of the United Nations Organization. The U.N. Commission on Human Rights drafted the more specific International Covenant on Economic, Social and Cultural Rights containing thirty-one articles that were approved by the General Assembly in 1966 for ratification by individual States. By 1985, more than eighty nations had ratified this more specific set of treaty obligations binding nation-states to certain human rights protections in various areas, including labor relations.

The ILO has played a major role in gradually building a body of law known as the **International Labor Code** through the development of conventions and recommendations to be adopted by member States. This body of law began with the adoption of six conventions and six recommendations by the first International Labor Conference in 1919 and today consists of more than 170 conventions and more than 180 recommendations. The United States has not been the most active

> **International Labor Code:** The body of law sponsored by the ILO that consists of more than 170 conventions and more than 180 recommendations limiting State practices in the field of labor relations.

supporter of these developments and has ratified only eleven of these conventions, whereas France, Spain, and Italy have ratified more than one hundred of them. The subjects covered by the International Labor Code are diverse, but they are considered a comprehensive charter of workers' rights. The most fundamental standards dealt with in the International Labor Code include the right to organize and bargain collectively, and prohibition of slavery or forced labor. The code also includes standards that regulate hours of work, wages, unemployment, worker's compensation benefits, and safety. Many parts of the code give protection to special categories of workers, especially women, young people, miners, and seamen. The number of new ratifications of these conventions is increasing rapidly. The current membership in the ILO is approximately 166 countries.

The International Covenant on Economic, Social and Cultural Rights is included in Appendix F of this text and should be read to gain an understanding of the various areas of labor interest that are included in this statement of general principles.

The United Nations has sponsored a draft Convention on the Elimination of All Forms of Discrimination Against Women, including employment discrimination. Some of these principles may be considered binding through the avenue of customary practice of nations regarded as legally binding. Hence, although the United States has never ratified these particular treaties, the U.S. Congress, through enactment of its trade laws, now requires the president to determine the existence of "internationally recognized workers' rights" before granting tariff and other benefits to a particular country. Some of these rights that are defined by U.S. statute include (a) a right of association, (b) a right of organization and

collective bargaining, (c) a right to be free of forced or compulsory labor, (d) minimum employment ages for children, and (e) acceptable working conditions.

The ILO has the primary goal of improving working conditions and living standards and ensuring the fair and equitable treatment of workers in all countries. It carries out its objectives by issuing recommended labor standards, organizing conferences to draft international labor conventions, monitoring compliance with its recommendations and its conventions, and providing technical assistance to member States. Its institutional structure is made up of the General Conference, which acts as a legislative body, approving conventions and adopting recommendations. The Governing Body serves as the executive authority, and there is an International Labor Office headed by a director-general who functions as the organization's secretariat. The membership of the General Conference is made up of the representatives of each member State. Each national delegation includes four representatives: two from government, one representing labor, and one representing employers.

ILO Compliance Procedures

ILO member States are required to provide annual reports to verify their compliance with the conventions they have ratified. Special reports may be required when solicited by the director-general to provide information on both recommendations and unratified conventions. These reports provide information concerning the statutory legislation and administrative regulations of the country, interpretation of these materials to show how they give effect to the provisions of international standards, and what actions are being taken to bring the country into compliance, including an explanation of the reasons for noncompliance.

The ILO Committee of Experts on the Application of Conventions and Recommendations evaluates these national reports and indicates the extent to which the parties have complied with their obligations. This committee includes individuals from the judiciary and academia who have a reputation for being impartial, independent, and knowledgeable of international labor law. The Committee of Experts prepares an annual summary of the national reports that is then reviewed by the General Conference.

A special list of governments that have defaulted on their obligations to the ILO is then prepared by the Conference Committee on the Application of Conventions and Recommendations. This list contains seven categories of deficiencies. Six deal with the failure of particular governments to submit reports, respond to requests for information, or participate in discussions concerning an alleged failure to comply with an ILO convention obligation. The seventh and most serious alleges that certain governments have failed to fully implement one or more of the ILO conventions they have ratified.

This **ILO compliance procedure** places pressure on individual States to make progress toward compliance with international labor standards. One of the most memorable sessions of the General Conference occurred in 1974 when the Soviet Union was named in Category 7 for an alleged breach of the 1930 Convention Concerning Forced or Compulsory Labor. The alleged reasons for this breach included the contention that the Soviet laws did not allow a collective farm laborer to quit work without the permission

> **ILO compliance procedure:** Requires annual reports from member States, evaluation of degree of compliance with international standards, and imposes sanctions designed to bring a member State into compliance.

of the farm's management. After lengthy and heated debate, the General Conference was unable to obtain a quorum when a vote was called and the special list was not adopted. This development ultimately led to the withdrawal of the United States from the ILO in protest in 1977.

This action on the part of the United States had a dramatic impact on the ILO. U.S. funding of the organization was also withdrawn, and this decline in resources led to some important changes. By 1980, when the United States rejoined the ILO, a strengthened functioning of the process had censured the Soviet Union, adopted the use of secret ballots, defeated an anti-Israeli resolution, begun screening out resolutions that violated ILO procedures, and reduced the number of meetings dealing with political affairs (Moy, 1988).

Ironically, the communist workers' States have been the most serious violators of basic international labor standards. The Western European countries have been the most protective of international labor standards and have developed innovative policies that support and enhance workers' rights. Advancements in the general field of human rights also include measures to protect the fundamental rights of workers. Outside the ILO framework, one of the major developments of the latter half of the twentieth century involved the **Conference on Security and Cooperation in Europe (CSCE),** which was convened in Helsinki in 1973. Two years later, the Final Act of the Conference was signed by 35 nations, including the countries of Western and Eastern Europe as well as the United States and Canada. Although

> **Conference on Security and Cooperation in Europe (CSCE):** Includes some thirty-five countries of Eastern and Western Europe, Canada, and the United States. It has become a consultative institution promoting cooperation between the East and West since the Helsinki Final Act in 1975.

the **Helsinki Final Act** was not a treaty and not meant by the parties to be legally binding, it represented a firm commitment on the part of the Soviet leadership to respect fundamental human rights. The analogy between the Final Act and the Universal Declaration of Human Rights is striking. Mikhail Gorbechev's commitment to respect human rights and to promote "the effective exercise of civil, political, economic, social, cultural and other rights and freedoms" (see Article 26[2] of the International Labor Organization Constitution) was taken as a signal by workers and other groups within the communist bloc countries that they would be permitted finally to exercise these basic rights. This development made a significant contribution to the ultimate breakup of the Soviet Union and the movements in the former communist countries of Eastern Europe to overthrow communist regimes.

Since the breakup of the USSR, the ILO has undertaken a major effort to revitalize the organization and develop more effective means of enforcement of the recognized standards of international labor law. A member State may file complaints "if it is not satisfied that any other member is securing the effective observance of any convention which both have ratified." The Governing Body may appoint a commission of inquiry to consider the complaint and to report its findings. Few such fact-finding commissions have been appointed, and even the obligation to comply requires that the State against whom the complaint is filed and the party making the complaint be parties to the two important labor conventions: the Convention Concerning Freedom of Association (No. 87) and the Convention Concerning the Application of Principles of the Right to Organize and to Bargain Collectively (No. 98). It is important to note that the United States has not ratified either of these major conventions.

The major device for encouraging adherence to the standards of the International Labor Code is to seek changes in national legislation to bring it into harmony with the code. Between 1964 and 1994, more than 1,850 changes in national legislation were attributed to efforts of national governments to bring national law into conformity with provisions of conventions in response to observations made by ILO supervisory bodies (Bennett, 1995, p. 360). The more advanced industrial countries are the most prominent contributors to development of the International Labor Code; however, the ILO's work in technical assistance and economic development is of primary significance to the developing nations. Developing nations now make up 70% of the ILO membership. More than half of all ILO activity is in the area of providing this needed technical assistance.

In the area of research and information the ILO is the only comprehensive organization capable of acting as a research and information agency in the field of labor data. The organization has also become heavily involved in the field of education and training. In its current program the ILO stresses the following themes: (a) standard setting and human rights, (b) employment promotion, (c) training, (d) industrial relations and labor administration, (e) working conditions and environment, (f) industrial sectoral activities, (g) social security, and (h) services to employers' and workers' organizations (Bennett, 1995, p. 362)

International labor regulation illustrates the unique concept of cooperative establishment of minimal international standards through institutionalized processes developed by international agencies (IGOs). These agencies have been created by legally binding treaty obligations, and their functions involve encouragement of compliance with international norms. Individual States are free to develop their own unique labor policies as long as they do not fall below the minimal international standards. Although the international norms developed through treaty obligations are the legal basis for these institutions and provide vague guidelines for the development of standards for regulatory practice, the "recommendations" of the ILO (or other IGOs) are similar to the **rulemaking** function familiar to domestic regulatory agencies.

Rule making: The rule-making process in the United States is characterized by authority given to regulatory agencies to spell out the detailed regulations and standards. This authority is limited by enabling acts, legislative grants of authority, and administrative procedures.

However, in the field of international regulation, there is an additional step in the regulatory process. Recommendations are not directly enforced by the IGO but must be adopted by individual States, either through changes in legislation or in alterations of their own domestic rule-making process. Involvement of specific representatives of the national regulatory agencies in international conferences dealing with areas of noncompliance and development of new standards ensures understanding of the problems involved both in implementation at the national level and the need to harmonize regulatory practices to meet international standards. Increasingly, this process also involves nongovernmental organizations (NGOs) in the deliberations of conferences in what could be considered **public comment sessions**. The detailed implementation of administrative decisions requires knowledge of how particular interests will be affected by these decisions, and the NGOs bring particular expertise to these deliberations.

Public comment sessions: Part of the typical procedure involved in the domestic rule-making process. This allows interested private parties to make input.

The pioneering achievements of the ILO in the field of international labor relations and the success of the functional unions in bringing about significant cooperation among nations has established a pattern, or model, that is now broadly used by most IGOs.

International Regimes and Soft Law

It is common to refer to the extraordinary development and proliferation of intergovernmental agencies as creating legal regimes that exemplify differentiated degrees of legally binding characteristics. Essentially, international law is created by treaty and specific agreement to accept legally binding limitations on individual State sovereignty. However, traditional international law also accepts customary practice of States regarded as legally binding as an instrument of change in the law. In the areas of international labor regulation and environmental regulation, as well as many others, a wide variety of instruments ranging from unratified treaties, some of which never enter into force, through executive agreements, to codes of practice, recommendations, guidelines, standards, and declarations of principles are involved. None of these instruments fits neatly into any of the established sources of international law. "They are often referred to as 'soft law,' as opposed to the binding 'hard law' represented by custom, treaty and established general principles of law" (Birnie & Boyle, 1992, p. 16).

The **soft-law** concept has inherent advantages in the evolving areas of labor and environmental regulation where States are thus able to tackle a problem collectively at a time when they do not want too strictly to shackle their freedom of action. This might be because scientific evidence is not conclusive or complete or because the economic costs are uncertain or overburdensome. Although enforcement of these soft-law instruments in a judicial sense may present difficulties, it is a more flexible approach to progressive development of State practices that promote defined goals. Some of these practices may rapidly become customary practice regarded as legally binding, and others may mature into specific treaty obligations.

> *Soft law:* A term used to describe practices of IGOs and individual States that are not necessarily legally binding but may be in the formative stages of law development (lex ferenda) as opposed to "hard law" (opinio juris).

Employment Laws in Other Countries

Laws of individual nations vary considerably, and U.S. investors are discovering that when they acquire a foreign business or engage in a joint venture, they must comply with restraints on employee dismissal that are completely unfamiliar in the U.S. context.

The European Community, now known as the European Union, has adopted the principle of equal pay for equal work, or **comparable worth,** which is an unsettled and very controversial issue in U.S. law. The People's Republic of China requires equal pay for foreign and Chinese managers of joint ventures located in China. For example, a foreign investor may enter into a joint venture by combining with a national of the host country to create a new entity or by acquiring a portion of an existing local entity. These and many more distinctions exist in comparative labor law in individual countries.

> *Comparable worth:* Various schemes to guarantee equal pay for all persons who do the same work regardless of sex, age, race, and so on.

Many nations require employee consultation or participation in management decisions. In many continental European countries, workers have been granted a right of consultation about or notice before the implementation of decisions resulting in workforce reductions.

The German development of its "Social Market Economy" after World War II provided a significant innovation in workers' rights through a policy known as *Mitbestemung,* or **codetermination.** By law, each plant with more than five employees must have a *Betriebsrat* (works council) to represent that plant's interest. These works councils are independent from trade unions.

> *Codetermination:* The national policy, initiated in Germany, that requires representation of workers on the boards of directors of most businesses.

Under the German Works Constitution Act, the employer has a duty to fully inform the works council in "due time" of any plant changes that might result in "substantial disadvantages for employees" and consult with it on such proposals. The German law also provides for mandatory employee representation on the boards of directors of most firms. Those employing more than two thousand workers must establish an *Aufsichtsrat* half composed of labor representatives and half of shareholder representatives. In companies with more than 500 workers, one-third of the *Aufsichtsrat* must be composed of workers. These policies have been instituted in the Netherlands and Luxembourg as well.

Europeans, as well as the Japanese, have adopted strong tendencies to regard workers as acquiring a **proprietary interest** in their jobs when held for a considerable length of time. Thus, the more senior the employee is, the greater the acquired proprietary interest. Severance pay is considered compensation for this proprietary interest. In the United Kingdom and Germany, an employer must consult with the appropriate trade union or works council about dismissals. In Germany, these decisions can be appealed to a labor court.

> **Proprietary interest:** The interest of an owner of property and the rights that an owner of property has by virtue of that ownership.

Regional Integration in the European Union

One of the most important aspects of the European Community treaties involves **freedom of movement** of workers and self-employed persons among the member States of the community. This concept also forms the very basis of the American union achieved by the U.S. Constitution in 1789. In Europe, the process of achievement of this basic goal has been accomplished gradually over the years since the Rome Treaty defined the ultimate objectives of an integrated economy. The European Coal and Steel Community Treaty forbids any restrictions based on nationality in the employment of qualified workers in the coal and steel industries, and similar provisions characterize the European Atomic Energy Community Treaty.

Much broader provisions are found in the treaty creating the European Economic Community (EEC). The EEC Treaty is meant to promote the comprehensive economic integration of its member States, and it accordingly provides that "freedom of movement for workers shall be secured within the Community," that "restrictions on the freedom of establishment (or entrepreneurs) shall be abolished," and that "restrictions on the freedom to provide services" by self-employed persons "shall be . . . abolished."

> **Freedom of movement:** The right to move across State borders to take up residence and seek employment.

Various directives by the Council of Ministers guarantee workers and their families the right to leave their own country and to enter any other member State, both to take up and to search for a job. These workers must produce an identity card or passport, but no exit or entry visa can be required. Moreover, Article 48(2) of the EEC Treaty states that workers who are citizens of a member State cannot be treated differently because of their nationality. Once a worker has found employment, the foreign worker is entitled to "enjoy the same social and tax advantages as national workers" and "to enjoy all the rights and benefits accorded to national workers in matters of housing, including the ownership of the housing he needs." Finally, foreign workers may not be treated differently in the manner in which they are dismissed or in their "reinstatement or re-employment" if they have become unemployed (Article 7).

There are three broad limitations on the right of workers to move freely across the borders of EU member States. They include restrictions on travel based on grounds of public policy, public security, and public health. These limitations apply only to the right to enter or leave a member State and not to the right of equal treatment once a worker has been admitted to a State.

The European Court of Justice has gradually narrowed the scope of these limitations and provided more precise meaning to them. Broad interpretation was at first noted in the case of *Van Duyn v. Home Office* in 1974. However, the very next year, in *Rutili v. French Minister of the Interior*, the Court stated that "restrictions cannot be imposed on the right of a national of any member State to enter the territory of another member State, to stay there [or] to move within it unless his presence or conduct constitutes a genuine and sufficiently serious threat to public policy." Then in 1977, the Court added that the genuine and serious threat had to affect "one of the fundamental interests of society." Finally, in 1981, the Court adopted the standards of the European Convention on Human Rights in defining the fundamental interest of society (August, 1993, p. 270).

An important limitation expressly recognized in the EEC Treaty, Article 48, is that "the provisions of this article shall not apply to employment in the public service." This does not prohibit foreign nationals from working in any job in public service, nor does it allow discrimination in such service areas. The public service limitation applies only to jobs that are related to the activity of governing. In an extended test case titled *Commission v. Belgium*, the European Court of Justice delivered its opinion in two parts. In Part I, 1980, the Court stated that "such posts in fact presume on the part of those occupying them the existence of a special relationship of allegiance to the State and reciprocity of rights and duties which form the foundation of the bond of nationality." Part 2 of the decision was delivered in 1982 and further delineated the division between service jobs and those related to the activity of governing by providing examples. Head technical office supervisor, principal supervisor, works supervisor, and stock controller for the municipalities of

Brussels and Auderghem fell within the group of governing employees exempted, and railway shunters, drivers, platelayers, signalmen and nightwatchmen, nurses, electricians, joiners, and plumbers employed by the same municipalities fell within the protected group.

Under the "right of establishment" and "freedom to provide services" these workers' rights were extended to the self-employed. These provisions of the EEC Treaty authorize a natural person or a company to settle in a member State and carry on a business. It includes the right to set up and carry on a business both as an individual and as an employer. The freedom to provide services relates to economic activity carried out on a temporary or nonpermanent basis. This provision covers consulting services that advise business in member States.

The European Court of Justice has interpreted these two provisions together and has generally regarded them as part of a general right of self-employed persons to pursue their activities throughout the community, regardless of the location of their principal office and regardless of the kind of economic endeavor they are involved in. The Council of Ministers has issued a number of directives to facilitate the free movement of self-employed persons. The EEC Treaty authorizes them to "issue directives for the mutual recognition of diplomas, certificates and other evidences of formal qualifications." Directives concerning persons engaged in the trades have been issued; however, the development of directives for the learned professions, such as law, medicine, and accounting, have been slow in finding agreement. Only in the medical field have directives appeared, setting minimum standards for medical training and requiring member States to recognize diplomas from other States satisfying those standards.

Guidelines for Multinational Enterprises and Termination of Employment

The Organization for Economic Cooperation and Development (OECD) has developed **Guidelines for Multinational Enterprises** (MNEs), establishing voluntary guidelines and minimal international standards. These guidelines include respect for employees' rights to be represented, organize, bargain collectively, and be informed. Employers are required to observe standards of the host country, to provide training and reasonable notice of layoffs and plant closures, to refrain from discriminatory practices, and to refrain from threats to close the plant while employees are exercising a right to organize. These guidelines have had some effect because they provide minimal international standards and put the company in an awkward position when dealing with local governments, local unions, and the international media.

> **Guidelines for Multinational Enterprises:** Developed by the OECD, which establishes voluntary guidelines and minimal international standards. Efforts have been made to make them mandatory by developing States but this has not yet been achieved.

The *Badger* case, which arose in 1979, has been considered a "historical precedent" in that it was the first time that the OECD guidelines were successfully used against an MNE operating in an OECD country. The case involved a U.S. MNE headquartered in Cambridge, Massachusetts, and owned by Raytheon, Inc. This corporation ordered the closure of its Belgian subsidiary, Badger Belgium N.V. The subsidiary did not supply adequate notice of the closing to the employees, and its assets

> **Badger case:** Illustrates successful implementation of OECD guidelines for MNEs through informal pressure and negotiated settlement.

were insufficient to satisfy the termination payments to which employees were entitled under Belgian law. As a result of international pressures, a successfully negotiated settlement was reached that was favorable to the Belgian employees.

In 1982, the ILO passed the **Convention on Termination of Employment**, which differs sharply from the common U.S. practices of management control. The convention promises to have a significant effect on MNE employee relations in countries outside the United States. Under the convention, employers must give dischargeable workers notice and a hearing before an impartial tribunal except in cases of criminal misconduct. Employers carry the burden of proof about reasons for the discharge and cannot terminate an employee because of race, sex, ethnic origin, affiliation with a union, or for protesting allegedly illegal MNE conduct. Workers are entitled to advice and counsel from unions, coverage for extended illness, access to certain business information, and prior consultation before certain MNE business judgments are made (see Folsom, Gordon, & Spanogle, 1992, pp. 295-296).

> **Convention on Termination of Employment:** Concluded in 1982 and promises to have significant effect on MNE employee relationships. Establishes legally binding obligations of member States. It has not been ratified by the United States.

U.S. Employment Discrimination Law

U.S. civil rights legislation creates the most comprehensive set of laws against employment discrimination. The reader will recall that in Chapter 5 the concept of treaty interpretation was illustrated. In *Sumitomo Shoji America, Inc. v. Avagliano*, the Supreme Court held that the Japan-United States Treaty of Friendship, Navigation and Commerce (FCN) could not be interpreted to exclude Japanese subsidiaries doing business in the United States from compliance with the 1964 Civil Rights Act prohibiting employment discrimination. However, Title VII of the Civil Rights Act, unlike most labor legislation, has been held on several occasions to apply extraterritorially to the foreign operations of U.S. employers.

Traditionally, most countries, including the United States, have refused to apply their labor laws extraterritorially. As long ago as 1804, in the case of *The Charming Betsy* (118 U.S. 64), the U.S. Supreme Court stated that the laws of the United States will not be interpreted to violate the laws of other nations unless no other interpretation is possible. Following this principle, the Supreme Court denied a Danish seaman's petition to have U.S. tort law apply to an injury he suffered on a Danish ship in Havana harbor (*Lauritzen v. Larsen* (345 U.S. 571 [1956]). The Court has also refused to give the National Labor Relations Board the authority to regulate collective bargaining among crewmen serving on foreign ships, and it has held that the Equal Pay Act does not apply outside the territorial jurisdiction of the United States.

Despite this body of case law to the contrary, the U.S. government, and particularly the Equal Employment Opportunity Commission (EEOC), began a concerted effort to apply U.S. labor laws to U.S. firms operating overseas. A confusing series of decisions in U.S. courts produced an interpretation that although Congress intended the Civil Rights Act not to apply to aliens employed by U.S. firms outside the territorial boundaries of the United States, that Congress must have meant to say that the act did apply to U.S. citizens employed abroad by U.S. firms. This "inferential logic" was adopted by several courts and by the EEOC in the 1980s. When the Fifth Circuit Court of Appeals expressly overruled this interpretation in *Ali Boureslan v. Arabian American Oil Company*, the EEOC appealed the decision to the Supreme Court.

In *EEOC v. Arabian American Oil Company*, the Court provided further clarification by upholding the Fifth Circuit's decision.

∎   ∎   ∎

Equal Employment Opportunity Commission v. Arabian American Oil Co. Et al.
United States Supreme Court, 1991.
499 U.S. 244.

CHIEF JUSTICE REHNQUIST delivered the opinion of the Court.

These cases present the issue whether Title VII applies extraterritorially to regulate the employment practices of United States employers who employ United States citizens abroad. The United States Court of Appeals for the Fifth Circuit held that it does not, and we agree with that conclusion.

Petitioner Boureslan is a naturalized United States citizen who was born in Lebanon. The respondents are two Delaware corporations, Arabian American Oil Company (Aramco), and its subsidiary, Aramco Service Company

(ASC). Aramco's principal place of business is Dhahran, Saudi Arabia, and it is licensed to do business in Texas. ASC's principal place of business is Houston, Texas.

In 1979, Boureslan was hired by ASC as a cost engineer in Houston. A year later he was transferred, at his request, to work for Aramco in Saudi Arabia. Boureslan remained with Aramco in Saudi Arabia until he was discharged in 1984. After filing a charge of discrimination with the Equal Employment Opportunity Commission (EEOC), he instituted this suit in the United States District Court for the Southern District of Texas against Aramco and ASC. He sought relief under both state law and Title VII of the Civil Rights Act of 1964, 78 Stat. 253, as amended, 42 U.S.C. § § 2000e17, on the ground that he was harassed and ultimately discharged by respondents on account of his race, religion, and national origin.

* * *

Both parties concede, as they must, that Congress has the authority to enforce its laws beyond the territorial boundaries of the United States. Cf. *Foley Bros., Inc. v. Filardo*, 336 U.S. 281, 284-285 (1949); *Benz v. Compania Naviera Hildalgo*, S.A., 353 U.S. 138, 147 (1957). Whether Congress has in fact exercised that authority in this case is a matter of statutory construction. It is our task to determine whether Congress intended the protections of Title VII to apply to United States citizens employed by American employers outside of the United States.

It is a long-standing principle of American law "that legislation of Congress, unless a contrary intent appears, is meant to apply only within the territorial jurisdiction of the United States." *Foley Bros.*, 336 U.S., at 285. This "canon of construction . . . is a valid approach whereby unexpressed congressional intent may be ascertained." Ibid. It serves to protect against unintended clashes between our laws and those of other nations which could result in international discord. See *McCulloch v. Sociedad Nacional de Marineros de Honduras*, 372 U.S. 10, 20-22 (1963).

In applying this rule of construction, we look to see whether "language in the [relevant act] gives any indication of a congressional purpose to extend its coverage beyond places over which the United States has sovereignty or has some measure of legislative control." *Foley Bros., supra*, at 285. We assume that Congress legislates against the backdrop of the presumption against extraterritoriality. Therefore, unless there is "the affirmative intention of the Congress clearly expressed," *Benz, supra*, at 147, we must presume it "is primarily concerned with domestic conditions." *Foley Bros., supra*, at 285.

Boureslan and the EEOC contend that the language of Title VII evinces a clearly expressed intent on behalf of Congress to legislate extraterritorially. They rely principally on two provisions of the statute. First, petitioners argue that the statute's definitions of the jurisdictional terms "employer" and "commerce" are sufficiently broad to include United States firms that employ American citizens overseas. Second, they maintain that the statute's "alien exemption" clause, 42 U.S.C. § 2000e1, necessarily implies that Congress intended to protect American citizens from employment discrimination abroad. Petitioners also contend that we should defer to the EEOC's consistently held position that Title VII applies abroad. We conclude that petitioners' evidence, while not totally lacking in probative value, falls short of demonstrating the affirmative congressional intent required to extend the protections of Title VII beyond our territorial borders.

* * *

. . . The language relied upon by petitioners—and it is they who must make the affirmative showing—is ambiguous, and does not speak directly to the question presented here. The intent of Congress as to the extraterritorial application of this statute must be deduced by inference from boilerplate language which can be found in any number of congressional Acts, none of which have ever been held to apply overseas. See, e.g., Consumer Product Safety Act, 15, U.S.C. § 2052(a)(12); Federal Food, Drug, and Cosmetic Act, 21 U.S.C. § 321(b); Transportation Safety Act of 1974, 49, U.S.C.A. § 1802(1); Labor-Management Reporting and Disclosure Act of 1959, 29 U.S.C.A. § 401 et seq.; Americans with Disabilities Act of 1990, 42, U.S.C.A. § 1201, et seq.

Petitioners' reliance on Title VII's jurisdictional provisions also finds no support in our case law; we have repeatedly held that even statutes that contain broad language in their definitions of "commerce" that expressly refer to "*foreign* commerce" do not apply abroad. . . .

Thus petitioner's argument based on the jurisdictional language of Title VII fails both as a matter of statutory language and of our previous case law. Many acts of Congress are based on the authority of that body to regulate commerce among the several states, and the parts of these acts setting forth the basis for legislative jurisdiction will obviously refer to such commerce in one way or another. If we were to permit possible, or even plausible interpretations of language such as that involved here to override the presumption against extraterritorial application, there would be little left of the presumption.

Petitioners argue that Title VII's "alien exemption provision," 42 U.S.C. § 2000e1, "clearly manifests an intention" by Congress to protect United States citizens with respect to their employment outside of the United States. The alien exemption provision says that the statute "shall not apply to an employer with respect to the employment of aliens outside any state." Petitioners contend that from this language a negative inference should be drawn that Congress intended Title VII to cover United States *citizens* working abroad for United States employers. There is "[n]o other plausible explanation [that] the alien exemption exists," they argue, because "[I]f Congress believed that the statute did not apply extraterritorially, it would have had no reason to include an exemption for a certain category of individuals employed outside the United States." . . . Since "[t]he statute's jurisdictional provisions cannot possibly be read to confer coverage only upon aliens employed outside the United States," petitioners conclude that "Congress could not rationally have enacted an exemption for the employment of aliens abroad if it intended to foreclose all potential extraterritorial applications of the statute." . . .

If petitioners are correct that the alien-exemption clause means that the statute applies to employers overseas, we see no way of distinguishing in its application between United States employers and foreign employers. Thus, a French employer of a United States citizen in France would be subject to Title VII—a result at which even petitioners balk. The EEOC assures us that in its view the term "employer" means only "American employer," but there is no such distinction in this statute, and no indication that EEOC in the normal course of its administration had produced a reasoned basis for such a distinction. Without clearer evidence of congressional intent to do so than is contained in the alien-exemption clause, we are unwilling to ascribe to that body a policy which would raise difficult issues of international law by imposing this country's employment-discrimination regime upon foreign corporations operating in foreign commerce.

This conclusion is fortified by the other elements in the statute suggesting a purely domestic focus. . . . [For example:] While Title VII consistently speaks in terms of "states" and state proceedings. it fails even to mention foreign nations or foreign proceedings.

Similarly, Congress failed to provide any mechanisms for overseas enforcement of Title VII. . . .

It is also reasonable to conclude that had Congress intended Title VII to apply overseas, it would have addressed the subject of conflicts with foreign laws and procedures. In amending the Age Discrimination in Employment Act of 1967 (ADEA), 81 Stat. 602, as amended, 29 U.S.C. § 621 et seq., to apply abroad, Congress specifically addressed potential conflicts with foreign law. . . . Title VII, by contrast, fails to address conflicts with the laws of other nations.

Finally, the EEOC, as one of the two federal agencies with primary responsibility for enforcing Title VII, argues that we should defer to its "consistent" construction of Title VII. . . .

In *General Electric Co. v. Gilbert*, 420 U.S. 125, 140-146 (1976), we addressed the proper deference to be afforded the EEOC's guidelines. Recognizing that "Congress, in enacting Title VII, did not confer upon the EEOC authority to promulgate rules or regulations," we held that the level of deference afforded "will depend upon the thoroughness evident in its consideration, the validity of its reasoning, its consistency with earlier and later pronouncements, and all those factors which give it power to persuade, if lacking power to control." Id., at 141, 142 (quoting *Skidmore v. Swift & Co.*, 323 U.S. 134, 140 (1944)).

The EEOC's interpretation does not fare well under these standards. As an initial matter, the position taken by the Commission "contradicts the position which [it] had enunciated at an earlier date, closer to the enactment of the governing statute." *General Electric Co., supra*, at 142. . . . As discussed above, it also lacks support in the plain language of the statute. . . .

Petitioners have failed to present sufficient affirmative evidence that Congress intended Title VII to apply abroad. Accordingly, the judgment of the Court of Appeals is *affirmed*.

Discussion Questions

1. Does international law recognize the extraterritorial effect of individual national labor laws? Why or why not?
2. What was the specific holding in the *EEOC v. Aramco* case? Do you agree or disagree with the majority opinion of the court? Why?
3. Would the United States accept the reciprocal application of the EEOC arguments and agree to the enforcement of Saudi Arabian labor law in the United States?

> *Comment:* Note that by special amendment in 1984, the Age Discrimination in Employment Act of 1967 applies extraterritorially. (29 U.S.C. § 623(g)) Congress has reacted to the *EEOC v. Aramco* decision by enacting the Civil Rights Act of 1991. This act extends the coverage of Title VII of the Civil Rights Act of 1964 and the Americans With Disabilities Act (ADA) to U.S. citizens employed in foreign countries by companies "controlled" by U.S. employers. However, such firms may engage in discrimination when the failure to do so would violate the law of the host country. See *Kern v. Dynalectron Corp.* (577 F.Supp. 1196 [N.D.Tex.1983], aff'd mem. 746 F.2d 810 [5th Cir.1984]). (Saudi requirement that pilots be Muslims merited religious discrimination.)

Movement of Workers Across National Borders

The movement of workers across national borders raises important issues of concern to most States. The fear that foreign workers may displace local workers is of major interest, and policies must be designed to balance the national interest in each State's domestic policy. It is frequently the policy of newly industrializing countries to require that a foreign investor educate local personnel to replace initial foreign personnel. In return for such human resource development, such countries may offer special tax exemptions or other benefits. The training of local personnel is often a requirement for investment permits. Indonesia, Ghana, Kenya, and Nigeria, for example, require training of indigenous labor. In Saudi Arabia, MNEs from the United States have established training centers in Yanbu and Jubail to train up to 1,000 persons at a time in essential technical skills.

Several countries have encountered major problems with foreign laborers. In Germany and Singapore, the economies of these countries at first needed foreign workers and then encountered an oversupply problem that has led to incentives to induce the return of these workers to their home nations. In 1983, Nigeria summarily expelled tens of thousand of foreign workers. In the absence of international treaty obligations, a country may expel aliens or deny them work permits.

The major problem in the United States relates to the entry of illegal aliens who have massively invaded the country seeking employment opportunities. The uncertain position of the United States toward "illegal alien" workers from Mexico has involved years of negotiations between the two countries. Congress passed the **Immigration Reform and Control Act** of 1986 as a response to the problem. This act allows aliens who have been in the United States since 1982 to obtain permanent residency status and, ultimately, citizenship. It establishes, for the first time, sanctions against employers who knowingly hire illegal aliens. The act also

> **Immigration Reform and Control Act:** *An act of the U.S. Congress in 1986 that reforms and regulates hiring practices concerning aliens. It subjects illegal aliens to deportation proceedings and imposes fines for hiring illegal aliens.*

creates a new "unfair immigration-related employment practice." It is now illegal to discriminate in employment because of the national origin or citizenship status of authorized aliens. Illegal aliens who came to the United States after 1982 now face deportation proceedings. This law affects many aliens from Ireland, Mexico, and many Central American countries.

National policies concerning passports, visas, and work permits vary considerably among nations. There is no customary international law concerning passports, visas, and work permits. In the United States, successive passport control acts have made passports the only means by which a U.S. citizen can lawfully leave the country and return to it, unless the president grants an exception. The U.S. Supreme Court has repeatedly held that the freedom to travel abroad with a U.S. passport is subordinate to national security and foreign policy considerations. Travel by U.S. passport holders to "enemy" countries such as Cuba, North Vietnam, and Iran has been periodically denied.

The U.S. Immigration and Nationality Act broadly distinguishes, for visa purposes, between aliens who are considered immigrants and those who are not. Whether a foreigner can even be employed in the United States now hinges on employer verification of visa eligibility to work and employer examination of required documents. Prior to the 1986 Immigration Reform and Control Act, U.S. employers regularly hired foreigners and then sought the necessary visas. Under the new law, employers face perjury penalties and prison terms if their verifications and examinations are not completed in advance and accurate. Moreover, parent companies are responsible for the hiring decisions of their subsidiaries and divisions. All decisions to hire foreigners must be fully documented through a company "employment verification system."

Government work permits are commonly required in industrial and developing countries. Special requirements may be attached to these permits, such as medical examinations and security deposits. There is a notable pattern of liberalization of work permit rules in European Community law. Various EC directives have removed permit requirements for EU nations but retained them for non-EU nationals. However, this pattern has not been duplicated in the new North American Free Trade Agreement (NAFTA) in which free movement of laborers and professionals is minimally covered (Folsom et al., 1992, p. 305).

▌   ▌   ▌

Chapter Summary

1. Unique forms of international regulation have been established in the areas of telecommunications, air transportation, human rights, labor, environmental protection, health, and many others. The pioneering International Labor Organization has developed a successful procedure for progressive implementation of international labor standards.

2. The International Labor Organization has played a major role in the development of the International Labor Code, which consists of more than 170 treaties and 180

recommendations. The ILO Labor Code is considered a comprehensive charter of minimal internationally recognized workers' rights.

3. ILO compliance procedure involves treaty commitment to a process that includes annual reports to verify compliance with the treaties and recommendations, review by a committee of experts that analyzes these reports and prepares an annual summary, and sanctions applied by the General Conference. Special lists of governments that have defaulted on their obligations are prepared by a special conference committee, and the General Conference decides on appropriate action.

4. The approach to enforcement that is used by the ILO is a flexible one that emphasizes cooperation and exploration of positive measures to bring about compliance rather than punitive sanctions. Progress toward compliance is encouraged even if full compliance is not being achieved.

5. ILO actions censuring the Soviet Union and the negotiated influence of the Helsinki Final Act commitments were influential in bringing about major changes in the Soviet Union and the former communist countries of Eastern Europe.

6. From 1964 to 1994, more than 1,850 changes in national legislation among member countries to ILO conventions have been attributed to the influence of regulatory pressures through the ILO compliance procedures.

7. The ILO experience has contributed to the general practices of other intergovernmental agencies and the proliferation of international regulatory regimes that now display a two-step regulatory function similar to the rule-making process in domestic regulation. The international standards, however, are not enforceable directly by the IGO but depend on incorporation into the municipal laws of the member State.

8. A wide variety of emerging legal standards in the form of unratified treaties, executive agreements, codes of practice, recommendations, guidelines, standards, and declarations of principle do not fit neatly into the established sources of international law. However, these soft-law instruments are frequently regarded as binding in practice and may mature into hard-law instruments of duly ratified treaties, customary practice regarded as binding, or general principles of law.

9. The soft-law approach is a more flexible contribution to the progressive development of State practices that promote legally defined goals and objectives.

10. Under international law, States are free to develop their own labor policies as long as they meet minimal international standards. This principle creates a wide variety of innovative labor practices that the foreign investor must be aware of when entering into business ventures abroad. Businesses located in a foreign country must comply with the municipal labor policies of the host State.

11. Employment and labor policies in other countries, especially Western Europe, may include equal pay for equal work provisions, codetermination, and recognized proprietary interest of employees based on longevity.

12. The countries of the European Union now include labor principles of freedom of movement of nationals and business enterprises among member States and nondiscrimination on the basis of national origin.

13. The OECD Guidelines for Multinational Enterprises establishes voluntary guidelines and minimal international standards that are beginning to have effect in international business practice.

14. The 1982 ILO Convention on Termination of Employment establishes new international standards in this area; however, the United States has not ratified the convention. This convention binds the parties to practices requiring notification and a hearing before workers can be discharged. It prohibits termination because of race, sex, ethnic origin, affiliation with a union, or protesting illegal conduct. Workers are entitled to union counsel, coverage for extended illness, access to business information, and prior consultation before closing plants.

15. The United States has attempted to apply its labor laws extraterritorially to U.S. citizens employed by U.S. firms abroad. This practice could be in violation of international law, if the host country is not limited by treaty obligation and it objects and finds the regulation in conflict with its own municipal laws.

16. The U.S. Immigration Reform and Control Act of 1986 attempts to provide more stringent controls over the employment of illegal aliens and has instituted a new employment verification system.

17. Under international law, each State has the right to control its own immigration, passports, visas, and work permits unless it has specifically agreed to treaty limitations.

Key Terms

International Labor Code
ILO compliance procedure
Conference on Security and Cooperation in Europe (CSCE)
Helsinki Final Act
rule making

public comment sessions
soft law
comparable worth
codetermination
proprietary interest
freedom of movement
Guidelines for Multinational Enterprises

Badger case
Convention on Termination of Employment
Immigration Reform and Control Act

■   ■   ■

Discussion Questions

1. What specific provisions of the International Covenant on Economic, Social and Cultural Rights might be objected to by the U.S. Senate? Should the United States ratify this treaty?

2. Why has the United States ratified only eleven of the 170 ILO treaties, whereas France, Italy, and Spain have ratified over one hundred of these treaties?

3. Does the ILO flexible compliance procedure offer any particular advantage over strict compliance measures that might be an alternative approach? What are these advantages or disadvantages?

4. What is the major distinction between "soft law" and "hard law" in international relations? Is there a similar distinction in the difference between regulations and legislation in domestic law?

5. Are many of the European concepts of workers' rights more advantageous to workers than U.S. policy now supports? Should these rights be protected in the United States?

6. Why does international law prohibit extraterritorial application of municipal labor laws that conflict with the laws of the host State? Do both the U.S. courts and the Congress indicate acceptance of this rule?

Suggested Readings

Bennett, A. L. (1995). *International organizations* (6th ed.). Englewood Cliffs, NJ: Prentice Hall.

Moy, L. L. (1988). The U.S. legal role in international labor organization conventions and recommendations. *International Lawyer, 22,* 768-769.

Organization for Economic Cooperation and Development. (1994). *Regulatory co-operation for an interdependent world.* Washington, DC: Author.

Internet Sources

Browse: Use U.N. Home Page (http://www.un.org) for ILO material.

OECD material can be accessed at (http://www.oecdwash.org/).

8 *International Environmental Regulation*

There is growing evidence of potentially irreversible degradation of the natural environment. Since World War II, the growth of population, the spread of industrialization, and the increase in automobile, air, and maritime traffic has produced a great increase in the pollution of land, air, and water. These developments have led to the realization that unilateral action by States to control pollution is insufficient and that international cooperation and regulation to protect the environment are necessary. The first global Conference on the Human Environment (UNCHE or Stockholm Conference) was held in Stockholm in 1972. This conference adopted the Stockholm Declaration on the Human Environment and an Action Plan. It also made proposals that led the General Assembly to establish the United Nations Environment Program (UNEP).

Principle 21 of the **Stockholm Declaration** provides a clear statement of the basic rights and responsibilities of States for environmental injury:

States have, in accordance with the Charter of the United Nations and the principles of international law, the Sovereign right to exploit their own resources pursuant to their own environmental policies

> **Stockholm Declaration:** *The statement of the basic rights and responsibilities of States concerning the environment resulting from the first global Conference on the Human Environment held in 1972.*

and the responsibility to ensure that activities within their jurisdiction or control do not cause damage to the environment of other states or of areas beyond the limits of national jurisdiction.

Principle 22 of the Stockholm Declaration further provides an obligation to cooperate in the development of international environmental law:

States shall co-operate to develop further the international law regarding liability and compensation for the victims of pollution and other environmental damage caused by activities within the jurisdiction or control of such States to areas beyond their jurisdiction.

These principles are rooted in customary international law and are fundamental in nature. They originated in rules relating to the responsibility of a State for injuries caused to another State or to its property, or to persons within another State's territory or their property. The International Court of Justice has noted that one of the "general and well-recognized principles" of international law is "every State's obligation not to allow knowingly its territory to be used for acts contrary to the rights of other States" (*Corfu Channel Case* [Merits] *[U.K. v. Albania*, 1949] [I.C.J. Rep. 4, 22]). The United Nations Survey of International Law concluded that "there has been general recognition of the rule that a State must not permit the use of its territory for purposes injurious to the interests of other States in a manner contrary to international law."

Customary International Environmental Law

These general principles have been applied to transfrontier air and marine pollution as well as to the pollution or alteration of international rivers. As early as 1911, the Institute of International Law expressed the opinion that where a river forms the boundary of two States, neither State may, "on its own territory, utilize or allow the utilization of the water in such a way as seriously to interfere with its utilization by the other State or by individuals, corporations, etc., thereof." The United States has accepted these principles in its practice and stated that "no State might claim to use the waters of an international river in such a way as to cause material injury to the interest of other States" (American Law Institute, 1987, pp. 100-101).

Perhaps the most frequently quoted opinion of an international tribunal regarding the general principle of transfrontier air pollution developed out of a dispute between the United States and Canada before World War II. The *Trail Smelter* case resulted from injuries caused in the state of Washington by large amounts of sulfur dioxide emitted since 1925 by a smelter plant at Trail, British Columbia. At that time, claims could not be brought in the courts of British Columbia under existing law. The courts of the state of Washington had no jurisdiction over the polluter, a Canadian company, since it was not engaged in any business in that state.

> **Trail Smelter case:** Precedent established through international arbitration that States are responsible for damages caused to other States by environmental pollution.

In 1928, the matter was referred to the International Joint Commission established under the Boundary Waters Treaty of 1909, but the commission's report was rejected by the United States. Further negotiations led to a convention in 1935 submitting to arbitration the major questions in dispute.

Trail Smelter Case *(United States v. Canada)*

Arbitral Tribunal, 1941.

3 U.N.Rep.Int'l Arb. Awards 1905, 1907 (1949).

CONVENTION FOR SETTLEMENT OF DIFFICULTIES ARISING FROM OPERATION OF SMELTER AT TRAIL, B.C.

* * *

ARTICLE III.

The Tribunal shall finally decide the questions, hereinafter referred to as "the Questions," set forth hereunder, namely:

(1) Whether damage caused by the Trail Smelter in the State of Washington has occurred since the first day of January, 1932, and, if so, what indemnity should be paid therefor?

(2) In the event of the answer to the first part of the preceding Question being in the affirmative, whether the Trail Smelter should be required to refrain from causing damage in the State of Washington in the future, and if so, to what extent?

(3) In the light of the answer to the preceding Question, what measures or regime, if any, should be adopted or maintained by the Trail Smelter?

(4) What indemnity or compensation, if any, should be paid on account of any decision or decisions rendered by the Tribunal pursuant to the next two preceding Questions?

ARTICLE IV.

The Tribunal shall apply the law and practice followed in dealing with cognate questions in the United States of America as well as international law and practice, and shall give consideration to the desire of the high contracting parties to reach a solution just to all parties concerned.

* * *

DECISION

REPORTED ON MARCH 11, 1941, TO THE GOVERNMENT OF THE UNITED STATES OF AMERICA AND TO THE GOVERNMENT OF THE DOMINION OF CANADA, UNDER THE CONVENTION SIGNED APRIL 15, 1935.

* * *

On April 16, 1938, the Tribunal reported its "final decision" on Question No. 1, as well as its temporary decisions on Questions No. 2 and No. 3, and provided for a temporary regime thereunder. The decision reported on April 16, 1938, will be referred to hereinafter as the "previous decision."

* * *

In conclusion (end of Part Two of the previous decision), the Tribunal answered Question No. 1 as follows:

> Damage caused by the Trail Smelter in the State of Washington has occurred since the first day of January, 1932, and up to October 1, 1937, and the indemnity to be paid therefor is seventy-eight thousand dollars ($78,000), and is to be complete and final indemnity and compensation for all damage which occurred between such dates.

In 1896, a smelter was started under American auspices near the locality known as Trail, B.C. In 1906, the Consolidated Mining and Smelting Company of Canada, Limited, obtained a charter of incorporation from the Canadian authorities, and that company acquired the smelter plant at Trail as it then existed. Since that time, the Canadian company, without interruption, has operated the Smelter, and from time to time has greatly added to the plant until it has become one of the best and largest equipped smelting plants on the American continent. In 1925 and 1927, two stacks of the plant were erected to 409 feet in height and the Smelter greatly increased its daily smelting of zinc and lead ores. This increased production resulted in more sulphur dioxide fumes and higher concentrations being emitted into the air. In 1916, about 5,000 tons of sulphur per month were emitted; in 1924, about 4,700 tons; in 1926, about 9,000 tons—an amount which rose near to 10,000 tons per month in 1930. In other words, about 300-350 tons of sulphur were being emitted daily in 1930. (It is to be noted that one ton of sulphur is substantially the equivalent of two tons of sulphur dioxide or SO2.)

From 1925, at least, to 1937, damage occurred in the State of Washington, resulting from the sulphur dioxide emitted from the Trail Smelter as stated in the previous decision.

* * *

The second question under Article III of the Convention is as follows:

> In the event of the answer to the first part of the preceding question being in the affirmative, whether the Trail Smelter should be required to refrain from causing damage in the State of Washington in the future and, if so, to what extent?
>   Damage has occurred since January 1, 1932, as fully set forth in the previous decision. To that extent, the first part of the preceding question has thus been answered in the affirmative.

The first problem which arises is whether the question should be answered on the basis of the law followed in the United States or on the basis of international law. The Tribunal, however, finds that this problem need not be solved here as the law followed in the United States in dealing with the quasi-sovereign rights of the States of the Union, in the matter of air pollution, whilst more definite, is in conformity with the general rules of international law.

Particularly in reaching its conclusions as regards this question as well as the next, the Tribunal has given consideration to the desire of the high contracting parties "to reach a solution just to all parties concerned."

As Professor Eagleton puts it (*Responsibility of States in International Law*, 1928, p. 80): "A State owes at all times a duty to protect other States against injurious acts by individuals from within its jurisdiction." A great number of such general pronouncements by leading authorities concerning the duty of a State to respect other States and their territory have been presented to the Tribunal. These and many others have been carefully examined. International decisions, in various matters, from the *Alabama* case onward, and also earlier ones, are based on the same general principle, and, indeed, this principle, as such, has not been questioned by Canada. But the real difficulty often arises rather when it comes to determine what, *pro subjecta materie*, is deemed to constitute an injurious act.

A case concerning, as the present one does, territorial relations, decided by the Federal Court of Switzerland between the Cantons of Soleure and Argovia, may serve to illustrate the relativity of the rule. Soleure brought a suit against her sister State to enjoin use of a shooting establishment which endangered her territory. The court, in granting the injunction, said: "This right (sovereignty) excludes . . . not only the usurpation and exercise of sovereign rights (of another State) . . . but also an actual encroachment which might prejudice the natural use of the territory and the free movement of its inhabitants." As a result of the decision, Argovia made plans for the improvement of the existing installations. These, however, were considered as insufficient protection by Soleure. The Canton of Argovia then moved the Federal Court to decree that the shooting be again permitted after completion of the projected improvements. This motion was granted. "The demand of the Government of Soleure," said the court, "that all endangerment be absolutely abolished apparently goes too far." The court found that all risk whatever had not been eliminated, as the region was flat and absolutely safe shooting ranges were only found in mountain valleys; that there was a federal duty for the communes to provide facilities for military target practice and that "no more precautions may be demanded for shooting ranges near the boundaries of two Cantons than are required for shooting ranges in the interior of a Canton." (R.O. 26, I, pp. 450, 451; R.O. 41, I, p. 137; see D. Schindler, "The Administration of Justice in the Swiss Federal Court in Intercantonal Disputes," *American Journal of International Law*, Vol. 15 (1921), pp. 172-174).

No case of air pollution dealt with by an international tribunal has been brought to the attention of the Tribunal nor does the Tribunal know of any such case. The nearest analogy is that of water pollution. But, here also, no decision of an international tribunal has been cited or has been found.

There are, however, as regards both air pollution and water pollution, certain decisions of the Supreme Court of the United States which may legitimately be taken as a guide in this field of international law, for it is reasonable to follow by analogy, in international cases, precedents established by that court in dealing with controversies between States of the Union or with other controversies concerning the quasi-sovereign rights of such States, where no contrary rule prevails in international law and no reason for rejecting such precedents can be adduced from the limitations of sovereignty inherent in the Constitution of the United States.

In the suit of the *State of Missouri v. the State of Illinois* (200 U.S. 496, 521) concerning the pollution, within the boundaries of Illinois, of the Illinois River, an affluent of the Mississippi flowing into the latter where it forms the boundary between that State and Missouri, an injunction was refused. "Before this court ought to intervene," said the court, "the case should be of serious magnitude, clearly and fully proved, and the principle to be applied should be one which the court is prepared deliberately to maintain against all considerations on the other side. (See *Kansas v. Colorado*, 185 U.S. 125.)" The court found that the practice complained of was general along the shores of the Mississippi River at that time, that it was followed by Missouri itself and that thus a standard was set up by the defendant which the claimant was entitled to invoke.

* * *

In the more recent suit of the State of New York against the State of New Jersey (256 U.S. 296, 309), concerning the pollution of New York Bay, the injunction was also refused for lack of proof. . . .

. . . What is true between States of the Union is, at least, equally true concerning the relations between the United States and the Dominion of Canada.

In another recent case concerning water pollution (283 U.S. 473), the complainant was successful. The City of New York was enjoined, at the request of the State of New Jersey, to desist, within a reasonable time limit, from the practice of disposing of sewage by dumping it into the sea, a practice which was injurious to the coastal waters of New Jersey in the vicinity of her bathing resorts.

In the matter of air pollution itself, the leading decisions are those of the Supreme Court in the *State of Georgia v. Tennessee Copper Company and Ducktown Sulphur, Copper and Iron Company, Limited*. Although dealing with a suit against private companies, the decisions were on questions cognate to those here at issue. Georgia stated that it had in vain sought relief from the State of Tennessee, on whose territory the smelters were located, and the court defined the nature of the suit by saying: "This is a suit by a State for an injury to it in its capacity of quasi-sovereign. In that capacity, the State has an interest independent of and behind the titles of its citizens, in all the earth and air within its domain."

On the question whether an injunction should be granted or not, the court said (206 U.S. 230):

> It (the State) has the last word as to whether its mountains shall be stripped of their forests and its inhabitants shall breathe pure air. . . . It is not lightly to be presumed to give up quasi-sovereign rights for pay and . . . if that be its choice, it may insist that an infraction of them shall be stopped. This court has not quite the same freedom to balance the harm that will be done by an injunction against that of which the plaintiff complains, that it would have in deciding between two subjects of a single political power. Without excluding the considerations that equity always takes into account . . . it is a fair and reasonable demand on the part of a sovereign that the air over its territory should not be polluted on a great scale by sulphurous acid gas, that the forests or its mountains, be they better or worse, and whatever domestic destruction they may have suffered, should not be further destroyed or threatened by the act of persons beyond its control, that the crops and orchards on its hills should not be endangered from the same source. . . . Whether Georgia, by insisting upon this claim, is doing more harm than good to her own citizens, is for her to determine. The possible disaster to those outside the State must be accepted as a consequence of her standing upon her extreme rights.

Later on, however, when the court actually framed an injunction, in the case of the Ducktown Company (237 U.S. 474, 477) (an agreement on the basis of an annual compensation was reached with the most important of the two smelters, the Tennessee Copper Company), they did not go beyond a decree "adequate to diminish materially the present probability of damage to its (Georgia's) citizens."

The Tribunal, therefore, finds that the above decisions, taken as a whole, constitute an adequate basis for its conclusions, namely, that, under the principles of international law, as well as of the law of the United States, no State has the right to use or permit the use of its territory in such a manner as to cause injury by fumes in or to the territory of another or the properties or persons therein, when the case is of serious consequence and the injury is established by clear and convincing evidence.

The decisions of the Supreme Court of the United States which are the basis of these conclusions are decisions in equity and a solution inspired by them, together with the regime hereinafter prescribed, will, in the opinion of the Tribunal, be "just to all parties concerned," as long, at least, as the present conditions in the Columbia River Valley continue to prevail.

Considering the circumstances of the case, the Tribunal holds that the Dominion of Canada is responsible in international law for the conduct of the Trail Smelter. Apart from the undertakings in the Convention, it is, therefore, the duty of the Government of the Dominion of Canada to see to it that this conduct should be in conformity with the obligation of the Dominion under international law as herein determined.

The Tribunal, therefore, answers Question No. 2 as follows: (2) So long as the present conditions in the Columbia River Valley prevail, the Trail Smelter shall be required to refrain from causing any damage through fumes in the State of Washington; the damage herein referred to and its extent being such as would be recoverable under the decisions of the courts of the United States in suits between private individuals. The indemnity for such damage should be fixed in such manner as the Governments, acting under Article XI of the Convention should agree upon.

The third question under Article III of the Convention is as follows: "In the light of the answer to the preceding question, what measures or regime, if any, should be adopted and maintained by the Trail Smelter?"

Answering this question in the light of the preceding one, since the Tribunal has, in its previous decision, found that damage caused by the Trail Smelter has occurred in the State of Washington since January 1, 1932, and since the Tribunal is of opinion that damage may occur in the future unless the operations of the Smelter shall be subject to some control, in order to avoid damage occurring, the Tribunal now decides that a regime or measure of control shall be applied to the operations of the Smelter and shall remain in full force unless and until modified in accordance with the provisions hereinafter set forth. . . .

* * *

Discussion Questions

1. What is the specific holding of the tribunal in the *Trail Smelter* case?
2. Why were the decisions of the U.S. Supreme Court and the Swiss Federal Court chosen for reliable precedents in this case?
3. How might this general principle be used to deal with other forms of air and water pollution injurious to other States?

Although there are only a few specific cases in the field of international environmental law, the *Gut Dam* case and the *Lake Lanoux* case provide important specific reference to State responsibility in this general area. The Gut Dam was built by Canada across the international boundary on the St. Lawrence River with the consent of the United States by actions occurring in 1902. However, after its completion, the dam raised the water levels of Lake Ontario between 1947 and 1952 and caused injury by erosion and inundation to property owners on the U.S. shore of the lake. These property owners were unsuccessful in their attempt to bring suit in the U.S. courts against Canada. The U.S. Congress then passed a statute authorizing the investigation of the Gut Dam claims by the Foreign Claims Settlement Commission (76 Stat. 387, 1962), but before any decisions were rendered, the United States and Canada agreed to establish an international arbitral tribunal to dispose finally of the claims of U.S. citizens. After the tribunal rendered several preliminary decisions in favor of the United States, Canada agreed to pay to the United States $350,000 in full settlement of all claims. The tribunal recorded the settlement and terminated the proceedings.

The *Lake Lanoux* case, or *Lac Lanoux* **arbitration**, between Spain and France, involved a dispute concerning whether or not States are required to cooperate with each other in mitigating transboundary environmental risks. In 1957, the tribunal held that France had complied in good faith before diverting a watercourse shared with Spain. The Court noted that conflicting interests must be reconciled by negotiation and mutual concession. This implied that France must inform Spain of its proposals, allow consultations, and give reasonable weight to Spain's interests, but it did not mean that it could act only with Spain's consent: "The risk of an evil use has so far not led to subjecting the possession of these means of action to the authorization of states which may possibly be threatened" (cited in Birnie & Boyle, 1992, p. 103). Spain's rights were thus of a procedural character only; it enjoyed no veto and no

> **Lac Lanoux arbitration:** *International precedent establishing that States sharing an international watercourse are entitled to notification and consultation concerning any plan to substantially alter that watercourse. They do not have a veto but are entitled to consultation.*

claim to insist on specific precautions. It was for France alone to determine whether to proceed with the project and how to safeguard Spain's rights. According to several International Court of Justice precedents, the obligation to negotiate is a real one, not a mere formality.

These early precedents have been supplemented by a large body of specific treaty law, especially since 1972 and the creation of UNEP. Specific cases of environmental adjudication have been rare because of major developments in treaty law, long-arm statutes that enable individuals to bring suit in State municipal courts, and the fact that Principles 21 and 22 of the Stockholm Declaration are widely accepted by States as customary international law.

The *Restatement (Third) of the Foreign Relations Law of the United States* (American Law Institute, 1987) provides a clear and inclusive statement of the general principles of State responsibility under customary international law:

> ### § 601. State Obligations with Respect to Environment of Other States and the Common Environment
>
> (1) A state is obligated to take such measures as may be necessary, to the extent practicable under the circumstances, to ensure that activities within its jurisdiction or control
> - (a) conform to generally accepted international rules and standards for the prevention, reduction, and control of injury to the environment of another state or of areas beyond the limits of national jurisdiction; and
> - (b) are conducted so as not to cause significant injury to the environment of another state or of areas beyond the limits of national jurisdiction.
>
> (2) A state is responsible to all other states
> - (a) for any violation of its obligations under Subsection (1)(a), and
> - (b) for any significant injury, resulting from such violation, to the environment of areas beyond the limits of national jurisdiction.

> (3) A state is responsible for any significant injury, resulting from a violation of its obligations under Subsection (1), to the environment of another state or to its property, or to persons or property within that state's territory or under its jurisdiction or control.

Remedies for Violation of Environmental Obligations

A State can fulfill its obligation to inhabitants of other States who suffer injuries by giving them access to its tribunals for adjudication of their claims. If such local remedies are available, the person who suffered injuries must exhaust these remedies before the State of which the private party is a national can bring an international claim on the private party's behalf. The two States, however, may agree at any time to settle the claim or include it in a lump sum settlement. Thus, most claims are handled in national courts, and the States that may be potential parties are only minimally involved.

The *Restatement (Third)* also includes a clear statement of the general principles of customary law on the subject of remedies for violations. The principle of nondiscrimination against foreign nationals requires that a State in which pollution originates avoid discrimination in the enforcement of applicable international rules and standards, as well as give to foreign victims the benefit of its own rules and standards for the protection of the environment, even if they are stricter than the international rules or standards. When environmental injury in one State results from private activity in another State, a remedy may be available in the courts of the victim State, or even a third State, and if the victim has received satisfaction by such a remedy the interstate remedy would abate.

> ### § 602. Remedies for Violation of Environmental Obligations
>
> (1) A state responsible to another state for violation of § 601 is subject to general interstate remedies (§ 902) to prevent, reduce, or terminate the activity threatening or causing the violation, and to pay reparation for injury caused.
> (2) Where pollution originating in a state has caused significant injury to persons outside that state, or has created a significant risk of such injury, the state of origin is obligated to accord to the person injured or exposed to such risk access to the same judicial or administrative remedies as are available in similar circumstances to persons within the state.

The remedies referred to in Subsection (1) usually begin with a protest against the violation, accompanied by a demand that the offending State terminate the violation, desist from further violations, and make reparation for past violations. If the matter is not resolved by diplomatic negotiations, the aggrieved State may resort to agreed third-party procedures, such as conciliation, mediation, arbitration, or adjudication. Some neighboring States have established international joint commissions to deal with transboundary problems, including pollution, but usually such commissions can only make recommendations. Strictly limited and reasonable measures of "self-help" may be permitted in special circumstances.

Remedies under this section of the *Restatement (Third)* are available for injury to a State's environmental interests within its territory as well as to interests beyond its territory, such as injury to its fishing interests on the high seas; it may pursue remedies, not only for injury to State interests but also to those of its political subdivisions or of its inhabitants or nationals. A State may also pursue appropriate remedies for injury to the common interest in the global commons, such as the high seas. Even where reparations for past injuries are not appropriate or feasible, a State may demand that violations be discontinued.

Major International Environmental Treaties

The major areas of international treaty law and regulation include international watercourses, international law of the sea, hazardous waste disposal, air pollution abatement, and protection of wildlife and biodiversity. Other environmental problems of international concern include the need to (a) improve habitat and human settlements; (b) protect archaeological treasures, cultural monuments, nature sanctuaries, endangered fauna and flora, and migratory birds; and (c) lessen the consequences of deforestation, overfishing, and weather modification. Hundreds of treaties of a bilateral and multilateral nature have been concluded in these areas of concern and many have created institutional arrangements for monitoring and regulating specific areas of concern.

In the United States, many international aspects of environmental problems, especially marine pollution, have been the subject of federal legislation. These acts of Congress include the acts relating, respectively, to National Environmental Policy, Clean Air, Federal Water Pollution Control, Toxic Substances Control, Oil Pollution, Ocean Dumping, Deepwater Ports, Rivers and Harbors, Coastal Zone Management, Outer Continental Shelf Lands, Submerged Lands, Fishery Conservation and Management, Deep Seabed Hard Mineral Resources, Resources Conservation and Recovery, Marine Mammals, Endangered Species, and Marine Sanctuaries (American Law Institute, 1987, pp. 202-203).

International Watercourses

An **international watercourse** is a convenient designation for rivers, lakes, or groundwater sources shared by two or more States. Such watercourses either form or straddle an international boundary or

> **International watercourse:** Rivers, lakes, or groundwater sources shared by two or more States.

flow through a succession of States. Early regulation of watercourses in Europe began with issues related to water use and navigation. The scope of the issues involved has progressed to create bilateral or regional institutions to achieve reasonable control of both pollution and water use. Most of the modern treaties use the basin approach to geographical definition of the watercourse. However, many new problems are emerging that relate to headwaters and tributary problems, and there is an emerging need to address the entire watershed, or international drainage basin.

The management of international watercourses through regional cooperation provides the most comprehensive basis for environmental protection and pollution control. Such schemes offer a forum for notification, consultation, and negotiation to take place; for coordinating responses to emergency situations; for data and information on environmental matters and water quality to be collected and disseminated; and for the coordination of research. In Northwestern Europe, the 1974 Paris Convention has become the main basis for regional control of river pollution, together with measures adopted by the EEC.

The International Commission for Protection of the Rhine was established in 1950 and reorganized in 1963. The Rhine flows north from Lake Constance on the Swiss border to the Netherlands where it empties into the sea. Initially, the commission's functions were to arrange for research into Rhine pollution and to make proposals and prepare guidelines for protection of the river from pollution. However, not until 1976 was it finally possible to negotiate, through the commission, framework conventions on chemicals and chloride pollution. Under the 1976 Rhine Chemicals Convention, the parties are committed to progressive elimination or strict regulation of specified groups of pollutants. Emission standards for chemicals and chlorides are controlled by a system of prior authorization by governments, and emission standards for eliminating the more serious pollutants are proposed by the commission. Standards for other pollutants are determined nationally. The development of EEC emission and water quality standards for most of the Rhine's riparian States (those having rights related to the watercourse) has helped the Rhine Commission in its task of coordinating national programs, receiving reports from governments, evaluating results, and proposing further measures.

The Rhine Chlorides Convention is intended to reduce French chloride discharges into the river and to prevent any increase in discharges by other parties. This treaty came into force in 1985 after a long delay on the part of France. The Rhine Commission's functions under the treaty include receiving national reports, making proposals for further limitations, and monitoring compliance with chloride levels set by the convention. This convention sets an unusual precedent in that it represents an attempt to provide a reasonable solution of the dispute between France and the Netherlands in which neither side pressed its legal rights to the full. The compromise was to allow a distribution of the costs of measures taken by France to control chloride pollution to all riparian States, including injured States downstream.

Although both Rhine treaties provide for compulsory unilateral arbitration, this method has not been used to deal with disputes. Instead, damage occurring in downstream States has been the subject of civil litigation in national courts or before the European Court of Justice. In 1987, the Rhine States were persuaded to adopt the Rhine Action Program to reduce structural pollution and minimize the risk of further accidents. The program is administered by the Rhine Commission and by regular ministerial conferences. It includes restoration of the living species of the river, the maintenance of its drinking quality, and the protection of the water quality of the North Sea. This program will be increasingly coordinated with the Paris Commission and the International North Sea Conference. "The Rhine now offers an example of significant progress in the regional management of watercourse pollution and the first to take account of the marine environment" (Birnie & Boyle, 1992, p. 245).

The U.S.-Canadian International Joint Commission was created by the 1909 Boundary Waters Treaty and has jurisdiction over all rivers and lakes along which the U.S.-Canadian border passes. It is not really a "basin treaty," since for most purposes its jurisdiction excludes tributaries or rivers flowing across the boundary, but it does cover the Great Lakes and transboundary pollution. The International Joint Commission (IJC) is unique in that it is more like an independent regulatory agency than an international conference. It is composed of independent experts who function quasi-judicially though public hearings, and its decisions are rendered by majority vote. This commission's approval is required before either State may permit the use, obstruction, or diversion of waters affecting the natural level or flow. Its primary function is to make binding determinations regarding the equitable use of the flow of the waters. The commission's decisions apportion those rights according to criteria that protect existing uses and give preference to domestic and sanitary purposes, navigation, power, and irrigation in that order.

The Boundary Waters Treaty does prohibit pollution of boundary waters and waters flowing across the boundary; however, in practice, this provision has been treated by the parties as a basis for compromise and balancing of interests rather than as an absolute prohibition. Environmental problems have been referred to the commission and have enabled it to fulfill some of the monitoring and policy formation functions of other more recently established bodies. The commission's research report on the Great Lakes resulted in the successful negotiation of two agreements on Great Lakes Water Quality in 1972 and 1978. The 1978 treaty was intended to replace the 1972 agreement, and its purpose is to restore and maintain the waters of the Great Lakes basin ecosystem; hence, its geographical coverage is broader than the 1909 treaty. As in Western Europe, equal access to national remedies is the preferred means of affording redress for damage caused by transboundary water pollution. However, the lack of a treaty comparable to the European Convention on the Recognition and Enforcement of Judgments precludes proceedings in the place of injury (Birnie & Boyle, 1992).

The most ambitious approach to environmental protection of a river basin involves the Zambezi in Africa. The Agreement on the Action Plan for the Environmentally Sound Management of the Common Zambezi River System was concluded in 1988 and is mainly concerned with river development. However, it exemplifies the potential for common management in addressing environmental problems. The agreement was drawn up with

UNEP assistance and based on recommendations of the Stockholm Conference, the Mar Del Plata Action Plan, and the Cairo Program for African Cooperation on the Environment. It forms part of UNEP's program for environmentally sound management of inland waters intended to ameliorate existing problems and prevent future conflicts.

These examples of regulation of international watercourses indicate potential for dealing with what will become increasingly difficult problems in the future.

International Law of the Sea and Regulation of Marine Pollution

The evolution of international law of the seas concerns the most important expanse of the international commons covering more than 75% of the earth's surface. As explained in Chapter 4, the international community has created a special regime for marine pollution because of the interdependent character of ocean waters (and air) and the cumulative effect of acts of pollution. Early in this century, pressure of international competition for living resources led to the first multilateral treaties on seals, fisheries, and whaling. However, it was only after World War II that problems of overexploitation of resources and the steady increase in the volume and effects of pollution from land and seaborne sources reached an intensity that required concerted international action. By the late 1960s, awareness of the impact of pollution on coastal environments, fisheries, and human populations had become widespread.

The Torrey Canyon disaster in 1967, involving the contamination of large areas of coastline by oil, alerted the world to the dangers posed by the daily transport of large quantities of toxic and hazardous substances at sea. Mercury emissions from a factory in Minamata in Japan had poisoned fish and endangered the lives and health of coastal communities. It became evident that the problem was not confined to the operation of ships but required comprehensive control of all potential pollution sources, including those on land.

Scientific studies conducted by international agencies have shown a steady increase in pollution of the sea by oil, chemicals, nuclear waste, and the effluent of urban, industrial society. The process of legal development was given substantial impetus by the 1972 Stockholm Conference on the Human Environment and the action plan adopted. The conference called on States to accept and implement existing legal instruments for the control of marine pollution and supported new conventions on dumping and pollution from ships. This led to the adoption of the 1972 London and Oslo Dumping Conventions and the 1973 International Convention for the Prevention of Pollution From Ships (MARPOL Convention), respectively.

The original MARPOL Convention was substantially revised in 1978. It is no longer confined to oil pollution but also regulates other types of ship-based pollution, including the bulk carriage of noxious liquids and garbage from ships. It also sets new construction standards for cargo ships, requiring, for example, double hulls for oil tankers, that will apply to new vessels. The **International Marine Organization (IMO)** is the principal regulatory agency involved in developing standards based on scientific evidence. The parties to the MARPOL Convention now include over 85% of the gross registered tonnage of the world's merchant

> *International Marine Organization (IMO):* The principal agency designed to conduct research and establish standards for regulation of the marine environment.

fleet and comprise the principal agency for development of the "generally accepted international rules and standards" prescribed by Article 211 of the 1982 UNCLOS.

The Stockholm Conference also called for stronger national controls over land-based pollution. Other recommendations dealt with support for research and monitoring programs at national and international levels using existing international institutions coordinated and stimulated by the proposed U.N. Environment Program. This led to a general set of principles for assessment and control of marine pollution that included a definition of "marine pollution" based on scientific findings and a series of general obligations to protect the marine environment from all sources of pollution. These developments form the basis for articles later incorporated in the 1982 UNCLOS and in UNEP's regional seas treaties.

The 1982 U.N. Law of the Sea Convention was intended to be a comprehensive restatement of almost all aspects of the Law of the Sea. One of its basic objectives is to establish protection of the environment. This aspect of the convention can be seen both "as a system for sustainable development and as a model for the evolution of international environmental law" (U.N. Doc. A/44/461, 1989, cited in Birnie & Boyle, 1992, pp. 252-253).

The *Restatement (Third)* incorporates the principles that have now become widely recognized in practice. Any State may complain to the offending State or to an appropriate international agency against violation of generally accepted international rules and standards for the protection of the marine environment by another State or its nationals or ships. Remedies are available to a particular State when pollution of the marine environment has caused injury to that State or its nationals.

§ 603. State Responsibility for Marine Pollution

(1) A state is obligated
  (a) to adopt laws and regulations to prevent, reduce, and control any significant pollution of the marine environment that are no less effective than generally accepted international rules and standards; and
  (b) to ensure compliance with the laws and regulations adopted pursuant to clause (a) by ships flying its flag, and, in case of a violation, to impose adequate penalties on the owner or captain of the ship.
(2) A state is obligated to take, individually and jointly with other states, such measures as may be necessary, to the extent practicable under the circumstances, to prevent, reduce, and control pollution causing or threatening to cause significant injury to the marine environment.

Most of the provisions of the 1982 Law of the Sea Convention concerning the protection of the marine environment reflect customary international law. However, the dispute settlement provisions are not customary law and will neither bind the United States nor will the United States be able to invoke them unless it becomes a party to the convention. Section 604 of *Restatement (Third)* restates the accepted customary obligations regarding remedies for marine pollution.

§ 604. Remedies for Marine Pollution

(1) A state responsible to another state for a violation of the principles of § 603 is subject to general interstate remedies (§ 902) to prevent, reduce, or terminate the activity threatening or causing pollution, and to pay reparation for injury caused.
(2) A state is obligated to ensure that a remedy is available, in accordance with its legal system, to provide prompt and adequate compensation or other relief for an injury to private interests caused by pollution of the marine environment resulting from a violation of § 603.
(3) In addition to remedies that may be available to it under Subsection (1):

(a) a coastal state may detain, and institute proceedings against, a foreign ship:
  (i) navigating in its territorial sea, for a violation therein of antipollution laws that the coastal state adopted in accordance with applicable international rules and standards; or
  (ii) navigating in its territorial sea or its exclusive economic zone, for a violation in that zone of applicable international antipollution rules and standards that resulted in a discharge causing or threatening a major injury to the coastal state;
(b) a port state may institute proceedings against a foreign ship that has voluntarily come into that state's port,
  (i) for a violation of the port state's antipollution laws adopted in accordance with applicable international rules and standards, if the violation had occurred in the port state's territorial sea or exclusive economic zone; or
  (ii) for a discharge in violation of applicable international antipollution rules and standards that had occurred beyond the limits of national jurisdiction of any state; and
(c) a port state is obligated to investigate, as far as practicable, whether a foreign ship that has voluntarily come into that state's port was responsible for a discharge in violation of applicable international antipollution rules and standards,
  (i) at the request of another state, where the discharge was alleged to have occurred in waters subject to that state's jurisdiction, or to have caused or threatened damage to that state; or
  (ii) at the request of the flag state, irrespective of where the violation was alleged to have occurred.

Regulation of Hazardous Waste

Land-based sources of marine pollution, dumping hazardous waste at sea, the transportation of such waste for transboundary disposal, and nuclear regulation are additional major concerns of the international community. Each of these topics is the subject of discrete legal regimes, and several major treaties have been concluded in an attempt to regulate international pollution and control the environmental risks involved.

In 1990, the second GESAMP (Group of Experts on the Scientific Aspects of Marine Pollution) report concluded that marine pollution had worsened since 1982. Sewage disposal and agricultural runoff were identified as the most urgent problems requiring international attention. Eutrophication (oxygen deficiency) had been occurring with increasing severity in enclosed waters in the Baltic Sea, North Sea, Mediterranean Sea, Northern Adriatic Sea, and off parts of the Japanese coast and the U.S. East Coast.

The **U.N. Environment Program (UNEP)** has launched a regional seas program, and the major areas covered by regional agreements on land-based sources of pollution are the Northeast Atlantic, the Baltic Sea, the Mediterranean Sea, the Persian Gulf, and the Southeast Pacific. All of these regional seas treaties require States to endeavor to control land-based pollution. However, only in the Mediterranean, Southeast Pacific, and Persian Gulf areas have protocols on land-based pollution been adopted.

> **U.N. Environment Program (UNEP):**
> Established after the Stockholm Conference in 1972 as a coordinating agency in the environmental protection area.

The London Dumping Convention was concluded in 1972 as a result of the Stockholm Conference and has been widely ratified. This convention covers dumping of hazardous waste from ships and distinguishes between different categories of pollutant. The dumping of more hazardous waste substances is absolutely prohibited, subject only to limited exceptions catering to warships and emergencies or if the substances appear as trace contaminants only or would be rapidly rendered harmless.

Dumping is subject to supervision by an international forum, the London Dumping Convention Consultative Meeting. This consultative body has been notably successful in generating international consensus on the development of policy for dumping at sea. It has facilitated the adoption of increasingly stringent standards and is widely regarded as one of the more successful regulatory treaties (Birnie & Boyle, 1992, p. 321).

The Basel Convention on the Control of Transboundary Movements of Hazardous Wastes and their Disposal, concluded in 1989, attempts to regulate transboundary shipments. This convention achieves a compromise that places important restrictions on the trade in hazardous waste. The African States have reserved the sovereign right to ban imports individually or regionally, and this right is recognized in the convention. The EEC, on the other hand, is committed to prohibit exports of radioactive and hazardous waste to any African, Caribbean, or Pacific States party to the convention. The Basel Convention recognizes the right to prohibit trade in waste by providing a requirement that import bans of individual parties be notified to other parties through the secretariat. No State may then permit transboundary movement in wastes to a party prohibiting their import, except by special agreement. Waste disposal at the source is thus strongly encouraged, and standards for disposal have been adopted. The more important agreement provides the following: (a) Trade that does take place requires the prior informed consent of transit and importing States; illegal trade is prohibited; (b) illegally imported waste must be accepted for re-import by the State of origin; and (c) ultimate disposal must be compatible with the protection of health, the environment, and the prevention of pollution (Birnie & Boyle, 1992, p. 334).

In 1996, the Basel Convention was amended to ban export of hazardous wastes from developed countries to developing nations. This ban took effect immediately, and the ban on wastes destined for final disposal, for recovery, or recycling operations will be phased in before taking complete effect after December 31, 1997 ("News Almanac," 1995b, p. 79).

The Chernobyl reactor accident in 1986 spread radioactive clouds to several European countries, which protested that the Soviet Union had not immediately notified them of the impending danger. As a result of this incident, the **International Atomic Energy Agency (IAEA)** prepared two conventions: one, the Convention on Early Notification of a Nuclear Accident, and the other, the Convention on Assistance in the Case of Nuclear Accident or Radiological Emergency. These agreements further commit States to notify and provide assistance in such disasters.

> *International Atomic Energy Agency (IAEA):* Established as a U.N. agency in 1956 and given extensive regulatory functions as a result of the nonproliferation treaty and other international developments.

The IAEA was created in 1956 with the object of encouraging and facilitating the spread of nuclear power. At the time, atomic energy was assumed to contribute to "peace, health and prosperity" (IAEA Statute, 1956, Article III) throughout the world. In 1968, the development of the Nuclear Non-Proliferation Treaty to limit possession of nuclear weapons to the five permanent members of the Security Council quickly became a means of arms control policy in the international community, and the IAEA assumed a new monitoring and regulatory role. The Stockholm Conference in 1972 called for a registry of emissions of radioactivity and international cooperation on radioactive waste disposal and reprocessing, adding new obligations to the IAEA.

Since the Chernobyl accident, the IAEA has acquired a new role to establish standards for protecting health and minimizing danger to life and property. The IAEA standards, regulations, codes of practice, guides, and other related instruments cover subjects such as radiation protection, transport and handling of radioactive materials, and radioactive waste disposal. The Nuclear Safety Standards Program (NUSS), revised in 1988, sets basic international minimum safety standards and guiding principles for regulating the design, construction, siting, and operation of nuclear power plants. What the agency lacks is the ability to give these standards obligatory force.

Other international regulatory bodies in the nuclear field include the institutions created by the EURATOM Treaty among the EEC member States, the Organization for Economic Cooperation and Development (OECD) Nuclear Energy Agency, and an ILO convention on protection of workers against radiation. The World Bank has also instituted an **environmental impact statement** requirement for development projects. The EURATOM agency is a regional regulatory agency with power to implement its standards. The EURATOM Treaty requires member States to implement safety directives and to ensure that they are enforced.

> *Environmental impact statement:* Scientific evaluation of the potential environmental impact of a proposed construction project.

Protecting the Atmosphere

Transboundary air pollution studies reveal perhaps the most dangerous and difficult-to-regulate area of environmental concerns. In addition to sulfur dioxide and nitrogen oxides, toxic fumes from vehicle emissions, chlorofluorocarbons (CFCs), halons, and other chlorine-based substances

produce conditions such as ozone depletion, acid rain, and potential global warm-
ing effects. The fear that further pollution
of the atmosphere could leave future generations a legacy of irreversible harm has
produced several important treaties and
worldwide conferences sponsored by the
United Nations in 1992 and 1995.

The U.N. Conference on Environment
and Development at Rio de Janeiro in 1992
produced the U.N. Framework Convention
on Climate Change, which has been ratified
by 120 nations. This convention envisioned
a reduction of greenhouse gas emissions to
1990 levels by the year 2000. A follow-up
conference among the parties to the framework convention, the U.N. Climate Conference, held in Berlin in 1995, considered the
principal issue of reconciling differences between developed and developing countries
concerning the pollution reduction targets
and procedures by additional protocols.
The delegates at this conference "agreed to
launch a new process to strengthen developed countries' commitments to combating
climate change after the year 2000, possibly
through the adoption of a new legal instrument" ("News Almanac," 1995a, p. 78). A
third session of the conference is scheduled
for 1997.

Measures to develop regional control of
transboundary air pollution are strongest in
Europe, where the problem of acid rain is
the most severe. Since 1975, the Conference
on Security and Cooperation in Europe
(CSCE) has provided the political momen-
tum for the adoption of a European policy
on control of air pollution. The 1979 Geneva
Convention on Long-Range Transboundary
Air Pollution came into force in 1983 and
has over thirty Northern Hemisphere parties in Western and Eastern Europe in addition to Russia, Canada, and the United
States. **Long-range transboundary air pollu-**
tion is defined as pol-
lution having effects
at such a distance
that it is not generally
possible to distin-
guish the contribu-
tions of individual
emission sources or
groups of sources.
Regulation requires
each State to instigate
policies that reduce
emission of pollutants.

> **Long-range transboundary air pollution:** Ambient air pollution having effects at such a distance that it is not generally possible to distinguish the sources; each State involved is required to instigate policies to reduce emissions.

The 1985 Vienna Convention for the
Protection of the Ozone Layer and the 1987
Montreal Protocol are responses to the
alarming finding that the protective ozone
in the upper layer of the earth's atmosphere
was depleting. The United States first instituted unilateral measures to reduce domestic production and consumption of CFCs as
a restraint on the use of ozone-depleting
substances. However, it became evident that
no regime would be likely to work unless
it was global, since the impact of ozone-
depleting substances is the same wherever
or however they originate and would affect
all States. The first
Ozone Convention
proceeded toward
preventive action in
advance of firm
proof of actual harm,
but by 1987, the sci-
entific evidence was
more conclusive, and
it was evident that

> **Ozone Convention:** A treaty that first established a commitment in 1987 to take action to reduce depletion of the earth's protective ozone layer and that has been supplemented by the Montreal Protocol in 1990.

stronger measures were needed. The Montreal Protocol, as revised in 1990, represents
a much more significant agreement than the
convention itself. It sets firm targets for
reducing and eventually eliminating consumption and production of a range of
ozone-depleting substances.

Protection of Wildlife and Biodiversity

Traditional international law regarded wildlife that migrated across borders as common property; however, these perceptions are beginning to change. Attention is being given to animal rights, and the common property doctrine is being overlaid with new concepts of "common heritage," "common interest," and "common concern." The first treaties concerning wildlife attempted to regulate common property. The 1885 Convention for the Uniform Regulation of Fishing on the Rhine was one of the first of such relevant treaties. Concern about the taking of species such as seals, birds, salmon, and whales were among the first to excite international concern.

The 1972 Stockholm Conference (UNCHE) produced the first of the emerging principles of customary international law. The relevant principles of the UNCHE Declaration included those safeguarding natural resources, including fauna, air, water, and land, for the benefit of present and future generations; requiring maintenance of renewable resources; and identifying humankind's special responsibility to safeguard the heritage of wildlife and its habitat and to improve it.

A large number of bilateral cooperative agreements on conservation of nature exist. The notable multilateral conventions include the 1979 Bonn Convention on the Conservation of Migratory Species of Wild Animals, the 1973 Convention on Trade in Endangered Species (CITES), and the Whaling Conventions, which created the International Whaling Commission. All of these treaties create significant regulatory agencies that are beginning to have important effects in protection of wildlife.

The most ambitious multilateral treaty is the Convention on Biological Diversity, concluded in 1992 as a result of the U.N. Environmental Conference at Rio de Janeiro. The purpose of this convention is to pursue the conservation of biological diversity, the sustainable use of its components, and the fair and equitable sharing of the benefits arising out of the use of genetic resources. The latter would include appropriate access to genetic resources and appropriate transfer of relevant technologies. **Biological diversity** is defined as "the variability among living organisms from all sources including terrestrial, marine and other aquatic ecosystems and the ecological complexes of which they are part, including diversity within species and between species and of ecosystems." By 1995, this convention had received the necessary sixty ratifications to bring it into force and create the relevant regulatory agencies involved.

> *Biological diversity:* Variability among living organisms from all sources, including terrestrial, marine, and other aquatic ecosystems and the ecological complexes of which they are part, including diversity within species and between species and of ecosystems.

The development of modern international environmental law has been one of the most remarkable exercises in international lawmaking, comparable only to the law of human rights in the scale and form it has taken. Birnie and Boyle (1992) conclude that "the system which has emerged from this process is neither primitive nor wholly without effect, though equally it has many weaknesses" (p. 549). What has been accomplished is a broad awareness of the importance of international cooperation in protection of the natural environment that sustains us all. Institutions for the progressive development of international law, resolution of disputes, and the adoption and harmonization of national environmental law have laid the foundation of a new system of global environmental order.

Global Regulatory Interdependence

Today, a comprehensive view of regulatory cooperation in the international community reveals a network of links between all levels of government in a multilayered regulatory system. This text has provided some details in only the areas of labor and environmental concerns; however, intergovernmental regulation has become a major part of development in an interdependent world. An interdependent world requires new forms of governance. In particular, OECD countries are finding that cooperative regulatory actions are more effective in bringing about change.

This conclusion is reached by the authors of a 1994 OECD publication titled *Regulatory Co-operation for an Interdependent World*. The quantitative data revealed in Figure 8.1 show three selected indicators of the enormous changes that are taking place in the international regulatory realm that reflect the magnitude of this dynamic development.

The International Standards Organization (ISO) is the major agency among some thirty similar organizations that set private and public international standards based on existing technology in a variety of fields, including products, chemicals, health, safety, labor, and environmental protection. The ISO has a membership of ninety-six national standards bodies who work with 460 other international organizations through 2,678 technical committees and subcommittees to write standards. These standards are used by government and industry in a variety of ways and influence the decisions made by national regulatory bodies (OECD, 1994, p. 26).

The OECD is composed of the twenty-four most developed countries of the world[1] and is charged with the function of promoting policies designed "to achieve the highest sustainable economic growth and employment and raising the standard of living in Member countries, while maintaining financial stability, and thus contribute to the development of the world economy" (OECD, 1994, p. 2).

∎   ∎   ∎

Chapter Summary

1. Growing evidence of potentially irreversible degradation of the natural environment has led to the development of international environmental regulatory regimes since the Stockholm Conference in 1972.

2. Widely accepted norms of customary international law establish an obligation of States to ensure that activities within their jurisdiction or control do not cause damage to the environment of other States or to the international commons, including ambient air and the marine environment.

3. The *Trail Smelter* and the *Lac Lanoux* arbitrations illustrate the customary principles of State responsibility to regulate transboundary pollution and to notify other States who share an international watercourse when engaging in significant alteration of such international waters.

International (ISO) standards in effect

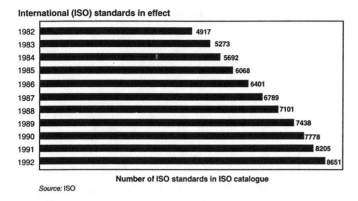

Number of ISO standards in ISO catalogue

Source: ISO

Substansive decisions and recomendations of the Council of the OECD, 1961-1992

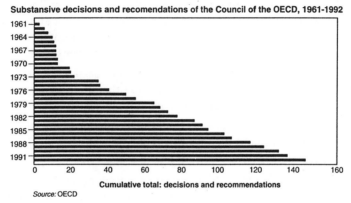

Cumulative total: decisions and recommendations

Source: OECD

Multilateral environmental Conventions signed or ratified by four or more OECD countries

Year that Convention was developed

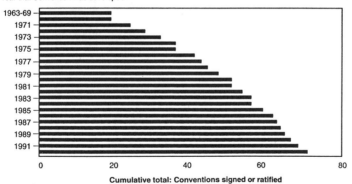

Cumulative total: Conventions signed or ratified

Figure 8.1. The Globization of Regulation: Three Selected Indicators
SOURCE: Organization for Economic Cooperation and Development (1994, p. 16). Used with permission.

4. The *Restatement (Third) of Foreign Relations Law of the United States* has produced clear statements of the principles of customary international law in the environmental area that are widely recognized today.

5. Remedies for injury caused by transboundary pollution and alteration of watercourses involve both private legal action for damages in domestic courts and public international legal remedies through negotiation, mediation, arbitration, and adjudication. Most

States have responded by liberalizing access to private legal remedies in their own courts.

6. Major international treaties, particularly since 1972, have created new regulatory regimes or strengthened older agencies in the effort to protect the environment in areas of international watercourses, marine pollution, hazardous waste disposal, ambient air pollution, and protection of wildlife.

7. The Rhine Commission has been strengthened by new Chemicals and Chlorides Conventions. The U.S. Canadian International Joint Commission, created by the Boundary Waters Treaty, has been strengthened by new agreements on Great Lakes water quality, and a new Zambezi River Commission has been established in Africa.

8. The regime established by the 1982 Law of the Convention is the most dramatic development in the area of marine pollution control and responsibility of States to enforce international standards adding new national jurisdiction and remedies. The International Marine Organization (IMO) has produced important international standards, and the major conventions regulate dumping of hazardous waste in the seas.

9. The International Atomic Energy Agency (IAEA) has been given new regulatory functions in regard to environmental pollution, and other regional regulatory bodies, such as EURATOM, have promoted the implementation of new international standards.

10. Major new conferences and treaties have established standards regarding long-range transboundary air pollution and measures to reduce the depletion of the protective ozone layer.

11. Important new treaties protecting wildlife and endangered species have been developed in regional areas. Trade in endangered species is being subjected to increasing controls. Particular species such as whales have made a comeback as a result of the regulatory efforts of the International Whaling Commission. A major new treaty protecting biological diversity has been established.

12. These developments illustrate the potential for international lawmaking in areas where the need for functional cooperation is clearly evident.

Key Terms

Stockholm Declaration (1972)
Trail Smelter case
Lac Lanoux arbitration
international watercourse
International Marine Organization
    (IMO)
U.N. Environment Program (UNEP)

International Atomic Energy Agency
    (IAEA)
environmental impact statement
long-range transboundary air pollution
Ozone Convention
biological diversity

▮   ▮   ▮

Discussion Questions

1. What are the basic customary principles of international environmental law? What private and public remedies are available under customary international law when violations occur?

2. How has the U.S. Congress acted to implement many of the standards of international environmental law? Is the United States more of a leader in the environmental field than in the labor field? Why or why not?

3. Why is the 1982 Law of the Sea Convention considered one of the most significant treaties providing a potential for more successful regulation and dispute settlement in the environmental area? Should the United States ratify this treaty? Why or why not?

4. What areas of international environmental regulation are of most interest to you? Does the brief summary in your text prompt additional questions to which you would like more complete answers? Discuss these areas of interest and questions in class.

Note

1. OECD member States include Australia, Austria, Belgium, Canada, Denmark, Finland, France, Germany, Greece, Iceland, Ireland, Italy, Japan, Luxembourg, Mexico, the Netherlands, New Zealand, Norway, Portugal, Spain, Sweden, Switzerland, Turkey, the United Kingdom, and the United States.

Suggested Readings

Birnie, P. W., & Boyle, A. E. (1992). *International law and the environment*. New York: Oxford University Press.

Gore, A. (1992). *Earth in the balance*. Boston: Houghton Mifflin.

Organization for Economic Cooperation and Development. (1994). *Regulatory co-operation for an interdependent world*. Washington, DC: Author.

Internet Sources

Browse: Use *environmental law* (http://www.un.org).

9 International Crimes and Extradition

This chapter may be considered a general summary of the individual nation-state's jurisdiction to prescribe the conduct of individuals under contemporary international law. Although State jurisdiction to prescribe theoretically includes both civil and criminal jurisdiction, the focus will be on jurisdiction to prescribe and adjudicate criminal activity.

The distinction between "private" and "public" law has not yet been clearly established in this text, but it becomes necessary to make the distinction at this point. **Private law** in general refers to the rules governing private parties in disputes that arise out of their private transactions. **Public law** involves governmental regulation of the society and is most clearly illustrated by the State's authority to define and punish individuals for crimes against the State. This distinction has become blurred in modern society where governmental authority to prescribe

Private law: As contrasted with public law, this term refers to that part of the law administered between private parties.

various aspects of private transactions is clearly recognized and increasingly regulated by the State. The major procedural distinction is that in matters of "public law," the party bringing the legal action is always the State; legal action cannot be brought by a private party. Public international law therefore includes governmental regulatory actions, such as taxation, antitrust legislation, securities regulation, labor laws, environmental regulation, and felony criminal actions.

Public law: A general classification of law, consisting of constitutional, administrative, criminal, and international law. It is concerned with the organization of the State; the relations between the State and the people who compose it; the responsibilities of public officers to the State, to each other, and to private persons; and the relations of States to one another.

International law has long recognized limitations on the authority of States to exercise jurisdiction to prescribe in circumstances affecting the interests of other States. Traditionally, it has been accepted that a State has jurisdiction to exercise its authority to prescribe individual conduct within its own territory and with respect to its own nationals abroad. This is the essential meaning of sovereignty. In the past, the jurisdiction of a State to make its law applicable in a transnational context was determined by formal criteria of conflict of law supposedly derived from concepts of State sovereignty and power. Ambiguous cases were seen as raising issues in the definition and application of these principles. As we have seen in the previous chapters of this text, these issues of conflict of law have given rise to new rules of reasonableness and reason as well as to treaty law that is better adapted to the complexities of international intercourse.

Jurisdiction to Prescribe

Jurisdiction to prescribe refers to the individual State's authority to define and punish acts of individuals. Such authority is limited by international law. Modern international law recognizes five principles on which the exercise of a State's jurisdiction to prescribe may be based: (a) the territoriality principle, (b) the nationality principle, (c) the protective principle, (d) the passive personality principle, and (e) the universal principle. Territoriality is the most fundamental of these principles, and the others are more extensively limited by international law. However, in regard to jurisdiction over crimes such as piracy, international law has expanded the universal jurisdiction of every State to prescribe a limited category of crimes. These crimes are subject to the jurisdiction of every State regardless of where the crime was committed or the accused's nationality.

The Principle of Territoriality

Any violation of a nation's criminal laws, committed within its sovereign territory, is subject to punishment by that State regardless of the nationality of the person accused. This is commonly referred to as the **territorial principle.** Thus, territoriality and nationality are discrete and independent bases of jurisdiction.

> **Territorial principle:** The most fundamental jurisdiction of a State to prescribe and punish criminal activity occurring within its territory.

The territorial principle is considered the normal, and nationality an exceptional, basis for the exercise of a State's jurisdiction. The territorial principle is by far the most common basis for the exercise of jurisdiction to prescribe, and it is generally undisputed. However, circumstances increasingly arise in which two or more States are involved in disputes over whether a person or property can properly be deemed present in the State asserting jurisdiction. Such a situation developed between France and Turkey in 1926 when a French mail steamer, the *S.S. Lotus*, bound for Constantinople, collided with a Turkish coal ship in international waters. Eight Turkish sailors and passengers were killed when the *Lotus* hit the Turkish vessel. When the *Lotus* arrived in Turkey, Turkish authorities arrested and prosecuted the French ship's watch officer, Lieutenant Demons, for involuntary manslaughter.

France objected to Turkey's exercise of jurisdiction, claiming that the action had occurred outside of Turkish territory and that any criminal action must be brought by France, the country of nationality of Lieutenant Demons. After diplomatic protests, France and Turkey decided to submit France's objection to the Permanent Court of International Justice (PCIJ) for resolution. In the following illustrative case, the PCIJ concluded that, in the absence of a treaty provision to the contrary, Turkey could prosecute France's citizen for involuntary manslaughter under the territorial principle, but France also had concurrent jurisdiction to prosecute under the nationality principle.

∎   ∎   ∎

The S.S. Lotus (France v. Turkey)

Permanent Court of International Justice, 1927.
P.C.I.J., Ser. A, No. 10.

* * *

By a special agreement signed at Geneva on October 12th, 1928, between the Governments of the French and Turkish Republics . . . , [France and Turkey] have submitted to the Permanent Court of International Justice the question of jurisdiction which has arisen between them following upon the collision which occurred on August 2nd, 1926, between the steamships *Boz-Kourt* and *Lotus*.

According to the special agreement, the Court has to decide the following questions:

(1) Has Turkey, contrary to Article 15 of the Convention of Lausanne of July 24th, 1923, respecting conditions of residence and business and jurisdiction, acted in conflict with the principles of international law—and if so, what principles—by instituting, following the collision which occurred on August 2nd, 1926, on the high seas between the French steamer *Lotus* and the Turkish steamer *Boz-Kourt* and upon the arrival of the French steamer at Constantinople—as well as against the captain of the Turkish steamship—joint criminal proceedings in pursuance of Turkish law against M. Demons, officer of the watch on board the *Lotus* at the time of the collision, in consequence of the loss of the *Boz-Kourt* having involved the death of eight Turkish sailors and passengers?

(2) Should the reply be in the affirmative, what pecuniary reparation is due to M. Demons, provided, according to the principles of international law, reparation should be made in similar cases?

* * *

On August 2nd, 1926, just before midnight, a collision occurred between the French mail steamer *Lotus*, proceeding to Constantinople, and the Turkish collier *Boz-Kourt*, between five and six nautical miles to the north of Cape Sigri (Mitylene). The *Boz-Kourt*, which was cut in two, sank, and eight Turkish nationals who were on board perished. After having done everything possible to succour the shipwrecked persons, of whom ten were able to be saved, the *Lotus* continued on its course to Constantinople, where it arrived on August 3rd.

At the time of the collision, the officer of the watch on board the *Lotus* was Monsieur Demons, a French citizen, lieutenant in the merchant service and first officer of the ship, whilst the movements of the *Boz-Kourt* were directed by its captain, Hassan Bey, who was one of those saved from the wreck.

* * *

On August 5th, Lieutenant Demons was requested by the Turkish authorities to go ashore to give evidence. The examination, the length of which incidentally resulted in delaying the departure of the *Lotus*, led to the placing under arrest of Lieutenant Demons—without previous notice being given to the French Consul-General—and Hassan Bey, amongst others. This arrest, which has been characterized by the Turkish Agent as arrest pending trial (*arrestation préventive*), was effected in order to ensure that the criminal prosecution instituted against the two officers, on a charge of manslaughter, by the Public Prosecutor of Stamboul, on the complaint of the families of the victims of the collision, should follow its normal course.

The case was first heard by the Criminal Court of Stamboul on August 28th. On that occasion, Lieutenant Demons submitted that the Turkish Courts had no jurisdiction; the Court, however, overruled his objection. When the proceedings were resumed on September 11th, Lieutenant Demons demanded his release on bail: this request was complied with. . . .

On September 15th, the Criminal Court delivered its judgment, the terms of which have not been communicated to the Court by the Parties. It is, however, common ground, that it sentenced Lieutenant Demons to eighty days' imprisonment and a fine of twenty-two pounds, Hassan Bey being sentenced to a slightly more severe penalty.

* * *

The action of the Turkish judicial authorities with regard to Lieutenant Demons at once gave rise to many diplomatic representations and other steps on the part of the French Government or its representatives in Turkey, either protesting against the arrest of Lieutenant Demons or demanding his release, or with a view to obtaining the transfer of the case from the Turkish Courts to the French Courts.

As a result of these representations, the Government of the Turkish Republic declared on September 2nd, 1926, that "it would have no objection to the reference of the conflict of jurisdiction to the Court at The Hague." The French Government having, on the 6th of the same month, given "its full consent to the proposed solution," the two Governments appointed their plenipotentiaries with a view to the drawing up of the special agreement to be submitted to the Court; this special agreement was signed at Geneva on October 12th, 1926, . . . and the ratifications were deposited on December 27th, 1926.

* * *

I

Before approaching the consideration of the principles of international law contrary to which Turkey is alleged to have acted—thereby infringing the terms of Article 15 of the Convention of Lausanne of July 24th, 1923, respecting conditions of residence and business and jurisdiction, it is necessary to define, in the light of the written and oral proceedings, the position resulting from the special agreement. . . .

1. The collision which occurred on August 2nd, 1926, between the *S.S. Lotus*, flying the French flag, and the *S.S. Boz-Kourt*, flying the Turkish flag, took place on the high seas: the territorial jurisdiction of any State other than France and Turkey therefore does not enter into account.

2. The violation, if any, of the principles of international law would have consisted in the taking of criminal proceedings against Lieutenant Demons. It is not therefore a question relating to any particular step in these proceedings—such as his being put to trial, his arrest, his detention pending trial or the judgment given by the Criminal Court of Stamboul—but of the very fact of the Turkish Courts exercising criminal jurisdiction. That is why the arguments put forward by the Parties in both phases of the proceedings relate exclusively to the question whether Turkey has or has not, according to the principles of international law, jurisdiction to prosecute in this case.

The Parties agree that the Court has not to consider whether the prosecution was in conformity with Turkish law; it need not therefore consider whether, apart from the actual question of jurisdiction, the provisions of Turkish law cited by Turkish authorities were really applicable in this case, or whether the manner in which the proceedings against Lieutenant Demons were conducted might constitute a denial of justice, and accordingly, a violation of international law. The discussions have borne exclusively upon the question whether criminal jurisdiction does or does not exist in this case.

3. The prosecution was instituted because the loss of the *Boz-Kourt* involved the death of eight Turkish sailors and passengers. . . . No criminal intention has been imputed to either of the officers responsible for navigating the two vessels; it is therefore a case of prosecution for involuntary manslaughter. . . . Moreover, the exact conditions in which these persons perished do not appear from the documents submitted to the Court; nevertheless, there is no doubt that their death may be regarded as the direct outcome of the collision, and the French Government has not contended that this relation of cause and effect cannot exist.

* * *

5. The prosecution was instituted in pursuance of Turkish legislation. The special agreement does not indicate what clause or clauses of that legislation apply. No document has been submitted to the Court indicating on what article of the Turkish Penal Code the prosecution was based; the French Government however declares that the Criminal Court claimed jurisdiction under Article 6 of the Turkish Penal Code, and far from denying this statement, Turkey, in the submissions of her Counter-Case, contends that that article is in conformity with the principles of international law. It does not appear from the proceedings whether the prosecution was instituted solely on the basis of that article.

Article 6 of the Turkish Penal Code, . . . runs as follows:

> [Translation] Any foreigner who, apart from the cases contemplated by Article 4, commits an offence abroad to the prejudice of Turkey or of a Turkish subject, for which offence Turkish law prescribes a penalty involving loss of freedom for a minimum period of not less than one year, shall be punished in accordance with the Turkish Penal Code provided that he is arrested in Turkey. . . .

* * *

Even if the Court must hold that the Turkish authorities had seen fit to base the prosecution of Lieutenant Demons upon the above mentioned Article 6, the question submitted to the Court is not whether that article is compatible with the principles of international law; it is more general. The Court is asked to state whether or not the principles of international law prevent Turkey from instituting criminal proceedings against Lieutenant Demons under Turkish law. Neither the conformity of Article 6 in itself with the principles of international law nor the application of that article by the Turkish authorities constitutes the point at issue; it is the very fact of the institution of proceedings which is held by France to be contrary to those principles.

* * *

II

Having determined the position resulting from the terms of the special agreement, the Court must now ascertain which were the principles of international law that the prosecution of Lieutenant Demons could conceivably be said to contravene.

It is Article 15 of the Convention of Lausanne of July 24th, 1923, respecting conditions of residence and business and jurisdiction, which refers the contracting Parties to the principles of international law as regards the delimitation of their respective jurisdiction.

This clause is as follows:

> Subject to the provisions of Article 16, all questions of jurisdiction shall, as between Turkey and the other contracting Powers, be decided in accordance with the principles of international law.
>
> . . . In these circumstances it is impossible—except in pursuance of a definite stipulation—to construe the expression "principles of international law" otherwise than as meaning the principles which are in force between all independent nations and which therefore apply equally to all the contracting Parties.

* * *

III

. . . The French Government contends that the Turkish Courts, in order to have jurisdiction, should be able to point to some title to jurisdiction recognized by international law in favour of Turkey. On the other hand, the Turkish Government takes the view that Article 15 allows Turkey jurisdiction whenever such jurisdiction does not come into conflict with a principle of international law.

* * *

International law governs relations between independent States. The rules of law binding upon States therefore emanate from their own free will as expressed in conventions or by usages generally accepted as expressing principles of law and established in order to regulate the relations between these co-existing independent communities or with a view to the achievement of common aims. Restrictions upon the independence of States cannot therefore be presumed.

Now the first and foremost restriction imposed by international law upon a State is that—failing the existence of a permissive rule to the contrary—it may not exercise its power in any form in the territory of another State. In this sense jurisdiction is certainly territorial; it cannot be exercised by a State outside its territory except by virtue of a permissive rule derived from international custom or from a convention.

It does not, however, follow that international law prohibits a State from exercising jurisdiction in its own territory, in respect of any case which relates to acts which have taken place abroad, and in which it cannot rely on some permissive rule of international law. Such a view would only be tenable if international law contained a general prohibition to States to extend the application of their laws and the jurisdiction of their courts to persons, property and acts outside their territory, and if, as an exception to this general prohibition, it allowed States to do so in certain specific cases. But this is certainly not the case under international law as it stands at present. Far from laying down a general prohibition to the effect that States may not extend the application of their laws and the jurisdiction of their courts to persons, property and acts outside their territory, it leaves them in this respect a wide measure of discretion which is only limited in certain cases by prohibitive rules; as regards other cases, every State remains free to adopt the principles which it regards as best and most suitable.

This discretion left to States by international law explains the great variety of rules which they have been able to adopt without objections or complaints on the part of other States; it is in order to remedy the difficulties resulting from such variety that efforts have been made for many years past, both in Europe and America, to prepare conventions the effect of which would be precisely to limit the discretion at present left to States in this respect by international law, thus making good the existing lacunae in respect of jurisdiction or removing the conflicting jurisdictions arising from the diversity of the principles adopted by the various States.

In these circumstances, all that can be required of a State is that it should not overstep the limits which international law places upon its jurisdiction; within these limits, its title to exercise jurisdiction rests in its sovereignty.

It follows from the foregoing that the contention of the French Government to the effect that Turkey must in each case be able to cite a rule of international law authorizing her to exercise jurisdiction, is opposed to the generally accepted international law to which Article 15 of the Convention of Lausanne refers. . . .

* * *

The Court therefore must, in any event, ascertain whether or not there exists a rule of international law limiting the freedom of States to extend the criminal jurisdiction of their courts to a situation uniting the circumstances of the present case.

IV

The Court will now proceed to ascertain whether general international law, to which Article 15 of the Convention of Lausanne refers, contains a rule prohibiting Turkey from prosecuting Lieutenant Demons.

For this purpose, it will in the first place examine the value of the arguments advanced by the French Government, without however omitting to take into account other possible aspects of the problem, which might show the existence of a restrictive rule applicable in this case.

The arguments advanced by the French Government [include the following]:

(1) International law does not allow a State to take proceedings with regard to offences committed by foreigners abroad, simply by reason of the nationality of the victim; and such is the situation in the present case because the offence must be regarded as having been committed on board the French vessel.

* * *

As regards the first argument, the Court feels obliged in the first place to recall that its examination is strictly confined to the specific situation in the present case, for it is only in regard to this situation that its decision is asked for.

As has already been observed, the characteristic features of the situation of fact are as follows: there has been a collision on the high seas between two vessels flying different flags, on one of which was one of the persons alleged to be guilty of the offence, whilst the victims were on board the other.

This being so, the Court does not think it necessary to consider the contention that a State cannot punish offences committed abroad by a foreigner simply by reason of the nationality of the victim. For this contention only relates to the case where the nationality of the victim is the only criterion on which the criminal jurisdiction of the State is based. Even if that argument were correct generally speaking—and in regard to this the Court reserves its opinion—it could only be used in the present case if international law forbade Turkey to take into consideration the fact that the offence produced its effects on the Turkish vessel and consequently in a place assimilated to Turkish territory in which the application of Turkish criminal law cannot be challenged, even in regard to offences committed there by foreigners. But no such rule of international law exists. No argument has come to the knowledge of the Court from which it could be deduced that States recognize themselves to be under an obligation towards each other only to have regard to the place where the author of the offence happens to be at the time of the offence. On the contrary, it is certain that the courts of many countries, even of countries which have given their criminal legislation a strictly territorial character, interpret criminal law in the sense that offences, the authors of which at the moment of commission are in the territory of another State, are nevertheless to be regarded as having been committed in the national territory, if one of the constituent elements of the offence, and more especially its effects, have taken place there. French courts have, in regard to a variety of situations, given decisions sanctioning this way of interpreting the territorial principle. Again, the Court does not know of any cases in which governments have protested against the fact that the criminal law of some country contained a rule to this effect or that the courts of a country construed their criminal law in this sense. Consequently, once it is admitted that the effects of the offence were produced on the Turkish vessel, it becomes impossible to hold that there is a rule of international law which prohibits Turkey from prosecuting Lieutenant Demons because of the fact that the author of the offence was on board the French ship. Since, as has already been observed, the special agreement does not deal with the provision of Turkish law under which the prosecution was instituted, but only with the question whether the prosecution should be regarded as contrary to the principles of international law, there is no reason preventing the Court from confining itself to observing that, in this case, a prosecution may also be justified from the point of view of the so-called territorial principle.

. . . The fact that the judicial authorities may have committed an error in their choice of the legal provision applicable to the particular case and compatible with international law only concerns municipal law and can only affect international law in so far as a treaty provision enters into account, or the possibility of a denial of justice arises.

* * *

The offence for which Lieutenant Demons appears to have been prosecuted was an act—of negligence or imprudence, having its origin on board the *Lotus*, whilst its effects made themselves felt on board the *Boz-Kourt*. These two elements are, legally, entirely inseparable, so much so that their separation renders the offence nonexistent. Neither the exclusive jurisdiction of either State, nor the limitations of the jurisdiction of each to the occurrences which took place on the respective ships would appear calculated to satisfy the requirements of justice and effectively to protect the interests of the two States. It is only natural that each should be able to exercise jurisdiction and to do so in respect of the incident as a whole. It is therefore a case of concurrent jurisdiction.

* * *

For These Reasons, the COURT, having heard both Parties, gives, by the President's casting vote—the votes being equally divided—judgment to the effect

(1) that, following the collision which occurred on August 2nd, 1926, on the high seas between the French steamship *Lotus* and the Turkish steamship *Boz-Kourt*, and upon the arrival of the French ship at Stamboul, and in consequence of the loss of the *Boz-Kourt* having involved the death of eight Turkish nationals, Turkey, by instituting criminal proceedings in pursuance of Turkish law against Lieutenant Demons, officer of the watch on board the *Lotus*

at the time of the collision, has not acted in conflict with the principles of international law, contrary to Article 15 of the Convention of Lausanne of July 24th, 1923, respecting conditions of residence and business and jurisdiction;

(2) that, consequently, there is no occasion to give judgment on the question of the pecuniary reparation which might have been due to Lieutenant Demons if Turkey, by prosecuting him as above stated, had acted in a manner contrary to the principles of international law.

* * *

[Separate and dissenting opinions omitted.]

Discussion Questions

1. Which State, France or Turkey, had the burden of proof that a principle of international law had been violated in this case? Why?
2. Does the decision in the *Lotus* case state (a) a rule of jurisdiction in international law or (b) the legal consequences of the lack of a rule of international law on the issue? Explain your answer.
3. If person *X* stands in country *Y* and shoots person *A* who is located in country *B*, under what conditions would country *B* have jurisdiction to prosecute person *X* according to the principle of law used to decide the *Lotus* Case?
4. Could France have exercised its jurisdiction over Lieutenant Demons if Turkey had agreed to extradite this person? Would Turkey have to extradite under the circumstances of this case?

> *Comment:* It must be clearly understood that the *Lotus* case represents the applicable rule in the absence of a specific provision of treaty law or customary principle regarded as limiting jurisdiction. Such rules have developed as international law progresses. Article 11 of the 1958 Convention on the High Seas and Article 97 of the 1982 LOS Convention, both provide:
>
>> In the event of a collision or of any other incident of navigation concerning a ship on the high seas, involving the penal or disciplinary responsibility of the master or of any person in the service of the ship, no penal or disciplinary proceedings may be instituted against such persons except before the judicial or administrative authorities either of the flag state or of the state of which such person is a national.

The *Restatement (Third) of the Foreign Relations Law of the United States* (American Law Institute, 1987) provides a clear statement of the basic principles of a State's jurisdiction to prescribe.

§ 402. *Bases of Jurisdiction to Prescribe*

Subject to § 403, a state has jurisdiction to prescribe law with respect to

(1) (a) conduct that, wholly or in substantial part, takes place within its territory;
   (b) the status of persons, or interests in things, present within its territory;
   (c) conduct outside its territory that has or is intended to have substantial effect within its territory;
(2) the activities, interests, status, or relations of its nationals outside as well as within its territory; and
(3) certain conduct outside its territory by persons not its nationals that is directed against the security of the state or against a limited class of other state interests.

The principles of territoriality and nationality are the bases of jurisdiction to prescribe. But these links are not sufficient in all cases: Not all activities within a State's territory, nor all activities of a State's nationals, may reasonably be subjected to its legislation. Section 403 of the *Restatement (Third)* relates to criteria of reasonableness that have become a part of international law on the subject of jurisdiction. The principles expressed in the basic statement above require considerable elaboration and will be illustrated by examples in the rest of this chapter.

However, after reading the *Lotus* case and the basic *Restatement (Third)* above, it should be evident that there is much potential for overlapping jurisdiction, and conflict that may call for the evaluation of competing interests by the standards of reasonableness.

The Effects Principle

Jurisdiction with respect to activity originating outside the State but having its effect (or intended to have effect) within the State's territory is an aspect of jurisdiction based on territoriality. The **effects principle** is universally accepted today with respect to acts such as shooting or even sending libelous publications across a boundary. It is generally accepted with respect to liability for injury in the State from products made outside the State and introduced into its stream of commerce. Conflict has arisen as a result of economic regulation when the conduct was lawful where carried out. The American Law Institute (1987) takes the position that a State may exercise jurisdiction based on effects in the State, when the effect or intended effect is substantial and the exercise of jurisdiction is reasonable under the reasonableness criteria listed in §403 (see p. 496).

> **Effects principle:** *Jurisdiction to prescribe activities having been initiated in one State but having a substantial effect in another State. Both States may have jurisdiction, but in criminal matters, the State exercising jurisdiction to adjudicate generally requires personal presence of the accused.*

The Nationality Principle

The nationality principle is an independent alternative basis of jurisdiction and may be asserted as a basis of jurisdiction to prescribe activities of a State's nationals wherever they may be located. Especially in tax matters, this authority is asserted by all States. However, many States assert that a crime committed by their nationals outside their territory is still subject to their jurisdiction even though there may be concurrent jurisdiction of the State where the crime was committed.

The **nationality principle** is applicable to juridical as well as to natural persons, and the nationality of a corporation or comparable juridical entity is generally that of the State under whose law it is organized.

> **Nationality principle:** *Jurisdiction to prescribe activities of a State's nationals wherever they may be located.*

With the major exception of application of its tax laws, the United States has applied the law to individuals residing abroad on the basis of their U.S. nationality in only a few types of cases. Such laws that have been applied by the United States in this manner include the treason statute (18 U.S.C. § 2381), the selective service law (50 U.S.C. App. § 453), and the regulations adopted under the Trading With the Enemy Act (50 U.S.C. App. § 5[b]).

A classic case of application of U.S. law on the basis of nationality is the following *Blackmer v. United States*, decided by the Supreme Court in 1932. This tax case arose out of the famous Teapot Dome scandal during the period of the administration of President Warren Harding in the 1920s. In litigation related to this scandal, the Supreme Court found that some high-ranking politicians had obtained oil leases through corrupt means. Blackmer was a U.S. citizen living in France. A U.S. consul in Paris served him with a notice to return to the District of Columbia to testify on behalf of the U.S. government during criminal and civil investigations of the scandal. After Blackmer refused the court order to return, the District Court judge found him in contempt and imposed a large fine. In this case, the Supreme Court upheld a subpoena, pursuant to statute, addressed to a U.S. national residing abroad, requiring his attendance in a U.S. court as a witness.

Blackmer v. United States
Supreme Court of the United States, 1932.
284 U.S. 421, 52 S.Ct. 252, 76 L.Ed. 375.

Mr. Chief Justice HUGHES delivered the opinion of the Court.

The petitioner, Harry M. Blackmer, a citizen of the United States resident in Paris, France, was adjudged guilty of contempt of the Supreme Court of the District of Columbia for failure to respond to subpoenas served upon him in France and requiring him to appear as a witness on behalf of the United States at a criminal trial in that court. Two subpoenas were issued, for appearances at different times, and there was a separate proceeding with respect to each. The two cases were heard together, and a fine of $30,000 with costs was imposed in each case, to be satisfied out of the property of the petitioner which had been seized by order of the court. The decrees were affirmed by the Court of Appeals of the District [49 F.2d 523], and this Court granted writs of certiorari . . .

The subpoenas were issued and served, and the proceedings to punish for contempt were taken under the provisions of the Act of July 3, 1926. . . . The statute provides that whenever the attendance at the trial of a criminal action of a witness abroad, who is "a citizen of the United States or domiciled therein," is desired by the Attorney General, or any assistant or district attorney acting under him, the judge of the court in which the action is pending may order a subpoena to issue, to be addressed to a consul of the United States and to be served by him personally upon the witness with a tender of traveling expenses. Sections 2, 3 of the act (28 U.S.C.A. §§ 712, 713). Upon proof of such service and of the failure of the witness to appear, the court may make an order requiring the witness to show cause why he should not be punished for contempt, and, upon the issue of such an order, the court may direct that property belonging to the witness and within the United States may be seized and held to satisfy any judgment which may be rendered against him in the proceeding. Sections 4, 5 (28 U.S.C.A. §§ 714, 715). Provision is made for personal service of the order upon the witness and also for its publication in a newspaper of general circulation in the district where the court is sitting. Section 6 (28 U.S.C.A. § 716). If, upon the hearing, the charge is sustained, the court may adjudge the witness guilty of contempt and impose upon him a fine not exceeding $100,000, to be satisfied by a sale of the property seized. Section 7 (28 U.S.C.A. § 717). This statute and the proceedings against the petitioner are assailed as being repugnant to the Constitution of the United States.

First. The principal objections to the statute are that it violates the due process clause of the Fifth Amendment. These contentions are: (1) That the "Congress has no power to authorize United States consuls to serve process except as permitted by treaty"; (2) that the act does not provide "a valid method of acquiring judicial jurisdiction to render personal judgment against defendant and judgment against his property"; (3) that the act "does not require actual or any other notice to defendant of the offense or of the Government's claim against his property"; (4) that the provisions "for hearing and judgment in the entire absence of the accused and without his consent" are invalid; and (5) that the act is "arbitrary, capricious and unreasonable."

While it appears that the petitioner removed his residence to France in the year 1924, it is undisputed that he was, and continued to be, a citizen of the United States. He continued to owe allegiance to the United States. By virtue of the obligations of citizenship, the United States retained its authority over him, and he was bound by its laws made applicable to him in a foreign country. Thus, although resident abroad, the petitioner remained subject to the taxing power of the United States. *Cook v. Tait*, 265 U.S. 47, 54, 56, 44 S.Ct. 444, 68 L.Ed. 895. For disobedience to its laws through conduct abroad, he was subject to punishment in the courts of the United States. *United States v. Bowman*, 260 U.S. 94, 102, 43 S.Ct. 39, 67 L.Ed. 149. With respect to such an exercise of authority, there is no question of international law, but solely of the purport of the municipal law which establishes the duties of the citizen in relation to his own government. While the legislation of the Congress, unless the contrary intent appears, is construed to apply only within the territorial jurisdiction of the United States, the question of its application, so far as citizens of the United States in foreign countries are concerned, is one of construction, not of legislative power. *American Banana Co, v. United Fruit Co.*, 213 U.S. 347, 357, 29 S.Ct. 511, 53 L.Ed. 826, 16 Ann.Cas. 1047; *United States v. Bowman, supra*. . . . Nor can it be doubted that the United States possesses the power inherent in sovereignty to require the return to this country of a citizen, resident elsewhere, whenever the public interest requires it, and to penalize him in case of refusal. . . . What in England was the prerogative of the sovereign in this respect pertains under our constitutional system to the national authority which may be exercised by the Congress by virtue of the legislative power to prescribe the duties of the citizens of the United States. It is also beyond controversy that one of the duties which the citizen owes to his government is to support the administration of justice by attending its courts and giving his testimony whenever he is properly summoned. . . . And the Congress may provide for the performance of this duty and prescribe penalties for disobedience.

In the present instance, the question concerns only the method of enforcing the obligation. The jurisdiction of the United States over its absent citizen, so far as the binding effect of its legislation is concerned, is a jurisdiction *in personam*, as he is personally bound to take notice of the laws that are applicable to him and to obey them. *United States v. Bowman, supra*. But for the exercise of judicial jurisdiction *in personam*, there must be due process, which requires appropriate notice of the judicial action and an opportunity to be heard. For this notice and opportunity the statute provides. The authority to require the absent citizen to return and testify necessarily implies the authority to give him notice of the requirement. As his attendance is needed in court, it is appropriate that the Congress should authorize the court to direct the notice to be given, and that it should be in the customary form of a subpoena. Obviously, the requirement would be nugatory, if provision could not be made for its communication to the witness in the foreign country. The efficacy of an attempt to provide constructive service in this country would rest upon the presumption that the notice would be given in a manner calculated to reach the witness abroad. *McDonald v. Mabee*, 243 U.S. 90, 92, 37 S.Ct. 343, 61 L.Ed. 608, L.R.A.1917F, 458. The question of the validity of the provision for actual service of the subpoena in a foreign country is one that arises solely between the government of the United States and the citizen. The mere giving of such a notice to the citizen in the foreign country of the requirement of his government that he shall return is in no sense an invasion of any right of the foreign government and the citizen has no standing to invoke any such supposed right. While consular privileges in foreign countries are the appropriate subjects of treaties, it does not follow that every act of a consul, as, e.g., in communicating with citizens of his own country, must be predicated upon a specific provision of a treaty. . . . The point raised by the petitioner with respect to the provision for the service of the subpoena abroad is without merit.

As the Congress could define the obligation, it could prescribe a penalty to enforce it. And, as the default lay in disobedience to an authorized direction of the court, it constituted a contempt of court, and the Congress could provide for procedure appropriate in contempt cases. The provision of the statute for punishment for contempt is applicable only "upon proof being made of the service and default." Section 4 (28 U.S.C.A. § 714). That proof affords a proper basis for the proceeding, and provision is made for personal service upon the witness of the order to show cause why he should not be adjudged guilty. For the same reasons as those which sustain the service of the subpoena abroad, it was competent to provide for the service of the order in like manner. It is only after a hearing pursuant to the order to show cause, and upon proof sustaining the charge, that the court can impose the penalty. The petitioner urges that the statute does not require notice of the offense, but the order to show cause is to be issued after the witness has failed to obey the subpoena demanding his attendance and the order is to be made by the court before which he was required to appear. This is sufficient to apprise the witness of the nature of the proceeding and he has full opportunity to be heard. The further contention is made that, as the offense is a criminal one, it is a violation of due process to hold the hearing, and to proceed to judgment, in the absence of the defendant. The argument misconstrues the nature of the proceeding. "While contempt may be an offense against the law and subject to appropriate punishment, certain it is that since the foundation of our government proceedings to punish such offenses have been regarded as *sui generis* and not 'criminal prosecutions' within the Sixth Amendment or common understanding." *Myers v. United States*, 264 U.S. 95, 104, 105, 44 S.Ct. 272, 273, 68 L.Ed. 577. . . . The requirement of due process in such a case is satisfied by suitable notice and adequate opportunity to appear and to be heard. . . .

The authorization of the seizure of the property belonging to the defaulting witness and within the United States, upon the issue of the order to show cause why he should not be punished for contempt . . . affords a provisional remedy, the propriety of which rests upon the validity of the contempt proceeding. As a witness is liable to punishment by fine if, upon the hearing, he is found guilty of contempt, no reason appears why his property may not be seized to provide security for the payment of the penalty. The proceeding conforms to familiar practice where absence or other circumstance makes a provisional remedy appropriate. . . . The order that is to be served upon the witness contains the direction for the seizure. The property is to be held pending the hearing, and is to be applied to the satisfaction of the fine imposed and unless it is paid. Given the obligation of the witness to respond to the subpoena, the showing of his default after service, and the validity of the provision for a fine in case default is not excused, there is no basis for objection to the seizure upon constitutional grounds. The argument that the statute creates an unreasonable classification is untenable. The disobedience of the defaulting witness to a lawful requirement of the court, and not the fact that he owns property, is the ground of his liability. He is not the subject of unconstitutional discrimination simply because he has property which may be appropriated to the satisfaction of a lawful claim. . . .

Third. The statute being valid, the question remains as to the procedure in its application against the petitioner. He insists that the showing for the issue of the subpoenas requiring him to attend was inadequate. But the "proper showing" required was for the purpose of satisfying the court that the subpoenas should issue. The petitions, in the instant cases, were presented to the judge of the court by the official representatives of the government, and their statement as to the materiality and importance of the testimony expected from the witness was unquestionably sufficient to give the court jurisdiction to issue the subpoenas, and, unless they were vacated upon proper application, the petitioner was bound to obey. . . .

Decrees affirmed.

Discussion Questions

1. What is the justification for the nationality principle as applied in the *Blackmer* case?
2. Does *Blackmer* provide a precedent for the proposition that a U.S. citizen summoned from abroad to stand trial for a crime may be tried in absentia if he refuses to return, with any fine collected out of that person's domestic assets? Discuss.
3. According to the U.S. Supreme Court, is service of legal process by the U.S. Embassy against a citizen of this country while he is in France a violation of French sovereignty? Why or why not?

> *Comment:* The statute applied against Blackmer was enacted hastily to meet the needs of the so-called "Teapot Dome scandal" in which Blackmer was involved. Improprieties in the leasing of federal oil lands led a Senate committee to investigate the matter in late 1923. This investigation had widespread repercussions, including the prosecution and conviction of a cabinet member to a prison term for accepting bribes. Blackmer's testimony was desired in various connections. After the subpoenas were served and he was found in contempt for not returning, the United States assessed him $8,500,000 for income taxes and penalties and unsuccessfully sought to extradite him for filing fraudulent tax returns. The statute involved in the *Blackmer* case has been revised and now appears in 28 U.S.C.A. § 1783. Also, there have been related changes in the provisions of F.R.C.P. 4(i) on service of subpoenas and of 28 U.S.C.A. § 1784 on contempt.
>
> In general, the U.S. Supreme court has refused to allow trials in absentia for "serious" criminal violations. In assessing the present accuracy of the *Blackmer* decision, it should be noted that recent decisions have gone far to impose on criminal contempt proceedings safeguards parallel to those in regular criminal proceedings (Steiner, Vagts, & Koh, 1994, pp. 836-837).
>
> Many other States provide that their nationals may be prosecuted for all crimes (or all serious crimes) wherever the crimes are committed. However, the use of the nationality principle alone is clearly the exception, and the territorial principle the rule. Prosecutions on the basis of nationality alone are infrequent in practice (American Law Institute, 1987, pp. 242-224).

The Protective and Passive Personality Principles

International law recognizes the right of a State to punish a limited class of offenses committed outside its territory by persons who are not its nationals when the offenses are directed against the security of the State or threaten the integrity of governmental functions that are generally recognized as crimes by developed legal systems. These crimes include espionage, counterfeiting of the State's seal or currency, falsification of official documents, as well as perjury before consular officials, and conspiracy to violate the immigration or customs laws. The **protective principle** may be seen as a special application of the effects principle, but it has been treated as an independent basis of jurisdiction. The protective principle does not support application to foreign nationals of laws against political expression, such as libel of the State or of the chief executive.

> **Protective principle:** *Jurisdiction to prescribe activity committed outside a State's territory when that activity is directed against the security of the State or threatens the integrity of governmental functions.*

The **passive personality principle** asserts that a State may apply law in criminal cases to an act committed outside its territory by a person not its national when the victim of the act was its national. The U.S. Congress applied this principle to a law directed at terrorism (§ 1202 of the Omnibus Diplomatic Security and Antiterrorism Act of 1986, 18 U.S.C. § 2231). The act makes it a crime to kill, to attempt or conspire to kill, or to cause serious bodily injury to a national of the United States

> **Passive personality principle:** *Jurisdiction of a State to prescribe acts committed outside its territory by a person not its national when the victim of the act is its national. This principle cannot be the sole basis of jurisdiction.*

outside the territory of the United States. Prosecution under this section, however, may be undertaken only on certification by the Attorney General that in his or her judgment the offense was intended to coerce, intimidate, or retaliate against a government or a civilian population.

The passive personality principle has not been generally accepted for ordinary torts or crimes, but it is increasingly accepted as applied to terrorist and other organized attacks on a State's nationals by reason of their nationality. It has also been applied to assassination of a State's diplomatic representatives or other officials.

These two principles, the protective and the passive personality principles, are derived from the more traditional territoriality and nationality principles and do not operate alone to provide a basis of jurisdiction. However, the complexity of jurisdictional bases implies vast potential for conflict in interpretation among modern nation-states. These conflicts are reduced somewhat by the principles of reasonableness, in application, that have emerged as a principle of international law (*Restatement [Third]*).

> **§ 403. Limitations on Jurisdiction to Prescribe**
>
> (1) Even when one of the bases for jurisdiction under § 402 is present, a state may not exercise jurisdiction to prescribe law with respect to a person or activity having connections with another state when the exercise of such jurisdiction is unreasonable.
> (a) Whether exercise of jurisdiction over a person or activity is unreasonable is determined by evaluating all relevant factors, including, where appropriate:
> (b) the link of the activity to the territory of the regulating state, i.e., the extent to which the activity takes place within the territory, or has substantial, direct, and foreseeable effect upon or in the territory;
> (c) the connections, such as nationality, residence, or economic activity, between the

regulating state and the person principally responsible for the activity to be regulated, or between that state and those whom the regulation is designed to protect;

(d) the character of the activity to be regulated, the importance of regulation to the regulating state, the extent to which other states regulate such activities, and the degree to which the desirability of such regulation is generally accepted;

(e) the existence of justified expectations that might be protected or hurt by the regulation;

(f) the importance of the regulation to the international political, legal, or economic system;

(g) the extent to which the regulation is consistent with the traditions of the international system;

(h) the extent to which another state may have an interest in regulating the activity; and

(i) the likelihood of conflict with regulation by another state.

(3) When it would not be unreasonable for each of two states to exercise jurisdiction over a person or activity, but the prescriptions by the two states are in conflict, each state has an obligation to evaluate its own as well as the other state's interest in exercising jurisdiction, in light of all the relevant factors, Subsection (2); a state should defer to the other state if that state's interest is clearly greater.

Universal Jurisdiction

The *Restatement (Third)* provides the following wording to describe the expanding class of universal offenses for which every State has jurisdiction regardless of where the crime was committed.

§ 404. Universal Jurisdiction to Define and Punish Certain Offenses

A state has jurisdiction to define and prescribe punishment for certain offenses recognized by the community of nations as of universal concern, such as piracy, slave trade, attacks on or hijacking of aircraft, genocide, war crimes, and perhaps certain acts of terrorism, even where none of the bases of jurisdiction indicated in § 402 is present.

This limited list of offenses is expanding, and some more recent additions to the class may be controversial; however, modern international law recognizes jurisdiction to prescribe and adjudicate to punish certain offenses although the State has no links of territory with the offense or of nationality with the offender (or even the victim).

The offenses listed previously in § 404 are subject to **universal jurisdiction** as a matter of customary international law. Universal jurisdiction for additional offenses is provided by international agreements, but it remains to be determined whether universal jurisdiction over a particular offense has become customary law for States not party to such an agreement. These offenses are not generally subject to time limitations.

> **Universal jurisdiction:** Jurisdiction to prescribe offenses even when there are no links of territory or nationality; applies to a limited class of offenses recognized by the community of nations as of universal concern.

There has been wide condemnation of *terrorism*, but the inability generally to agree on an acceptable definition of that term seems to require a more precise definition. In 1976, the United States and six other States in Latin America adopted the Convention to Prevent and Punish the Acts of Terrorism Taking the Form of Crimes Against Persons and Related Extortion. Universal jurisdiction is increasingly accepted for certain acts of terrorism, such as assaults on the life or physical integrity of diplomatic personnel, kidnapping, and indiscriminate violent assaults on people at large.

Piracy and Slavery

Piracy and slavery have been recognized as offenses against the law of nations and are well-established crimes in the U.S. Constitution and laws of the United States. The original U.S. Constitution, in Article I, Section 8, gives Congress the power "to define and punish Piracies and Felonies committed on the High Seas, and Offences against the Law of Nations." Although international law is part of the law of the United States, a person cannot be tried in the federal courts for an international crime unless Congress adopts a statute to define and punish the offense. The act of Congress, however, may define the offense by reference to international law. The crime of piracy is defined in Admiralty Law, and the Thirteenth Amendment prohibits slavery and gives Congress the power to enact laws to enforce this provision. The Alien Tort Statute of the United States was discussed in Chapter 5, and it should be recalled that universal jurisdiction has civil application as well (see discussion of the *Filartiga* Case in Chapter 5 of this text).

Genocide

Genocide and war crimes became subject to universal jurisdiction after World War II. Universal jurisdiction to punish the crime of **genocide**, which involves "intent to destroy, in whole or in part, a national, ethnical, racial or religious group" is widely accepted as a principle of customary law. The Convention on the Prevention and Punishment of the Crime of Genocide was drafted in 1948 by the U.N. General Assembly and opened for ratification by the individual States. Although the U.S. ratification of this convention did not come into force until 1989, it has now been ratified by the overwhelming majority of nations. It is included in Appendix H of this text and

> **Genocide:** *A universal crime involving intent to destroy a national, ethnic, racial, or religious group.*

should be consulted for a definition of the concept.

Apparently, since World War II, no State has exercised jurisdiction to punish genocide or war crimes in circumstances for which no other basis for jurisdiction under the *Restatement (Third)* § 402 was present. This lack of enforcement has ultimately led to major recent developments that seek to address this deficiency. In 1993, the U.N. Security Council, acting under Chapter VII of the U.N. Charter, created a special international tribunal to try persons for international crimes committed in the former Yugoslavia. In 1994, the International Law Commission of the United Nations produced a draft for a permanent international criminal court. These major international developments will be the subject of more complete discussion in later chapters dealing with international tribunals.

In several notable cases, national courts have made decisions that recognize the existence of universal jurisdiction to try and punish individuals as common enemies of mankind. In the *Eichmann* case involving the principal executioner of Hitler's "final solution" during World War II, Israel relied on universal jurisdiction as well as other bases for prosecution of Adolf Eichmann. His abduction from Argentina will be discussed later in this chapter; however, in 1961, the Jerusalem District Court of Israel held that the crime of genocide was a crime against humanity, and therefore, the Court had the right to hear the case even though Eichmann was a resident of Argentina and the crimes had been committed on German territory. The case is highly controversial in its invocation of the Genocide Convention, because Article 6 indicates that an individual charged with such an act is to be tried by the courts in the territory where the act took place or before an international tribunal empowered to have such jurisdiction.

The Israeli courts justified jurisdiction partly on the protective principle and not entirely on universal jurisdiction.

In the *Matter of Barbie*, a person who had been a Gestapo officer in occupied France challenged his arrest and prosecution in France for offenses committed during the wartime occupation, on the ground that he had been unlawfully transported to France from Bolivia and that the statute of limitations had expired. The Supreme Court of France rejected this challenge in 1983, ruling that the charges against Barbie transcended internal French rules of procedure, since they involved crimes against all humanity.

War Crimes

The concept of **war crimes** consists of (a) crimes against peace, (b) crimes against humanity, and (c) war crimes. These principles were instigated by the United Nations during World War II to prosecute individuals for these crimes. This historic precedent was attempted by the Treaty of Versailles after World War I, in providing for the trial and punishment of the German emperor, although the Allies never carried out the trials. Some trials were conducted by individual States, but the results were unsatisfactory. During World War II, the major powers agreed that an international tribunal would be necessary. The London Agreement of 1946 created an International Military Tribunal, representing Britain, France, the Soviet Union, and the United States. Twenty-two Germans accused of war crimes were tried at Nuremberg in 1945 by this Tribunal. Twelve defendants were sentenced to death,

> **War crimes:** Universal crimes against peace, crimes against humanity, and war crimes. More specifically involving violations of the law of war.

three were acquitted, and the rest were imprisoned for crimes against peace, crimes against humanity, and war crimes. Similar proceedings took place in Tokyo, where Japanese war criminals were tried before the International Military Tribunal for the Far East, consisting of the eleven States at war with Japan. All twenty-five defendants were found guilty, and seven of them were sentenced to death.

Scholarly evaluation of the legality of the Nuremberg and Tokyo trials has been mixed, with general agreement that decisions based on long-standing customary and treaty law regarding war crimes were well-founded but that judgments based on crimes against the peace and crimes against humanity were open to interpretation as ex post facto judgments, although there is no rule of international law against ex post facto legislation. The Kellogg-Briand Pact of 1928, outlawing war as an instrument of national policy, was used as the basis of these trials, since both Germany and Japan had ratified this treaty prior to World War II. In 1946, the U.N. General Assembly adopted unanimously the principles of the Nuremberg Charter and Judgment. The following statement of the principles adopted by the General Assembly was prepared by the International Law Commission:

> *Principles of International Law Recognized in the Charter and Judgment of the Nuremberg Tribunal*
>
> *Report of the International Law Commission, 2nd Session, 1950.*
>
> *U.N., G.A.O.R., 5th Session, Supp. No. 12 (A/1316), p. 11.*
>
> Principle I. Any person who commits an act which constitutes a crime under international law is responsible therefore and liable to punishment.

Principle II. The fact that international law does not impose a penalty for an act which constitutes a crime under international law does not relieve the person who committed the act from responsibility under international law.

Principle III. The fact that a person who committed an act which constitutes a crime under international law acted as Head of State or responsible Government official does not relieve him from responsibility under international law.

Principle IV. The fact that a person acted pursuant to order of his Government or of a superior does not relieve him from responsibility under international law, provided a moral choice was in fact possible to him.

Principle V. Any person charged with a crime under international law has the right to a fair trial on the facts and law.

Principle VI. The crimes hereinafter set out are punishable as crimes under international law:

a. Crimes against peace:
   (i) Planning, preparation, initiation or waging of a war of aggression or a war in violation of international treaties, agreements or assurances:
   (ii) Participation in a common plan or conspiracy for the accomplishment of any of the acts mentioned under (i).

b. War crimes:
   Violations of the laws or customs of war which include, but are not limited to, murder, ill-treatment or deportation to slave-labor or for any other purpose of civilian population of or in occupied territory, murder or ill-treatment of prisoners of war or persons on the seas, killing of hostages, plunder of public or private property, wanton destruction of cities, towns, or villages, or devastation not justified by military necessity.

c. Crimes against humanity:
   Murder, extermination, enslavement, deportation and other inhuman acts done against any civilian population, or persecution on political, racial or religious grounds, when such acts are done or such persecutions are carried on in execution of or in connexion with any crime against peace or any war crime.

Principle VII: Complicity in the commission of a crime against peace, a war crime, or a crime against humanity as set forth in Principle VI is a crime under international law.

The series of Hague Conventions before World War I concerning the rules of land and naval warfare have been supplement by the Geneva Conventions drafted in 1949 with protocols added in 1977. These conventions have codified prior practice and dealt with the new problems imposed by new military technology. These rules now cover not only the rules of traditional warfare but also those relevant to undeclared hostilities.

One method of enforcement of these rules of the law of war is for the armed forces in which the individual is serving to make violations of these rules a crime. Indeed, under some of these conventions, the parties are obligated to do so under the treaty provisions. The U.S. Army field manual, *The Law of Land Warfare, FM 27-10*, in force at the time of the hostilities in Vietnam specifically defined crimes against peace, crimes against humanity, and war crimes. The U.S. Uniform Code of Military Justice provides in Article 18 (10 U.S.C.A. § 818) that general courts-martial "have jurisdiction to try any person who by the law of war is subject to trial by a military tribunal and may adjudge any punishment permitted by the law of war."

A controversial case that aroused analogies to the Nuremberg trials was the court-martial of Lieutenant Calley in 1973 for his role in the massacre of Vietnamese civilians in My Lai. However, he was prosecuted simply for murder under Article 118 (10 U.S.C.A. § 918) and was found guilty and, initially, sentenced to life imprisonment. Later, the sentence was reduced to 10 years.

Other Universal Offenses

The Hague Convention for the Suppression of Unlawful Seizure of Aircraft of 1971, the 1973 Montreal Convention for the Suppression of Unlawful Acts Against the Safety of Civil Aviation, the 1975 Convention on the Prevention and Punishment of Crimes against Internationally Protected Persons Including Diplomatic Agents, and the 1985 International Convention Against the Taking of Hostages include an obligation on the parties to punish or extradite offenders, even when the offense was not committed within their territory or by a national. The United States is a party to all of these agreements.

The International Convention on the Suppression and Punishment of the Crime of Apartheid came into force in 1976. This treaty declares that **apartheid** is a crime against humanity and subject to universal jurisdiction (see Appendix I). Although the anti-apartheid treaty has been ratified by a large number of States, the United States has not become a party. The Convention Against Torture and Other Cruel, Inhuman and Degrading Treatment or Punishment also provides for universal jurisdiction in the Introductory Note to Part VII.

> **Apartheid:** Universal crime involving inhumane acts committed for the purpose of establishing and maintaining domination by one racial group of persons over any other racial group of persons and systematically oppressing them.

All of these agreements are effective only among the parties, unless customary law comes to accept them as subject to universal jurisdiction. Ultimately, this decision is a matter of judicial opinion and must be argued on an individual basis. The draft Articles on State Responsibility, prepared by the International Law Commission and intended to codify customary law on this subject, would include a provision that an international crime may result from "a serious breach on a wide-spread scale of an international obligation of essential importance for safeguarding the human being, such as those prohibiting slavery, genocide and apartheid."

Jurisdiction to Tax and Regulate

Basically, taxation and regulation are administrative actions of governments. These actions may result in criminal prosecutions in extreme cases, but governmental agencies may seize property located within their territorial jurisdiction, investigate alleged infractions, and require reports and accounting procedures of private parties who are neither their nationals nor present in their territorial jurisdiction. Therefore, jurisdiction to regulate is even broader than jurisdiction to adjudicate for criminal prosecution. The general principles of tax jurisdiction are stated in § 412 of the *Restatement (Third)*:

§ 412. Jurisdiction to Tax: Basic Rule Applied

(1) A state may exercise jurisdiction to tax the income of
  (a) a person, whether natural or juridical, who is a national, resident, or domiciliary of the state, whether the source of the income is within or without the state;
  (b) a natural or juridical person who is not a national, resident, or domiciliary of the state but who is present or does business in the state, but only with respect to income derived from or associated with presence or doing business within the state; and
  (c) a natural or juridical person who is not a national, resident or domicilary of the state and is not present or doing business therein, with respect to income derived from property located in the territory of the state.

(2) A state may exercise jurisdiction to tax property located within its territory, without regard to the nationality, domicile, residence, or presence of the owner of the property.

(3) A state may exercise jurisdiction to tax transfer of wealth
  (a) if the wealth consists of property located in its territory, or

(b) if the transfer is made by or to a national, resident, or domiciliary of the state.

(4) A state may exercise jurisdiction to tax a transaction that occurs, originates, or terminates in its territory or that has a substantial relation to the state, without regard to the nationality, domicile, residence, or presence of the parties to such a transaction.

An interesting tax case involving several of the principles mentioned and illustrating the importance of ties of nationality took place in 1977, in the case of *United States v. Rexach*. This case involves a person who was denied citizenship under the Nationality Act of 1940, which was later held unconstitutional.

▮ ▮ ▮

United States v. Rexach
United States Court of Appeals, First Circuit, 1977.
558 F.2d 37.

INGRAHAM, Circuit Judge.

This case and related lawsuits reflect the United States' efforts to tax income earned in the 1940's and 1950's by Felix Benitez Rexach, husband of Lucienne D'Hotelle de Benitez Rexach. The deaths of Lucienne and Felix have not halted the litigation. We hold that the district court erred in ruling that Lucienne was not liable for taxes on one-half the income earned by Felix from November 10, 1949 to May 20, 1952. . . .

Facts

Lucienne D'Hotelle was born in France in 1909. She became Lucienne D'Hotelle de Benitez Rexach upon her marriage to Felix in San Juan, Puerto Rico in 1928. She was naturalized as a United States citizen on December 7, 1942. The couple spent some time in the Dominican Republic, where Felix engaged in harbor construction projects. Lucienne established a residence in her native France on November 10, 1946 and remained a resident until May 20, 1952. During that time § 404(b) of the Nationality Act of 1940 provided that naturalized citizens who returned to their country of birth and resided there for three years lost their American citizenship. On November 10, 1947, after Lucienne had been in France for one year, the American Embassy in Paris issued her a United States passport valid through November 9, 1949. Soon after its expiration Lucienne applied in Puerto Rico for a renewal. By this time she had resided in France for three years. Nevertheless, the Governor of Puerto Rico renewed her passport on January 20, 1950 for a two year period beginning November 10, 1949. Three months after the expiration of this passport, Lucienne applied to the United States Consulate in Nice, France for another one. On May 20, 1952, the Vice-Consul there signed a Certificate of Loss of Nationality, citing Lucienne's continuous residence in France as having automatically divested her of citizenship under § 404(b). Her passport from the Governor of Puerto Rico was confiscated, cancelled and never returned to her. The State Department approved the certificate on December 23, 1952. Lucienne made no attempt to regain her American citizenship; neither did she affirmatively renounce it.

In October 1952 the Dominican Republic (then controlled by the dictator Rafael Trujillo) extended citizenship to Lucienne retroactive to January 2, 1952. Trujillo was assassinated in May 1961. The provisional government which followed revoked Lucienne's citizenship on January 20, 1962. On June 5, 1962 the French government issued her a passport.

For the years 1944 to 1958, Felix earned millions of dollars from harbor construction in the Dominican Republic. He was aided by Trujillo's favor and by his own undeniable skills as an engineer. Felix, an American citizen since 1917 was sued by the United States for income taxes. The court held that Lucienne had a vested one-half interest in Felix's earnings under Dominican law, which established that such income was community property. Since the law of the situs where the income was earned determined its character, Felix could be sued only for his half of the earnings. *United States v. Rexach*, 185 F.Supp. 465 (D.P.R.1960).

Predictably, the United States eventually sought to tax Lucienne for her half of that income. Whether by accident or design, the government's efforts began in earnest shortly after the Supreme Court invalidated the successor statute to § 404(b). In *Schneider v. Rusk*, 377 U.S. 163, 84 S.Ct. 1187, 12 L.Ed.2d 218 (1964), the Court held that the distinction drawn by the statute between naturalized and native-born Americans was so discriminatory as to violate due process. In January 1965, about two months after this suit was filed, the State Department notified Lucienne by letter that her expatriation was void under *Schneider* and that the State Department considered her a citizen. Lucienne replied that she had accepted her denaturalization without protest and had thereafter considered herself not to be an American citizen.

Lucienne died on January 18, 1968. . . .

* * *

The district court found that Lucienne was liable for taxes on her half of Felix's income from 1944 through November 9, 1949 * * *. The district court absolved Lucienne of liability for taxes on income earned after November 9, 1949. . . .

The United States appealed the denial of liability for the period November 10, 1949 to May 20, 1952. . . .

Lucienne's Citizenship

The government contends that Lucienne was still an American citizen from her third anniversary as a French resident until the day the Certificate of Loss of Nationality was issued in Nice. This case presents a curious situation, since usually it is the individual who claims citizenship and the government which denies it. But pocketbook considerations occasionally reverse the roles. . . . The government's position is that under either *Schneider v. Rusk, supra*, or *Afroyim v. Rusk*, 387 U.S. 253, 87 S.Ct. 1660, 18 L.Ed.2d 757 (1967), the statute by which Lucienne was denaturalized is unconstitutional and its prior effects should be wiped out. *Afroyim* held that Congress lacks the power to strip persons of citizenship merely because they have voted in a foreign election. The cornerstone of the decision is the proposition that intent to relinquish citizenship is a prerequisite to expatriation.

Section 404(b) would have been declared unconstitutional under either *Schneider* or *Afroyim*. The statute is practically identical to its successor, which *Schneider* condemned as discriminatory. Section 404(b) would have been invalid under *Afroyim* as a congressional attempt to expatriate regardless of intent. Likewise it is clear that the determination of the Vice-Consul and the State Department in 1952 would have been upheld under then prevailing case law, even though Lucienne had manifested no intent to renounce her citizenship.

* * *

We think the principles governing retrospective application dictate that either *Schneider* or *Afroyim* apply to this case. . . .

* * *

Retroactive application of constitutional decisions is not automatic. . . . The Supreme Court has opted for a flexible approach. Equitable principles control in deciding whether cases should be applied retrospectively. . . .

The district court accurately summarized the law:

> [T]he general principles that govern retroactivity should be applied on a case by case basis taking into consideration such factors as the reliance placed by the parties on the legislation in question, the balancing of the equities of the particular situation, and the fore-seeability or lack thereof, that the legal doctrine or statute in question would be declared unconstitutional. 411 F.Supp. at 1293.

However, the district court went too far in viewing the equities as between Lucienne and the government in strict isolation from broad policy considerations which argue for a generally retrospective application of *Afroyim* and *Schneider* to the entire class of persons invalidly expatriated. . . . The rights stemming from American citizenship are so important that, absent special circumstances, they must be recognized even for years past. Unless held to have been citizens without interruption, persons wrongfully expatriated as well as their offspring might be permanently and unreasonably barred from important benefits. Application of *Afroyim* or *Schneider* is generally appropriate.

Of course, American citizenship implies not only rights but also duties, not the least of which is the payment of taxes. *Cook v. Tait*, 265 U.S. 47, 44 S.Ct. 444, 68 L.Ed. 895 (1924). . . . We do think that the balance of the equities mandates that back income taxes be collectible for periods during which the involuntarily expatriated persons affirmatively exercised a specific right of citizenship. This is precisely the position taken by the Internal Revenue Service. As to such periods, neither the government nor the expatriate can be said to have relied upon the constitutionality of § 404. Since the expatriate in fact received benefits of citizenship, the equities favor the imposition of federal income tax liability.

We now focus upon Lucienne's status. The years for which the government sought to collect taxes can be divided into three discrete periods: 1944 through November 9, 1949; November 10, 1949 through May 20, 1952; and May 21, 1952 through 1958. The district court's ruling that Lucienne was liable for taxes during the first period is not appealed. The district court refused to distinguish between the two remaining periods.

During the interval from late 1949 to mid-1952, Lucienne was unaware that she had been automatically denaturalized. In fact, she applied for, obtained and used an American passport for most of that period. On the passport application she stated that her travel outside the United States had consisted of "vacations," and her signature appeared below an oath that she had neither been naturalized by a foreign state nor declared her allegiance to a foreign state. Her subsequent application on February 11, 1952, which was eventually rejected, included an affidavit in which she stated that her mother's death and other business obligations caused her to remain in France. Ironically, on that same application, the following line appears:

"I (do/do not) pay the American Income Tax at ————." Lucienne scratched out the words "do not" and filled in the blank with "San Juan, Puerto Rico."

As late as February 1952 Lucienne regarded herself as an American citizen and no one had disabused her of that notion. The ViceConsul reported that Lucienne had told him "she was advised (by the State Department) that she could remain in France without endangering her American citizenship."

Fairness dictates that the United States recover income taxes for the period November 10, 1949 to May 20, 1952. Lucienne was privileged to travel on a United States passport; she received the protection of its government.

Although the government has not appealed the decision with respect to taxes from mid-1952 through 1958, the district court was presented with the issue. We wish to explain why the government should be allowed to collect taxes for the two and one-half year interval but not for the subsequent period. The letter from Lucienne to the Department of State official in 1965, which appears in English translation in the record, states that after the Certificate of Loss of Nationality, "I have never considered myself to be a citizen of the United States." We think that in this case this letter can be construed as an acceptance and voluntary relinquishment of citizenship. Lucienne cannot be dunned for taxes to support the United States government during the years in which she was denied its protection. . . . Here, Lucienne severed her ties to this country at the direction of the State Department. The right hand will not be permitted to demand payment for something which the left hand has taken away. However, until her citizenship was snatched from her, Lucienne should have expected to honor her 1952 declaration that she was a taxpayer.

* * *

The case is reversed and remanded for a proper determination of taxes for the period November 10, 1949 to May 20, 1952. . . .

Discussion Questions

1. For what period of time does the United States claim that the defendant owed taxes? Who is the defendant in this case, since the couple, Felix and Lucienne Rexach, died before the case was decided?
2. How did the district court decide this case? What is being appealed?
3. How did the appeals court decide this case? Why?
4. What principles of the *Restatement (Third)* § 412 are involved in this case?

Jurisdiction to tax seldom raises issues between States, but according to the *Restatement (Third)*, an example of unreasonable exercise of jurisdiction would involve a tax on a nonresident alien temporarily present within a State, measured by his or her worldwide income. This exercise could be challenged as a violation of international law by both the taxpayer and the State of the taxpayer's nationality.

Some states in the United States have assessed taxation by attributing a portion of the total worldwide business income of the enterprise and its subsidiaries to determine the portion of that income attributed to the taxing state. This practice has been protested by other countries, particularly when the corporation has a nationality status outside the United States. The U.S. Supreme Court has held that such "unitary taxation" violates neither the U.S. Constitution nor international law, at least when the parent corporation is organized in the United States, provided that the enterprise has a substantial nexus to the taxing State, that the foreign affiliated companies are part of an integrated business, and that the apportionment formula is not shown to be unfair (*Japan Line, Ltd. v. County of Los Angeles;* 441 U.S. 434, 99 S.Ct. 1813, 60 L.Ed. 2d 336 [1979]).

Taxation on the basis of differently defined links does not violate customary international law, even if the result is double taxation. The avoidance of **double taxation** has been the subject of numerous international agreements. The Organization for Economic Cooperation and Development (OECD) has adopted the Model Double Taxation Convention on Income and Capital, and the U.N. Model Double Taxation Convention Between Developed and Developing Countries seeks to avoid double taxation by determining domicile to be in one of the States involved. These efforts have not produced uniformity. Instead, a network of some four hundred bilateral and multilateral agreements form the basis of obligations to avoid double taxation. States have been reluctant to admit a general obligation to avoid double taxation except on the basis of specific agreements and in accordance with its terms. The details of existing tax agreements differ, but they all aim at avoiding double taxation.

Under U.S. law and agreements to which the United States is a party, when a State exercises jurisdiction to tax the income of a person by reason of nationality, residence, or domicile, and the State imposes its tax on income derived from presence in or from property located in another State, the taxing State must give appropriate recognition to any comparable tax imposed by the other State. Such recognition may take the form of either an exemption of such income from its tax or of an appropriate credit or deduction against its tax (see *Restatement [Third]*).

> **Double taxation:** Taxing of the same item or piece of property twice to the same person or taxing it as the property of one person and again as the property of another.

Jurisdiction to Adjudicate in Criminal Cases

A court in the United States may try a person only for violation of U.S. law, not for violation of the penal law of a foreign State. However, under international law, a State may exercise jurisdiction through its courts to enforce its criminal laws that punish universal crimes or other nonterritorial offenses within the State's jurisdiction to prescribe. A court in the United States may not try a person unless he or she is before the court at the time the trial begins (see §§ 422 and 423 of the *Restatement* [Third]).

Indictments may be returned by a grand jury against a person not within the United States, but under existing law, a warrant or summons on that indictment may be served only within the jurisdiction of the United States or in connection with a request for extradition by the United States.

The U.S. constitutional "due process" guarantees preclude trials in absentia and trials of persons for the criminal violations of the laws of another country. However, some civil law States have adopted a practice of trying persons whom they could not extradite to another country for crimes committed in that country. Agreements with other countries permit the United States to exercise authority to adjudicate in limited areas of criminal jurisdiction, such as over its military and other defense personnel for acts committed by them in those countries. In *Reid v. Covert* (354 U.S. 1 [1957]) the U.S. Supreme Court held that a civilian tried abroad under the authority of the United States must be provided with all the constitutional safeguards, including a jury trial.

By agreement with other countries, the United States has secured the provision of reciprocal transfer of prisoners convicted in other countries, with the prisoner's consent.

These bilateral treaties exist with Canada and Mexico, and the United States has signed the Council of Europe's multilateral treaty governing transfers of prisoners. These agreements raised issues whether the United States could hold in penal custody a person who had never had a trial affording the safeguards of the U.S. Constitution. The drafters sought to defuse that problem by providing that the prisoner's consent was a prerequisite to any transfer. The constitutionality of such treaty provisions has been upheld in a number of cases (*Velez v. Nelson*, 621 F.2d 1179, 2d Cir.1980; *Pfeifer v. Bureau* of Prisons, 468 F.Supp. 920, S.D.Cal.1979, aff'd 615 F.2d 873, 9th Cir.1980).

Abduction and Limits on Jurisdiction to Enforce

It is universally recognized, as a corollary of State sovereignty, that officials of one State may not exercise their functions in the territory of another State without the latter's consent. If a State's law enforcement officials exercise their functions in the territory of another State without that State's consent, the offended State is entitled to protest, and, in appropriate cases, to receive reparation from the offending State. If the unauthorized action includes abduction of a person, the State from which the person was abducted may demand return of the person, and international law requires that he or she be returned.

Nearly all States, however, have followed the rule that, absent protest from other States, they will try persons brought before their courts through irregular means, even though the abduction from the other State is in violation of international law. English cases going back to the early nineteenth century have followed this rule. The U.S. Supreme Court has followed the leading case of *Ker v. Illinois* (119 U.S. 436) since 1886. The French Supreme Court also accepted this principle in 1964. These decisions were based in part on the principle that only States, and not individuals, may raise objections to violations of international law and in part on the grounds that the international law was merely customary.

According to the *Restatement (Third)*, both of these propositions have been largely abandoned as general principles, and many commentators have criticized the rule. The Draft Convention on Jurisdiction With Respect to Crime proposed by Harvard Research in International Law includes a rule that would have provided that "no State shall prosecute or punish any person who has been brought within its territory . . . by recourse to measures in violation of international law or international convention without first obtaining the consent of the State or States whose rights have been violated by such measures" (from the *American Journal of International Law*, 1935, cited in *Restatement [Third]*, American Law Institute, 1987). In prevailing practice, however, States ordinarily refrain from trying persons illegally brought from another State only if that State demands the person's return.

In a number of cases, such protests by offending States have resulted in the release or return of the accused person. In the *Jacob* case of 1935, Nazi agents kidnapped a former German journalist from Switzerland and took him to Germany for trial for treason. Switzerland protested and succeeded in having the matter submitted to an international arbitral tribunal. Before the issue could be adjudicated, Germany decided to return the kidnapped person and punish the kidnappers. In a number of instances, bounty hunters from the United States have pursued a bail jumper to a foreign State and forcibly returned him or her to the place of trial in the United States. In several cases, the trial of the fugitive proceeded despite the circumstances of the bail jumper's return, but the bounty hunters were extradited to the foreign State on a charge of kidnapping (*Kear v. Hinton* (699 F.2d 181, 4th Cir. [1983]).

The Eichmann abduction from Argentina by agents of the State of Israel produced a protest on the part of Argentina, and the U.N. Security Council adopted a resolution declaring that such acts, "which affect the sovereignty of a Member State and therefore cause international friction, may, if repeated, endanger international peace and security." Following these actions, Argentina and Israel reached a settlement that did not call for Eichmann's return.

In *United States v. Alvarez-Machain* (1992), the U.S. Supreme Court seems to ignore the modern international legal developments that have just been described. Humberto Alvarez Machain, a citizen and resident of Mexico, was indicted for participating in the kidnap and murder, in Mexico, of a special agent of the Drug Enforcement Administration (DEA). He was believed to have helped prolong the agent's life so that others could torture and interrogate him. DEA agents, after attempts to negotiate delivery of Alvarez with Mexican officials, offered a reward for his delivery to the United States. He was kidnapped from his medical office in Guadalajara, Mexico, and flown to El Paso, Texas, where he was delivered to DEA officials who arrested him. Alvarez claimed that because of the abduction, the U.S. courts lacked jurisdiction to try him; the district court discharged him and ordered his repatriation to Mexico; the court of appeals affirmed. The Supreme Court, in an opinion by Chief Justice Rehnquist, reversed and remanded for further proceedings.

United States v. Alvarez-Machain
Supreme Court of the United States, 1992.
U.S. 655, 112 S.Ct. 218H, 119 L,.Ed.Bd 441.

REHNQUIST, C. J., delivered the opinion of the Court, in which WHITE, SCALIA, KENNEDY, SOUTER, and THOMAS, JJ., joined.

The issue in this case is whether a criminal defendant, abducted to the United States from a nation with which it has an extradition treaty, thereby acquires a defense to the jurisdiction of this country's courts. We hold that he does not, and that he may be tried in federal district court for violations of the criminal law of the United States.

Respondent, Humberto Alvarez-Machain, is a citizen and resident of Mexico. He was indicted for participating in the kidnap and murder of United States Drug Enforcement Administration (DEA) special agent Enrique Camarena-Salazar and a Mexican pilot working with Camarena, Alfredo Zavala-Avelar. The DEA believes that respondent, a medical doctor, participated in the murder by prolonging agent Camarena's life so that others could further torture and interrogate him. On April 2, 1990, respondent was forcibly kidnapped from his medical office in Guadalajara, Mexico, to be flown by private plane to El Paso, Texas, where he was arrested by DEA officials. The District Court concluded that DEA agents were responsible for respondent's abduction, although they were not personally involved in it.

Respondent moved to dismiss the indictment, claiming that his abduction constituted outrageous governmental conduct, and that the District Court lacked jurisdiction to try him because he was abducted in violation of the extradition treaty between the United States and Mexico. Extradition Treaty, May 4, 1978, [1979] United States—United Mexican States, 31 U.S.T. 5059, T.I.A.S. No. 9656 (Extradition Treaty or Treaty). The District Court rejected the outrageous governmental conduct claim, but held that it lacked jurisdiction to try respondent because his abduction violated the Extradition Treaty. The district court discharged respondent and ordered that he be repatriated to Mexico.

The Court of Appeals affirmed the dismissal of the indictment and the repatriation of respondent, relying on its decision in *United States v. Verdugo-Urquidez*, 939 F.2d 1341 (CA9 1991), cert. pending, No. 91-670, 946 F.2d 1466 (1991). In *Verdugo*, the Court of Appeals held that the forcible abduction of a Mexican national with the authorization or participation of the United States violated the Extradition Treaty between the United States and Mexico. Although the Treaty does not expressly prohibit such abductions, the Court of Appeals held that the "purpose" of the Treaty was violated by a forcible abduction which, along with a formal protest by the offended nation, would give a defendant the right to invoke the Treaty violation to defeat jurisdiction of the district court to try him. Court of Appeals further held that the proper remedy for such a violation would be dismissal of the indictment and repatriation of the defendant to Mexico.

* * *

Although we have never before addressed the precise issue raised in the present case, we have previously considered proceedings in claimed violation of an extradition treaty, and proceedings against a defendant brought before a court by means of a forcible abduction. We addressed the former issue in *United States v. Rauscher*, 119 U.S. 407, 7 S.Ct. 234, 30 L.Ed. 425 (1886); more precisely, the issue of whether the Webster-Ashburton Treaty of 1842, which governed extraditions between England and the United States, prohibited the prosecution of defendant Rauscher for a crime other than the crime for which he had been extradited. Whether this prohibition, known as the doctrine of *specialty*, was an intended part of the treaty had been disputed between the two nations for some time. Justice Miller delivered the opinion of the Court, which carefully examined the terms and history of the treaty; the practice of nations in regards to extradition treaties; the case law from the states; and the writings of commentators, and reached the following conclusion: "[A] person who has been brought within the jurisdiction of the court by virtue of proceedings under an extradition treaty, can only be tried for one of the offences described in that treaty, and for the offence with which he is charged in the proceedings for his extradition, until a reasonable time and opportunity have been given him, after his release or trial upon such charge, to return to the country from whose asylum he had been forcibly taken under those proceedings." In addition, Justice Miller's opinion noted that any doubt as to this interpretation was put to rest by two federal statutes which imposed the doctrine of *specialty* upon extradition treaties to which the United States was a party. Unlike the case before us today, the defendant in Rauscher had been brought to the United States by way of an extradition treaty; there was no issue of a forcible abduction.

In *Ker v. Illinois*, 119 U.S. 436, 7 S.Ct. 225, 30 L.Ed. 421 (1886), also written by Justice Miller and decided the same day as *Rauscher*, we addressed the issue of a defendant brought before the court by way of a forcible abduction. Frederick Ker had been tried and convicted in an Illinois court for larceny; his presence before the court was procured by means of forcible abduction from Peru. A messenger was sent to Lima with the proper warrant to demand Ker by virtue of the extradition treaty between Peru and the United States. The messenger, however, disdained reliance on the treaty processes, and instead forcibly kidnapped Ker and brought him to the United States. We distinguished Ker's case from Rauscher, on the basis that Ker was not brought into the United States by virtue of the extradition treaty between the United States and Peru, and rejected Ker's argument that he had a right under the extradition treaty to be returned to this country only in accordance with its terms. We rejected Ker's due process argument more broadly, holding in line with "the highest authorities" that "such forcible abduction is no sufficient reason why the party should not answer when brought within the jurisdiction of the court which has the right to try him for such an offence, and presents no valid objection to his trial in such court."

In *Frisbie v. Collins*, 342 U.S. 519, 72 S.Ct. 509, 96 L.Ed. 541, rehearing denied, 343 U.S. 937, 72 S.Ct. 768, 96 L.Ed. 1344 (1952), we applied the rule in *Ker* to a case in which the defendant had been kidnapped in Chicago by Michigan officers and brought to trial in Michigan. We upheld the conviction over objections based on the due process clause and the Federal Kidnapping Act and stated: "This Court has never departed from the rule announced in [*Ker*] that the power of a court to try a person for crime is not impaired by the fact that he had been brought within the court's jurisdiction by reason of a 'forcible abduction.' No persuasive reasons are now presented to justify overruling this line of cases. They rest on the sound basis that due process of law is satisfied when one present in court is convicted of crime after having been fairly apprized of the charges against him and after a fair trial in accordance with constitutional procedural safeguards. There is nothing in the Constitution that requires a court to permit a guilty person rightfully convicted to escape justice because he was brought to trial against his will."

The only differences between *Ker* and the present case are that *Ker* was decided on the premise that there was no governmental involvement in the abduction, and Peru, from which Ker was abducted, did not object to his prosecution. Respondent finds these differences to be dispositive, as did the Court of Appeals in *Verdugo*, contending that they show that respondent's prosecution, like the prosecution of Rauscher, violates the implied terms of a valid extradition treaty. The Government, on the other hand, argues that *Rauscher* stands as an "exception" to the rule in *Ker* only when an extradition treaty is invoked, and the terms of the treaty provide that its breach will limit the jurisdiction of a court. Therefore, our first inquiry must be whether the abduction of respondent from Mexico violated the extradition treaty between the United States and Mexico. If we conclude that the Treaty does not prohibit respondent's abduction, the rule in *Ker* applies, and the court need not inquire as to how respondent came before it.

In construing a treaty, as in construing a statute, we first look to its terms to determine its meaning. The Treaty says nothing about the obligations of the United States and Mexico to refrain from forcible abductions of people from the territory of the other nation, or the consequences under the Treaty if such an abduction occurs. . . .

More critical to respondent's argument is Article 9 of the Treaty which provides: "1. Neither Contracting Party shall be bound to deliver up its own nationals, but the executive authority of the requested Party shall, if not prevented by the laws of that Party, have the power to deliver them up if, in its discretion, it be deemed proper to do so. 2. If extradition is not granted pursuant to paragraph 1 of this Article, the requested Party shall submit the case to its competent authorities for the purpose of prosecution, provided that Party has jurisdiction over the offense." According to respondent, Article 9 embodies the terms of the bargain which the United States struck: if the United States wishes to prosecute a Mexican national, it may request that individual's extradition. Upon a request from the United States, Mexico may either extradite the individual, or submit the case to the proper authorities for prosecution in Mexico. In this way, respondent reasons, each nation preserved its right to choose whether its nationals would be tried in its own courts or by the courts of the other nation. This preservation of rights would be frustrated if either nation were free to abduct nationals of the other nation for the purposes of prosecution. More broadly, respondent reasons, as did the Court of Appeals, that all the processes and restrictions on the obligation to extradite established by the Treaty would make no sense if either nation were free to resort to forcible kidnapping to gain the presence of an individual for prosecution in a manner not contemplated by the Treaty.

We do not read the Treaty in such a fashion. Article 9 does not purport to specify the only way in which one country may gain custody of a national of the other country for the purposes of prosecution. . . .

The history of negotiation and practice under the Treaty also fails to show that abductions outside of the Treaty constitute a violation of the Treaty. As the Solicitor General notes, the Mexican government was made aware, as early as 1906, of the Ker doctrine, and the United States' position that it applied to forcible abductions made outside of the terms of the United States-Mexico extradition treaty. Nonetheless, the current version of the Treaty, signed in 1978, does not attempt to establish a rule that would in any way curtail the effect of *Ker*. Moreover, although language which would grant individuals exactly the right sought by respondent had been considered and drafted as early as 1935 by a prominent group of legal scholars sponsored by the faculty of Harvard Law School, no such clause appears in the current treaty.

Thus, the language of the Treaty, in the context of its history, does not support the proposition that the Treaty prohibits abductions outside of its terms. The remaining question, therefore, is whether the Treaty should be interpreted so as to include an implied term prohibiting prosecution where the defendant's presence is obtained by means other than those established by the Treaty.

Respondent contends that the Treaty must be interpreted against the backdrop of customary international law, and that international abductions are "so clearly prohibited in international law" that there was no reason to include such a clause in the Treaty itself. The international censure of international abductions is further evidenced, according to respondent, by the United Nations Charter and the Charter of the Organization of American States. Respondent does not argue that these sources of international law provide an independent basis for the right respondent asserts not to be tried in the United States, but rather that they should inform the interpretation of the Treaty terms.

The Court of Appeals deemed it essential, in order for the individual defendant to assert a right under the Treaty, that the affected foreign government had registered a protest. *Verdugo*, 939 F.2d, at 1357 ("in the kidnapping case there must be a formal protest from the offended government after the kidnapping"). Respondent agrees that the right exercised by the individual is derivative of the nation's right under the Treaty, since nations are authorized, notwithstanding the terms of an extradition treaty, to voluntarily render an individual to the other country on terms completely outside of those provided in the Treaty. The formal protest, therefore, ensures that the "offended" nation actually objects to the abduction and has not in some way voluntarily rendered the individual for prosecution. Thus, the Extradition Treaty only prohibits gaining the defendant's presence by means other than those set forth in the Treaty when the nation from which the defendant was abducted objects.

This argument seems to us inconsistent with the remainder of respondent's argument. The Extradition Treaty has the force of law, and if, as respondent asserts, it is self-executing, it would appear that a court must enforce it on behalf of an individual regardless of the offensiveness of the practice of one nation to the other nation. In *Rauscher*, the Court noted that Great Britain had taken the position in other cases that the Webster-Ashburton Treaty included the doctrine of *specialty*, but no importance was attached to whether or not Great Britain had protested the prosecution of Rauscher for the crime of cruel and unusual punishment as opposed to murder.

More fundamentally, the difficulty with the support respondent garners from international law is that none of it relates to the practice of nations in relation to extradition treaties. In *Rauscher*, we implied a term in the Webster-Ashburton Treaty because of the practice of nations with regard to extradition treaties. In the instant case, respondent would imply terms in the extradition treaty from the practice of nations with regards to international law more generally. Respondent would have us find that the Treaty acts as a prohibition against a violation of the general principle of international law that one government may not "exercise its police power in the territory of another state." There are many actions which could be taken by a nation that would violate this principle, including waging war, but it cannot seriously be contended an invasion of the United States by Mexico would violate the terms of the extradition treaty between the two nations.

In sum, to infer from this Treaty and its terms that it prohibits all means of gaining the presence of an individual outside of its terms goes beyond established precedent and practice. In *Rauscher*, the implication of a doctrine of *specialty* into the terms of the Webster-Ashburton Treaty which, by its terms, required the presentation of evidence establishing probable cause of the crime of extradition before extradition was required, was a small step to take. By contrast, to imply from the terms of this Treaty that it prohibits obtaining the presence of an individual by means outside of the procedures the Treaty establishes requires a much larger inferential leap, with only the most general of international law principles to support it. The general principles cited by respondent simply fail to persuade us that we should imply in the United States-Mexico Extradition Treaty a term prohibiting international abductions.

Respondent and his amici may be correct that respondent's abduction was "shocking," and that it may be in violation of general international law principles. Mexico has protested the abduction of respondent through diplomatic notes, and the decision of whether respondent should be returned to Mexico, as a matter outside of the Treaty, is a matter for the Executive Branch. We conclude, however, that respondent's abduction was not in violation of the Extradition Treaty between the United States and Mexico, and therefore the rule of *Ker v. Illinois* is fully applicable to this case. The fact of respondent's forcible abduction does not therefore prohibit his trial in a court in the United States for violations of the criminal laws of the United States.

* * *

Justice STEVENS, with whom Justice BLACKMUN and Justice O'CONNOR join, dissenting.

. . . The case is unique for several reasons. It does not involve an ordinary abduction by a private kidnaper, or bounty hunter, as in *Ker v. Illinois*, nor does it involve the apprehension of an American fugitive who committed a crime in one State and sought asylum in another, as in *Frisbie v. Collins*. Rather, it involves this country's abduction of another country's citizen; it also involves a violation of the territorial integrity of that other country, with which this country has signed an extradition treaty.

A Mexican citizen was kidnapped in Mexico and charged with a crime committed in Mexico; his offense allegedly violated both Mexican and American law. Mexico has formally demanded on at least two separate occasions that he be returned to Mexico and has represented that he will be prosecuted and punished for his alleged offense. It is clear that Mexico's demand must be honored if this official abduction violated the 1978 Extradition Treaty between the United States and Mexico. In my opinion, a fair reading of the treaty in light of our decision in *United States v. Rauscher*, and applicable principles of international law, leads inexorably to the conclusion that the District Court, and the Court of Appeals for the Ninth Circuit, correctly construed that instrument.

The Extradition Treaty with Mexico is a comprehensive document containing 23 articles and an appendix listing the extraditable offenses covered by the agreement. The parties announced their purpose in the preamble: The two Governments desire "to cooperate more closely in the fight against crime and, to this end, to mutually render better assistance in matters of extradition." From the preamble, through the description of the parties' obligations with respect to offenses committed within as well as beyond the territory of a requesting party, the delineation of the procedures and evidentiary requirements for extradition, the special provisions for political offenses and capital punishment, and other details, the Treaty appears to have been designed to cover the entire subject of extradition. Thus, Article 22, entitled "Scope of Application" states that the "Treaty shall apply to offenses specified in Article 2 committed before and after this Treaty enters into force," and Article 2 directs that "[e]xtradition shall take place, subject to this Treaty, for willful acts which fall within any of [the extraditable offenses listed in] the clauses of the Appendix."

Petitioner's claim that the Treaty is not exclusive, but permits forcible governmental kidnapping, would transform these, and other, provisions into little more than verbiage. . . .

It is true, as the Court notes, that there is no express promise by either party to refrain from forcible abductions in the territory of the other Nation. Relying on that omission, the Court, in effect, concludes that the Treaty merely creates an optional method of obtaining jurisdiction over alleged offenders, and that the parties silently reserved the right to resort to self help whenever they deem force more expeditious than legal process. If the United States, for example, thought it more expedient to torture or simply to execute a person rather than to attempt extradition, these options would be equally available because they, too, were not explicitly prohibited by the Treaty. That, however, is a highly improbable interpretation of a consensual agreement, which on its face appears to have been intended to set forth comprehensive and exclusive rules concerning the subject of extradition.

II

* * *

Although the Court's conclusion in *Rauscher* was supported by a number of judicial precedents, the holdings in these cases were not nearly as uniform as the consensus of international opinion that condemns one Nation's violation of the territorial integrity of a friendly neighbor. It is shocking that a party to an extradition treaty might believe that it has secretly reserved the right to make seizures of citizens in the other party's territory. Justice Story found it shocking enough that the United States would attempt to justify an American seizure of a foreign vessel in a Spanish port:

> "But, even supposing, for a moment, that our laws had required an entry of the *Apollon*, in her transit, does it follow, that the power to arrest her was meant to be given, after she had passed into the exclusive territory of a foreign nation? We think not. It would be monstrous to suppose that our revenue officers were authorized to enter into foreign ports and territories, for the purpose of seizing vessels which had offended against our laws. It cannot be presumed that Congress would voluntarily justify such a clear violation of the laws of nations." *The Apollon*, 9 Wheat. 362, 370-371, 6 L.Ed. 111(1824).

The law of Nations, as understood by Justice Story in 1824, has not changed. Thus, a leading treatise explains:

"A State must not perform acts of sovereignty in the territory of another State."

"It is . . . a breach of International Law for a State to send its agents to the territory of another State to apprehend persons accused of having committed a crime. Apart from other satisfaction, the first duty of the offending State is to hand over the person in question to the State in whose territory he was apprehended." 1 Oppenheim's International Law 295, and n. 1 (H. Lauterpacht 8th ed. 1955).*

Commenting on the precise issue raised by this case, the chief reporter for the American Law Institute's Restatement of Foreign Relations used language reminiscent of Justice Story's characterization of an official seizure in a foreign jurisdiction as "monstrous": "When done without consent of the foreign government, abducting a person from a foreign country is a gross violation of international law and gross disrespect for a norm high in the opinion of mankind. It is a blatant violation of the territorial integrity of another state; it eviscerates the extradition system (established by a comprehensive network of treaties involving virtually all states)."

In the *Rauscher* case, the legal background that supported the decision to imply a covenant not to prosecute for an offense different from that for which extradition had been granted was far less clear than the rule against invading the territorial integrity of a treaty partner that supports Mexico's position in this case. If *Rauscher* was correctly decided—and I am convinced that it was—its rationale clearly dictates a comparable result in this case.

III

A critical flaw pervades the Court's entire opinion. It fails to differentiate between the conduct of private citizens, which does not violate any treaty obligation, and conduct expressly authorized by the Executive Branch of the Government, which unquestionably constitutes a flagrant violation of international law, and in my opinion, also constitutes a breach of our treaty obligations. Thus, at the outset of its opinion, the Court states the issue as "whether a criminal defendant, abducted to the United States from a nation with which it has an extradition treaty, thereby acquires a defense to the jurisdiction of this country's courts." *Ante*, at 2190. That, of course, is the question decided in *Ker v. Illinois*, 119 U.S. 436, 7 S.Ct. 225, 30 L.Ed. 421 (1886); it is not, however, the question presented for decision today.

* * *

IV

As the Court observes at the outset of its opinion, there is reason to believe that respondent participated in an especially brutal murder of an American law enforcement agent. That fact, if true, may explain the Executive's intense interest in punishing respondent in our courts. Such an explanation, however, provides no justification for disregarding the Rule of Law that this Court has a duty to uphold. That the Executive may wish to reinterpret the Treaty to allow for an action that the Treaty in no way authorizes should not influence this Court's interpretation. Indeed, the desire for revenge exerts "a kind of hydraulic pressure . . . before which even well settled principles of law will bend," *Northern Securities Co. v. United States*, 193 U.S. 197, 401, 24 S.Ct. 436, 468, 48 L.Ed. 679 (1904)

(Holmes, J., dissenting), but it is precisely at such moments that we should remember and be guided by our duty "to render judgment evenly and dispassionately according to law, as each is given understanding to ascertain and apply it." *United States v. Mine Workers*, 330 U.S. 258, 342, 67 S.Ct. 677, 720, 91 L.Ed. 884 (1947) (Rutledge, J., dissenting). The way that we perform that duty in a case of this kind sets an example that other tribunals in other countries are sure to emulate.

* * *

I respectfully dissent.

Discussion Questions

1. Do you agree with the majority opinion in this case or with the dissenters? Why?
2. Had this situation been reversed and the person involved in the alleged crime been a U.S. citizen abducted in this country and forcibly brought to Mexico for trial, how would the United States have reacted? Discuss.
3. Why does the majority opinion indicate that the matter of Alvarez's return is within the executive's discretion? How are the roles of the courts and the executive different in matters of international law?
4. How would the International Court of Justice have decided this case if it were properly submitted to it for adjudication? Would it have approached the issue in the same way? Discuss.
5. Would an international criminal court be useful in dealing with matters similar to the *Alvarez* case? Discuss.

Comment: The *Alvarez* case was remanded back to the District Court in Texas where a preliminary hearing did not produce sufficient evidence (probable cause) to warrant holding Alvarez for trial according to the trial judge. Alvarez was released and allowed to return to Mexico (O'Brien, 1995, pp. 249-250).

The notable exception to the **Ker-Frisbie rule**, relied on to decide the *Alvarez* case, involved both abduction and torture on the part of U.S. government officials. In *United States v. Toscanino* (1974) the Court of Appeals for the Second Circuit held that allegations of brutal treatment in the course of an abduction from abroad, coupled with active participation by United States government officials in the abduction and torture, if proved to have occurred, would support discharge of the prisoner (500 F.2d 267). *Toscanino* has not been followed in cases involving conduct by United States officials abroad not amounting to torture and "shocking brutality," although inconsistent with the standards of the Fourth, Fifth, or Sixth Amendment. Some

> **Ker-Frisbie rule:**
> The rule in U.S. courts that allows individuals to be prosecuted in U.S. courts regardless of how they were brought into the territorial jurisdiction of that court.

decisions have upheld convictions resulting from arrest or search and seizure by improper police measures abroad, where the court found that the participation by U.S. law enforcement officers was subordinate to that of foreign officials (see *Restatement [Third] § 433, Reporter's Note 3*).

Extradition Treaties

The practice of **extradition** is the most widespread example of cooperation among States in criminal matters. Grotius, in his *De Jure Belli ac Pacis*, thought that according to the law and usage of civilized nations, every State was obliged to grant extradition freely and

> **Extradition:** The surrender of one State to another of an individual accused or convicted of an offense outside its own territory and within the territorial jurisdiction of another when the other State is competent to try and punish him or her and/or demands his or her surrender.

without qualification or restriction or to punish the wrongdoer itself. The influence of the positivist school of jurisprudence in the nineteenth century caused State practice to yield to the view that delivery of persons charged with or convicted of crimes in another State was at most a moral duty, not required by customary international law but generally governed by treaty and subject to various limitations. Today, a network of treaties, mostly bilateral, has been developed to create a body of law with substantial uniformity in major respects but differing in detail. The network of treaties, however, has not created a principle of customary law requiring extradition.

Under most treaties, laws, and State practice, particularly since World War II, the following general principles can be found:

1. That extradition of a person sought for prosecution requires some showing that there is cause for holding the person for trial for the offense charged
2. That the offense is one for which extradition has been provided by treaty or statute
3. That the offense is considered a crime in both the requested and the requesting State
4. That the offense committed was within the jurisdiction to prescribe of the requesting State
5. That extradition would not violate an applicable principle of double jeopardy

The requested State retains an interest in the fate of a person whom it has extradited and may insist that the person be tried only for the crime for which that person was extradited. The accused may not be given a more severe punishment than the one applicable at the time of the request.

These general features of modern treaties express what they have in common. There are also many differences in details of the individual agreements. As a matter of policy, some States will not extradite their own nationals, although the United States and the United Kingdom do not draw this distinction. However, reciprocity is also a general feature of all treaties. Some States, including the United States, Canada, and the United Kingdom, will grant extradition only on the basis of a preexisting treaty; other States will sometimes extradite without a treaty obligation to do so.

By the end of the nineteenth century, a general rule in treaty provisions developed that political offenders would not be extradited. This rule is now undergoing a process of alteration in response to the worldwide rise of terrorism. States have moved to narrow the definition of "political offense" to distinguish between "pure" political offenses, such as unlawful speech or assembly, and crimes of violence committed from political motive or against political leaders.

Many States have also been concerned to ensure that any person extradited from their territory will not be subject to persecution in the requesting State and will be accorded a fair trial. For this reason, nearly all extradition treaties leave some room, at least by implication, for discretion by the requested State not to extradite in certain cases.

The United States is a party to nearly one hundred bilateral extradition treaties. It is also a party to the 1933 Montevideo Convention on Extradition, involving a number of Latin American States. Extradition procedure is governed by the terms of the particular treaty and by statutory provisions that eliminate controversy over whether or not these treaties are self-executing. The judge is therefore limited by the statute and the treaty provisions. These rules provide for the issue of warrants for wanted persons, for their arrest and commitment, for a public hearing as to the sufficiency of the evidence that their cases come within the terms of the relevant treaty, and for their surrender to agents of the foreign government.

U.S. extradition treaties are less standardized than the typical foundation treaties of friendship and commerce (FCN treaties) and are therefore quite difficult to characterize. These treaties generally stipulate that the accused is not to be tried for an offense other than that designated in the request for his or her extradition (the doctrine of "speciality.") The general concept of "double criminality" (i.e., that one can be extradited only if the acts alleged constitute a crime in both countries) is a standard feature. There is an exception for "political crimes" that is increasingly subject to refined wording that more narrowly defines this term.

More difficult problems emerge in drafting treaties that include countries with longstanding policies that prohibit the extradition of their own nationals. Some countries are limited in this respect by their constitutions. This results in variation among U.S. treaties. For example, the treaty with Brazil prohibits extradition of its nationals, the one with Sweden leaves it to executive discretion whether to extradite nationals, and the treaty with Israel provides that extradition may not be refused on the basis that the fugitive is a national.

The traditional approach has allowed extradition only for crimes committed within the territory of the requesting State. This raises important questions about prosecution under the protective principle. Some recent treaties have provided for extradition in cases of perjury or counterfeiting if the laws of both States authorize the application of criminal sanctions despite the degree of extraterritoriality involved.

The application of capital punishment in the United States raises additional problems. Most other States, particularly of Western Europe, have abolished the death penalty. In the *Soering* case, the European Court of Human Rights held that it would violate the convention for the United Kingdom to extradite a German national to the United States for trial in Virginia because of the mental torture inherent in the long-continued death sentence litigation process (*Soering v. United Kingdom*, 161 Eur.Ct.H.R., 1989). A Netherlands court also refused to extradite or turn over to the U.S. army an American soldier accused of murder until the court was assured that the United States would not seek the death penalty. Both of these cases terminated in commitments by the United States not to seek the death penalty.

One of the most complicated cases of extradition from the United States is the *Matter of Demjanjuk* involving a person accused of being "Ivan the Terror" of the Treblinka death camp during World War II. The U.S. District Court in Ohio approved a request by Israel for extradition of a person who had lived in the United States for 40 years and had become a U.S. citizen. The request charged Demjanjuk with murder, manslaughter, and related offenses alleged to have been committed in Nazi concentration camps in Eastern Europe (603 F.Supp. 1468, N.D. Ohio, affirmed, 776 F.2d 571, 6th Cir.1985). Nearly ten years later in 1992, Demjanjuk was tried in Israel and found guilty of murder under circumstances that raised important questions about mistaken identity by witnesses to crimes allegedly committed nearly a half century earlier. Discovery that Demjanjuk was not the famous "Ivan the Terror" of the Treblinka death camp but a guard at another death camp led to attempts to try him under different charges than those for which he was extradited. The United States asserted its interest in the original extradition and demanded his return. Ultimately, the Israeli

Supreme Court reversed his conviction, and he was finally allowed to return to the United States.

There is some indication that because of the complexities associated with extradition, it may be easier to institute deportation proceedings in some circumstances; however, there is considerable evidence of increasing cooperation among governments in the area of transnational law enforcement regarding drug enforcement and terrorist investigations. Extradition of persons who are fleeing felons or who are wanted for serious crimes are increasingly approved on the basis of the principles outlined in this chapter. Attempts to develop multilateral extradition treaties have had only limited success, but a notable exception is the European Convention on Extradition. This multilateral treaty was concluded under the auspices of the Council of Europe in 1960, and by 1986, nineteen States were parties.

Law Enforcement Cooperation

At an informal level, there is considerable cooperation and interchange of information and data between national police forces. A permanent structure for such interchanges is provided by the International Criminal Police Organization (INTERPOL), which links national police departments in some 136 States. It receives and distributes lists and descriptions of fugitives wanted by member States for use at airports, border crossings, and similar places where a fugitive might be identified and apprehended. If a State seeking arrest of a fugitive gives assurances that his or her arrest will be followed by a request for extradition, the person's name and description will be circulated on a "red individual notice." Some States authorize provisional arrest of a person on the basis of an INTERPOL notice, pending notification to the State at whose behest the notice was issued. A person so arrested must be discharged if a request for extradition is not received from that State promptly.

The United States has concluded a number of agreements for exchange of information and even use of U.S. agents abroad serving with the other State's authorities (see Nadelmann, 1985, p. 467). The notable Treaty on Mutual Assistance in Criminal Matters Between the United States and Switzerland entered into force in 1977, and the Bank Secrecy Act of 1970 (31 U.S.C.A. §§ 5311-5322) gives law enforcement officers more authority to investigate individual bank accounts where probable cause can be demonstrated. This act of Congress requires reports on various transactions by U.S. banks, reports on the export or import of money in excess of $10,000, and reports on transactions between U.S. citizens and foreign banks. The treaty requires each party, subject to various safeguards in the interest of its sovereignty or security, to assist the other in obtaining evidence needed for criminal prosecutions in a wide variety of situations. It now enables authorities to penetrate Swiss bank secrecy in the case of serious offenses where the evidence is shown to be important and where other efforts at obtaining it have failed.

Chapter Summary

1. Jurisdiction to prescribe refers to the individual State's authority to define and punish acts of individuals. International law has long recognized limitations on this authority in circumstances affecting the interests of other States.

2. The modern internationally recognized bases of individual State jurisdiction to prescribe include the territorial principle, the nationality principle, the protective principle, the passive personality principle, and the universal principle.

3. The territorial principle is the most fundamental and by far the most common basis for the exercise of a State's jurisdiction. Any violation of a nation's criminal laws, committed within its sovereign territory, is subject to punishment by that State regardless of the nationality of the person accused.

4. As illustrated in the *Lotus* case, situations arise that include transnational behavior that may originate in one State but have its effect in another State. Such situations create concurrent jurisdiction, and both States may have jurisdiction to define and punish violations of their laws.

5. The effects principle is an extension of the principle of territorial jurisdiction and is universally recognized today as a proper basis for jurisdiction.

6. The nationality principle is an independent alternative basis of jurisdiction and may be asserted as a basis of jurisdiction to prescribe activities of a State's nationals wherever they may be located. Especially in tax matters, this authority is asserted by all States. However, many States assert that a crime committed by their nationals outside their territory is still subject to their jurisdiction even though there may be concurrent jurisdiction of the State where the crime was committed.

7. The protective principle is derived from the territorial principle but is recognized as a distinct class of offenses that may be committed outside its territory by persons who are not its nationals when the offenses are directed against the security of the State or threatens the integrity of governmental functions of the State asserting jurisdiction. This situation also produces concurrent jurisdiction over the offender.

8. The passive personality principle asserts jurisdiction over persons who commit certain criminal acts when the victim of the crime is a national of the State claiming jurisdiction, even though the crime was committed in another country by individuals who are not nationals of the State in question. This principle is the most controversial and requires additional links to a universal crime or some other recognized basis of jurisdiction.

9. A limited, but expanding, class of crimes is of universal concern to the international community, which accepts the principle that any State has jurisdiction to prescribe punishment in relationship to these crimes even where there are no links to territoriality or nationality.

10. The modern principles of reasonableness stated in § 403 of the *Restatement (Third)* have been developed by the international community to reduce the amount of conflict that must inevitably occur as a result of the extraordinary amount of overlapping jurisdiction in our increasingly interdependent world.

11. In cases of concurrent jurisdiction, a State has an obligation to weigh all the relevant factors involving the interests of other States and should defer to the other State if that State's interest is clearly greater.

12. Disputes over how to interpret these rules are frequent, and the most significant practical factor in criminal cases is more directly related to which State has personal jurisdiction over the accused.

13. Jurisdiction to tax and regulate is even broader than in criminal matters, and a State may tax or seize property located within its territory, investigate alleged violations, and require reports and accounting procedures of private parties who are neither their nationals nor present in their territorial jurisdiction.

14. Efforts have been made to prevent double taxation, but multilateral treaties have had little success in this area. States have been reluctant to accept a general obligation to avoid double taxation except on the basis of specific agreements.

15. Jurisdiction to adjudicate in criminal cases is generally restricted because the person accused must be present to answer criminal charges. U.S. constitutional guarantees prevent trials in absentia except for lesser regulatory offenses.

16. However, indictments are frequently brought against individuals who are not located within the court's jurisdiction. Resulting warrants and summons for the person to appear may be served only within the jurisdiction of the State and cannot be exercised in another country. This must be done by consent of the other State to exercise its authority to apprehend and extradite the individual in question.

17. Jurisdiction to enforce involves the exercise of the sovereign authority of the State. One State may not exercise its governmental functions in the territory of another State without that State's consent.

18. Abductions of individuals who are forcibly removed from one State and brought to another State without the consent of the State where the abduction occurs are violations of international law. However, nearly all States follow the rule that in the absence of protest from other States, they will try such persons even though they have been brought before their courts by irregular means.

19. In *United States v. Alvarez-Machain* the U.S. Supreme Court went one step further than prevailing State practice and accepted jurisdiction even though there was protest by Mexico, the individual was alleged to have committed a crime in Mexico, and he was a Mexican national.

20. There is, however, precedent in U.S. courts that supports refusal to try individuals who have been abducted abroad with active participation by U.S. government officials involving torture and "shockingly brutal" conduct.

21. Extradition is the process that is the legal method of obtaining personal jurisdiction over individuals located in another country. There is no generally recognized principle of customary international law requiring extradition. Such obligations are achieved by specific treaty agreement.

22. The United States is a party to nearly one hundred bilateral extradition treaties and a few multilateral treaties of this nature. Judicial authority is required to grant extradition, and the specific treaty provisions are used as a basis for the judge to make a decision based on the reasonableness criteria used in cases of conflict. There is nearly always some degree of discretionary authority left to the judge.

23. Clauses that exclude "political offenses" are generally included; both States must recognize the crime (double criminality); and the accused cannot be tried for an offense other than that for which the person is extradited (doctrine of specialty).

24. Some progress has been made in securing greater cooperation between States in controlling international crime; however, there are sensitive issues of national sovereignty involved.

Key Terms

private law	protective principle	war crimes
public law	passive personality	apartheid
territorial principle	principle	double taxation
effects principle	universal jurisdiction	Ker-Frisbie rule
nationality principle	genocide	extradition

■   ■   ■

Discussion Questions

1. What are the most important areas of potential conflict among nations in regard to areas of concurrent criminal jurisdiction?

2. Are the rules of reasonableness outlined by the *Restatement (Third)* adequate to resolve these conflicts? Why or why not?

3. Is there a need for a permanent international criminal court to resolve these issues? Why or why not?

4. What specific areas of jurisdiction to adjudicate might produce sufficient consensus among the international community to achieve agreement? Discuss.

5. What specific areas of jurisdiction to adjudicate might produce the least consensus among the international community?

6. Is it more likely that a State would agree to extradite a person to an international tribunal for adjudication than to another State? Why or why not?

Suggested Readings

Appendix H: Convention on the Prevention and Punishment of the Crime of Genocide

Appendix I: International Convention on the Suppression and Punishment of the Crime of "Apartheid"

Nadelmann, E. A. (1985). Negotiations in criminal law assistance treaties. *American Journal of Comparative Law, 33,* 467-504.

Steiner, H. J., Vagts, D. F., & Koh, H. H. (1994). *Transnational legal problems* (4th ed.). New York: Foundation Press.

Internet Sources

Browse: Use *international law* and *human rights* (http://www.un.org) and (http://hrweb.org).

10 Diplomatic and Sovereign Immunity

This chapter deals with the most fundamental limitations on sovereignty and individual State jurisdiction imposed by international law. Diplomatic immunity and the prohibition of one State to sit in judgment of another State's actions, when these actions are truly acts of State, are exceptions to the general law provided for territorial jurisdiction. The general principles of diplomatic immunity and sovereign immunity (or State immunity) thus provide an understanding of the limits of individual State courts in their jurisdiction over transnational legal questions. Issues relating to these acts become the primary concern of international tribunals and are beyond the scope of individual State jurisdiction. However, domestic courts must deal with problems of diplomatic immunity on a frequent basis and determine the existence of acts of State that are immune from its jurisdiction.

The decentralized system of international law derives from the mutual respect for State sovereignty of its constituent parts. The purpose of diplomatic immunity is to allow representatives of sovereign States to carry out their communicative functions within a framework of necessary security and confidentiality. Generally, diplomats are required to comply with local law but are immune from the local jurisdiction to apply and enforce such law. The international legal rules protecting foreign diplomats are some of the oldest in history, and generally, they have been the most respected rules of international law. The major innovations in modern international law that will be emphasized in this chapter relate to the codification of the rules of diplomatic immunity and the development of restrictive immunity for acts of State as opposed to commercial transactions of modern nations.

Diplomatic Immunity

Professor I. Brownlie (1979), of Oxford University, explains the existence of diplomatic immunity in international law as flowing from a license extended from the host State to the receiving State allowing the

289

exercise of State functions within the host State. He explains:

> The essence of diplomatic relations is the exercise by the sending government of state functions on the territory of the receiving state by license [permission] of the latter. Having agreed to the establishment of diplomatic relations, the receiving [host] state must take steps to enable the sending state to benefit from the content of the license. The process of giving full faith and credit to the license results in a body of privileges and immunities. (pp. 346-347)

Therefore, diplomatic immunity is not given to all sovereign entities, and international law does not require it. However, once given, in specific agreements to establish diplomatic relations, the host State accepts the customary international legal obligation to respect the rules of diplomatic immunity. The rules of diplomatic immunity have evolved from common practice of States that date back to the beginning of recorded history. Even the ancient Greeks recognized that it was wrong to punish the messenger for bringing bad news from an alien power. The temptation to "kill the messenger" or to subject the representative of a foreign sovereign to intimidation, coercion, or abuse has always existed. The rules of modern diplomacy have been developed to facilitate diplomatic communications.

One of the first areas of traditional international law to be considered by the U.N. International Law Commission (ILC) for codification was the subject of diplomatic intercourse and immunities. At its seventh session, in 1952, the General Assembly passed a resolution requesting the commission to develop a draft convention. The preliminary work of the commission was completed in 1959 when the General Assembly called for an international confer-

ence to complete the drafting process. The U.N. Conference on Diplomatic Intercourse and Immunities met in Vienna in 1961 and completed three instruments: (a) the Vienna Convention of Diplomatic Relations, (b) the Optional Protocol Concerning Acquisition of Nationality, and (c) the Optional Protocol Concerning the Compulsory Settlement of Disputes.

Diplomatic immunity rests on two grounds: (a) It ensures the effective performance by the diplomatic agent, and (b) it protects the diplomatic agent's person and dignity (see Oliver, Firmage, Blankesley, Scott, & Williams, 1995, pp. 950-951).

The **Vienna Convention on Diplomatic Relations** is particularly noteworthy because it brought together the diverse elements of customary practice concerning diplomatic law and especially diplomatic privileges and immunities. Previous partial attempts at codification included diplomatic ranks and precedence that were established by the Congress of Vienna in 1815 and the Conference of Aix-la-Chappelle in 1818. The Sixth International Conference of American States in 1928 drafted a convention on diplomatic privileges and immunities that had the effect of regional international law. However, the Vienna Convention compiled and delineated these norms, making them clearer and less subject to State interpretation. The 1961 convention also bridged the gap between States that had previously accepted only functional immunity for diplomats. The 1961 convention makes a clear distinc-

> **Vienna Convention on Diplomatic Relations:** *General treaty, concluded in 1961, that codifies diplomatic law and the privileges and immunities of diplomatic agents. It includes clear definitions of rules concerning diplomatic functions, accreditation, agreement, classes of heads of missions, precedence, and breaking off of diplomatic relations.*

tion between diplomatic and consular functions.

The 1961 convention is comprehensive in regard to diplomatic, as opposed to consular, relations or those related to State representation in international organizations. These latter subjects have been dealt with in separate conventions. The Vienna Convention on Consular Relations was concluded in 1963, and the Vienna Convention on the Representation of States in Their Relations With International Organizations of a Universal Character was concluded in 1975. The Vienna Convention on Diplomatic Relations (1961) covers diplomatic functions, accreditation, agreement, classes of heads of missions, precedence, breaking off of diplomatic relations, and similar matters. It should be noted that those portions of the convention that codify customary practices are also binding on nonsignatory States, since custom is a source of international law. The final paragraph of the preamble to the convention declares that the signatory States affirm "that the rules of customary international law should continue to govern questions not expressly regulated by the provisions of the present Convention."

The Vienna Convention on Diplomatic Relations entered into force in 1964. As of 1995, 174 States were parties to the convention. It was ratified by the United States and entered into force in 1972. Congressional review of existing legislation, which dated from the eighteenth century, revealed considerable compatibility with the new convention. However, the **Diplomatic Relations Act of 1978** repealed the previous legislation and gave effect to the convention as controlling

> *Diplomatic Relations Act of 1978:*
> The act of Congress that repealed previous legislation and gave effect to the Vienna Convention on Diplomatic Relations as controlling domestic law.

domestic law (22 U.S.C. §§ 254a-254e, 28 U.S.C. § 1364).

Establishing Diplomatic Relations

The establishment of diplomatic relations with another nation is a political act subject to the municipal laws of the States involved. The U.S. Constitution gives this power to the president ("to send and receive ambassadors"). The president, therefore, has the discretionary power to establish and to terminate diplomatic relations with other States. The establishment of diplomatic missions in other countries is an expensive decision, and even the United States does not maintain embassies in every country. Some States can afford embassies in only a few countries, and the U.N. Organization in New York serves as a means to promote their diplomatic interests. The United States maintains about 140 embassies abroad and hosts about 130 foreign embassies in Washington, D.C.

Once a decision has been made to send and receive ambassadors between two States, the process of receiving a **diplomatic agent** (head of mission or a member of the diplomatic staff of the mission) involves review of credentials, and individuals may be refused diplomatic status if unacceptable to the host State. Even after accredited, the diplomatic agent may be asked to leave at any time but must be given reasonable time to leave the country. Full diplomatic immunity is usually granted only to persons defined as diplomatic agents by the Vienna Conven-

> *Diplomatic agent:*
> The head of a diplomatic mission or a member of the diplomatic staff of the mission. These political officers are given full diplomatic immunity that protects the diplomat from arrest, detention, criminal process, and in general, civil process in the receiving State.

tion. This group of diplomats does not include many other lesser officials and employees of an embassy who may be granted less than full immunity, usually referred to as functional immunity.

The *Restatement (Third) of the Foreign Relations Law of the United States* (American Law Institute, 1987) provides a brief statement of the immunity afforded such diplomatic agents, often referred to as full diplomatic immunity:

§ *464. Immunity of Diplomatic Agents of Other States*

A diplomatic agent of a state, accredited to and accepted by another state, is immune

(1) from the exercise by the receiving state of jurisdiction to prescribe in respect of acts or omissions in the exercise of the agent's official functions, as well as from other regulation that would be incompatible with the agent's diplomatic status; and

(2) from arrest, detention, criminal process, and, in general, civil process in the receiving state.

Diplomatic functions are defined by the Vienna Convention of 1961 as:

(a) representing the sending State in the receiving State;

(b) protecting in the receiving State the interests of the sending State and of its nationals, within the limits permitted by international law;

(c) negotiating with the Government of the receiving State;

(d) asserting by all lawful means conditions and developments in the receiving State, and reporting thereon to the Government of the sending State;

(e) promoting friendly relations between the sending State and the receiving State, and developing their economic, cultural and scientific relations.

Consular Functions and Immunities

There is a basic distinction between diplomatic functions and consular functions. Although they are official agents of the sending State, consuls are not diplomatic representatives, nor are they accredited to the host State. Consular officers may conduct diplomatic negotiations, but these negotiations are confined to international trade matters. In general, consuls promote commercial, economic, cultural, and scientific relations between the sending State and the receiving State; issue passports and travel documents; assist nationals and business entities from the sending State; prepare official documents; safeguard the interests of their nationals and assist them in securing appropriate representation; and a number of other administrative functions.

The **Vienna Convention on Consular Relations** of 1963 was the product of a U.N. conference attended by ninety-two States in 1963 called to codify the norms pertaining to consular functions, privileges, and immunities. This convention was also based on a draft prepared by the ILC. The 1963 convention outlines the immunities to be accorded consular officials, including freedom from arrest until trial (except for grave offenses) and from imprisonment until final judgment by the court, freedom of travel and communication, free access to the consul's nationals held in the jails of the host country, and immunity from jurisdiction in cases arising from the consul's performance of official duties. In addition, the consular premises are inviolable as are its archives and documents. This convention also represents the first global multilateral agreement to establish norms governing the status, privileges, and immunities of consular officials. It has been ratified by the United States and generally entered into force in 1967 (for the U.S., 1969); as of 1995, 153 States were parties.

Vienna Convention on Consular Relations: A general treaty, concluded in 1963, codifying the functions and immunities of consular officials who perform important administrative functions.

Diplomatic and consular immunities differ substantially in that the consular officer is not immune from all legal process: "He must respond to any process and plead and prove immunity on the ground that the act or omission underlying the process was in the performance of his official functions" (American Law Institute, 1987, p. 475). Hence, this form of immunity is frequently referred to as **functional immunity**. In the mid-1980s, concern about potential abuse of these immunities in the United States, in the aftermath of the "shoot-out" at the Libyan Peoples' Bureau in London and other developments, prompted Congress to order a State Department study and report on the issue. Congressional hearings were held in the spring of 1988. The State Department reported that there were at that time 26,282 persons with criminal immunity (full immunity) and 29,689 with official acts (functional) immunity in the United States. The State Department concluded that of the total, 55,971, the number of crimes committed by those persons was "very small" and that there was not a "diplomatic crime wave" (cited in Oliver et al., 1995, p. 953). As a consequence, draft legislation before the Congress to tighten procedures was not adopted.

> *Functional immunity:* Nonaccredited embassy officials and consular staff are given protection from criminal prosecution only to the extent that it affects the performance of official functions. Such officials must respond to any process and prove immunity on basis of their function.

Inviolability of the Diplomatic and Consular Premises

"The premises, archives, documents, and communications of an accredited diplomatic mission or consular post are inviolable, and are immune from any exercise of jurisdiction by the receiving State that would interfere with their official use" (American Law Institute, 1987, p. 483). Officials may not enter the premises of a diplomatic or consular mission without consent. The private residence of a diplomatic agent or of a member of the administrative and technical staff of a diplomatic mission also enjoy the same status and protection as the premises of the mission. The residence of the consular officials and other mission personnel is not inviolable, but persons and papers located there may enjoy immunities. That the premises are inviolable does not mean that they are extraterritorial. Acts committed on those premises are within the territorial jurisdiction of the receiving State. The mission is required to observe local law as well as fire and police codes.

Both the diplomatic and consular conventions require the receiving State to permit and protect freedom of communication by the mission or consular post for all official purposes. The diplomatic or consular bag (pouch) may not be opened or detained. However, if the competent authorities of the receiving State have "serious reason to believe" that a consular bag contains something other than correspondence, documents, or articles for official use, the authorities may ask that the bag be opened in the presence of the responsible official. If the request is refused, the bag must be returned to its place of origin (Consular Convention, Article 35[3]). There is no such provision in the Diplomatic Convention, but the same rules may apply to a diplomatic bag.

These conventions also provide for protection of the diplomat and his or her family in transit through the territory of a third State that may be required to ensure transit to the diplomat's post or return. Both diplomatic agents and consular personnel may be declared *persona non grata* and be required to return to their State of origin, but

> **Persona non grata:**
> A person not wanted; the host government may withdraw accreditation from diplomats and require them to leave within a reasonable time.

the receiving State, even in case of armed conflict, has an obligation to allow them to leave at the earliest possible moment and in case of need must provide the necessary means of transport for them and their property. In the event of breaking diplomatic relations between two States, these conventions require the respect and protection of the premises of the mission, together with its property and archives.

The revolutionary overthrow of the Shah of Iran in 1979 produced the most serious violations of diplomatic and consular immunity since the "defenstration of Prague," which touched off the Thirty Years War. On November 4, 1979, the U.S. embassy in Tehran, Iran, was overrun by several hundred of the three thousand Iranians who had been demonstrating at the embassy gates. The demonstrators seized diplomats, consuls, and Marine personnel in the embassy and occupied the embassy premises. Again, on November 22, several hundred thousand demonstrators converged on the embassy in Tehran, and the Iranian government made no effort to intervene or to assist the hostages.

After the taking of the U.S. Embassy in Tehran by Iranian militants and the holding as hostages of members of the U.S. diplomatic and consular staff, the United States instituted proceedings against Iran before the International Court of Justice (ICJ). The United States contended that by encouraging, adopting, and exploiting the conduct of Iranian citizens toward the embassy and hostages, Iran had violated international legal obligations to the United States set forth in several treaties to which both countries were parties. The treaties included the Vi-

enna Convention on Diplomatic Relations of 1961, the Vienna Convention on Consular Relations of 1963, and the Treaty of Amity, Economic Relations, and Consular Rights of 1955 between the United States and Iran. Compulsory jurisdiction of the ICJ rested on jurisdictional submissions in protocols to the two Vienna Conventions to which both countries were parties and in the 1955 Treaty.

The government of Iran filed no pleadings and was not represented in the oral proceedings. However, the position of the Iranian government was defined in a letter to the Court by its Minister of Foreign Affairs. The letter urged the court not to take cognizance of the case and attempted to excuse the events as only "a marginal and secondary aspect of an overall problem [involving] more than 25 years of continual interference by the United States in the internal affairs of Iran, the shameless exploitation of our country . . . contrary to and in conflict with all international and humanitarian norms."

The United States sought restoration of possession of the embassy, release of the hostages, and compensation for the wrongs done.

The ICJ issued an order dated December 15, 1979, indicating provisional measures in the case to be taken by Iran. In its final judgment, the Court decided (with one, two, or three dissenting votes on several of the decisions) that Iran had violated conventions in force with the United States "as well as . . . long-established rules of general international law," that Iran must release the hostages, that Iran must return possession of the U.S. Embassy and its related documents, and that Iran must make reparations to the United States, the form and amount thereof to be settled by the parties or the Court.

Case Concerning United States Diplomatic and Consular Staff in Tehran *(United States of America v. Iran)*
International Court of Justice, 1980.
[1980] I.C.J. Rep. 3.

[Selected excerpts from the Court's opinion]

* * *

22. The persons still held hostage in Iran include, according to the information furnished to the Court by the United Stares, at least 28 persons having the status, duly recognized by the Government of Iran, of "member of the diplomatic staff" within the meaning of the Vienna Convention on Diplomatic Relations of 1961; at least 20 persons having the status, similarly recognized, of "member of the administrative and technical staff" within the meaning of that Convention; and two other persons of United States nationality not possessing either diplomatic or consular status. Of the persons with the status of member of the diplomatic staff, four are members of the Consular Section of the Mission.

23. Allegations have been made by the Government of the United States of inhumane treatment of hostages; the militants and Iranian authorities have asserted that the hostages have been well treated, and have allowed special visits to the hostages by religious personalities and by representatives of the International Committee of the Red Cross. The specific allegations of ill treatment have not however been refuted. Examples of such allegations, which are mentioned in some of the sworn declarations of hostages released in November 1979, are as follows: at the outset of the occupation of the Embassy some were paraded bound and blindfolded before hostile and chanting crowds; at least during the initial period of their captivity, hostages were kept bound, and frequently blindfolded, denied mail or any communication with their government or with each other, subjected to interrogation, threatened with weapons.

24. Those archives and documents of the United States Embassy which were not destroyed by the staff during the attack on 4 November have been ransacked by the militants. Documents purporting to come from this source have been disseminated by the militants and by the Government-controlled media.

* * *

36. The Court, however, in its Order of 15 December 1979, made it clear that the seizure of the United States Embassy and consulates and the detention of internationally protected persons as hostages cannot be considered as something "secondary" or "marginal," having regard to the importance of the legal principles involved. It also referred to a statement of the Secretary-General of the United Nations, and to Security Council resolution 457 (1979), as evidencing the importance attached by the international community as a whole to the observance of those principles in the present case as well as its concern at the dangerous level of tension between Iran and the United States. The Court, at the same time, pointed out that no provision of the Statute or Rules contemplates that the Court should decline to take cognizance of one aspect of a dispute merely because that dispute has other aspects, however important. It further underlined that, if the Iranian Government considered the alleged activities of the United Stares in Iran legally to have a close connection with the subject-matter of the United States' Application, it was open to that Government to present its own arguments regarding those activities to the Court either by way of defence in a Counter-Memorial or by way of a counter-claim.

46. The terms of Article I, which are the same in the two Protocols, provide:

> "Disputes arising out of the interpretation or application of the Convention shall lie within the compulsory jurisdiction of the International Court of Justice and may accordingly be brought before the Court by an application made by any party to the dispute being a Party to the present Protocol."

The United States' claims here in question concern alleged violations by Iran of its obligations under several Articles of the Vienna Conventions of 1961 and 1963 with respect to the privileges and immunities of the personnel, the inviolability of the premises and archives, and the provision of facilities for the performance of the functions of the United States Embassy and Consulates in Iran. In so far as its claims relate to two private individuals held hostage in the Embassy, the situation of these individuals falls under the provisions of the Vienna Convention of 1961 guaranteeing the inviolability of the premises of embassies, and of Article 5 of the 1963 Convention concerning the consular functions of assisting nationals and protecting and safeguarding their interests. By their very nature all these claims concern the interpretation or application of one or other of the two Vienna Conventions.

47. The occupation of the United States Embassy by militants on 4 November 1979 and the detention of its Personnel as hostages was an event of a kind to provoke an immediate protest from any government, as it did from the United States Government, which dispatched a special emissary to Iran to deliver a formal protest. Although the special emissary, denied all contact with Iranian officials, never entered Iran, the Iranian Government was left in no doubt as to the reaction of the United States to the taking over of its Embassy and detention of its diplomatic and consular staff as hostages. Indeed, the Court was informed that the United States was meanwhile making its views known to the Iranian Government through its Chargé d'affaires, who has been kept since 4 November 1979 in the Iranian Foreign Ministry itself, where he happened to be with two other members of his mission during the attack on the Embassy. In any event, by a letter of 9 November 1979, the United States brought the situation in regard to its Embassy before the Security Council. The Iranian Government did not take any part in the debates on the matter in the Council, and it was still refusing to enter into any discussions on the subject when, on 29 November 1979, the United States filed the present Application submitting its claims to the Court. It is clear that on that date there existed a dispute arising out of the interpretation or application of the Vienna Conventions and thus one falling within the scope of Article 1 of the protocols.

* * *

61. The conclusion just reached by the Court, that the initiation of the attack on the United States Embassy on 4 November 1979, and of the attacks on the Consulates at Tabriz and Shiraz the following day, cannot be considered as in itself imputable to the Iranian State does not mean that Iran is, in consequence, free of any responsibility in regard to those attacks; for its own conduct was in conflict with its international obligations. By a number of provisions of the Vienna Conventions of 1961 and 1963, Iran was placed under the most categorical obligations, as a receiving State, to take appropriate steps to ensure the protection of the United States Embassy and Consulates, their staffs, their archives, their means of communication and the freedom of movement of the members of their staffs.

62. Thus, after solemnly proclaiming the inviolability of the premises of a diplomatic mission, Article 22 of the 1961 Convention continues in paragraph 2:.

> *"The receiving State is under a special duty to take all appropriate steps to protect the premises of the mission against any* [italics added] *intrusion or damage and to prevent any disturbance of the peace of the mission or impairment of its dignity."*

So too, after proclaiming that the person of a diplomatic agent shall be inviolable, and that he shall not be liable to any form of arrest or detention, Article 29 provides:

> *"The receiving State shall treat him with due respect and shall take all appropriate steps to prevent any attack on his person, freedom or dignity."* [italics added]

The obligation of a receiving State to protect the inviolability of the archives and documents of a diplomatic mission is laid down in Article 24, which specifically provides that they are to be "inviolable at any time and wherever they may be." Under Article 25, it is required to "accord full facilities for the performance of the functions of the mission," under Article 26, to "ensure to all members of the mission freedom of movement and travel in its territory," and under Article 27, to "permit and protect free communication on the part of the mission for all official purposes." Analogous provisions are to be found in the 1963 Convention regarding the privileges and immunities of consular missions and their staffs (Article 31, paragraph 3, Articles 40, 33, 28, 34 and 35). In the view of the Court, the obligations of the Iranian Government here in question are not merely contractual obligations established by the Vienna Conventions of 1961 and 1963, but also obligations under general international law.

63. The facts set out in paragraphs 14 to 27 above establish to the satisfaction of the Court that on 4 November 1979 the Iranian Government failed altogether to take any "appropriate steps" to protect the premises, staff and archives of the United States' mission against attack by the militants, and to take any steps either to prevent this attack or to stop it before it reached its completion. They also show that on 5 November 1979 the Iranian Government similarly failed to take appropriate steps for the protection of the United States Consulates at Tabriz and Shiraz. In addition they show, in the opinion of the Court, that the failure of the Iranian Government to take such steps was due to more than mere negligence or lack of appropriate means. 12

* * *

77. In the first place, these facts constituted breaches additional to those already committed of paragraph 2 of Article 22 of the 1961 Vienna Convention on Diplomatic Relations which requires Iran to protect the premises of the mission against any intrusion or damage and to prevent any disturbance of its peace or impairment of its dignity. Paragraphs 1 and 3 of that Article have also been infringed, and continue to be infringed, since they forbid agents of a receiving State to enter the premises of a mission without consent or to undertake any search, requisition, attachment or like measure on the premises. Secondly, they constitute continuing breaches of Article 29 of the same Convention which forbids any arrest or detention of a diplomatic agent and any attack on his person, freedom or dignity. Thirdly, the Iranian authorities are without doubt in continuing breach of the provisions of Articles 25, 26 and 27 of the 1961 Vienna Convention and of pertinent provisions of the 1963 Vienna Convention concerning facilities for performance of functions, freedom of movement and communications for diplomatic and consular staff, as well as of Article 24 of the former Convention and Article 33 of the latter, which provide for the absolute inviolability of the archives and documents of diplomatic missions and consulates. This particular violation has been made manifest to the world by repeated statements by the militants occupying the Embassy, who claim to be in possession of documents from the archives, and by various government authorities, purporting to specify the contents thereof. Finally, the continued detention as hostages of the two private individuals of United States nationality entails a renewed breach of the obligations of Iran under Article II, paragraph 4, of the 1955 Treaty of Amity, Economic Relations, and Consular Rights.

78. Inevitably, in considering the compatibility or otherwise of the conduct of the Iranian authorities with the requirements of the Vienna Conventions, the Court has focussed its attention primarily on the occupation of the Embassy and the treatment of the United States diplomatic and consular personnel within the Embassy. It is however evident that the question of the compatibility of their conduct with the Vienna Conventions also arises in connection with the treatment of the United States Chargé d'affaires and two members of his staff in the Ministry of Foreign Affairs on 4 November 1979 and since that date. The facts of this case establish to the satisfaction of the Court that on 4 November 1979 and thereafter the Iranian authorities have withheld from the Chargé d'affaires and the two members of his staff the necessary protection and facilities to permit them to leave the Ministry in safety. Accordingly it appears to the Court that with respect to these three members of the United States' mission the Iranian authorities have committed a continuing breach of their obligations under Articles 26 and 29 of the 1961 Vienna Convention on Diplomatic Relations. It further appears to the Court that the continuation of that situation over a long period has, in the circumstances, amounted to detention in the Ministry. 12

79. The Court moreover cannot conclude its observations on the series of acts which it has found to be imputable to the Iranian State and to be patently inconsistent with its international obligations under the Vienna Conventions of 1961 and 1963 without mention also of another fact. This is that judicial authorities of the Islamic Republic of Iran and the Minister for Foreign Affairs have frequently voiced, or associated themselves with, a threat first announced by the militants, of having some of the hostages submitted to trial before a court or some other body. These threats may at present merely be acts in contemplation. But the Court considers it necessary here and now to stress that, if the intention to submit the hostages to any form of criminal trial or investigation were to be put into effect, that would constitute a grave breach by Iran of its obligations under Article 31, paragraph 1, of the 1961 Vienna Convention. This paragraph states in the most express terms: "A diplomatic agent shall enjoy immunity from the criminal jurisdiction of the receiving State." Again, if there were an attempt to compel the hostages to bear witness, a suggestion renewed at the time of the visit to Iran of the Secretary-General's Commission, Iran would without question be violating paragraph 2 of that same Article of the 1961 Vienna Convention which provides that "A diplomatic agent is not obliged to give evidence as a witness."

* * *

85. In any case, even if the alleged criminal activities of the United States in Iran could be considered as having been established, the question would remain whether they could be regarded by the Court as constituting a justification of Iran's conduct and thus a defence to the United States' claims in the present case. The Court, however, is unable to accept that they can be so regarded. This is because diplomatic law itself provides the necessary means of defence against, and sanction for, illicit activities by members of diplomatic or consular missions.

84. The Vienna Conventions of 1961 and 1963 contain express provisions to meet the case when members of an embassy staff, under the cover of diplomatic privileges and immunities, engage in such abuses of their functions as espionage or interference in the internal affairs of the receiving State. It is precisely with the possibility of such abuses in contemplation that Article 41, paragraph 1, of the Vienna Convention on Diplomatic Relations, and Article 55, paragraph 1, of the Vienna Convention on Consular Relations, provide.

> "Without prejudice to their privileges and immunities, it is the duty of all persons enjoying such privileges and immunities to respect the laws and regulations of the receiving State. They also have a duty not to interfere in the internal affairs of that State."

Paragraph 3 of Article 41 of the 1961 Convention further states "The premises of the mission must not be used in any manner incompatible with the functions of the mission . . ."; an analogous provision, with respect to consular premises is to be found in Article 55, paragraph 2 of the 1963 Convention.

85. Thus, it is for the very purpose of providing a remedy for such possible abuses of diplomatic functions that Article 9 of the 1961 Convention on Diplomatic Relations stipulates:

> "1. The receiving State may at any time and without having to explain its decision, notify the sending State that the head of the mission or any member of the diplomatic staff of the mission is *persona non grata* or that any other member of the staff of the mission is not acceptable. In any such case, the sending State shall, as appropriate, either recall the person concerned or terminate his functions with the mission. A person may be declared *non grata* or—not acceptable before arriving in the territory of the receiving State.
>
> 2. If the sending State refuses or fails within a reasonable period to carry out its obligations under paragraph 1 of this Article, the receiving State may refuse to recognize the person concerned as a member of the mission."

The 1963 Convention contains, in Article 23, paragraphs 1 and 4, analogous provisions in respect to consular officers and consular staff. Paragraph 1 of Article 9 of the 1961 Convention, and paragraph 4 of Article 23 of the 1963 Convention, take account of the difficulty that may be experienced in practice of proving such abuses in every case or indeed, of determining exactly when exercise of the diplomatic function, expressly recognized in Article 3(1)(*d*) of the 1961 Convention, of "ascertaining by all lawful means conditions and developments in the receiving State" may be considered as involving such acts as "espionage" or "interference in internal affairs." The way in which Article 9, paragraph 1, takes account of any such difficulty is by providing expressly in its opening sentence that the receiving State may "at any time and without having to explain its decision" notify the sending State that any particular member of its diplomatic mission is "*persona non grata*" or "not acceptable" (and similarly Article 23, paragraph 4, of the 1963 Convention provides that "the receiving State is not obliged to give to the sending State reasons for its decision"). Beyond that remedy for dealing with abuses of the diplomatic function by individual members of a mission, a receiving State has in its hands a more radical remedy if abuses of their diplomatic function by members of a mission reach serious proportions. This is the power which every receiving State has, at its own discretion, to break off diplomatic relations with a sending State and to call for the immediate closure of the offending mission.

86. The rules of diplomatic law, in short, constitute a self-contained régime which, on the one hand, lays down the receiving State's obligations regarding the facilities, privileges and immunities to be accorded to diplomatic

missions and, on the other, foresees then possible abuse by members of the mission and specifies the means at the disposal of the receiving State to counter any such abuse. These means are by their nature, entirely efficacious, for unless the sending State recalls the member of the mission objected to forthwith, the prospect of the almost immediate loss of his privileges and immunities, because of the withdrawal by the receiving State of his recognition as a member of the mission, will in practice compel that person, in his own Interest, to depart at once. But the principle of the inviolability, of the persons of diplomatic agents and the premises of diplomatic missions is one of the very foundations of this long-established régime, to the evolution of which the traditions of Islam made a substantial contribution. The fundamental character of the principle of inviolability is, moreover, strongly underlined by the provisions of Articles 44 and 45 of the Convention of 1961 (cf. also Articles 26 and 27 of the Convention of 1963). Even in the case of armed conflict or in the case of a breach in diplomatic relations those provisions require that both the inviolability of the members of a diplomatic mission and of the premises, property and archive of the mission must be respected by the receiving State. Naturally, the observance of this Principle does not mean—and this the Applicant Government expressly acknowledges—that a diplomatic agent caught in the act of committing an assault or other offence may not, on occasion, be briefly arrested by the police of the receiving State in order to prevent the commission of the particular crime. But such eventualities bear no relation at all to what occurred in the present case.

87. In the present case, the Iranian Government did not break off diplomatic relations with the United States; and in response to a question put to him by a Member of the Court, the United States Agent informed the Court that at no time before the events of 4 November 1979 had the Iranian Government declared, or indicated any intention to declare, any member of the United States diplomatic or consular staff in Tehran *persona non grata*. The Iranian Government did not, therefore, employ the remedies placed at its disposal by diplomatic law specifically for dealing with activities of the kind of which it now complains. Instead, it allowed a group of militants to attack and occupy the United States Embassy by force, and to seize the diplomatic and consular staff as hostages; instead, it has endorsed that action of those militants and has deliberately maintained their occupation of the Embassy and detention of its staff as a means of coercing the sending State. It has, at the same time, refused altogether to discuss this situation with representatives of the United States. The Court, therefore, can only conclude that Iran did not have recourse to the normal and efficacious means at its disposal, but resorted to coercive action against the United States Embassy and its staff.

Discussion Questions

1. How was it possible for the ICJ to exercise jurisdiction over this case despite the objections of the Iranian government?
2. Does the refusal of the Iranian government to participate in the Court proceedings reduce the potential for implementation of the Court's judgment? What power does the Court have to implement its judgment?
3. Would the Court have ruled differently on the merits of the case if Iran had not been a party to the Vienna Conventions?
4. What does the Court mean when it describes the rules of diplomatic law as constituting "a self-contained regime?"

Comment: Iran did not comply with the Court's Judgment immediately; however, the matter was ultimately settled through negotiations between the two parties in the Algiers Accord. President Carter had frozen the assets of the Iranian government in the United States, amounting to more than $13 billion. The 1980 Hostage Treaty resolved the most important aspects of the hostage crisis and resulted in the release of the embassy personnel and citizens of the United States that Iran had held for fifteen months. That agreement also established the Iran-United States Claims Tribunal and set aside a fund from a portion of the frozen assets of Iran to settle claims of U.S. nationals against Iran. Three separate dollar accounts were established. Two were in the Bank of England to cover bank loans; they amounted to about $5 billion. The third dollar account, amounting to $1 billion (plus interest) was deposited in the Central Bank of the Netherlands and was to be used to pay nonbank claims by U.S. claimants for awards made by the Arbitral Tribunal.

Diplomatic Asylum ~Part II~

The inviolability of the embassy premises under international law has produced a practice of granting diplomatic asylum in foreign embassies. There are hundreds of celebrated occasions when this grant of asylum was made, mainly to protect political refugees. The practice raises important questions concerning whether there is a "right" to diplomatic asylum. Latin American States assert that a right to grant asylum in the diplomatic premises exists by virtue of a regional custom particular to them. However, most States take the position that the practice of granting asylum is an unwarranted intervention in the internal affairs of the host State.

The following case concerns the institution of diplomatic asylum in Latin America. This case also provides important insight into the opinions of the ICJ as to what constitutes "customary" international law. In 1949, a Peruvian political leader, Victor Raul Haya de la Torre, was given asylum in the Colombian Embassy in Lima, Peru. The Colombian Ambassador requested the government of Peru to allow Haya de la Torre to leave the country on the grounds that the Colombian government qualified him as a political refugee. Peru refused to accept the right of Colombia to define unilaterally the nature of Haya de la Torre's offense. After diplomatic correspondence, the case was referred to the ICJ.

In its submission, Colombia claimed the right to characterize the nature of the offense by unilateral decision that would be binding on Peru. It based its claim on certain international agreements among Latin American States and in addition on "American international law."

Haya de la Torre, a Peruvian national, led an unsuccessful rebellion against Peru in 1948. When the Peruvian government issued a warrant for his arrest for criminal charges related to the political uprising, Haya de la Torre went to the Colombian Embassy in Lima, Peru. He was granted asylum by the Colombian ambassador on behalf of the government of Colombia, which then requested permission for de la Torre's safe conduct out of the embassy, through Peru, and into Colombia. Peru refused.

Colombia brought this suit against Peru in the ICJ, asking the Court to declare that Colombia had properly granted asylum and that Peru should thus grant Haya de la Torre safe passage out of the Colombian Embassy. Peru's lawyers argued that Colombia could not unilaterally grant asylum over the objection of Peru. Peru's position was that Haya de la Torre had committed a common crime subjecting him to prosecution by Peru and that Colombia had no right to characterize his conduct as a political act to justify a grant of asylum. Colombia countered that Peru must recognize the right of diplomatic asylum and allow Haya de la Torre to leave Peru.

Asylum Case (*Columbia v. Peru*)

International Court of Justice.
1950 International Court of Justice Reports 266.

In the case of diplomatic asylum, the refugee is within the territory of the State where the offence was committed. A decision to grant diplomatic asylum involves a derogation from the sovereignty of that State. It withdraws the offender from the jurisdiction of the territorial State and constitutes an intervention in matters which are exclusively within the competence of that State. Such a derogation from territorial sovereignty cannot be recognised unless its legal basis is established in each particular case.

* * *

The Havana Convention on Asylum of 1928 . . . lays down certain rules relating to diplomatic asylum, but does not contain any provision conferring on the State granting asylum a unilateral competence to qualify the offence with definitive and binding force for the territorial State. . . .

A competence of this kind is of an exceptional character. It involves a derogation from the equal rights of qualification which, in the absence of any contrary rule, must be attributed to each of the States concerned; it thus aggravates the derogation from territorial sovereignty constituted by the exercise of asylum. Such a competence is not inherent in the institution of diplomatic asylum. This institution would perhaps be more effective if a rule of unilateral and definitive qualification were applied. But such a rule is not essential to the exercise of asylum.

* * *

The Colombian Government has finally invoked "American [regional] international law in general." In addition to the rules arising from agreements, . . . it has relied on an alleged regional or local custom peculiar to Latin-American States.

The Party which relies on a custom of this kind must prove that this custom is established in such a manner that it has become binding on the other Party, . . . that it is in accordance with a constant and uniform usage practiced by the States in question, and that this usage is the expression of a right appertaining to the State granting asylum and a duty incumbent on the territorial State. This follows from Article 38 of the Statute of the Court, which refers to international custom "as evidence of a general practice accepted as law."

3

* * *

The Colombian Government has referred to a large number of particular cases in which diplomatic asylum was in fact granted and respected. But it has not shown that the alleged rule of unilateral and definitive qualification was invoked or . . . that it was, apart from conventional stipulations, exercised by the States granting asylum as a right appertaining to them and respected by the territorial states as a duty incumbent on them and not merely for reasons of political expediency. The facts brought to the knowledge of the Court disclose so much uncertainty and contradiction, so much fluctuation and discrepancy in the exercise of diplomatic asylum and in the official views expressed on various occasions, there has been so much inconsistency in the rapid succession of conventions on asylum, ratified by some States and rejected by others, and the practice has been so much influenced by considerations of political expediency in the various cases, that it is not possible to discern in all this any constant and uniform usage, accepted as law, with regard to the alleged rule of unilateral and definitive qualification of the offence.

The Court cannot therefore find that the Colombian Government has proved the existence of such a custom. But even if it could be supposed that such a custom existed between certain Latin-American States only, it could not be invoked against Peru which, far from having by its attitude adhered to it, has, on the contrary, repudiated it by refraining from ratifying the Montevideo Conventions of 1933 and 1939 which were the first to include a rule concerning the qualifications of the offence in matters of diplomatic asylum.

* * *

Article 2 lays down in precise terms the conditions under which asylum shall be granted to [political] offenders by the territorial State. All these conditions are designed to give guarantees to the territorial State and appear, in the final analysis, as the consideration for the obligation which that State assumes to respect asylum, that is, to accept its principle and its consequences as long as it is regularly maintained.

At the head of the list of these conditions appears Article 2, paragraph 2. It is certainly the most important of them, the essential justification for asylum being in the imminence or persistence of a danger for the person of the refugee. It was incumbent upon the Government of Colombia to submit proof of facts to show that [this] condition was fulfilled.

* * *

Asylum may be granted on humanitarian grounds . . . to protect political offenders against the violent and disorderly action of irresponsible sections of the population. It has not been contended . . . that Haya de la Torre was in such a situation at the time when he sought refuge in the Colombian Embassy at Lima.

* * *

In principle, it is inconceivable that the Havana Convention could have intended the term "urgent cases" to include the danger of regular prosecution to which the citizens of any country lay themselves open by attacking the institutions of that country, nor can it be admitted that in referring to "the period of time strictly indispensable for the person who has sought asylum to ensure in some other way his safety," the Convention envisaged protection from the operation of regular legal proceedings. . . .

In principle, asylum cannot be opposed to the operation of justice. An exception to this rule can occur only if, in the guise of justice, arbitrary action is substituted for the rule of law. Such would be the case if the administration of justice were corrupted by measures clearly prompted by political aims. Asylum protects the political offender against any measures of a manifestly extra-legal character which a Government might take or attempt to take against its political opponents. The word "safety," which determines the specific effect of asylum granted to political offenders, means that the refugee is protected against arbitrary action by the Government, and that he enjoys the benefits of the law. On the other hand, the safety which arises out of asylum cannot be construed as a protection against the regular application of the laws and against the jurisdiction of legally constituted tribunals. Protection thus understood would authorise the diplomatic agent to obstruct the application of the laws of the country whereas it is his duty to respect them; it would in fact become the equivalent of an immunity, which was evidently not within the intentions of the draftsmen of the Havana Convention.

It has not been shown that the existence of a state of siege [in Peru] implied the subordination of justice to the executive authority, or that the suspension of certain constitutional guarantees entailed the abolition of judicial guarantees. . . .

The Court cannot admit that the States signatory to the Havana Convention intended to substitute for the practice of the Latin-American republics, in which considerations of courtesy, good-neighbourliness and political expediency have always held a prominent place, a legal system which would guarantee to their own nationals accused of political offences the privilege of evading national jurisdiction. Such a conception, moreover, would come into conflict with one of the most firmly established traditions of Latin-America, namely, nonintervention.

* * *

[The court must] reject the argument that the Havana Convention was intended to afford a quite general protection to any person prosecuted for political offences, either in the course of revolutionary events or in the more or less troubled times that follow, for the sole reason that it must be assumed that such events interfere with the administration of justice. It is clear that the adoption of such a criterion would lead to foreign interference of a particularly offensive nature in the domestic affairs of States; besides which no confirmation of this criterion can be found in Latin-American practice, as this practice has been explained to the Court.

In thus expressing itself, the Court does not lose sight of the numerous cases of asylum which have been cited.

* * *

In the absence of precise data, it is difficult to assess the value of such cases as precedents tending to establish the existence of a legal obligation upon a territorial State to recognise the validity of asylum which has been granted against proceedings instituted by local judicial authorities. In a number of cases, the persons who had enjoyed asylum were not, at the moment at which asylum was granted, the object of any accusation on the part of the judicial authorities. In a more general way, considerations of convenience or simple political expediency seem to have led the territorial State to recognise asylum without that being dictated by any feeling of legal obligation.

If these remarks tend to reduce considerably the value as precedents of the cases of asylum cited . . ., they show none the less, that asylum as practised in Latin-America is an institution which, to a very great extent, owes its development to extra-legal factors. The good-neighbour relations between the republics, the different political interests of the Governments, have favoured the mutual recognition of asylum apart from any clearly defined juridical system. Even if the Havana Convention, in particular, represents an indisputable reaction against certain abuses in practice, it in no way tends to limit the practice of asylum as it may arise from agreements between interested Governments inspired by mutual feelings of toleration and goodwill.

* * *

The Court considers that . . . there did not exist a danger constituting a case of urgency within the meaning of Article 2, paragraph 2, of the Havana Convention.

Discussion Questions

1. Is there a general right of diplomatic asylum recognized in international law? Discuss.
2. If such a regional right existed in customary law, how could it be documented to the satisfaction of the Court?
3. What humanitarian exceptions does the Court indicate as being within the reasonable authority of embassies to grant?
4. What constitutes customary international law?

Comment: Although the court refused to accept Colombia's arguments, de la Torre was effectively sheltered because Peru could not enter the Colombian Embassy to force his surrender. The proceeding before the ICJ was also unsuccessful in enabling Colombia to force Peru to grant de la Torre safe passage out of Peru. However, Colombia and Peru ultimately negotiated an arrangement permitting de la Torre to leave Peru. Four years later, Peru ratified the Caracas Convention on Diplomatic Asylum. Article 2 provides that "every State has the right to grant asylum." Article 4 adds that "it shall rest with the State granting asylum to determine the nature of the offense [common crime versus political act] or the motives for the persecution."

The policy of the United States has been fairly consistent over many decades. Diplomatic agents have been instructed not to grant asylum except temporarily to persons whose lives were threatened by mob violence. However, there have been notable exceptions.

Perhaps the most notorious of these exceptions involved Hungary's Cardinal Jozset Mendszenty. He had been arrested for antigovernment activities in 1948, jailed in 1949, and freed for several days during the Hungarian revolt that occurred in 1956. During this period, he sought refuge in the U.S. Embassy in Budapest, Hungary. In this exceptional case, the United States granted asylum. Mendszenty remained in the Embassy for fifteen years (1956 to 1971) and was finally allowed by Hungary to return to the Vatican.

More recent instances of diplomatic asylum occurred during the Iran hostage crisis when the Canadian government quietly granted diplomatic asylum to five U.S. consular employees and one U.S. agricultural attaché who had escaped via a back door of the U.S. Embassy when it was seized on November 4, 1979.

A rare example of diplomatic refuge granted by the United States was that of Fang Lizhi and his wife. Fang was a Chinese astrophysicist and dissenter who had fled to the U.S. Embassy in Beijing during the demonstrations at Tiananmen Square in June of 1989. A year later, the Fangs were allowed to leave China for England aboard a U.S. Air Force jet. A heart attack suffered a month earlier by Fang turned out to be the face-saving event that permitted the Chinese government to cite "humanitarian reasons" for allowing the Fangs to leave.

A situation of even greater complexity occurred when General Manuel Antonio Noriega sought refuge in the Vatican Embassy (Papal Nonciature) in Panama. The invasion of Panama in 1989 had a major objective of capturing Noriega. He had been indicted in Miami on federal drug-related charges. Panama and the Vatican are not parties to an extradition treaty, and Noriega's extradition to the United States would have been forbidden by the Panamanian constitution. After discovering Noriega's whereabouts, U.S. troops surrounded the embassy and set up loudspeakers blaring rock and roll music to harass the embassy personnel. Finally, Noriega left the Vatican Embassy and turned himself over to U.S. troops. U.S. authorities claimed that he was technically not under arrest until the aircraft provided for him was in international airspace. He was taken to a plane and ferried from the U.S. Howard Air Force Base in Panama to Florida and eventually tried and found guilty.

During the invasion of Panama ("Operation Just Cause") U.S. troops had encircled the Cuban and Peruvian Embassies in Panama, searched the Nicaraguan Embassy, and the Papal Noncio's car several times. These violations of diplomatic immunity resulted in countermeasures taken by Nicaragua. Nicaragua expelled twenty of the twenty-eight U.S. diplomats accredited to Managua and reduced from 120 to 100 the non-diplomatic members of the U.S. Embassy.

Sovereign Immunity

The doctrine of sovereign immunity is one of the most fundamental principles of law in the modern nation-state system. **Sovereign immunity** shields the government in domestic courts from suit for monetary damages without the government's prior consent. In international law, as well, the principles of sovereign immunity shield foreign governments (sovereigns) from the exercise of jurisdiction by other State's courts in cases in which the sovereign has not given consent to such jurisdiction. This principle allows the governmental authority to act within its legitimate area of discretion without fear that its actions will be subject to adjudication by its own courts or those of another State. Its purpose also is to ensure that the public property of the foreign State remains available for public purposes, free from the constraints of the forum State's powers of attachment and execution.

> **Sovereign immunity:** A principle of law that shields government from suit for monetary damages without that government's prior consent.

Modern doctrines of foreign sovereign immunities are a product of the dynamic evolution of customary international law, domestic legislation, court decisions, and efforts to codify international law through the treaty process. This area of the law is one of the most complex and dynamic of the principles of international law. Controversies are frequently in evidence, and when an immunity exists under international law, its denial by municipal law of one country may create a claim for violation of international law by the other country. Consequently, in determining the jurisdictional immunities to which an international legal person is entitled, both international and municipal law must be studied.

Further complexity exists because jurisdiction may be exercised on the legislative, the judicial, and the enforcement levels, and immunities also operate on these three levels.

Traditional international law regarded jurisdictional immunities as absolute. A State could invoke them, regardless of the nature of the sovereign activity in question. This position was asserted by Chief Justice Marshall in *Schooner Exchange v. M'Faddon* in 1812 (11 U.S. 116, 3 L.Ed. 287). The concept of **absolute immunity** was developed in the eighteenth and nineteenth centuries when governments were involved in few commercial activities that raised questions as to the necessity of such claims. As States have become increasingly involved in commercial activities, the pressure toward limiting (restricting) immunity has grown. This has led to numerous legal actions in domestic courts over questions of sovereign immunity, and the international legal rules on sovereign immunity are still not free from dispute and uncertainty. In general, it can be said that today, immunity is more restrictive and can be justified only on the basis of the most compelling considerations of public policy.

The international community has evolved toward a more realistic and pragmatic approach to sovereign immunity known as **restrictive immunity**. Under this functional approach, the problems that may be encountered in potential interference

> **Absolute immunity:** *The traditional theory of sovereign immunity that could be invoked regardless of the nature of the sovereign activity in question.*

with the conduct of foreign relations are balanced against the propriety of denying persons the benefits of exercising jurisdiction that they would enjoy if their claims were asserted against a private person rather than a foreign State. The restrictive doctrine denies immunity claimed by a foreign State in regard to an activity or property that is commercial rather than public. The legal terminology used with great frequency in these cases makes a distinction between *acta jure gestionis* and *acta jure imperii*. Commercial activities of governmental entities are considered *acta jure gestionis*, and those, in general, that are acts that can be performed only by recognized governmental entities are considered *acta jure imperii*. This generalization is subject to many problems of interpretation and controversy, primarily because a satisfactory delineation between these two concepts has not been found.

> **Restrictive immunity:** *The modern theory of sovereign immunity that restricts immunity to those functions that can be performed only by recognized sovereign authority.*

Around the turn of the century, Italy and Belgium became the first countries to adopt restrictive immunity. However, since the 1950s, an increasing number of States began to move toward the restrictive doctrine. Today, absolute immunity finds only minority support among the community of nations. The major exceptions are among the communist countries and a number of Third World States that still embrace it. The restrictive practices are not uniform, and uncertainty exists among and within many countries:

More erosion of the traditional doctrine may be reasonably foreseen. The former socialist countries of central and eastern Europe, among the last bastions of the absolute principle, may find that, as they move to market economies, they will have the same incentives as in traditional market economy countries to find ways of limiting sovereign immunity. They may adopt the "restrictive principle" which relaxes the immunity for commercial and a number of other specified activities. (Oliver et al., 1995, p. 581)

Transition From Absolute to Restrictive Immunity

In the United States, American jurisprudence regarding State immunity doctrines derived from those that had developed in England. By the mid-nineteenth century, Supreme Court decisions had established the immunity of the United States from suits by private parties seeking compensation for harm. The Eleventh Amendment of the Constitution specifically excludes suits against individual states by citizens of other states or of a foreign State. This has been interpreted by the Supreme Court as excluding suits for monetary damages, not actions in judicial review of constitutional standards that the states of the union must follow. Valid acts of Congress also limit state authority as expressed in the "supremacy clause" of the U.S. Constitution. However, a body of unique law based on historical and political considerations control suits against states in the federal courts (see *Cohens v. Virginia*, 6 Wheaton 264 [1821]; *Fitzpatrick v. Blitzer*, 427 U.S. 445 [1976]; *Maine v. Thiboutot*, 448 U.S. 1 [1980]; *Pennhurst State School and Hospital v. Halderman*, 104 S.Ct. 900 [1984]; and *Nevada v. Hall*, 440 U.S. 410 [1979]).

The first legislative inroads on the immunity doctrines occurred in the contract field. An act of 1855 first created the Court of Claims, which has now become the U.S. Claims Court, and conferred on it jurisdiction over certain kinds of money damages against the United States. This legislation has extended the consent of the federal government to allow suit for monetary damages in designated areas to be found in 28 U.S.C.A. §§ 1346(a) and 1491. Smaller claims are handled by the district courts, and larger ones must be brought in the U.S. Claims Court. The provisions on contract claims contain the widest and most unequivocal waivers of sovereign immunity.

Special doctrines of federal common law have developed with respect to government contracts with private parties that distinguish actions on them in some important respects from private-party litigation. Many disputes over governmental contracts, and particularly those relating to defense procurement, are handled, at least initially, through administrative processes.

In 1946, Congress enacted the **Federal Tort Claims Act (FTCA)**, which can be found in its updated form in 28 U.S.C.A. §§ 1346(b), 2671-2680. This act confers jurisdiction on the district courts over claims against the United States for money damages

> **Federal Tort Claims Act (FTCA):** *Congressional act of 1946 providing consent to bring legal action for monetary claims against the federal government when private persons would be liable.*

for injury or loss of property, or personal injury or death caused by the negligent or wrongful act or omission of any employee of the Government while acting within the scope of his office or employment, under circumstances where the United States, if a private person, would be liable to the claimant in accordance with the law of the place where the act or omission occurred.

Section 2680 provides various exceptions that strongly qualify the waiver of immunity. Court interpretation of this legislation provides further areas of court discretion. In a leading case, *Dalehite v. United States* (346 U.S. 15, 73 S.Ct. 956, 97 L.Ed. 1427 [1953]), the Supreme Court held that the acts of the United States in preparing for export shipment a fertilizer that exploded, causing the Texas City disaster, were on a "planning" rather than an "operational" level. This resulted in holding the exception applicable and rendering the government immune. In other cases, the Court has taken a more restrictive view of the application of the statute producing a domestic distinction between "governmental" and "proprietary" conduct similar to the relationship between acts *jure imperii* and acts *jure gestionis*.

Foreign Policy and the Tate Letter

In transnational law, there is the further complexity that involves the discretionary authority given to the executive branch to conduct the foreign policy of the United States. If a court decision offends the sovereignty of another State, the U.S. State Department will be concerned about diplomatic protests and potential retaliatory action. This raises issues involving the "political question" doctrine that the courts have developed. In law, a political question is one that relates to the legitimate discretionary authority given to the legislative and executive branches of government. Prior to 1952, the courts sought to comply with executive requests to avoid embarrassment in the conduct of U.S. foreign relations when cases arose involving other countries. However, in 1952, the famous **Tate Letter** indicated a willingness on the

> **Tate Letter:** *Communication from the U.S. State Department declaring a policy to follow the restrictive theory of sovereign immunity in requests to grant such immunity (1952).*

part of the U.S. Department of State to move toward the restrictive theory of sovereign immunity. After conducting a thorough study of evolving practices of most trading States, the State Department concluded that "it will hereafter be the Department's policy to follow the restrictive theory of sovereign immunity in the consideration of requests of foreign governments for a grant of sovereign immunity" (26 Department of State Bulletin 984 [1952]).

The Tate Letter made it clear that the State Department would decline immunity to any friendly sovereign in suits arising from private or commercial activity, but it offered no guidelines or criteria for differentiating between a sovereign's private and public acts. Various tests were attempted by the courts, but most agreed that they were unsatisfactory, and court confusion remained in several areas. However, it was generally agreed that immunity should be granted if the activity in question falls within one of the categories of strictly political or public acts about which sovereigns have traditionally been quite sensitive. Such acts are generally limited to the following categories:

1. Internal administrative acts, such as expulsion of an alien
2. Legislative acts, such as nationalization
3. Acts concerning the armed forces
4. Acts concerning diplomatic activity
5. Public loans

The Foreign Sovereign Immunities Act of 1976

Finally, the U.S. Congress enacted the **Foreign Sovereign Immunities Act of 1976 (FSIA)**, which is found in Appendix J of this volume. It is important that the reader take a look at the specific wording of this statute,

> **Foreign Sovereign Immunities Act of 1976 (FSIA):** An act of Congress providing access to the federal courts to bring civil legal actions against foreign sovereigns in their commercial activities and limiting sovereign immunity to only those areas of recognized sovereign authority that can be performed only by governments.

which attempts to reduce the confusion and express legislative intent. The FSIA is codified in Title 28, U.S.C.A., principally at §§ 1602-11 where updated annotations may be found. The act was amended in relatively minor respects in 1988. It provides detailed instructions concerning service of process on a foreign sovereign, permits execution of judgment, within strict limits, and denies a right of withdrawal of waivers. It also denies the right of trial by jury in such civil legal actions, which is questionably in conflict with the Seventh Amendment. The courts have sustained this denial in the face of Seventh Amendment claims (see *Williams v. Shipping Corp. of India*, 653 F.2d 875 [4th Cir. 1981]; *Ruggiero v. Cia. Peruana De Vapores*, 639 F.2d 872 [2d Cir. 1981]).

The most significant provision of the FSIA deals with the drawing of the line between acts *jure gestionis* and acts *jure imperii*. Section 1603(d) of the statute provides a definition based on the nature and not the purpose of the activity. However, the wording of the statute provides in § 1605(a)(5) that even acts *jure imperii*, if done within the United States, can be the basis for a suit. In an important decision by the Supreme Court, *Weltover, Inc. v. Republic of Argentina* (112 S.Ct. 2160 [1992]), the Court affirmed lower court rulings that public debt of foreign States may be characterized as commercial activity and provide the necessary nexus required to satisfy the "direct effect" requirements of the FSIA. The Court states that the FSIA definition of "commercial activity" by reliance on the nature of the activity rather than its purpose

"leaves the critical term 'commercial' largely undefined."

Efforts in other countries to restrict sovereign immunity from judicial jurisdiction are increasingly taking legislative form. The United Kingdom enacted its State Immunity Act in 1978, and Canada, Pakistan, Singapore, and South Africa enacted similar statutes in 1982. The Council of Europe has developed a European Convention on State Immunity and Additional Protocol of 1972. The International Law Commission also has produced a draft convention patterned after the European Convention. The International Law Association Draft Convention on Foreign Sovereign Immunity: A Comparative Approach is reported in the *Virginia Journal of International Law* (see Vol. 23, 1983, p. 635). In a recent article by Georges Delaume, the author concludes that there appears to be considerable consistency in the *Weltover* decision in the United States and those that prevail in European countries (Delaume, 1994, p. 277).

Despite the difficulties in interpretation, the near universal acceptance of the restrictive principle of sovereign immunity over the past thirty years has greatly increased the access of private parties to the domestic courts of individual States in civil litigation regarding monetary damages against governmental entities, foreign and domestic. This development does not mean that private parties have equal access to sue sovereign entities in domestic courts on the same basis that private parties may sue other private parties. Sovereign immunity is still an important consideration, and a State cannot be sued without its consent in domestic courts. Consent, however, has been greatly altered by these developments.

One of the most interesting cases to arise out of the Iran hostage crisis involves important questions about restrictive sovereign immunity as well as the president's authority to conduct the foreign policy of the United States. This case illustrates why the rights of private parties are limited by the exercise of legitimate governmental authority. Sovereign immunity protects both foreign and domestic governmental actions. It places the legitimate exercise of governmental authority above the private rights of individuals or corporations to recover damages in civil legal actions.

In legal actions prior to the case included below, a private corporation sought satisfaction of a judgment by a federal district court in the United States against Iran in a contract dispute with the government of that country. This issue clearly fell within the "commercial activity" meaning of the FSIA and was not subject to immunity under the modern concept of restrictive immunity. However, winning a judgment in court does not necessarily mean that damages will be recovered. The phrase "satisfaction of judgment" refers to the payment of the award. Suits against foreign sovereigns are conditioned on the ability to attach property to enforce satisfaction of judgment. This ability also is restricted by the FSIA (see Appendix J).

President Carter's actions in response to the hostage crisis in Iran included the use of his powers under the **International Emergency Economic Powers Act (IEEPA)** to declare an emergency and to block the removal of "all property and interests of the government of Iran, its instrumentalities," and so on. Under the president's authority, the Treasury Office of Foreign Assets Control issued a regulation providing that "[unless] licensed or authorized . . . any attachment, judgment, decree, lien, execution, garnish-

> *International Emergency Economic Powers Act (IEEPA):* An act of Congress granting and limiting the president's authority to deal with foreign policy issues in the economic area (1977).

ment, or other judicial process is null and void with respect to any property" in which Iran had an interest. It also made it clear that any license or authorizations could be "amended, modified, or revoked at any time." On November 26, 1979, the president granted a general license allowing certain judicial proceedings against Iran but not the "entry of any judgment or of any decree or order of similar or analogous effect." A later regulation said that prejudgment attachments were authorized thereby. Dames & Moore filed their suit against the government of Iran on December 19, 1979, while the blocking order was in effect but before agreement was reached in the **Hostage Treaty** providing for the disposal of these assets. More specifically, the suit involved not only the Iranian government but the Atomic Energy Organization of Iran and some Iranian banks. It alleged

> *Hostage Treaty:* Term used to describe the executive agreements reached at the Algiers Accord in 1980 between the United States and Iran.

that petitioner was owed $3.4 million for services performed under a contract for nuclear power plant site studies before the organization canceled it. Orders of attachment directed to property of some Iranian banks were issued by the district court.

The district court granted summary judgment in this case on January 27, 1981. The petitioner, Dames & Moore, then commenced proceedings to satisfy the judgment, but on May 28, the district court issued a stay and vacation of all attachments because of the solution reached by the two countries in the Algiers Accord and the subsequent executive orders of the president of the United States revoking all licenses permitting dealing with the frozen Iranian accounts. This action also nullified all non-Iranian interests in these frozen assets. The international settlement stated that the parties intended to terminate all litigation by their nationals and the other government and to submit such matters to arbitration before the Iranian-United States Claims Tribunal that was to be established. The United States was to terminate all suits against Iran and its State enterprises, to nullify all attachments and judgments, and to terminate such claims through arbitration.

The action that is reported hereafter, *Dames & Moore v. Regan*, was initiated by the petitioner against the Secretary of the Treasury of the United States seeking an injunction to prevent enforcement of the presidential orders pursuant to the Hostage Treaty. The district court dismissed the complaint and the petitioner appealed to the Court of Appeals. In the meantime, the Treasury ordered the Federal Reserve Bank to turn over all financial assets of Iran by noon on June 19. Because of the importance of prompt resolution of these issues, the Supreme Court granted certiorari before judgment by the Court of Appeals and heard oral argument on June 24, 1981. On July 2, 1981, the Supreme Court affirmed the district court decision in the opinion below drafted by Justice Rehnquist.

Claims by U.S. citizens against foreign countries have frequently been settled in American history by **claims settlement agreements** similar to that reached by the United States and Iran. Although the president has implied powers to conduct the foreign policy of the United States, the Constitution grants few specific powers exclusively to the executive office in this regard. The president has vast emergency powers to conduct foreign policy that have been granted in specific acts of Congress. The IEEPA of 1977 is one of these specific acts of Congress granting, and lim-

> **Claims settlement agreements:** Negotiated settlement of claims of U.S. citizens against foreign countries. These agreements have taken the form of both formal treaties and executive agreements.

iting, the president's authority. This act was one of many revisions of the president's emergency powers stimulated by powerful congressional reaction against the "Imperial Presidency" and the perceived abuses of executive authority in the Vietnam conflict. These reform acts were intended to subject the president to stringent procedural constraints in the exercise of the president's delegated foreign affairs powers.

As further background, the reader should be made aware of the leading decisions in this area of constitutional interpretation of executive authority. In *U.S. v. Curtiss-Wright Export Corp.* (299 U.S. 304 [1936]), the Supreme Court upheld the validity of a joint resolution of Congress that delegated broad powers to the president to prohibit arms shipments to foreign belligerents. In question was a presidential proclamation levying an embargo on shipment of war materiel to either side in the Gran Chaco war between Bolivia and Paraguay. In this case, the Court distinguished between permissible delegations of congressional lawmaking power in domestic areas and those in foreign affairs. The Court noted, "As a member of the family of nations, the right and power of the United States . . . are equal to the right and power of the other nations of the international family. Otherwise, the United States is not completely sovereign." This has been variously described as the **inherent powers doctrine**.

> **Inherent powers doctrine:** Powers attributed to the president in foreign policy matters that are more extensive than in domestic affairs (see opinion in U.S. v. Curtiss-Wright Export Corp.).

In *Youngstown Sheet and Tube Co. v. Sawyer* (343 U.S. 579 [1952]), the Court struck down the president's executive order that had authorized the seizure of steel mills and their operation by the national government. President Harry S. Truman acted to seize the steel mills under his inherent power as chief executive and commander in chief to safeguard the nation's security during the Korean war, when a strike in the steel mills threatened the supply of weapons. The Court held that the president has no author-ity under the Constitution to seize private property unless Congress authorizes the seizure and that the Constitution does not permit the president to legislate.

Dames & Moore v. Regan

Supreme Court of the United States 1981.
453 U.S. 654, 101 S.Ct. 2972, 69 L.Ed.2d 918.

JUDGE REHNQUIST

* * *

II

The parties and the lower courts confronted with the instant questions have all agreed that much relevant analysis is contained in *Youngstown Sheet & Tube Co. v. Sawyer.*

. . . Justice Jackson himself recognized that his three categories represented "a somewhat over-simplified grouping," 343 U.S., at 635, 72 S.Ct., at 870, and it is doubtless the case that executive action in any particular instance falls, not neatly in one of three pigeon-holes, but rather at some point along a spectrum running from explicit congressional authorization to explicit congressional prohibition. This is particularly true as respects cases such as the one before us, involving responses to international crises the nature of which Congress can hardly have been expected to anticipate in any detail.

III

In nullifying post-November 14, 1979, attachments and directing those persons holding blocked Iranian funds and securities to transfer them to the Federal Reserve Bank of New York for ultimate transfer to Iran, President Carter cited five sources of express or inherent power. The Government, however, has principally relied on § 1702 of the IEEPA as authorization for these actions. . . .

The Government contends that the acts of "nullifying" the attachments and ordering the "transfer" of the frozen assets are specifically authorized by the plain language of the above statute. The two Courts of Appeals that have considered the issue agreed with this contention. [Discussion of cases omitted.]

Petitioner contends that we should ignore the plain language of this statute because an examination of its legislative history as well as the history of § 5(b) of the Trading With the Enemy Act (hereinafter "TWEA," 50 U.S.C.App. § 5(b), from which the pertinent language of § 1702 is directly drawn, reveals that the statute was not intended to give the President such extensive power over the assets of a foreign state during times of national emergency. According to petitioner, once the President instituted the November 14, 1979, blocking order, § 1702 authorized him "only to continue the freeze or to discontinue controls."

We do not agree and refuse to read out of § 1702 all meaning to the words "transfer," "compel," or "nullify." Nothing in the legislative history of either § 1702 or § 5(b) of the TWEA requires such a result. To the contrary, we think both the legislative history and cases interpreting the TWEA fully sustain the broad authority of the Executive when acting under this congressional grant of power. . . . Although Congress intended to limit the President's emergency power in peacetime, we do not think the changes brought about by the enactment of the IEEPA in any way affected the authority of the President to take the specific actions taken here. We likewise note that by the time petitioner instituted this action, the President had already entered the freeze order. Petitioner proceeded against the blocked assets only after the Treasury Department had issued revocable licenses authorizing such proceedings and attachments. The Treasury regulations provided that "unless licensed" any attachment is null and void, 31 CFR, § 535.203(e), and all licenses "may be amended, modified, or revoked at any time." 31 CFR § 535.805. As such, the attachments obtained by petitioner were specifically made subordinate to further actions which the President might take under the IEEPA. Petitioner was on notice of the contingent nature of its interest in the frozen assets.

This Court has previously recognized that the congressional purpose in authorizing blocking orders is "to put control of foreign assets in the hands of the President. . . ." *Propper v. Clark*, 337 U.S. 472, 493, 69 S.Ct. 1333, 1345, 93 L.Ed. 1480 (1949). Such orders permit the President to maintain the foreign assets at his disposal for use in negotiating the resolution of a declared national emergency. The frozen assets serve as a "bargaining chip" to be used by the President when dealing with a hostile country. Accordingly, it is difficult to accept petitioner's argument because the practical effect of it is to allow individual claimants throughout the country to minimize or wholly eliminate this "bargaining chip" through attachments, garnishments or similar encumbrances on property. Neither the purpose the statute was enacted to serve nor its plain language supports such a result.

Because the President's action in nullifying the attachments and ordering the transfer of the assets was taken pursuant to specific congressional authorization, it is "supported by the strongest of presumptions and the widest latitude of judicial interpretation, and the burden of persuasion would rest heavily upon any who might attack it." *Youngstown*, 343 U.S., at 637, 72 S.Ct., at 871 (Jackson, J., concurring). Under the circumstances of this case, we cannot say that petitioner has sustained that heavy burden. A contrary ruling would mean that the Federal Government as a whole lacked the power exercised by the President, see Id., at 636-637, 72 S.Ct., at 870-871, and that we are not prepared to say.

IV

Although we have concluded that the IEEPA constitutes specific congressional authorization to the President to nullify the attachments and order the transfer of Iranian assets, there remains the question of the President's authority to suspend claims pending in American courts. Such claims have, of course, an existence apart from the attachments which accompanied them. In terminating these claims through Executive Order No. 12294 the President purported to act under authority of both the IEEPA and 22 U.S.C. § 1732, the so-called "Hostage Act." . . .

We conclude that although the IEEPA authorized the nullification of the attachments, it cannot be read to authorize the suspension of the claims. The claims of American citizens against Iran are not in themselves transactions involving Iranian property or efforts to exercise any rights with respect to such property. An *in personam* lawsuit, although it might eventually be reduced to judgment and that judgment might be executed upon, is an effort to establish liability and fix damages and does not focus on any particular property within the jurisdiction. The terms of the IEEPA therefore do not authorize the President to suspend claims in American courts. The Hostage Act, passed in 1868, provides:

> "Whenever it is made known to the President that any citizen of the United States has been unjustly deprived of his liberty by or under the authority of any foreign government, it shall be the duty of the President forthwith to demand of that government the reasons of such imprisonment; and if it appears to be wrongful and in violation of the rights of American citizenship, the President shall forthwith demand the release of such citizen, and if the release so demanded is unreasonably delayed or refused, the President shall use such means, not amounting to acts of war, as he may think necessary and proper to obtain or effectuate the release; and all the facts and proceedings relative thereto shall as soon as practicable be communicated by the President to Congress." 22 U.S.C. § 1732.

We are reluctant to conclude that this provision constitutes specific authorization to the President to suspend claims in American courts. Although the broad language of the Hostage Act suggests it may cover this case, there are several difficulties with such a view. The legislative history indicates that the Act was passed in response to a situation unlike the recent Iranian crisis. Congress in 1868 was concerned with the activity of certain countries refusing to recognize the citizenship of naturalized Americans traveling abroad, and repatriating such citizens against their will. . . . These countries were not interested in returning the citizens in exchange for any sort of ransom. This also explains the reference in the Act to imprisonment "in violation of the rights of American citizenship." Although the Iranian hostage taking violated international law and common decency, the hostages were not seized out of any refusal to recognize their American citizenship—they were seized precisely *because of* their American citizenship. The legislative history is also somewhat ambiguous on the question whether Congress contemplated presidential action such as that involved here or rather simply reprisals directed against the offending foreign country and its citizens.

* * *

Concluding that neither the IEEPA nor the Hostage Act constitutes specific authorization of the President's action suspending claims, however, is not to say that these statutory provisions are entirely irrelevant to the question of the validity of the President's action. We think both statutes highly relevant in the looser sense of indicating congressional acceptance of a broad scope for executive action in circumstances such as those presented in this case. As noted above in Part III, . . . the IEEPA delegates broad authority to the President to act in times of national emergency with respect to property of a foreign country. The Hostage Act similarly indicates congressional willingness that the President have broad discretion when responding to the hostile acts of foreign sovereigns. . . .

Although we have declined to conclude that the IEEPA or the Hostage Act directly authorizes the President's suspension of claims for the reasons noted, we cannot ignore the general tenor of Congress' legislation in this area in trying to determine whether the President is acting alone or at least with the acceptance of Congress. As we have noted, Congress cannot anticipate and legislate with regard to every possible action the President may find it necessary to take or every possible situation in which he might act. Such failure of Congress specifically to delegate authority does not, "especially . . . in the areas of foreign policy and national security," imply "congressional disapproval" of action taken by the Executive. *Haig v. Agee*, 453 U.S. 280, 291, 101 S.Ct. 2766, 2774, 68 L.Ed.2d 640 (1981). On the contrary, the enactment of legislation closely related to the question of the President's authority in a particular case which evinces legislative intent to accord the President broad discretion may be considered to "invite" "measures on independent presidential responsibility," *Youngstown*, 343 U.S., at 637 72 S.Ct., at 871 (Jackson, J., concurring). At least this is so where there is no contrary indication of legislative intent and when, as here, there is a history of congressional acquiescence in conduct of the sort engaged in by the President. It is to that history which we now turn.

Not infrequently in affairs between nations, outstanding claims by nationals of one country against the government of another country are "sources of friction" between the two sovereigns. *United States v. Pink*, 315 U.S. 203, 225, 62 S.Ct. 552, 563, 86 L.Ed. 796 (1942). To resolve these difficulties, nations have often entered into agreements settling the claims of their respective nationals. As one treatise writer puts it, international arrangements settling claims by nationals of one state against the government of another "are established international practice reflecting traditional international theory." L. Henkin, *Foreign Affairs and the Constitution* 262 (1972). Consistent with that principle, the United States has repeatedly exercised its sovereign authority to settle the claims of its nationals against foreign countries. Though those settlements have sometimes been made by treaty, there has also been a longstanding practice of settling such claims by executive agreement without the advice and consent of the Senate. Under such agreements, the President has agreed to renounce or extinguish claims of United States nationals against foreign governments in return for lump sum payments or the establishment of arbitration procedures. To be sure, many of these settlements were encouraged by the United States claimants themselves, since a claimant's only hope of obtaining any payment at all might lie in having his government negotiate a diplomatic settlement on his behalf. But it is also undisputed that the "United States has sometimes disposed of the claims of citizens without their consent, or even without consultation with them, usually without exclusive regard for their interests, as distinguished from those of the nation as a whole." Henkin, *supra*, at 263. It is clear that the practice of settling claims continues today. Since 1952, the President has entered into at least 10 binding settlements with foreign nations, including an $80 million settlement with the People's Republic of China.

Crucial to our decision today is the conclusion that Congress has implicitly approved the practice of claim settlement by executive agreement. This is best demonstrated by Congress' enactment of the International Claims Settlement Act of 1949, 22 U.S.C. § 1621 et seq., as amended (1980). The Act had two purposes: (1) to allocate to United States nationals funds received in the course of an executive claims settlement with Yugoslavia, and (2) to provide a procedure whereby funds resulting from future settlements could be distributed. To achieve these ends Congress created the International Claims Commission, now the Foreign Claims Settlement Commission, and gave it jurisdiction to make final and binding decisions with respect to claims by United States nationals against settlement funds. 22 U.S.C. § 1623(a). By creating a procedure to implement future settlement agreements, Congress placed its stamp of approval on such agreements. Indeed, the legislative history of the Act observed that the United States was seeking settlements with countries other than Yugoslavia and stated that the bill "contemplates that settlements of a similar nature are to he made in the future." H.R.Rep. No. 81-770, 81st Cong., 1st Sess., 4, 8 (1949).

Over the years Congress has frequently amended the International Claims Settlement Act to provide for particular problems arising out of settlement agreements, thus demonstrating Congress' continuing acceptance of the President's claim settlement authority. [References to legislation on claims agreements with the People's Republic of China, East Germany, and Vietnam are omitted.]

. . . Finally, the legislative history of the IEEPA further reveals that Congress has accepted the authority of the Executive to enter into settlement agreements. Though the IEEPA was enacted to provide for some limitation on the President's emergency powers, Congress stressed that "nothing in this Act is intended to interfere with the authority of the President to [block assets], or to impede the settlement of claims of United States citizens against foreign countries." S.Rep. No. 95-466, 95th Cong., 2d Sess., 6 (1977), U.S.Code Cong. & Admin.News, 1977, pp. 4540, 4544; 50 U.S.C. § 1706(a)(1).

In addition to congressional acquiescence in the President's power to settle claims, prior cases of this Court have also recognized that the President does have some measure of power to enter into executive agreements without obtaining the advice and consent of the Senate. [Discussion of United States v. Pink, p. 572, infra, omitted.]

* * *

Petitioner . . . asserts that Congress divested the President of the authority to settle claims when it enacted the Foreign Sovereign Immunities Act of 1976 (hereinafter "FSIA"), 28 U.S.C. §§ 1330, 1602 et seq. The FSIA granted personal and subject matter jurisdiction in the federal district courts over commercial suits brought by claimants against those foreign states which have waived immunity. 28 U.S.C. § 1330. Prior to the enactment of the FSIA, a foreign government's immunity to suit was determined by the Executive Branch on a case-by-case basis. According to petitioner, the principal purpose of the FSIA was to depoliticize these commercial lawsuits by taking them out of the arena of foreign affairs—where the Executive Branch is subject to the pressures of foreign states seeking to avoid liability through a grant of immunity—and by placing them within the exclusive jurisdiction of the courts. Petitioner thus insists that the President, by suspending its claims, has circumscribed the jurisdiction of the United States courts in violation of Art. III of the Constitution.

We disagree. In the first place, we do not believe that the President has attempted to divest the federal courts of jurisdiction. Executive Order No. 12294 purports only to "suspend" the claims, not divest the federal court of "jurisdiction." As we read the Executive Order, those claims not within the jurisdiction of the Claims Tribunal will "revive" and become judicially enforceable in United States courts. This case, in short, illustrates the difference between modifying federal court jurisdiction and directing the courts to apply a different rule of law. See *United States v. Schooner Peggy*, 5 U.S. 1, 103, 1 Cranch 103, 2 L.Ed. 49 (1801). The President has exercised the power, acquiesced in by Congress, to settle claims and, as such, has simply effected a change in the substantive law governing the lawsuit. Indeed, the very example of sovereign immunity belies petitioner's argument. No one would suggest that a determination of sovereign immunity divests the federal courts of "jurisdiction." Yet, petitioner's argument, if accepted, would have required courts prior to the enactment of the FSIA to reject as an encroachment on their jurisdiction the President's determination of a foreign state's sovereign immunity.

Petitioner also reads the FSIA much too broadly. The principal purpose of the FSIA was to codify contemporary concepts concerning the scope of sovereign immunity and withdraw from the President the authority to make binding determinations of the sovereign immunity to be accorded foreign states. . . . The FSIA was thus designed to remove one particular barrier to suit, namely sovereign immunity, and cannot be fairly read as prohibiting the President from settling claims of United States nationals against foreign governments. It is telling that the Congress which enacted the FSIA considered but rejected several proposals designed to limit the power of the President to enter into executive agreements, including claims settlement agreements. It is quite unlikely that the same Congress that rejected proposals to limit the President's authority to conclude executive agreements sought to accomplish that very purpose *sub silentio* through the FSIA. And, as noted above, just 1 year after enacting the FSIA, Congress enacted the IEEPA, where the legislative history stressed that nothing in the IEEPA was to impede the settlement of claims of United

States citizens. It would be surprising for Congress to express this support for settlement agreements had it intended the FSIA to eliminate the President's authority to make such agreements.

In light of all of the foregoing—the inferences to be drawn from the character of the legislation Congress has enacted in the area, such as the IEEPA and the Hostage Act, and from the history of acquiescence in executive claims settlement—we conclude that the President was authorized to suspend pending claims pursuant to Executive Order No. 12294. As Justice Frankfurter pointed out in *Youngstown*, 343 U.S. at 610-611, 72 S.Ct. at 897-898, "a systematic, unbroken executive practice, long pursued to the knowledge of Congress and never before questioned . . . may be treated as a gloss on 'Executive Power' vested in the President by § 1 of Art. II." Past practice does not, by itself, create power, but "long-continued practice, known to and acquiesced in by Congress, would raise a presumption that the [action] has been [taken] in pursuance of its consent. . . ." *United States v. Midwest Oil Co.*, 236 U.S. 459, 474, 35 S.Ct. 309, 313, 59 L.Ed. 673 (1915). See *Haig v. Agee*, 453 U.S., at 291, 101 S.Ct., at 2774. Such practice is present here and such a presumption is also appropriate. In light of the fact that Congress may be considered to have consented to the President's action in suspending claims, we cannot say that action exceeded the President's powers.

Our conclusion is buttressed by the fact that the means chosen by the President to settle the claims of American nationals provided an alternate forum, the Claims Tribunal, which is capable of providing meaningful relief. The Solicitor General also suggests that the provision of the Claims Tribunal will actually enhance the opportunity for claimants to recover their claims, in that the Agreement removes a number of jurisdictional and procedural impediments faced by claimants in United States courts. . . . Although being overly sanguine about the chances of United States claimants before the Claims Tribunal would require a degree of naivete which should not be demanded even of judges, the Solicitor General's point cannot be discounted. Moreover, it is important to remember that we have already held that the President has the statutory authority to nullify attachments and to transfer the assets out of the country. The President's power to do so does not depend on his provision of a forum whereby claimants can recover on those claims. The fact that the President has provided such a forum here means that the claimants are receiving something in return for the suspension of their claims, namely, access to an international tribunal before which they may well recover something on their claims. Because there does appear to be a real "settlement" here, this case is more easily analogized to the more traditional claim settlement cases of the past.

Just as importantly, Congress has not disapproved of the action taken here. Though Congress has held hearings on the Iranian Agreement itself, Congress has not enacted legislation, or even passed a resolution, indicating its displeasure with the Agreement. Quite the contrary, the relevant Senate Committee has stated that the establishment of the Tribunal is "of vital importance to the United States." S.Rep. No. 97-71, 97th Cong., 1st Sess., 5 (1981). We are thus clearly not confronted with a situation in which Congress has in some way resisted the exercise of presidential authority.

Finally, we re-emphasize the narrowness of our decision. We do not decide that the President possesses plenary power to settle claims, even as against foreign governmental entities. As the Court of Appeals for the First Circuit stressed, "the sheer magnitude of such a power, considered against the background of the diversity and complexity of modern international trade, cautions against any broader construction of authority than is necessary." *Chas. T. Main Int'l, Inc, v. Khuzestan Water & Power Authority*, 651 F.3d, at 814. But where, as here, the settlement of claims has been determined to be a necessary incident to the resolution of a major foreign policy dispute between our country and another, and where, as here, we can conclude that Congress acquiesced in the President's action, we are not prepared to say that the President lacks the power to settle such claims.

V

We do not think it appropriate at the present time to address petitioner's contention that the suspension of claims, if authorized, would constitute a taking of property in violation of the Fifth Amendment to the United States Constitution in the absence of just compensation. Both petitioner and the Government concede that the question whether the suspension of the claims constitutes a taking is not ripe for review. . . . However, this contention, and the possibility that the President's actions may effect a taking of petitioner's property, makes ripe for adjudication the question whether petitioner will have a remedy at law in the Court of Claims under the Tucker Act, 28 U.S.C. § 1491, in such an event. . . .

* * *

It has been contended that the "treaty exception" to the jurisdiction of the Court of Claims, 28 U.S.C. § 1502, might preclude the Court of Claims from exercising jurisdiction over any takings claim the petitioner might bring. At oral argument, however, the Government conceded that § 1502 would not act as a bar to petitioner's action in the Court of Claims. . . . Accordingly, to the extent petitioner believes it has suffered an unconstitutional taking by the suspension of the claims, we see no jurisdictional obstacle to an appropriate action in the United States Court of Claims under the Tucker Act.

The judgment of the District Court is accordingly affirmed, and the mandate shall issue forthwith.

* * *

JUSTICE POWELL, concurring and dissenting in part.

I join the Court's opinion except its decision that the nullification of the attachments did not effect a taking of property interests giving rise to claims for just compensation. The nullification of attachments presents a separate question from whether the suspension and proposed settlement of claims against Iran may constitute a taking. I would leave both "taking" claims open for resolution on a case-by-case basis in actions before the Court of Claims. The facts of the hundreds of claims pending against Iran are not known to this Court and may differ from the facts in this case. I therefore dissent from the Court's decision with respect to attachments. The decision may well be erroneous, and it certainly is premature with respect to many claims.

I agree with the Court's opinion with respect to the suspension and settlement of claims against Iran and its instrumentalities. The opinion makes clear that some claims may not be adjudicated by the Claims Tribunal and that others may not be paid in full. The Court holds that parties whose valid claims are not adjudicated or not fully paid may bring a "taking" claim against the United States in the Court of Claims, the jurisdiction of which this Court acknowledges. The Government must pay just compensation when it furthers the Nation's foreign policy goals by using as "bargaining chips" claims lawfully held by a relatively few persons and subject to the jurisdiction of our courts. The extraordinary powers of the President and Congress upon which our decision rests cannot, in the circumstances of this case, displace the Just Compensation Clause of the Constitution.

Discussion Questions

1. What is the specific holding in the *Dames & Moore* case?

2. Does the Court address the issue of the president's action resulting in a "taking" of petitioner's property in violation of the Fifth Amendment?

3. What is the dissenter's position on the "taking" in violation of the Fifth Amendment issue?

4. Is the president's authority under the IEEPA and the inherent foreign policy powers of the chief executive as exercised in this case necessary for the proper exercise of the foreign policy of this country? Discuss.

5. What further recourse does the private party, Dames & Moore, have in pursuit of satisfaction of judgment made by the district court in their suit against the government of Iran, the Atomic Energy Organization of Iran, and the Iranian banks?

> *Comment*: Dames & Moore did file a claim with the Iranian-United States Claims Tribunal following the judgment of the Supreme Court in *Dames & Moore v. Regan*. That claim on behalf of Dames & Moore was denied in part because of a clause in the contract that said "the matter shall be decided finally by resort to the courts of Iran." That clause brought the claim within a provision in the Algiers Declaration that excluded claims arising under a contract "provided that any disputes thereunder shall be within the sole jurisdiction of the competent Iranian courts" (*Dames & Moore v. Iran*, 4 Rep. Iran-U.S. Claims Trib. 212 [1983]).
>
> The *Dames & Moore* decision has been criticized for not demanding a "clear statement" that Congress had authorized the president to suspend individual claims. There is no such specific statement in the IEEPA. The president's actions had an undeniable impact on individual rights. It is argued that this decision is inconsistent with other decisions that demand specific authority for the suspension of

such rights. The decision is criticized also for its refusal to inquire more deeply into the legislative history of the IEEPA, which provides evidence of intent to narrow presidential power, rather than expand it, as resulted in the *Dames & Moore* decision (see Steiner, Vagts, & Koh, 1994, pp. 122-124).

The Act of State Doctrine

The **act of State doctrine** complements and often interacts with the doctrine of sovereign immunity. In general, municipal courts have adopted the rule that a State's executive, legislative, or judicial acts, having effect within that State's own territory, are not subject to judicial inquiry by other States. This act of State doctrine is both linked with the sovereign immunity doctrine and differs from it in substantial respects. Both doctrines have at least one purpose in common: preventing domestic courts from becoming involved in disputes that might lead to friction between a foreign State and their own. However, in other aspects the two doctrines differ:

> **Act of State doctrine:** Another defense in civil litigation that prevents the questioning of acts of other foreign sovereigns in suits between private parties, even if the parties are not sovereign States themselves.

> [Sovereign immunity] applies only where a foreign State or its instrumentality is sought to be made a party to litigation or where its property is involved. On the other hand, the act of State doctrine focuses entirely on the action taken by that State, and may be applicable to litigation between two private parties to which that action is relevant. (Steiner et al., 1994, p. 781)

The Sabbatino Case

The act of State doctrine is widely supported by both Anglo-American law countries and communist States as well as by many noncommunist civil law countries that prefer to deal with such issues through conflict of laws (private international law). The doctrine raises several sets of issues, particularly those in which acts may be contrary to international law or when they are contrary to the public policy of another State affected by such acts. In the controversial opinion *Banco National de Cuba v. Sabbatino* (376 U.S. 398 [1964]), the Supreme Court upheld the act of State doctrine despite lower court rulings that the "act of State" in question was a violation of international law. The act of State doctrine became a subject of controversy when it was applied to preclude scrutiny by U.S. courts of acts of foreign States alleged to be in violation of international law.

In retaliation for a U.S. reduction in the import quota for Cuban sugar by the U.S. Congress, the Cuban government nationalized many companies in which U.S. nationals held interests. Farr, Whitlock, a U.S. commodities broker, had contracted to buy a shipload of sugar from Compania Azucarera Vertientes (CAV). To obtain the now-nationalized sugar, Farr, Whitlock entered into a new agreement to buy the shipload from the Cuban government, which assigned the bills of lading to its shipping agent, Banco Nacional. Farr, Whitlock gained possession of the shipping documents and negotiated them to its customers, but protected by CAV's promise of indemnification, Farr, Whitlock turned the proceedings over to CAV instead of Cuba. CAV was a Cuban firm in which U.S. citizens held interest.

In the following case, Banco Nacional sued Farr, Whitlock for conversion of the bills of lading and also sought to enjoin Sabbatino, the temporary receiver of CAV's New York assets, from disposing of the proceeds. Farr, Whitlock defended on the ground that title to the sugar never passed to Cuba because the expropriation violated international law.

In this case, the federal district court had acknowledged the continuing vitality of the act of State doctrine but held it inapplicable when the questioned foreign act is in violation of international law. Proceeding on the basis that a taking invalid under international law does not convey good title, the district court found the Cuban expropriation decree to violate such law in three separate respects: It was motivated by a retaliatory and not a public purpose; it discriminated against U.S. nationals; and it failed to provide adequate compensation. Summary judgment against petitioner was accordingly granted.

The Court of Appeals affirmed the decision on similar grounds. It also relied on two letters that were not before the district court, written by State Department officers, which it took as evidence that the executive branch had no objection to a judicial testing of the Cuban decree's validity. The appeals court was unwilling to declare that any one of the infirmities found by the district court rendered the taking invalid under international law but was satisfied that in combination they had that effect.

The U.S. Supreme Court granted certiorari "because the issues involved bear importantly on the conduct of the country's foreign relations and more particularly on the proper role of the Judicial Branch in this sensitive area." The majority opinion upheld the classic U.S. statement of the act of State doctrine found in *Underhill v. Hernandez* (168 U.S. 250) to the effect that

every sovereign state is bound to respect the independence of every other sovereign state, and the courts of one country will not sit in judgment on the acts of the government of another, done within its own territory. Redress of grievances by reason of such acts must be obtained through the means open to be availed of by sovereign powers as between themselves.

The majority opinion of the court went to great lengths to explain the historic importance of this doctrine in preserving the discretionary authority of the executive branch of government to pursue the foreign policy of the United States. It implied that the State Department letters were "intended to reflect no more than the Department's . . . wish not to make any statement bearing on this litigation." The majority opinion also found that

international law does not require application of the [act of state] doctrine is evidenced by the practice of nations. Most of the countries rendering decisions on the subject fail to follow the rule rigidly. No international arbitral or judicial decision discovered suggests that international law prescribes recognition of sovereign acts of foreign governments . . . and apparently no claim has ever been raised before an international tribunal that failure to apply the act of state doctrine constitutes a breach of international obligation.

Nonetheless, the majority reversed the decisions of the District Court and the Court of Appeals in the *Sabbatino* case because of the uncertainty of the international law on the subject of a State's power to expropriate the property of aliens and because of its unwillingness to deviate from precedent.

Justice White wrote a very convincing dissent in the *Sabbatino* case stating in part:

I am dismayed that the Court has, with one broad stroke, declared the ascertainment and application of international law beyond the competence of the courts of the United States in a large and important category of cases. I am also disappointed in the Court's declaration that the acts of a sovereign state with regard to the property of aliens within its borders are beyond the reach of international law in the courts of this country. However clearly established that law may be, a sovereign may violate it with impunity, except insofar as the political branches of the government may provide a remedy. This backward-looking doctrine, never before declared in this Court, is carried a disconcerting step further: not only are the courts powerless to question acts of state proscribed by international law but they are likewise powerless to refuse to adjudicate the claim founded upon a foreign law; they must render judgment and thereby validate the lawless act. Since the Court expressly extends its ruling to all acts of state expropriating property, however clearly inconsistent with the international community, all discriminatory expropriations of the property of aliens, as for example the taking of properties of persons belonging to certain races, religions or nationalities, are entitled to automatic validation in the courts of the United States. No other civilized country has found such a rigid rule necessary for the survival of the executive branch of its government; the executive of no other government seems to require such insulation from international law adjudications in its courts; and no other judiciary is apparently so incompetent to ascertain and apply international law.

This controversial decision prompted much criticism of the Supreme Court, prompting the Congress to intervene by passing legislation intended to reverse the decision. The act of State doctrine as reaffirmed in *Sabbatino* was thus limited by an act of Congress in "the Second Hickenlooper Amendment," and the ruling in the *Sabbatino* case itself was remanded to the district court and thereby effectively reversed. The district court, interpreting the Hickenlooper Amendment, dismissed the complaint in *Banco Nacional de Cuba v. Farr*, 243 F.Supp. 957 (S.D.N.Y.1965). This decision was affirmed at the appeals level, 383 F.2d 166 (2d Cir 1967), and certiorari was denied by the Supreme Court, 390 U.S. 956 (1968). Thus, the Supreme Court refused to rule on the application of the Hickenlooper Amendment by allowing the lower court decision to stand.

The specific wording of the **Hickenlooper Amendment** that follows is intended to have the effect of reversing the presumption expressed in the *Sabbatino* decision that any adjudication as to the lawfulness under international law of the act of a foreign State would embarrass the conduct of foreign policy unless the president says it would not. Under the amendment, the Court would presume that it may proceed with an adjudication on the merits unless the president states officially that such an adjudication in the particular case would embarrass the conduct of foreign policy.

> *Hickenlooper Amendment:* An act of Congress that attempted to reverse the decision in Banco Nacional de Cuba v. Sabbatino by reversing the presumption of the Court and that requires positive determination by the State Department that court action would embarrass foreign policy. It attempts to prevent courts from enforcing foreign acts of State that are in violation of international law.

Lower courts have been unanimous in holding that the act of State doctrine does not apply to a taking by a foreign State of property outside of its territory at the time of taking but have been divided as to how the territorial limitations should be applied to tangible property. The Supreme Court has not passed on the applicability of the doctrine to an act of a foreign government in respect of property outside that State's territory, to an act of a government not recognized by the United States, or to an act alleged to violate a provision of a law not in dispute. Hence, the application of exceptions to the act of State doctrine have taken place in lower courts where there is considerable confusion about exactly how the courts will treat the doctrine in specific cases.

The act of State doctrine was held not to apply in the case of a claim based on an act alleged to be in violation of a treaty between the United States and Ethiopia (*Kalamazoo Spice Extraction Co. v. Government of Socialist Ethiopia*, 729 F.2d 422 [6th Cir.1984]).

The Second Hickenlooper Amendment

Pul.L. 89-171, 79 Stat. 653 (1964), 22 U.S.C. S 2370(e)(2).

Notwithstanding any other provision of law, no court in the United States shall decline on the ground of the federal act of state doctrine to make a determination on the merits giving effect to the principles of international law in a case in which a claim of title or other right to property is asserted by any party including a foreign state (or a party claiming through such state) based upon (or traced through) a confiscation or other taking after January 1, 1959, by an act of that state in violation of the principles of international law including the principles of compensation and the other standards set out in this subsection: *Provided*, That this subparagraph shall not be applicable (1) in any case in which an act of a foreign state is not contrary to international law or with respect to a claim of title or other right to property acquired pursuant to an irrevocable letter of credit of not more than 180 days duration issued

in good faith prior to the time of the confiscation or other taking, or (2) in any case with respect to which the President determines that application of the act of state doctrine is required in that particular case by the foreign policy interests of the United States and a suggestion to this effect is filed on his behalf in that case with the court.

The controversy over the proper application of the act of State doctrine and the Hickenlooper Amendment continues without definitive resolution. Professor Henkin (Henkin, Pugh, Schachter, & Smit, 1987) asserts that the amendment framers did not have a clear idea of the act of State doctrine and its relation to general conflicts principles. Hence, he concludes

that the statute does not give a clear idea as to what is left after the Supreme Court is overruled. Did the statute intend to remove act of state from these cases? If so, are the courts left to traditional conflicts principles, and *Erie R. R. v. Tompkins?* Did Congress, instead, intend to prescribe new federal substantive law to govern these cases? If so, what exactly is the new law? And may Congress properly prescribe law for these transactions? (p. 179)

These are all questions left unanswered.

Professor Henkin (Henkin et al., 1987) further asserts that the proposition that international law is part of our law (see *Paquete Habana*) means that international law will be applied to give effect to limitations that international law imposes on the U.S. government. According to Henkin,

Congress could declare that regardless of any principles of conflicts, or of the act of state doctrine, it is the policy of the United States not to allow its courts to apply foreign law that contravenes international law. Or Congress could pass a statute providing that in Sabbatino-type cases, courts shall not apply the substantive law designated either by act of state or by traditional conflicts principles, but shall apply instead a new federal substantive law, which incorporates by reference the principles of international law as Congress saw them. (p. 180)

The courts in *Farr*, he asserts, "in effect, treated the Second Hickenlooper Amendment as though it were one of these two possible Congressional enactments" (p. 180).

∎   ∎   ∎

Chapter Summary

1. The general principles of diplomatic and sovereign immunity provide an understanding of the limits of individual State courts in their jurisdiction over transnational legal questions.

2. The establishment of diplomatic relations between two countries is a political act governed by the municipal law of the countries involved. However, the host State then accepts the customary international legal obligation to respect the rules of diplomatic immunity.

3. These rules have been codified and extended by the Vienna Conventions on Diplomatic Relations (1961) and Consular Relations (1963).

4. Diplomatic agents are given full diplomatic immunity that covers immunity from arrest, detention, criminal process, and in general, civil process in the receiving State.

5. Embassy personnel and consular officials are given functional immunity that requires them to respond to any criminal or civil process and to prove immunity on the basis of their official functions.

6. Diplomatic and consular premises are considered inviolable and may not be entered by officials of the host State without consent, nor may the diplomatic or consular bag be opened or detained without permission of the receiving State.

7. Other rules of diplomatic immunity protect the premises of the diplomat, his family, transit to and from his post, and the official records of the mission.

8. The rules for breaking diplomatic relations require respect for the protection and return of the personnel, the property of the mission, and its archives. A host State may declare diplomatic agents *persona non grata* and require them to return to their home State but must give them safe passage out of the country or require them to return within a reasonable time. Nondiplomatic personnel may also be required to leave within a reasonable time.

9. The Iran hostage crisis illustrates the further requirement that the host State must protect the rights of diplomats from being violated by mob action that is within their capacity to prevent.

10. Diplomatic asylum results from the rule of inviolability of the embassy premises under international law and is generally considered to be an unwarranted intervention in the internal affairs of the host State.

11. The *Asylum* case illustrated the opinion of the International Court of Justice that diplomatic asylum is not a customary right of international law, even among Latin American States, unless stipulated in positive treaty law.

12. Sovereign immunity shields foreign and domestic governments from suit in the municipal courts of a particular nation without their prior consent.

13. Traditional international law regarded sovereign immunity as absolute and could be invoked regardless of the nature of the governmental activity involved. This practice has given way to the modern theory of restrictive sovereign immunity that allows sovereign States to be sued in civil legal actions that are commercial in nature.

14. Most modern nations now make a distinction between commercial activities (acts *jure gestionis*), which are subject to suit, and exercises of sovereign authority that can only be performed by recognized governmental authority (acts *jure imperii*).

15. However, this distinction has proven difficult to define precisely, and there remains much that is unsettled in this area of law.

16. In the United States, the Foreign Sovereign Immunities Act (FSIA) of 1976 attempts to clarify these issues but remains vague in some respects and subject to varying interpretation.

17. Consideration of legitimate exercise of executive responsibility in the conduct of foreign policy adds complexity to the issues of application of sovereign immunity in particular cases, as illustrated in the *Dames & Moore* case.

18. Claims settlement agreements are treaty responsibilities between sovereigns that take precedence over private rights when legitimately exercised. U.S. courts have upheld such executive agreements with appropriate Congressional support.

19. The U.S. courts have held that the president has inherent powers in foreign policy to enable the executive to exercise broader powers in foreign policy than in domestic policy areas.

20. The act of State doctrine, generally, prevents the questioning of acts of foreign authority (*jure imperii*) done within the territorial jurisdiction of that State when relied on by parties in civil legal actions before the courts of a particular State.

21. Controversy exists as to the granting of respect for foreign acts of State that may violate international law, as illustrated in the *Sabbatino* case.

22. The Hickenlooper Amendment attempts to reverse the view of the act of State doctrine as expressed in *Sabbatino* by the U.S. Supreme Court. However, this legislative action is controversial and subject to varied interpretation. It has influenced subsequent decisions and resulted in the reversal of the *Sabbatino* decision. The effect seems to strengthen the rule that foreign acts in violation of international law will not be given effect in U.S. courts.

Key Terms

Vienna Convention on Diplomatic
    Relations
Diplomatic Relations Act of 1978
diplomatic agent
Vienna Convention on Consular
    Relations
functional immunity
persona non grata
sovereign immunity
absolute immunity
restrictive immunity

Federal Tort Claims Act (FTCA)
Tate Letter
Foreign Sovereign Immunities Act
    of 1976 (FSIA)
International Emergency Economic
    Powers Act (IEEPA)
Hostage Treaty
claims settlement agreements
inherent powers doctrine
act of State doctrine
Hickenlooper Amendment

▮   ▮   ▮

Discussion Questions

1. Do the principles of diplomatic immunity provide for adequate measures to prevent abuse?

2. What are the most important purposes of the rules of diplomatic immunity?

3. What are the most important effects of the modern principles of restrictive sovereign immunity? How does this development affect the private rights of individuals and corporations?

4. How does the act of State doctrine illustrate the dividing line between private international law and public international law?

Suggested Readings

Appendix J: Foreign Soverign Immunities Act
    of 1976
Delaume, G. R. (1994). The Foreign Sovereign
    Immunities Act and Public Debt Litigation:

Some fifteen years later. *American Journal of
International Law, 88*(2), 257-279.
Higgins, R. (1994). *Problems and process: Inter-
national law and how we use it*. New York:
Oxford University Press.

Internet Sources

Browse: Use *international law*, U.N. Home Page (http://www.un.org/) and U.N. Treaty Database (http://www.un.org/Depts/Treaty/).

American Society of International Law (http://www.asil.org).

U.S. State Department. *The Bulletin (Dispatch)*. Washington, D.C. Government Printing Office. (Newsletter of the State Department and a primary source of department policies and positions on various issues.) The new title is *Dispatch*. Hard copy is available in most libraries, but it is also available through the Internet: U.S. Department of State (http://www.state.gov/).

III Law on the International Plane

Part III will discuss those aspects of international law that are the core principles of the system of public international law. On the international plane, only those entities possessing attributes of sovereignty may bring legal actions against each other. States and intergovernmental organizations are considered the principal subjects of international law with rights and duties vis-à-vis each other. On this international plane, individuals and private entities are not considered subjects of the law of nations.

Only states can possess territory and exercise territorial sovereignty in these defined areas. Chapter 12 will explain the basic principles of acquiring statehood, the rights and duties of states, the methods of acquiring territory, and the extent of the exercise of territorial sovereignty. IGOs that exercise some attributes of sovereignty are now considered subjects of international law with limited international personality.

Only sovereign entities may negotiate and conclude treaties with other sovereign entities. In Chapter 13, the basic principles of the law of treaties will be explained. This body of public international law includes the treaty formation process, treaty practice, the general principles of treaty observance, and rules concerning termination and suspension of treaty obligations. As a general rule, only states may bring legal actions in international tribunals. In Chapter 14, the principles of adjudication of international disputes will be discussed. Finally, Part III includes a chapter explaining the basic concepts involved in the development of compliance measures under international law (Chapter 14).

11 The Legal Status of States and Intergovernmental Organizations

The traditional concept of international law recognized only the nation-state as a subject of that particular body of law among nations. However, in modern times, there has been a widening of the concept of international legal personality beyond the State to include other international entities that may not have all the attributes of the historical nation-state. Professor Henkin considers this broadening of international legal personality one of the more significant features of contemporary international law (see Henkin, Pugh, Schachter, & Smit, 1987, p. 229). Although international organizations and even insurgent communities may possess limited international personality, the nation-state is still the primary and predominant legal entity of the international community.

The nation-state system that has evolved over the past three and a half centuries accepts the State as the repository of legitimate authority over peoples and territories. As so eloquently expressed by Wolfgang Friedman in 1964,

It is only in terms of state powers, prerogatives, jurisdictional limits and law-making capabilities that territorial limits and jurisdiction, responsibility for official actions, and a host of other questions of coexistence between nations can be determined. It is by virtue of their law-making power and monopoly that states enter into bilateral and multilateral compacts, that wars can be started or terminated, that individuals can be punished or extradited. (pp. 213-214)

Friedman goes on to state that "this basic primacy of the state as a subject of international relations and law could be superseded only if national entities were absorbed into a world state" (p. 214). This has definitely not happened. In fact, the opposite trend is evidenced by the massive proliferation of new States. The most significant achievement of the United Nations Organization has been to promote self-determination of peoples from the empires of the colonial past. The proliferation of sovereign States now approaches four times that of the immediate post-World War II system of national identities.

Statehood and Recognition

The *Restatement (Third) of the Foreign Relations Law of the United States* (American Law Institute, 1987) includes the following definition of a State:

> ### § 201.   State Defined
>
> Under international law, a state is an entity that has a defined territory and a permanent population, under the control of its own government, and that engages in, or has the capacity to engage in formal relations with other such entities.

These criteria of **Statehood** that define the primary sovereign entities of the international community have been used to justify the existence of a State even in the absence of **recognition** by other States. They are derived from the 1933 Montevideo Inter-American Convention on the Rights and Duties of States. In 1936, the prestigious *Institut de Droit International* stated, "The existence of a new State with all the legal consequences attaching to this existence is not affected by the refusal of recognition by one or more states." This means that the issues of Statehood and diplomatic recognition must be treated differently; however, they are interrelated and often confused.

There are two basic theories of the effect of recognition on Statehood: the *constitutive* and the *declaratory* views. These distinctions are becoming more unified in con-

Statehood: *Acquiring the status of a State, which is the primary legal (juridical) person and subject in international law.*

Recognition: *The discretionary function exercised unilaterally by the government of a State officially acknowledging the existence of another State or government or belligerent community.*

temporary practice, but they are useful in an introductory explanation of one of the most fundamental concepts of international law.

The **constitutive theory** asserts that the act of recognition by other States confers international personality on an entity purporting to be a State. This means that States exist because the international community has admitted them into the community of nations. The historical development of Western civilization and law is associated with this concept. The charter members of the international community may be said to be those participating in the peace settlement at the end of the Thirty Years War in Europe in 1648. Only Christian nations were admitted into the group of States subject to international law until 1856. The Concert of Europe took actions to admit the Ottoman Empire into the "public law and system of Europe," but it also declared Africa south of the Sahara subject to European colonization.

Constitutive theory: *Asserts that recognition by other States confers international personality on an entity seeking to become a State.*

The opposing **declaratory theory** asserts that the existence of a State depends on the facts and on whether those facts meet the criteria of Statehood laid down in international law. According to this theory, a State may exist without being recognized. Recognition is merely declaratory, and the function of recognition is to acknowledge the fact of the State's political existence and the willingness of the recognizing State to treat that entity as an international person.

Declaratory theory: *Asserts that the existence of a State depends on whether or not the entity in question meets the criteria of Statehood laid down in international law.*

The more traditional authorities, such as Lauterpacht (1946), adopt the constitutive theory but contend that States have an obligation to recognize an entity that meets the qualifications of Statehood. The American Law Institute's *Restatement (Third)* accepts the declaratory view but indicates that although a State is not required to accord formal recognition to any other State, it is required to treat an entity that meets the requirements of Statehood as a State unless it has attained the qualifications of Statehood in violation of international law, in which case it is required not to recognize or treat the entity as a State (Lauterpacht, 1946, cited in Henkin et al., 1987, p. 231).

Controversies as to whether an entity should be considered a State arise in many different contexts. An individual State may decide to recognize a new State by sending and receiving ambassadors, or it may break off diplomatic relations with a State because it disagrees with the particular government. These actions, usually performed by the executive branch, have particular consequences for municipal courts, but international organizations and international tribunals must use different criteria for determining Statehood. However, even the U.S. Supreme Court must ascertain whether or not the particular entity in question meets the standards of international law. This calls for the determination of difficult questions of fact and law. Both States and international bodies will generally give weight to recognition by other States. Thus, acts of recognition or refusals to recognize may have a significant and sometimes decisive role in determining controversial legal questions.

In contemporary practice, it is clear that an entity that meets the conditions of Statehood, as defined in § 201 of the *Restatement (Third)*, can neither be denied the rights conferred on States by international law nor evade the duties and responsibilities of the law among nations. In fact, nonrecognized States are frequently charged with violations of international law and are the object of international claims by the very States refusing recognition.

U.N. membership is actively sought by all aspirants to Statehood today. However, a State does not have to be a member of that organization to be recognized legally as a State. Switzerland is the primary remaining example of a State that chooses to remain a nonmember. Swiss voters have rejected several recent referenda on the subjects of entrance into both the United Nations and the European Union. Switzerland nonetheless participates in the United Nations with a permanent mission in Observer Status, and it is a party to the Statute of the International Court of Justice (ICJ).

The remaining nonmember States include Kiribati (formerly the Gilbert Islands), Nauru, New Caldonia, Niue (freely associated with New Zealand), Serbia and Montenegro, Taiwan, Tonga, the Holy Sea (Vatican City), Western Sahara, and Palestine-PLO (Gaza/West Bank). There are still more entities that aspire, or may aspire, to Statehood and may eventually seek membership in the United Nations.

The Rights and Duties of States

The Charter of the United Nations Organization is the most fundamental lawmaking treaty that defines the modern rights and duties of States. This document is admittedly vague in the specific provisions that relate to rights and duties. However, it defines the composition and authority of the institutions of this nearly universal organization of modern nation-states. The actions of these institutions, pursuant to the charter, are the basic means of clarification of the general principles of international law.

The difficulties of codification of the rights and duties of States and State responsibility are illustrated by the failure of the International Law Commission (ILC) to secure the necessary ratifications for draft treaties on these subjects. The U.N. General Assembly asked the ILC to prepare a draft declaration of the rights and duties of States in 1947. The work of the commission did produce a draft document delineating four rights (independence, territorial jurisdiction, equality in law, and self-defense) and ten duties. However, the document was severely criticized on numerous counts and was unable to secure enough ratifications to go into force.

After a decade of debate and negotiation, the General Assembly, by consensus, adopted the Friendly Relations Declaration in 1970. This document represents a clarification of the principles of the U.N. Charter relating to the rights and duties of States. "It has become the international lawyer's favorite example of an authoritative U.N. resolution" (Schachter, 1994, p. 3).

This rather complete list of rights and duties of States has proven quite useful in providing clarification for a number of vague concepts that create difficulties of interpretation in the daily activities of the major organs of the U.N. system. It is particularly helpful in regard to the concept of <u>self-determination of peoples</u>. The undefined concept could become, and some may argue has already become, an encouragement to the "Balkanization" of the world's recognized political units. This potential source of instability could undermine the entire purpose of the U.N. system to promote international peace and security.

> **Self-determination of peoples:** *A controversial concept expressed vaguely in the U.N. Charter and generally accepted as the right of States to self-determination from colonial rule.*

Self-Determination of Peoples

The debate over the specific meaning of self-determination of peoples has a long history going back to World War I and beyond. However, the U.N. Charter mentions the concept in only a few places. Article 2(1) provides that one of the purposes of the United Nations is "to develop friendly relations among nations based on respect for the principle of equal rights and self-determination of peoples." Elsewhere, this same phrase connects equal rights and self-determination and appears to relate them to "equal rights" of States, not of individuals (see Cassese, 1995, pp. 34–42).

In the most pertinent sections of the U.N. Charter dealing with dependent territories, Chapters XI and XII, there is no reference to a duty to provide self-determination on the basis of independence. Chapter XI, which is concerned with non-self-governing territories, refers in Article 73(b) to the duty of the governing State to "develop self-government, to take due account of the political aspirations of the peoples, and to assist them in the progressive development of their free political institutions, according to the particular circumstances of each territory and its peoples and the varying stages of advancement." In Chapter XII, concerning the basic objective of the trusteeship system, a statement in Article 76 provides some clarification. The basic objective of the trusteeship shall be "to promote . . . their progressive development toward self-government or independence as may be appropriate to the particular circumstances of each territory and its peoples and the freely expressed wishes of the peoples concerned." Professor Rosalyn Higgins (1994, p. 112) asserts that there is still no use of the term *self-determination,* and independence was not assumed as the only proper outcome.

The issues in the debate over self-determination have to do with the extent of that right and whether it requires independence. Does it apply to tribes and groups living within a particular established State, and if it does, may a particular group assert such a right alone, or is it subordinate to the will of the majority of the entire electorate of the State in question?

Separatist movements have become endemic in the post-Cold War era, and these questions will require more definitive answers in the future. The U.N. Declaration on Friendly Relations contains a clear statement that bears repeating here, since it helps to answer these questions:

> Nothing in the foregoing paragraphs shall be construed as authorizing or encouraging any action which would dismember or impair, totally or in part, the territorial integrity or political unity of sovereign or independent States conducting themselves in compliance with the principle of equal rights and self-determination of peoples as described above and thus possessed of a government representing the whole people belonging to the territory without distinction as to race, creed or colour.

This statement implies a negative answer to the question of whether particular groups within an existing State are governed by the same rules that apply to the former mandates and trust territories. However, it does not settle the debate, and, as Higgins (1994) points out, important elements of compliance with human rights conventions require States to respect the cultural rights of minority groups. Article 27 of the International Covenant on Civil and Political Rights, for example, provides the following:

> In those states in which ethnic, religious or linguistic minorities exist, persons belonging to such minorities shall not be denied the right, in community with other members of their group, to enjoy their own culture, to profess and practice their own religion, and to use their own language.

Higgins (1994) asserts that international law does not support a right of self-determination of minorities as such. "That means, in effect, that they have no right to secession, to independence, or to join with comparable groups in other states" (p. 124).

The post-Cold War era has witnessed some of the most astounding changes in the composition of States in the history of international relations. The success of the trusteeship system in moving former colonial territories to a status of "equal rights and self-determination" has resulted most frequently in movement toward independence. However, there are notable exceptions.

The people of Gibraltar decided by referendum to maintain their present constitutional arrangement with the United Kingdom. Puerto Rico has had several elections indicating that the people wish to remain as a territory of the United States. Quebec has also expressed its voters' determination not to become a separate nation, although the vote in 1995 was very close. Canada may well have demanded that a national referendum decide the issue of independence of Quebec, had the separatist referendum in that province succeeded. In 1992, the Canadian government signed an accord with Eskimo leaders that would create an autonomous or native-run territory in Canada's Northwest Territories, to be called Nunavut. The Arctic Eskimos ratified a land claim agreement by way of a referendum, which resulted in the Canadian government's passing legislation establishing Nunavut in 1999.

The breakup of the Soviet Union and rejection of communist international control over the Eastern European countries ultimately produced many changes in State status. East and West Germany voluntarily merged in 1990; the fifteen autonomous republics of the former Soviet Union seceded from that recognized State in 1991; Slovenia, Croatia, Macedonia, and Bosnia-Herzegovina seceded from the former Yugoslavia during a two-year period beginning in 1992; and the Czech Republic and Slovakia became separate States by peaceful agreement in 1993. Separatist movements within these newly formed independent States are creating major conflicts and civil war situations that confound the international community.

Ultimately, the solutions to these complex problems will have to be achieved by the warring factions themselves. However, international legal principles of succession and secession are being tested as never before.

Succession of States

According to the International Law Commission, **State succession** "means the replacement of one State by another in the responsibility for the international relations of territory." The ten-year effort of the commission in drafting two treaties on State succession, the Convention on Succession of States in Respect of Treaties (Vienna, 1978) and the Convention on Succession of States in Respect of State Property, Archives and Debts (Vienna, 1983), has been of some

> **State succession:** Replacement of one State by another in the responsibility for the international relations of the territory.

help in understanding customary practice; however, these treaties have never received sufficient ratifications to enter into force.

Succession occurs in a variety of circumstances, including breakups and mergers as well as total and partial succession. The problems of treaty obligations have been the most serious international concerns along with those of representation in the United Nations. The Community of Independent States (CIS) formed by seven of the fifteen former constituent republics of the Soviet Union asserted that the "States' members . . . undertake to discharge the international obligations incumbent on them under treaties and engagements entered into by the former Union of Soviet Socialist Republics." They also expressed their intention to support the inviolability of existing territorial borders and to "set up lawfully constituted democratic States." The document was carefully conveyed to the United Nations, expressing regional solidarity favoring the Russian Federation as the entity to occupy the former seat held by the Soviet Union in the Security Council's permanent seat. This change was recognized by the Security Council in 1991.

This action recognized the Russian Federation as the largest unit of the former USSR and would seem to follow from the general concept of State succession, that loss of some part of a State's territories does not change existing treaty obligations unless these changes result in impossibility of performance. New States, on the other hand, are not bound to maintain in force treaties applicable to the predecessor State. They start with a "clean slate" with regard to political treaties. However, new States are bound by customary practices of States regarded as legally binding and all those lawmaking treaties that express the specific content of the body of customary law among nations.

The total extinction of the legal personality of a State, as in the case of the former Democratic Republic of Germany (East), traditionally results in an abrogation of all political and military treaties previously concluded between the now extinct entity and other States. If succession involves only a portion of the original owner's territory, the remaining State is still bound by treaties with other countries because such a State's legal personality continues alive, as with the Russian Federation. Only those provisions of treaties relating to lost parts of the territory no longer bind the former sovereign.

The unratified 1983 Vienna Convention concerning State property, archives, and debts provides that the successor State is entitled to the property of the former State, including responsibility for its debts. Therefore, succession "does not as such affect the rights . . . of creditors" (Article 36).

The issue of claims against an extinct State, such as the German Democratic Republic, Czechoslovakia, and the Soviet Union are uncertain. However, an agreement reached on May 13, 1992, between the Federal Republic of Germany and the United States resulted in the payment of U.S. claims for damages. A total of $190 million was to cover claims filed by U.S. individual and corporate nationals. In theory, such claims should be treated the same as debts. However, all of these general principles are subject to agreement among the parties concerning settlement.

The Duty Not to Recognize

Recognition in international relations takes many forms and is generally regarded by legal authorities as a *political act with legal consequences*. The president of the United States is constitutionally authorized

to "send and receive ambassadors" and to conduct the foreign policy of the nation. Such action is therefore interpreted as a political decision within the discretion of the president, and the courts in the United States have indicated respect for the president's authority by seeking the position of the executive when legal issues have arisen.

One form of recognition is recognition of governments. A classic example of the internal legal consequences of recognition is illustrated in the *Bank of China v. Wells Fargo Bank* (104 F.Supp.59 [1952]). The Chinese communist overthrow of the Nationalist Government of China, in 1949, produced the refusal of the U.S. government to recognize the People's Republic of China for over twenty years. In 1952, the only Chinese government recognized by the United States was the nationalist government that had retreated to the island of Formosa (now called Taiwan). The government-directed Bank of China at Shanghai had deposited money in the Wells Fargo bank in San Francisco before the takeover was completed in 1949. The legal issue before the federal district court in California was, which government was entitled to the assets of the State of China in the United States amounting to some $800,000. Although the court indicated that it did not have to follow the policy of the executive in this matter and that there was precedent for other options, the judge nonetheless decided in favor of the Nationalist Government out of deference to the executive authority (see also *United States v. Belmont* [1937] and *United States v. Pink*, 315 U.S. 203 [1942]).

The political nature of acts of recognition are more evident in the acts of governments that recognize the existence of States before the elements of Statehood are reasonably achieved. In 1988, when the Palestine Liberation Organization (PLO) declared the independence of the State of Palestine, twenty-three countries of the Middle East recognized the State of Palestine, and by 1989, about seventy States had done so. Since the PLO possessed neither a defined territory nor a functioning government, these actions are clearly expressions of political policy and willingness to support the cause of Statehood for Palestine.

Situations involving internal conflict *within a State* are more serious concerns of the international community, and traditional international law recognizes a duty to refrain from intervention in such conflicts. Traditional international law recognizes a series of developments involving rather specific elements of recognition first of insurgency and then of belligerency before extending full recognition to the new State, if it is established.

Local uprisings or civil disturbances in a particular country are internal matters, and other States have a duty to refrain from participation in such activities or from prematurely extending recognition to such groups that may be involved. When such internal conflicts become more widespread, other States may declare an intermediate measure recognizing **insurgency** and thus restrict travel or business dealings in that country in the interest of protecting the safety of their own citizens. However, the recognition of a state of belligerency requires specific criteria and carries with it important legal consequences.

> **Insurgency:** *A state of rebellion or revolt within a country that has not yet reached the proportions warranted for extension to the status of belligerency.*

The traditional conditions of **belligerency** required the internal conflict to be extensive, involving the following

> **Belligerency:** *The existence of a state of war between a State's central government and a portion of that State.*

criteria: (a) A government and military organization had to have been established and be operative in the rebel-controlled area; (b) the rebellion had to have reached a stage of warfare equivalent to conflicts between States; and (c) the rebel government had to, in fact, control a reasonable portion of the territory of the parent State or overseas territory. When this condition exists, other States may grant a limited measure of personality by recognizing a status of belligerency (von Glahn, 1996, p. 71).

The consequences of a State of belligerency places both the parent State and the insurgent group(s) under responsibility for all violations of the laws of war and for the treatment of foreign property and citizens. Rights acquired by the belligerents then include the rights of blockade, visitation, search and seizure of contraband articles on the high seas, and abandonment of claims for reparation on account of "damages suffered" through the conflict by foreign citizens (*The Three Friends*, 166 U.S. 1, 1897, at 63).

Under traditional international law, the recognition of the status of belligerency by the parent State or other States was necessary for the legal creation of that status. Other States are expected to remain neutral until the belligerency is resolved. The **premature recognition** of the insurgent community has been taken as an act of war, as was France's recognition of the

> **Premature recognition:** *Considered a violation of the duty to remain neutral until the belligerency is resolved.*

United States in 1778, which was soon followed by an expected declaration of war by Great Britain against France.

During the American Civil War, England recognized the Confederate States of the United States as "belligerents" at the beginning of the war in 1861. However, Great Britain failed to remain neutral as required under international law. The *Alabama Claims* tribunal awarded the United States $15 million in damages resulting from British violation of the duty to remain neutral. The major violation was in allowing ships for the Confederacy to be built in British ports and prepared for war with the Union forces in the United States.

The customary practice of **neutrality** has been changed somewhat by the United Nations Charter, which prohibits military intervention unless authorized by the Security Council. During the Cold War, the practice of neutrality seemed to have been forgotten by the major powers who intervened repeatedly in the civil war situations that existed, since the Security Council could be effectively blocked from action by the veto. In the post-Cold War era, the Security Council has attempted to prohibit outside intervention in civil war situations such as those in the former Yugoslavia.

> **Neutrality:** *The legal status of a State during a war (external or internal) that creates rights and duties under international law.*

Acquisition of territory by a State in violation of international law is prohibited by the U.N. Charter, and States have a duty at least to refrain from recognizing such acquisitions. In 1965, British-controlled Rhodesia declared its independence after staging an illegal coup. The Ian Smith government in that territory was condemned by the U.N. Security Council as a usurpation of power by a racist settler minority and regarded the declaration of independence as having no legal validity. The Security Council called on all States to refrain from any action that would assist and encourage the illegal regime (November 20, 1965). At the time of this resolution, the government of Rhodesia met all the traditional requirements of Statehood and independence. Its government was clearly the effective authority, and it had capacity to enter into foreign relations. Although the Security Council does not have the authority to recognize governments, its action was effective in branding the government of Rhodesia illegal, and it was subsequently not recognized as a State by any government or treated as a State by any international organization. Ultimately, the Rhodesian problem was resolved in 1979-1980 with the establishment of the State of Zimbabwe, which is generally recognized and which became a member of the United Nations in 1980.

There is a growing tendency in the international community to ensure not only that the remnants of colonialism are transferred to independent status but that the newly independent countries are governed by representative governments. Evidence of recent State practice indicates an emerging recognition of an international right to a representative form of government. The European Union has developed Guidelines on Recognition of States that refer to a representative form of government; the Organization of American States has, since the 1994 Haitian crisis, taken even stronger action in amending its charter to expel any State whose democratically elected government has been overthrown; and several scholarly studies all point in this direction (see Damrosch, 1993b; Franck, 1992; Higgins, 1994).

Every ratifying party to the International Covenants on Humanitarian Rights acknowledges the right of peoples to self-determination. As Higgins (1994) asserts, "That commitment will, as we approach the twenty-first century, require the international community to harness every means at its disposal to encourage democracy and free choice" (p. 44).

State Responsibility

Once Statehood has been achieved, the new State is required under customary international law to assume the obligations of Statehood and to make reparations for any international wrongdoing to other States for injuries they may have sustained. The concept of **State responsibility** is fundamental to the concept of international law. When any State commits a wrongful act in violation of international law against another State, its breach of the law requires that it make reparations for that harm.

> **State responsibility:** The obligation of the State to make reparation for damages arising from a failure to comply with an obligation under international law.

Three fundamental elements establish State responsibility under international law: (a) the existence of a legal obligation recognized by international law, (b) an act or omission that violates that obligation, and (c) some loss or damage caused by the breach of the obligation. The violation in question must also be *imputable* (attributable) to the government involved and not merely due to private injuries beyond the reasonable control of the government (see *Iran Hostage* case in Chapter 10).

State responsibility has generally been considered analogous to "strict liability" in a civil legal action; therefore, fault and intent do not have to be proven. Although there is a great body of customary law on the subject of State responsibility, efforts to codify and clarify this body of law in a lawmaking treaty have failed to produce drafts that have received widespread agreement.

Methods of Acquiring Territory

Many States have come into existence without having settled territorial boundaries, but sovereignty over a specific territorial area is an essential element of Statehood. Each State has had to deal with boundary disputes with its neighbors, and historically, these have been settled by agreements with other States. Unraveling the claims of various States to their existing territorial jurisdictions is an impossible task for an introductory text. The great bulk of the recognized States today have settled borders that have been agreed to by their neighbors, and this legal status allows them to live in peaceful conditions of settled and secure borders. However, many States do not enjoy this condition, and boundary disputes are some of the most serious problems contributing to international conflict.

Western concepts of property have contributed to the division of the world into categories of territory that have important historical significance and help to explain many aspects of territorial sovereignty today. These categories include the following:

- Territory owned by a sovereign State
- Trust territories
- *Terra nullius* (territory capable of ownership but owned by no State)
- *Res communis* (territory belonging to the community of nations)

The concept of State sovereignty is limited by the territorial boundaries of that State, and hence the establishment of stable and secure borders is an integral part of the protection of sovereignty. The particular aspects of these boundaries contribute to the protection of the sovereign entity by securing borders that present natural barriers to military threats from their neighbors, or the lack of these features present a threat to their security.

Trust territories have been established over particular areas, ostensibly to provide protection of areas thought to be too weak

Trust territories: *Territories to be administered by a State, or the United Nations itself, under the supervision of the Trusteeship Council.*

and underdeveloped to protect their own sovereignty. The U.N. trusteeship system was established to ensure that the former colonial powers lived up to their commitment to move these areas toward freedom of choice and self-determination. The mandates set up under the League of Nations were transferred by the Mandatory Powers to the Trusteeship Council after it was created, with one notable exception. The South African mandate over Southwest Africa (now known as Namibia) was not transferred, and South Africa refused to relinquish it. It was South Africa's contention that with the demise of the League of Nations, the mandate lapsed and South Africa could incorporate the mandate into its own territory. This position was refuted in the *International Status of South-West Africa* advisory opinion by the ICJ in 1950. This opinion will be presented in Chapter 12 in connection with the discussion of the Law of Treaties. Namibia became an independent State in 1990.

In addition to the former mandates that were transferred, the Trusteeship Council administered territories previously under control of the defeated powers of World War II. A total of eleven territories under the control of seven States were placed under the trusteeship system. The United States trust over the Marianas, Carolines, and Marshall Islands produced an unusual relationship, because these were classified as strategic trust areas in view of their geopolitical importance. The strategic trust territories came under the supervision of the Security Council rather than the Trusteeship Council and the General Assembly. Although the U.N. Trusteeship Council declared its mandate completed in 1994, there are still many problems involving territorial borders that have their origin in the colonial experiences of many parts of the world.

The method of acquiring original title to territory involves a claim to land not previously owned, or *terra nullius*. The concept of *terra nullius* involves territory capable of being legally owned but owned by no State. The modes of original acquisition of territory, adopted from Roman law, include discovery and occupation, prescription, and accretion. *Discovery* of unclaimed land confers only an inchoate (vague) claim that must be followed by occupation, or effective control, to constitute valid title. *Prescription* involves abandonment of a claim of territory by failure to protest occupation by another State, and *accretion* refers to the accumulation of new land from the sea or change in watercourse boundaries.

The modes of acquisition of territory include not only the **original title** mode just mentioned but also **derivative title,** acquired by cession (voluntary or forcible) and conquest. Cession is usually based on a treaty. Consequently, it is a formal procedure for changing sovereignty over territory, in contrast to forcible annexation without formalization by treaty. Cession can be effected by purchase, exchange, a gift or dowry, voluntary merger, or other voluntary manner, or it can be a result of use of force against the State ceding the territory. Conquest is the acquisition of territory through force, occupation, and annexation. If all the territory of a defeated nation is annexed, then it is called *subjugation.* If only a part of the State is annexed,

Terra nullius: *Territory capable of being legally owned but owned by no State.*

Original title: *A claim to sovereignty over territory that has not previously been claimed by any State.*

Derivative title: *Title acquired from a previous owner by cession, conquest, or both.*

then forcible cession of territory has taken place. Forcible annexation, or subjugation, of territory by States is prohibited by the U.N. Charter and by the Kellogg-Briand Pact of 1928 that preceded it. However, disputed claims of territory may go back to periods when international law recognized acquisition of territory by conquest.

Res communis refers to community property belonging to all States and that must remain available for all to use. Such community property is incapable of ownership or control. The clearest examples of *res communis* are the high seas and outer space. We have already discussed some of the history of these concepts in previous chapters. However, it is important to note that modern technology has made exploitation of the resources of even the most remote areas of this planet a possibility, and even outer space may present similar opportunities. International lawmaking treaties on these subjects have anticipated the future potential for conflict involving the areas of *res communis* that will be discussed in this chapter.

> **Res communis:**
> Community property belonging to all States and incapable of being under State ownership or control.

The use of the basic principles of territorial acquisition will be illustrated in the following cases. They provide illustrations of the opinions of international tribunals in a sequence that demonstrates the changing nature of international law. The circumstances of each case must be taken into consideration as well as the time element of the specific claim.

As a result of the Spanish-American War of 1898, Spain was forced into cession of the Philippines. After taking possession of the various islands comprising the Philippine archipelago, the United States discovered a Dutch presence on the Island of Palmas (situated midway between the Philippines and the Dutch East Indies), which had been included in the Spanish transfer of title. The Dutch contended that they had exercised sovereignty over the island since the latter part of the seventeenth century without Spanish protest and that the Spanish claim was nullified by abandonment, since discovery was not followed by continued and effective display of State authority, namely occupation. The two countries accepted a Swiss jurist, Max Huber, as the sole arbitrator in this dispute.

■   ■   ■

Island of Palmas Case (United States v. The Netherlands)
Permanent Court of Arbitration, 1928.
2 U.N.Rap.Int'l Arb.Awards 829.

[The Island of Palmas (also known as Miangas) is an isolated island of less than two square miles in area, lying about half way between Mindanao in the Philippine Islands and the most northerly of the Nanusa group in the former Dutch East Indies. It lies within the boundaries of the Philippines as ceded by Spain to the United States in 1898 (by the Treaty of Paris). U.S. authorities learned in 1906 that the island was considered by The Netherlands to form a part of the Dutch possessions in that part of the world. After diplomatic correspondence, the United States and the Netherlands agreed in 1925 to submit to a member of the Permanent Court of Arbitration the question "whether the Island of Palmas (or Miangas) in its entirety forms a part of territory belonging to the United States of America or of Netherlands territory."]

HUBER, Arbitrator:

. . . The United States, as successor to the rights of Spain over the Philippines, bases its title in the first place on discovery.

The Netherlands Government's main argument endeavours to show that the Netherlands, represented for this purpose in the first period of colonization by the East India Company, have possessed and exercised rights of sovereignty from 1677, or probably from a date prior even to 1648, to the present day. . . .

* * *

Titles of acquisition of territorial sovereignty in present-day international law are either based on an act of effective apprehension, such as occupation or conquest, or, like cession, presuppose that the ceding and the cessionary Powers, or at least one of them, have the faculty of effectively disposing of the ceded territory. In the same way natural accretion can only be conceived of as an accretion to a portion of territory where there exists an actual sovereignty capable of extending to a spot which falls within its sphere of activity. It seems therefore natural that an element which is essential for the constitution of sovereignty should not be lacking in its continuation. So true is this, that practice, as well as doctrine, recognizes—though under different legal formulae and with certain differences as to the conditions required—that the continuous and peaceful display of territorial sovereignty (peaceful in relation to other States) is as good as a title. The growing insistence with which international law, ever since the middle of the 18th century, has demanded that the occupation shall be effective would be inconceivable, if effectiveness were required only for the act of acquisition and not equally for the maintenance of the right. If the effectiveness has above all been insisted on in regard to occupation, this is because the question rarely arises in connection with territories in which there is already an established order of things.

Territorial sovereignty, as has already been said, involves the exclusive right to display the activities of a State. This right has as corollary a duty: the obligation to protect within the territory the rights of other States, in particular their right to integrity and inviolability in peace and in war, together with the rights which each State may claim for its nationals in foreign territory. Without manifesting its territorial sovereignty in a manner corresponding to circumstances, the State cannot fulfill this duty. Territorial sovereignty cannot limit itself to its negative side, i.e. to excluding the activities of other States; for it serves to divide between nations the space upon which human activities are employed, in order to assure them at all points the minimum of protection of which international law is the guardian.

* * *

Manifestations of territorial sovereignty assume, it is true, different forms, according to conditions of time and place. Although continuous in principle, sovereignty cannot be exercised in fact at every moment on every point of a territory. The intermittence and discontinuity compatible with the maintenance of the right necessarily differ according as inhabited or uninhabited regions are involved, or regions enclosed within territories in which sovereignty is incontestably displayed or again regions accessible from, for instance, the high seas. . . .

It is admitted by both sides that international law underwent profound modifications between the end of the Middle-Ages and the end of the 19th century, as regards the rights of discovery and acquisition of uninhabited regions or regions inhabited by savages or semi-civilised peoples. Both Parties are also agreed that a juridical fact must be appreciated in the light of the law contemporary with it, and not of the law in force at the time when a dispute in regard to it arises or fails to be settled. The effect of discovery by Spain is therefore to be determined by the rules of international law in force in the first half of the 16th century.

* * *

If the view most favourable to the American arguments is adopted—with every reservation as to the soundness of such view—that is to say, if we consider as positive law at the period in question the rule that discovery as such, i.e. the mere fact of seeing land, without any act, even symbolical, of taking possession, involved *ipso jure* territorial sovereignty and not merely an "inchoate title," a *jus ad rem*, to be completed eventually by an actual and durable taking of possession within a reasonable time, the question arises whether sovereignty yet existed at the critical date, i.e. the moment of conclusion and coming into force of the Treaty of Paris.

As regards the question which of different legal systems prevailing at successive periods is to be applied in a particular case (the so-called intertemporal law), a distinction must be made between the creation of rights and the existence of rights. The same principle which subjects the act creative of a right to the law in force at the time the right arises, demands that the existence of the right, in other words its continued manifestation, shall follow the conditions required by the evolution of law. International law in the 19th century, having regard to the fact that most parts of the globe were under the sovereignty of States members of the community of nations, and that territories without a master had become relatively few, took account of a tendency already existing and especially developed since the middle of the 18th century, and laid down the principle that occupation, to constitute a claim to territorial sovereignty, must be effective, that is, offer certain guarantees to other States and their nationals. It seems therefore incompatible with this rule of positive law that there should be regions which are neither under the effective sovereignty of a State, nor without a master, but which are reserved for the exclusive influence of one State, in virtue solely of a title of acquisition which is no longer recognized by existing law, even if such a title ever conferred territorial sovereignty. For these reasons, discovery alone, without any subsequent act, cannot at the present time suffice to prove sovereignty over the Island of Palmas (or Miangas); and in so far as there is no sovereignty, the question of an abandonment properly speaking of sovereignty by one State in order that the sovereignty of another may take its place does not arise.

If on the other hand the view is adopted that discovery does not create a definitive title of sovereignty, but only an "inchoate" title, such a title exists, it is true without external manifestation. However, according to the view that has prevailed at any rate since the 19th century, an inchoate title of discovery must be completed within a reasonable period by the effective occupation of the region claimed to be discovered. This principle must be applied in the present case, for the reasons given above in regard to the rules determining which of successive legal systems is to be applied (the so-called intertemporal law). Now, no act of occupation nor, except as to a recent period, any exercise of sovereignty at Palmas by Spain has been alleged. But even admitting that the Spanish title still existed as inchoate in 1898 and must be considered as included in the cession under Article III of the Treaty of Paris, an inchoate title could not prevail over the continuous and peaceful display of authority by another State; for such display may prevail even over a prior, definitive title put forward by another State.

In the last place there remains to be considered *title arising out of contiguity*. Although States have in certain circumstances maintained that islands relatively close to their shores belonged to them in virtue of their geographical situation, it is impossible to show the existence of a rule of positive international law to the effect that islands situated outside territorial waters should belong to a State from the mere fact that its territory forms the *terra firma* (nearest continent or island of considerable size). . . .

The Netherlands' arguments contend that the East India Company established Dutch sovereignty over the Island of Palmas (or Miangas) as early as the 17th century, by means of conventions with the princes of Tabukan (Taboekan) and Taruna (Taroena), two native chieftains of the Island of Sangi (Groot Sangihe), the principal island of the Talautse Isles (Sangi Islands), and that sovereignty has been displayed during the past two centuries. . . .

The questions to be solved in the present case are the following:

Was the Island of Palmas (or Miangas) in 1898 a part of territory under Netherlands' sovereignty?

Did this sovereignty actually exist in 1898 in regard to Palmas (or Miangas) and are the facts proved which were alleged on this subject? . . .

. . . Since the contract of 1885 with Taruna and that of 1899 with Kandahar-Taruna comprise Palmas (or Miangas) within the territories of a native State under the suzerainty of the Netherlands and since it has been established that in 1906 on the said island a state of things existed showing at least certain traces of display of Netherlands sovereignty, it is now necessary to examine what is the nature of the facts invoked as proving such sovereignty, and to what periods such facts relate. This examination will show whether or not the Netherlands have displayed sovereignty over the Island of Palmas (or Miangas) in an effective continuous and peaceful manner at a period at which such exercise may have excluded the acquisition of sovereignty, or a title to such acquisition, by the United States of America. . . .

[After a detailed examination of the acts of the Dutch East India Company and the Netherlands State tending to establish a display of sovereignty over the Island of Palmas, the arbitrator continued:]

The claim of the United States to sovereignty over the Island of Palmas (or Miangas) is derived from Spain by way of cession under the Treaty of Paris. The latter Treaty, though it comprises the island in dispute within the limits of cession, and in spite of the absence of any reserves or protest by the Netherlands as to these limits, has not created in favour of the United States any title of sovereignty such as was not already vested in Spain. The essential point is therefore to decide whether Spain had sovereignty over Palmas (or Miangas) at the time of the coming into force of the Treaty of Paris. . . .

The acts of indirect or direct display of Netherlands sovereignty at Palmas (or Miangas), especially in the 18th and early 19th centuries are not numerous, and there are considerable gaps in the evidence of continuous display. But apart from the consideration that the manifestations of sovereignty over a small and distant island, inhabited only by natives, cannot be expected to be frequent, it is not necessary that the display of sovereignty should go back to a very far distant period. It may suffice that such display existed in 1898, and had already existed as continuous and peaceful before that date long enough to enable any Power who might have considered herself as possessing sovereignty over the island, or having a claim to sovereignty, to have, according to local conditions, a reasonable possibility for ascertaining the existence of a state of things contrary to her real or alleged rights.

It is not necessary that the display of sovereignty should be established as having begun at a precise epoch; it suffices that it had existed at the critical period preceding the year 1898. It is quite natural that the establishment of sovereignty may be the outcome of a slow evolution, of a progressive intensification of State control. This is particularly the case, if sovereignty is acquired by the establishment of the suzerainty of a colonial Power over a native State, and in regard to outlying possessions of such a vassal State.

Now the evidence relating to the period after the middle of the 19th century makes it clear that the Netherlands Indian Government considered the island distinctly as a part of its possessions and that, in the years immediately preceding 1898, an intensification of display of sovereignty took place.

Since the moment when the Spaniards in withdrawing from the Moluccas in 1666, made express reservations as to the maintenance of their sovereign rights, up to the contestation made by the United States in 1906, no contestation or other action whatever or protest against the exercise of territorial rights by the Netherlands over the Talautse (Sangi) Isles and their dependencies (Miangas included) has been recorded. The peaceful character of the display of Netherlands sovereignty for the entire period to which the evidence concerning acts of display relates (1700-1906) must be admitted. . . .

The conditions of acquisition of sovereignty by the Netherlands are therefore to be considered as fulfilled. It remains now to be seen whether the United States as successors of Spain are in a position to bring forward an equivalent or stronger title. This is to be answered in the negative.

The title of discovery, if it had not been already disposed of by the Treaties of Muenster and Utrecht would, under the most favourable and most extensive interpretation, exist only as an inchoate title, as a claim to establish sovereignty by effective occupation. An inchoate title however cannot prevail over a definite title founded on continuous and peaceful display of sovereignty.

The title of contiguity, understood as a basis of territorial sovereignty, has not foundation in international law. . . .

The Netherlands title of sovereignty, acquired by continuous and peaceful display of State authority during a long period of time going probably back beyond the year 1700, therefore holds good. . . .

Discussion Questions

1. How was prescription used by Judge Huber to decide the dispute in this case?

2. What is the significance of the rule of "intertemporal law" as expressed by the arbitrator in this case? Must good title depend on the law at the time of acquisition? Why or why not?

3. Does the law expounded in 1928 concerning a dispute arising in 1898, before the most significant changes in modern international law, still have relevance today? Discuss the Western European nature of these nineteenth-century rules of acquisition of territory.

Comment: Some scholars dispute the acquisition of territory by prescription. There is no set time rule concerning the length of time that occupation without protest becomes a basis of title. However, in contrast to the two-hundred-year claim of the Netherlands in the *Palmas Island* case, the ICJ awarded the area surrounding a sacred temple on the Siamese-Cambodian border to Cambodia on the basis of a sixty-year occupation without protest from Thailand (see *Case Concerning the Temple of Preah Vihear*, 1962, I.C.J. Rep. 6).

In another case, this time before the Permanent Court of International Justice in 1933, two countries that were once united under the same monarch were in dispute over the very different geographic and climatic area of Eastern Greenland. After a proclamation that Norway had placed portions of Eastern Greenland under Norwegian sovereignty in 1931, Denmark brought this action under the compulsory jurisdiction (optional clause) of the Court's Statute to which both States had adhered. Denmark founded its title on the same principle used to support the Palmas Island decision.

■   ■   ■

Legal Status of Eastern Greenland Case (Denmark v. Norway)

Permanent Court of International Justice, 1933.
P.C.I.J., Ser. A/B, No. 53, 3 Hudson, World Ct.Rep. 148.

[A Norwegian proclamation of 1931 purported to place portions of Eastern Greenland under Norwegian sovereignty, on the theory that the territory was *terra nullius*, rather than Danish territory. Denmark thereupon instituted proceedings against Norway in the Permanent Court of International Justice, both states being bound by the "optional clause" of the Court's Statute, asking that the Court declare the Norwegian decree invalid.

The Court first discussed the history of Greenland, as well as the history of the Danish and Norwegian monarchies, noting that the crowns of the two countries had been united from 1380 to 1814 AD. By the Treaty of Kiel of 1814, the King of Denmark ceded to Sweden the Kingdom of Norway, excluding, however, his rights in Greenland and other territories.]

[The Court's Opinion:]

* * *

The first Danish argument is that the Norwegian occupation of part of the East coast of Greenland is invalid because Denmark has claimed and exercised sovereign rights over Greenland as a whole for a long time and has obtained thereby a valid title to sovereignty. The date at which such Danish sovereignty must have existed in order to render the Norwegian occupation invalid is the date at which the occupation took place, viz., July 10th, 1931.

The Danish claim is not founded upon any particular act of occupation but alleges—to use the phrase employed in the Palmas Island decision of the Permanent Court of Arbitration, April 4th, 1928—a title "founded on the peaceful and continuous display of State authority over the island." It is based upon the view that Denmark now enjoys all the rights which the King of Denmark and Norway enjoyed over Greenland up till 1814. Both the existence and the extent of these rights must therefore be considered, as well as the Danish claim to sovereignty since that date.

It must be borne in mind, however, that as the critical date is July 10th, 1931, it is not necessary that sovereignty over Greenland should have existed throughout the period during which the Danish Government maintains that it was in being. Even if the material submitted to the Court might be thought insufficient to establish the existence of that sovereignty during the earlier periods, this would not exclude a finding that it is sufficient to establish a valid title in the period immediately preceding the occupation.

Before proceeding to consider in detail the evidence submitted to the Court, it may be well to state that a claim to sovereignty based not upon some particular act or title such as a treaty of cession but merely upon continued display of authority, involves two elements each of which must be shown to exist: the intention and will to act as sovereign, and some actual exercise or display of such authority.

Another circumstance which must be taken into account by any tribunal which has to adjudicate upon a claim to sovereignty over a particular territory, is the extent to which the sovereignty is also claimed by some other Power. In most of the cases involving claims to territorial sovereignty which have come before an international tribunal, there have been two competing claims to the sovereignty, and the tribunal has had to decide which of the two is the stronger. One of the peculiar features of the present case is that up to 1931 there was no claim by any Power other than Denmark to the sovereignty over Greenland. Indeed, up till 1921, no Power disputed the Danish claim to sovereignty.

It is impossible to read the records of the decisions in cases as to territorial sovereignty without observing that in many cases the tribunal has been satisfied with very little in the way of the actual exercise of sovereign rights, provided that the other State could not make out a superior claim. This is particularly true in the case of claims to sovereignty over areas in thinly populated or unsettled countries.

[The Court described the establishment of Nordic colonies in Greenland as early as the 10th century, and acknowledgments by these colonies of the sovereignty of the King of Norway. It then held that, although the original colonies disappeared at an early date, there was no abandonment by the King of his rights in Greenland. The Court then noted that a reawakening of interest in Greenland during the 18th century led to the reestablishment of colonies in 1721, and that thereafter there was "a manifestation and exercise of sovereign rights." The Court rejected Norway's contention that in the legislative and administrative acts of the 18th century the term "Greenland" was not used in the geographic sense but only in reference to the colonized areas of western Greenland. As evidence supporting this conclusion, the Court relied on Danish treaties in which the other contracting party had agreed to the exclusion of Greenland from the scope of the treaty: this showed, said the Court, "a willingness on the part of the States with which Denmark has contracted to admit her right to exclude Greenland. . . . To the extent that these treaties constitute evidence of recognition of her sovereignty over Greenland in general, Denmark is entitled to rely upon them." After discussing Danish activity in Greenland from 1814 to 1915, the Court summarized:]

In view of the above facts, when taken in conjunction with the legislation she had enacted applicable to Greenland generally, the numerous treaties in which Denmark, with the concurrence of the other contracting Party, provided for the non-application of the treaty to Greenland in general, and the absence of all claim to sovereignty over Greenland by any other Power, Denmark must be regarded as having displayed during this period of 1814 to 1915 her authority over the uncolonized part of the country to a degree sufficient to confer a valid title to the sovereignty.

[The Court then discussed the effect of various communications which Denmark had addressed to other states between 1915 and 1921, asking recognition of Denmark's rights in Greenland, and rejected the Norwegian contentions that Denmark thereby admitted that it possessed no sovereignty over uncolonized parts of Greenland and that it was "estopped" from claiming a long-established sovereignty over the whole island.]

The period subsequent to the date when the Danish Government issued the Decree of May 10th, 1921, referred to above, witnessed a considerable increase in the activity of the Danish Government on the eastern coast of Greenland. . . .

Even if the period from 1921 to July 10th, 1931, is taken by itself and without reference to the preceding periods, the conclusion reached by the Court is that during this time Denmark regarded herself as possessing sovereignty over all Greenland and displayed and exercised her sovereign rights to an extent sufficient to constitute a valid title to sovereignty. When considered in conjunction with the facts of the preceding periods, the case in favour of Denmark is confirmed and strengthened.

It follows from the above that the Court is satisfied that Denmark has succeeded in establishing her contention: that at the critical date, namely, July 10th, 1931, she possessed a valid title to the sovereignty over all Greenland.

This finding constitutes by itself sufficient reason for holding that the occupation of July 10th, 1931, and any steps taken in this connection by the Norwegian Government, were illegal and invalid.

[The Court also held, as separate and independent grounds for its conclusion, that: (1) Norway had "debarred herself from contesting Danish sovereignty over the whole of Greenland" by becoming a party to various bilateral and multilateral agreements in which Greenland had been described as Danish or in which Denmark had excluded Greenland from the operation of the agreement, and (2) Norway had given express undertakings to the Danish government by which it promised not to contest Danish sovereignty over the whole of Greenland.]

Discussion Questions

1. How is prescription used by the Permanent Court of International Justice to decide this case?
2. Is the interest in the exploitation of fishery resources more important to the protagonists in this dispute than control over territory and population?
3. How does the situation in Eastern Greenland, as described by the Court, differ from the conditions present in the *Palmas Island* case? If Spain had protested Dutch sovereignty over the Palmas Islands would it have affected the outcome of that decision?
4. Why must the court use a balancing test in such disputes to determine by the weight of the evidence which State has the stronger claim?

After the significant developments of the establishment of the U.N. Charter, the passage of the 1970 Friendly Relations Declaration 2625 (XXV), and coming into force of various human rights covenants, a dispute arose over the status of the territory known as Western Sahara.

The legal controversy addressed in this advisory opinion is essentially between Spain and Morocco. The dispute began in the General Assembly where it had lingered from 1966 to 1974. Western Sahara has had little contact with Western colonialism. However, in 1884 Spain proclaimed a protectorate over the coast. Beginning in 1912, the territory was a Spanish protectorate. In 1958, Spain declared it a Spanish province called Spanish Sahara. Both Mauritania and Morocco acknowledged the applicability of the principle of self-determination, but neither country abandoned their respective claims to Western Sahara. This particular phase of the controversy became evident when Morocco directly presented its legal claim to Spanish authorities in 1974.

In 1975 the General Assembly requested this advisory opinion from the ICJ. The members of the assembly hoped to advance the right of Western Sahara's peoples to self-determination. The General Assembly had previously resolved that the inhabitants possessed a right to self-determination, specifically finding that there should be a referendum conducted so that they could vote to determine the status of Western Sahara.

The general right to self-determination was being prevented by the maintenance of the colonial status of Western Sahara. After Mauritania became a member of the United Nations in 1960, it claimed Western Sahara as a part of its national territory. In 1975, when this case was decided, Mauritania was prepared to acquiesce to the will of the peoples of Western Sahara. It did not wish to confront Spain with a direct legal claim, but Morocco did.

Spain's position in this matter before the U.N. General Assembly was that a judicial decision was unnecessary and impractical. Before the ICJ, the issue raised by Spain was that the Court should decline to render an opinion on this matter because it would circumvent the principle that jurisdiction to settle a territorial dispute requires the consent of the parties. This is a very significant issue and one that the Court dealt with in the first part of the opinion.

Since the matter was not subject to compulsory jurisdiction, the possibility of submitting this case to the Court was the only other alternative for the General Assembly "in order to guide the United Nations towards a final solution of the problem of Western Sahara" (from the General Assembly's request for an advisory opinion). The disclosed purpose of the opinion was to provide guidance to the General Assembly. The real purpose was to provide an authoritative analysis to demonstrate the absence of any genuine legal claim that could hinder the right of the Western Sahara inhabitants to self-determination. The ICJ's opinion nevertheless defined and confirmed the parameters of self-determination as it exists since the decolonization of the rest of Africa.

The court's narrow task was to determine the presence of any legal claims to this territory by the various nations involved. These claims would interfere with the inhabitants' right to exercise their right of self-determination.

▌　　　　　　▌　　　　　　▌

Western Sahara
International Court of Justice, Advisory Opinion, 1975.

[The Court first considers two important preliminary issues before addressing the specific questions for which the General Assembly has requested an advisory opinion. The first concerns the objections of Spain to the General Assembly's request.]

The Court:

* * *

25. Spain has made a number of observations relating to the lack of its consent to the proceedings, which, it considers, should lead the Court to decline to give an opinion. These observations may be summarized as follows:

(a) In the present case the advisory jurisdiction is being used to circumvent the principle that jurisdiction to settle a dispute requires the consent of the parties.

(b) The questions, as formulated, raise issues concerning the attribution of territorial sovereignty over Western Sahara.

(c) The Court does not possess the necessary information concerning the relevant facts to enable it to pronounce judicially on the questions submitted to it.

26. The first of the above observations is based on the fact that on 23 September 1974 the Minister for Foreign Affairs of Morocco addressed a communication to the Minister for Foreign Affairs of Spain recalling the terms of a statement by which His Majesty King Hassan II had on 17 September 1974 proposed the joint submission to the ICJ of an issue expressed in the following terms:

"You, the Spanish Government, claim that the Sahara was *res nullius*. You claim that it was a territory or property left uninherited, you claim that no power and no administration had been established over the

Sahara: Morocco claims the contrary. Let us request the arbitration of the International Court of Justice at The Hague. . . . It will state the law on the basis of the titles submitted."

Spain has stated before the Court that it did not consent and does not consent now to the submission of this issue to the jurisdiction of the Court.

27. Spain considers that the subject of the dispute which Morocco invited it to submit jointly to the Court for decision in contentious proceedings, and the subject of the questions on which the advisory opinion is requested, are substantially identical; thus the advisory procedure is said to have been used as an alternative after the failure of an attempt to make use of the contentious jurisdiction with regard to the same question. Consequently, to give a reply would, according to Spain, be to allow the advisory procedure to be used as a means of bypassing the consent of a State, which constitutes the basis of the Court's jurisdiction. If the Court were to countenance such a use of its advisory jurisdiction, the outcome would be to obliterate the distinction between the two spheres of the Court's jurisdiction, and the fundamental principle of the independence of States would be affected, for States would find their disputes with other States being submitted to the Court, by this indirect means, without their consent; this might result in compulsory jurisdiction being achieved by majority vote in a political organ. Such circumvention of the well established Principle of consent for the exercise of international jurisdiction would constitute, according to this view, a compelling reason for declining to answer the request.

28. In support of these propositions Spain has invoked the fundamental rule, repeatedly reaffirmed in the Court's jurisprudence, that a State cannot, without its consent, be compelled to submit its disputes with other States to the Court's adjudication. It has relied, in particular, on the application of this rule to the advisory jurisdiction by the Permanent Court of International Justice in the *Status of Eastern Carelia* case (P.C.I.J., Series B, No. 5), maintaining that the essential principle enunciated in that case is not modified by the decisions of the present Court in the cases concerning the Interpretation of Peace Treaties with Bulgaria, Hungary and Romania, First Phase (I.C.J. Reports 1950, p. 65) and the Legal Consequences for States of the Continued Presence of South Africa in Namibia (South West Africa) notwithstanding Security Council Resolution 276 (1970) (I.C.J. Reports 1971, p. 16). Morocco and Mauritania, on the other hand, have maintained that the present case falls within the principles applied in those two decisions and that the *ratio decidendi* of the *Status of Eastern Carelia* case is not applicable to it.

* * *

31. In the proceedings concerning the Interpretation of Peace Treaties with Bulgaria, Hungary and Romania, First Phase, this Court had to consider how far the views expressed by the Permanent Court in the *Status of Eastern Carelia* case were still pertinent in relation to the applicable provisions of the Charter of the United Nations and the Statute of the Court. It stated, *inter alia:*

"This objection reveals a confusion between the principles governing contentious procedure and those which are applicable to Advisory Opinions.

"The consent of States, parties to a dispute, is the basis of the Court's jurisdiction in contentious cases. The situation is different in regard to advisory proceedings even where the Request for an Opinion relates to a legal question actually pending between States. The Court's reply is only of an advisory character: as such it has no binding force. It follows that no State, whether a Member of the United Nations or not, can prevent the giving of an Advisory Opinion which the United Nations considers to be desirable in order to obtain enlightenment as to the course of action it should take. The Court's Opinion is given not to the States, but to the organ which is entitled to request it; the reply of the Court, itself an 'organ of the United Nations', represents its participation in the activities of the organization, and, in principle, should not be refused." (I.C.J. Reports 1956, p. 71)

32. The Court, it is true, affirmed in this pronouncement that its competence to give an opinion did not depend on the consent of the interested States, even when the case concerned a legal question actually pending between them. However, the Court proceeded not merely to stress its judicial character and the permissive nature of Article 65, paragraph 1, of the Statute but to examine, specifically in relation to the opposition of some of the interested States, the question of the judicial propriety of giving the opinion. Moreover, the Court emphasized the circumstances differentiating the case then under consideration from the *Status of Eastern Carelia* case and explained the particular

grounds which led it to conclude that there was no reason requiring the Court to refuse to reply to the request. Thus the Court recognized that lack of consent might constitute a ground for declining to give the opinion requested if, in the circumstances of a given case, considerations of judicial propriety should oblige the Court to refuse an opinion. In short, the consent of an interested State continues to be relevant, not for the Court's competence, but for the appreciation of the propriety of giving an opinion.

33. In certain circumstances, therefore, the lack of consent of an interested State may render the giving of an advisory opinion incompatible with the Court's judicial character. An instance of this would be when the circumstances disclose that to give a reply would have the effect of circumventing the principle that a State is not obliged to allow its disputes to be submitted to judicial settlement without its consent. If such a situation should arise, the powers of the Court under the discretion given to it by Article 65, paragraph 1, of the Statute, would afford sufficient legal means to ensure respect for the fundamental principle of consent to jurisdiction.

* * *

39. The above considerations are pertinent for a determination of the object of the present request. The object of the General Assembly has not been to bring before the Court, by way of a request for advisory opinion, a dispute or legal controversy, in order that it may later, on the basis of the Court's opinion, exercise its powers and functions for the peaceful settlement of that dispute or controversy. The object of the request is an entirely different one: to obtain from the Court an opinion which the General Assembly deems of assistance to it for the proper exercise of its functions concerning the decolonization of the territory.

40. The General Assembly, as appears from paragraph 3 of resolution 3292 (XXIX), has asked the Court for an opinion so as to be in a position to decide "on the policy to be followed in order to accelerate the decolonization process in the territory . . . in the best possible conditions, in the light of the advisory opinion. . . ." The true object of the request is also stressed in the preamble of resolution 3292 (XXIX), where it is stated "that it is highly desirable that the General Assembly, in order to continue the discussion of this question at its thirtieth session, should receive an advisory opinion on some important legal aspects of the problem."

* * *

42. Furthermore, the origin and scope of the dispute, as above described, are important in appreciating, from the point of view of the exercise of the Court's discretion, the real significance in this case of the lack of Spain's consent. The issue between Morocco and Spain regarding Western Sahara is not one as to the legal status of the territory today, but one as to the rights of Morocco over it at the time of colonization. The settlement of this issue will not affect the rights of Spain today as the administering Power, but will assist the General Assembly in deciding on the policy to be followed in order to accelerate the decolonization process in the territory. It follows that the legal position of the State which has refused its consent to the present proceedings is not "in any way compromised by the answers that the Court may give to the questions put to it" (Interpretation of Peace Treaties with Bulgaria, Hungary and Romania. First Phase, I.C.J. Reports 1950, p. 72).

43. A second way in which Spain has put the objection of lack of its consent is to maintain that the dispute is a territorial one and that the consent of a State to adjudication of a dispute concerning the attribution of territorial sovereignty is always necessary. The questions in the request do not however relate to a territorial dispute, in the proper sense of the term, between the interested States. They do not put Spain's present position as the administering Power of the territory in issue before the Court: resolution 3292 (XXIX) itself recognizes the current legal status of Spain as administering Power. Nor is in issue before the Court the validity of the titles which led to Spain's becoming the administering Power of the territory, and this was recognized in the oral proceedings. The Court finds that the request for an opinion does not call for adjudication upon existing territorial rights or sovereignty over territory. Nor does the Court's Order of 22 May 1975 convey any implication that the present case relates to a claim of a territorial nature.

44. A third way in which Spain, in its written statement, has presented its opposition to the Court's pronouncing upon the questions posed in the request is to maintain that in this case the Court cannot fulfil the requirements of good administration of justice as regards the determination of the facts. The attribution of territorial sovereignty, it argues, usually centres on material acts involving the exercise of that sovereignty, and the consideration of such acts and of the respective titles inevitably involves an exhaustive determination of facts. In advisory proceedings

there are properly speaking no parties obliged to furnish the necessary evidence, and the ordinary rules concerning the burden of proof can hardly be applied. That being so, according to Spain, the Court should refrain from replying in the absence of facts which are undisputed, since it would not be in possession of sufficient information such as would be available in adversary proceedings.

45. Considerations of this kind played a role in the case concerning the *Status of Eastern Carelia*. In that instance, the non-participation of a State concerned in the case was a secondary reason for the refusal to answer. The Permanent Court of International Justice noted the difficulty of making an enquiry into facts concerning the main point of a controversy when one of the parties thereto refused to take part in the proceedings.

46. Although in that case the refusal of one State to take part in the proceedings was the cause of the inadequacy of the evidence, it was the actual lack of "materials sufficient to enable it to arrive at any judicial conclusion upon the question of fact" (P.C.I.J., Series B, No. 5, p. 28) which was considered by the Permanent Court, for reasons of judicial propriety, to prevent it from giving an opinion. Consequently, the issue is whether the Court has before it sufficient information and evidence to enable it to arrive at a judicial conclusion upon any disputed questions of fact the determination of which is necessary for it to give an opinion in conditions compatible with its judicial character.

47. The situation in the present case is entirely different from that with which the Permanent Court was confronted in the *Status of Eastern Carelia* case. Mauritania, Morocco and Spain have furnished very extensive documentary evidence of the facts which they considered relevant to the Court's examination of the questions posed in the request, and each of these countries, as well as Algeria and Zaire, have presented their views on these facts and on the observations of the others. The Secretary-General has also furnished a dossier of documents concerning the discussion of the question of Western Sahara in the competent United Nations organs. The Court therefore considers that the information and evidence before it are sufficient to enable it to arrive at a judicial conclusion concerning the facts which are relevant to its opinion and necessary for replying to the two questions posed in the request.

* * *

[The Court's opinion concerning self-determination follows.]

52. Extensive argument and divergent views have been presented to the Court as to how, and in what form, the principles of decolonization apply in this instance, in the light of the various General Assembly resolutions on decolonization in general and on decolonization of the territory of Western Sahara in particular.

* * *

55. The principle of self-determination as a right of peoples, and its application for the purpose of bringing all colonial situations to a speedy end, were enunciated in the Declaration on the Granting of Independence to Colonial Countries and Peoples, General Assembly resolution 1514 (XV). In this resolution the General Assembly proclaims the necessity of bringing to a speedy and unconditional end colonialism in all its forms and manifestations. . . . To this end the resolution provides *inter alia:*

* * *

2. All peoples have the right to self-determination; by virtue of that right they freely determine their political status and freely pursue their economic, social and cultural development.

* * *

5. Immediate steps shall be taken, in Trust and Non-Self-Governing Territories or all other territories which have not yet attained independence, to transfer all powers to the peoples of those territories, without any conditions or reservations, in accordance with: their freely expressed will and desire, without any distinction as to race, creed or colour, in order to enable them to enjoy complete independence and freedom.

The above provisions, in particular paragraph 2, thus confirm and emphasize that the application of the right of self-determination requires a free and genuine expression of the will of the peoples concerned.

* * *

57. General Assembly resolution 1514 (XV) provided the basis for the process of decolonization which has resulted since 1960 in the creation of many States which are today Members of the United Nations. It is complemented in certain of its aspects by General Assembly resolution 1541 (XV), which has been invoked in the present proceedings. The latter resolution contemplates for non-self-governing territories more than one possibility, namely:

    (a) emergence as a sovereign independent State;

    (b) free association with an independent State;

        or

    (c) integration with an independent State.

At the same time, certain of its provisions give effect to the essential feature of the right of self-determination as established in resolution 1514 (XV). Thus principle VII of resolution 1541 (XV) declares that: 'Free association should be the result of a free and voluntary choice by the peoples of the territory concerned expressed through informed and democratic processes.' Again, principle IX of resolution 1541 (XV) declares [in part] that:

* * *

    (b) The integration should be the result of the freely expressed wishes of the territory's peoples acting with full knowledge of the change in their status, their wishes having been expressed through informed and democratic processes, impartially conducted and based on universal adult suffrage. The United Nations could, when it deems it necessary, supervise these processes.

58. General Assembly resolution 2625 (XXV), 'Declaration on Principles of International Law concerning Friendly Relations and Co-operation among States in accordance with the Charter of the United Nations,'—to which reference was also made in the proceedings—mentions other possibilities besides independence, association or integration. But in doing so it reiterates the basic need to take account of the wishes of the people concerned:

The establishment of a sovereign and independent State, the free association or integration with an independent State or the emergence into any other political status freely determined by a people constitute modes of implementing the right of self-determination by that people.

Resolution 2625 (XXV) further provides that:

Every State has the duty to promote, through joint and separate action, realization of the principle of equal rights and self-determination of peoples in accordance with the provisions of the Charter, and to render assistance to the United Nations in carrying out the responsibilities entrusted to it by the Charter regarding the implementation of the principle.

* * *

60. Having set out the basic principles governing the decolonization policy of the General Assembly, the Court now turns to those resolutions which bear specifically on the decolonization of Western Sahara. . . . In particular it is pertinent to compare the different ways in which the General Assembly resolutions adopted from 1966 to 1969 dealt with the questions of . . . Western Sahara.

61. In 1966, in the Special Committee on the Situation With Regard to the Implementation of the Declaration on the Granting of Independence to Colonial Countries and Peoples, Spain expressed itself in favour of the decolonization of Western Sahara through the exercise by the population of the territory of their right to self-determination. At that time this suggestion received the support of Mauritania and the assent of Morocco.

* * *

In the case of Western Sahara, the resolution:

* * *

4. Invites the administering Power to determine at the earliest possible date, in conformity with the aspirations of the indigenous people of Spanish Sahara and in consultation with the Governments of Mauritania and Morocco and any other interested party, the procedures for the holding of a referendum under United Nations auspices with a view to enabling the indigenous population of the Territory to exercise freely its right to self-determination. . . .

In respect of this territory the resolution also set out conditions designed to ensure the free expression of the will of the people, including the provision by the administering Power of facilities to a United Nations mission so that it may be able to participate actively in the organization and holding of the referendum.

* * *

64. In subsequent years [after 1966], the General Assembly maintained its approach to the question of Western Sahara, and reiterated in more pressing terms the need to consult the wishes of the people of the territory as to their political future. Indeed resolution 2983 (XXVII) of 1972 expressly reaffirms the responsibility of the United Nations in all consultations intended to lead to the free expression of the wishes of the people. Resolution 3162 (XXVIII) of 1973, while deploring the fact that the United Nations mission whose active participation in the organization and holding of the referendum had been recommended since 1966 had not yet been able to visit the territory, reaffirms the General Assembly's:

attachment to the principle of self-determination and its concern to see that principle applied with a framework that will guarantee the inhabitants of the Sahara under Spanish domination free and authentic expression of their wishes, in accordance with the relevant United Nations resolutions on the subject.

65. All these resolutions from 1966 to 1973 were adopted in the face of reminders by Morocco and Mauritania of their respective claims that Western Sahara constituted an integral part of their territory. At the same time Morocco and Mauritania assented to the holding of a referendum. These States, among others, alleging that the recommendations of the General Assembly were being disregarded by Spain, emphasized the need for the referendum to be held in satisfactory conditions and under the supervision of the United Nations.

* * *

70. In short, the decolonization process to be accelerated which is envisaged by the General Assembly in this provision is one which will respect the right of the population of Western Sahara to determine their future political status by their own freely expressed will. This right is not affected by the present request for an advisory opinion, nor by resolution 3292 (XXIX); on the contrary, it is expressly reaffirmed in that resolution. The right of that population to self-determination constitutes therefore a basic assumption of the questions put to the Court.

71. . . . The right of self-determination leaves the General Assembly a measure of discretion with respect to the forms and procedures by which that right is to be realized.

[After having considered the preliminary questions the Court proceeded to deal with the specific opinions requested by the General Assembly.]

75. Having established that it is seised of a request for advisory opinion which it is competent to entertain and that it should comply with that request, the Court will now examine the two questions which have been referred to it by General Assembly resolution 3292 (XXIX). These questions are so formulated that an answer to the second is called for only if the answer to the first is in the negative:

"I. Was Western Sahara (Rio de Oro, and Sakiet El Hamra) at the time of colonization by Spain a territory belonging to no one *(terra nullius)*?

"If the answer to the first question is in the negative,

"II. What were the legal ties between this territory and the Kingdom of Morocco and the Mauritanian entity?"

* * *

77. In the view of the Court, for the purposes of the present Opinion. "the time of colonization by Spain" may be considered as the period beginning in 1884, when Spain proclaimed a protectorate over the Rio de Ore.

* * *

79. Turning to Question I, the Court observes that the request specifically locates the question in the context of "the time of colonization by Spain," and it therefore seems clear that the words "Was Western Sahara . . . a territory belonging to no one (*terra nullius*)?" have to be interpreted by reference to the law in force at that period. The expression *"terra nullius"* was a legal term of art employed in connection with "occupation" as one of the accepted legal methods of acquiring sovereignty over territory. "Occupation" being legally an original means of peaceably acquiring sovereignty over territory otherwise than by cession or succession, it was a cardinal condition of a valid "occupation" that the territory should be *terra nullius*—a territory belonging to no-one—at the time of the act alleged to constitute the "occupation" (cf. Legal Status of Eastern Greenland, P.C.I.J. Series A/B, No. 53, pp. 44 f. and 63 f.). In the view of the Court, therefore, a determination that Western Sahara was a "terra nullius" at the time of colonization by Spain would be possible only if it were established that at that time the territory belonged to no-one in the sense that it was then open to acquisition through the legal process of "occupation."

80. Whatever differences of opinion there may have been among jurists, the State practice of the relevant Period indicates that territories inhabited by tribes or peoples having a social and political organization were not regarded as *terra nullius*. It shows that in the case of such territories the acquisition of sovereignty was not generally considered as effected unilaterally through "occupation" of *terra nullius* by original title but through agreements concluded with local rulers. On occasion, it is true, the word "occupation" was used in a non-technical sense denoting simply acquisition of sovereignty; but that did not signify that the acquisition of sovereignty through such agreements with authorities of the country was regarded as an "occupation" of a *"terra nullius"* in the proper sense of these terms. On the contrary, such agreements with local rulers, whether or not considered as an actual "cession" of the territory, were regarded as derivative roots of title, and not original titles obtained by occupation of *terra nullius*.

81. In the present instance, the information furnished to the Court shows that at the time of colonization Western Sahara was inhabited by peoples which, if nomadic, were socially and politically organized in tribes and under chiefs competent to represent them.

82. Before the Court, differing views were expressed concerning the nature and legal value of agreements between a State and local chiefs. But the Court is not asked by Question I to pronounce upon the legal character or the legality of the titles which led to Spain becoming the administering Power of Western Sahara. It is asked only to state whether Western Sahara (Rio de Oro and Sakiet El Hamra) at the time of colonization by Spain was "a territory belonging to no one (*terra nullius*)." As to this question, the Court is satisfied that, for the reasons which it has given, its answer must be in the negative.

83. The Court's answer to Question I is, therefore, in the negative and, in accordance with the terms of the request, it will now turn to Question II.

84. Question II asks the Court to state "what were the legal ties between this territory"—that is, Western Sahara—"and the Kingdom of Morocco and the Mauritanian entity." The scope of this question depends upon the meaning to be attached to the expression "legal ties" in the context of the time of the colonization of the territory by Spain. That expression, however, unlike *"terra nullius"* in Question I, was not a term having in itself a very precise meaning. Accordingly, in the view of the Court, the meaning of the expression "legal ties" in Question II has to be found rather in the object and purpose of General Assembly resolution 3292 (XXIX), by which it was decided to request the present advisory opinion of the Court.

85. Analysis of this resolution, as the Court has already pointed out, shows that the two questions contained in the request have been put to the Court in the context of proceedings in the General Assembly directed to the decolonization of Western Sahara in conformity with resolution 1514 (XV) of 14 December 1960. During the discussion of this item, according to resolution 3292 (XXM), a legal controversy arose over the status of Western Sahara at the time of its colonization by Spain; and the records of the proceedings make it plain that the "legal controversy" in question concerned pretensions put forward, on the one hand, by Morocco that the territory was then a part of the Sherifian State and, on the other, by Mauritania that the territory then formed part of the Bilad Shinguitti or Mauritanian entity. Accordingly, it appears to the Court that in Question II the words "legal ties between this territory and the Kingdom of Morocco and the Mauritanian entity" must be understood as referring to such

"legal ties" as may affect the policy to be followed in the decolonization of Western Sahara. In this connection, the Court cannot accept the view that the legal ties the General Assembly had in mind in framing Question II were limited to ties established directly with the territory and without reference to the people who may be found in it. Such an interpretation would unduly restrict the scope of the question, since legal ties are normally established in relation to people.

86. The Court further observed that, inasmuch as Question II had its origin in the contentions of Morocco and Mauritania, it was for them to satisfy the Court in the present proceedings that legal ties existed between Western Sahara and the Kingdom of Morocco or the Mauritanian entity at the time of the colonization of the territory by Spain.

87. Western Sahara (Rio de Oro and Sakiet El Hamra) is a territory having very special characteristics which, at the time of colonization by Spain, largely determined the way of life and social and political organization of the peoples inhabiting it. In consequence, the legal regime of Western Sahara, including its legal relations with neighbouring territories, cannot properly be appreciated without reference to these special characteristics. The territory forms part of the great Sahara desert which extends from the Atlantic coast of Africa to Egypt and the Sudan. At the time of its colonization by Spain, the area of this desert with which the Court is concerned was being exploited, because of its low and spasmodic rainfall, almost exclusively by nomads, pasturing their animals or growing crops as and where conditions were favourable. It may be said that the territory, at the time of its colonization, had a sparse population that, for the most part, consisted of nomadic tribes the members of which traversed the desert on more or less regular routes dictated by the seasons and the wells or water-holes available to them. In general, the Court was informed, the right of pasture was enjoyed in common by these tribes; some areas suitable for cultivation, on the other hand, were subject to a greater degree to separate rights. Perennial water-holes were in principle considered the property of the tribe which put them into commission, though their use also was open to all, subject to certain customs as to priorities and the amount of water taken. Similarly, many tribes were said to have their recognized burial grounds, which constituted a rallying point for themselves and for allied tribes. Another feature of life in the region, according to the information before the Court, was that inter-tribal conflict was not infrequent.

88. These various points of attraction of a tribe to particular localities were reflected in its nomadic routes. But what is important for present purposes is the fact that the sparsity of the resources and the spasmodic character of the rainfall compelled all those nomadic tribes to traverse very wide areas of the desert. In consequence, the nomadic routes of none of them were confined to Western Sahara; some passed also through areas of southern Morocco, or of present-day Mauritania or Algeria, and some even through further countries. All the tribes were of the Islamic faith and the whole territory lay within the Dar al-Islam. In general, authority in the tribe was vested in a sheikh, subject to the assent of the "Juma'a," that is, of an assembly of its leading members, and the tribe had its own customary law applicable in conjunction with the Koranic law. Not infrequently one tribe had ties with another, either of dependence or of alliance, which were essentially tribal rather than territorial, ties of allegiance or vassalage.

89. It is in the context of such a territory and such a social and political organization of the population that the Court has to examine the question of the "legal ties" between Western Sahara and the Kingdom of Morocco and the Mauritanian entity at the time of colonization by Spain. At the conclusion of the oral proceedings, as will be seen, Morocco and Mauritania took up what was almost a common position on the answer to be given by the Court on Question II. The contentions on which they respectively base the legal ties which they claim to have had with Western Sahara at the time of its colonization by Spain are, however, different and in some degree opposed.

* * *

129. The inferences to be drawn from the information before the Court concerning internal acts of Moroccan sovereignty and from that concerning international acts are, therefore, in accord in not providing indications of the existence, at the relevant period, of any legal tie of territorial sovereignty between Western Sahara and the Moroccan State. At the same time, they are in accord in providing indications of a legal tie of allegiance between the Sultan of Morocco and some, though only some, of the tribes of the territory, and in providing indications of some display of the Sultan's authority or influence with respect to those tribes. Before attempting, however, to formulate more precisely its conclusions as to the answer to be given to Question II in the case of Morocco, the Court must examine the situation in the territory at the time of colonization in relation to the Mauritanian entity. This is so because the "legal ties" invoked by Mauritania overlap with those invoked by Morocco.

130. The Court will therefore now take up the question of what were the legal ties which existed between Western Sahara, at the time of its colonization by Spain, and the Mauritanian entity. As the very formulation of Question II implies, the position of the Islamic Republic of Mauritania in relation to Western Sahara at that date differs from that of Morocco for the reason that there was not then any Mauritanian State in existence. In the present proceedings Mauritania has expressly accepted that the "Mauritanian entity" did not then constitute a State; and also that the present statehood of Mauritania "is not retroactive." Consequently, it is clear that it is not legal ties of State sovereignty with which the Court is concerned in the case of the "Mauritanian entity" but other legal ties.

[After having summarized the contentions of Mauritania and Spain on this question, the Court continued:]

148. In the case concerning Reparation for Injuries Suffered in the Service of the United Nations, the Court observed: "The subjects of law in any legal system are not necessarily identical in their nature or in the extent of their rights, and their nature depends upon the needs of the community" (I.C.J. Reports 1949, p. 178). In examining the propositions of Mauritania regarding the legal nature of the Bilad Shinguitti or Mauritanian entity, the Court gives full weight both to that observation and to the special characteristics of the Saharan region and peoples with which the present proceedings are concerned. Some criterion has, however, to be employed to determine in any particular case whether what confronts the law is or is not legally an "entity." The Court, moreover, notes that in the *Reparation* case the criterion which it applied was to enquire whether the United Nations Organization—the entity involved—was in "such a position that it possesses, in regard to its Members, rights which it is entitled to ask them to respect" (ibid.). In that Opinion, no doubt, the criterion was applied in a somewhat special context. Nevertheless, it expresses the essential test where a group, whether composed of States, of tribes or of individuals, is claimed to be a legal entity distinct from its members.

149. In the present case, the information before the Court discloses that, at the time of the Spanish colonization, there existed many ties of a racial, linguistic, religious, cultural and economic nature between various tribes and emirates whose Peoples dwelt in the Saharan region which today is comprised within the Territory of Western Sahara and the Islamic Republic of Mauritania. It also discloses, however, the independence of the emirates and many of the tribes in relation to one another and, despite some forms of common activity, the absence among them of any common institutions or organs, even of a quite minimal character. Accordingly, the Court is unable to find that the information before it provides any basis for considering the emirates and tribes which existed in the region to have constituted, in another phrase used by the Court in the *Reparation* case, "an entity capable of availing itself of obligations incumbent upon its Members" (ibid.). Whether the Mauritanian entity is described as the Bilad Shinguitti, or as the Shinguitti "nation," as Maruritania suggests, or as some form of league or association, the difficulty remains that it did not have the character of a personality or corporate entity distinct from the several emirates and tribes which composed it. The proposition, therefore, that the Bilad Shinguitti should be considered as having been a Mauritanian "entity" enjoying some form of sovereignty in Western Sahara is not one that can be sustained.

150. ... The Court must conclude that at the time of colonization by Spain there did not exist between the territory of Western Sahara and the Mauritanian entity any tie of sovereignty, or of allegiance of tribes, or of "simple inclusion" in the same legal entity.

151. This conclusion does not, however, mean that the reply to Question II should necessarily be that at the time of colonization by Spain no legal ties at all existed between the territory of Western Sahara and the Mauritanian entity. The language employed by the General Assembly in Question II does not appear to the Court to confine the question exclusively to those legal ties which imply territorial sovereignty. On the contrary, the use of the expression "legal ties" in conjunction with "Mauritanian entity" indicates that Question II envisages the possibility of other ties of a legal character. To confine the question to ties of sovereignty would, moreover, be to ignore the special characteristics of the Saharan region and peoples to which reference has been made in paragraphs 87 and 88 above; and also to disregard the possible relevance of other legal ties to the various procedures concerned in the decolonization process.

152. The information before the Court makes it clear that the nomadism of the great majority of the peoples of Western Sahara at the time of its colonization gave rise to certain ties of a legal character between the tribes of the territory and those of neighbouring regions of the Bilad Shinguitti. The migration routes of almost all the nomadic tribes of Western Sahara, the Court was informed, crossed what were to become the colonial frontiers and traversed, *inter alia*, substantial areas of what is today the territory of the Islamic Republic of Mauritania. The tribes, in their

migrations, had grazing pastures, cultivated lands, and wells or water-holes in both territories, and their burial grounds in one or other territory. These basic elements of the nomads' way of life, as stated earlier in this Opinion, were in some measure the subject of tribal rights, and their use was in general regulated by customs. Furthermore, the relations between all the tribes of the region in such matters as inter-tribal clashes and the settlement of disputes were also governed by a body of inter-tribal custom. Before the time of Western Sahara's colonization by Spain, those legal ties neither had nor could have any other source than the usages of the tribes themselves or Koranic law. Accordingly, although the Bilad Shinguitti has not been shown to have existed as a legal entity, the nomadic peoples of the Shinguitti country should, in the view of the Court, be considered as having in the relevant period possessed rights, including some rights relating to the lands through which they migrated. These rights, the Court concludes, constituted legal ties between the territory of Western Sahara and the "Mauritanian entity," this expression being taken to denote the various tribes living in the territories of the Bilad Shinguitti which are now comprised within the Islamic Republic of Mauritania. They were ties which knew no frontier between the territories and were vital to the very maintenance of life in the region.

[Having stated Morocco's and Mauritania's views on the nature of their overlapping ties to the territory, the Court said:]

158. The Court, as has already been indicated, concurs in the view that Question II does not envisage any form of territorial delimitation by the Court. It is also evident that the conclusions reached by the Court concerning the ties which existed between Western Sahara and the Kingdom of Morocco or the Mauritanian entity, as defined above, at the time of colonization lead also to the conclusion that there was a certain overlapping of those ties.

159. The overlapping arose simply from the geographical locations of the migration routes of the nomadic tribes; and the intersection and overlapping of those routes was a crucial element in the complex situation found in Western Sahara at that time. To speak of a "north" and a "south" and an overlapping with no void in between does not, therefore, reflect the true complexity of that situation. This complexity was, indeed, increased by the independence of some of the nomads, notably the Regheibat, a tribe prominent in Western Sahara. The Regheibat, although they may have had links with the tribes of the Bilad Shinguitti, were essentially an autonomous and independent people in the region with which these proceedings are concerned. Nor is the complexity of the legal relations of Western Sahara with the neighbouring territories at that time fully described unless mention is made of the fact that the nomadic routes of certain tribes passed also within areas of what is present-day Algeria.

160. In the view of the Court, therefore, the significance of the geographical overlapping is not that it indicates a "north" and a "south" without a "no-man's land." Its significance is rather that it indicates the difficulty of disentangling the various relationships existing in the Western Sahara region at the time of colonization by Spain.

161. . . . The General Assembly has made it clear, in resolution 3292 (XXIX), that the right of the population of Western Sahara to self-determination is not prejudiced or affected by the present request for an advisory opinion, nor by any other provision contained in that resolution. It is also clear that, when the General Assembly asks in Question II what were the legal ties between the territory of Western Sahara and the Kingdom of Morocco and the Mauritanian entity, it is addressing an enquiry to the Court as to the nature of these legal ties. This question, as stated in paragraph 85 above, must be understood as referring to such legal ties as may affect the policy to be followed in the decolonization of Western Sahara. In framing its answer, the Court cannot be unmindful of the purpose for which its opinion is sought. Its answer is requested in order to assist the General Assembly to determine its future decolonization policy and in particular to pronounce on the claims of Morocco and Mauritania to have had legal ties with Western Sahara involving the territorial integrity of their respective countries.

162. The materials and information presented to the Court show the existence, at the time of Spanish colonization, of legal ties of allegiance between the Sultan of Morocco and some of the tribes living in the territory of Western Sahara. They equally show the existence of rights, including some rights relating to the land, which constituted legal ties between the Mauritanian entity, as understood by the Court, and the territory of Western Sahara On the other hand, the Court's conclusion is that the materials and information presented to it do not establish any tie of territorial sovereignty between the territory of Western Sahara and the Kingdom of Morocco or the Mauritanian entity. Thus the Court has not found legal ties of such a nature as might affect the application of resolution 1514 (XV) in the decolonization of Western Sahara and, in particular, of the principle of self-determination through the free and genuine expression of the will of the peoples of the Territory. . . .

[Separate and dissenting opinions have been omitted.]

Discussion Questions

1. Can advisory opinions be used to circumvent the requirement that territorial issues require the consent of the parties concerned? What is the effect of advisory opinions?

2. Does Spain have an obligation to allow self-determination for the people of Western Sahara? Does the ICJ have authority to order such action?

3. How does this case illustrate the fundamental changes in international law concerning the rights of indigenous inhabitants of areas once considered *terra nullius* by Western jurists? Compare statements in the *Palmas Island* case.

4. What rights do Morocco and Mauritania have with regard to self-determination of the peoples of Western Sahara?

Comment: The opinion by the ICJ did not end the controversy over the Western Sahara. On November 14, 1975, Spain, Morocco, and Mauritania agreed to a Spanish decolonization formula under which the Western Sahara would be partitioned between Morocco and Mauritania in exchange for an award of mineral and fishing rights to Spain. The U.N. General Assembly confirmed both the need for self-determination (G.A.Res 3458(A) (XXX 1975) p. 116), and the three-power agreement (G.A.Res. 3458(B) p. 117) (for a criticism of U.N. handling of this matter, see Franck, 1976, p. 694).

The Spaniards departed in February 1976; two-thirds of the territory was then occupied by Morocco and the rest by Mauritania. Algeria protested the partition and supported the Popular Front for the Liberation of Saguia el Hamra and Rio de Oro (Polisario), a nationalist group seeking to transform the former Spanish Sahara into an independent country. The Polisario staged several guerrilla raids into Mauritania and Morocco from 1976 through 1978.

When Mauritania surrendered its portion and made peace with the Polisario in 1979, Morocco laid claim to all of Western Sahara and continued the war alone. The Polisario-backed Sahrawi Arab Democratic Republic received the recognition of the Organization of African Unity in February 1982, when it was admitted as a member. Under a U.N.-sponsored peace plan, a truce took effect in Western Sahara in September 1991, with a referendum on self-determination to follow. The U.N. Mission for the Referendum in Western Sahara (MINURSO) was to organize a referendum on the future of the area. Originally, 74,000 Saharans were to constitute the body of voters, but Morocco had allegedly added by June 1992 some 120,000 names of pro-Moroccan voters by moving supporters into the Western Sahara. The 1995 estimate of population in the territory is 217,212. As of the time of this writing, self-determination remains uncertain. The referendum has been delayed to verify the authenticity of the potential voters. This is an extremely difficult task among nomadic tribes that live in such a remote area.

The Extent of Territorial Sovereignty

State territories have been historically delineated by special geographical features that provide some means of defense. Mountain ranges, rivers, lakes, and oceans are some of these characteristic features that have frequently been used as territorial boundaries. However, modern technology has produced new threats to national security with regard to airspace and outer space, sea boundaries, and the exploitation of natural resources of the seas. The general principles of customary international law and lawmaking treaties will be discussed under this topic of extent of territorial sovereignty.

Land Territory

The boundary separating the land areas of two States is determined by acts of the States expressing their consent to its location. Such decisions may also establish boundaries by renunciation of prior claims, joint decisions through negotiation, or by adjudication. When the boundary between two States is a navigable river, its location is in the middle of the channel of navigation, or the *thalweg*. When the boundary between two States is a nonnavigable river or a lake, its location is the middle of the river or lake.

These general principles are rules of customary practice and may be altered by treaty agreement. Many boundary disputes have been settled by peaceful means, including boundary conventions and arbitration. Most of the boundary disputes involving the United States have been settled in this manner. Because in the majority of cases, the location of land boundaries between States is defined by agreement (frequently as interpreted by arbitration), few specific principles of international law have developed in this field.

The principle of *uti possidetis (juris)* is an interesting concept that is being used in connection with disputes involving former boundaries between colonial jurisdictions and the implementation of the concept of self-determination. The concept developed in the Latin American region where consent has assumed an indirect form. By the practice of the successor States of Spain after independence, there emerged a principle concerning settlement of boundary disputes that preserved the former colonial divisions that were used to constitute new States.

> **Uti possidetis:** Originally applied to the status of movable public property. Each State retains such property as was in the possession of each party on the day of cessation of hostilities. The term is used here to explain a practice with regard to recognition of former colonial territorial borders when a former colonial territory gains independence.

When the common sovereign power was withdrawn, it became indispensably necessary to agree on a general principle of demarcation, since there was a universal desire to avoid resort to force, and the principle adopted was a *colonial uti possidetis* [italics added], that is, the principle involving the preservation of the demarcations under the colonial regimes corresponding to each of the colonial entities that was constituted as a State. (Brownlie, 1990, pp. 134-135)

Many of the newly emerging States that have developed out of the former Soviet Union have specifically agreed to this principle in treaty form. However, the breakup of Yugoslavia and many of the African and Asian conflicts have resulted from the failure to respect this principle. Brownlie (1990) says that it must be emphasized that the principle is "by no means mandatory and the states concerned are free to adopt other principles as a basis of settlement" (p. 135; Brownlie cites the *Guatemala-Honduras Boundary* arbitration, 1933).

In 1964, at the height of African decolonization, the Organization of African Unity (OAU) adopted a resolution accepting the inheritance of colonial boundaries. In a celebrated Cairo resolution, the OAU affirmed that the status quo was to be preserved on African boundaries and that these would mark the international frontiers within Africa as States emerged to independence. It has been used in various African cases before international tribunals and has been viewed as consistent with the general international law on treaty succession. It has also been used in various Asian cases (see Brownlie, 1990, p. 135; Higgins, 1994, pp. 122-123).

The practice of designating river boundaries as the frontiers of States has led to the development of rules of **accretion** and **avulsion,** under which the boundary between two States shifts with the gradual shifting of the channel caused by erosion and deposit of alluvium (accretion) but does not shift

> **Accretion:** *Land acquired through the process of creating land by natural development, volcanic action, or action of water, such as river currents and ocean tides. Such acquisition constitutes original title.*
>
> **Avulsion:** *A rapid change in the course of a river or the banks of bodies of water caused by some natural force or disaster, such as floods, tidal waves, or hurricanes. The alteration of territory as a consequence of avulsion does not affect title to territory.*

when the river is suddenly diverted from the previous channel (avulsion).

The famous *Chamizal Arbitration*, involving a dispute between the United States and Mexico over the Rio Grande border, illustrates both of these principles. These practices have been applied by the U.S. Supreme Court in cases involving the river boundaries of various states within the United States (see *Nebraska v. Iowa*, 143 U.S. 359 [1892] and *Arkansas v. Tennessee*, 246 U.S. 158, [1918]).

Treaties in 1848 and 1853 fixed the Rio Grande as the international boundary at a point further north than that which existed at the time of the arbitration in 1911. During the interim period, the gradual southward movement of the Rio Grande exposed a tract of land that was formerly within the river depression, thus adding to U.S. territory by accretion. And in 1864, the river flooded, causing a sudden diversion of the river flow that cut off a much larger tract from Mexican territory.

The arbitrators decided the resulting dispute according to the applicable international rules explained earlier. They decided that the United States was entitled to the smaller area developed by gradual accretion and that Mexico was entitled to the much larger area produced by the sudden shift in the river flow caused by the flood of 1864. They thus fixed the border along the old river bed existing prior to the flood of 1864. However, the award was not finalized until 1967 when the United States put an end to the matter by formally transferring this portion of the Chamizal Tract to Mexico.

Airspace

The development of the aircraft is a twentieth-century phenomenon, and technological advancement in this area has led to one of the most rapidly developed bodies of international law. Prior to World War I, there were no international norms concerning international flight. The 1919 Paris Convention first extended the principle of State sovereignty into the dimension of airspace by providing that "every Power [State] has complete and exclusive sovereignty over the airspace above its territory."

The 1944 **Chicago Convention on International Civil Aviation** is the more comprehensive contemporary basis for reference to international air law. This lawmaking instrument created the International Civil Aviation Organization (ICAO), which regulates international commercial aviation. The

> **Chicago Convention on International Civil Aviation:** *Basic multilateral treaty creating the International Civil Aviation Organization (ICAO) and defining air zones (1944).*

basic treaty provisions "recognize that every State has complete and exclusive sovereignty over the airspace above its territory." It further defines this zone to include "the land areas and territorial waters adjacent thereto under the sovereignty . . . of such State."

Article 3 of the Chicago Convention does not specifically regulate public aircraft operated by the military, customs, and police authorities. However, it contains a clause that "no State aircraft . . . shall fly over the territory of another State or land thereon without authorization by special agreement." Unlike nonscheduled private aircraft, government aircraft cannot enter another State's airspace without the express prior agreement of the receiving State. These agreements are made either on a case-by-case basis or by treaty arrangement between friendly countries. Before making an emergency landing in another State, a military pilot must seek permission to enter that State's airspace or to land.

The U-2 incident involving Francis Gary Powers in 1960 is the most often cited example of violation of these rules. The U-2 military reconnaissance aircraft was shot down over the Soviet Union. The Soviet Union tried and convicted Powers for espionage involved in the "spy flight," which the court considered an aggressive act of the United States that "created a threat to universal peace." The Soviet Union also held Pakistan (the country of origin of the flight) as well as the countries of Iran, Turkey, and Norway (the country of destination) responsible as "accomplices in the aggression against the Soviet Union."

In light of the modern technology of space age military spy satellites, the Soviet Union may have been exaggerating the threat of the unarmed reconnaissance aircraft. However, the principle is broadly accepted as a violation of law today, and within the authority of the sovereign State to punish violators. More recent agreements allow overflights for inspection purposes with the consent of the parties involved. Francis Gary Powers was released from custody in exchange for Soviet espionage agent Col. Rudolf Able on February 10, 1962.

French denial of permission to allow U.S. aircraft to fly over its territory on a retaliatory bombing mission into Libya in 1986 is further evidence of the sensitivity with which States regard their legal obligation to respect airspace and the prohibition against unilateral use of military force. The Reagan administration action thus required U.S. aircraft to fly a rather circuitous route around France's territorial airspace and through the Straits of Gibraltar to gain access to Libya via the western entrance to the Mediterranean Sea.

The breakup of the Soviet Union and agreements to reduce military forces between Eastern and Western European countries have produced agreement to the Treaty on Open Skies, which was signed by twenty-five countries in March of 1992 and ratified by the United States in August of 1993. This agreement permits surveillance flights over North America, Europe, and the former Soviet Union to ensure compliance with arms control agreements. It established an annual quota of overflights for each country (see Nash, 1994, p. 96).

Noncommercial private aircraft have a general right to fly into or over foreign State territory but must file a flight plan at the flight's point of origin, and when they refuel in a particular State, they may be required to alter their flight plan according to the regulations of the State they are traversing. Commercial aircraft are subject to restrictive regulations and may not fly over or land in the territory of another country without advance routing or landing arrangements. The ICAO regulates international commercial aviation by scheduling air routes, cargo delivery, and passenger service. This public intergovernmental organization (IGO) has limited regulatory authority to promote safe and orderly growth of international civil aviation throughout the world. Article 84 of the Chicago Convention provides that States may appeal ICAO decisions "to an *ad hoc* arbitral tribunal agreed upon with the other parties to the dispute or to the Permanent Court of International Justice."

The ICJ assumed this role for the first time in 1972 when it accepted an appeal to review an ICAO decision brought by member States (see *Jurisdiction of the ICAO Council [India v. Pakistan]* [1972] I.C.J. Rep. 46). The ICJ accepted another case in 1989 requesting the review of an ICAO decision that the United States was not legally responsible when one of its naval vessels shot down an Iranian commercial aircraft over the Persian Gulf. Iran filed a suit, asking the court to declare the ICAO's decision erroneous. The parties ultimately dismissed this suit in 1994 after a number of delays in the pleading phase.

There is also a private organization called the International Air Transport Association (IATA), which has been formed by the commercial air carriers themselves. This nongovernmental organization (NGO) attempts to coordinate scheduling and unreasonable competition. It has been criticized for possible implication in the anticompetitive behavior of many of its members in the Laker Airways failure discussed in Chapter 6 of this text. Many of the members of this organization are countries that own and operate their own airlines.

There have been several international incidents involving commercial aircraft being shot down because of actual or presumed violations of airspace. A major incident in 1955 involved an Israeli commercial plane that flew into Bulgarian airspace while en route from Austria to Israel. A Bulgarian military aircraft shot it down over Bulgaria, killing all fifty-eight passengers. Israel instituted proceedings in the ICJ. The court decided, however, that it could not hear the case because Bulgaria had not consented to the court's jurisdiction. Bulgaria finally agreed to pay a total of $195,000, which excluded compensation for the loss of the aircraft.

One of these major disasters occurred in 1983 when the Soviet military shot down a Korean passenger jet that veered from its course and flew over sensitive Soviet territory. Eight Soviet military aircraft monitored the movement of the KAL Flight 007. After the airliner had turned away from the Soviet mainland, and while in Soviet airspace, one of the Soviet military jets shot it down. All 269 passengers and crew of Flight 007 were killed, including a U.S. congressman. The Soviet pilots claimed they had been unable to communicate with the Korean plane, which normally involves tipping the wings of the pursuit aircraft to signal the intruding aircraft to follow and land, when radio communication fails. The nighttime conditions in bad weather played some role in this communication failure. However, this incident generated a number of diplomatic protests, stimulating investigations by the ICAO and the U.N. Security Council. Both of these U.N. agencies condemned the use of deadly force and called for amendments to the Chicago Convention to prevent recurrence of this type of tragedy.

The tragic accidents involving both the KAL Flight 007 (1983) and the mistaken destruction of an Iranian passenger jet by the United States in the Strait of Hormus in 1988 during the Gulf Oil Crisis, demonstrated that both superpowers were capable of mistakes. The ending of Cold War tensions and refined procedures have reduced the potential for such accidents. However, issues related to terrorist threats to international air travel have taken on a more urgent character.

Jurisdiction over criminal activity onboard aircraft engaged in international travel was not adequately regulated before the 1963 Tokyo Convention on Offenses and Certain Other Acts Committed on Board Aircraft. This major convention became effective in 1969 and has been ratified by most nations of the world. The **Tokyo Convention** established a framework for punishing individuals who commit violent crimes during international flights. The air-

Tokyo Convention: Basic convention establishing priority jurisdiction of flag States for prosecution of crimes committed during international flights (1963).

craft's State of registration is given primary jurisdiction to prosecute such offenses. However, other States retain potential jurisdiction under the principles discussed in Chapter 9 (see concepts of criminal jurisdiction). Article 4 of the Tokyo Convention provides that a State that is *not* the State of registration cannot generally interfere on the basis that its otherwise applicable territorial criminal jurisdiction applies in its own airspace. Exceptions to this general rule include the effects principle, when the offense was committed by or against a national or permanent resident of such State, and the offense is against the security of such State.

In 1970, the Hague Convention for the Suppression of Unlawful Seizure of Aircraft added to the universal principle the crime of "aircraft hijacking." And the related 1971 Montreal Sabotage Convention extended the universal crimes to include those who bomb or sabotage (rather than merely seize) commercial aircraft. The parties to these treaties agree to prosecute or extradite persons accused of such crimes.

The terrorist bombing of Pan Am Flight 103 over Lockerbie, Scotland, in 1988 triggered the criminal liability of the Libyan individuals accused of being responsible for the deaths of the 230 passengers and crew members. Libya has the responsibility to prosecute these individuals or turn them over for trial in Scotland or the United States, where they have been indicted. U.N. Security Council Resolution 731 of 1992 resolved that Libya must release them for trial.

Libya responded with a suit in the ICJ, claiming that the United States and the United Kingdom had themselves breached the Montreal Convention by threatening the use of force. It requested that the ICJ issue a preliminary order prohibiting these countries from acting in any way that would further threaten peaceful relations. The ICJ refused jurisdiction, noting that another U.N. organ, the Security Council, had already demanded that Libya turn over the terrorists for trial elsewhere. The Court did not want to be placed in the awkward position of rendering an injunction against permanent members of the Security Council while action is pending in that body.

This is another good example of an area left to the "political discretion" of the Security Council under the U.N. Charter. The court therefore supported the Security Council and rejected Libya's claim that the Security Council had exceeded its authority under the charter. Judge Shahabuddeen (Guyana) stated:

> This [denial] results not from any collision between the competence of the Security Council and that of the Court, but from a collision between the obligations of Libya under the decision of the Security Council and any obligation it may have under the Montreal Convention. The [UN] Charter says that the former [must] prevail. ("Official Documents," 1992, p. 651)

Outer Space and Environmental Concerns

The upper extent of a nation's airspace has not been defined precisely by international law. The vague concept of where inner and outer space converge, or where the earth's atmosphere ends, is not very helpful. Some have suggested a twelve-mile limit corresponding to the extent of the territorial sea under the 1982 U.N. Convention on Law of the Sea (UNCLOS III; see von Glahn, 1996, p. 335).

As explained in Chapter 4 of this text, the status of outer space is declared to be analogous to the historical maritime concept of *res communis*. In the 1967 U.N. Treaty on Principles Governing the Activities of States in the Exploration and Use of Outer Space, Including the Moon and Other Celestial Bodies, States have declared that the "exploration and use of outer space . . . shall be carried out for the benefit and in the interests of all countries, irrespective of their degree of economic or scientific development, and shall be the province of all mankind."

The Outer Space Treaty also demilitarizes outer space by declaring a ban on nuclear weapons or any other kinds of weapons of mass destruction and by stating that the moon and other celestial bodies shall be used by all States party to the treaty exclusively for peaceful purposes. The treaty does permit a limited military presence in space. Article IV provides that the "use of military personnel for scientific research or for any other peaceful purposes shall not be prohibited."

The Convention of the Prohibition of the Development, Production, Stockpiling and Use of Chemical Weapons and on their Destruction was ratified by the United States in April 1997 and entered into force on that date as well. On September 10, 1996, the Comprehensive Nuclear-Test-Ban Treaty was adopted by the General Assembly and opened for signature and ratification. The United States signed this treaty on September 24, 1996, however, as of May 1997 it had not been ratified by the U.S. nor had it obtained sufficient adherents to enter into force. These important treaties have important consequences which limit the sovereignty of individual states.

Law of the Sea Extensions of Territorial Sovereignty

UNCLOS III (or the 1982 LOS treaty) was initially discussed in Chapter 3 of this text. There, the general features of the law involving the most extensive expanse of the earth's surface and beneath its surface was explained. The concept of *res communis* (community property) has been its central feature; however, the new treaty that went into force in 1994 and that has been signed by the United States will effectively expand the territory of the sea, subject to individual State jurisdiction, and thus contract the area of exclusive territory belonging to no State.

The International Law of the Sea is a vast body of law that creates many regimes to regulate the enormously important aspects of the world's oceans. Rather than attempt to discuss this body of law in a single chapter, this text recognizes that the law of the sea has many implications in almost all areas of the law among nations. The implications for what some have called the "territorialization" of the world's oceans deserves elaboration and explanation. The sea zones laid down in UNCLOS III were briefly discussed and illustrated in Figure 3.1 of this text. The extension of State sovereignty and development of international regimes implicit in these vast changes are discussed next.

Internal Waters. **Internal waters** are defined as the "waters on the landward side of the baseline of the territorial sea," and the baseline is defined as the point where the sea intersects with the coast. These waters include bays, rivers, and other internal waters that contain ocean water and are subject to the full sovereign authority of the individual State. Ports have a special status in international law because they are the areas of most frequent international contact.

States have developed special port authorities to deal with the regulation of

> **Internal waters:**
> Waters on the landward side of the baseline of the territorial sea subject to the full authority of that State. Bays, rivers, and inland seas are included.

individual ports. In general, these areas are required by international law to offer emergency assistance to vessels in distress but may refuse permission to enter such internal waters. However, warships, when allowed to enter with permission, are usually immune from inspection and the port authorities do not board them, for mutual security reasons. Merchant ships and other private vessels registered in another country are given some consideration as flagships of foreign States concerning crimes committed by persons on board in port. However, serious and violent crimes that may disturb what is called "port tranquility" are exceptions to the primary jurisdiction of the flag State.

Bays. Most **bays** consist of only internal waters and are most sensitive to regulation by the contiguous State. A bay, as defined in Article 10 of the 1982 treaty is "a well marked indention whose penetration . . . constitute[s] more than a mere curvature of the coast. An indention . . . [must be] as large as, or larger than, that of a semicircle whose diameter is a line drawn across the mouth of that indentation." The mouth of the bay consists of its natural entrance points.

> **Bays:** *Inlets that constitute internal waters when they are larger than the diameter of a semicircle taken from the width of the mouth of the bay and are less than twenty-four nautical miles apart. Historic bays also are recognized by customary law.*

The 1982 LOS treaty provisions concerning the *territorial sea* fixes the limitation of this zone at twelve nautical miles from the coastal baseline. However, in the case of a bay, if the semicircle's diameter of the bay is less than twenty-four miles between each side of the mouth of the bay, its waters consist solely of internal waters. If the diameter is greater than twenty-four miles, the bay also contains *high seas* in the center of the mouth and territorial waters up to twelve miles from the entire coastline that forms the land boundary of the bay.

Historic bays are an exception for which the State can show that over a long period of time customary practice has regarded that particular bay as completely within the internal waters of that State even though the bay is wider than twenty-four miles. The United States thus claims the Chesapeake Bay as completely within the territorial waters of the country even though the semicircle's diameter for that bay is greater than twenty-four miles.

Examples of disputed claims to historic bays include Canada's Hudson Bay and the Gulf of Sidra claimed by Libya. An incident in the Gulf of Sidra resulted in the shooting down of Libyan aircraft by the U.S. military conducting naval maneuvers in the area in 1986. Libya's leader, Muammar Qaddafi, had proclaimed the "Line of Death" across the mouth of this gulf, which is approximately three hundred miles across. Libya considers the entire gulf to be internal waters subject to its exclusive control. The United States disputes this claim, and when Libyan aircraft attacked, they were shot down to protect the U.S. fleet.

The Territorial Sea. The expansion of the **territorial sea** from the "cannon shot" theory of traditional international law to the twelve-mile limit of the 1982 LOS treaty is an important change. The range of national claims to their territorial seas before

> **Territorial sea:** *Limited to twelve nautical miles from the low-water baseline of the coast that includes nearly full exercise of sovereignty by the coastal State and extends the airspace of the State to this limit.*

the new treaty was enormous and provided no real norm. Now the rule is generally accepted that a State may extend its territorial sea only to the extent of twelve nautical miles from its coastal baseline. Within its territorial sea, a State exercises sovereignty over this territory essentially to the same extent that it does over its land mass, and this includes its airspace above the territorial sea.

The minimal exercise of this zone includes charting of the waters this close to its coast to provide warning of navigational hazards. The coastal State's baseline is defined under Article 5 of the 1982 LOS treaty as the "low-water line along the coast as marked on large-scale charts officially recognized by the coastal State." The baseline thus marks the inner boundary of the various coastal sea zones. Coastal baselines must follow the general direction of the coast, and the ICJ has recognized the drawing of straight baselines connecting the rocks and islets constituting unusual geological configurations (*Anglo-Norwegian Fisheries* case [1951]).

The U.S. objection to the extension of the territorial sea from three to twelve miles is illustrated by the Bering Strait separating Alaska and Russian territory. This strait is only nineteen miles wide at its narrowest point. Ships pass through it when going between the Arctic and the northern Pacific oceans. The former Soviet Union claimed a twelve-mile territorial sea. Prior to 1988, 24 the U.S. three-mile territorial sea claim left (?) a four-mile slice of high seas at the narrowest point of passage. The new twelve-mile limit claimed by the United States in 1988 left no area for "transit passage." This is of major concern to the military and commercial interests involved.

To solve this and other similar problems, Article 38.2 provides that ships and aircraft may transit through such territorial-water straits formerly containing international waters "solely for the purpose of continuous and expeditious transit of the strait between one part of the high seas . . . and another part of the high seas." This special "transit passage" provision exists independently of the more general concept of "innocent passage."

Innocent Passage. Under the new LOS treaty, **innocent passage** means passage that is "not prejudicial to the peace, good order, or security of the coastal State." The passing vessel may not stop or anchor unless incidental to ordinary navigation or undertaken for the purpose of the authorized entry into a foreign port. Such vessels may thus proceed to or from port and render assistance to persons, ships, or aircraft needing emergency assistance. The coastal State's rules of innocent passage are restricted by the new LOS treaty by Article 24, which prohibits discrimination against the ships or cargo of a particular nation or ships carrying cargo to or from certain nations.

> **Innocent passage:** Vessels are entitled to passage through various zones that is not prejudicial to the peace, good order, or security of the coastal state. The LOS treaty prohibits discrimination against ships or cargo from particular nations.

The Contiguous Zone. A coastal State may exercise limited jurisdiction in the **contiguous zone** (CZ) extending twenty-four nautical miles from its coastal baseline. These limited sovereign rights allow it to enforce "customs, fiscal, immigration, or sanitary laws." The United States and many other States had declared varying zones beyond the territorial sea as subject to "hovering laws" that enabled that State to exercise jurisdiction to stop a vessel and inspect for evidence of violations of its domestic laws. This provision of the LOS treaty codifies such prac-

> **Contiguous zone (CZ):** A sea zone not to exceed twenty-four nautical miles from the baseline, which allows limited exercise of sovereignty to enforce the coastal State's customs and fiscal, immigration, and sanitary laws. The coastal State may stop and inspect vessels in this zone for evidence of violation of its domestic laws.

tices and provides a uniform designation of the extent of the zone. Innocent passage must be allowed in these zones even for military vessels.

The Exclusive Economic Zone. The 1958 U.N. Law of the Sea Convention concerning the Continental Shelf extended coastal jurisdiction "to where the depth of the superjacent waters admits of the exploitation of natural resources." This provision effectively permitted coastal States to monopolize the marine resources in and over their continental shelves. The United States had declared such a rule applicable to exploitation of natural resources during the administration of President Harry S. Truman in 1946.

Other States, such as Chile, Ecuador, and Peru, which are not blessed with extensive continental shelves because the ocean suddenly drops off near the coast, then began declaring two-hundred-mile territorial sea zones to protect their fishing interests. Advances in technology had also progressed to the point that exploitation and mining of the deep seabed might become a reality. These controversies led to compromise solutions in the creation of the two-hundred-nautical-mile limit designated the exclusive economic zone (EEZ) in the new LOS treaty.

> **Exclusive economic zone (EEZ):** *A sea zone extending up to two hundred nautical miles from the coastal baseline. In this zone, a State may claim exclusive rights to exploration and exploitation of the resources of this area.*

Article 56 provides that the coastal State enjoys sovereign rights in the EEZ for the purposes of "exploring and exploiting, conserving and managing the natural resources . . . of the waters superjacent to the sea-bed and its subsoil, and with regard to other activities for the economic exploitation and exploration of the zone, such as the production of energy from the water." Although the coastal State enjoys primary economic rights in this area, Article 58 provides that all States retain the right to navigate, overfly, lay submarine cables and pipelines "compatible with . . . this Convention."

This area includes fishery rights and responsibility to protect and conserve fisheries by designating the "allowable catch" to be taken by other States from its EEZ. Landlocked States are given the right "to participate, on an equitable basis, in the exploitation of an appropriate part of the surplus of the living resources of the [EEZ] of coastal States of the same subregion or region, taking into account the relevant economic and geographical circumstances of all the States concerned" (Article 70).

The High Seas. Article 86 of the new LOS treaty defines the **high seas** as "all parts of the sea that are not included in the exclusive economic zone, in the territorial sea, or in the internal waters of a State." Freedom of navigation on the high seas is assured

> **High seas:** *All parts of the sea that are not included in the exclusive economic zone, in the territorial sea, or the internal waters of a state. Freedom of navigation on the high seas is protected by the LOS treaty.*

by the new treaty; however, the new Deep Seabed Authority created by the treaty has been the subject of great controversy (see Chapter 3 for details).

Deep Seabed Authority. The 1994 Special Agreement has now removed many of the obstacles to ratification regarding the **Deep Seabed Authority** asserted by the developed nations. The United States will be able to

> **Deep Seabed Authority:** *A special regime created by the 1982 LOS treaty and given authority to regulate the exploration and exploitation of the deep seabed resources beneath the high seas.*

block decisions of the Seabed Authority in matters of finance and budget. "The Enterprise" (the mineral exploration and exploitation organ of the authority) will not have to be funded by the developed countries alone. Mining already licensed under U.S. law will be allowed to operate on the same favorable terms as those previously granted by the authority to French, Japanese, Indian, and Chinese companies whose mine site claims have already been registered. Certain financial obligations otherwise imposed on mining nations at the exploration stage are eliminated under the 1994 Special Agreement.

The 1982 LOS Convention had received 112 ratifications by January of 1997, and having 158 signatory States to this treaty, including the United States, indicates that it will have overwhelming support. For some observers, this "territorialization" of the world's oceans represents a quadrupling of the nations' territorial seas, a doubling of the size of the CZs, and adds a two-hundred-mile EEZ for each coastal nation. This may create as many problems at it solves in terms of new disputes over vague provisions and determining issues where these zones overlap.

However, when seen from a different perspective, coastal States now have increased responsibility to prevent pollution and promote conservation of the ocean resources (see Chapter 8), a new tribunal will be established to adjudicate disputes (see Chapter 13), and the limits of functional aspects of the exercise of territorial sovereignty will be more clearly defined.

The Legal Status of Intergovernmental Organizations

One of the more important developments of the twentieth century is the recognition that not only States but also IGOs have legal personality under modern public international law. This means that under certain conditions IGOs can perform many of the functions formerly attributed to States alone under traditional international law. IGOs created by treaty obligations that transfer some element of sovereign authority to that multinational body have functional capacity as legal entities with rights and duties under public international law.

According to Professor Brownlie (1990), of Oxford University, the general criteria of an organization that possesses legal personality include the following:

1. A permanent association of states, with lawful objectives, equipped with organs [with distinctive decision-making powers]
2. A distinction, in terms of legal powers and purposes, between the organization and its member states
3. The existence of legal powers exercisable on the international plane and not solely within the national systems of one or more states (pp. 681-682)

Application of these criteria requires determination of delicate issues of law and fact that are not always apparent. However, many important IGOs undoubtedly have **international legal personality**, such as the specialized agencies of the United Nations and the institutions of the European Community. On the other hand, an organization that lacks international personality is the British Commonwealth, which does not meet the three criteria above (Brownlie, 1990, p. 682).

> *International legal personality:* Entities having limited rights and duties under public international law. They could be termed juridical States just as corporations are treated as juridical persons in private law.

In 1949, the U.N. General Assembly called on the ICJ for an advisory opinion on the subject of whether or not the United Nations had the legal right to sue for damages on the international plane in its capacity as an international organization. The ICJ opinion in the *Reparation for Injuries Suffered in the Service of the United Nations* represents an explanation of the basic concept of the legal personality of IGOs.

The background for this request for an advisory opinion involved the U.N. General Assembly Resolution 181 partitioning the former British mandate referred to as "Palestine" to create new Jewish and Arab States in that territory. Shortly after Israel declared

its Statehood in May of 1948, hostilities began in and around what is now the State of Israel. After the U.N. Security Council had called for a cessation of hostilities, a Norwegian, Count Bernadotte, was appointed the U.N. mediator in Palestine for the purpose of negotiating a settlement. He was killed while pursuing this objective in the Palestinian territory. The issue before the ICJ was whether or not the U.N. Charter gave the United Nations the legal capacity, as an international organization, to seek reparations from the responsible State or States involved in the death of U.N. agents.

▮   ▮   ▮

Reparation for Injuries Suffered in the Service of the United Nations
International Court of Justice, Advisory Opinion, 1949.
2949 I.C.J. 174.

THE COURT.

. . . The first question asked of the Court is as follows:

> "In the event of an agent of the United Nations in the performance of his duties suffering injury in circumstances involving the responsibility of a State, has the United Nations, as an Organization, the capacity to bring an international claim against the responsible *de jure* or *de facto* government with a view to obtaining the reparation due in respect of the damage caused (a) to the United Nations, (b) to the victim or to persons entitled through him?"

It will be useful to make the following preliminary observations:

(a) The Organization of the United Nations will be referred to usually, but not invariably, as "the Organization."

(b) Questions I(a) and I(b) refer to "an international claim against the responsible de jure or de facto government." The Court understands that these questions are directed to claims against a State, and will, therefore, in this opinion, use the expression "State" or "defendant State."

(c) The Court understands the word "agent" in the most liberal sense, that is to say, any person who, whether a paid official or not, and whether permanently employed or not, has been charged by an organ of the Organization with carrying out, or helping to carry out, one of its functions—in short, any person through whom it acts.

(d) As this question assumes an injury suffered in such circumstances as to involve a State's responsibility, it must be supposed, for the purpose of this Opinion, that the damage results from a failure by the State to perform obligations of which the purpose is to protect the agents of the Organization in the performance of their duties.

(e) The position of a defendant State which is not a member of the Organization is dealt with later, and for the present the Court will assume that the Defendant State is a Member of the Organization.

* * *

Competence to bring an international claim is, for those possessing it, the capacity to resort to the customary methods recognized by international law for the establishment, the presentation and the settlement of claims. Among these methods may be mentioned protest, request for an enquiry, negotiation, and request for submission to an arbitral tribunal or to the Court in so far as this may be authorized by the Statute.

This capacity certainly belongs to the State; a State can bring an international claim against another State. Such a claim takes the form of a claim between two political entities, equal in law, similar in form, and both the direct subjects of international law, it is dealt with by means of negotiation, and cannot, in the present state of the law as to international jurisdiction, be submitted to a tribunal, except with the consent of the States concerned.

When the Organization brings a claim against one of its Members, this claim will be presented in the same manner, and regulated by the same procedure. It may, when necessary, be supported by the political means at the disposal of the Organization. In these ways the Organization would find a method for securing the observance of its rights by the Member against which it has a claim.

But, in the international sphere, has the Organization such a nature as involves the capacity to bring an international claim? In order to answer this question, the Court must first enquire whether the Charter has given the Organization such a position that it possesses, in regard to its Members, rights which it is entitled to ask them to respect. In other words, does the Organization possess international personality? This is no doubt a doctrinal expression, which has sometimes given rise to controversy. But it will be used here to mean that if the Organization is recognized as having that personality, it is an entity capable of availing itself of obligations incumbent upon its Members.

To answer this question, which is not settled by the actual terms of the Charter, we must consider what characteristics it was intended thereby to give to the Organization.

The subjects of law in any legal system are not necessarily identical in their nature or in the extent of their rights, and their nature depends upon the needs of the community. Throughout its history, the development of international law has been influenced by the requirements of international life, and the progressive increase in the collective activities of States has already given rise to instances of action upon the international plane by certain entities which are not States. This development culminated in the establishment in June 1946 of an international organization whose purposes and principles are specified in the Charter of the United Nations. But to achieve these ends the attribution of international personality is indispensable.

The Charter has not been content to make the Organization created by it merely a centre "for harmonizing the actions of nations in the attainment of these common ends" (Article 1, pare. 4). It has equipped that centre with organs, and has given it special tasks. It has defined the position of the Members in relation to the Organization by requiring them to give it every assistance in any action undertaken by it (Article 2, para. 5), and to accept and carry out the decisions of the Security Council; by authorizing the General Assembly to make recommendations to the Members; by giving the Organization legal capacity and privileges and immunities in the territory of each of its Members; and by providing for the conclusion of agreements between the Organization and its Members. Practice—in particular the conclusion of conventions to which the Organization is a party—has confirmed this character of the Organization, which occupies a position in certain respects in detachment from its Members, and which is under a duty to remind them, if need be, of certain obligations. It must be added that the Organization is a political body, charged with political tasks of an important character, and covering a wide field, namely, the maintenance of international peace and security, the development of friendly relations among nations, and the achievement of international cooperation in the solution of problems of an economic, social, cultural or humanitarian character (Article 1); and in dealing with its Members it employs political means. The "Convention on the Privileges and Immunities of the United Nations" of 1946 creates rights and duties between each of the signatories and the Organization (see, in particular, Section 35). It is difficult to see how such a convention could operate except upon the international plane and as between parties possessing international personality.

In the opinion of the Court, the Organization was intended to exercise and enjoy, and is in fact exercising and enjoying, functions and rights which can only be explained on the basis of the possession of a large measure of international personality and the capacity to operate upon an international plane. It is at present the supreme type of international organization, and it could not carry out the intentions of its founders if it was devoid of international personality. It must be acknowledged that its Members, by entrusting certain functions to it, with the attendant duties and responsibilities, have clothed it with the competence required to enable those functions to be effectively discharged.

Accordingly, the Court has come to the conclusion that the Organization is an international person. That is not the same thing as saying that it is a State, which it certainly is not, or that its legal personality and rights and duties are the same as those of a State. Still less is it the same thing as saying that it is "a super-State," whatever that expression may mean. It does not even imply that all its rights and duties must be upon the international plane, any more than all the rights and duties of a State must be upon that plane. What it does mean is that it is a subject of international law and capable of possessing international rights and duties, and that it has capacity to maintain its rights by bringing international claims.

The next question is whether the sum of the international rights of the Organization comprises the right to bring the kind of international claim described in the Request for this Opinion. That is a claim against a State to obtain reparation in respect of the damage caused by the injury of an agent of the Organization in the course of the performance of his duties. Whereas a State possesses the totality of international rights and duties recognized by international law, the rights and duties of an entity such as the Organization must depend upon its purposes and functions as specified or implied in its constituent documents and developed in practice. The functions of the Organization are of such a character that they could not be effectively discharged if they involved the concurrent action, on the international plane, of fifty-eight or more Foreign Offices, and the Court concludes that the Members have endowed the Organization with capacity to bring international claims when necessitated by the discharge of its functions.

Discussion Questions

1. What type of international personality do IGOs possess according to the implications of this advisory opinion of the ICJ? Why?
2. Since the U.N. Charter prohibits its employees from seeking or receiving instructions from any government, is legal action by the United Nations in public international law necessary to protect its interests? Why is the right of the State of nationality of the employee insufficient?
3. What elements of Statehood are not present with regard to IGOs? How are they different from States?
4. Do States that are not members of the United Nations have duties and rights under international law?

Intergovernmental organizations have concluded treaties, made use of the high seas with ships flying their own flags, created international peace forces, convened international conferences, sent diplomatic representatives to member and nonmember States, received permanent missions from member States, undertaken administrative tasks in certain territories, presented protests to States, and brought claims on the international plane. These activities were all once considered the exclusive activities of sovereign nation-states. Functional sovereign immunity for "acts of State" of IGOs from private legal actions in municipal courts is also broadly recognized in the courts of individual States (see Convention on the Privileges and Immunities of the United Nations and *Broadbent v. Organization of American States*, 628 F.2d 27, [1980]).

NGOs (nongovernmental organization) have not been accorded the status of international legal persons. They may bring legal actions in municipal courts that concern issues of private international law. However, they cannot bring legal actions in international tribunals. Nonetheless, they play an active role on the international scene, and in some cases have a recognized legal status under treaties and other international arrangements.

Many of these organizations have been accorded the right to express their views to official international bodies, and in some circumstances, they perform functions delegated to them by international instruments or governmental decision. The International Committee of the Red Cross, for example, is an NGO that has been given important functions under the Geneva Conventions on the Laws of War.

This chapter has attempted to describe the modern subjects, or entities, possessing international personality and their rights and responsibilities under international law. The attributes of Statehood, the range of State jurisdiction, and the limited functional capacity of IGOs have been discussed. The next chapter will provide a deeper understanding of the general principles of the Law of Treaties.

▊   ▊   ▊

Chapter Summary

1. The basic criteria for Statehood under international law include a defined territory, a permanent population, an independent government, and the capacity to fulfill international obligations. Entities that fulfill these qualifications have international personality, including rights and duties, whether they are recognized by all States or not.

2. As a practical matter, recognition by other governments is also a significant factor in achieving full status as a nation entitled to equality of treatment and all the rights and duties of Statehood. All new nations today have sought membership in the United Nations Organization to achieve this status.

3. However, a State, such as Switzerland, that is not a U.N. member has full status as an equal member of the international community of nations. Other nonmember States may lack some of the factual attributes of Statehood or legitimacy in the international community.

4. A complete list of the rights and duties of States under international law has not been codified. However, the U.N. General Assembly document adopted by consensus in 1970 known as the Friendly Relations Declaration provides an authoritative clarification of the U.N. Charter understanding of these basic principles.

5. These principles include a duty to refrain from the threat or use of force against the territorial integrity or political independence of any State, a duty to settle disputes by peaceful means, a duty not to intervene in another State's domestic jurisdiction, an agreement that all States have equal rights, and an agreement that all States must cooperate to fulfill the obligations assumed under the U.N. Charter.

6. The principle of self-determination of peoples is given a greater degree of clarification in the Friendly Relations Declaration, indicating that it applies principally to the colonial territories or to situations in which an established State is not conducting itself in compliance with the principles of "equal rights and self-determination of peoples." However, the debate over the precise meaning of "self-determination" remains an area of considerable confusion.

7. General principles of State succession have not been codified but include the customary practice that loss of some part of a State's territory does not change existing treaty obligations unless these changes result in impossibility of performance. New States, however, start with a clean slate and are not bound by the political treaties of the predecessor State. New States must accept existing customary principles of international law.

8. Recognition takes many forms and is generally regarded as a political act with legal consequences. Recognition of governments in relation to internal conflict within a State is limited by traditional principles involving a duty to refrain from premature recognition of revolutionary governments. There is a duty to refrain from recognition of acquisition of territory in violation of international law.

9. The basic concept of State responsibility requires that States make reparations for any damages to other States or their nationals in violation of international law, and new States must assume these obligations. State responsibility is generally analogous to "strict liability" in civil legal action and fault or intent does not have to be proven.

10. Achieving settled borders agreed to by a State's neighbors contributes to international stability. The methods of acquisition of territory include those associated with original title and derivative title.

11. The basic method of acquiring original title involves a claim to land not previously owned, or *terra nullius*. Discovery and occupation, prescription, and accretion are the basic concepts derived from Roman law.

12. The basic methods of acquiring derivative title are by cession and conquest. Forcible annexation, or subjugation, of territory by States is prohibited under the U.N. Charter. However, claims to territory acquired before this fundamental change in the law may be recognized as a basis of good title in international law.

13. *Res communis* refers to territory belonging to all States which must remain available for all to use. Such community property includes the high seas and outer space.

14. The *Island of Palmas* case illustrates the application of the principle of prescription involving uncontested peaceful and continuous occupation of territory as a basis of title even when there are competing claims.

15. The *Legal Status of Eastern Greenland* case illustrates the necessity of comparing competing claims and awarding title to the State with superior claims.

16. The complex *Western Sahara* advisory opinion illustrates the difficulty of dealing with not only competing claims of States regarding a territory but also the complex issues involved in carrying out the U.N. mandate to allow self-determination of peoples in colonial territories.

17. Territorial boundaries are fixed by agreement between the States involved expressing the location of these frontiers. When the boundary between two States is a navigable river, its location is in the middle of the channel of navigation, or the *thalweg*. When the boundary water is nonnavigable or is a lake, its location is the middle of the river or lake.

18. The principle of *colonial uti possidetis* has been used to settle disputes arising between former colonial States. This concept assumes that the former colonial borders are to be used in the absence of agreement between the disputing parties.

19. Water boundaries are somewhat unstable since they meander or shift, usually gradually, but sometimes in dramatic ways. The *Chamizal Arbitration* illustrates the legal principles of both accretion and avulsion. Accretion is the shifting of a river channel or the accumulation of soil deposits on one side of the river thus adding territory to that State. Avulsion refers to the sudden shift of the river boundary due to floods or natural diversion that results in the boundary remaining in the old river channel.

20. States have sovereignty over the airspace above their territory, including the territorial waters of maritime states. The upward limits of territorial airspace are uncertain but generally conceded to be limited by outer space where the earth's atmosphere ends. Outer space is considered *res communis*.

21. The 1944 Chicago Convention codified basic air law and created the ICAO, which regulates international commercial aviation. The ICJ has accepted jurisdiction to review significant decisions of the ICAO.

22. The Tokyo Convention of 1963 established a framework for deciding questions of jurisdiction concerning individuals who commit violent crimes during international flights. The State of registration has primary jurisdiction to prosecute such offenses.

23. The 1982 LOS treaty extends the jurisdiction of States to include a limit of twelve miles of territorial sea, twenty-four miles of contiguous zone (CZ) of regulation, and two hundred miles of exclusive economic zone (EEZ), all measured from the maritime State's low-water baseline. Internal waters, bays, territorial waters, transit passage in international straits, innocent passage, limitations of sovereignty in the CZ, limitations of the EEZ, and development of the Deep Seabed Authority are all defined in the treaty.

24. The extension of sovereign authority of States over significant aspects of the world's oceans is the basic effect of the new lawmaking treaty defining the law of the sea. However, it also extends State responsibility and provides for a new international tribunal to decide disputes.

25. IGOs, created by treaty obligations that transfer some element of sovereign authority to such multinational bodies, have functional capacity as legal entities with rights and duties under public international law. This principle is illustrated in the ICJ advisory opinion in the *Reparations* case.

26. Today, many intergovernmental organizations perform functions that were once exclusively reserved for States. Even NGOs have been given important functions as legal entities for vary limited purposes. NGOs, however, cannot bring claims under public international law.

Key Terms

Statehood
recognition
constitutive theory
declaratory theory
self-determination
   of peoples
State succession
insurgency
belligerency
premature recognition
neutrality
State responsibility
trust territories

terra nullius
original title
derivative title
res communis
uti possidetis
accretion
avulsion
Chicago Convention on
   International Civil
   Aviation (1944)
Tokyo Convention
   (1963)
internal waters

bays
territorial sea
innocent passage
contiguous zone (CZ)
exclusive economic
   zone (EEZ)
high seas
Deep Seabed
   Authority
international legal
   personality

■   ■   ■

Discussion Questions

1. What is required for the achievement of the legal status of Statehood in international law?

2. What are the basic rights and duties of States in international law?

3. What is meant by the legal concept of "self-determination of peoples" as used in the U.N. Charter?

4. What are the basic rules of international law on State succession?

5. When do States have a duty not to recognize the existence of particular States or acquisition of territory?

6. What is meant by the fundamental concept of State responsibility under international law?

7. What are the basic methods of acquiring territory by a State?

8. How have the methods of acquiring legitimate title to territory been changed by the U.N. Charter? Is there an emerging rule requiring a representative form of government?

9. What are the customary rules of international law concerning river and lake boundaries?

10. What are the basic rules regarding territorial airspace and jurisdiction of persons who have committed crimes of violence on board aircraft in flight?

11. What are the basic rules concerning sea zones in the 1982 LOS treaty? How has this treaty extended territorial jurisdiction of States?

12. Under what conditions do intergovernmental organizations have status as subjects of international law with capacity to bring legal claims against States?

Suggested Readings

Appendix K: Declaration on Principles of International Law Concerning Friendly Relations and Co-operation Among States in Accordance With the Charter of the United Nations

Cassese, A. (1995). *Self-determination of peoples: A legal reappraisal*. New York: Cambridge University Press.

Damrosch, L. F. (Ed.). (1993). *Enforcing restraint: Collective intervention in internal conflicts*. New York: Council on Foreign Relations Press.

Franck, T. M. (1976). The stealing of the Sahara. *American Journal of International Law, 70,* 694-721.

Franck, T. M. (1992). The emerging right to democratic governance. *American Journal of International Law, 86,* 96 46-91.

Internet Sources

Browse: U.N. Home Page (http://www.un.org/) and U.N. Treaty Database (http://www.un.org/Depts/Treaty/)

The American Society of International Law (http://www.asil.org)

12 *The Law of Treaties*

Treaties are a principal source of obligation in international law. Although customary practice, recognized by nation-states as legally binding, is a major source of international law, the treaty instrument is a method of creating and altering the binding obligations recognized by such law. Thus, both customary practice and treaties are the principal sources of international law accepted in the Statute of the International Court of Justice (Article 38). The "general principles of law recognized by civilized nations" is the only other specific source of international law recognized by the statute.

This chapter will discuss the general principles of the law of treaties that characterize the process by which treaties are formulated and interpreted by authoritative international tribunals. The treaty formation process will be discussed in the first section of this chapter, with the Vienna Convention on the Law of Treaties (1969) serving as the basis for this discussion. Approval of these international treaty obligations is subject to particular national or municipal limitations.

Some of the most important issues of U.S. treaty practice will be used to illustrate these differences. However, on the international plane, a State may not use a conflict with its own laws as a valid means of abrogating a binding obligation under international law. The basic principles of treaty observance, validity, and termination will be illustrated.

In earlier chapters (particularly Chapter 3), it has been noted that treaties may create (a) particular obligations binding two States (bilateral agreements), (b) general obligations binding more than two States (multilateral agreements); or (c) universally binding obligations that are "lawmaking" in character. Treaties may also vary in their intended effect on the municipal law of the parties to the treaty obligation. Some treaty provisions are intended to have direct effect in municipal law, conferring rights and duties on individuals in the municipal courts of each State that is a party to the treaty. To ensure this intended effect, some treaties employ the requirement of enactment into the municipal law of each State by legislative act as well as the conclusion of the formal treaty obligation. Most treaties are not "self-executing" in the sense described above but are intended to bind only the parties to the extent of their authority. Some are even personal commitments to work for intended goals and objectives made on the international plane.

Because treaties serve such a wide variety of functions, they have been given perhaps an even wider variety of names, or appellations. The term *treaty* is generally used to refer to all binding forms of agreements between subjects of international law. The terms used in these agreements themselves and attached to them in news stories include *convention, pact, protocol, charter, covenant, declaration, treaty*, and *international agreement*. Other terms are *act, statute, accord, modus vivendi, exchange of notes*, and *communiqué*, and *agreed statement*. The particular term used to refer to an agreement has, in itself, no legal effect. The legal effect of the agreement must be ascertained by the intent of the parties as expressed in the particular agreement.

Some actions that are the result of negotiations between sovereign States and that appear to be agreements are really intended to create only political or moral, as opposed to legal, commitments. These are often referred to as "gentlemen's agreements" and are nonbinding in the legal sense.

Difficulty in defining a treaty has produced some specific language usage that attempts to reduce misunderstanding. The League of Nations Covenant and the U.N. Charter both require treaty registration. However, the specific wording in these documents illustrates the attempt to gain more precision. Article 18 of the League of Nations Covenant contained an outright bar that voided the potential effects of any unregistered treaty. The U.N. Charter, in Article 102, however, provides that a party to an unregistered treaty may not "invoke that treaty or agreement before any organ of the United Nations." The most authoritative lawmaking treaty on the subject, the Vienna Convention on the Law of Treaties (1969), adds a requirement to the definition of a treaty: The agreement must be "governed by international law."

The **Vienna Convention on the Law of Treaties (VCLT)** was prepared by the U.N. International Law Commission through the laborious process described in Chapter 3 of this text, which in this case took twenty-six years to complete. The convention is

> **Vienna Convention on the Law of Treaties (VCLT):** The principal authoritative source of the law of treaties. It was concluded in Vienna in 1969 and entered into force in 1980.

generally declaratory of existing customary principles of international law and has been invoked and applied by tribunals and by States even prior to its entry into force. These aspects of the treaty may be considered "restatements" providing clarification of principles developed by custom and may be invoked by States that have not formally ratified it.

The 1969 VCLT Convention will be used as the basis for the discussion in this chapter. However, it has been supplemented by the 1986 **Vienna Convention on the Law of Treaties Between States and International Organizations or Between International Organizations**, which provides clarification of another facet of international treaty law. The VCLT Convention is limited to agreements between States and came into force in 1980 when the thirty-fifth State ratified it. It was signed by the president of the United States and submitted to the Senate in 1971, when the Department of State declared that the VCLT Convention "is al-

Vienna Convention on the Law of Treaties Between States and International Organizations or Between International Organizations (1986): *This convention provides clarification for another dimension to the law of treaties and was deliberately separated from the original document of 1969 to recognize this distinction. The general principles are the same, but details dealing with the special character of IGOs, as entities having legal personality, are dealt with separately.*

ready recognized as the authoritative guide to current treaty law and practice." Thus, while the treaty has not been ratified by the United States, it has applicable importance as a clarification of customary principles. The newer convention relating to agreements involving intergovernmental organizations (IGOs) has not yet entered into force.

The basic convention (VCLT) involves treaties concluded between States (as opposed to IGOs) and applies to agreements in written form. This convention expressly recognizes that agreements in nonwritten form and other general principles of the customary law of treaties are not prejudiced by the document. It is clearly stated that the parties affirm "that the rules of customary international law will continue to govern questions not regulated by the provisions of the present Convention." Thus, a State that is not a party to this intended universal convention can reasonably argue that any innovative provision of the VCLT does not bind such a State, and it can invoke evidence of other customary practice regarded as legally binding. The distinction between the declaratory and the "new" law of the convention is not readily apparent from the text and is sometimes subject to conflicting assessments. However, there is a general tendency for States to refer to all of the provisions of the VCLT as an authoritative source of law (Henkin, Pugh, Schachter, & Smit, 1987, p. 387).

The Treaty Formation Process

Bilateral treaties are formulated through individual negotiations between two States and may vary considerably in the manner by which these negotiations are undertaken. However, multilateral treaties have developed a fairly standardized series of steps that may be referred to as the treaty formation process. The basic steps are negotiation, signature (or accession), ratification, reservations (if any), entry into force, and registration.

Negotiation

The preparatory process of lawmaking conferences for treaties sponsored by the United Nations was discussed in Chapter 3. This usually involves research by the International Law Commission (ILC). The work of the ILC is sometimes augmented by other more political commissions, as it was with the International Law of the Sea Convention of 1982. Other multilateral preparatory procedures are developed outside the auspices of the United Nations that serve the same basic function of doing the groundwork for a more formal negotiation process when there is indication of potential general agreement.

If State representatives reach a general consensus, they will agree to activate an international conference of representatives who possess the authority to negotiate on behalf of their respective States. These representatives, who are vested with "full powers" to negotiate, adopt, authenticate, and sign a completed document include heads of State, heads of government, ministers of foreign affairs, heads of diplomatic missions, and representatives accredited by States to an international conference. Other representatives are required to present credentials to the chairperson or conference committee to verify their specific authority.

It is important to the negotiation process to have a clear understanding of the limits of the authority of the State delegates at such a conference. Presentation of documentary powers at the inception of a conference notifies all participants of the extent of a particular delegate's powers, which may in some cases be limited by the competent authority of the State. The conference verification process and Article 8 of the VCLT address situations in which the claimed absence of such authority may arise. Article 8 provides that any "act relating to the conclusion of a treaty performed by a person who cannot be considered . . . as authorized to represent a State for that purpose is without legal effect unless afterwards confirmed by the competent authority of the State."

Such formal treaty conferences offer an opportunity for objections and clarifications to take place in the final wording of the document before it is adopted. **Adoption** does not mean that the treaty has been signed. The adoption of the text takes place by the consent of the States participating in the drawing up of the text. At large international conferences, the adoption of the text of the negotiated treaty takes place by a vote. The VCLT suggests a two-thirds majority, but any special rules of the international organization within which the conference is held may apply to the adoption.

Authentication is a distinct procedural step in the conclusion of a treaty whereby the de-

> **Adoption:** *A formal act whereby the form and content of the text of a proposed treaty are settled.*

> **Authentication:** *A distinct procedural step in the conclusion of a treaty whereby the definitive text of the treaty is established as correct and authentic and not subject to alteration.*

finitive text of the treaty is established as correct and authentic and not subject to alterations. The specific procedure may be stipulated in the text of the treaty itself or by agreement of the negotiating States. Failing any such prescribed or agreed-on procedure, authentication takes place by **signature**, signature *ad referendum* (that is, a signature given provisionally and subject to confirmation by the respective governments), or initialing of the text by the representatives of the negotiating States or, alternatively, of the final act of the conference incorporating the text.

> **Signature:** *The official fixing of names to the text of a treaty by the representatives of the negotiating States either as a means of expressing the definitive consent of a State to be bound by a treaty or as an expression of provisional consent subject to ratification, acceptance, or approval.*

Signature or Accession

Signature of a treaty signals that the negotiating States have agreed in principle to the general wording of the articles appearing in the text of the final draft of the treaty. Many treaties provide that they go into force on the date of signature. When ratification, acceptance, or approval is necessary, the treaty enters into force only after the exchange or deposit of instruments of ratification, acceptance, or approval by all or a certain minimum number of States. Multilateral treaties usually provide that they will enter into force following the date of the deposit of a specified number of instruments of ratification, acceptance, approval, or accession.

Accession refers to acceptance of a treaty by a State that did not take part in negotiating and sign-

> **Accession:** *Formal acceptance of a treaty by a State that did not take part in negotiating and signing it.*

ing it. Accession is possible only if it is provided for in the treaty, if agreement of the negotiating States can otherwise be established, or if all the parties have subsequently agreed to a State's accession. Although it was once a controversial matter, recent practice allows a State to accede to a treaty that is not yet in force. The terms *adherence* or *adhesion* are considered to have the same meaning as *accession* in modern practice.

A signatory State to a multilateral treaty that requires ratification undertakes an obligation not to defeat the object and purpose of the treaty prior to its entry into force (VCLT Article 18). The final process of acceptance of the full obligations of the treaty may take considerable time to accomplish, particularly in States such as the United States where Senate agreement by a two-thirds majority is required.

Ratification

The word *ratification* is confusing because it has two different meanings. As explained by the ILC, **ratification** refers only to ratification on the international plane. It is distinct and separate from the procedural act of ratification under municipal law, such as parliamentary ratification or approval. Post-conference ratification is the typical mode for full acceptance of a treaty. Ratification means essentially that the conference delegate has submitted the provisionally accepted treaty text to the proper authority in his or her State for final approval—to be determined in accordance with that State's internal laws on treaty acceptance.

> **Ratification:** *An international act whereby a State establishes on the international plane its definitive consent to be bound by a treaty.*

Some States require a constitutional procedure that vests all, or part, of the treaty-making power in some organ that must be consulted for its approval before a formal treaty obligation is accepted. In these States, municipal constitutional law vests the treaty-making power in some organ that cannot delegate it to the plenipotentiaries (representatives with "full power"), and yet that organ cannot itself carry on negotiations with other States. For example, in the United Kingdom, Parliament must approve formal treaties, and in the United States the power is vested in the president but is subject to the advice and consent of the Senate.

In other States where such municipal treaty approval institutions are not required, or where, as in the United States, the presidential powers are the basis of the authority to enter the agreement (executive agreements), the signature of the competent authority is considered ratification and completes the obligation in international law for that State becoming party to the agreement.

Reservations

A **reservation** is a unilateral variation, submitted at the time of acceptance of the treaty. It attempts to exclude or modify the legal effect of certain provisions as applied to that State. The State normally agrees with the text generally but does not wish to become a party to the treaty on all details.

> **Reservation:** *A unilateral statement made by a State when approving a treaty, whereby it purports to exclude or to modify the legal effect of certain provisions of the treaty in their application to that State.*

There is considerable controversy about the permissibility of reservations. Many treaties contain clauses expressly prohibiting reservations or limiting them to certain aspects of the agreement only. Other treaties contain clauses requiring approval of the other parties to reservations or a required number of acceptances among the parties to allow reservations. In regard to *bilateral* treaties, reservations are normally not used. When one party attempts a reservation during the municipal acceptance process, it identifies a new proposal that reopens the joint negotiations over what terms will be in the ultimate agreement. Both States must agree on all terms of a bilateral treaty.

Multilateral treaties present more difficulties in regard to reservations. There has been much confusion regarding the acceptability of reservations to multilateral treaties in the absence of a specific clause designating the acceptance of reservations. Traditional practice would suggest that reservations would not be allowed unless all parties agreed to allow them. This issue arose in regard to the U.N. Genocide Convention. The Genocide Convention was drafted by the Legal Committee of the General Assembly (Sixth Committee) in 1948, before a thorough research effort of the ILC could be undertaken. It was unanimously adopted by all U.N. members by General Assembly resolution in the aftermath of the Holocaust in Nazi Germany. However, during the ultimate ratification process, many States were reluctant to ratify without knowing what specific obligations it entailed. They faced the dilemma of their willingness to accept this treaty's obligations in general yet feared that the absence of a reservation

provision might one day subject them to scrutiny under the convention on grounds that they had never contemplated; allowing reservations would enable them to clarify the acceptance of the obligation.

In 1950, the U.N. General Assembly requested an advisory opinion of the International Court of Justice (ICJ) on this subject. The Genocide Convention had just received the minimum number of ratifications, and the treaty had entered into force. There was no provision on the very sensitive question of whether reservations were permitted. If reservations were permitted, States could theoretically exclude certain forms of genocide from their consent to be bound by the treaty.

Some parties to the Genocide Convention were concerned that allowing reservations would enable such States to exempt themselves from its general provisions. They wanted to know the effect of objections by States who were already parties to any reservations that might be tendered by newly ratifying States. Other States, such as the United States, wanted to ratify the convention but would not do so without reservations limiting and clarifying the broad terms in the 1948 draft. The General Assembly thus turned to the ICJ for guidance.

In the following opinion, the Court delivered a very general and abstract answer to this sensitive question. The conclusion of the court is that this treaty would permit reservations as long as they are not incompatible with the language and purpose of the treaty.

Reservations to the Convention on Genocide
International Court of Justice, Advisory Opinion, 1951.
1951 I.C.J. 15.

[After a dispute had arisen concerning the legal effect of reservations made by several States to the Genocide Convention of 1948 (78 U.N.T.S. 277), the General Assembly adopted a resolution on November 16, 1950, G.A. Res. 478 (V 1950), asking the International Court of Justice for an advisory opinion on the questions, *inter alia:*

Insofar as concerns the Convention on the Prevention and Punishment of the Crime of Genocide in the event of a State's ratifying or acceding to the convention subject to a reservation made either on ratification or on accession or on signature followed by ratification:

    I. Can the reserving State be regarded as being a party to the convention while still maintaining its reservation, if the reservation is objected to by one or more of the parties to the convention but not by others?

    II. If the answer to Question I is in the affirmative, what is the effect of the reservation as between the reserving State and

        (a) the parties that object to the reservation?

        (b) those that accept it?

In answering these questions, the Court stated the following:]

All three questions are expressly limited by the terms of the Resolution of the General Assembly to the Convention on the Prevention and Punishment of the Crime of Genocide. . . . [T]he replies which the Court is called upon to give to them are necessarily and strictly limited to that Convention. The Court will seek these replies in the rules of law relating to the effect to be given to the intention of the parties to multilateral conventions. . . .

It is well established that in its treaty relations a State cannot be bound without its consent, and that consequently no reservation can be effective against any State without its agreement thereto. It is also a generally recognized principle that a multilateral convention is the result of an agreement freely concluded upon its clauses and that consequently none of the contracting parties is entitled to frustrate or impair, by means of unilateral decisions or particular agreements, the purpose and *raison d'être* of the convention. To this principle was linked the notion of the integrity of the convention as adopted, a notion which in its traditional concept involved the proposition that no reservation was valid unless it was accepted by all the contracting parties without exception, as would have been the case if it had been stated during the negotiations.

This concept, which is directly inspired by the notion of contract, is of undisputed value as a principle. However, as regards the Genocide Convention, it is proper to refer to a variety of circumstances which would lead to a more flexible application of this principle. Among these circumstances may be noted the clearly universal character of the United Nations under whose auspices the Convention was concluded, and the very wide degree of participation envisaged by Article XI of the Convention. Extensive participation in conventions of this type has already given rise to greater flexibility in the international practice concerning multilateral conventions. More general resort to reservations, very great allowance made for tacit assent to reservations, the existence of practices which go so far as to admit that the author of reservations which have been rejected by certain contracting parties is nevertheless to be regarded as a party to the convention in relation to those contracting parties that have accepted the reservations—all these factors are manifestations of a new need for flexibility in the operation of multilateral conventions.

It must also be pointed out that although the Genocide Convention was finally approved unanimously, it is nevertheless the result of a series of majority votes. The majority principle, while facilitating the conclusion of multilateral conventions, may also make it necessary for certain States to make reservations. This observation is confirmed by the great number of reservations which have been made of recent years to multilateral conventions. . . .

The Court . . . must now determine what kind of reservations may be made and what kind of objections may be taken to them.

The solution of these problems must be found in the special characteristics of the Genocide Convention. . . . The Genocide Convention was . . . intended by the General Assembly and by the contracting parties to be definitely universal in scope. It was in fact approved on December 9th, 1948, by a resolution which was unanimously adopted by fifty-six States.

The objects of such a convention must also be considered. The Convention was manifestly adopted for a purely humanitarian and civilizing purpose. It is indeed difficult to imagine a convention that might have this dual character to a greater degree, since its object on the one hand is to safeguard the very existence of certain human groups and on the other to confirm and endorse the most elementary principles of morality. In such a convention the contracting States do not have any interests of their own; they merely have, one and all, a common interest, namely, the accomplishment of those high purposes which are the *raison d'être* of the convention. Consequently, in a convention of this type one cannot speak of individual advantages or disadvantages to States, or of the maintenance of a perfect contractual balance between rights and duties. The high ideals which inspired the Convention provide, by virtue of the common will of the parties, the foundation and measure of all its provisions. . . .

The object and purpose of the Genocide Convention imply that it was the intention of the General Assembly and of the States which adopted it that as many States as possible should participate. The complete exclusion from the Convention of one or more States would not only restrict the scope of its application, but would detract from the authority of the moral and humanitarian principles which are its basis. It is inconceivable that the contracting parties readily contemplated that an objection to a minor reservation should produce such a result. But even less could the contracting parties have intended to sacrifice the very object of the Convention in favour of a vain desire to secure as many participants as possible. The object and purpose of the Convention thus limit both the freedom of making reservations and that of objecting to them. It follows that it is the compatibility of a reservation with the object and Purpose of the Convention that must furnish the criterion for the attitude of a State in making the reservation on accession as well as for the appraisal by a State in objecting to the reservation. . . .

Any other view would lead either to the acceptance of reservations which frustrate the purposes which the General Assembly and the contracting parties had in mind, or to recognition that the parties to the Convention have the power of excluding from it the author of a reservation, even a minor one, which may be quite compatible with those purposes.

It has nevertheless been argued that any State entitled to become a party to the Genocide Convention may do so while making any reservation it chooses by virtue of its sovereignty. The Court cannot share this view. It is obvious that so extreme an application of the idea of State sovereignty could lead to a complete disregard of the object and purpose of the Convention.

On the other hand, it has been argued that there exists a rule of international law subjecting the effect of a reservation to the express or tacit assent of all the contracting parties. This theory rests essentially on a contractual conception of the absolute integrity of the convention as adopted. This view, however, cannot prevail if, having regard to the character of the convention, its purpose and its mode of adoption, it can be established that the parties intended to derogate from that rule by admitting the faculty to make reservations thereto.

It does not appear, moreover, that the conception of the absolute integrity of a convention has been transformed into a rule of international law. The considerable part which tacit assent has always played in estimating the effect which is to be given to reservations scarcely permits one to state that such a rule exists, determining with sufficient precision the effect of objections made to reservations. In fact, the examples of objections made to reservations appear to be too rare in international practice to have given rise to such a rule. It cannot be recognized that the report which was adopted on the subject by the Council of the League of Nations on June 17th, 1927, has had this effect. At best, the recommendation made on that date by the Council constitutes the point of departure of an administrative practice which, after being observed by the Secretariat of the League of Nations, imposed itself, so to speak, in the ordinary course of things on the Secretary-General of the United Nations in his capacity of depositary of conventions concluded under the auspices of the League. But it cannot be concluded that the legal problem of the effect of objections to reservations has in this way been solved.

It results from the foregoing considerations that Question I, on account of its abstract character, cannot be given an absolute answer. The appraisal of a reservation and the effect of objections that might be made to it depend upon the particular circumstances of each individual case.

Having replied to Question I, the Court will now examine Question II

* * *

[E]ach State which is a party to the Convention is entitled to appraise the validity of the reservation, and it exercises this right individually and from its own standpoint. As no State can be bound by a reservation to which it has not consented, it necessarily follows that each State objecting to it will or will not, on the basis of its individual appraisal within the limits of the criterion of the object and purpose stated above, consider the reserving State to be a party to the Convention. . . .

The disadvantages which result from this possible divergence of views—which an article concerning the making of reservations could have obviated—are real; they are mitigated by the common duty of the contracting States to be guided in their judgment by the compatibility or incompatibility of the reservation with the object and purpose of the Convention. It must clearly be assumed that the contracting States are desirous of preserving intact at least what is essential to the object of the Convention; should this desire be absent, it is quite clear that the Convention itself would be impaired both in its principle and in its application.

It may be that the divergence of views between parties as to the admissibility of a reservation will not in fact have any consequences. On the other hand, it may be that certain parties who consider that the assent given by other parties to a reservation is incompatible with the purpose of the Convention, will decide to adopt a position on the jurisdictional plane in respect of this divergence and to settle the dispute which thus arises either by special agreement or by the procedure laid down in Article IX of the Convention.

Finally, it may be that a State, whilst not claiming that a reservation is incompatible with the object and purpose of the Convention, will nevertheless object to it, but that an understanding between that State and the reserving State will have the effect that the Convention will enter into force between them, except for the clauses affected by the reservation.

Such being the situation, the task of the Secretary-General would be simplified and would be confined to receiving reservations and objections and notifying them. . . .

For these reasons,

The Court is of Opinion,

In so far as concerns the Convention on the Prevention and Punishment of the Crime of Genocide, in the event of a State ratifying or acceding to the Convention subject to a reservation made either on ratification or on accession, or on signature followed by ratification,

On Question I:

by seven votes to five,

that a State which has made and maintained a reservation which has been objected to by one or more of the parties to the Convention but not by others, can be regarded as being a party to the Convention, if the reservation is compatible with the object and purpose of the Convention; otherwise, that State cannot be regarded as being a party to the Convention.

On Question II:

by seven votes to five,

(a) that if a party to the Convention objects to a reservation which it considers to be incompatible with the object and purpose of the Convention, it can in fact consider that the reserving State is not a party to the Convention;

(b) that if, on the other hand, a party accepts the reservation as being compatible with the object and purpose of the Convention, it can in fact consider that the reserving State is a party to the Convention. . . .

Discussion Questions

1. In answering the question of whether or not reservations to a treaty may be accepted in the absence of a clause concerning reservations, why does the Court caution that its decision specifically relates to the Genocide Convention?

2. Why is a reservation that attempts to defeat the object and purpose of the treaty unacceptable?

3. What effect does a reservation have when there is an objection by one or more of the parties to the Genocide Convention (a) when the objecting State considers the reservation incompatible with the object and purpose of the Convention, and (b) when a party to the Convention accepts the reservation as being compatible with the object and purpose of the Convention?

> *Comment:* Four of the fifteen judges on the ICJ joined in a dissenting opinion in this decision, arguing that the majority should have answered the question concerning reservations in the negative. They attempted to show that "the practice of governments [had] resulted in a rule of law requiring the unanimous consent of all parties to a treaty before a reservation can take effect and the State proposing it can become a party." These dissenters also criticized the Court's distinction between "compatible" and "incompatible" reservations on the grounds that it represented an innovation in the law of treaties and that the subjective nature of the distinction made it unworkable (1951 I.C.J. 32).
>
> Both the U.S.S.R. (and, by succession, the Russian Federation) and the United States have since ratified the Genocide Convention with reservations. Both superpowers have reservations to the dispute settlement clause in Article IX of the Convention. These reservations provide that the specific consent of the reserving party shall be required before a dispute may be submitted to the Court. The United States, however, included another reservation in its consent to ratification of the Genocide Convention in 1986. This reservation states "that nothing in the Convention requires or authorizes legislation or other action by the United States of America prohibited by the Constitution of the United States as interpreted by the United States."

The Legal Effect of Reservations

The international law on the question of the validity and effects of reservations is not settled, but in general, the rules of the Vienna Convention (1969) reflect the position of the great majority of States. Under Section 2, the Vienna Convention provides some clarification concerning reservations. A reservation by a particular State must be formulated in writing and communicated to the dispositary of the treaty or directly to the contracting States and other States entitled to become parties to the treaty. This stipulation is also required of the opposing or accepting States in communicating their reactions to the reservation. Reservations when signing a treaty must be confirmed on ratification.

The effect of a reservation is to modify certain provisions of the treaty in the reserv-

ing State's relations with the other parties without, however, modifying the provisions of the treaty for those parties *inter se*—that is, in their relations with each other. If a State objecting to a reservation has not opposed the entry into force of the treaty between itself and the reserving State, its treaty relations vis-à-vis the reserving State are modified by the reservation (Article 21 VCLT).

The Vienna Convention recognizes the general freedom to make reservations except in three cases: (a) reservations expressly prohibited, (b) those not falling within provisions in the treaty permitting specified reservations and not other reservations, and (c) reservations incompatible with the object and purpose of the treaty (Article 19). Reservations expressly authorized by the treaty do not require any subsequent acceptance by the other contracting States.

> When it appears from the limited number of negotiating states and the object and purpose of a treaty that the application of the treaty in its entirety between all the parties is an essential condition of the consent of each one to be bound by the treaty, a reservation requires acceptance by all parties. (Article 20, VCLT)

Similarly, unless the treaty provides otherwise, reservations to treaties establishing an international organization require acceptance by the competent organ of the organization (Article 20).

In all other multilateral treaties, a more flexible, relative approach applies under which a reserving State may become a party to the treaty in relation to States accepting the reservation, whereas an objection to a reservation does not preclude the entry into force of the treaty as between the objecting and reserving States unless a contrary intention is expressed by the objecting State. The Vienna Convention recognizes the tacit (implied) acceptance of a reservation by a State if it has raised no objections within a year of the notification of the reservation or its ratification of the treaty, whichever occurs later (see Article 20).

The modern trend toward acceptance of reservations to multilateral treaties is designed to encourage broader participation under the assumption that minor reservations that do not defeat the object and purpose of the major provisions allow flexibility that is necessary under the varying circumstances of individual State ratification procedures. A study of reservations concerning multilateral conventions that entered into force between 1919 and 1971 found that 85% of the 1,164 conventions had no reservations at all. Even fewer reser-

vations were found in the 839 conventions (over the same period) that were limited to certain States because of the subject matter or regional geography. Of these more limited conventions, 92% were without reservations (Gamble, 1980, p. 379).

Most reservations do not deal with the substantive provisions of the treaties. They relate mainly to dispute settlement, nonrecognition of other parties, compatibility with specific domestic laws, and colonial territories. The category of human rights treaties demonstrate the greatest tendency to promote reservations. For example, the Convention on Discrimination Against Women has drawn reservations from over thirty countries. Treaties dealing with private law and judicial procedure also attract reservations, nearly always on narrow points (Gamble, 1980, p. 386).

The International Covenant on Civil and Political Rights (ICCPR) is one of the most significant of the human rights covenants. The extensive use of reservations by States that have ratified this treaty, and objections raised by other parties, illustrate the issues involved in the more recent flexibility in the use of reservations. The United States ratified the ICCPR in 1992 with five reservations and a rather lengthy list of understandings and declarations clarifying U.S. interpretation of certain provisions of the document. By 1996, there were 132 parties to the ICCPR agreement and forty-nine States had included some form of reservation in their ratification, accession, or succession to the obligations of the treaty. Thus, the United States was not the only State to make use of the flexibility of the new rules allowing reservations.

Most of the reservations by the United States and the forty-eight other countries that expressed some form of reservation or clarification could be regarded as reasonable efforts to harmonize the unique conditions of the ratifying State with the letter of the wording of the ICCPR and were not objected to by other parties as incompatible with the spirit of the major provisions of the document. However, the U.S. reservation concerning capital punishment for minors was objected to by eleven States as incompatible with the covenant. These States included Belgium, Denmark, Finland, France, Germany, Italy, the Netherlands, Norway, Portugal, Spain, and Sweden. The only other reservations objected to as incompatible with the covenant were those submitted by Trinidad and Tobago and by the Republic of Korea, which drew considerably fewer objections than the U.S. reservation concerning capital punishment for minors.

The U.S. reservation concerning capital punishment for minors was the most important reservation that drew consistent objections from other parties of great significance in the European Union. The wording of this reservation is as follows:

> 2) That the United States reserves the right, subject to its Constitutional constraints, to impose capital punishment on any person (other than a pregnant woman) duly convicted under existing or future laws permitting the imposition of capital punishment, including such punishment for crimes committed by persons below eighteen years of age.

The objection raised by France is typical of the objections stated by the other ten members of the European Union that declared the U.S. reservation incompatible with the covenant. They all state in more or less the same words the following objection:

> At the time of the ratification of [the said Covenant], the United States of America expressed a reservation relating to article 6,

paragraph 5, of the Covenant, which prohibits the imposition of the death penalty for crimes committed by persons below 18 years of age.

> France considers that this United States Reservation is not valid, inasmuch as it is incompatible with the object and purpose of the Convention.

> Such objection does not constitute an obstacle to the entry into force of the Covenant between France and the United States.

These objections leave the U.S. reservation concerning capital punishment for minors in doubt as to its validity in a contested case. Most states within the United States prohibit execution of persons who were below the age of eighteen at the time they committed acts punishable by execution. However, the U.S. Supreme Court has ruled in a five-to-four decision that a state that imposes such a penalty is not in violation of the U.S. Constitution's "cruel and unusual punishment" prohibition (see *Stanford v. Kentucky* and *Wilkins v. Missouri*, 109 S.Ct. 2969, [1989]).

Other U.S. reservations to the ICCPR include reference to Article 20 of the covenant, which prohibits "propaganda for war." This provision is clarified to avoid conflict with "freedom of speech and association protected by the Constitution and laws of the United States." Another reservation seeks to exempt the United States from the provision in the covenant (Article 15,1) that requires retroactive application of changes in criminal penalties to the benefit of prisoners already sentenced. A reservation to allow treatment of juveniles as adults is included along with an attempt to use U.S. definitions of "cruel and unusual" punishment in the Fifth, Eighth, and/or Fourteenth Amendments as limiting the binding effects of Article 7 of the covenant. The *declarations* by the United States include the statement "that the provisions of articles 1 through 27 of the Covenant are not self-executing." This means that they do not directly extend rights to individuals in the courts of the United States.

In the Senate debate that concluded these reservations, Senator Moynihan attempted to excuse the effect of the Senate's action by asserting that the selective nature of the reservations indicated the seriousness with which the United States approached its new obligations. Unlike "nations of the totalitarian block [that] ratified obligations without reservation—obligations that they had no intention of carrying out."

However, in contrast to this assessment, Professor Schachter (1979) provides the following characterization of the proposed reservations:

> The critical legal issue raised is not whether specific reservations are admissible. It is rather whether a whole series of reservations admittedly designed to avoid any need to modify U.S. law can be regarded as in conformity with the object and purpose of the Covenant. . . . The proposed U.S. group of reservations . . . thus turns upside down the .. general principle of treaty law that a party may not invoke its internal law as justification for failure to perform a treaty. (p. 462)

Other general multilateral conventions of a lawmaking character have included provisions prohibiting reservations. This was done in regard to the 1982 U.N. Convention on the Law of the Sea. The relevant provisions of the treaty are specified in Articles 309 and 310 below:

Article 309

No reservations or exceptions may be made to this Convention unless expressly permitted by other articles of this Convention.

Article 310

Article 309 does not preclude a State, when signing, ratifying or acceding to this Convention, from making declarations or statements, however phrased or named, with a view, *inter alia*, to the harmonization of its laws and regulations with the provisions of this Convention, provided that such declarations or statements do not purport to exclude or to modify the legal effect of the provisions of this Convention in their application to that State.

The report of the U.S. delegation to the Law of the Sea (LOS) Convention explained this restrictive clause in the following manner:

> Since the Convention is an overall "package" reflecting different priorities of different states, to permit reservations would inevitably permit one State to eliminate the "quid" of another State's "quo." Thus there was general agreement in the Conference that in principle reservations could not be permitted.

This reasoning reflects a strategy that places greater priority on complete reciprocity and consistency of agreement than on encouraging broader participation at the expense of universality in all details.

Thus, problems relating to interpreting the legal effects of reservations can be at least partially remedied by a careful drafting of the text of the treaty to achieve genuine consensus and by making explicit provisions on the subject of reservations, such as providing for decisions on the incompatibility of reservations to be made by majority rule. Under the Convention on the Elimination of All Forms of Racial Discrimination (1966), for example, a reservation is incompatible if at least two-thirds of the contracting parties object to it.

Entry Into Force

The parties that have drafted the treaty specify the manner and date of the entry into force of the substantive obligations of the treaty. Failing such a provision that specifies these matters, the treaty enters into force as soon as all negotiating States have consented to be bound. Many treaties provide for their entry into force on the date of signature.

Multilateral treaties, for which ratification, acceptance, or approval is necessary, enter into force only after the exchange or deposit of the instruments of ratification. It would normally be unreasonable to wait for ratification, acceptance, or approval by all the signatory States, and accordingly, such treaties usually provide that they will enter into force following the date of the deposit of a specified number of instruments of ratification. For example, the U.N. Charter specifies that it enters into force when all permanent members of the Security Council and one-half of the signatory States have deposited their instruments of ratification.

The extensive development and use of the multilateral treaty instrument in modern times has required the explicit rule in Article 24(4) of the Vienna Convention that negotiating States in agreeing to the adoption of the text of a treaty are legally bound by the provisions of the draft treaty concerning authentication, signature and ratifications, depositary functions, reservations, or entry into force that have to be dealt with prior to the treaty's coming into force. Thus, even before instruments of ratification have been exchanged, there is some degree of assumed obligation by the States that have adopted the text of a treaty.

Another of these provisional obligations that exists during the interval between signature and entry into force (when instruments of ratification are required) is that each signatory State has an obligation to refrain from acts that would defeat the object and purpose of the treaty until it has made clear its intention not to become a party to the treaty.

The fixing of the date on which a treaty enters into force is essential for ascertaining the rights and obligations of the parties with regard to the treaty. Modern treaties usually specify such a date. A typical formula for a multilateral treaty is provided in the VCLT, which stipulates that "the Convention shall enter into force on the thirtieth day following the date of the deposit of the thirty-fifth instrument of ratification or accession."

Registration

Treaty registration is required under the U.N. Charter in order to be given legally binding effect by any organ of the United Nations. Over 33,000 bilateral and multilateral treaties have been registered with the U.N. Secretariat and are published in the U.N. publication titled the *United Nations Treaty Series*.

An international agreement carrying some forms of obligation does not have to be published or registered to have some binding effect. But individual nations usually have municipal provisions requiring publication. The U.S. Congress therefore requires publication in the comprehensive *United States Statutes at Large*. Congressional action requiring publication states that once published, those statutes "shall be legal evidence of laws . . . treaties, and international agreements [executive agreements] other than treaties."

U.S. Treaty Practice

The difficulty of defining precisely what the term *treaty* includes is a problem on both the municipal and international planes of consideration. Article II, § 2, clause 2 of the U.S. Constitution states that the president "shall have power, by and with the advice and consent of the Senate, to make treaties, provided two-thirds of the Senators present concur." However, the Constitution does not define precisely what it means by a treaty. Other aspects of the Constitution appear to recognize that there are international agreements other than treaties that may be concluded without the advice and consent of two-thirds of the Senate. The president's power to conclude "executive agreements" that are obligations under international law, without the advice and consent of two-thirds of the Senate, has become broadly accepted. Nonetheless, there is considerable controversy over the limitations of this executive authority.

In U.S. treaty practice, there are three methods of concluding binding international agreements: (a) the formal treaty procedure defined in Article II of the Constitution, (b) the *executive-legislative* agreement, and (c) the *sole executive* agreement. These methods are frequently available to the president for optional choice in discharging the obligations of the executive in conducting the foreign relations of the United States.

There is an often overlooked fourth method available to the states under Article I, Section 10, of the Constitution. Although this provision prohibits states of the union from entering into any "treaty, alliance or confederation," it also says that "No state shall, without the consent of Congress . . . enter into any agreement or compact with another state, or with a foreign power." This provision indicates that the framers of the Constitution recognized international agreements other than treaties dealt with specifically in Article II. But again, there is no other specific definition in the document

that clarifies the distinction between a treaty and an agreement or compact.

Early practice of the United States made use of all of these methods of concluding agreements that were intended to have legally binding effect in international law. However, there has always been some controversy over the proper use of these varying instruments, especially with regard to the use of the sole executive agreement. Although the U.S. Constitution distinguishes between the two categories of agreement—treaties and executive agreements—international law does not. The VCLT provides in Article 2 that a treaty is an international agreement concluded between States in written form and governed by international law, whether embodied in a single instrument or in two or more related instruments and whatever its particular designation. "Thus," according to the State Department's letter of submittal to Congress in 1971, "it applies not only to formal treaties but to agreements in simplified form, such as exchange of notes."

Although the VCLT came into effect on January 27, 1980, the United States has not ratified it. This impasse exists primarily because the Senate Foreign Relations Committee has "sought to equate 'treaties' as used in the Convention with 'treaties' in the U.S. Constitution, and to declare that every agreement that is a 'treaty' under the Convention can be concluded by the United States only by the process prescribed for 'treaties' in the Constitution. That position has been rejected by the Executive Branch" (American Law Institute, 1987, Part III, Introductory Note 146, n. 4).

Article II Treaties

One of the most important issues arising under the Articles of Confederation, which prompted the Constitutional Convention of 1787, was the weakness of the treaty power of the union of former colonial states. The Articles of Confederation conferred on Congress "the sole and exclusive right and power of . . . entering into treaties and alliances." However, the newly independent former colonies were eager to retain the commercial freedom and political control they had gained as a result of the revolution and stipulated in Article II that "each State retains its sovereignty, freedom, and independence, and every power, jurisdiction, and right, which is not by this Confederation expressly delegated to the United States in Congress assembled." This loose confederation gave the union the authority to conclude treaties and alliances with other countries, but it had little authority to ensure that the treaties concluded would be fulfilled by the independent states of the union.

As the war of independence ended, it became evident that the new confederate government was at a distinct disadvantage in negotiating a multilateral peace settlement. There was no executive authority under the Articles of Confederation, and Congress was ill equipped to conduct these negotiations. Members of Congress appointed plenipotentiaries to represent them in Paris, the site of the peace conference; however, their communications with the Congress were leaked by the congressional delegates. This lack of secrecy in the negotiations no doubt had an influence on the decision to exclude congressional representatives from any part in treaty negotiation when the new Constitution was drafted.

More important, under the Articles of Confederation, Congress was unable to compel the states to execute the provisions in the peace treaty. Because of this weakness, the states refused to return property of British citizens promised in the treaty, and the British government retaliated by retaining her forts in the Northwest Territory. When John Adams, American ambassador

to Britain, sought to conclude a commercial treaty with that country, the British Foreign Secretary contemptuously suggested that ambassadors from the thirteen states ought to be present, since Congress had no authority over the subject. This led to British actions to close the West Indies to American trade. It was almost impossible for Congress to negotiate commercial treaties with foreign States because they realized that Congress could not guarantee compliance by the states with any commercial policy agreed to. Even France and Holland hesitated to negotiate treaties with a nation that could not meet its commitments (Kelly, Harbison, & Belz, 1983, p. 87).

These recognized weaknesses led to the creation of a powerful and independent executive authority under the new Constitution. Article II of the Constitution says simply, "The executive Power shall be vested in a President of the United States." This article may be deceptive in that it gives the president few other specific powers, but it also denies that office few powers. The Constitution makes the president "Commander in Chief" of the military forces when called into service of the United States. It also gives the president power to send and receive ambassadors and negotiate treaties, as well as extensive appointment powers.

The **supremacy clause** in Article VI of the Constitution is the heart of the efforts of the framers to "create a more perfect union." It states:

> **Supremacy clause:** Article VI, paragraph 2 makes the U.S. Constitution, acts of Congress, and treaties the "supreme law of the land."

This Constitution, and the Laws of the United States which shall be made in Pursuance thereof; and all Treaties made, or which shall be made, under the Authority of the United States, shall be the supreme Law of the land; and the Judges in every State shall be bound thereby, any Thing in the Constitution or Laws of any State to the Contrary notwithstanding.

Thus, certainly an **Article II treaty** negotiated by the president and ratified with the advice and consent of two-thirds of the Senate has the force of law within the United States as well as creating a binding international legal obligation.

> **Article II treaty:**
> An international agreement concluded by and with the advice and consent of two-thirds of the Senate.

Although the principles of British government were highly regarded by the framers and frequently referred to as a model in the construction of the U.S. Constitution, the treaty power differs from that of Great Britain. An Article II treaty does not require full congressional approval for it to become the "law of the land." The British practice now, and at the time of the Constitutional Convention, was that Parliament must assent to a treaty before it becomes a part of the internal law of that land. However, British practice also accepted the authority of the Crown to engage in internationally binding agreements as long as they are not intended to become a part of the municipal law. The primary criterion that determines the necessity for legislative assent to an international agreement is a royal desire for the treaty to have the sanction of internal law.

Certain internationally binding commitments are accepted by the negotiating representatives of any government of necessity before approval of the agreement can be concluded according to the municipal laws of that country. The British practice of use of executive agreements was thus well-known and accepted by the framers of the Constitution. The U.S. Constitution does not rule out executive-legislative agreements that were used under the Articles of Confederation. What the new Constitution added was the alternative route of Article II treaties that may become the law of the land by agreement between the president and two-thirds of the Senate.

Executive-Legislative Agreements

The president of the United States may choose to pursue legislative support for an international obligation by securing its enactment into the "law of the land" by the ordinary lawmaking procedure or by joint resolution of both houses of Congress. President Truman's message to Congress in 1947 concerning the Trusteeship Agreement for the Territory of the Pacific Islands indicated that joint approval of both houses of Congress would have the same effect internationally and domestically as the Article II treaty process. The following statement from his 1947 message explains Truman's position:

> I am satisfied that either method is constitutionally permissible, and that the agreement resulting will be of the same effect internationally, and under the supremacy clause of the Constitution whether advised and consented to by the Senate or whether approval is authorized by a joint resolution. The interest of both Houses of Congress in the execution of this agreement is such, however, that I think it would be appropriate for the Congress, in this instance, to take action by a joint resolution in authorizing this Government to bring the agreement into effect.

The **executive-legislative treaty** has been used many times by the president to secure agreement particularly in areas that require the sustained support of both houses of Congress. This alternative gives

> **Executive-legislative treaty:** *A treaty concluded by executive agreement and enacted into law by a majority vote of both houses of Congress. This option removes any question as to whether the treaty is self-executing and avoids the two-thirds requirement in Senate approval of an Article II treaty.*

the president flexibility and has raised little controversy. It should be noted that the executive-legislative treaty removes any question about whether or not it is self-executing since it complies with the domestic lawmaking criteria *(People of Saipan v. U.S. Department of Interior*, 502 F.2d 90, [1974]). The approval of the North American Free Trade Agreement (NAFTA) was secured by joint resolution of Congress, which enacted the agreement into law in 1992.

The Sole Executive Agreement

The U.S. Supreme Court has attributed to the president "inherent powers" in foreign policy. In the 1936 case, *United States v. Curtiss-Wright*, the Court upheld the validity of the president to declare an embargo of arms shipments to the belligerents in the Chaco War between Bolivia and Paraguay (1932-1935). Prior to the president's action, Congress had enacted a joint resolution providing that if the president made certain findings and issued a proclamation to the effect that a ban on arms sales to certain countries would serve the cause of regional peace, such arms sales would be illegal. The issue in the *Curtiss-Wright* case was whether the joint resolution amounted to delegation of the lawmaking power. Justice Sutherland's majority opinion concluded that in the "vast external realm [foreign relations], with its important, complicated, delicate and manifold problems, the President alone has the power to speak or listen as a representative of the nation." He further explains the decision:

It is important to bear in mind that we are here dealing not alone with an authority vested in the President by an exertion of legislative power, but with such an authority plus the very delicate, plenary and exclusive power of the President as the sole organ of the federal government in the field of international relation—a power which does not require as a basis for its exercise an act of Congress. *(United States v. Curtiss-Wright Corp.*, 299 U.S. 304, [1936])

Sutherland asserts that the inherent powers of the British sovereign in foreign policy matters never passed to the former colonies as independent states but were exercised by the U.S. government under the Articles of Confederation and then by the president under the provisions of the U.S. Constitution. The reasoning of this decision has been subject to much scholarly criticism for historical accuracy and bias; however, the decision has never been overruled.

In the *Steel Seizure* case, during the Truman administration, the Court struck down an action by the president ordering seizure of the private steel mills threatened by a general strike during the Korean War *(Youngstown Sheet & Tube Co. v. Sawyer*, 343 U.S. 579, [1952]). These two cases are generally considered illustrative of the dividing line between permissible presidential action under the Constitution and that which is prohibited. The Congress had earlier refused to authorize the president to take such action as seizing the steel mills even in time of undeclared war. The *Steel Seizure* case is further distinguished from the *Curtiss-Wright* case by the characterization of the president's action as within the "external realm" in declaring the arms embargo as opposed to the "internal realm" in seizing the steel mills.

The **sole executive agreement** refers to those agreements with foreign countries or intergovernmental agencies pursuant to the exercise of the president's sole powers under the Constitution. This authority does not require the prior specific authorization of Congress or the approval of two-thirds of the Senate. It is clear from the decisions of the Supreme Court that follow that the president has such authority to commit the United States to certain forms of international agreements. The vagueness of the president's "sole plenary powers under the Constitution" is the basic source of the conflict between the Congress and the president. This vagueness has often been described by constitutional scholars such as Laurence H. Tribe as "beneficent ambiguity."

Domestic Issues Concerning U.S. Treaty Practice

One of the most important domestic issues concerning the treaty-making power relates to the federal system in which responsibilities for lawmaking are distributed between the national and State governments. Although the United States was one of the first federal systems, today, at least a dozen significant countries also have genuine federal systems; among the more important federal States are Switzerland, the United States, Canada, the Russian Federation, India, Australia, Brazil, and Germany. However, the overwhelming majority of nation-states today have unitary systems in which there is only one lawmaking authority.

The federal features of those States that divide their lawmaking authority between the central government and quasi-autonomous regions profoundly affect their participation in the international treaty-making system. These issues were less evident in a treaty system characterized mainly by bilateral agreements of peace, alliance, commerce, and navigation when there was little effect on domestic laws. Today, multilateral conventions regulate a far wider range of subjects, such as child labor, human rights, copyrights, and environmental issues that raise a number of concerns for the national authority. May the federal government enter into treaties that deal with matters wholly, or in part, assigned to the states? Do such treaties automatically become part of the law of the land, even to the extent of repealing inconsistent legislation of the states and barring future inconsistent legislation by the local units of government? Could this expansion of treaty commitments change the character of the federal system of division of authority?

The issues raised in the classic case of *Missouri v. Holland*, which follows, have produced severe criticism and fear that the treaty system may not be bound by constitutional considerations. Here, the Supreme Court upheld an act of Congress pursuant to an Article II treaty. Note that the same statute was previously held unconstitutional in the lower federal courts before the treaty was adopted. The earlier congressional act was restricted by the constitutional division between federal and state authority. After a treaty was concluded with Canada, the same regulation was passed by Congress but this time pursuant to a treaty.

Missouri v. Holland
Supreme Court of the United States, 1920.
252 U.S. 416, 40 S.Ct. 382, 64 L.Ed. 641.

Ultra Vires — Beyond Authority

MR. JUSTICE HOLMES delivered the opinion of the Court.

This is a bill in equity brought by the State of Missouri to prevent a game warden of the United States from attempting to enforce the Migratory Bird Treaty Act of July 3, 1918, c. 128, 40 Stat. 755, and the regulations made by the Secretary of Agriculture in pursuance of the same. The ground of the bill is that the statute is an unconstitutional interference with the rights reserved to the States by the Tenth Amendment, and that the acts of the defendant done and threatened under that authority invade the sovereign right of the State and contravene its will manifested in statutes. The State also alleges a pecuniary interest, as owner of the wild birds within its borders and otherwise, admitted by the Government to be sufficient, but it is enough that the bill is a reasonable and proper means to assert the alleged quasi sovereign rights of a State. *Kansas v. Colorado*, 185 U.S. 125, 142, 22 Sup.Ct. 552, 46 L.Ed. 838; *Georgia v. Tennessee Copper Co.*, 206 U.S. 230, 237, 27 Sup.Ct. 618, 51 L.Ed. 1038, 11 Ann.Cas. 488; *Marshall Dental Manufacturing Co. v. Iowa*, 226 U.S. 460, 462, 33 Sup.Ct. 168, 57 L.Ed. 300. A motion to dismiss was sustained by the District Court on the ground that the Act of Congress is constitutional. 258 Fed. 479. Acc. *United States v. Thompson* (D.C.) 258 Fed. 257; *United States v. Rockefeller* (D.C.) 260 Fed. 346. The State appeals.

On December 8, 1916, a treaty between the United States and Great Britain was proclaimed by the President. It recited that many species of birds in their annual migrations traversed many parts of the United States and of Canada, that they were of great value as a source of food and in destroying insects injurious to vegetation, but were in danger of extermination through lack of adequate protection. It therefore provided for specified closed seasons and protection in other forms, and agreed that the two powers would take or propose to their lawmaking bodies the necessary measures for carrying the treaty out. 39 Stat. 1702. The above mentioned act of July 3, 1918, entitled an act to give effect to the convention, prohibited the killing, capturing or selling any of the migratory birds included in the terms of the treaty except as permitted by regulations compatible with those terms, to be made by the Secretary of Agriculture. Regulations were proclaimed on July 31, and October 25, 1918. 40 Stat.1812, 1863. It is unnecessary to go into any details, because, as we have said, the question raised is the general one whether the treaty and statute are void as an interference with the rights reserved to the States.

To answer this question it is not enough to refer to the Tenth Amendment, reserving the powers not delegated to the United States, because by Article 2, Section 2, the power to make treaties is delegated expressly, and by Article 6 treaties made under the authority of the United States, along with the Constitution and laws of the United States made in pursuance thereof, are declared the supreme law of the land. If the treaty is valid there can be no dispute about the validity of the statute under Article 1, Section 8, as a necessary and proper means to execute the powers of the Government. The language of the Constitution as to the supremacy of treaties being general, the question before us is narrowed to an inquiry into the ground upon which the present supposed exception is placed.

It is said that a treaty cannot be valid if it infringes the Constitution, that there are limits, therefore, to the treaty-making power, and that one such limit is that what an act of Congress could not do unaided, in derogation of the powers reserved to the States, a treaty cannot do. An earlier act of Congress that attempted by itself and not in pursuance of a treaty to regulate the killing of migratory birds within the States had been held bad in the District Court. *United States v. Shauver*, 214 Fed. 154. *United States v. McCullagh*, 221 Fed. 288. Those decisions were supported by arguments that migratory birds were owned by the States in their sovereign capacity for the benefit of their people, and that under cases like *Geer v. Connecticut*, 161 U.S. 519, 16 Sup.Ct. 600, 40 L.Ed. 793, this control was one that Congress had no power to displace. The same argument is supposed to apply now with equal force.

Whether the two cases cited were decided rightly or not they cannot be accepted as a test of the treaty power. Acts of Congress are the supreme law of the land only when made in pursuance of the Constitution, while treaties are declared to be so when made under the authority of the United States. It is open to question whether the authority of the United States means more than the formal acts prescribed to make the convention. We do not mean to imply that there are no qualifications to the treaty-making power; but they must be ascertained in a different way. It is obvious that there may be matters of the sharpest exigency for the national well-being that an act of Congress could not deal with but that a treaty followed by such an act could, and it is not lightly to be assumed that, in matters requiring national action, "a power which must belong to and somewhere reside in every civilized government" is not to be found. *Andrews v. Andrews*, 188 U.S. 14, 33, 23 Sup.Ct. 237, 47 L.Ed. 366. What was said in that case with regard to the powers of the States applies with equal force to the powers of the nation in cases where the States individually are incompetent to act. We are not yet discussing the particular case before us but only are considering the validity of the test proposed. With regard to that we may add that when we are dealing with words that also are a constituent act, like the Constitution of the United States, we must realize that they have called into life a being the development of which could not have been foreseen completely by the most gifted of its begetters. It was enough for them to realize or to hope that they had created an organism; it has taken a century and has cost their successors much sweat and blood to prove that they created a nation. The case before us must be considered in the light of our whole experience and not merely in that of what was said a hundred years ago. The treaty in question does not contravene any prohibitory words to be found in the Constitution. The only question is whether it is forbidden by some invisible radiation from the general terms of the Tenth Amendment. We must consider what this country has become in deciding what that amendment has reserved.

The State as we have intimated founds its claim of exclusive authority upon an assertion of title to migratory birds, an assertion that is embodied in statute. No doubt it is true that as between a State and its inhabitants the State may regulate the killing and sale of such birds, but it does not follow that its authority is exclusive of paramount powers. To put the claim of the State upon title is to lean upon a slender reed. Wild birds are not in the possession of anyone; and possession is the beginning of ownership. The whole foundation of the State's rights is the presence within their jurisdiction of birds that yesterday had not arrived, tomorrow may be in another State and in a week a thousand miles away. If we are to be accurate we cannot put the case of the State upon higher ground than that the treaty deals with creatures that for the moment are within the state borders, that it must be carried out by officers of the United States within the same territory, and that but for the treaty the State would be free to regulate this subject itself.

As most of the laws of the United States are carried out within the States and as many of them deal with matters which in the silence of such laws the State might regulate, such general grounds are not enough to support Missouri's claim. Valid treaties of course "are as binding within the territorial limits of the States as they are elsewhere throughout the dominion of the United States." *Baldwin v. Franks*, 120 U.S. 678, 683, 7 Sup.Ct. 656, 657, 32 L.Ed. 766. No doubt the great body of private relations usually fall within the control of the State, but a treaty may override its power. We do not have to invoke the later developments of constitutional law for this proposition; it was recognized as early as *Hopkirk v. Bell*, 3 Cranch, 454, 2 L.Ed. 497, with regard to statutes of limitation, and even earlier, as to confiscation, in *Ware v. Hylton*, 3 Dall. 199, 1 L.Ed. 568. It was assumed by Chief Justice Marshall with regard to the escheat of land to the State in *Chirac v. Chirac*, 2 Wheat. 259, 275, 4 L.Ed. 234; *Hauenstein v. Lynham*, 100 U.S. 483, 25 L.Ed. 628; *DeGeofroy v. Riggs*, 133 U.S. 258, 10 Sup.Ct. 295, 33 L.Ed. 642; *Blythe v. Hinckley*, 180 U.S. 333, 340, 21 Sup.Ct. 390, 45 L.Ed. 557. So as to a limited jurisdiction of foreign consuls within a State. *Wildenhus' Case*, 120 U.S. 1, 7 Sup.Ct. 385, 30 L.Ed. 565. *See Boss v. McIntyre*, 140 U.S. 453, 11 Sup.Ct. 897, 35 L.Ed. 581. Further illustration seems unnecessary, and it only remains to consider the application of established rules to the present case.

Here a national interest of very nearly the first magnitude is involved. It can be protected only by national action in concert with that of another power. The subject matter is only transitorily within the State and has no permanent habitat therein. But for the treaty and the statute there soon might be no birds for any powers to deal with. We see nothing in the Constitution that compels the Government to sit by while a food supply is cut off and the protectors of our forests and our crops are destroyed. It is not sufficient to rely upon the States. The reliance is vain, and were it otherwise, the question is whether the United States is forbidden to act. We are of opinion that the treaty and statute must be upheld. *Carey v. South Dakota*, 250 U.S. 118, 39 Sup.Ct. 403, 63 L.Ed. 886.

Decree affirmed.

MR. JUSTICE VAN DEVANTER and MR. JUSTICE PITNEY dissent.

Discussion Questions

1. Does this decision imply that the treaty-making authority is not limited by the provisions of the Constitution? Discuss.
2. How does the U.S. Constitution divide the lawmaking authority between the national government and the states?
3. Is the treaty-making power an exclusive power of the national government and denied to the states?
4. Is there a danger that extensive use of the treaty authority by the national government could change the character of American federalism?

Comment: The Bricker Amendment, proposed by Senator Bricker in the early 1950s, represents the most serious threat to alter the treaty-making power under the U.S. Constitution. For Bricker and his colleagues, the Holmes' dictum in *Missouri v. Holland* suggested that treaties are not bound by constitutional limitations and when combined with the ability of treaties to be self-executing, seriously threatened the federal character of U.S. sovereignty. Senator Bricker announced that his amendment would "prohibit the use of the treaty as an instrument of domestic legislation," and would "prevent its use as a vehicle for surrendering national sovereignty." The amendment went through a series of modifications, but it attempted to specify in some form that treaties are subservient to the Constitution. The proposed amendment usually made all treaties non-self-executing and sometimes advocated further restriction by limiting treaty subject matter to that which Congress "could enact under its delegated powers in the absence of such treaty." In 1954, a floor vote in the Senate on a similar version of the amendment fell one vote short of the two-thirds majority needed. After this defeat, the interest in this issue has declined, especially after the decision in *Reid v. Covert* in 1957.

The issue in *Missouri v. Holland* did not quite reach the more important issue raised by the fears of the supporters of the Bricker amendment. Can treaties supersede rights established by the Constitution? This is the more specific issue that was dealt with in **Reid v. Covert**, at least when there is a conflict between a sole executive agreement and the criminal due process rights to indictment by a grand jury and trial by jury in the Fifth and Sixth Amendments to the U.S. Constitution.

In the *Reid* Case, two wives of military personnel (one in Japan and the other in Great Britain) were alleged to have murdered their husbands on military bases while the couples were stationed abroad. Although the wives were civilians, they were court-marshaled, without ability to exercise the Fifth and Sixth Amendment guarantees to a grand jury indictment and trial by jury. The executive agreements that had been concluded with Japan and Great Britain permitted U.S. military courts to exercise exclusive jurisdiction over such offenses committed in those countries.

The Supreme Court found that the necessary and proper clause of Article I, Section 8, could not be stretched to validate military jurisdiction over a person not a member of the military described in Clause 14, providing for the "land and naval forces." No treaty or executive agreement could confer on Congress or any other branch of government powers that it does not possess under the Constitution. Nor could the executive, or the executive and Senate combined, effectively amend the Constitution by means other than the process prescribed in Article V to change the Constitution, which re-

> *Reid v. Covert:* U.S. Supreme Court decision in 1957 holding that the president could not abrogate the criminal due process rights of dependents of military personnel overseas even though the crime alleged was committed in a foreign country and the defendants were convicted by court-marshal according to an executive agreement between the president and the host country.

quires ratification by three-fourths of the states. ⟩

The Court further found that trial by jury in a court of law and in accordance with traditional modes of procedure after an indictment by grand jury, as guaranteed by Article II, Section 2, and by the Fifth and Sixth Amendments, was a vital barrier to government arbitrariness. These constitutional provisions could not be abrogated by an agreement with a foreign power. The Court therefore concluded that the executive agreements in question were inconsistent with the Constitution, that military tribunals could have no jurisdiction over civilian dependents of military personnel in contravention of these rights, and finally, that the two women were entitled to trials in civil courts of law with the full panoply of constitutional rights (see *Reid v. Covert,* 354 U.S. 1, 1957).

Thus, it is clear that the courts of the United States will not enforce a treaty that is in direct conflict with the provisions of the U.S. Constitution. However, this does not abrogate the international obligations of the United States to Japan and Great Britain under international law. This aspect of the dispute had to be worked out on the international plane. U.S. treaty practice is also ambiguous with regard to whether or not a treaty supersedes an act of Congress. The supremacy clause appears to place them both on the same plane, and this is the interpretation that has become known as the "last in time" doctrine.

In an early case establishing the "last in time" doctrine

> ***"Last in time" doctrine:*** A rule established by early Supreme Court decisions that when a treaty and an act of Congress are in direct conflict, the act that is last in time prevails, based on the assumption that treaties and acts of Congress are on an equal plane.

the Supreme Court was faced with a conflict between rights asserted under Article 10 of an 1866 treaty between the United States and the Cherokee Indian Nation and the Internal Revenue Act (two years later) of July 20, 1868. The Court concluded as follows:

> Undoubtedly one or the other must yield. The repugnancy is clear and cannot stand together. . . . The effect of treaties and acts of Congress, when in conflict, is not settled by the Constitution. But the question is not involved in any doubt as to its proper solution. A treaty may supersede a prior act of Congress, and an act of Congress may supersede a prior treaty. (*The Cherokee Tobacco,* 78 U.S. [11 Wall.] 616, 1870 at 620-21)

The "last in time" doctrine has been used in several subsequent cases by the Supreme Court and the lower federal courts. These court decisions have indicated reluctance to give acts of Congress precedence over treaties and have made every effort to avoid construing the existence of a direct conflict. In *Whitney v. Robertson* (1888), the Supreme court added, "When the two [treaty and statute] relate to the same subject, the courts will always endeavor to construe them so as to give effect to both, if that can be done without violating the language of either; but if the two are inconsistent, the one last in date will control the other; provided, always, the treaty on the subject is self-executing" (*Whitney v. Robertson,* 124 U.S. 190, [1888]).

The Supreme Court's opinion in *Weinberger v. Rossi*, drafted by Justice Rehnquist, illustrates this careful attempt to avoid conflict with the president's conduct of foreign affairs. The opinion also explains the inconsistent usage of the term *treaty*.

Weinberger v. Rossi
Supreme Court of the United States, 1982.
456 U.S. 25, 102 S.Ct. 1510, 71 L.Ed.2d 715.

Justice REHNQUIST delivered the opinion of the Court.

In 1944, Congress authorized the President, "by such means as he finds appropriate," to acquire, after negotiation with the President of the Philippines, military bases "he may deem necessary for the mutual protection of the Philippine Islands and of the United States." 58 Stat. 626, 22 U.S.C. § 1392. Pursuant to this statute, the United States and the Republic of the Philippines in 1947 entered into a 99-year Military Bases Agreement (MBA), Mar. 14, 1947, 61 Stat. 4019, T.I.A.S. No. 1775. The MBA grants the United States the use of various military facilities in the Philippines. It does not, however, contain any provisions regarding the employment of local nationals on the base. In 1968, the two nations negotiated a Base Labor Agreement (BLA), May 27, 1968, [1968] 19 U.S.T. 5892, T.I.A.S. No. 6542, as a supplement to the MBA. The BLA, *inter alia*, provides for the preferential employment of Filipino citizens at United States military facilities in the Philippines.

In 1971, Congress enacted § 106 of Pub.L. 92-129, the employment discrimination statute at issue in this case. At the time § 106 was enacted, 12 agreements in addition to the BLA were in effect providing for preferential hiring of local nationals on United States military bases overseas. Since § 106 was enacted, four more such agreements have been concluded. None of these agreements were submitted to the Senate for its advice and consent pursuant to Art. II, § 2, cl. 2, of the Constitution.

In 1978, respondents, all United States citizens residing in the Philippines, were notified that their jobs at the United States Naval Facility at Subic Bay were being converted into local national positions in accordance with the BLA, and that they would be discharged from their employment with the Navy. After unsuccessfully pursuing an administrative remedy, respondents filed suit in the United States District Court for the District of Columbia, alleging that the preferential employment provisions of the BLA violated, *inter alia*, § 106. The District Court granted summary judgment for petitioners, *Rossi v. Brown*, 467 F. Supp. 960 (1979), but the Court of Appeals reversed. *Rossi v. Brown*, 206 U.S.App.D.C 148, 642 F.2d 553 (1980). We in turn reverse the Court of Appeals.

II

* * *

We naturally begin with the language of § 106, which provides in relevant part as follows:

> "*Unless prohibited by treaty* [italics added], no person shall be discriminated against by the Department of Defense or by any officer or employee thereof, in the employment of civilian personnel at any facility or installation operated by the Department of Defense in any foreign country because such person is a citizen of the United States or is a dependent of a member of the Armed Forces of the United States." 85 Stat. 355, note following 5 U.S.C. § 7201 (1976 ed., Supp. IV)

* * *

The word "treaty" has more than one meaning. Under principles of international law, the word ordinarily refers to an international agreement concluded between sovereigns, regardless of the manner in which the agreement is brought into force. 206 U.S.App.D.C., at 151, 642 F.2d, at 556.5 Under the United States Constitution, of course, the word "treaty" has a far more restrictive meaning. Article II, § 2, cl. 2, of that instrument provides that the President "shall have Power, by and with the Advice and Consent of the Senate, to make Treaties, provided two thirds of the Senators present concur."

Congress has not been consistent in distinguishing between Art. II treaties and other forms of international agreements. For example, in the Case Act, 1 U.S.C. § 112b(a) (1976 ed., Supp.IV), Congress required the Secretary of State to "transmit to the Congress the text of any international agreement, . . . other than a treaty, to which the United States is a party" no later than 60 days after "such agreement has entered into force." Similarly, Congress has explicitly referred to Art. II treaties in the Fishery Conservation and Management Act of 1976, 16 U.S.C. § 1801 *et seq.* (1976 ed. and Supp.IV), and the Arms Control and Disarmament Act, 22 U.S.C. § 2551 *et seq.* (1976 ed. and Supp.IV). On the other hand, Congress has used "treaty" to refer only to international agreements other than Art. II treaties. In 39 U.S.C. § 407(a), for example, Congress authorized the Postal Service, with the consent of the President, to "negotiate and conclude postal treaties or conventions." A "treaty" which requires only the consent of the President is not an Art. II treaty. Thus it is not dispositive that Congress in § 106 used the term "treaty" without specifically including international agreements that are not Art. II treaties.

The fact that Congress has imparted no precise meaning to the word "treaty" as that term is used in its various legislative Acts was recognized by this Court in *B. Altman & Co. v. United States*, 224 U.S. 583, 32 S.Ct. 593, 56 L.Ed. 894 (1912). There this Court construed "treaty" in § 5 of the Circuit Court of Appeals Act of 1891, ch. 517, 26 Stat. 826, to include international agreements concluded by the President under congressional authorization. 224 U.S., at 601, 32 S.Ct., at 597. The Court held that the word "treaty" in the jurisdictional statute extended to such an agreement, saying: "If not technically a treaty requiring ratification, nevertheless it was a compact authorized by the Congress of the United States, negotiated and proclaimed under the authority of its President. We think such a compact is a treaty under the Circuit Court of Appeals Act." . . . Ibid.

The statute involved in the *Altman* case in no way affected the foreign policy of the United States, since it dealt only with the jurisdiction of this Court. In the case of a statute such as § 106, that does touch upon the United States' foreign policy, there is even more reason to construe Congress' use of "treaty" to include international agreements as well as Art. II treaties. At the time § 106 was enacted, 13 executive agreements provided for preferential hiring of local nationals. *Supra*, at 1513. Thus, if Congress intended to limit the "treaty exception" in § 106 to Art. II treaties, it must have intended to repudiate these executive agreements that affect the hiring practices of the United States only at its military bases overseas. One would expect that Congress would be aware that executive agreements may represent a *quid pro quo*: the host country grants the United States base rights in exchange, *inter alia*, for preferential hiring of local nationals. See n. 17, infra.

It has been a maxim of statutory construction since the decision in *Murray v. The Charming Betsy*, 2 Cranch 64, 118, 2 L.Ed. 208 (1804), that "an act of congress ought never to be construed to violate the law of nations, if any other possible construction remains. . . ." In *McCulloch v. Sociedad Nacional de Marineros de Honduras*, 372 U.S. 10, 20-21, 83 S.Ct. 671, 677-678, 9 L.Ed.2d 547 (1963), this principle was applied to avoid construing the National Labor Relations Act in a manner contrary to State Department regulations, for such a construction would have had foreign policy implications. The *McCulloch* Court also relied on the fact that the proposed construction would have been contrary to a "well-established rule of international law." Id., at 21, 83 S.Ct., at 677-678. While these considerations apply with less force to a statute which by its terms is designed to affect conditions on United States enclaves outside of the territorial limits of this country than they do to the construction of statutes couched in general language which are sought to be applied in an extraterritorial way, they are nonetheless not without force in either case.

At the time § 106 was enacted, there were in force 12 agreements in addition to the BLA providing for preferential hiring of local nationals on United States military bases overseas. Since the time of the enactment of § 106, four more such agreements have been concluded, and none of these were submitted to the Senate for its advice and consent. *Supra*, at 1513. We think that some affirmative expression of congressional intent to abrogate the United States' international obligations is required in order to construe the word "treaty" in § 106 as meaning only Art. II treaties. We therefore turn to what legislative history is available in order to ascertain whether such an intent may fairly be attributed to Congress.

The legislative history seems to us to indicate that Congress was principally concerned with the financial hardship to American service-men which resulted from discrimination against American citizens at overseas bases. As the Conference Committee Report explains:

> "The purpose of [§ 106] is to correct a situation which exists at some foreign bases, primarily in Europe, where discrimination in favor of local nationals and against American dependents in employment has contributed to conditions of hardship for families of American enlisted men whose dependents are effectively prevented from obtaining employment." H.R.Conf.Rep. No. 92433, p. 31 (1971).

The Conference Report, however, is entirely silent as to the scope of the "treaty" exception. Similarly, there is no mention of the 13 agreements that provided for preferential hiring of local nationals. Thus, the Conference Report provides no support whatsoever for the conclusion that Congress intended in some way to limit the President's use of international agreements that may discriminate against American citizens who seek employment at United States military bases overseas.

On the contrary, the brief congressional debates on this provision indicate that Congress was not concerned with limiting the authority of the President to enter into executive agreements with the host country, but with the ad hoc decision making of military commanders overseas. In early 1971, Brig. Gen. Charles H. Phipps, Commanding General of the European Exchange System, issued a memorandum encouraging the recruitment and hiring of local nationals instead of United States citizens at the system's stores. The hiring of local nationals, General Phipps reasoned, would result in lower wage costs and turnover rates. Senator Schweiker, a sponsor of § 106, complained of General Phipps' policy.

* * *

While the question is not free from doubt, we conclude that the "treaty" exception contained in § 106 extends to executive agreements as well as to Art. II treaties. The judgment of the Court of Appeals is reversed, and the case is remanded for proceedings consistent with this opinion.

It is so ordered.

Discussion Questions

1. Is there a direct conflict between the Base Labor (executive) Agreement (BLA) of 1968, and Section 106 of employment discrimination statute enacted by Congress in 1971?
2. Should the "last in time" doctrine prevail in this case?
3. What are the consequences of Congressional meddling in foreign affairs by attempting to abrogate executive agreements and treaties by subsequent acts of Congress?

In 1988, the decision of a federal district court in New York demonstrates how narrowly a court can construe a later-in-time congressional enactment in order to harmonize it with a treaty. Congress passed the Anti-Terrorism Act of 1987 (ATA) in an attempt to close the office of the Palestine Liberation Organization (PLO) Observer Mission to the United Nations. The statute provides, *inter alia*, that

it shall be unlawful, if the purpose be to further the interests of the PLO . . . notwithstanding any provision of law to the contrary, to establish or maintain an office, headquarters, premises, or other facilities or establishments within the jurisdiction of the United States at the behest or direction of, or with funds provided by the PLO. (22 U.S.C.A. §§ 5202, 5202[3])

In 1947, the United States had concluded the Agreement Between the United States and the United Nations Regarding the Headquarters of the United Nations (U.N.T.S. 11, No. 147, 1947). The U.N. headquarters in New York was established as an international enclave by the Agreement Between the United States and the United Nations (an executive-legislative agreement) found in 22 U.S.C.A. § 287 note. Under the Headquarters Agreement, the United States is obligated to provide unimpeded transit, entry, and access to the United Nations for representatives of members and persons invited to the headquarters district by the United Nations. Invited persons include permanent observers, a practice conducted for forty years and specifically recognized for the PLO by the State Department when the

PLO was invited to become a permanent observer and maintain a mission in 1974.

After the U.S. Anti-Terrorism Act was passed, the United Nations called for an advisory opinion from the ICJ. The ICJ determined that the Anti-Terrorism Act had created a dispute between the United States and the United Nations concerning obligations owed by the United States under the Headquarters Agreement. In the opinion of the international tribunal on the international plane, Section 21 of the Headquarters Agreement required the United States to participate in arbitration with the United Nations (*Applicability of the Obligation to Arbitrate Under Section 21 of the United Nations Headquarters Agreement of 26 June 1947, Advisory Opinion* [1988], I.C.J. 12).

In *United States v. Palestine Liberation Organization*, the following opinion of the federal district court illustrates how this issue was dealt with on the municipal plane in the United States. This decision also illustrates the differences between the functions of international tribunals and the municipal courts in the United States.

▮　　　　　▮　　　　　▮

United States v. Palestine Liberation Organization
United States District Court, Southern District of New York, 1988.
695 F.Supp. 1456.

ORDER AND OPINION

PALMIERI, DISTRICT JUDGE.

The Anti-terrorism Act of 1987 (the "ATA"), is the focal point of this lawsuit. At the center of controversy is the right of the Palestine Liberation Organization (the "PLO") to maintain its office in conjunction with its work as a Permanent Observer to the United Nations. The case comes before the court on the government's motion for an injunction closing this office and on the defendants' motions to dismiss.

I

Background

The United Nations' Headquarters in New York were established as an international enclave by the *Agreement Between the United States and the United Nations Regarding the Headquarters of the United Nations* (the "Headquarters Agreement"). This agreement followed an invitation extended to the United Nations by the United States, one of its principal founders, to establish its seat within the United States.

As a meeting place and forum for all nations, the United Nations, according to its charter, was formed to:

> maintain international peace and security . . . ; to develop friendly relations among nations, based on the principle of equal rights and self-determination of peoples . . . ; to achieve international cooperation in solving international problems of an economic, social, cultural or humanitarian character and be a centre for harmonizing the actions of nations in the attainment of these common ends. U.N. Charter art. 1

Today, 159 of the United Nations members maintain missions to the United Nations in New York. U.N. Protocol and Liaison Service, *Permanent Missions to the United Nations* No. 262 3-4 (1988) (hereinafter "Permanent Missions No. 262"). In addition, the United Nations has, from its incipiency, welcomed various non-member observers to participate in its proceedings. See *Permanent Missions to the United Nations: Report of the Secretary-General* (hereinafter Permanent Missions: Report of the Secretary-General). Of these, several nonmember nations, intergovernmental organizations, and other organizations currently maintain "Permanent Observer Missions" in New York. The PLO falls into the last of these categories and is present at the United Nations as its invitee. See Headquarters Agreement, ¶ 11 (22 U.S.C. § 287 note). The PLO has none of the usual attributes of sovereignty. It is not accredited to the United States and does not have the benefits of diplomatic immunity. There is no recognized state it claims to govern. It purports to serve as the sole political representative of the Palestinian people. The PLO nevertheless considers itself to be the representative of a state, entitled to recognition in its relations with other governments, and is said to have diplomatic relations with approximately one hundred countries throughout the world.

In 1974, the United Nations invited the PLO to become an observer at the United Nations, to "participate in the sessions and the work of the General Assembly in the capacity of observer." The right of its representatives to admission to the United States as well as access to the United Nations was immediately challenged under American law. Judge Costantino rejected that challenge in *Anti-Defamation League of B'nai B'rith v. Kissinger*. The court upheld the presence of a PLO representative in New York with access to the United Nations, albeit under certain entrance visa restrictions which limited PLO personnel movements to a radius of 25 miles from Columbus Circle in Manhattan. It stated from the bench:

> This problem must be viewed in the context of the special responsibility which the United States has to provide access to the United Nations under the Headquarters Agreement. It is important to note that a primary goal of the United Nations is to provide a forum where peaceful discussions may displace violence as a means of resolving disputed issues. At times our responsibility to the United Nations may require us to issue visas to persons who are objectionable to certain segments of our society. . . .

Since 1974, the PLO has continued to function without interruption as a permanent observer and has maintained its Mission to the United Nations without trammel, largely because of the Headquarters Agreement, which we discuss below.

II

The Anti-Terrorism Act

In October 1986, members of Congress requested the United States Department of State to close the PLO offices located in the United States. That request proved unsuccessful, and proponents of the request introduced legislation with the explicit purpose of doing so. The result was the ATA, 22 U.S.C. §§ 5201-5203. It is of a unique nature. We have been unable to find any comparable statute in the long history of Congressional enactments. The PLO is stated to be "a terrorist organization and a threat to the interests of the United States, its allies, and to international law and should not benefit from operating in the United States." 22 U.S.C. § 5201(b). The ATA was added, without committee hearings, as a rider to the Foreign Relations Authorization Act for Fiscal Years 1988-89, which provided funds for the operation of the State Department, including the operation of the United States Mission to the United Nations. The bill also authorized payments to the United Nations for maintenance and operation. Id., § 102(a)(1); see also id. § 143.

The ATA, which became effective on March 21, 1988, forbids the establishment or maintenance of "an office, headquarters, premises, or other facilities or establishments within the jurisdiction of the United States at the behest or direction of, or with funds provided by" the PLO, if the purpose is to further the PLO's interests. 22 U.S.C. § 5202(3). The ATA also forbids spending the PLO's funds or receiving anything of value except informational material from the PLO, with the same *mens rea* requirement.

* * *

The United States commenced this lawsuit the day the ATA took effect, seeking injunctive relief to accomplish the closure of the Mission. The United States Attorney for this District has personally represented that no action would be taken to enforce the ATA pending resolution of the litigation in this court.

* * *

[Section III omitted.]

IV

Counsel for the PLO and for the United Nations and the Association of the Bar of the City of New York, as *amici curiae*, have suggested that the court defer to an advisory opinion of the International Court of Justice. Applicability of the Obligation to Arbitrate Under Section 21 of the United Nations Headquarters Agreement of 26 June 1947, 1988 I.C.J. 12 (April 26, 1988) (U.N. v. U.S.). That decision holds that the United States is bound by Section 21 of the Headquarters Agreement to submit to binding arbitration of a dispute precipitated by the passage of the ATA. Indeed, it is the PLO's position that this alleged duty to arbitrate deprives the court of subject matter jurisdiction over this litigation. In June 1947, the United States subscribed to the Headquarters Agreement, defining the privileges and immunities of the United Nations' Headquarters in New York City, thereby becoming the "Host Country"—a descriptive title that has followed it through many United Nations proceedings. The Headquarters Agreement was brought into effect under United States law, with an annex, by a Joint Resolution of Congress approved by the President on August 4, 1947. The PLO rests its argument, as do the amici, on Section 21(a) of the Headquarters Agreement, which provides for arbitration in the case of any dispute between the United Nations and the United States concerning the interpretation or application of the Headquarters Agreement. Because interpretation of the ATA requires an interpretation of the Headquarters Agreement, they argue, this court must await the decision of an arbitral tribunal yet to be appointed before making its decision.

Section 21(a) of the Headquarters Agreement provides, in part:

> "Any dispute between the United Nations and the United States concerning the interpretation or application of this agreement or of any supplemental agreement, which is not settled by negotiation or other agreed mode of settlement, shall be referred for final decision to a tribunal of three arbitrators. . . ."

. . . Because these proceedings are not in any way directed to settling any dispute, ripe or not, between the United Nations and the United States, Section 21, is, by its terms, inapplicable. The fact that the Headquarters Agreement was adopted by a majority of both Houses of Congress and approved by the President, see 61 Stat. at 768, might lead to the conclusion that it provides a rule of decision requiring arbitration any time the interpretation of the Headquarters Agreement is at issue in the United States Courts. That conclusion would be wrong for two reasons.

First, this court cannot direct the United States to submit to arbitration without exceeding the scope of its Article III powers. What sets this case apart from the usual situation in which two parties have agreed to binding arbitration for the settlement of any future disputes, requiring the court to stay its proceedings, . . . is that we are here involved with matters of international policy. This is an area in which the courts are generally unable to participate. These questions do not lend themselves to resolution by adjudication under our jurisprudence. See generally *Baker v. Carr*, . . . The restrictions imposed upon the courts forbidding them to resolve such questions (often termed "political questions" derive not only from the limitations which inhere in the judicial process but also from those imposed by Article III of the Constitution. *Marbury v. Madison*, . . . (Marshall, C.J.) ("The province of the court is, solely, to decide on the right of individuals, not to inquire how the executive, or executive officers, perform duties in which they have a discretion. Questions in their nature political, or which are, by the constitution and laws, submitted to the executive can never be made in this Court."). The decision in *Marbury* has never been disturbed.

The conduct of the foreign relations of our Government is committed by the Constitution to the executive and legislative—the "political"—departments of the government. As the Supreme Court noted in *Baker v. Carr*, . . . not all questions touching upon international relations are automatically political questions. Nonetheless, were the court to order the United States to submit to arbitration, it would violate several of the tenets to which the Supreme Court gave voice in *Baker v. Carr*, . . . Resolution of the question whether the United States will arbitrate requires "an initial policy determination of a kind clearly for nonjudicial discretion"; deciding whether the United States will or ought to submit to arbitration, in the face of a determination not to do so by the executive, would be impossible without the court "expressing lack of the respect due coordinate branches of government;" and such a decision would raise not only the "potentiality" but the reality of "embarrassment from multifarious pronouncements by various departments on one question." It is for these reasons that the ultimate decision as to how the United States should honor its treaty obligations with the international community is one which has, for at least one hundred years, been left to the executive to decide. *Goldwater v. Carter*, 444 U.S. 996, 996-97, 100 S.Ct. 533, 533, 62 L.Ed.2d 428 (1979) (vacating, with instructions to dismiss, an attack on the President's action in terminating a treaty with Taiwan);

Clark v. Allen, 331 U.S. 503, 509, 67 S.Ct. 1431, 1435, 91 L.Ed. 1633 (1947) ("President and Senate may denounce a treaty and thus terminate its life") (quoting *Techt v. Hughes*, 229 N.Y. 222, 243, 128 N.E. 185 (Cardozo, J.), cert. denied, 254 U.S. 643, 41 S.Ct. 14, 65 L.Ed. 454(1920)); *Oetjen v. Central Leather Co.*, 246 U.S. 297, 302, 38 S.Ct. 309, 310, 62 L.Ed. 726 (1918) (redress for violation of international accord must be sought via executive); *Chae Chan Ping v. United States (The Chinese Exclusion Case)*, 130 U.S. 581, 602, 9 S.Ct. 623, 628, 32 L.Ed. 1068 ("the question whether our government is justified in disregarding its engagements with another nation is not one for the determination of the courts") (1889); accord *Whitney v. Robertson*, 124 U.S. 190, 194-95, 8 S.Ct. 456, 458, 31 L.Ed. 386 (1888).Consequently the question whether the United States should submit to the jurisdiction of an international tribunal is a question of policy not for the courts but for the political branches to decide.

Section 21 of the Headquarters Agreement cannot provide a rule of decision regarding the interpretation of that agreement for another reason: treating it as doing so would require the courts to refrain from undertaking their constitutionally mandated function. The task of the court in this case is to interpret the ATA in resolving this dispute between numerous parties and the United States. Interpretation of the ATA, as a matter of domestic law, falls to the United States courts. In interpreting the ATA, the effect of the United States' international obligations—the United Nations Charter and the Headquarters Agreement in particular—must be considered. As a matter of domestic law, the interpretation of these international obligations and their reconciliation, if possible, with the ATA is for the courts. It is, as Chief Justice Marshall said, "emphatically the province and duty of the judicial department to say what the law is." *Marbury v. Madison* That duty will not be resolved without independent adjudication of the effect of the ATA on the Headquarters Agreement. Awaiting the decision of an arbitral tribunal would be a repudiation of that duty.

Interpreting Section 21 as a rule of decision would, at a minimum, raise serious constitutional questions. We do not interpret it in that manner. *NLRB v. Catholic Bishop of Chicago*, 440 U.S. 490, 500-01, 99 S.Ct. 1313, 1319, 59 L.Ed.2d 533 (1979). It would not be consonant with the court's duties for it to await the interpretation of the Headquarters Agreement by an arbitral tribunal, not yet constituted, before undertaking the limited task of interpreting the ATA with a view to resolving the actual dispute before it. In view of the foregoing, the court finds that it is not deprived of subject matter jurisdiction by Section 21 of the Headquarters Agreement and that any interpretation of the Headquarters Agreement incident to an interpretation of the ATA must be done by the court.

V

The Anti-Terrorism Act and the Headquarters Agreement

If the ATA were construed as the government suggests, it would be tantamount to a direction to the PLO Observer Mission at the United Nations that it close its doors and cease its operations *instanter*. Such an interpretation would fly in the face of the Headquarters Agreement, a prior treaty between the United Nations and the United States, and would abruptly terminate the functions the Mission has performed for many years. This conflict requires the court to seek out a reconciliation between the two.

* * *

We believe the ATA and the Headquarters Agreement cannot be reconciled except by finding the ATA inapplicable to the PLO Observer Mission.

A. The Obligations of the United States under the Headquarters Agreement.

The obligation of the United States to allow transit, entry and access stems not only from the language of the Headquarters Agreement but also from forty years of practice under it. Section 11 of the Headquarters Agreement reads, in part: "The federal, state or local authorities of the United States shall not impose any impediments to transit to or from the headquarters district of: (1) representatives of Members . . . , (5) other persons invited to the headquarters district by the United Nations . . . on official business." (22 U.S.C. § 287 note). These rights could not be effectively exercised without the use of offices. The ability to effectively organize and carry out one's work, especially as a liaison to an international organization, would not be possible otherwise. It is particularly significant that Section 13 limits the application of United States law not only with respect to the entry of aliens, but also their residence. The Headquarters Agreement thus contemplates a continuity limited to official United Nations functions and is entirely consistent with the maintenance of missions to the United Nations. The exemptions of Section 13 are not limited to members, but extend to invitees as well.

There can be no dispute that over the forty years since the United States entered into the Headquarters Agreement it has taken a number of actions consistent with its recognition of a duty to refrain from impeding the functions of observer missions to the United Nations. It has, since the early days of the United Nations's presence in New York, acquiesced in the presence of observer missions to the United Nations in New York. See Permanent Missions: Report of the Secretary-General.

After the United Nations invited the PLO to participate as a permanent observer, the Department of State took the position that it was required to provide access to the United Nations for the PLO. The State Department at no time disputed the notion that the rights of entry, access and residence guaranteed to invitees include the right to maintain offices.

* * *

In sum, the language of the Headquarters Agreement, the long-standing practice under it, and the interpretation given it by the parties to it leave no doubt that it places an obligation upon the United States to refrain from impairing the function of the PLO Observer Mission to the United Nations. The ATA and its legislative history do not manifest Congress' intent to abrogate this obligation. We are therefore constrained to interpret the ATA as failing to supersede the Headquarters Agreement and inapplicable to the Mission.

* * *

VI

Conclusions

The Anti-Terrorism Act does not require the closure of the PLO Permanent Observer Mission to the United Nations nor do the act's provisions impair the continued exercise of its appropriate functions as a Permanent Observer at the United Nations. The PLO Mission to the United Nations is an invitee of the United Nations under the Headquarters Agreement and its status is protected by that agreement. The Headquarters Agreement remains a valid and outstanding treaty obligation of the United States. It has not been superseded by the Anti-Terrorism Act, which is a valid enactment of general application.

* * *

The motion of the United States for summary judgment is denied, and summary judgment is entered for the defendants, dismissing this action with prejudice.

Discussion Questions

1. Why does the court decide not to give direct effect to the ICJ advisory opinion?
2. How does this decision deviate from the "last in time" doctrine?
3. How would the U.S. Supreme Court have decided this question if the issue had been properly before it?

> *Comment:* On August 29, 1988, the U.S. Department of Justice announced that the administration would not appeal this decision in the *PLO* case. "The Administration based its decision on foreign policy considerations. Specifically, the State Department expressed concern that the closure of the mission would violate the U.S. obligations as the host country under the United Nations Headquarters Agreement" (28 I.L.M. 1704, 1988).
>
> Some commentators have questioned the "last in time" doctrine, calling for a rule that more clearly establishes the superiority of international law over domestic legislation that is reflected in more modern constitutions, such as those of France and the Netherlands (see Article 55 of the Constitution of France [1958] and Article 94 of the Constitution of the Netherlands [1983]; see also *Restatement (Third) of the Foreign Relations Law of the United States* § 115 Reporters' Notes 1 [1987]).

The Case Act

The use of sole executive agreements has generated the most controversy with Congress and elements of the public. In an attempt to regulate itself, the Department of State has issued directives that executive agreements ought to be subject to certain limitations. In its Circular No. 175 (1955 as revised in 1966), the department stated the following:

> Executive agreements shall not be used when the subject matter should be covered by a treaty. The executive agreement form shall be used only for agreements which fall into one or more of the following categories:
>
> a. Agreements which are made pursuant to or in accordance with existing legislation or a treaty;
>
> b. Agreements which are made subject to Congressional approval or implementation; or
>
> c. Agreements which are made under and in accordance with the President's Constitutional Power.

If an executive agreement has not been authorized by prior legislation or does not fall within the sphere of constitutional presidential authority, the agreement is regarded as void (see *United States v. Guy W. Capps, Inc.*, 204 F.2d 655; for the problem of a conflict between an executive agreement and State law, see *United States v. Pink*, 315 U.S. 293).

Nonetheless, Congress has long been concerned with the idea of curbing the use of sole executive agreements. Various resolutions of the Senate Foreign Relations Committee attempt to curb the use of sole executive agreements and recognize only agreements having the support of the legislative branch. These actions were not intended to have lawmaking force. However, in 1972, Congress adopted a bill to limit the use of "sole" executive agreements.

The **Case Act** (1 U.S.C.A. § 112b) requires the president to transmit to Congress all international agreements other than treaties within sixty days of the time they were concluded. If the

> **Case Act:** *An act of Congress requiring the president to report all international agreements, written or oral, within sixty days of their being concluded.*

president feels that public disclosure would jeopardize national security, the agreement could be transmitted to the foreign affairs committees of both houses of Congress under injunction of secrecy.

The Case Act was amended in 1977 to apply to agreements made by any department or agency of the U.S. government. It was again amended in 1978 to apply to oral as well as written agreements.

Treaty Validity, Observance, and Termination

—duty to observe treaties in good faith (page 5)

The principle of *pacta sunt servanda* was described as the fundamental postulate of international law in Chapter 1 of this text. The binding effect of treaties is therefore an assumption of the international legal order required of necessity, if such an order is to exist. Good faith performance of treaty obligations is the responsibility of the parties. This means that the basic intent of these obligations must be followed and not be evaded by a merely literal application of the clauses. The term *good faith* is used also to refer to the acceptance of minor deviations that are reasonable under the circumstances.

The most serious challenge to the traditional international law of treaties was the acceptance of the validity of treaties that were "unequal" (provided benefits to only one party) and negotiated under duress. The modern law of treaties as expressed in the Vienna Convention reflects the fundamental changes in international law resulting from the U.N. Charter prohibition against the threat or use of force in violation of the principles of international law.

Invalidity of Treaties

The newly created nations of Africa and Asia had long experience with unequal treaties that they rightfully contended, in the 1960s, were no longer acceptable under international law. The general argument is that since Article 2(4) of the U.N. Charter requires all members "to refrain in their international relations from the threat or use of force . . . inconsistent with the purposes of the United Nations," then coercion in the treaty process should invalidate the legality of a treaty made under duress.

The resulting provisions of the Vienna Convention incorporate two articles that concern the invalidity of treaties concluded under (a) coercion of the representative of the State and (b) treaties that have been concluded under coercion of the State.

Article 51

The expression of a State's consent to be bound by a treaty which has been procured by the coercion of its representative through acts or threats directed against him shall be without any legal effect.

Article 52

A treaty is void if its conclusion has been procured by the threat or use of force in violation of the principles of international law embodied in the Charter of the United Nations.

These provisions were the subject of much debate and negotiation at the Vienna Conference where a number of Eastern communist bloc and African States advocated the view that prohibition against force should expressly include economic, military, and political coercion. Their attempts were resisted by Western representatives who argued that such a definition would be too difficult to determine in practice. Article 52 therefore does not contain a specific definition of force. Instead, it generally prohibits the threat or use of force in violation of the principles of international law embodied in the U.N. Charter. This leaves the language purposefully vague and subject to some flexibility of interpretation.

As part of the compromise on the issue of defining the term *force*, the delegates at the Vienna Convention adopted a separate Declaration on the Prohibition of Military, Political or Economic Coercion in the Conclusion of Treaties. This declaration states that the U.N. Conference on the Law of Treaties "solemnly condemns the threat or use of pressure in any form, whether military, political, or economic, by any State in order to coerce another State to perform any act relating to the conclusion of a treaty in violation of the principles of the sovereign equality of States and freedom of consent" (UN Doc. A/CONF. 39/26, Documents of the Conference [1969], 285).

The issue of entry into force of Article 52 is equally vague in that it can be argued that treaties concluded under duress are void if concluded after the ratification of the U.N. Charter. The most certain date is the date of entry into force of the Vienna Convention (January 27, 1980). However, in the *Fisheries Jurisdiction* case (*U.K. v. Iceland*, 1973), the ICJ stated there "can be little doubt, as is implied in the Charter of the United Nations and recognized in Article 52 of the Vienna Convention on the Law of Treaties, that under contemporary international law an agreement concluded under the threat or use of force is void."

Fraud and corruption of a representative of a State does not automatically invalidate the treaty but may be invoked by a party as invalidating its consent to be bound by the treaty (Articles 49 and 50). Errors that result in misunderstandings of the essential basis of a party's consent, as long as that party did not contribute to the error, is another basis for invoking invalidity. However, an error relating only to the wording of the text of a treaty does not affect its validity (Article 48; Article 79 provides a procedure for correcting such errors).

Article 53 of the Vienna Convention also provides that "a treaty is void if, at the time of its conclusion, it conflicts with a peremptory norm of general international law." A **peremptory norm** of general international law is defined as a "norm accepted and recognized by the international community of States as a whole as a norm from which no derogation is permitted and which can be modified only by a subsequent norm of general international law having the same character." The concept of *jus cogens* is still subject to some controversy but would generally include the prohibition of the use or threat of force and aggression and the prevention and repression of genocide, piracy, slave trade, racial discrimination, terrorism or the taking of hostages, and torture. The evolving nature of these principles does not allow a conclusive definition (see *Siderman v. Republic of Argentina* in Chapter 4).

> *Peremptory norm:* A norm of general international law (jus cogens) *from which States cannot deviate. New States must accept such a norm, and it cannot be changed without the approval of the international community as a whole. A treaty in conflict with such a universal norm is therefore void (Article 53 VCLT).*

Treaty Observance

In international law, a State may not invoke its internal law as justification for failure to perform a treaty (Article 27 VCLT). However, Article 46 of the Vienna Convention does provide for a carefully worded exception in circumstances in which the question of constitutional competence to conclude a treaty arises. According to Henkin et al. (1987), that provision "permits a state to assert as a ground of invalidity of a treaty the fact that its consent to be bound was expressed in violation of a provision of its internal law concerning the competence to conclude treaties" (p. 459).

The Vienna Convention provides that "A treaty shall be interpreted in good faith in accordance with the ordinary meaning to be given to the terms of the treaty in their context and in the light of its object and purpose" (Article 31). The convention further provides guidance for such interpretation and in Article 32 allows for recourse to "preparatory work" to confirm the meaning of treaty provision when the document leaves the meaning ambiguous or obscure or leads to a result that is "manifestly absurd or unreasonable."

Termination or Suspension of Treaties

Most modern treaties contain clauses fixing (a) their duration, (b) the date of termination, (c) an event or condition to bring about termination, or (d) a right to denounce or withdraw from the treaty. Therefore, it is self-evident that a treaty may be terminated in accordance with its own provisions (Article 54 VCLT). It also provides that a treaty may be terminated at any time by consent of all its parties.

A typical clause in many treaties will provide that if "after the expiration of ten (or X number) of years, one party requests its termination, it must so notify the other party one year in advance and in written form; and the present treaty shall be terminated one year after the tendering of such notification." A clause in the Mutual Defense Treaty between the United States and the Republic of China (Taiwan) provided that it would remain in force "indefinitely [although] either Party may terminate it one year after notice has been given to the other Party." This clause was used when President Carter gave notice in 1978 that he intended to terminate the treaty with Taiwan. One year later, the United States recognized the People's Republic of China (mainland China) and terminated its treaty with Taiwan.

Such modern treaty provisions have reduced the need for the highly controversial doctrine of *rebus sic stantibus* (fundamental change of circumstance) that will be discussed later. However, many older treaties used language that precluded subsequent change. The Panama Canal Treaty between Panama and the United States of 1903 granted the United States rights "in perpetuity" to construct, operate, maintain, and protect the Panama Canal. Panamanian opposition to U.S. presence in the zone and the general change in the attitude of the international community toward treaties secured under duress contributed to the conclusion of a new treaty signed in 1979 repealing the 1903 treaty and providing for the continued U.S. maintenance, operation, and defense of the canal; Panama would increase its share of responsibility and assume complete control of the canal in the year 2000.

Subsequent treaties between the same parties may, by implication, terminate or suspend previous agreements. This method

of termination is referred to as *termination by implied consent*. Such implied consent is also possible when there is failure of compliance. A treaty can be negated by implication when all of the parties ignore it, since the absence of objections constitutes an implied understanding that the treaty is no longer in force (see Article 59 VCLT).

Material Breach

A more complex problem of interpretation exists when violations of treaties occur and the injured party, or parties, allege that the violation abrogates the treaty or allows the injured party to suspend the performance of its own obligations under the treaty. A violation of a treaty obligation may give rise to a right of the other party to take nonforcible reprisals that may properly include suspension of the benefits of the treaty obligations.

"A material breach of a bilateral treaty by one of the parties entitles the other to invoke the breach as a ground for terminating the treaty or suspending its operation in whole or in part" (Article 60, para. 1 VCLT). However, multilateral treaties have been deemed to require exceptions in excluding conventions of a humanitarian character that protect the "human person." It was considered desirable to make it clear that a material breach in these cases should not lead to abrogation or suspension of the treaty.

Other complexities are dealt with in the Vienna Convention regarding multilateral treaties that require respect for the rights of parties other than the offending nation. All parties, other than the party responsible for the material breach, may act together in suspending or terminating the agreement with that State. In certain situations, such as in disarmament treaties, where a breach by one party tends to undermine the whole regime of the treaty as between all the parties, any party must be permitted without first obtaining the agreement of the other parties to suspend the operation of the treaty with respect to itself generally in its relations with all the other parties (see Article 60, para. 2, 3, and 4 VCLT).

A **material breach** is defined as repudiation of the treaty in violation of the provisions of the Vienna Convention or the violation of a provision of the treaty essential to the accomplishment of the object or purpose of the treaty (Article 60, para. 3). Many jurists were concerned with the possibility that a State may allege a trivial or even fictitious breach simply to furnish a pretext for denouncing a treaty that it now finds embarrassing. The ILC was unanimous in asserting that the right to terminate or suspend must be limited to cases in which the breach is of a serious character. The Commission preferred the term *material* to *fundamental* to express the kind of breach that is required. The word *fundamental* might be understood as meaning that only the violation of a provision directly touching the central purposes of the treaty can ever justify the other party in terminating the treaty (see ILC Report, 1966, pp. 253-255).

The interpretation of these provisions by the ICJ can be observed in the *Namibia* case (1971). Here, the ICJ makes specific use of the provisions of the VCLT, although the convention had not yet entered into force (the VCLT entered into force in 1980). One of the issues involved in the *Namibia* case concerned the authority of the United Nations to terminate the mandate for misconduct of the mandatory State.

The background of the *Namibia* case began in 1915, during World War I, when the German colony was conquered by military forces of the Union (now Republic) of South Africa. Germany renounced sovereignty over the region in the Treaty of Versailles, and in 1920 the League of Nations granted South Africa a Class C mandate over the territory. In 1946, the U.N. General Assembly requested South Africa to submit a trusteeship agreement to the United Nations to replace the mandate of the defunct League of Nations; South Africa refused to do so. In 1949 a South African constitutional amendment extended parliamentary representation to South-West Africa (the territory now known as Namibia). The ICJ however, ruled in 1950 that the status of the mandate could be changed only with the consent of the United Nations. South Africa agreed to discuss the trusteeship question with a special committee of the General Assembly, but the negotiations ended in failure in 1951. South Africa subsequently refused to accede to U.N. demands concerning a trusteeship arrangement, but it permitted a U.N. committee to enter Namibia in 1962 to investigate charges of atrocities committed against the indigenous peoples. The committee found the charges against South Africa to be baseless.

Aroused by steps that the government of South Africa was taking to establish apartheid in the mandated territory, Ethiopia and Liberia took the case to the ICJ, but the court dismissed the complaint in 1966 on technical grounds. In October of that year, the apartheid laws of South Africa were

> **Material breach:** *A serious violation of a provision essential to the accomplishment of the object of the treaty, which entitles the other party or parties to invoke the breach as a ground for terminating the treaty or suspending its operation in whole or in part. A material breach does not ipso facto rescind the treaty; it only gives the injured party or parties the right to invoke the breach as a ground for termination or suspension.*

extended to the country. The United Nations continued to debate the question, and in 1966 the General Assembly adopted a resolution that decided that South Africa's Mandate be terminated (G.A.Res. 2145 [XXI 1966]). This resolution was unsuccessful and on January 30, 1970, the Security Council reaffirmed the General Assembly resolution declaring "that the continued presence of South African authorities in Namibia is illegal and that consequently all acts taken by the Government of South Africa on behalf of or concerning Namibia after the termination of the Mandate are illegal and invalid" (S.C.Res. 276, U.N.Doc. S/INF/25, at 1).

South Africa remained adamant and refused to cooperate with the U.N. Council for Namibia, which had been set up by the General Assembly in 1967. The U.N. Council for Namibia began to issue travel documents and identity certificates for the inhabitants of Namibia. On July 29, 1970, the Security Council adopted a resolution submitting the issue to the ICJ for an advisory opinion seeking an answer to the following question: "What are the legal consequences for States of the continued presence of South Africa in Namibia, notwithstanding Security Council resolution 276 (1970)?" (S.C.Res. 284).

The Namibia Case

Legal Consequences for States of the Continued Presence of South Africa in Namibia (South West Africa) notwithstanding Security Council Resolution 276 (1970).
International Court of Justice, Advisory Opinion, 1971.
1971 I.C.J. 16.

[On June 21, 1971, the Court answered this question as follows:

by 13 votes to 2,

(1) that, the continued presence of South Africa in Namibia being illegal, South Africa is under obligation to withdraw its administration from Namibia immediately and thus put an end to its occupation of the Territory;

by 11 votes to 4,

(2) that States Members of the United Nations are under obligation to recognize the illegality of South Africa's presence in Namibia and the invalidity of its acts on behalf of or concerning Namibia, and to refrain from any acts and in particular any dealings with the Government of South Africa implying recognition of the legality of, or lending support or assistance to, such presence and administration;

(3) that it is incumbent upon States which are not Members of the United Nations to give assistance, within the scope of subparagraph (2)

In the course of its reasoning, the Court rejected South Africa's suggestion that Class C Mandates were "in their practical effect not far removed from annexation," as well as the contention that such Mandates were not terminable without the Mandatory's consent. Excerpts from the Court's opinion are as follows:]

* * *

93. In paragraph 3 of the operative part of the resolution the General Assembly "Declares that South Africa has failed to fulfill its obligations in respect of the administration of the Mandated Territory and to ensure the moral and material well-being and security of the indigenous inhabitants of South West Africa and has, in fact, disavowed the Mandate." In paragraph 4 the decision is reached, as a consequence of the previous declaration "that the Mandate conferred upon His Britannic Majesty to be exercised on his behalf by the Government of the Union of South Africa is *therefore* terminated . . . [italics added]. It is this part of the resolution which is relevant in the present proceedings.

94. In examining this action of the General Assembly it is appropriate to have regard to the general principles of international law regulating termination of a treaty relationship on account of breach. For even if the mandate is viewed as having the character of an institution, as is maintained, it depends on those international agreements which created the system and regulated its application. As the Court indicated in 1962 "this Mandate, like practically all other similar Mandates" was "a special type of instrument composite in nature and instituting a novel international regime. It incorporates a definite agreement . . ." (I.C.J. Reports 1962, p. 331). The Court stated conclusively in that Judgment that the Mandate ". . . in fact and in law, is an international agreement having the character of a treaty or convention" (I.C.J. Reports 1962, p. 330). The rules laid down by the Vienna Convention on the Law of Treaties concerning termination of a treaty relationship on account of breach (adopted without a dissenting vote) may in many respects be considered as a codification of existing customary law on the subject. In the light of these rules, only a material breach of a treaty justifies termination, such breach being defined as:

(a) a repudiation of the treaty not sanctioned by the present Convention; or

(b) the violation of a provision essential to the accomplishment of the object or purpose of the treaty (Art. 60, para. 3).

95. General Assembly resolution 2145 (XXI) determines that both forms of material breach had occurred in this case. By stressing that South Africa "has, in fact, disavowed the Mandate," the General Assembly declared in fact that it had repudiated it. The resolution in question is therefore to be viewed as the exercise of the right to terminate a relationship in case of a deliberate and persistent violation of obligations which destroys the very object and purpose of that relationship.

* * *

96. It has been contended that the Covenant of the League of Nations did not confer on the Council of the League power to terminate a mandate for misconduct of the mandatory and that no such power could therefore be exercised by the United Nations, since it could not derive from the League greater powers than the latter itself had. For this objection to prevail it would be necessary to show that the mandates system, as established under the League, excluded the application of the general principle of law that a right of termination on account of breach must be presumed to exist in respect of all treaties, except as regards provisions relating to the protection of the human person contained in treaties of a humanitarian character (as indicated in Art. 60, para. 5, of the Vienna Convention). The silence of a treaty as to the existence of such a right cannot be interpreted as implying the exclusion of a right which has its source outside of the treaty, in general international law, and is dependent on the occurrence of circumstances which are not normally envisaged when a treaty is concluded.

* * *

101. It has been suggested that, even if the Council of the League had possessed the power of revocation of the Mandate in an extreme case, it could not have been exercised unilaterally but only in cooperation with the mandatory Power. However, revocation could only result from a situation in which the mandatory had committed a serious breach of the obligations it had undertaken. To contend, on the basis of the principle of unanimity which applied in the League of Nations, that in this case revocation could only take place with the concurrence of the mandatory, would not only run contrary to the general principle of law governing termination on account of breach, but also postulate an impossibility. For obvious reasons, the consent of the wrongdoer to such a form of termination cannot be required.

Discussion Questions

1. How does the mandate system create a special regime? Does it have the character of a treaty or convention as the Court asserts?
2. Since South Africa never agreed to place South-West Africa under the Trusteeship Council, is it fair to apply the changing nature of developments under the trusteeship system?
3. What implications does this decision have for the application of evolving principles of international law?

Comment: South Africa did not immediately comply with the Court's decision and continued to govern the territory. As a result, the South-West African People's Organization (SWAPO), a black African nationalist movement led by Sam Nujoma, escalated its guerrilla campaign to oust the South Africans. The major Western powers, principally the United States, Great Britain, Canada, and West Germany became deeply involved in the Namibian question in the late 1970s. South Africa continued to resist eviction until December 1988, when it agreed to allow Namibia to become independent in exchange for the removal of Cuban troops from Angola. Open elections for a seventy-two-member constituent assembly were held under U.N. supervision in November of 1989, with SWAPO emerging as the majority party. After the assembly approved a new constitution and elected Nujoma as the first president, Namibia attained independence on March 21, 1990.

Impossibility of Performance

A party to a treaty may invoke impossibility of performance as the basis for suspending or terminating its obligations under that treaty. Article 61 of the Vienna Convention provides that impossibility "results from the permanent disappearance or destruction of an object indispensable for the execution of the treaty." Examples such as the submergence of an island that is the object of a treaty relationship, the drying up of a river, and the destruction of a dam or hydroelectric installation indispensable for the execution of a treaty were provided by the drafters. These circumstances would terminate (or temporarily suspend) rights and obligations arising under a treaty governing their use (see "Official Documents," 1967).

The extinction of a State would also fit this definition of impossibility of performance. These subjects were dealt with in Chapter 11 concerning State succession. Treaty obligations may not be terminated merely because there has been a political change in the government or governing structure. A fundamental change that radically alters the nature of treaty obligations has been characterized by some jurists as impossibility of performance. However, the Vienna Convention draws a specific distinction between impossibility of performance and *rebus sic stantibus* (fundamental change of circumstances).

Fundamental Change of Circumstances

The controversial issues involving the doctrine of *rebus sic stantibus* have been debated within the legal community since the time of Hugo Grotius. The ILC concluded, however, that almost all jurists reluctantly admit the existence in international law of the doctrine. The concept is derived from the analogy of municipal contract law that recognizes both impossibility of performance and that contracts may become inapplicable through a fundamental change of circumstances. Most jurists express concern for the risk to the security of treaties that the doctrine presents in the absence of any general system of compulsory jurisdiction of the courts and express the need to confine the scope of the doctrine within narrow limits and to regulate the conditions under which it may be invoked (ILC Report, 1966, pp. 256-258).

The ILC concluded that the term *rebus sic stantibus* should not be used in the Vienna Convention so as to avoid the doctrinal implications of the term that had been used as a tacit condition implied in every "perpetual" treaty. Thus the specific wording of Article 62 is identified as "fundamental change of circumstances" and contains the following provisions:

> ### Article 62
>
> 1. A fundamental change of circumstances which has occurred with regard to those existing at the time of the conclusion of a treaty, and which was not foreseen by the parties, may not be invoked as a ground for terminating or withdrawing from the treaty unless:
>   (a) the existence of those circumstances constituted an essential basis of the consent of the parties to be bound by the treaty; and
>   (b) the effect of the change is radically to transform the extent of obligations still to be performed under the treaty.
> 2. A fundamental change of circumstances may not be invoked as a ground for terminating or withdrawing from a treaty.

> (a) if the treaty establishes a boundary; or
> (b) if the fundamental change is the result of a breach by the party invoking it either of an obligation under the treaty or of any other international obligation owed to any other party to the treaty.

Note that the wording of the Vienna Convention expressly excludes a treaty establishing boundaries from the application of the principle of fundamental change of circumstances.

International tribunals have generally avoided giving effect to the principle of fundamental change of circumstances, usually on the ground that it was not applicable to the facts at hand. In the *Case of the Free Zones* between France and Switzerland decided by the Permanent Court of International Justice in 1932, the Court found that the circumstances that had changed were not those on the basis of which the parties entered into the treaty. The ICJ had occasion to consider the argument of fundamental change of circumstances in the *Fisheries Jurisdiction* case between the United Kingdom and Iceland in 1973. In the case excerpts that follow, the Court considers the applicability of the principle of fundamental change of circumstances in light of the Vienna Convention, which had not yet gone into effect.

The Fisheries Jurisdiction Case (United Kingdom v. Iceland)
International Court of Justice, 1973.
1973 I.C.J. 3.

[On April 14, 1972, the United Kingdom filed an Application before the International Court of Justice instituting proceedings against Iceland challenging the proposed extension of Iceland's exclusive fisheries jurisdiction from 12 to 50 miles around its shores. The United Kingdom founded the Court's jurisdiction on Article 36, paragraph 1, of the Court's Statute and a March 11, 1961, Exchange of Notes between the two countries under which the United

Kingdom recognized Iceland's claim to a 12-mile fisheries limit in return for Iceland's agreement that any dispute as to the extension of Icelandic fisheries jurisdiction beyond the 12-mile limit "shall, at the request of either party, be referred to the International Court of Justice."

The Government of Iceland notified the Court by letter dated May 29, 1972 that Iceland was not willing "to confer" jurisdiction on the Court and would not appoint an Agent. Thereupon, the Government of the United Kingdom requested the Court to grant interim measures of protection under Article 41 of the Court's Statute, which the Court proceeded to do, while ordering hearings on the question of its jurisdiction to deal with the merits.

In its decision of February 2, 1973, the Court, finding by 14 to 1 that it had jurisdiction, regretted the absence of Iceland in the proceedings, noted its obligations under the Statute to establish its own jurisdiction, and observed that in so doing it would "consider those objections which might, in its view, be raised against its jurisdiction."

With respect to questions relating to fundamental change of circumstances, the decision of the Court contained the following paragraphs:]

31. It should be observed at the outset that the compromissory clause has a bilateral character, each of the parties being entitled to invoke the Court's jurisdiction; it is clear that in certain circumstances it could be to Iceland's advantage to apply to the Court. The argument of Iceland appears, however, to be that, because of the general trend of development of international law on the subject of fishery limits during the last ten years, the right of exclusive fisheries jurisdiction to a distance of 12 miles from the baselines of the territorial sea has been increasingly recognized and claimed by States, including the applicant State itself. It would then appear to be contended that the compromissory clause was the price paid by Iceland for the recognition at that time of the 12-mile fishery limit by the other party. It is consequently asserted that if today the 12-mile fishery limit is generally recognized, there would be a failure of consideration relieving Iceland of its commitment because of the changed legal circumstances. It is on this basis that it is possible to interpret the Prime Minister's statement to the Althing [Iceland's parliament] on 9 November 1971, to the effect that it was unlikely that the agreement would have been made if the Government of Iceland had known how these matters would evolve.

32. While changes in the law may under certain conditions constitute valid grounds for invoking a change of circumstances affecting the duration of a treaty, the Icelandic contention is not relevant to the present case. The motive which induced Iceland to enter into the 1961 Exchange of Notes may well have been the interest of obtaining an immediate recognition of an exclusive fisheries jurisdiction to a distance of 12 miles in the waters around its territory. It may also be that this interest has in the meantime disappeared, since a 12-mile fishery zone is now asserted by the other contracting party in respect of its own fisheries jurisdiction. But in the present case, the object and purpose of the 1961 Exchange of Notes, and therefore the circumstances which constituted an essential basis of the consent of both parties to be bound by the agreement embodied therein, had a much wider scope. That object and purpose was not merely to decide upon the Icelandic claim to fisheries jurisdiction up to 12 miles, but also to provide a means whereby the parties might resolve the question of the validity of any further claims. This follows not only from the text of the agreement but also from the history of the negotiations, that is to say, from the whole set of circumstances which must be taken into account in determining what induced both parties to agree to the 1961 Exchange of Notes.

* * *

34. It is possible that today Iceland may find that some of the motives which induced it to enter into the 1961 Exchange of Notes have become less compelling or have disappeared altogether. But this is not a ground justifying the repudiation of those parts of the agreement the object and purpose of which have remained unchanged. Iceland has derived benefits from the executed provisions of the agreement, such as the recognition by the United Kingdom since 1961 of a 12-mile exclusive fisheries jurisdiction, the acceptance by the United Kingdom of the baselines established by Iceland and the relinquishment in a period of three years of the pre-existing traditional fishing by vessels registered in the United Kingdom. Clearly it then becomes incumbent on Iceland to comply with its side of the bargain, which is to accept the testing before the Court of the validity of its further claims to extended jurisdiction. Moreover, in the case of a treaty which is in part executed and in part executory, in which one of the parties has already benefited from the executed provisions of the treaty, it would be particularly inadmissible to allow that party to put an end to obligations which were accepted under the treaty by way of *quid pro quo* for the provisions which the other party has already executed.

35. In his letter of 29 May 1972 to the Registrar, the Minister for Foreign Affairs of Iceland refers to "the changed circumstances resulting from the ever-increasing exploitation of the fishery resources in the seas surrounding Iceland." Judicial notice should also be taken of other statements made on the subject in documents which Iceland has brought to the Court's attention. Thus, the resolution adopted by the Althing on 15 February 1972 contains the statement that "owing to changed circumstances the Notes concerning fishery limits exchanged in 1961 are no longer applicable."

36. In these statements the Government of Iceland is basing itself on the principle of termination of a treaty by reason of change of circumstances. International law admits that a fundamental change in the circumstances which determined the parties to accept a treaty, if it has resulted in a radical transformation of the extent of the obligations imposed by it, may, under certain conditions, afford the party affected a ground for invoking the termination or suspension of the treaty. This principle, and the conditions and exceptions to which it is subject, have been embodied in Article 62 of the Vienna Convention of the Law of Treaties, which may in many respects be considered as a codification of existing customary law on the subject of the termination of a treaty relationship on account of change of circumstances.

37. One of the basic requirements embodied in that Article is that the change of circumstances must have been a fundamental one. In this respect the Government of Iceland has, with regard to developments in fishing techniques, referred in an official publication on Fisheries Jurisdiction in Iceland, enclosed with the Foreign Minister's letter of 29 May 1972 to the Registrar, to the increased exploitation of the fishery resources in the seas surrounding Iceland and to the danger of still further exploitation because of an increase in the catching capacity of fishing fleets. The Icelandic statements recall the exceptional dependence of that country on its fishing for its existence and economic development. In his letter of 29 May 1972 the Minister stated:

> "The Government of Iceland, considering that the vital interests of the people of Iceland are involved, respectfully informs the Court that it is not willing to confer jurisdiction on the Court in any case involving the extent of the fishery limits of Iceland. . . ."

In this same connection, the resolution adopted by the Althing on 16 February 1972 had contained a paragraph in these terms:

> "That the Governments of the United Kingdom and the Federal Republic of Germany be again informed that because of the vital interests of the nation and owing to changed circumstances the Notes concerning fishery limits exchanged in 1961 are no longer applicable and that their provisions do not constitute an obligation for Iceland."

38. The invocation by Iceland of its "vital interests," which were not made the subject of an express reservation to the acceptance of the jurisdictional obligation under the 1961 Exchange of Notes, must be interpreted, in the context of the assertion of changed circumstances, as an indication by Iceland of the reason why it regards as fundamental the changes which in its view have taken place in previously existing fishing techniques. This interpretation would correspond to the traditional view that the changes of circumstances which must be regarded as fundamental or vital are those which imperil the existence or vital development of one of the parties.

39. The Applicant, for its part, contends that the alterations and progress in fishing techniques have not produced in the waters around Iceland the consequences apprehended by Iceland and therefore that the changes are not of a fundamental or vital character. In its Memorial, it points out that, as regards the capacity of fishing fleets, increases in the efficiency of individual trawlers have been counterbalanced by the reduction in total numbers of vessels in national fleets fishing in the waters around Iceland, and that the statistics show that the total annual catch of demersal species has varied to no great extent since 1960.

40. The Court, at the present stage of the proceedings, does not need to pronounce on this question of fact, as to which there appears to be a serious divergence of views between the two Governments. If, as contended by Iceland, there have been any fundamental changes in fishing techniques in the waters around Iceland, those changes might be relevant for the decision on the merits of the dispute, and the Court might need to examine the contention at that stage, together with any other arguments that Iceland might advance in support of the validity of the extension of

its fisheries jurisdiction beyond what was agreed to in the 1961 Exchange of Notes. But the alleged changes could not affect in the least the obligation to submit to the Court's jurisdiction, which is the only issue at the present stage of the proceedings. It follows that the apprehended dangers for the vital interests of Iceland, resulting from changes in fishing techniques, cannot constitute a fundamental change with respect to the lapse or subsistence of the compromissory clause establishing the Court's jurisdiction.

* * *

43. Moreover, in order that a change of circumstances may give rise to a ground for invoking the termination of a treaty it is also necessary that it should have resulted in a radical transformation of the extent of the obligations still to be performed. The change must have increased the burden of the obligations to be executed to the extent of rendering the performance something essentially different from that originally undertaken. In respect of the obligation with which the Court is here concerned, this condition is wholly unsatisfied; the change of circumstances alleged by Iceland cannot be said to have transformed radically the extent of the jurisdictional obligation which is imposed in the 1961 Exchange of Notes. The compromissory clause enabled either of the parties to submit to the Court any dispute between them relating to an extension of Icelandic fisheries jurisdiction in the waters above its continental shelf beyond the 12-mile limit. The present dispute is exactly of the character anticipated in the compromissory clause of the Exchange of Notes. Not only has the jurisdictional obligation not been radically transformed in its extent; it has remained precisely what it was in 1961.

44. In the United Kingdom Memorial it is asserted that there is a flaw in the Icelandic contention of change of circumstances: that the doctrine never operates so as to extinguish a treaty automatically or to allow an unchallengeable unilateral denunciation by one party; it only operates to confer a right to call for termination and, if that call is disputed, to submit the dispute to some organ or body with power to determine whether the conditions for the operation of the doctrine are present. In this connection the Applicant alludes to Articles 65 and 66 of the Vienna Convention on the Law of Treaties. Those Articles provide that where the parties to a treaty have failed within 12 months to achieve a settlement of a dispute by the means indicated in Article 33 of the United Nations Charter (which means include reference to judicial settlement) any one of the parties may submit the dispute to the procedure for conciliation provided in the Annex to the Convention.

45. In the present case, the procedural complement to the doctrine of changed circumstances is already provided for in the 1961 Exchange of Notes, which specifically calls upon the parties to have recourse to the Court in the event of a dispute relating to Iceland's extension of fisheries jurisdiction. Furthermore, any question as to the jurisdiction of the Court, deriving from an alleged lapse through changed circumstances, is resolvable through the accepted judicial principle enshrined in Article 36, paragraph 6, of the Court's Statute, which provides that "in the event of a dispute as to whether the Court has jurisdiction, the matter shall be settled by the decision of the Court." In this case such a dispute obviously exists, as can be seen from Iceland's communications to the Court, and to the other Party, even if Iceland has chosen not to appoint an Agent, file a Counter-Memorial or submit preliminary objections to the Court's jurisdiction; and Article 53 of the Statute both entitles the Court and, in the present proceedings, requires it to pronounce upon the question of its jurisdiction. This it has now done with binding force.

Discussion Questions

1. In light of the changed circumstances of the entry into force of the 1982 Law of the Sea Treaty allowing a State to claim a two-hundred-mile fisheries jurisdiction, is Iceland's claim any more valid? Discuss.

2. Could Iceland have foreseen the potential for extension of the Law of the Seas and fisheries jurisdiction in 1962? How could Iceland have protected itself in the exchange of notes with the United Kingdom?

3. What conditions essential to the exception of fundamental change of circumstances, as defined in the Vienna Convention, did Iceland have to prove in order to have succeeded?

Chapter Summary

1. The Vienna Convention on the Law of Treaties (1969) represents the codification of the general principles of the customary law of treaties and is therefore the most authoritative source of law used in international legal practice, particularly since its entry into force in 1980.

2. The normal treaty formation process for multilateral treaties involves a negotiation phase, adoption, authentication, signature, and ratification. This procedure is quite detailed and may extend for decades, allowing States that did not participate in all phases to adhere to the agreement when the agreement so stipulates. This process may be used to bring about change in concepts of customary international law through "law-making treaties" that have this general intent.

3. The adoption of the text of a treaty at an international conference generally requires the approval of two-thirds of the States present and voting.

4. Ratification is defined in international law as an act whereby a State establishes its definitive consent to be bound by a treaty. Some forms of treaties that bind only the executive authority may be ratified by signature of that authority. However, some States require a constitutional procedure that vests all, or part, of the treaty-making power in some other institution that must be consulted before a formal treaty obligation is accepted.

5. Reservations to multilateral treaties are unilateral variations, submitted at the time of acceptance of the treaty, attempting to exclude or modify the legal effect of certain provisions as applied to that State. In the absence of a treaty provision to the contrary, reservations are allowed as long as they are not objected to by all the parties, if the reservation is compatible with the object and purpose of the Vienna Convention.

6. Although the effect of reservations is not conclusively defined, it depends on the particular treaty in question. If a party to the Vienna Convention objects to a reservation that it considers to be incompatible with the object and purpose of the VCLT, it may consider the reserving State not to be a party. In practice, States often object to certain reservations but accept such States as parties to the convention. This leaves the effect of the reservation in doubt.

7. Modern multilateral treaties stipulate whether or not reservations will be allowed or limit them to narrow points of differences. The most extensive use of reservations that have drawn objections appear in connection with human rights treaties. The United States has made more extensive use of reservations in this area that have drawn objections than any other State and seems to be unwilling to ratify any agreement that affects interpretation of the U.S. Constitution.

8. Multilateral treaties provide additional complexity with regard to the manner and date of entry into force. In the absence of a specific provision, all negotiating parties must ratify to effect entry into force. However, most treaties specify a given number of ratifications necessary for entry into force. For lawmaking treaties in which the intent is to clarify or modify customary international law, the minimum of one-third of the negotiating States is the practice, but there appears to be no definite number or percentage of States required.

9. Registration of a treaty is required under the U.N. Charter in order to be given legally binding effect by any organ of the United Nations. Thus far, over 33,000 bilateral and multilateral treaties have been so registered with the Secretariat and published in the *U.N. Treaty Series.*

10. In U.S. treaty practice, there are several different methods of concluding binding international agreements. They include the formal treaty procedure defined in Article II of the Constitution, the executive-legislative agreement, the sole executive agreement, and a method defined in Article I, Section 10 of the Constitution that allows states of the union to conclude agreements with the consent of Congress.

11. The formal treaty procedure requires the advice and consent of the Senate by a two-thirds vote. The executive-legislative agreement may accomplish the same objectives by enacting the executive-negotiated agreement into the municipal law. The sole executive agreement is always involved in the treaty negotiation process and may be used when the president already has the authority under the Constitution, a treaty, or an act of Congress. The "interstate compact" allows states a limited method of concluding agreements with the approval of Congress.

12. In the international realm, the president has inherent powers as the sole representative of the nation to exercise its foreign policy powers *(United States v. Curtiss-Wright Corp.).* However, in the internal realm of domestic affairs, the president must have clear authority under the Constitution, a treaty, or an act of Congress *(Youngstown Sheet & Tube Co. v. Sawyer).*

13. In *Missouri v. Holland,* the Supreme Court upheld an act of Congress pursuant to a formal Article II treaty even though that same act of Congress had been held unconstitutional as a violation of the Tenth Amendment (reserve powers of the states) before enactment of the treaty. The treaty power is an exclusive national power under the U.S. Constitution, whereas the domestic powers are shared between the states and the national government.

14. In *Reid v. Covert,* a sole executive agreement was held by the Supreme Court to be in conflict with Constitutional criminal due process guarantees. The executive agreements with Japan and the United Kingdom provided for military court-marshal proceedings for criminal offenses committed on U.S. military installations. Two wives accused of murdering their husbands were released after a court-marshal had found them guilty. The Court held that the executive agreement could not abrogate guarantees to grand jury indictment and trial by jury to U.S. dependents.

15. The "last in time" doctrine of the U.S. Supreme Court was established in the nineteenth century and is based on the assumption that treaties and acts of Congress are on an equal plane. Hence, when an act of Congress squarely conflicts with a treaty provision, the act or treaty that is the last in time shall prevail. The Court has also fashioned the doctrine that it will always endeavor to construe such acts so as to give effect to both, if that can be done without violating the language of either *(Weinberger v. Rossi* or *United States v. Palestine Liberation Organization).*

16. In an attempt to control sole executive agreements, Congress has enacted the Case Act, which requires the president to report all international agreements, written or oral, within sixty days of their being concluded.

17. The fundamental principle of *pacta sunt servanda* requires that the parties to legally binding obligations perform the basic intent of these obligations in good faith. The Vienna Convention now provides that treaties that have been procured by coercion of either the negotiating representative or the State are void and without legal effect. The specific language used to define such treaties is "procured by the threat or use of force in violation of the principles embodied in the Charter of the United Nations."

18. A treaty is void if, at the time of its conclusion, it conflicts with a peremptory norm *(jus cogens)* of general international law, which is defined as a norm accepted by the international community as a whole from which no derogation is permitted.

19. In international law, a State may not invoke its internal law as justification for failure to perform in accordance with a treaty. A treaty shall be interpreted in good faith in accordance with the ordinary meaning to be given to the terms of the treaty in their context and in the light of its object and purpose.

20. A material breach of a treaty by one of the parties generally entitles the other party to invoke the breach as grounds for terminating the treaty or suspending its operation in whole or in part. The Vienna Convention excludes multilateral treaties of a humanitarian character from this means of enforcement. Multilateral treaties generally require concurrent action by all parties against the violator, except in narrowly defined instances, such as disarmament treaties, where the material breach by one party radically changes the position of every party with respect to further performance.

21. A party to a treaty may invoke impossibility of performance as a basis for suspending or terminating its obligations under the treaty. This provision is distinguished from the doctrine of "fundamental change of circumstances" *(rebus sic stantibus)* by a provision of the Vienna Convention limiting the application of the latter doctrine and prohibiting its use in boundary treaties or when the fundamental change is the result of a breach by that party.

Key Terms

Vienna Convention on
  the Law of Treaties
  (VCLT, 1969)
Vienna Convention on
  the Law of Treaties
  Between States and
  International Organi-
  zations or Between
  International
  Organizations (1986)

adoption
authentication
signature
accession
ratification
reservation
supremacy clause
Article II treaty
executive-legislative
  treaty

sole executive
  agreement
Reid v. Covert
"last in time"
  doctrine
Case Act
peremptory norm
material breach

Discussion Questions

1. Why is the codification of the law of treaties fundamental to the progressive development of international law?

2. What are the basic steps involved in the multilateral treaty formation process? Under what conditions can this process result in a method of changing customary international law?

3. What is the difference between signature and ratification of a treaty? What obligations does signature entail?

4. What are the legal consequences of reservations made to multilateral treaties?

5. Why have reservations been most prevalent in regard to human rights treaties?

6. In U.S. treaty practice, what are the different methods of engaging in a binding international agreement? What advantages do each of these methods provide?

7. Why is an act of Congress pursuant to a treaty more powerful than an act of Congress alone, as illustrated in *Missouri v. Holland*? Does this mean that a treaty is superior to the Constitution? Discuss.

8. Assuming that the U.S. Constitution is a treaty, what would it take to change the Constitution by another treaty?

9. How has the "last in time" doctrine been interpreted when there is a chance of construing the statute so as not to conflict with a treaty obligation?

10. Under what conditions can a treaty obligation be considered invalid?

11. What constitutes a material breach of a treaty, and what rights are available to the opposing parties?

12. How does "impossibility of performance" differ from "fundamental change of circumstances?"

13. What conditional limitations have been placed on the exception of fundamental change of circumstances by the Vienna Convention?

Suggested Readings

Higgins, R. (1994). *Problems and process: International law and how we use it*. New York: Oxford University Press.

Steiner, H. J., Vagts, D. F., & Koh, H. H. (1994). *Transnational legal problems* (4th ed.). New York: Foundation Press.

Internet Sources

Browse: Use U.N. Treaty Database (http://www.un.org/Depts/Treaty/)

American Society of International Law (http://www.asil.org)

13

The Function and Process of International Tribunals

The substantive chapters of this text have attempted to outline the basic principles of contemporary international law. These fundamental norms have grown out of the practices of States that have ripened into principles regarded as legally binding by States themselves. Thus, unlike modern domestic legislation, international law has been formed by consent and not imposed from any central authority. This process is similar to the original development of English common law, which emerged as a functioning body of law before there were legislative institutions to impose so-called positive law.

This chapter on the function and process of international tribunals undertakes the task of explaining the basic function of law in dispute settlement and describing the variety of fora (institutions of dispute settlement) on the international plane. International tribunals are fundamentally different from domestic courts in that they deal with a different sphere of authority involving disputes between sovereign entities having international personality. Municipal courts, as has been illustrated in the previous chapters, are increasingly available to private parties when a cause of action as a matter of right results from an obligation of international law. The various alternatives available to individuals and to States to pursue legal remedies for injuries of a transnational character will be discussed. However, this chapter will be confined to legal remedies.

The more important issues of a political nature will be discussed in the subsequent chapter. The issues that are more directly related to war and peace are essentially political issues. As vaguely defined earlier, political issues are *nonjusticiable* and represent situations in which the parties are unwilling to submit to decisions according to established law. This chapter will set the stage for the later discussion of compliance measures and enforcement of international law.

The Function of Law in Dispute Settlement

The term *law* is often misunderstood and subject to many confusing definitions. Most people confuse law with law enforcement and the imposition of penalties. Often, *law* is equated with criminal litigation and the imposition of criminal penalties. A local lawyer recently told me that he believes that international law is not truly law because there is no means of enforcing it. "What are you going to do? Go to war to enforce it?" he asked. This is a widespread perception about international law that deserves more elaboration at this point in this text, because the student now has become exposed to some of the legal materials available on the subject.

The issue of enforcement is certainly salient to the efficacy of law in society because it demonstrates that sanctions will be taken against one who violates the law. However, violations of law occur without the imposition of sanctions, perhaps more frequently in national societies than among the members of the international community of nation-states. The record of reported violations of even felony crimes of violence in the United States reveals that only about 5% of these crimes are "solved" in the sense that persons are arrested and ultimately punished for the crimes they have committed. Does this mean that law in the United States is not truly law because it is not fully enforced?

It may reflect that the law is not as effective in deterring violations as in other societies where the ratio of persons brought to justice for the crimes committed in that society is higher. Law enforcement serves to deter crime among individuals when there is a reasonably high expectation that if one commits a prohibited act, that person will be caught and punished. The law itself defines the act prohibited and regulates the government's use of authority to apprehend and punish the person accused of having committed the crime. Thus the law itself serves to develop rules of behavior that provide a reasonable means of settlement of disputes, in the case of crimes, between the government and the person accused of the crime.

In the evolution of modern society, institutional specialization within government has produced the functional concept of separation of powers more clearly to define the separate roles of lawmaking, law application, and law enforcement. This concept is fundamental to understanding the potential for the development of the rule of law. For, as was clearly understood by the framers of the U.S. Constitution, only a dynamic system of checks and balances among these institutions could prevent tyranny, defined as the concentration of governmental power in the hands of any individual or group of individuals. Only independent legislative, executive, and judicial departments of government could promote the rule of law under the limitations of a constitutional order. It is the particular province of the judicial department to determine what the law is and how it is to be applied to the specific set of facts before the court when a dispute arises within the jurisdiction of the court.

This method of protecting the rule of law in society is particularly pronounced in the United States, but we inherited the concept from British governmental experience, and the overwhelming majority of modern countries of the world have come to accept its essential functional nature. Although the functional concept of separation of powers is broadly accepted today in principle, any society can only approximate the achievement of this ideal in practice. Thus, it is possible to win a legal action against a government that admittedly possesses overwhelming military and coercive power.

Another measure of the effectiveness of law might be to count the number of times individuals or weaker parties are able to protect themselves against stronger opponents. The fact that over two-thirds of the world's nations today possess extremely weak economic and military potential in comparison with the other one-third indicates that international law must have some effect. In fact, most of these nations owe their existence to the principles of international law that have emerged in the twentieth century. This refutes the notion that might always makes right.

Anthony D'Amato, a professor of international law at Northwestern Law School and practicing international lawyer, provides interesting insight into these questions. The more contemporary notion that might makes right may contribute to a self-fulfilling prophecy that requires the Orwellian view of the "brave new world." If "law" is something that only works when a policeman is standing by ready to enforce it physically, then it would require the ultimate police state to maintain it. Most people obey the law most of the time because they think it is the right thing to do. Law serves as a guide to the prevention of conflict in society, and when conflict does occur, it serves to provide rules for the pacific settlement of disputes, to preserve peace and order as well as justice (fairness). "Law indeed is something that is opposed to force. Right is not the same thing as might" (D'Amato, 1995, p. 5).

In a broader sense, law consists of a bundle of rights and obligations. This is true for the individual as well as for States. However, the State administers this bundle of rights and duties on a different plane than the bundle of rights and duties administered by international law. Punishments for viola-

tions of municipal law consist of withdrawing rights from individuals and groups that violate the duties imposed by the law. This does not always mean imprisonment or execution. In fact, the great body of municipal law is civil in nature (noncriminal), involving the rights and duties of private parties. Administrative law encompasses the entire body of relationships between the citizen and government, including constitutional rights and duties of the government itself.

International law is more analogous to private and administrative law within the municipal sphere; however, it operates on a higher plane (or sphere of authority), involving the rights and duties of sovereign political entities. It is a highly decentralized system of law that displays only weak organizational specialization and a much narrower range of centralized authority than that associated with domestic societies. However, *international law is still capable of imposing punishment in the form of withdrawing corresponding rights when duties are violated.*

Traditional international law has been developed through a more fundamental method of law development associated with early societies. As opposed to the modern notion of the State as the creator of law that is imposed on individuals from above, international law developed out of State practice, providing evidence of consensus within the international community to consent to be bound by certain restraints. Even the notion of modern lawmaking treaties is still controversial but rests on the assumption of consent to change traditional customary practice by consensus. D'Amato asks in vain for an answer to the question of why lawmaking treaties are binding on States that refuse to ratify them or how the validity of this proposition might be proved (see D'Amato, 1995, p. 185). There is no adequate answer except that in the interest of peace and order, the few noncontracting States must ultimately voluntarily submit to the change in the face of overwhelming opposition.

The voluntary nature of international law, based on prior consent of the individual State or the community of nations, has produced rules that are more likely to be obeyed because they represent mutual self-interest of the contracting parties. As Louis Henkin (1979) has observed, *"Almost all nations observe almost all principles of international law and almost all of their obligations almost all of the time* [italics added]" (p. 47).

This is true in part because there are relatively few rights and obligations of international law when compared with the enormous volumes of municipal law for the individual nation-state. It is also true in part because there are so few nation-states in comparison with individuals within any particular nation-state. The increasing interdependence of the international community due to increased technology, transportation, and communications makes it in the mutual self-interest of States to settle their differences by peaceful means and to "refrain from the use of force against the territorial integrity of any other state" (Article 2[4], U.N. Charter).

Peaceful Settlement of International Disputes

Both individuals and States have a wide variety of methods of settling their disputes by peaceful means and are prohibited from use of force to settle their differences. Article 33 of the U.N. Charter provides that national parties to any dispute "shall, first of all, seek a solution by negotiation . . . arbitration, judicial settlement [or] resort to regional agencies or arrangements, or any

other means of their own choice." As Brownlie (1990) points out, "there is no obligation in general international law *to settle* disputes, and procedures for settlement by formal and legal procedures rest on the consent of the parties" (p. 708).

The overwhelming majority of disputes between individuals within municipal societies as well as international disputes between States are settled by negotiation and mutual accommodation. Even in the United States, which is reported to be the most litigious society in the world, over 90% of the civil complaints filed in courts are ultimately settled out of court. Indeed, the modern trend toward encouragement of the use of alternative dispute settlement techniques such as mediation, conciliation, and arbitration is considered essential to the problems of handling the increasing caseload of the courts.

Diplomatic Negotiation

The oldest and most practical of the great variety of methods available for peaceful settlement of disputes is that of **diplomatic negotiation**. It is also the least encumbered with procedural details and provides great flexibility in arriving at a reasonable solution to a problem. Communication—at least, stating the nature of the grievance and listening to the reply of the government involved—is required as a minimum condition for proceeding to further actions.

> *Diplomatic negotiation:* The oldest and most practical of the methods of peaceful settlement of disputes. It is considered a prerequisite before international adjudication.

Since the days of ancient Rome, when the College of Fetials sent agents or heralds who presented the demands of Rome to the other party in a dispute, governments have accepted the need for negotiation before engaging in the use of force. The concept of "just war" during the medieval period began to include the obligation of negotiation before the use of force. In later centuries, this ripened into an obligation as a matter of practice and was deemed to constitute one of the prior conditions necessary to grant any designation of justice to the use of force.

Traditional international law considered resort to force without prior negotiation as an attack without warning, and it was consistently condemned. Aside from being morally and legally wrong, it was considered foolish to engage in the risks of war when a State might conceivably achieve its aims without going to the risks and expenses of war.

In the modern era, and particularly since the development of the United Nations Organization, permanent institutions of negotiation and communications are available almost immediately. Even when the parties to the dispute have already broken diplomatic relations, avenues of negotiation are still available and more easily maintained than in the past.

Countless diplomatic communications and face-to-face meetings of the representatives occur daily around the world. The vast diplomatic network, described in Chapter 10 of this text, where the routine business of achieving diplomatic understanding constantly takes place, is conducted in secrecy or at least in relative privacy. These quiet negotiations are perhaps the most effective dispute settlement techniques. Only the disputes that cannot be solved by this method get into the press reports.

There are many levels above that of the basic country-to-country communications. These involve multilateral communications in permanent institutional settings within the intergovernmental organizations (IGOs),

including the widest of these at the United Nations itself. The realization that the United States alone concludes about two hundred treaties and executive agreements each year is some indication of the volume of this form of dispute settlement and preventive diplomacy.

As von Glahn (1996) observes, almost every one of the many international treaties for the peaceful settlement of disputes restricts its applicability to disputes that have been impossible to settle by diplomatic negotiation (see p. 495). International tribunals have insisted that "before a dispute can be made the subject of action at law, its subject matter should have been clearly defined by means of diplomatic negotiations" (*Mavromatis Palestine Concessions* [*Jurisdiction*] P.C.I.J., 1922, Ser. A, No. 2).

Mediation and Good Offices

The technique of engaging a neutral third party in the negotiations of international disputes is a particularly effective technique that often leads to solutions when direct negotiations between the parties has broken down. The use of **good offices** may be distinguished from *mediation* by such third party *intercession*, in that mediation goes further than merely providing a suitable setting for further negotiation. **Mediation** refers to a procedure in which the third party actively participates in the settle-

> *Good offices:* A peaceful settlement technique whereby a third party acting with the consent of the disputants serves as a friendly intermediary without necessarily offering the disputing parties substantive suggestions for settlement.
>
> *Mediation:* A peaceful settlement technique whereby a third party acting with the agreement of the disputants actively participates in the negotiations, offering suggestions concerning the terms of settlement and, in general, trying to reconcile the opposite claims and appeasing any feelings of resentment between the parties.

ment itself. The mediator is expected to offer concrete proposals for settling substantive questions instead of merely making negotiation possible. Both of the Hague Conventions for the Pacific Settlement of Disputes (1899 and 1907) emphasized that the right to offer good offices "can never be regarded by either of the parties in dispute as an unfriendly act" (Article III).

Intervention is a professional term used in a specialized sense in international relations to refer to the use of armed force, and the use of good offices or mediation is properly called *intercession*. Both good offices and mediation require the approval of the parties to be effective, and the proposals submitted are considered advice from the mediator that cannot be taken as having any binding force on either party to the dispute.

The intercession of mediation or good offices may proceed at the request of the parties or may be offered by the third party. The third party that intercedes in the conflict may vary widely from an individual State to a group of States or may even be an individual. In medieval times, the Pope often performed these functions in European disputes. Today, the secretary-general of the United Nations is frequently called on, or attempts, to intercede in these capacities. Modern examples of third-party efforts are numerous, and they frequently succeed in bringing the disputants together, inducing them to start or resume negotiations.

Most of the major conflicts of the post-Cold War era involved numerous attempts to use mediation to effect settlement. Recent examples include such actions in the major conflicts of Central America (involving the Contradora peace plan to end the international conflict associated with the civil war in El Salvador), the Iraq-Iran peace settlement in 1990, and the Dayton Peace Agreements concerning Bosnia in 1995.

In 1983, the Contradora peace plan, proposed by Costa Rica, Nicaragua, Honduras, and Guatemala, called for free elections and total removal of all foreign troops and advisers, coupled with continuing efforts on the part of the four countries involved to ensure peace. This effort was thwarted by lack of cooperation from the United States and by Nicaragua's rejection of the plan as long as the U.S.-backed Contra insurgency continued. The effort widened to include thirteen States that supported the Contradora plan.

Then Costa Rica put forth a full-fledged peace plan in 1987, which was supported by the United States and the four Central American States. This plan was still rejected by Nicaragua as long as the U.S.-backed Contra insurgency continued. Finally, Nicaragua's President Ortega offered a peace proposal of his own, based on a monthlong cease-fire and amnesty. The Organization of American States (OAS) ultimately assigned a team of mediators to achieve a democratic transfer of power following a democratic election in Nicaragua.

Mediation by the U.N. secretary-general was considered a key element in bringing about the cease-fire in the eight-year-old war involving Iraq and Iran in 1988. The secretary-general had the backing of the 1987 Security Council's Resolution 598 demanding a cease-fire and bringing the two belligerents to meet and discuss an end to the war. In July of 1990, Iran and Iraq agreed to seek a permanent peace settlement through mediation by the U.N. secretary-general.

The Dayton Peace Agreements, in 1995, were the culmination of repeated efforts by the United Nations and the European Union (EU) to resolve the conflict in Bosnia. Many States, acting separately or in groups, attempted to resolve the Balkan conflict through negotiations since it began in 1991.

The EU mediator Lord David Owen and U.N. mediator Cyrus Vance (former U.S. Secretary of State) proposed a draft constitution organizing Bosnia into a decentralized federation. This became known as the "Vance-Owen" plan of 1992. In February of 1993, the United States named the first U.S. special envoy to the United Nations-European Union joint negotiations, Ambassador Reginald Bartholomew. This U.S. effort helped gain the parties' agreement to the Vance-Owen plan in 1993, but the Bosnian Serbs subsequently renounced the accord.

In March of 1994, the new U.S. envoy, Ambassador Charles Redman, and other U.S. officials led negotiations between Bosnia's Muslims and Croats that resulted in a cease-fire, the formation of a bicommunal federation, and improved relations with neighboring Croatia. Later in the spring of 1994, the United States, Russia, Britain, France, and Germany established a five-nation contact group, with the goal of brokering a settlement between the federation and Bosnian Serbs. The contact group based its efforts on three principles: (a) Bosnia would remain a single State; (b) that State would consist of the federation and a Bosnian Serb entity; and (c) these two entities would be linked via mutually agreed-on constitutional principles, which would also spell out relationships with Serbia and Croatia proper.

In July of 1994, the contact group put forward a proposed map representing a 51% to 49% territorial compromise between the federation and Bosnian Serbs. The Bosnian, Croatian, and Serbian governments all accepted the proposal. The Bosnian Serbs repeatedly rejected it. However, all of its key principles were accepted as the basis for negotiations at the November 1995 proximity peace talks in Dayton. In the fall of 1994, Serbia announced that it was withdrawing support for the Bosnian Serbs, would seal them off economically, and would allow a United Nations-European Union team to monitor the border closure. The U.N. Security Council then offered a temporary suspension of some of the economic sanctions that had been in place against Serbia since 1992.

In the summer of 1995, a series of events changed the situation on the ground in Bosnia. The two U.N.-declared safe areas, Srebrenica and Zepa, were overrun by Bosnian Serb forces, Croatia retook most of the territory held for three years by separatist Krajina Serbs, and NATO threatened broad-based air strikes if the safe areas were attacked again. In mid-August, U.S. negotiators, led by Assistant Secretary of State Richard Holbrooke, began intensive shuttle diplomacy with the parties to the conflict. After a Bosnian Serb shell killed thirty-seven people in a Sarajevo market, NATO and the United Nations issued an ultimatum to the Bosnian Serbs to stop the shelling of Sarajevo and the remaining safe areas, withdraw heavy weapons from around Sarajevo, and allow road and air access to that city. After the Bosnian Serbs refused to comply, NATO began heavy and continuous air strikes against the Bosnian Serb military targets. The Bosnian Serbs finally complied with the U.N. ultimatum.

At meetings sponsored by the contact group in Geneva and New York, in September of 1995, the foreign ministers of Bosnia, Croatia, and Serbia (now also representing the Bosnian Serbs) agreed to basic principles for a settlement in Bosnia:

* The preservation of Bosnia as a single State
* An equitable division of territory between the Muslim-Croat Federation and a Bosnian Serb entity based on the contact group's 51%-49% formula

* Constitutional structures
* Free and fair elections
* Respect for human rights

In early October, the United States helped broker a cease-fire, now holding throughout Bosnia. The United States and the other contact group countries convened the parties in Dayton, Ohio, to begin "proximity peace talks" on November 1, 1995. On November 21, the parties initialed the Dayton Peace Accords, which were signed in Paris on December 14, 1995. These agreements call for extensive procedures to ensure the observance of human rights. The agreement on human rights calls for the close monitoring of the human rights situation by intergovernmental missions and cooperation with the International Criminal Tribunal for the Former Yugoslavia and with any other organization authorized by the U.N. Security Council with a mandate concerning human rights or humanitarian law (Annex 6: Agreement on Human Rights).

These negotiations involved very delicate situations in which violations of clearly established international law have occurred and civil war conditions include international implications. The resolution of such conflicts become part of international law, but they could not be resolved by reference to international tribunals because of the unwillingness of the parties to accept a solution based on previously established law. They may argue that the law was uncertain or inconclusive on particular subjects, but such negotiations are conducted with reference to establishment or clarification of international law.

Commissions of Inquiry and Conciliation

Many of the more serious international disputes involve an inability or unwilling-ness of the parties concerned to agree on points of fact. Commissions of inquiry may be concluded by agreement between the parties to allow a neutral commission to investigate and report to the parties in question on the disputed facts.

> **Commissions of inquiry:** Independent or party-initiated agreement to allow a neutral commission to investigate and report to the parties in question on the disputed facts.

The Hague Peace Conference of 1899 established commissions of inquiry as a formal institution for Pacific Settlement of International Disputes. It called for the maintenance of a permanent panel of names, from which five were to be selected for specific cases. Each party to a dispute was entitled to select two commissioners, only one of whom was to be taken from its own appointees to the panel; the fifth commissioner was to be named by the other four. The commission's report was to be limited to a finding of facts and had in no way the character of an award.

There are numerous examples of the use of this technique, such as in the *Dogger Bank* case (1904) involving a dispute between Great Britain and Russia arising when Russian warships attacked British fishing vessels under the misapprehension that the fishing vessels were Japanese torpedo boats. Also, the Latin-American countries have concluded treaties calling for inquiry into disputes; these instruments were used successfully to investigate and report on the facts in the Gran Chaco conflict between Bolivia and Paraguay in the 1930s.

The League of Nations made use of commissions of inquiry on at least six occasions involving the infamous Lytton Commission, which investigated the dispute between China and Japan over the Mukden incident in 1931. The commission's report came too late, and the Japanese had already secured their aggression in Manchuria. This failure of will on the part of the League members, explained in Chapter 2 of this text, may account for the infrequent use of reference to commissions of inquiry in the U.N. era. If fact-finding comes too late and no action is taken to deter aggression, this is simply another form of appeasement.

The successful uses of fact-finding commissions of inquiry involve some action resulting from the investigative report that brings about an equitable solution to the conflict. The procedure of **conciliation** involves submitting a given dispute to an already established commission or a single conciliator for the purpose of examining all facets of the dispute and suggesting a solution to the parties concerned.

> *Conciliation:* A procedure whereby a third party is appointed with the agreement of the disputants to conduct fact-finding procedures and recommend a concrete solution for settlement. The recommendation is not binding on the parties.

In the U.N. era, fact-finding and conciliation procedures have been institutionalized in the areas of international labor law and human rights law, as discussed in Chapters 4 and 7 of this text. The procedures of the International Labor Commission and the International Human Rights Commission are essentially modern forms of the fact-finding and conciliation commissions originally conceived by the Hague Conventions of 1899 and 1907. These fact-finding and conciliation recommendations are not judicial decisions, but they may contribute to bringing about changes, or they may aid the Security Council in making binding decisions in extreme cases that are considered to represent threats to the peace.

More *ad hoc* (after the fact) commissions of this nature were established in 1969 involving the federation of Anguilla and the inhabitants of the island of Anguilla. A U.N. fact-finding mission appointed in November 1970 investigated the charge by the Republic of Guinea that Portuguese forces based on Portuguese Guinea had repeatedly invaded the republic's territory (von Glahn, 1996, pp. 500-501).

The International Civil Aviation Organization (ICAO) conducted fact-finding efforts in regard to the tragic accident involving the shooting down of KAL Flight 007 by Russia in 1983 that led to clarification of ICAO policy concerning passenger aircraft that mistakenly fly over restricted airspace. The report of the ICAO fact-finding investigation of the mistaken destruction of an Iranian passenger jet by the United States in the Strait of Hormus in 1988 is another example (see "Excerpts from Report," 1989). Iran filed a legal action before the International Court of Justice (ICJ) on May 17, 1989, styled the *Case Concerning the Aerial Incident of 3 July 1988 (Iran v. United States of America)*. On March 4, 1991, the United States filed preliminary objections challenging the Court's jurisdiction. However, the proceedings were suspended following the announcement by both parties on August 8, 1994, that they had entered into negotiations with a view to reaching a friendly settlement of the matter.

On February 23, 1996, the Registry of the International Court of Justice announced that proceedings in the case brought by Iran against the United States had been discontinued. This action followed the joint notification of the two parties that their governments had entered into "an agreement in full and final settlement of all disputes, differences, claims, counterclaims and matters directly or indirectly raised by or capable of arising out of, or directly or indirectly related to or connected with, this case" (*ASIL* Newsletter, June-Aug., 1996).

These kinds of solutions are preferred by most States in international dispute resolution because the more formal legal actions in the form of ICJ **adjudication** are less flexible and often regarded as an unfriendly act. Negotiation, mediation, and conciliation graduate in terms of more outside restrictions on the negotiating parties, but they all resemble domestic alternative dispute resolution (ADR) techniques. Arbitration is the most restrictive of these ADR techniques, short of formal adjudication.

> **Adjudication:** *The process of bringing a dispute before a judicial tribunal for resolution according to established rules of law.*

Arbitration

The informal methods of peaceful settlement of disputes have traditionally included arbitration. However, in modern practice **arbitration** has evolved into a sophisticated procedure similar to judicial settlement. It is a peaceful method of legally binding settlement of international disputes by judges of the parties' choice, according to the rules set forth by them, and on the basis of voluntary submission and respect for law. It differs from judicial settlement only in that the disputing parties normally have the freedom to select arbitrators and, to some extent, determine the procedure and the law to be applied. The result, nonetheless, is a legally binding award as in a judicial settlement.

> **Arbitration:** *In modern international practice, a more formal method of legally binding settlement of disputes by judges of the parties' choice, agreed-on rules of procedure, and law.*

In both national and international practice, judicial processes have developed out of relatively informal administrative and political procedures. Today, arbitration is a widely practiced form of authoritative settlement of disputes between private parties (see Brownlie, 1990, p. 709). In municipal practice, there is opportunity for appeal to court jurisdictions to order enforcement of the awards resulting from arbitration. However, in international law, this process of review generally does not exist. Although the U.N. General Assembly adopted the Model Rules of Arbitral Procedure in 1958, it rejected an International Law Commission (ILC) draft of these rules that given the parties' consent to submit to arbitration, would have provided for compulsory jurisdiction of the ICJ to review and even to revise or annul the arbitral award (see Bledsoe & Boczek, 1987, p. 283).

Consent to submit to arbitration is formalized by an international agreement known as a ***compromis*** or *compromis d'arbitrage*. This is a formal agreement stipulating the terms under which the tribunal will function, such as the applicable rules of law and any other provisions deemed desirable by the parties. Questions not dealt with in the *compromis*, including the tribunal's competence to determine its own jurisdiction, must be settled by the tribunal itself.

> **Compromis:** *The formal agreement of parties to a dispute to submit the matter to arbitration or adjudication.*

Arbitration clauses have been included as a part of treaties since antiquity, as was explained earlier in Chapter 1. However, modern arbitration within the nation-state system begins with the Jay Treaty of 1794 between the United States and Great Britain, which provided for arbitration, by mixed United States-British commissions, of various legal issues arising from the Revolutionary War. This precedent led to its widespread practice in the nineteenth century. State responsibility for injury to aliens was the most common subject matter of arbitration by mixed claims commissions.

The *Alabama Claims* award, in 1872, of $15,500,000 to the United States was an innovative development involving a truly independent arbitral tribunal. The award was against Great Britain for injuries arising out of damages resulting from the Confederate cruiser, *The Alabama,* and some other ships supplied to the southern states by British interests in violation of international law. The departure from mixed claims commissions to truly independent tribunals was then supported by the first Hague Peace Conference in creating the Permanent Court of Arbitration in 1899. In the early stage of the history of arbitration, mixed commissions were often invited by the parties to resort to "principles of justice and equity" and to propose extralegal compromises. However, by the end of the nineteenth century, arbitration was primarily, if not exclusively, associated with a process of decision according to law and supported by appropriate procedural standards (see Brownlie, 1990, pp. 709-710).

After the establishment of the Permanent Court of Arbitration in 1900, it became the major organization for arbitration for the next twenty years. It is not really a court but consists of machinery for the calling into being of tribunals. The Permanent Administrative Council and the International Bureau act as a secretariat or registry for the setting up of tribunals. The essential element is a panel of arbitrators from which parties may nominate a maximum of four persons. When parties to the Hague Convention agree to submit a dispute to the "Court," each appoints two arbitrators from the panel, and the four arbitrators select a fifth arbitrator to act as umpire.

Prior to 1931, the Permanent Court of Arbitration heard twenty-four cases (Slomanson, 1995, p. 361). However, since then, it nearly became defunct because of disuse. It has been given a new image by the very significant use of this machinery in the Iran-U.S. Claims Tribunal. Seventy-five countries still participate in appointing four individuals to provide arbitration services for a fixed number of years. The immediate availability of this machinery and its neutrality, given the very sensitive atmosphere surrounding the hostage crisis, provided an ideal choice for the selection by the parties. The resources of the Permanent Court of Arbitration could immediately begin to consider the difficult compensation issues arising out of this dispute.

Still, the Permanent Court of Arbitration is underused and has heard only three cases since 1931. This can be explained in part because the functions of arbitration have been integrated into various IGOs and because the use of chambers (panels) by the ICJ has further limited the need for a pool of arbitrators. The ICJ chambers concept makes it possible today to choose a panel of judges with the agreement of the parties and the Court. The chambers concept functions much like the Permanent Court of Arbitration was intended to function. Ad hoc arbitral tribunals may be more easily constituted today for specific types of disputes involving particular expertise.

Since World War II, there have been several significant ad hoc arbitration settlements, such as the *Rann of Kutch* case between India and Pakistan (1968) and the *Delimitation of the Continental Shelf* arbitration between the United Kingdom and France (1977). The *Beagle Channel* dispute between Argentina and Chile produced an interesting hybrid arbitration-adjudication solution involving remnants of the past processes. The issue was first decided in 1977 by an arbitral award of the Queen of England as nominal arbitrator (the actual tribunal consisted of five judges of the ICJ), but Argentina rejected the award as null and void. Subsequently, the two countries agreed to papal mediation, leading to agreement on the Pope's arbitration, which was accepted by the parties in 1984 (see Bledsoe & Boczek, 1987, p. 283).

A significant trend in international arbitration has been in the area of commercial disputes between States and private corporations. These have included the *Abu Dhabi* arbitration of 1951 between Abu Dhabi and Petroleum Development (Trucial Coast), Ltd.; the *Texaco-Libya* arbitration of 1977; the awards delivered within the framework of the International Center for the Settlement of Investment Disputes, set up under the Convention of 1965; and the International Chamber of Commerce Court of Arbitration awards.

These disputes in transnational law do not clearly fit within the traditional dual interpretation of international law. They involve instances in which sovereign immunity has been waived, as does the Iran-U.S. Claims Tribunal. Here, private corporations are given rights to bring actions against sovereign entities. The general liberalization of foreign sovereign immunities in the area of commercial activities makes possible direct actions in municipal courts. Through private arbitration, contract disputes may be resolved and the resulting judgments enforced through municipal court orders.

The new World Trade Organization (WTO) has just established a thorough system of dispute settlement within that comprehensive organization adhered to by over 130 countries. The WTO Understanding on Rules and Procedures Governing the Settlement of Disputes is "a central element in providing security and predictability to the multilateral trading system" (WTO Agreement, 1995). WTO members commit themselves not to take unilateral action against perceived violations of the trade rules but to seek recourse in the multilateral dispute settlement system and to abide by its rules and findings.

This process involves the WTO General Council, which convenes as the Dispute Settlement Board (DSB) to deal with disputes arising from any agreement contained in the Final Act of the Uruguay Round. Thus, the whole council acting as the DSB has the sole authority to establish panels, adopt panel and appellate reports, maintain surveillance of implementation of rulings and recommendations, and authorize retaliatory measures in cases of nonimplementation of recommendations. Thus there is a complete system of dispute settlement (involving complaint filing, panel argumentation and fact-finding, appeal, and implementation procedure) similar to that associated with municipal administrative law in the United States.

The WTO Understanding on Rules and Procedures emphasizes that prompt settlement of disputes is essential to the effective functioning of the organization. It sets out the following detailed procedures and the timetable to be followed in resolving disputes.

The First Stage. This requires bilateral discussions between the disputing parties. Once the parties have determined that such consultations have failed, they can bring the dispute to the WTO director-general, who, acting in an *ex officio* capacity, will offer good offices, conciliation, or mediation to settle the dispute.

The Panel Process. If consultations fail to arrive at a solution after sixty days, the complainant can ask the DSB to establish a panel to examine the case. The establishment of the panel is almost automatic. Procedures require the DSB to establish a panel no later than the second time it considers the panel request, unless there is a consensus against the decision.

• The panel's function is to make findings that will assist the DSB in making recommendations or in giving rulings provided for in the agreement. The panel may operate under different terms of reference, if the parties concerned so agree.

• The panel must be constituted within thirty days of its establishment. The WTO Secretariat will suggest the names of three potential panelists to the parties to the dispute, drawing as necessary on a list of qualified persons. If there is real difficulty in the choice, the director-general can appoint the panelists. The panelists serve in their individual capacities and are not subject to government instructions.

• Normally, the panel's final report should be given to the parties to the dispute within six months. In cases of urgency, including those related to perishable goods, the time frame is shortened to three months.

Fact-Finding and Argumentation. The main stages of the panel's detailed working procedures are set out in the Understanding of Rules and Procedures. They include the following:

• In advance of the first substantive meeting, each party to the dispute transmits to the panel its submission on the facts and arguments in the case.

• At that first meeting, the complainant presents its case and the responding party its defense. Third parties that notify their interest in the dispute may also present views. Formal rebuttals are made at the second substantive meeting.

• In cases in which a party raises scientific or other technical matters, the panel may appoint an expert review group to provide an advisory report.

• The panel submits descriptive (factual and argument) sections of its report to the parties, giving them two weeks to comment. The panel then submits an interim report, including its findings and conclusions, to the parties, giving them one week to request a review. The period of review is not to exceed two weeks, during which the panel may hold additional meetings with the parties.

• A final report is submitted to the parties, and three weeks later, it is circulated to all WTO members.

• Should the panel decide that the measure in question is inconsistent with the terms of the relevant WTO agreement, the panel recommends that the member concerned bring the measure into conformity with that agreement. It may also suggest ways in which the member could implement the recommendation.

• Panel reports are adopted by the DSB within sixty days of issuance, unless one party notifies its decision to appeal or a consensus emerges against the adoption of the report.

The Opportunity for Appeal. Either party may appeal; however, any such appeal must be limited to issues of law covered in the panel report and the legal interpretation developed by the panel:

• Appeals are heard by a standing appellate body established by the DSB. This appellate body is composed of seven persons—broadly representative of the WTO membership—who will serve four-year terms. They are required to be persons of recognized standing in the field of law and international trade and not affiliated with any government.

• Three members of the appellate body sit at any one time to hear appeals. They can uphold, modify, or reverse the legal findings and conclusions of the panel. As a general rule, the appeal proceedings are not to exceed sixty days, but in no case shall they exceed ninety days.

• Thirty days after it is issued, the DSB adopts the report of the appellate body, which is unconditionally accepted by the parties to the dispute—unless there is a consensus against the adoption of the report.

Implementing Dispute Decisions. At a DSB meeting held within thirty days of the adoption of the panel or appellate report, the party concerned must state its intentions in respect of the implementation of the recommendations. If it is impractical to comply immediately, the member will be given a "reasonable period of time," to be set by the DSB, to do so. If it fails to act within this period, it is obliged to enter into negotiations with the complainant to determine a mutually acceptable compensation—for instance, tariff reductions in areas of particular interest to the complainant.

• If after twenty days no satisfactory compensation is agreed upon, the complainant may request authorization from the DSB to suspend concessions or obligations against the other party. The DSB should grant this authorization within thirty days of the expiration of the "reasonable period of time" unless there is a consensus against the request.

• In principle, concessions should be suspended in the same sector as that in issue in the panel case. If this is not practicable or effective, the suspension can be made in a different sector of the same agreement. In turn, if this is not effective or practicable and if the circumstances are serious enough, the suspension of concessions may be made under another agreement. In any case, the DSB will keep under surveillance the implementation of adopted recommendations or rulings, and any outstanding case will remain on its agenda until the issue is resolved.

This procedure is the most extensive ever developed in international law, and it incorporates all of the informally developed procedures for peaceful dispute settlement described in this subsection of the text. It is highly analogous to municipal law procedures in the administrative area. However, it is too early to attempt any analysis of its effects, because it began taking cases only in 1995. The North American Free Trade Agreement (NAFTA) dispute settlement agreements offer a similar procedure involving a smaller number of States (United States, Canada, and Mexico).

As of January 14, 1997, the WTO procedure described here involved some forty-four distinct matters. Two of these cases had been completed and fourteen settled prior to completion of the process. Ten cases, involving a variety of issues, were active at the time of this writing. Several of the complaints filed during this period (1995-97) were against the United States. The most prominent of these issues involved the Helms-Burton (the Cuban Liberty and Democratic Solidarity) Act of 1996 regarding trade sanctions against Cuba. Congress passed this legislation after Cuban military aircraft shot down two civilian planes flown by members of the counterrevolutionary group "Brothers to the Rescue." Cuba contends that these planes had violated Cuban airspace; however, they were shot down in international waters. The sanctions imposed by the Helms-Burton Act of 1996 involve tightening the U.S. economic blockade of Cuba. Many countries around the world have condemned the act as a violation of international law. The major issue is a provision of the Helms-Burton Act that allows U.S. citizens to sue foreign companies that invest in or profit from Cuban property or businesses that the Cuban people expropriated after the revolution in 1959. Another section of the act will establish a list of these same companies and individuals who will then be barred from entering the

United States. The European Community (EC) requested consultations with the United States over this issue through the WTO procedures on June 13, 1996. The EC claims that U.S. trade restrictions on the goods of Cuban origin, as well as through the possible refusal of visas and the exclusion of non-U.S. nationals from U.S. territory, are inconsistent with the U.S. obligations under the WTO agreement. After unsatisfactory outcome of the consultation, the EC requested the establishment of a panel on October 3, 1996. The DSB established a panel at its meeting on November 20, 1996. The issue has broader implications than the WTO dispute settlement process and will provide an interesting opportunity for students of international law to follow these multiple ramifications in future developments. Mexico and Canada consider the Helms-Burton Act an interference in their internal affairs and a violation of NAFTA. Many other countries have threatened to retaliate with their own countermeasures.

International Adjudication of Disputes

As Professor Brownlie (1990) notes, no sharp line can be drawn between arbitration and judicial settlement: Judicial settlement "can properly be applied to the work of any **international tribunal** settling disputes between States in accordance with rules of international law" (p. 712). This method of classification could therefore include most of the modern actions of ad hoc tribunals and those drawn from arbitral institutions that have been discussed in the previous subsection as well as the ICJ.

> **International tribunal:** An institutional body set up for the purpose of providing judicial settlement of disputes by judges selected independently of the parties.

Additional mixed commissions, and specialized tribunals of a semipermanent character include the U.N. Tribunal in Libya, the U.N. Tribunal in Eritrea, the Supreme Restitution Court of the German Federal Republic, the Arbitral Commission on Property Rights and Interests in Germany, the Arbitral Tribunal and Mixed Commission for the Agreement on German External Debts, the Property Commissions set up as a consequence of Article 15(a) of the Peace Treaty with Japan, and the Austrian-German Arbitral Tribunal (see Brownlie, 1990, p. 712). The regional courts also fit this broad definition of international tribunals, as does the Law of the Sea Tribunal. The particular process associated with the use of international regional tribunals, criminal tribunals, and the new Law of the Sea Tribunal will be discussed later in this chapter.

The World Court

The Permanent Court of International Justice (PCIJ) and its predecessor, the ICJ, or the "World Court" as these institutions are collectively called, is usually associated with the concept of international adjudication. This is accepted because it is today the official judicial organ of the United Nations and all members of that organization must become a party to the Statute of the Court to become members. Its advisory opinions and contentious cases have developed a continuity of jurisprudence that is worldwide in scope. Adherence to the Statute of the Court is even broader than U.N. membership since it is possible to adhere to the statute and not be a member of the United Nations.

This text has provided many examples of the Court's decisions and legal opinions. Its historical development has been outlined in earlier chapters. However, the World Court is in many ways a product of nineteenth-century thinking and the then-predominant dualist theory of international law (see D'Amato, 1995). There were few changes from the PCIJ Statute of the League of Nations era. One major defect of the PCIJ Statute, which came into force in 1921, was that it contained no provision for amendment and all changes required unanimous approval from the parties. This was corrected in the new statute. The new Court after 1945 is more closely related to the United Nations than the old Court had been with the League of Nations. The U.N. Charter provides that the ICJ is "the principal judicial organ" of the United Nations. "In substance if not in form, the new Court is a continuation of the old: the Statute is virtually the same; jurisdiction under instruments referring to the old Court has been transferred to the new; and there is continuity in the jurisprudence of the Court" (Brownlie, 1990, p. 716).

Jurisdiction and Organization

The ICJ has jurisdiction in contentious cases between States, on the basis of the consent of the parties in dispute. Article 34(1) provides that "only states may be parties in cases before the Court." The advisory jurisdiction of the Court is also a rather unique feature of the ICJ that distinguishes it from other regional tribunals having compulsory jurisdiction for the parties adhering to the treaty instruments creating them, and generally, they do not have advisory jurisdiction.

The organization of the Court is intended to create a standing international tribunal in which States may have confidence; therefore, its statute goes far toward maintaining the independence of judges

once appointed. No member of the Court may exercise any political or administrative function, engage in any other occupation of a professional nature (Article 16[1]), act as agent or counsel in any case, or participate in the decision of a case with which he or she has previously been connected in some other capacity (Article 17). Dismissal can occur only on the basis of the unanimous opinion of the other members of the Court (Article 18[1]). Members engaged on business of the Court have diplomatic privileges and immunities (Article 19). Salaries are fixed by the General Assembly and may not be decreased during the term of office. The judges' salaries are free of all taxation (Article 32).

Nonetheless, the conditions governing the appointment of judges and the machinery of nomination and election are political in character. Article 2 of the statute provides that

the Court shall be composed of a body of independent judges, elected regardless of their nationality from among persons of high moral character, who possess the qualifications required in their respective countries for appointment to the highest judicial offices, or are juris-consultants of recognized competence in international law.

They are selected for nine-year terms in independent actions by majority vote of both the General Assembly and the Security Council of the United Nations.

The ICJ is composed of fifteen judges, each from a different U.N. member State. To preserve continuity, the judges are divided into groups of five that are subject to election every three years as their terms expire. There is no limit to the number of times they can be reelected. Vacancies are filled by the U.N. Security Council and General Assembly to hold office for the remainder of that judge's nine-year term.

The election process begins with the U.N. secretary-general inviting State groups that are parties to the Permanent Court of Arbitration to submit names of judicial candidates. Members of the United Nations not so represented may create national groups for this purpose. This system was an attempt to have independent persons nominated and to remove the process from individual State nominations. The statute provides that no two members may be nationals of the same State (Article 3[1]), and Article 9 requires electors to bear in mind "that in the body as a whole the representation of the main forms of civilization and the principal legal systems of the world should be assured." In practice, the system of election ensures that the composition of the Court reflects voting strength and political alliances in the Security Council and General Assembly. The permanent members of the Security Council normally have judges on the Court. The national groups are themselves nominated by governments, and nominations are sent through Foreign Ministries.

The system of election involves independent, simultaneous voting by the Security Council and the General Assembly. Nonmembers of the United Nations are allowed to participate when they are adherents of the Statute of the Court. Candidates must obtain an absolute majority in both organs to be elected (Article 10). In practice, there is more or less discreet consultation between the organs to prevent resort to a joint conference. The statute does provide procedures to deal with deadlock (see Articles 11 and 12).

These methods have produced highly respected judges. About one-third of the judges have been judicial officers in their own countries. Most have been law professors and practicing lawyers. Some of the judges have been senior government administrators, and two were heads of State.

As a further concession to potentially contentious parties that may not have a representative on the Court, Article 31 of the statute provides that a party to a case before the Court has a right, in effect, to representation on the Court by a judge ad hoc. The judge ad hoc is appointed by the party concerned and does not have to be of the same nationality as the party. This is a political concession to induce States to agree to adjudication and is justified on the basis of expediency alone. As could be expected, ad hoc judges commonly support the views of the party appointing them.

Consent to the Court's Jurisdiction

Ratification of the Statute of the Court does not constitute consent to adjudicate a specific dispute. Consent to the Court's contentious jurisdiction may take various forms, including these:

1. Bilateral or multilateral treaty clauses before development of a dispute (*ante hoc*), providing for limited subject matter jurisdiction of the Court to decide disputes

2. Adherence to the optional clause (ante hoc) providing for compulsory jurisdiction subject to reservations

3. Consent after the fact (ad hoc), which may be in the form of a *compromis* involving agreement between the parties or may be a situation in which the plaintiff State has accepted the jurisdiction by a unilateral application followed by a separate act of consent by the other party, either by a communication to the Court or by taking part in the initiation of proceedings.

As has been illustrated in several cases in this text, the competence of the Court to deal with the merits of a claim may be challenged on a number of grounds. Even advisory opinions can be challenged on the ground that the Court's opinion may jeopardize a party's position on a potentially contentious case (see *Eastern Carelia* case P.C.I.J., 1923, Ser. B, No. 5). An objection to the admissibility of a claim on the grounds that local remedies have not been exhausted involves a challenge to the validity of a claim distinct from issues as to jurisdiction or merits. The issues of admissibility and those concerning the nationality of the claimant on whose behalf the plaintiff State brings a claim are normally considered when jurisdiction has been assumed. These issues may be closely connected with the merits of the case (see *Nottebohm* in Chapter 4 and *Barcelona Traction*, in Chapter 5).

Thus, it is possible for cases to go through three phases, involving distinct proceedings concerned successively with preliminary objections to jurisdiction, preliminary objections to admissibility, and the ultimate merits of the case. Objections to jurisdiction may involve issues that cannot be pronounced on without prejudging the merits.

Ratification of the Statute of the Court alone does have some important consequences. Article 36(6) provides that "in the event of a dispute as to whether the Court has jurisdiction, the matter shall be settled by the decision of the Court." In addition, Article 41 supports preliminary actions of the Court in the form of "interim measures of protection" and "provisional measures" (specific performance orders or cease and desist orders) to preserve the respective rights of the parties before the merits and final action of the Court are concluded.

In *The Case of Military and Paramilitary Activities in and Against Nicaragua (Nicara-gua v. United States)* the ICJ upheld its compulsory jurisdiction in the matter on the basis of the 1956 Treaty of Friendship, Commerce and Navigation between the two countries. Nicaragua filed an application to the Court against the United States seeking reparation for damages and to stop alleged military activities of the United States in the form of mining its harbors and organizing and equipping the contra insurgents based in Honduras.

The United States filed a *counter-memorial* to the Court on August 17, 1984. The United States argued strenuously that Nicaragua was engaged in an armed attack against its neighbors, carried out not only by supporting armed groups engaged in military and paramilitary activities in and against El Salvador (and on a smaller scale against Costa Rica, Honduras, and Guatemala) but also by direct armed incursions across its border into Honduras and Costa Rica. Any military activity by the United States in response was within the exercise of its "inherent right of self-defense."

The major defense of the United States was that the dispute was a political question to be resolved by the Security Council and not suitable for adjudication by the ICJ. In its judgment on jurisdiction, the Court unanimously rejected the political question (nonjusticiability) argument. It pointed out that Article 24 of the U.N. Charter gives to the Security Council "primary" responsibility for the maintenance of international peace and security but that "primary" does not mean "exclusive" (I.C.J. Rep., para. 95, *Judgment on Jurisdiction and Admissibility* of November 26, 1984). It also reminded the United States that the Court was capable of dealing with the "legal" aspects of a case embedded necessarily within a "political" context, which was what the United States had successfully argued was the Court's proper role in the *Iran Hostages* case.

In April of 1984, just before Nicaragua *seized* (notified) the ICJ of its action, the United States announced that it rejected the authority of the ICJ over Central American questions for the next two years. In its jurisdictional phase, the Court then ruled that the U.S. decision to reject the Court's jurisdiction was invalid. The Court reminded the United States that the Statute of the Court gave it authority to decide on the jurisdiction of the Court in cases of dispute (Article 36[6]) and cited the requirement of first giving the Court six months' notice, an element that had been accepted by the United States in its ratification of the optional clause.

The U.S. ratification of the **optional clause** included reservations stating that it rejected jurisdiction of the Court when the issue was under consideration by another tribunal, involved a multilateral treaty, or had to do with "disputes with regard to matters which are essentially within the domestic jurisdiction of the United States of America as determined by the United States of America." The Court, in the *Nicaragua* case, ultimately accepted the U.S. objection to jurisdiction on the multilateral treaty grounds; however, it found authority to go to the merits of the case on the basis of the 1956 Treaty of Friendship between the two countries and customary international law.

> **Optional clause:**
> One of three methods of consent to compulsory jurisdiction of the ICJ. Article 36(2) of the Statute of the Court provides for States to agree in advance to a specified list of matters subject to compulsory jurisdiction in disputes with any other State accepting the same obligation.

The United States then refiled its intent (October 1985) to withdraw from the Court's jurisdiction and refused to participate in arguments on the merits in the second phase of the Court's proceedings. The ICJ issued its judgment *against* the United States in 1986, awarding Nicaragua reparations for all injuries caused by breaches of the 1956 Treaty of Friendship and Commerce.

The *Nicaragua* case has many implications with regard to the issues of political versus legal questions that will be discussed in the next chapter of this text. Here, the issues of jurisdiction and the optional clause providing compulsory jurisdiction before the fact (ante hoc) were illustrated. The ICJ took a courageous stand in this case and, for many, indicated that it would insist on the rule of law even against a permanent member of the U.N. Security Council. At the present time, the United States remains withdrawn from the compulsory jurisdiction of the Court. However, specific treaty obligations requiring the Court's jurisdiction remain operative.

The United Kingdom is the only permanent member of the Security Council that still accepts the optional clause. France has also withdrawn its declaration; Russia and China have never accepted it. Nonetheless, in 1996, sixty-two States accepted the compulsory jurisdiction as stipulated in Article 36(2) of the Court's Statute.

Advisory Jurisdiction

The function of the **advisory jurisdiction** of the Court is to assist the political organs in settling disputes and to provide authoritative guidance on points of law arising from the function of organs and specialized agencies. Thus, Article 65(1) of the statute authorizes advisory opinions "on any le-

> **Advisory jurisdiction:** Article 65(1) of the ICJ Statute provides for the court to assist the political organs of the United Nations by providing authoritative guidance on points of law. Article 96 of the U.N. Charter authorizes the General Assembly and the Security Council to request such legal opinions. Any other organs or special agencies authorized by the General Assembly may also make such requests.

gal question . . . in accordance with the Charter of the United Nations to make such a request." The U.N. Charter, in Article 96, empowers the General Assembly and the Security Council to make such requests. It also provides that on the authorization of the General Assembly, this power may be given to other organs and to specialized agencies.

The issue of "political questions" has often been raised before the Court, challenging the power of the Court to deal with political questions. "The Court has taken the view that, however controversial and far reaching in their implications, issues of treaty interpretation, arising in the context of the United Nations Charter, are legal questions" (Brownlie, 1990, p. 732). The Court may decline jurisdiction on grounds of judicial propriety (see the *Northern Cameroons* case, ICJ Reports, cited in Brownlie, 1990). The issue of interference with actions of other organs of the United Nations may become clearer after the Court has made its decision in the *Lockerbie* case *(Libya v. the United Kingdom and United States)* now pending before the Court as of May 1996.

The Caseload of the Court

The World Court has not been overloaded with cases throughout its 75 years of existence. Between 1922 and 1946 the PCIJ dealt with thirty-three contentious cases and twenty-eight requests for advisory opinions. The ICJ handled sixty contentious cases and twenty requests for advisory opinions between 1946 and 1988 (Brownlie, 1990, p. 733). For the World Court combined record, the total therefore includes 141 contentious and advisory decisions between 1922 and 1988. This averages two to three cases a year in the aggregate. Since 1988,

the Court's caseload has substantially increased, with its highest yearly caseload ever in 1995 of thirteen pending cases (Bekker, 1996, p. 328).

Any quantitative analysis of the caseload suffers from lack of consideration of the importance or complexity of the issues before the Court. The caseload has fluctuated considerably since 1946, but there has been a definite increase since the *Nicaragua* case opinion on the merits announced in 1986 and the end of the Cold War. The Court, at the time of this writing, seems quite fully used and may be in danger of exceeding its capacity. The use of ad hoc chambers of three or five judges since 1982 has aided in the Court's ability to handle the expanding caseload and may also contribute to its expanding use. Articles 26 through 29 of the Court's statute authorizes such smaller chambers, but that authorization was not used until the case of *Delimitation of the Maritime Boundary in the Gulf of Main Area* in 1982. The statute provides that the Court may from time to time form one or more chambers, composed of three or more judges, dealing with particular categories of cases, or it may form a chamber to deal with a particular case. A judgment by the chamber is considered as rendered by the Court. The chambers may sit in locations other than the Hague with the consent of the parties, and they may annually form a chamber composed of five judges who, at the request of the parties, may hear and determine cases by summary procedure.

The Revised Rules adopted by the Court provide that a request for the formation of a chamber may be filed at any time until the closure of the written proceedings. With the other party's agreement, a chamber may be formed. The parties are to be consulted to determine their views regarding the composition of the chamber; however, the Court decides in cases of dispute. This development increases the flexibility of the Court in ways that are also advantageous to the parties. It enables the Court to handle a much greater caseload than would otherwise be possible, and it makes it possible to allow the chamber to sit close to the litigants, making its location more convenient.

The Trial Process in Contentious Cases

The process of formal argument before the Court in contested cases is similar to that of a trial in civil proceedings. The Court is *seized* of a **contentious case** by the plaintiff State's complaint by either application or a *compromis* between the contentious parties. This action is followed by the plaintiff's **memorial**, a detailed written legal argument of the party, and the defending State files a counter-memorial. Oral arguments and evidence (both in the form of witness testimony and documentation) are presented. Thus, the Court serves as a trial court but must also perform the functions of a court of last resort. This places the Court in a far more difficult position than domestic courts, where fact-finding is the central focus of the trial court and the higher appellate tribunal devotes itself more exclusively to the legal issues applicable to predetermined facts (see Lillich, 1991; see particularly Franck, 1991).

Generally, the Court must depend on the parties to produce the facts in evidence within their own jurisdiction, and the Court has no authority to order discovery powers within the national jurisdiction of the opposing parties. The Court may call on the public international organizations for information relevant to cases under its consideration, and such organizations may present such information at their initiative. Article 62(1) of the Court's statute provides for third-party intervention similar to "friend of the court briefs" in appeals court procedures in the United States. This provision of the statute is limited to States and does not include private parties. Intervention is, of course, subject to the approval of the Court.

There is no issue of guilt; only questions of liability are pursued. There is no jury, and the tribunal makes findings of fact and liability by majority vote. For panels, it is a majority of the panel; and for the full Court, nine justices may constitute a *quorum*, in which the majority of those judges present decide. Majority opinions are not identified by the author of the opinion, but the opinion must contain the names of the judges that have taken part in the decision. The presiding judge does not vote unless there is an equal division of the chamber. Dissenting opinions are allowed but used sparingly.

There is no hierarchy within the system, as there is in domestic court structures. Hence, the judgment of the Court is final and without appeal. A revision of judgment is possible only when new facts that are decisive are discovered subsequent to the decision and were not considered by the Court in its judgment (von Glahn, 1996, p. 515).

The Court makes decisions in cases where the opposing party refuses to participate by nonappearance. This reduces the effectiveness of the fact-finding process in an adversarial relationship dependent on the parties to produce relevant facts (see Franck, 1991; Schwebel, 1991, p. 11). The actual procedure is a mixture of the adversarial and inquisitorial systems associated

> **Contentious case:** A case before the ICJ that involves States as parties, as opposed to a request for an advisory opinion.
>
> **Memorial:** The detailed written legal argument of the party bringing the dispute before the ICJ presenting the case for that party. The defending State prepares a counter-memorial.

with both the common law countries and the civil law countries. The judges therefore are more active in the process than in the common law tradition. They may question witnesses at length and seek out expert advice on technical matters. However, the opposing counsel members are called on to make oral and written arguments.

The provisions of Article 38 dealing with the sources of law designated by the Statute of the Court have been discussed throughout this text. They include treaties, customary practice regarded as legally binding, general principles of law, and subsidiary means of determining these rules by reference to judicial decisions and the teaching of publicists. In addition to these sources, the statute provides for agreement by the parties to decide a case *ex aequo et bono*. The familiar concept of *equity* in Anglo-American legal practice is not exactly what the Latin phrase above means in the jurisprudence of civil law countries. In international law, it apparently means that the Court can use its own judgment, even if this means disregarding the existing rules of law, to arrive at a fair decision.

A decision by the Court has no binding force except between the parties and in respect of the particular case in question (Article 59 of the statute). However, decisions are considered evidence of what the law is, which is the civil law concept on the use of court opinions, as opposed to the common law tradition accepting the doctrine of *stare decisis* and rather strict adherence to precedent.

Finally, there is the weakness of the Court in enforcing its judgments. This is basically a function performed by other governmental agencies in municipal actions, and the courts merely order performance. Article 94(2) of the U.N. Charter provides for such enforcement of the Court's judgments by the Security Council. However, thus far, no actual precedent has been established by the Security Council implementing such a decision of the Court.

Enforcement of International Law in National Courts

The highly decentralized system of the international community must depend substantially on national governments and their courts for enforcement of the bundle of rights and duties that have been described in this text as international law; just as in the United States, the federal government must depend on the state governments through their courts to enforce national law.

It may be surprising to note that the state courts in the United States handle some thirty-three million civil, criminal, and juvenile court cases of a serious nature annually, whereas the federal court system handles only about 300,000 similar cases each year (National Center for State Courts, 1991). State courts in the United States must serve two sovereigns and are sworn to uphold the U.S. Constitution and their own state constitutions. The supremacy clause of the U.S. Constitution makes it clear that state *and* federal judges are to uphold the *U.S. Constitution, acts of Congress* pursuant to the Constitution, and all *treaties*. It is also clear from the wording of the U.S. Constitution and Court interpretation that international law is a part of our law and, under certain conditions, may be applied by our courts, both state *and* federal. The federal courts have the ultimate authority over the three areas stipulated in the supremacy clause that constitute "federal question jurisdiction."

The overwhelming majority of modern nation-states do not have this complex federal structure that has just been described for the United States. They have unitary systems characterized by only one legislative, executive, and court system. However, almost all of them recognize and apply international law in their own courts under certain conditions. For this reason, international tribunals require the exhaustion of local remedies before accepting jurisdiction on the international plane.

Thus, in the *Interhandel* case, Judge Winiarski instructs that

> when a State adopts the cause of its nationals as against a respondent State in a dispute which originally was one of national law, it is important to obtain the ruling of the local courts with regard to the issues of fact and law involved, before international aspects are dealt with by an international tribunal. It [the defendant State] . . . should have a fair opportunity to rectify the position [asserted by the plaintiff] through its own tribunals. (*Switzerland v. United States*, 1959 I.C.J. Rep. 6)

Most States have adopted modern constitutions containing clauses that recognize international law, and many contain more specific clauses that recognize the superiority of treaty obligations over national legislation that may be in conflict. Most States, like the United States, require that for treaties to provide a private remedy in the form of a cause of legal action in their courts, the parties to the treaty must have intended that effect, or the State's legislature must incorporate the treaty into national law by specific enactment.

The United States recognizes even customary international law that is not in conflict with an act of Congress or constitutional exercise of the president's authority (see *Paquete Habana* case in Chapter 4). The body of federal common law is extensively reported by the *Restatement (Third) of the Foreign Relations Law of the United States* (American Law Institute, 1987).

However, it must be noted that in the event of a direct conflict between an act of Congress and a treaty, the "last in time" doctrine appears to require U.S. courts to uphold the most recent act. This may produce a conflict of obligations in which the national courts will uphold an act of Congress over a treaty obligation. The resulting obligation on the international plane must then be pursued by State-versus-State action through the processes available internationally. The national courts will decline jurisdiction on the basis of the political question doctrine. Nonetheless, the courts have been very reluctant to find important treaties in conflict with more recent statutes. They have taken judicial notice of the seriousness of such actions and will, if at all possible, construe the statute and treaty not to be in conflict (*Weinberger v. Rossi* and *United States v. Palestine Liberation Organization* in Chapter 12).

National courts provide important access for individuals to seek remedies under international law. Normally, private parties may not bring actions in international law on the international plane. Access to national courts to seek remedies for injuries in transnational disputes involving citizens of two different States is increasingly available. Private parties, corporations, or governments acting in their commercial capacities may be sued as long as an act of State is not involved. Even when an act of State is involved but that act is in violation of international law, there may be a remedy through national courts (see *Siderman v. Republic of Argentina* in Chapter 4).

The major limitations to private actions in national courts involve the *political question doctrine, the act of State doctrine,* and the *doctrine of standing.* Sufficient discussion of the act of State doctrine and the political question doctrine has been developed throughout this text. The political question doctrine is justified on reasonable grounds of deference to the political institutions of each nation that have constitutionally defined discretionary authority. The act of State doctrine is justified out of respect for the sovereign equality of nations and on the basis of deference to other governments as a matter of comity in international affairs.

The doctrine of standing deserves greater elaboration in this summary. **Standing** relates to the issue of whether or not there is applicability of a legal right in a particular situation. This may involve access to the courts to bring a legal action in which the plaintiff must show a cause of action in the form of a legal right. It may also involve a defendant who asserts a defense based on law. The defendant must likewise show a legal right to such a claim. Thus, the issue of standing is a challenge to the right asserted by either party. The claim to a right by a private party based on international law must demonstrate that the treaty is self-executing and intended by the parties to confer a legal right that is applicable to individuals in national courts.

The unusual circumstances surrounding the apprehension and conviction of General Manuel Noriega after the U.S. invasion of Panama raised some significant issues involving the doctrine of standing, which precludes a criminal defendant from asserting the rights of a third party who is not present in the litigation. The following excerpts from the district court's opinion concerning the issues of standing illustrate the related questions of whether or not the particular treaties in question are self-executing.

> *Standing:* The doctrine requiring that a party bringing suit before a court, or offering a defense, must have a legal right to do so.

United States v. Noriega
746 F.Supp (S.D.Fla.) 1990.

OMNIBUS ORDER
HOEVELER, District Judge.

* * *

Violations of International Law

In addition to his due process claim, Noriega asserts that the invasion of Panama violated international treaties and principles of customary international law—specifically, Article 2(4) of the United Nations Charter, Article 20(17) of the Organization of American States Charter, Articles 23(b) and 25 of the Hague Convention, Article 3 of Geneva Convention I, and Article 6 of the Nuremberg Charter.

Initially, it is important to note that individuals lack standing to assert violations of international treaties in the absence of a protest from the offended government. Moreover, the *Ker-Frisbie* doctrine establishes that violations of international law alone do not deprive a court of jurisdiction over a defendant in the absence of specific treaty language to that effect. *United States v. Postal*, 589 F.2d at 875-76 n. 19; *Cook v. United States*, 288 U.S. 102, 53 S.Ct. 305, 77 L.Ed. 641 (1933); *Ford v. United States*, 273 U.S. at 611, 47 S.Ct. at 537. To defeat the Court's personal jurisdiction, Noriega must therefore establish that the treaty in question is self-executing in the sense that it confers individual rights upon citizens of the signatory nations, and that it by its terms expresses "a self-imposed limitation on the jurisdiction of the United States and hence on its courts." *United States v. Postal, supra.*

As a general principle of international law, individuals have no standing to challenge violations of international treaties in the absence of a protest by the sovereign involved. *United States v. Hensel*, 699 F.2d 18, 30 (1st Cir.), *cert. denied*, 461 U.S. 958, 103 S.Ct 2431, 77 L.Ed.2d 1317 (1983); *Matta-Ballesteros v. Henman*, 896 F.2d at 263; *United States v. Williams*, 617 F.2d 1063, 1090 (5th Cir. 1980) (*en banc*) ("[R]ights under international common law must belong to the sovereigns, not to individuals"); *United States v. Rosenthal*, 793 F.2d at 1232 ("Under international law, it is the contracting foreign government that has the right to complain about a violation."). The rationale behind this rule is that treaties are "designed to protect the sovereign interests of nations, and it is up to the offended nations to determine whether a violation of sovereign interests occurred and requires redress." *United States v. Zabaneh*, 837 F.2d 1249, 1261 (5th Cir.1988). See also *United States v. Cadena*, 585 F.2d at 1261; *United States v. Davis*, 767 F.2d 1025, 1030 (2d Cir.1985); *United States v. Cordero*, 668 F.2d 32, 37-38 (1st Cir.1981); *United States v. Valot*, 625 F.2d 308, 310 (9th Cir.1980); *Lujan v. Gengler*, 510 F.2d at 67 (under international law, "individual rights are only derivative through the states") (quoting *Restatement (Second) of the Foreign Relations Law of the United States*, § 115, comment e (1965)). Consistent with that principle, a treaty will be construed as creating enforceable private rights only if it expressly or impliedly provides a private right of action. *Head Money Cases*, 112 U.S. 580, 598-99, 5 S.Ct 247, 253-54, 28 L.Ed. 798 (1884).

No such rights are created in the sections of the U.N. Charter, O.A.S. Charter, and Hague Convention cited by Noriega. Rather, those provisions set forth broad general principles governing the conduct of nations toward each other and do not by their terms speak to individual or private rights. See *Frolova v. Union of Soviet Socialist Republics*, 761 F.2d at 374 (articles phrased in "broad generalities" constitute "declarations of principles, not a code of legal rights"); *Tel-Oren v. Libyan Arab Republic*, 726 F.2d 774, 809 (D.C.Cir. 1984) (Bork, J., concurring) (Articles 1 and 2 of the United Nations Charter "contain general 'purposes and principles,' some of which state mere aspirations and none of which can be sensibly thought to have been intended to be judicially enforceable at the behest of individuals."), *cert. denied*, 470 U.S. 1003, 105 S.Ct. 1354, 84 L.Ed.2d 377 (1985); *Lujan v. Gengler*, 510 F.2d at 66-67 (individuals may not invoke Article 2(4) of the U.N. Charter or Article 20[17] of the O.A.S. Charter if the sovereign state involved does not protest); 33 *Handel v. Artukovic*, 601 F.Supp. 1421, 1425 (C.D.Cal. 1985) (Hague Convention confers no private right of action on individuals); *Dreyfus v. von Finck*, 534 F.2d 24, 30 (2d Cir.) (same), *cert. denied* 429 U.S. 835, 97 S.Ct 102, 50 L.Ed.2d 101,(1976); *Tel-Oren v. Libyan Arab Republic*, supra at 810 (same). Thus, under the applicable international law, Noriega lacks standing to challenge violations of these treaties in the absence of a protest by the Panamanian government that the invasion of Panama and subsequent arrest of Noriega violated that country's territorial sovereignty.

It can perhaps be argued that reliance on the above body of law, under the unusual circumstances of this case, is a form of legal bootstrapping. Noriega, it can be asserted, is the government of Panama or at least its de facto head of state, and as such he is the appropriate person to protest alleged treaty violations; to permit removal of him and his associates from power and reject his complaint because a new and friendly government is installed, he can further urge, turns the doctrine of sovereign standing on its head. This argument is not without force, yet there are more persuasive answers in response. First, as stated earlier, the United States has consistently refused to recognize the Noriega regime as Panama's legitimate government, a fact which considerably undermines Noriega's position. Second, Noriega nullified the results of the Panamanian presidential election held shortly before the alleged treaty violations occurred. The suggestion that his removal from power somehow robs the true government of the opportunity to object under the applicable treaties is therefore weak indeed. Finally, there is no provision or suggestion in the treaties cited which would permit the Court to ignore the absence of complaint or demand from the present duly constituted government of Panama. The current government of the Republic of Panama led by Guillermo Endara is therefore the appropriate entity to object to treaty violations. In light of Noriega's lack of standing to object, this Court therefore does not reach the question of whether these treaties were violated by the United States military action in Panama.

Article 3 of Geneva Convention I, which provides for the humane treatment of civilians and other non-participants of war, applies to armed conflicts "not of an international character," i.e., internal or civil wars of a purely domestic nature. 6 U.S.T. at 3116. See *American Baptist-Churches v. Meese*, 712 F.Supp. 756, 769 (N.D.Ca1.1989); L. Oppenheim, *International Law*, Vol. II at 370 (7th ed. 1952). Accordingly, Article 3 does not apply to the United States' military invasion of Panama.

Finally, Defendant cites Article 6 of the Nuremberg Charter, which proscribes war crimes, crimes against peace, and crimes against humanity. The Nuremberg Charter sets forth the procedures by which the Nuremberg Tribunal, established by the Allied powers after the Second World War, conducted the trials and punishment of major war criminals of the European Axis. The Government maintains that the principles laid down at Nuremberg were developed solely for the prosecution of World War II war criminals, and have no application to the conduct of U.S. military forces in Panama. The Court cannot agree. As Justice Robert H. Jackson, the United States Chief of Counsel at Nuremberg, stated: "If certain acts in violation of treaties are crimes, they are crimes whether the United States does them or whether Germany does them, and we are not prepared to lay down a rule of criminal conduct against others which we would not be willing to have invoked against us." Nonetheless, Defendant fails to establish how the Nuremberg Charter or its possible violation, assuming any, has any application to the instant prosecution. As stated above, the *Ker-Frisbie* doctrine makes clear that violations of treaties or customary international law alone do not deprive the court of jurisdiction over the defendant in the absence of limiting language to that effect. See *United States v. Winter*, 509 F.2d at 989. Defendant has not cited any language in the Nuremberg Charter, nor in any of the above treaties, which limits the authority of the United States to arrest foreign nationals or to assume jurisdiction over their crimes. The reason is apparent; the Nuremberg Charter, as is the case with the other treaties, is addressed to the conduct of war and international aggression. It has no effect on the ability of sovereign states to enforce their laws, and thus has no application to the prosecution of Defendant for alleged narcotics violations. "The violation of international law, if any, may be redressed by other remedies, and does not depend upon the granting of what amounts to an effective immunity from criminal prosecution to safeguard individuals against police or armed forces misconduct." *United States v. Cadena*, 585 F.2d at 1261. The Court therefore refrains from reaching the merits of Defendant's claim under the Nuremberg Charter.

* * *

[Motion to dismiss denied.]

Discussion Questions

1. Does the Court in this case attempt to decide the issue of whether or not the United States violated international law in invading Panama? Why is this issue relevant or irrelevant?
2. Does the Court "avoid" a conflict between national and international law in its decision, or is it simply recognizing two separate spheres of authority and jurisdiction? Discuss.
3. What arguments could be raised for and against the application of the act of State doctrine in the Noriega case?
4. Would an international criminal tribunal be a more appropriate court for prosecuting such cases analogous to the Noriega case? Why or why not?

International Regional Tribunals

This text has provided a brief description of the major regional organizations and their appropriate international tribunals (Chapter 3 and other chapters). This subsection will attempt some comparative analysis of their varied jurisdictions and procedures. What distinguishes regional tribunals is that they are limited to relationships between smaller groups of States within a particular region and do not attempt to provide worldwide jurisdiction.

Article 33 of the U.N. Charter provides that the "parties to any dispute" shall, first of all, seek a solution by the peaceful means discussed earlier in this chapter, including "resort to regional agencies or arrangements, or other peaceful means of their own choice." However, the U.N. Charter establishes no **hierarchy of courts**, an important and characteristic feature of national court systems. There is no general formal relationship between the ICJ and the regional

Hierarchy of courts: *The division of functional aspect of court jurisdiction providing for trial-level courts that are overseen by appellate courts. Courts of original jurisdiction are trial courts that focus on the fact-finding tasks, and appeals courts exercise the functions of error correction and law development.*

courts. Theoretically, international litigation could be filed in both a regional court and the ICJ at the same time. Various States have included reservations in their acceptance of the ICJ's compulsory jurisdiction under the optional clause to exclude jurisdiction of the global body while a case is pending in a regional tribunal, but there is no general rule regarding this potential conflict. The ICJ's rulings that litigants must first exhaust local remedies in *national* courts has not been extended to litigation in *regional* courts, perhaps because this question has not been squarely faced by the Court.

A lack of uniformity results from this failure to clearly define a hierarchy between regional courts and global courts. In general, regional courts operate independently of national courts, the ICJ, and each other. Thus, like the ICJ, regional international courts function as *trial* courts, from which there is no appeal; nor is there any forum to which an appeal could be taken. This problem can be partially rectified by filing a new case in a different court; however, it promotes lack of uniformity of decision within the international community's overall legal structure. Nations have never ceded appellate powers to regional or global courts. States appear, therefore, to have deliberately avoided creating appellate jurisdiction in international litigation.

The jurisdictional authority of regional courts is specified by the particular treaty arrangements creating them; therefore, such courts vary considerably in the extent of their methods of determining jurisdiction, standing of individuals, court composition, procedure, and implementation authority.

Most commentators consider the largely unsuccessful Central American Court as the first regional international court created in 1907. However, this institution is basically only an agreement to decide disputes among the five presidents of the Central American Republics and does not really operate as a court in the modern sense. An Arab Court of Justice has been proposed but has never been brought into existence. The major regional courts that will be compared in this section include the Court of Justice of the European Communities and its associated Court of First Instance, the European Court of Human Rights, the Inter-American Court of Human Rights, and the Andean Court of Justice.

Jurisdiction of Regional Courts

The European Court of Justice (ECJ) is the most fully developed regional court. It has broad jurisdictional authority in all questions related to the treaties of economic integration. The associated Court of First Instance has been created to relieve the ECJ of many of the problems of fact-finding, making it possible to allow participation on the part of individuals and corporations. The caseload of the ECJ is substantial; it handles over two hundred cases a year, comparable to the U.S. Supreme Court.

The European Court of Human Rights (ECHR) and the Inter-American Court of Human Rights (IACHR) have commissions that must first review complaints filed by individuals and make a decision concerning whether or not to bring charges before the Court. This also serves fact-finding functions that relieve the final court action of much of the trial court complexity of international tribunals. None of these regional courts have appellate jurisdiction with regard to disputes originating in State courts. The ECJ may have legal questions referred to it by national courts, which are more in the form of interlocutory appeals. Ultimately, the regional courts are restricted to hearing cases involving only States as parties.

The Court of First Instance (CFI) associated with the ECJ allows individuals who have been fined by an administrative body of the EU to appeal to the ECJ. The jurisdiction of the CFI is limited to direct actions or proceedings by individuals or legal persons except antidumping complaints. There is a right of appeal on points of law from the CFI to the ECJ. Thus, the regional courts are limited to **subject matter jurisdiction** specified in the treaties creating them.

> **Subject matter jurisdiction:** Limitation of a court's jurisdiction to decide disputes within a given subject matter area, which is specified in the legal instrument creating the court or tribunal.

The ECJ and CFI are limited to the economic areas of regulation within the EU. The Andean Court of Justice is likewise limited to the areas of economic regulation created by the "Andean Pact" (the Treaty of Bogota in 1969, the subsequent Cartagena Agreement, and most recently, the Quito Protocol of 1989). Although the Andean Court of Justice has not been extensively used, the Quito Protocol now commits the five nations fully to implement the Andean Common Market in an attempt to achieve a European-style economic integration. Judges of national courts within the five nations involved may request rulings on interpretation of the Andean Pact's economic provisions, when such issues are litigated in their own courts.

The two regional human rights courts, the ECHR and the IACHR, are limited to human rights subject matter areas of jurisdiction defined in their respective treaties. These rights and responsibilities are spelled out in the European Human Rights Convention and the OAS Human Rights Convention. Both of these courts have a human rights commission that conducts investigations and refers cases to the court for adjudication.

Composition of Regional Courts

The European Court of Justice and its Court of First Instance, as well as the European Court of Human Rights and the Andean Court of Justice, have followed a common pattern of allowing one justice from each member State. An additional judge may be added to prevent even numbers in the European Courts; however, they sit in panels of three to five judges to hear cases. The ECJ also adds a president of the Court to this number. Thus, the current fifteen-member EU has resulted in the expansion of the ECJ to seventeen members. There are twenty-three member States of the European Human Rights Convention, and an equal number of judges sit on the ECHR.

The IACHR does not include all the members of the OAS, even though it is a part of that regional organization. The American Convention on Human Rights' "Pact of San Jose, Costa Rica," includes twenty-five ratifying States as of 1996. It has *not* been ratified by the United States.

The IACHR deviates from the pattern of other regional courts in several ways. It has six part-time judges and one full-time president. Whereas all other regional courts have instituted measures to ensure a more permanent and professional judiciary, the IACHR provides for a unique body of part-time judges who are free to practice law, teach, and engage in whatever other occupations they may have in their native countries. A

U.S. professor of international law has even served in this capacity, even though the United States has not ratified or become a party to the Court's statute. The Pact of San Jose, Costa Rica, includes creation of the Inter-American Court and the Inter-American Commission of Human Rights. The Court is located in San Jose, Costa Rica, and began operation in 1979. It did not try its first case until 1981 but has become more active in recent years, increasing its caseload of contentious cases and advisory opinions (see the *Velásquez Rodriguez* case in Chapter 4 for an example).

Practice and Procedures of Regional Courts

The other regional courts differ considerably from the familiar procedures of the U.S. Supreme Court. Even though, generally, they are trial courts of last resort, there is a definite emphasis on written (versus oral) procedures. These courts are patterned after the civil law procedures of continental Europe, and the court assumes an active role in the development of evidence. Witnesses are questioned by the court, not predominantly by attorneys. Therefore, these proceedings are more analogous to those of the ICJ than to U.S. courts.

The application by a member State serves as a "complaint" for notice purposes and thereby limits (in most cases) the issues and evidence that can be raised in the proceeding. In the ECJ, the State against which the application is filed has one month to file a written "defense." The plaintiff State may file replies and the defense rejoinders, providing the court with written documentation that may resemble full evidentiary and legal briefs more than pleadings. Member States, the Commission of the EU, and (where appropriate) the EU Council may

submit written briefs to the Court. In general, the member States and the EU institutions (including Parliament) always have the right to intervene in cases before the Court. Individuals and enterprises with an interest in the litigation have the same right.

In oral arguments during the second phase of the proceedings, the ECJ hears the advocate-general, a special lawyer employed by the EU to analyze and evaluate all cases before the Court and give public opinions on the proper result under EU law. Other parties to the dispute are also heard, and the Court finally decides by majority vote in opinions that are written in a terse and summary fashion. Dissenting opinions are not allowed, in an attempt to shelter the judges from nationalistic pressures and critics. Interested parties may request clarification of the Court's rulings (see Folsom, 1995, pp. 120-125).

The ECHR does not allow individuals to be parties to the formal dispute. However, individuals may petition the European Commission to correct State action that fails to comply with the Human Rights treaty. This court has even allowed an individual whose rights were allegedly violated to appear before the Court and present his own case directly, although he was technically not a party to the international proceeding (see *Lawless v. Ireland*, 31 Int'l L. Rep. 290 [1960]).

Implementation

The EU member State courts enforce the decisions of the ECJ with regard to the economic directives contained in the EU's self-executing treaties. Thus, individuals and corporations may seek enforcement orders in the ordinary courts in the same manner as a national court may require compliance with its internal law. Likewise,

ECHR judgments are directly enforceable in the national courts of the parties to the European Convention on Human Rights. This eliminates a major enforcement problem plaguing the International Court of Justice.

The ECHR has demonstrated its capacity, in effect, to reverse a decision of the British House of Lords, the court of last resort in the United Kingdom. In the *Sunday Times* case, the ECHR ruled that the government of the United Kingdom violated European human rights law when actions were brought against the *Sunday Times* prohibiting the newspaper from printing an article detailing how the Thalidomide tragedy occurred.

The article claimed that the injuries arose from lack of proper testing of the drug before it was deemed safe for mothers carrying children. The drug produced severe deformities in children born after their mothers had used it as a sedative during pregnancy. The British argument, which had been upheld in the House of Lords, was that the internal law prohibits "trial by newspaper" and is justified so as to avoid pretrial publicity that would adversely affect pending litigation (see Mann, 1979, pp. 348-349).

The Inter-American Court of Human Rights has demonstrated more difficulty in implementation of its decisions (see notes after the *Velásquez Rodriguez* case in Chapter 4). This court handles far fewer cases than its European counterpart, which is possibly explained by the lack of regional solidarity and the prevalence of Latin-American military dictatorships in the past. The democratic changes in Latin-American countries in recent years have increased the number of states officially ratifying the Inter-American Convention on Human Rights, and more cases are being processed by the IACHR.

The New International Law of the Sea Tribunal

Although this new tribunal is something more than a regional tribunal, its assured development at the time of this writing requires at least brief mention. The International Law of the Sea Tribunal (ILST) is an integral part of the U.N. Convention on the Law of the Sea. At the time of this writing, eighty-five states have ratified the rights and obligations associated with this important developing legal regime. France and the United Kingdom are also close to completing their ratification processes.

The States Parties to the Convention elected twenty-one members of the Tribunal for the Law of the Sea on August 2, 1996. Hamburg, Germany, will be the site of the new Court, and over $6 million has been approved for its first year's budget. The Federal Republic of Germany and the city of Hamburg will spend some $100 million to build the facilities to house the Court.

The Tribunal Statute (Annex VI to the LOS Convention) sets out its method of function and composition. This new international tribunal promises to be one of the most important developments in this century and will create an important new area of international dispute settlement by adjudication.

International Criminal Courts

The historical development of the concept of universal crimes, and the acceptance of the legal right of every State to prosecute persons accused of such crimes, was discussed in Chapter 9 of this text. It is now important that the reader be brought up to date on the significant developments of the new international tribunals designed to indict, bring to trial, and punish individuals for humanitarian atrocities committed in the former Yugoslavia since 1991 and in the genocide that occurred in Rwanda in 1994. These developments have created the first international criminal tribunals since the post-World War II trials at Nuremberg.

The Ad Hoc Criminal Tribunals

Responding to the overwhelming evidence of "ethnic cleansing" and genocidal activity in the ongoing war in the former Yugoslavia, the U.N. Security Council voted to create the International Tribunal for the Prosecution of Persons Responsible for Serious Violations of International Humanitarian Law Committed in the Territory of the Former Yugoslavia Since 1991. This Security Council action took place by adoption of Resolution 827 of May 1993. In November of 1994, the Security Council voted again to create the International Tribunal for Rwanda.

These tribunals are quite different from the International Military Tribunal created to prosecute Nazi atrocities fifty years earlier. They were created in the explicit belief that accountability would "contribute to the restoration and maintenance of peace." The new tribunals are truly international exercises. The countries that supply judges, prosecutors, and staff are not parties to the conflict. They are also committed to the investigation and prosecution of persons responsible for serious violations of humanitarian crimes committed by persons on each side in the respective conflicts. The Yugoslavia Tribunal has its seat in the Hague, Netherlands, and the Rwanda Tribunal will take place in Arusha, Tanzania.

The two tribunals will share resources. The Yugoslavia Tribunal is composed of eleven judges from eleven different States, divided into two trial chambers and an appellate chamber. The Rwanda Tribunal has a similar structure and mandate to that of the court originally created for the former Yugoslavia. To maximize the efficient sharing of resources, avoid conflicting legal approaches, and minimize start-up time, the two tribunals share their chief prosecutor and their appellate chamber. The respective rules of evidence and procedure are virtually identical. A deputy prosecutor directs a team of investigators and criminal attorneys in Kigali, the capital of Rwanda, and the trials for this tribunal will be held in Tanzania.

The charters of the two international tribunals recognize a domestic component of responsibility for prosecuting the offenders and provide concurrent jurisdiction with national courts over the crimes in question. The numbers of potential cases that must be investigated and screened is astounding. The Bosnian State Commission on War Crimes currently has some twenty thousand cases in its files, and various Bosnian officials suggest that as many as five thousand may be appropriate for domestic prosecution. Croat and Serb authorities each have their war crimes cases as well. In Rwanda, where up to one million Rwandan Tutsis and moderate Hutus were brutally slaughtered in just fourteen weeks in 1994, some seventy thousand Rwandans are detained, on allegations of involvement in the genocide, in prisons built to house a fraction of that number (Kritz, 1996).

The Bosnian government has already designated six special judicial panels around the country, and one appellate panel in Sarajevo, to deal exclusively with war crimes and genocide cases. The Dayton Accords adopted a screening approach to classify those accused of humanitarian crimes. It includes, roughly, the following priority categories:

Category 1. These are the leaders who gave the orders to commit war crimes, and those who actually carried out the worst offenses. The warring parties have committed themselves to full cooperation and assistance to the international tribunal as it prosecutes those who perpetrated the most heinous offenses.

Category 2. This includes persons not falling in the first category but "persons in military, paramilitary, and police forces, and other public servants constituting a second tier of culpability." The parties to the Dayton Accords agreed to undertake immediate "prosecution, dismissal or transfer" of those "responsible for serious violations of basic rights of persons belonging to ethnic or minority groups."

Category 3. Finally, those charged with any crime related to the conflict "other than a serious violation of international humanitarian law" are guaranteed amnesty for their offenses. (see Dayton Agreement, Annex 7, Para. 3[e] and Article VI)

In Rwanda, legislation is under consideration by the government of that State to create a similar four levels of culpability for genocide:

1. The planners and leaders of the genocide, those in positions of authority who fostered these crimes, and killers of more than fifty people—all subject to full prosecution and punishment
2. Others who killed
3. Those who committed other crimes against persons, such as rape
4. Those who committed offenses against property

Those in Categories 2 and 3 who voluntarily provide a full confession of their crimes, information on accomplices or co-conspirators, and importantly, an apology to the victims of their crimes will benefit from an expedited process and a signifi-

cantly reduced schedule of penalties. Those in Category 4 will not be subject to any criminal penalties (Kritz, 1996).

The creation of the international criminal tribunals are calculated to convey a clear message that the international community will not tolerate such atrocities, in hope of deterring future carnage of this nature both in the country in question and worldwide. Such tribunals can be staffed by experts able to apply and interpret evolving international standards in this field of international law, which can do more to advance the development and enforcement of international criminal norms than the national governments can alone. The superior resources of the international community can be focused more quickly than the shattered judicial system of a country emerging from genocide or other mass atrocities, and it can function on the basis of independence and impartiality rather than retribution. Finally, in a situation in which the majority of the senior planners and perpetrators of these atrocities have left the territory where the crimes were committed, an international tribunal stands a greater chance of obtaining their physical custody and extradition.

This international component requires the cooperation of the entire international community. The one-and-a-half-year delay in getting the tribunals up and running was mostly because individual States had to agree to cooperate by passing new legislation to allow extradition to the new tribunals. The funding of these new agencies was uncertain, and the difficulty of hiring staff and conducting thorough investigations to identify persons accused of these crimes were problems that had to be overcome.

The recognition of a domestic component by the international tribunals is significant and justified on several grounds. Prosecution of war crimes before domestic courts can enhance the legitimacy and credibility of a fragile new government, demonstrating its determination to hold individuals accountable for their crimes. The public attention from the local population and foreign observers can provide an important focus for rebuilding the domestic judiciary and criminal justice system. This rebuilding can establish the courts as a credible forum for the redress of grievances in a nonviolent manner. Finally, as has been noted by the U.N. commission investigating the Rwanda genocide, domestic courts can be more sensitive to the nuances of local culture and the resulting decision "could be of greater and more immediate symbolic force because verdicts would be rendered by courts familiar to the local community."

How these ad hoc international criminal tribunals will discharge their responsibilities, whether or not the international community will sustain its commitment to enforcing humanitarian law, and what effect these international and domestic criminal courts will have on the deep resentments felt by the victims of these crimes are questions that must be answered by future developments. Indictments of over fifty major leaders accused of humanitarian crimes have been issued by the tribunals, and trials have already begun as of the time of this writing.

Plans for a Permanent International Criminal Tribunal

New precedents are being established in various countries that are finally beginning to seriously prosecute persons accused of humanitarian crimes within their national jurisdictions. Atrocities committed in Ethiopia in connection with the decades of civil war that have gone on there are finally being prosecuted. The new Ethiopian government has created a Special Prosecutor's Office established for the purpose of bringing persons accused of atrocities committed by the ousted Mengistu regime. The United Nations and various countries have provided technical and financial assistance to this process.

Although international tribunals may not be needed in every case involving humanitarian crimes, the end of the Cold War and the experience of establishing the two ad hoc tribunals has led to a serious effort to create a permanent international criminal authority. In 1993, the U.N. General Assembly requested the ILC to produce a detailed draft statute for such a court. The draft report was refined in 1994 and is being deliberated on by a preparatory committee established by the General Assembly. The issues being deliberated include the role of the Security Council as a gatekeeper for referral of cases to the Court; possible jurisdiction over crimes such as terrorism, aggression, and drug trafficking; the authority of the prosecutor to initiate investigations; and questions of extradition and procedure.

There is broad consensus that the Court should have jurisdiction over individuals for the core crimes of genocide, war crimes, and crimes against humanity. The principle of shared responsibility for prosecution of those accused of humanitarian crimes by both the international community and the national government is included in this draft under discussion. The experience in regard to the two ad hoc criminal tribunals will definitely affect the willingness of the international community to ratify a new convention. Its major advantage would be to reduce the delays that have hampered the commencement of these tribunals. By 1997, or more likely 1998, the process can be expected to move to a plenipotentiary conference for the final drafting and adoption of a treaty establishing a permanent international criminal court.

Chapter Summary

1. International law and municipal law are not necessarily in conflict. Each system of law is supreme within its own sphere of authority. A conflict of obligations may occur when municipal courts rule that municipal law takes priority over international law within the domestic sphere. The consequences of this action may invoke subsequent legal action on the international plane.

2. Most people obey the law most of the time because they think it is the right thing to do. Law serves as a guide to the prevention of conflict in society, and when conflict does occur, it serves to provide rules for the peaceful settlement of disputes.

3. International law, like domestic law, consists of a bundle of rights and obligations enforced through punishments that involve withdrawing rights from those who violate their obligations.

4. International law is a highly decentralized system of law that displays only weak organizational specialization and a much narrower range of centralized authority, but it is still capable of imposing punishment in the form of withdrawing corresponding rights when duties are violated.

5. Almost all nations observe almost all principles of international law and almost all of their obligations almost all of the time because it is in their mutual self-interest to do so since they have participated in the development of these rules.

6. States have a duty under modern international law to settle their disputes by peaceful means. These basic methods include negotiation, mediation, conciliation, arbitration, and adjudication. They graduate progressively in the degree of procedural restraints, reducing the flexibility of the parties in the order listed above.

7. Diplomatic negotiation is the least encumbered with procedural details restricting the parties and is the most flexible and effective means of dispute settlement.

8. Mediation and good offices allow the intercession of third parties who may be able to assist in overcoming barriers to diplomatic negotiation. Mediation offers positive alternatives for a solution that may bring the opposing parties to agreement.

9. Commissions of inquiry and conciliation provide investigation of factual questions that may cause disagreement between the disputing parties. Conciliation involves proposing solutions after agreement on the facts has been reached. The parties still must agree to the solution.

10. Arbitration, in modern times, has become a sophisticated procedure similar to judicial settlement in that it offers a binding award based on legal rulings of an independent tribunal chosen by the parties.

11. Adjudication refers the dispute to an established international tribunal for authoritative decision on the basis of law, for which the judges are selected by independent authority.

12. The procedural rules of the World Court are the most extensive, and the potential jurisdiction of the Court is the broadest of all the international tribunals. The ICJ has both contentious and advisory jurisdiction to decide disputes.

13. The fifteen ICJ judges are selected for staggered nine-year terms by the U.N. General Assembly and the Security Council. Their independence is protected by requiring professional qualifications, they cannot be dismissed except by the Court itself, they have diplomatic immunities, and their salaries cannot be decreased during their term in office.

14. These methods have produced highly respected judges who decide issues of fact and law by majority vote of the panel or full court. A panel (or chamber) consists of three to five judges, and the full court may operate with a quorum of nine judges. The presiding judges do not vote except to break a tie.

15. Although all U.N. members must also accept the statute of the ICJ, disputes in contentious cases must be submitted by consent of the parties. This consent may be expressed either before the dispute arises (ante hoc) or after the dispute arises (ad hoc). Bilateral agreements to refer disputes to the ICJ are one form of ante hoc consent, and adherence to the optional clause of the Court's statute providing for compulsory jurisdiction is another method.

16. The dispute before the ICJ may go through several phases, with decisions of the Court announced at each phase, including a jurisdiction and admission phase in addition to the final decision on the merits of the case. The decision in the *Nicaragua* case went against the United States in both the jurisdictional and the merits phases. The Court uses its authority to determine its own jurisdiction in cases of dispute.

17. The ICJ has increased its caseload since the *Nicaragua* case and the end of the Cold War. A record thirteen cases were considered in 1996 through its chambers and full-court procedures. However, the trial process in contentious cases demonstrates weaknesses in its inability to subpoena witnesses and evidence within the jurisdiction of sovereign States and lack of effective power to enforce its judgments.

18. The system of international law enforcement includes national court application of rules of international law, particularly in relation to access for private parties to assert rights under international law. Private parties may not bring actions before international tribunals but may, under limited circumstances, assert such rights in national courts. The major limitations to private actions involve the political question, acts of State, and standing doctrines of national courts.

19. When sovereign States bring actions on behalf of their citizens before international tribunals, the Court requires that they first exhaust local remedies before they are considered on the international plane.

20. There is no hierarchy uniting the great variety of international tribunals. Generally, they are all courts of last resort and provide no appeal opportunity. There is also no appeal from national courts to international tribunals. Cases must be initiated *de novo* (anew) on the international plane. The relationship between the European Court of Justice and its Court of First Instance is the one exception to this rule.

21. The existing regional international tribunals are limited by subject matter jurisdiction. They are limited to issues involving interpretation of the treaties of economic integration or human rights treaties.

22. The European regional courts have been the most successful in developing an extensive caseload involving compulsory jurisdiction for the parties to their treaty instruments of creation and in the effectiveness of enforcement of their judgments.

23. The new International Law of the Sea Tribunal will have extensive jurisdiction over interpretation of the Law of the Sea Convention, which went into effect in 1995. Its growing number of ratifications now include some eighty-five nations that are proceeding to elect twenty-one judges and complete administrative and procedural details to bring the tribunal into being.

24. The two extensive ad hoc international criminal courts created by the U.N. Security Council have jurisdiction to indict, bring to trial, and punish persons accused of humanitarian violations in the former Yugoslavia and Rwanda. This concept includes both international and national responsibility to bring the most serious violators to justice for their crimes.

25. Plans for a permanent international criminal court of justice are well underway in the U.N. General Assembly, which expects to bring the matter to an international conference for approval of its final draft by 1998. Jurisdiction will involve genocide, war crimes, crimes against humanity, and possibly, terrorism and drug trafficking.

Key Terms

diplomatic negotiation
good offices
mediation
commissions of inquiry
conciliation
adjudication

arbitration
compromis
international tribunal
optional clause
advisory jurisdiction
contentious case

memorial
standing
hierarchy of courts
subject matter
  jurisdiction

■ ■ ■

Discussion Questions

1. What is the function of law in dispute settlement? Is there a difference between law, lawmaking, and law enforcement? What is the difference?

2. How do the lawmaking functions in international law differ from those in modern domestic societies?

3. How do legal systems use the basic method of withdrawal of rights from those who have violated the duties expected in that community as a form of punishment?

4. What are the major methods of peaceful settlement of disputes in international relations? How are they related to each other?

5. How does the WTO dispute settlement system illustrate the combined value of the basic methods of peaceful settlement of disputes?

6. How does adjudication in international law differ from adjudication in national courts?

7. Should the ICJ have exercised compulsory jurisdiction over the dispute in the *Nicaragua* case? Discuss.

8. How has the ICJ contributed to the clarification of international law?

9. How do national courts contribute to the adjudication and enforcement of international law? What are the limitations of national courts in this regard?

10. How do regional tribunals contribute to the development of international law? What innovative aspects of these courts could be developed by the ICJ?

11. What major contributions to the development of the international legal system are represented by the new Law of the Sea Tribunal?

12. Are international criminal courts really needed?

Suggested Readings

Appendix L: Statute of the International Court of Justice

D'Amato, A. (1995). *International law: Process and prospect* (2nd ed.). Irvington, NY: Transnational.

Lillich, R. B. (Ed.). (1991). *Fact-finding before international tribunals*. Ardsley-on-Hudson, NY: Transnational.

Internet Sources

Browse: Use any of the net search programs such as Compuserve explorer or web crawler. The term *international law* will provide many current sources for your investigation.

U.N. Home Page (http://www.un.org) will be useful as well as the U.S. Department of State (http://www.state.gov/)

The American Society of International Law has a home page (http://www.asil.org) that provides excellent information on publications and legal materials. This source will provide information on new developments analyzed by competent experts in international law.

International Court of Justice (http://www.law.cornell.edu/icj/) will give you access to information about the ICJ, including text of recent opinions.

International Criminal Tribunal (ICTY/ICTR) Internet address (http://www.cij.org/tribunal).

14 Compliance and Enforcement Measures

The right to go to war was regarded for hundreds of years as not only a lawful course of action for a sovereign State but the ultimate method of enforcement of international law. Acquisition of territory by conquest was accepted as a part of traditional law. War provided an effective method of self-help in the absence of competent international governmental authority. It also supplied States with a method of changing the rules of international law, analogous to a domestic revolution carried on to change laws no longer considered tolerable.

Traditional international law made a clear distinction between the law of peace and the law of war. It did not prohibit war but viewed military force as part of the normal function of sovereign States. The functions of international law were conceived of as dealing primarily with the relations of States in time of peace, emphasizing the independent equality of States under those conditions.

However, once a state decided to go to war, it was regarded as having been released from the obligations imposed by the law, except those few that regulated the conduct of armed conflicts, and could proceed 'lawfully' to impair or even to extinguish the same independence of the opponent that had been preserved so jealously in time of peace under the rules of the law. (von Glahn, 1996, p. 555)

This textbook has emphasized the very significant changes that have occurred in the twentieth century in an attempt on the part of the world community to alter the traditional concepts of *just* and *unjust* wars and *trial by combat* that characterized earlier forms of law. However, nineteenth-century thinking still permeates our historical understanding of the world.

The Kellogg-Briand Pact (or Pact of Paris) of 1928 was considered by the "realist" school of thought as proof of the ultimate fantasy of the "idealists," in that it purported to outlaw war as an instrument of national policy. It was styled the General Treaty for the Renunciation of War, negotiated by fifteen States on August 27, 1928, and eventually ratified or adhered to by sixty-five nations. The key provisions of this famous document read as follows:

Art. 1. The High Contracting Parties solemnly declare in the names of their respective peoples that they condemn recourse to war for the solution of international controversies, and renounce it as an instrument of national policy in their relations with one another.

Art. 2. The High Contracting Parties agree that the settlement or solution of all disputes or conflicts of whatever nature or of whatever origin they may be, which may arise among them, shall never be sought except by pacific means.

The only provision for implementation of this agreement was that all the contracting parties were free to go to war with any party violating it. This is implied from the statement that any State violating the treaty would be absolved of the benefits of its provisions. The customary right of self-defense was not to be restricted or impaired in any way. The pact contained no provisions for denunciation and did not state a date of termination. Hence, it is still in effect; although, for all practical purposes, it has been superseded by the U.N. Charter, specifically its Article 2 (3, 4).

The circumstances under which this agreement was reached should be explained. It was instigated and named after the U.S. Secretary of State at the time and the French Foreign Minister who negotiated the pact. The United States was unable to join the League of Nations and the Permanent Court of International Justice because the Senate refused to ratify these initial attempts to create the institutions that might have provided a means of enforcement of this admittedly idealistic change in the cus-

tomary practice of States. The pact was an advance over the Covenant of the League of Nations, which had gaps allowing resort to war under certain circumstances. In addition, the pact allowed the United States to join in a general outlawry of war.

Although critics have seen this treaty as a primary example of futility and excessive idealism, all changes in law must begin with some sense of idealism. The positivist school of jurisprudence, as opposed to the natural law school, believes that any rule, to be effective, must correspond to the practice of States. Law cannot be built on a heedless sacrifice to reality; it must contain some sense of idealism rooted in the interests of States as well as in humanitarian values. If international law is merely what States do, it would have no functional purpose. No law is an expression of objective reality; it is a standard, or norm, expressing a desired goal.

It may be true that the premature declaration of the banishing of war may have caused a failure to prepare for acts of aggression that became obvious in the decade after its entry into force in 1929. It may have contributed to the failure of the League of Nations to take effective action against Japanese, Italian, and German aggression under the mistaken assumption that the pact outlawed the use of force. However, it was used by the United Nations to prosecute the war and by the Nuremberg Tribunal as the basis for punishing those who planned and waged aggressive war. The tribunal declared in 1945, "War for the solution of international controversies includes a war of aggression, and such a war is therefore outlawed by the Pact."

In 1945, the U.N. Charter clarified the obvious intent of the Kellogg-Briand Pact, which had been to prohibit the use of military force as a means of self-help or to change existing rights in international law.

Although the charter language pulled back from the broad sweeping language of the pact, its wording is still broad and subject to considerable controversy. The charter declares that the purpose of the organization it creates is

> to maintain international peace and security, and to that end: to take effective collective measures for the prevention and removal of *threats to the peace*, and for the suppression of *acts of aggression* or other *breaches of the peace* [italics added] and to bring about by peaceful means, and in conformity with principles of justice and international law, adjustment or settlement of international disputes or situations which might lead to a breach of the peace" (Article 1). Article 2(3)(4) provides the basic norm change of the charter:

> 3. All Members shall settle their international disputes by peaceful means in such a manner that international peace and security, and justice, are not endangered.

> 4. All Members shall refrain in their international relations from the threat or use of force against the territorial integrity or political independence of any state, or in any other manner inconsistent with the Purposes of the United Nations.

It further declares that "the organization shall ensure that states which are not Members of the United Nations act in accordance with these Principles" and that nothing in the charter "shall authorize the United Nations to intervene in matters which are essentially within the domestic jurisdiction of any state," except for the application of enforcement measures under Chapter VII (see Paragraphs 6 and 7 of Article 2).

Chapter VII gives the Security Council primary responsibility for determining what constitutes a threat to the peace, an act of aggression, or a breach of the peace and what actions are required to maintain the peace (Articles 39, 40, and 41).

Article 51 preserves the "inherent right of individual or collective self-defense if an armed attack occurs against a Member of the United Nations" until the Security Council "has taken measures necessary to maintain international peace and security." Such action in self-defense must be reported to the Security Council, which may take such action as it deems necessary to maintain or restore international peace and security.

These key articles are subject to much controversy and varied interpretation. However, it is clear that the U.N. Charter intended to change a fundamental rule of traditional international law in a more realistic manner than that attempted by the Kellogg-Briand Pact. The charter provided for the creation of institutions for the specialized purposes of making authoritative decisions intended to have binding effect on members and nonmembers alike backed by collective military force, if that became necessary.

Still, many critics argue that the United Nations has failed to fulfill the obligations essential to making the enormous change from a decentralized system of self-help to one of *effective* collective security. They point to the failure of the nations involved to carry out the intent of Article 47 of the charter, which provides for the establishment of a Military Staff Committee composed of the permanent members of the Security Council "to advise and assist the Security Council on all questions relating to . . . military requirements . . . , the employment and command of forces placed at its disposal, the regulation of armaments, and possible disarmament." The Cold War conditions of deep suspicion and tension between the superpowers have made these objectives unrealistic for the last forty years.

This chapter will examine the very controversial issues related to this major transitional period in world history. It will discuss the variety of methods available to induce compliance with international law through unilateral actions by individual States, coalitions of States, regional intergovernmental organizations (IGOs), and agencies of the United Nations Organization.

These are the political agencies of the international community that seek to deal with the most significant problems involving not only threats to the peace, acts of aggression, or breaches of the peace but also potential problems that could lead to these conditions. By facilitating the development of international law, these institutions seek to replace the ancient system of trial by combat. Elements of that older system still prevail, but much has been changed.

Self-Defense and Unilateral Self-Help Measures

The bundle of rights and duties that constitute modern international law are allocated to States when they become recognized by the community of nations as having the attributes of sovereignty. Anthony D'Amato (1995) refers to these rights and duties as "entitlements" and asserts in his "reciprocal entitlements" argument "that international law is enforceable in the same way that domestic law is enforceable" (p. 13).

Since a person is entitled to "life, liberty, and property" under domestic law, the law may in turn deprive a person of those entitlements as punishments for violation of the law. In international law, D'Amato (1995) asserts, a nation may be deprived of its entitlements as punishment for violations of

the law as well. This enforcement process he calls "reciprocal-entitlement violation." By this, he means that a violation of international law is enforced by a system of retaliation or deprivation of entitlements commensurate with the deprivation caused by the initial violators (see pp. 13-26).

Some forms of retaliation are still retained by the individual State in the modern system of international law enforcement. But the unilateral use of military force is limited by the U.N. Charter. D'Amato (1995) makes a distinction between *force* and *enforcement* action. "An unjustified use of military force against another nation is illegal. The other nation would be justified in retaliating, and that retaliation would not legally be justification of counter-retaliation." The retaliatory action in this case would be an enforcement action. This is a modern formulation of the ancient concept of *just* and *unjust* war, or use of military force. D'Amato concludes:

> The use of force, I contend, is only legal under international law if it is an *enforcement* action or if it is undertaken in self-defense. All other uses of force are ruled out by the U.N. Charter and other instruments evidencing customary international law. (p. 28)

Every State has the inherent right to self-defense—that is, to protect its existence and most vital interests against actions by other States that would deny to it these attributes of sovereignty. Thus, international law is not a mutual suicide pact, as some may try to assert. In the United States, some have asked why this country should attend to the law since others do not. Clearly, a direct attack may be responded to by the victim State and that action becomes an enforcement action entitling the victim State to compensation for the damages caused.

This traditional system, as described by D'Amato, is, of course, riddled with serious questions about who is to judge whether or not an action is illegal use of force or legitimate self-defense. The unilateral determination of nation-states themselves leads to anarchy and escalates to potential worldwide destruction, given the modern technology of today.

The questions involved in some of the basic legal tests acknowledged by D'Amato (1995) are these:

1. Was the enforcement carried out by the appropriate party?
2. Was the enforcement proportional to the harm?
3. Was the enforcement of limited duration?
4. Was there an attempt to use enforcement to effect a change in the territorial integrity or political independence of the country that was attacked?

Other important questions result from the ambiguity of the language of the U.N. Charter provisions. May unilateral military force be used to prevent a threat to a nation's vital interests, in the form of a nuclear or biological threat, when the action it takes is not intended to deprive the opposing State of territory? May such force be used for humanitarian intervention to protect the lives of its own citizens held hostage by another State? These questions are not answered in the charter, but the institutions of the organization are given the authority to answer them, particularly when they present a threat to the peace, an act of aggression, or a breach of the peace.

Sanctions Short of the Use of Force

Countermeasures short of the use of military force are a form of sanctions that can be legally imposed by States unilaterally.

The variety and expanding potential for the use of countermeasures in the modern world of increasing economic interdependence of nations is often overlooked in the debate over the use of force.

States cultivate friendly relations and cooperation with other nations for their mutual benefit and to prevent the development of conflict among them. Inducement, in the form of economic or financial aid, may be used to develop or maintain friendly relations. Trading concessions and reductions of tariffs in the form of treaties of friendship, commerce, and navigation are standard types of preventive diplomacy. When conflicts or problems arise, States attempt first of all to negotiate reasonable solutions to these problems. Failing to reach a mutual accommodation of the conflict, a State may issue a formal protest indicating that a duty under international law has been violated.

Diplomatic protests are unilateral expressions of a complaint that has some of the attributes of civil complaints filed in private litigation. Such protests are made from one government to another and require a response in the form of a convincing answer to the complaint. The consequences of failure to reply or provide a convincing answer will likely lead to deterioration of the friendly relations between the two States. A material breach of a treaty agreement will result in retaliation in the form of suspension of the duties of the protesting State and a possible legal action in arbitration or before an international tribunal, if the parties agree that they have a legal dispute that can be settled by authoritative interpretation.

> *Diplomatic protests:* A complaint communicated to another nation through diplomatic channels, alleging violations of international law and establishing an official record of such complaint.

Disputes over political issues or extreme violations of the vital interests of a State that involve fundamental entitlements in international law are likely to require more extreme forms of action. These include breaking of diplomatic relations, deportation of the offending State's nationals, and the seizure of property belonging to the offending state that is located in the protesting State. The Iran Hostage Crisis facing President Carter in 1979 illustrates the potential for unilateral enforcement action in such extreme cases.

The threat to perhaps the oldest of international legal entitlements, that of diplomatic immunity, posed by the events in Iran, constituted a threat to the existence of that entitlement throughout the entire international legal system. The violation of the U.S. Embassy premises, documents, and papers and the seizing of diplomatic personnel as hostages by a revolutionary regime that did nothing to stop radical students from taking such actions and then ratified them by participating in the holding of these diplomatic hostages, could not go unpunished. The practical situation, however, was one of great delicacy.

The international legal community could have justified a wide range of retaliatory responses on the part of the United States. It could have seized the Iranian diplomatic personnel in the United States in retaliation. However, this may have been counterproductive. This "tit-for-tat" style would only have weakened the institution of diplomatic immunity and may not have provided any inducement to cause the release of the U.S. hostages in Iran. The Iranian diplomats in the United States were the representatives of the ousted Shah anyway, and the revolutionary government did not care about what happened to them.

The action that was taken by the Carter administration was to freeze approximately $13 billion of Iranian deposits in U.S. banks and in various European banks where the United States, through U.S. corporations, had the authority to act. This innovative and rather sophisticated response was fortuitously available as leverage to eventually gain release of the hostages unharmed as well as to confiscate the interest that such vast assets could have earned. The setting aside of $1 billion of these assets to compensate private interests for their losses through the U.S.-Iran Claims Tribunal was another form of countermeasure that aided in the enforcement of international law.

This solution was more advantageous to the enforcement of international law than was direct military action. Although such action was attempted, it was unsuccessful. The planned military rescue would have more than likely resulted in getting the hostages killed, escalating the situation into full-scale military conflict.

As it turned out, President Jimmy Carter lost his bid for reelection in the United States, largely due to the adverse publicity generated by the hostage crisis, but the international community applauded the restraint demonstrated by a superpower. There was no condemnation of the United States by the international community, whereas governments all over the world expressly condemned Iran's seizure of the U.S. embassy.

Unilateral countermeasures must be proportional to the harm caused by the alleged violation and may not involve the use of military force, except for humanitarian interventions for which the criteria include greater potential for saving human lives than for destroying them. Drop-

> **Countermeasures:** *Actions in response to violations of international law that may be taken by nations unilaterally, withdrawing entitlements that are subject to that nation's discretion under international law. These unilateral sanctions must be proportional to the harm caused by the alleged violation and, generally, may not involve the use of military force.*

ping an atomic bomb on Iran or initiation of a full-scale invasion would not meet these criteria. Breaking diplomatic relations was used as a countermeasure in the Iran Hostage crisis, but it was neither a decisive factor nor perceived as punitive. Lower levels of countermeasures include deportation of the nationals of the offending State or expulsion of particular diplomats by declaring them *persona non grata*.

There are few examples of *opinio juris* as interpreted by international tribunals on the subject of countermeasures. However, two of the fifteen judges on the International Court of Justice (ICJ) felt that the blocking of Iranian assets should be set off against any reparations owing to the United States, but all fifteen members of the court agreed that Iran's initial detention of the U.S. diplomatic and consular personnel was unlawful (see *U.S. Diplomatic and Consular Staff in Tehran [United States v. Iran]* 1980 I.C.J. 3, 51).

The International Law Commission's draft article on State responsibility acknowledges the legal acceptability of proportional countermeasures at the direction of a U.N. organ that is responding to an international offense in violation of U.N. Charter principles. Arbitral tribunals have confirmed the proportionality concept and upheld countermeasures after examining both quality and quantity criterion for judging proportionality of the countermeasures in question (Zoller, 1984, p. 23 and the *Air Service Agreement [United States v. France]*, in Zoller, 1984, pp. 166-167, both cited in D'Amato, 1995).

International law is not a straitjacket that requires stiff adherence to the letter of the law. Its interpretation must change with the development of new technologies and changing circumstances. The spirit of the law is the more important element, and international precedent may begin to establish exceptions to the written rules of law. Although the use of force is prohibited by the U.N. Charter, self-defense is a unilateral written and inherent customary defense in cases of the use of force. The term *armed attack* in Article 51 of the charter suggests a territorial trespass. The controversial line between legal and illegal self-help measures might allow financial aid and moral support to revolutionary groups within another country; however, an attack by the same revolutionary group from another State's territory can amount to an armed attack.

The doctrine of **self-defense** does not permit an excessive response to even an armed attack. The response must be necessary and proportional, in that the magnitude of the response must be related to the magnitude of the attack. The legal tests for the conditions under which self-defense may be successfully demonstrated are as vague in domestic law as they are in international law. However, in international law, the decisions are made by the political institutions of the international community more frequently than by tribunals.

> *Self-defense:* The doctrine in international law that allows a nation to defend itself against attack. It may use military force to do so, but that force must be proportional to the magnitude of the attack.

The *Caroline* case involving a dispute between Great Britain and the United States began in 1837. A rebellion in Canada against the British government, which held dominion over that territory, was being suppressed. Some of the Canadian insurgents obtained American support in Buffalo, New York, and about 1,000 persons, mostly Americans, took over Navy Island, lying in the Niagara River on the Canadian side of the border. Navy Island was then used as a base for raids on the Canadian shore. The steamer *Caroline* was used to ship arms and supplies to the group on the island.

Since the U.S. authorities did nothing about this, the British commander, across the river, decided that the only way to cut off the traffic in supplies was to destroy the *Caroline*. English soldiers conducted a nighttime raid on the steamer while it was anchored at Fort Schlosser in New York. They boarded the ship and started shooting, killing two Americans and taking two others prisoner temporarily in Canada. They then set fire to the *Caroline*, cutting it loose and sending it over Niagara Falls.

After diplomatic protest by the United States and numerous exchanges of communications in which many legal points were raised, the matter came to a head when one of the English soldiers who took part in the raid was caught in the United States and tried for murder and arson. Although the English soldier was eventually acquitted, his trial stimulated interest in the *Caroline* affair and led to the famous exchange between Daniel Webster, then U.S. Secretary of State, and the British Foreign Minister in 1841.

Webster's diplomatic note set forth a powerful statement of the conditions necessary to claim self-defense in such a situation that has been frequently quoted in political as well as judicial opinions. The U.S. position was that the British were responsible unless the British government could show

> necessity of self-defense, instant, overwhelming, leaving no choice of means, and no moment for deliberation. It will be for it to show, also that the local authorities of Canada, even supporting the necessity of the moment authorized them to enter the territories of the United States at all, did nothing unreasonable or excessive; since the act, justified by the necessity of self-defense, must be limited by that necessity, and kept clearly within it. It must be shown that admonition or remonstrance to the persons on board the *Caroline* was impracticable, or would have

> been unavailing; it must be shown that daylight could not be waited for; that there could be no attempt at discrimination between the innocent and the guilty; that it would not have been enough to seize and detain the vessel; but that there was a necessity, present and inevitable, for attacking her in the darkness of the night, while moored to the shore, and while unarmed men were asleep on board, killing some and wounding others, and then drawing her into the current, above the cataract, setting her on fire, and careless to know whether there might not be in her the innocent with the guilty, or the living with the dead, committing her to a fate which fills the imagination with horror. A necessity for all this, the Government of the United States cannot believe to have existed. (cited in D'Amato, 1995, pp. 34-35)

Lord Ashburton's reply accepted all the principles stated by Webster but argued that the facts of the case fitted into the circumstances described by Webster. In his judgment, the act was not excessive—the ship was set adrift so that the U.S. property in the port would not be burned, and the attack took place in nighttime for the greatest efficiency of the attack and the least loss of life.

This agreement on the law involved set a powerful precedent that has been frequently quoted. Ashburton apologized for the fact that the act necessitated a violation of U.S. territory, but the matter was amicably concluded as a part of the overall Webster-Ashburton agreements.

"Anticipatory" Self-Defense

The Cuban Missile Crisis of 1962 demonstrated another form of self-defense argument for many observers. It has been frequently cited as an example of "anticipatory self-defense"; however, the United States argued its position on different grounds and did not invoke Article 51 of the U.N. Charter. Self-defense in the absence of an armed attack by the other side is, according to Henkin (1979), "unfounded, its reasoning is fallacious, its doctrine pernicious" (p. 141).

After the successful Cuban revolution in 1959, the communist-inspired Castro regime negotiated economic and military agreements with the Soviet Union. President Eisenhower broke diplomatic relations with Cuba in 1961. Even before that, however, the Central Intelligence Agency had been training antirevolutionary Cuban exiles for a possible invasion of the island. The invasion plan was approved by Eisenhower's successor, John F. Kennedy. On April 17, 1961, about thirteen hundred exiles, armed with U.S. weapons, landed at the Bay of Pigs on the south coast of Cuba. By the time the fighting had stopped, two days later, ninety had been killed and the rest taken prisoner by the Cuban Army, commanded by Fidel Castro. The invasion was probably a clear violation of international law. However, the invasion was squashed, and the United States did not provide the air cover that apparently was promised to the insurgents. Nonetheless, threatening behavior on the part of the United States was part of the background for the events that ensued.

U.S. intelligence flights over Cuba discovered clear evidence of preparation for the installation of missile-launching sites for offensive nuclear weapons on Cuban territory, one hundred miles from the U.S. mainland. Such weapons posed an obvious threat to the United States, but U.S. missiles of a similar nature had already been installed by the United States in Turkey within one hundred miles of Soviet territory. This new initiative by Nikita Khruschev was the occa-

sion for the most dangerous nuclear crisis of the Cold War.

U.S. intelligence further established that the nuclear warheads for the missiles were en route to Cuba on Soviet freighters. This gave the Kennedy administration thirteen days to devise a plan to meet the nuclear threat. He decided on the Cuban quarantine of 1962 that would establish a completely new type of maritime blockade, the legality of which is highly controversial. The United States deliberately described the action as a "quarantine" and not a "blockade" since, under traditional international law, interference with shipping of third States would imply that it was a belligerent blockade.

It was definitely a coercive measure short of war applied by the U.S. naval and air forces for four weeks during the Cuban Missile Crisis in 1962. It was not, however, entirely unilateral. The Cuban quarantine was based on a resolution of the Council of the Organization of American States (OAS) acting as the Provisional Organ of Consultation. It was carried out, as designed, to interdict on the high seas the delivery to Cuba of specified offensive weapons carried by ships and craft of whatever nationality.

President Kennedy's orders were to halt "All ships of any kind bound for Cuba from whatever nation or port" and "if found to contain cargoes of offensive weapons, [to] be turned back. This quarantine will be extended, if needed, to other types of cargo and carriers" (as quoted in Slomanson, 1995, p. 435).

The "quarantine" displayed features of both a *pacific* and a *belligerent* blockade as well as other unique features. **Pacific blockades** were common in the nineteenth century but controversial as a contradiction in terms. Most authorities considered them illegal unless undertaken by way of "reprisal" for prior illegal offenses. It was pacific since a state of war did not exist and none

of the parties mani-
fested any belligerent
intent *(animus bel-
lirerendi).* Unlike a traditional blockade, it
was not intended to
block the coast of a
State as such but only to
interdict the supply of
certain specific weap-
ons to Cuba. Entry and
exit of other ships not
bound for Cuba were
not barred. Vessels en
route to Cuba were subject to visit and
search, with possible exercise of force but
were subject only to "custody" and not to
capture for any breach of quarantine. Finally, the quarantine was proclaimed pursuant to a resolution of a regional IGO (see
Bledsoe & Boczek, 1987, pp. 324-325).

Abram Chayes (1963), legal adviser to
the Department of State during the Cuban
Missile Crisis, explained that the overriding
object of international law is to keep and
defend the peace. He argued the legality of
the Cuban quarantine entirely on the basis
of considerations relating to the Charter of
the United Nations, without reference to
doctrines such as the traditional concepts of
pacific blockade or belligerent blockade. He
dismissed these more traditional arguments
as having little to do with international law
after the U.N. Charter (p. 552).

The issue was presented to the United
Nations by Adali Stevenson, the U.S. ambassador, who argued the case forcefully. The
Soviet Union was embarrassed by Nikita
Khruschev's brash action, and his reckless-
ness in fomenting the Cuban Missile Crisis
became one of the major reasons for his
ouster in 1964. However, the successful
outcome of the Cuban Missile Crisis involved an agreement by President Kennedy
to remove the U.S. missiles in Turkey that
threatened the Soviet Union, as well as some
assurance that the United States would respect Cuban sovereignty.

Scholarly criticism of the U.S. action includes assertions that it was a threat of force
in breach of the U.N. Charter and violated
the principle of freedom of the seas. It has
been further pointed out that the OAS
lacked charter authority to authorize use of
force, which required the authority of the
U.N. Security Council. The Security Council did discuss the quarantine without condemning it or adopting any resolution on
the subject.

This event demonstrated the flexibility of
the U.N. Charter, which is dedicated to
preservation of world peace rather than to
a rigid system of legalities. The consensus
view of the charter is that its priority is to
prevent large-scale war, not primarily to
impose sanctions for minor violations of the
law. This political function differs considerably from the legal criteria of a court in its
mandate to decide issues on the basis of
opinio juris and established principles of
law.

Hostage Rescue Missions

Since the adoption of the U.N. Charter,
any transboundary use of military force is
subject to condemnation as a violation of
Article 2(4). The specific wording of that
article is therefore extremely important.
The specific terms, "territorial integrity"
and "political independence" found in this
article acquire their meaning from previous
usage in international instruments and
documents that were accessible to the signatories of the charter. They were chosen for
specific purposes and allow certain exceptions to the prohibition of the use of force.

This language refers to the intentions and purpose of the party using force and may be interpreted to allow certain actions involving the use of force not intended "against the territorial integrity or political independence of any state." These exceptions, however, must be consistent with the purposes of the United Nations.

Humanitarian interventions have been widely asserted by enough States in traditional international law to provide support for a *limited right* of unilateral intervention to protect human lives under certain conditions. Unilateral humanitarian intervention is less justifiable than collective intervention; however, both have support in customary international law. Nonetheless, the debate over precisely how to limit such a right has been the subject of controversy for many centuries (see Chapter 4, Protection of Aliens).

In general, **humanitarian intervention** involves forcible intervention by one State in another State's territory for the purpose of protecting individuals from threats to their lives, inhumane and cruel treatment, or persecution. Such a right has been asserted both for the protection of the nationals of the intervening State and for protection of foreign nationals, including those of the State in which the intervention takes place. The potential for this form of intervention to provide a legal pretext for the pursuit of *national* rather than *humanitarian* interests of the intervening State poses a danger to the basic entitlement of sovereign equality of States.

> **Humanitarian intervention:** *Use of force within another State's territory for the purpose of protecting individuals from threats to their lives, inhumane and cruel treatment, or persecution. This right has been severely limited in modern international law as a unilateral practice but is more easily justified as a collective action by U.N. Security Council authority.*

In the era of "gunboat diplomacy," many Western powers used the relatively unrestrained excuse of humanitarian intervention on many occasions. The United States alone is attributed with having used this exception some seventy times between 1813 and 1927 (von Glahn, 1996, p. 97). In modern international law, the practice has become considerably refined and subject to numerous limitations, particularly when used unilaterally. Rescue missions to protect nationals in hostage situations have been the more frequent situation in modern times.

The Entebbe Raid, undertaken by Israel in 1976 against the territory of Uganda, is perhaps the classic illustration of the claim to unilateral humanitarian intervention. On June 28, 1976, an Air France passenger plane, with a crew of twelve and 256 passengers aboard, was hijacked in Athens, while en route from Israel to France, by a Middle East terrorist organization. After a detour to Libya, the plane was finally landed at Entebbe airport in Uganda. Although 164 passengers were released, the remaining ninety-six passengers and twelve crew members were held hostage. The hijackers demanded the release of over 150 terrorists jailed in several European countries, Israel, and in Kenya. Most of the hostages were Israeli nationals. The hijackers threatened systematically to kill the hostages unless their demands were met. Uganda's President, Idi Amin, whose dictatorial regime was accused of humanitarian atrocities itself, refused to help the hostages and did nothing to assist the crew to gain control of the aircraft.

A daring nighttime commando raid staged on July 3 by Israeli military forces then liberated the surviving hostages (three had died) and flew them to Israel. During the raid, one Israeli soldier, seven terrorists, and a number of Ugandan military personnel were killed. The Entebbe airport was wrecked, and several Ugandan military aircraft were destroyed.

The chairman of the Organization of African Unity (OAU) initiated a complaint in the United Nations. On July 12, 1976, two draft resolutions were introduced in the Security Council. One of these was introduced by Tanzania, Libya, and Benin, condemning Israel for violating the territorial integrity and sovereignty of Uganda. The other draft resolution was sponsored by the United Kingdom and the United States, condemning hijacking but affirming the need to respect the territorial integrity and sovereignty of all States.

The two-day debate in the Security Council produced much heated discussion from the members. The representative from Guyana called the raid a modern-day version of gunboat diplomacy. The Soviet representative also condemned the Israeli raid, calling it an act of aggression that should require Israel to pay for material damage done in connection with the attack. Even the Swedish representative could not reconcile the Israeli action with the strict rules of the U.N. Charter but could not find it possible to join in a condemnation in such a case. Japan reserved its opinion as to whether the action by Israel had met the conditions required to exercise the right of unilateral self-defense in these circumstances.

The U.S. position was that Israel had acted within the limited right to use force to protect its nationals from "an imminent threat of injury or death in a situation where the State in whose territory they were located was either unwilling or unable to protect them" (Excerpts from the U.N. Security Council debate on the Entebbe incident, 1976, as reported in Slomanson, 1995, p. 459). In the end, neither of the two draft resolutions were passed by the necessary nine votes. The U.K.-U.S. resolution failed to obtain the nine affirmative votes needed, and the African resolution was not pressed to a vote.

In a similar action, two hundred U.S. Marines had rescued the crew of a U.S. containership, the *Mayaquez*, on May 14, 1975, which had been seized by the Khmer Rouge in Cambodian waters and held on Tang Island, off the shores of Cambodia. The United States likened the Cambodian action to piracy, and the counteraction was characterized as legitimate self-defense against the seizure of its citizens. There was almost no international protest over this affair. Most recently, an analogous situation occurred in 1992, when a U.S. Navy sea, air, and land (SEAL) team conducted a secret rescue mission in Haiti. They rescued a handful of former Haitian officials aligned with ousted President Aristide. This action was criticized in Congress but has been supported by the events explained in Chapter 4 of this text.

The failed attempt to rescue the U.S. hostages held in Iran during the Iran Hostage Crisis is another example of unilateral self-defense based on the humanitarian exception. However, one of the major criteria for such intervention is that the action must be intended to save more lives than might be destroyed. The aborted rescue mission of April 24-25, 1980, ran into a sandstorm in the Iranian desert that destroyed much of the equipment. The attempt produced no protest by Iran or other countries, and the international reaction in general focused on criticism of strategy and tactics and seemed to say little about legality. The ICJ, which was at the time considering the case before the tribunal, stated in its judgment that it "cannot fail to express its concern in regard to the United States' incursion into Iran." However, the Court then made it clear that its concern was that the incursion could "undermine respect for the judicial process," since it took place while the Court was deliberating (Tehran Hostages Case 19 *Int'l. Legal Materials*, 553 [1980] Judgment of May 24).

Unilateral humanitarian intervention was taken by France and Belgium in the form of military troops to protect their respective citizens living in Zaire in 1991. Then in Rwanda, in 1994, the French government sought to intervene to protect human life from the genocide taking place in that country.

UN action was considerably delayed in doing anything about the tragedy in Rwanda. France attempted to act unilaterally but was accused of employing this convenient basis for intervening in the affairs of its former French colony rather than truly seeking an end to the massacres. However, ultimately, with U.N. Security Council approval, France formed a safety zone for Hutu refugees during Rwanda's civil war, and the five hundred French troops protecting it withdrew on August 22, 1994, as stipulated in the U.N. mandate.

Preemptive Strikes

Weapons of mass destruction involving nuclear and biological capabilities could not have been clearly understood by the drafters of the U.N. Charter in 1945. These weapons and their modern delivery techniques symbolize the problem of new technology producing factual situations that require new legal interpretations. The Cuban Missile Crisis posed one set of circumstances that was met with an innovative quarantine that was a unique response. The Israeli **preemptive strike** launched against an Iraqi nuclear reactor in 1981 posed a very different set of circumstances.

On the morning of June 7, 1981, Israeli planes using conventional weapons engaged in a "surgical strike" on an Iraqi nuclear reactor allegedly being used to make weapons-grade materials near Baghdad. The attack occurred without warning at a time when the personnel were mainly away from the plant. Four of these workers were killed in the raid and the nuclear reactor destroyed. The Israeli planes had to make unauthorized flights over the territory of Syria and Jordan to reach their target, but otherwise they completed their mission without incident and returned.

> **Preemptive strike:**
> An action taken in response to a threat to a nation's security in the form of an attack before the threat can be fully mobilized. This form of action is clearly prohibited by international law but has some support under very narrow circumstances when executed in a very limited manner. As a collective security measure authorized by the Security Council, it might be justified.

The immediate reaction of the Security Council was to condemn the Israeli raid as a violation of international law. Resolution 487 of June 19, 1981, "*strongly condemn*[ed] the military attack by Israeli in clear violation of the Charter of the United Nations and the norms of international conduct" (see Vol. 75 of *American Journal of International Law,* 1981, pp. 724-725).

However, an action in self-defense is always a violation of the law until the defense asserted is proven. The Security Council resolution omitted any mention of punishment; no reparations were called for, and no enforcement machinery under the U.N. Charter was set in motion. Anthony D'Amato (1995) interprets this action as a slap on the wrist indicating an excusable violation of some sort. He explains that Security Council resolutions cannot be interpreted in the same way as decisions in a court of law. Decisions are made in the Security Council with "a wink and a nod," often on the basis of secret deals of accommodation between the member States rather than on strict legal criteria.

This incident is the first unilateral use of military force to neutralize a potential nuclear attack by a modern nation. After the Persian Gulf War in 1991, the United States made similar strikes in Iraq but under very different conditions, in which sanctions were imposed by the U.N. Security Council and Iraq was under specific order to eliminate its mass destruction capabilities, both biological and nuclear. There is little question that the Security Council may authorize elimination of such a threat.

However, in the case of unilateral action by Israel in 1981, there would be very serious consequences if this type of action were considered permissible. After all, this was the rationale for the von Schlieffen Plan, which caused World War I. During the height of the Cold War, either side could have made such an argument for a first strike that would have made the doctrine of "anticipatory self-defense" a recipe for global disaster. One might review the criteria outlined in Webster's letter to Ashburton concerning the *Caroline* incident and explore the consequences in a nuclear age. D'Amato (1995) does this in great detail and comes out in favor of Israel but would require Israel to pay for the damages and loss of life (see pp. 73–85).

The political decision of the Security Council in its resolution condemning Israel is probably more reasonable given the priority purpose of the organization to protect international peace and security rather than to act as an institution for law development. Politics has been realistically defined as compromise and the art of the possible. This political flexibility is essential to the maintenance of world order, and the flexibility would be sacrificed to a stiffer legal system involving only legal criteria. Such a judicial-dominated order may create more problems than it solves. This is perhaps the major fear of the realists who see premature development of compulsory jurisdiction of legal institutions as a mistake.

The Limits of Legitimate Self-Defense

The legal authority under the U.N. Charter prohibits the unilateral use of military force in the form of **reprisals** to enforce international law. This authority was given to the U.N. Security Council, where the veto power of the permanent members applies. International tribunals may have overlapping jurisdiction in these matters when the parties to the dispute are willing to submit to judicial settlement. However, the court is bound by the existing law and must make its decisions according to law, not political expediency.

> **Reprisals:** *The unilateral use of military force in an attempt to enforce international law. This is prohibited under the U.N. Charter and can be used legally only by the U.N. Security Council, where the veto applies.*

The ICJ, in one of its first cases, made this clear in the *Corfu Channel* case *(United Kingdom v. Albania* [1949]). In this case, the Court rejected Great Britain's argument that Albania's violations of international law gave it a right to take reprisals in the form of use of force to clear mines in Albanian territorial waters. The Court held that this act was a violation of the fundamental rule of the U.N. Charter on the prohibition of force, even though it may have been a reprisal for Albanian violations.

However, since both States were in violation of international law, the Court ultimately awarded damages to Great Britain to compensate for the initial damage caused by the mines set in a strait where innocent passage had been customary practice.

An earlier Soviet veto had been cast in the U.N. Security Council on this issue, preventing similar action by the political body. The ICJ is therefore also capable of making some forms of compromise in deciding such disputes. However, it must be careful to interpret the law accurately or lose respect for its decisions. The Court must justify its decisions, whereas the Security Council does not have to explain why it made a political decision. Court decisions are used as a subsidiary means of determining what the law is on a particular subject; therefore, the Court must be careful in its law development role of interpretation.

The U.N. General Assembly also plays a role in the law development function by its resolutions, particularly if unanimously adopted. The 1970 Declaration on Principles of International Law Concerning Friendly Relations and Cooperation Among States in Accordance With the Charter of the United Nations has become a further guide to appropriate interpretation that has been used by the ICJ. The General Assembly resolution, adopted unanimously, further defines the threat or use of force in the following designated categories:

1. Wars of aggression
2. Propaganda for wars of aggression
3. Threat of use of force to violate international boundaries or international lines of demarcation
4. Acts of reprisal involving the use of force
5. Forcible action to deprive peoples of self-determination, freedom, and independence
6. Organizing armed bands for incursion into another State's territory
7. Organizing, instigating, assisting, or participating in acts of civil strife or terrorist acts in another State or acquiescing in organized activities within its territory directed toward the commission of such acts of force
8. Acquisition of foreign territory by the threat or use of force (see Appendix K in this text)

The ICJ provides further clarification of the international law of use of force in the *Nicaragua* case in its judgment on the merits, issued in 1986. The principle argument made during the jurisdictional phase was that the issues raised by Nicaragua were political issues not subject to the Court's jurisdiction. The argument of self-defense was also raised in the jurisdictional phase. The Court rejected these arguments as not constituting a bar to the Court's jurisdiction. The Court accepted the U.S. reservation against multilateral treaties raised by the United States in the jurisdiction and acceptance phase and based its decisions on customary international law developing from the practices of States (see discussion in Chapter 13).

In the merits phase of the *Nicaragua* case, the United States had refused to participate in the arguments before the Court. This deprived the United States, and the Court, of important factual material that may have been presented. However, the Court rendered the following judgments against the United States on the basis of international law. These are important precedents that help to more clearly define the law of force in the U.N. Charter era and may be used as evidence of what the customary law is on these subjects, given the particular circumstances examined by the Court.

Military and Paramilitary Activities in and Against Nicaragua *(Nicaragua v. United States of America)*

I.C.J. Reports 14, 1986.

OPERATIVE PART OF THE COURT'S JUDGMENT

The Court

(1) By eleven votes to four,

Decides that in adjudicating the dispute brought before it by the Application filed by the Republic of Nicaragua on 9 April 1984, the Court is required to apply the "multilateral treaty reservation" contained in proviso (c) to the declaration of acceptance of jurisdiction made under Article 36, paragraph 2, of the Statute of the Court by the Government of the United States of America deposited on 26 August 1946;

(2) By twelve votes to three,

Rejects the justification of collective self-defence maintained by the United States of America in connection with the military and paramilitary activities in aid against Nicaragua the subject of this case;

(3) By twelve votes to three,

Decides that the United States of America, by training, arming, equipping, financing and supplying the *contra* forces or otherwise encouraging, supporting and aiding military and paramilitary activities in and against Nicaragua, has acted, against the Republic of Nicaragua, in breach of its obligation under customary international law not to intervene in the affairs of another State;

(4) By twelve votes to three,

Decides that the United States of America, by certain attacks on Nicaraguan territory in 1983-1984, namely attacks on Puerto Sandino on 13 September and 14 October 1983; an attack on Corinto on 10 October 1983; an attack on Potosi Naval Base on 4/5 January 1984; an attack on San Juan del Sur on 7 March 1984; attacks on patrol boats at Puerto Sandino on 28 and 30 March 1984; and an attack on San Juan del Norte on 9 April 1984; and further by those acts of intervention referred to in subparagraph (3) hereof which involve the use of force, has acted, against the Republic of Nicaragua, in breach of its obligation under customary international law not to use force against another State;

(5) By twelve votes to three,

Decides that the United States of America, by directing or authorizing overflights in Nicaraguan territory, and by the acts imputable to the United States referred to in subparagraph (4) hereof, has acted, against the Republic of Nicaragua, in breach of its obligation under customary international law not to violate the sovereignty of another State;

(6) By twelve votes to three,

Decides that, by laying mines in the internal or territorial waters of the Republic of Nicaragua during the first months of 1984, the United States of America has acted against the Republic of Nicaragua, in breach of its obligations under customary international law not to use force against another State, not to intervene in its affairs, not to violate its sovereignty and not to interrupt Peaceful maritime commerce;

(7) By fourteen votes to one,

Decides that, by the acts referred to in subparagraph (6) hereof, the United States of America has acted against the Republic of Nicaragua, in breach of its obligations under Article XIX of, the Treaty of Friendship, Commerce and Navigation between the United States of America and the Republic of Nicaragua signed at Managua on 21 January 1956;

(8) By fourteen votes to one,

Decides that the United States of America, by failing to make known the existence and location of the mines laid by it, referred to in subparagraph (6) hereof, has acted in breach of its obligations under customary international law in this respect;

(9) By fourteen votes to one,

Finds that the United States of America, by producing in 1983 a manual entitled "Operaciones sicológicas an guerra de guerrillas," and disseminating it to *contra* forces, has encouraged the commission by them of acts contrary to general principles of humanitarian law; but does not find a basis for concluding that any such acts which may have been committed are imputable to the United States of America as acts of the United States of America;

(10) By twelve votes to three,

Decides that the United States of America, by the attacks on Nicaraguan territory referred to in subparagraph (4) hereof, and by declaring a general embargo on trade with Nicaragua on 1 May 1985, has committed acts calculated to deprive of its object and purpose the Treaty of Friendship, Commerce and Navigation between the Parties signed at Managua on 21 January 1956;

(11) By twelve votes to three,

Decides that the United States of America, by the attacks on Nicaraguan territory referred to in subparagraph (4) hereof, and by declaring a general embargo on trade with Nicaragua on 1 May 1985, has acted in breach of its obligations under Article XIX of the Treaty of Friendship, Commerce and Navigation between the Parties signed at Managua on 21 January 1956;

(12) By twelve votes to three,

Decides that the United States of America is under a duty immediately to cease and to refrain from all such acts as may constitute breaches of the foregoing legal obligations;

(13) By twelve votes to three,

Decides that the United States of America is under an obligation to make reparation to the Republic of Nicaragua for all injury caused to Nicaragua by the breaches of obligations under customary international law enumerated above;

(14) By fourteen votes to one,

Decides that the United States of America is under an obligation to make reparation to the Republic of Nicaragua for all injury caused to Nicaragua by the breaches of the Treaty of Friendship, Commerce and Navigation between the Parties signed at Managua on 21 January 1956;

(15) By fourteen votes to one,

Decides that the form and amount of such reparation, failing agreement between the Parties, will be settled by the Court, and reserves for this purpose the subsequent procedure in the case;

(16) Unanimously,

Recalls to both Parties their obligation to seek a solution to their disputes by peaceful means in accordance with international law.

* * *

The Facts Imputable to the United States (paras. 75 to 125)

1. The Court examines the allegations of Nicaragua that the mining of Nicaraguan ports or waters was carried out by United States military personnel or persons of the nationality of Latin American countries in the pay of the United States. After examining the facts, the Court finds it established that, on a date in late 1983 or early 1984, the President of the United States authorized a United States Government agency to lay mines in Nicaraguan ports; that in early 1984 mines were laid in or close to the ports of El Bluff, Corinto and Puerto Sandino, either in Nicaraguan internal waters or in its territorial sea or both, by persons in the pay and acting on the instructions of that agency, under the supervision and with the logistic support of United States agents; that neither before the laying of the mines, nor subsequently, did the United States Government issue any public and official warning to international shipping of the existence and location of the mines; and that personal and material injury was caused by the explosion of the mines, which also created risks causing a rise in marine insurance rates.

2. Nicaragua attributes to the direct action of United States personnel, or persons in its pay, operations against oil installations, a naval base, etc., listed in paragraph 81 of the Judgment. The Court finds all these incidents except three, to be established. Although it is not proved that any United States military personnel took a direct part in the operations, United States agents participated in the planning, direction and support. The imputability to the United States of these attacks appears therefore to the Court to be established.

3. Nicaragua complains of infringement of its airspace by United States military aircraft. After indicating the evidence available, the Court finds that the only violations of Nicaraguan airspace imputable to the United States on the basis of the evidence are high altitude reconnaissance flights and low altitude flights on 7 to 11 November 1984 causing "sonic booms."

With regard to joint military manoeuvres with Honduras carried out by the United States on Honduran territory near the Honduras/Nicaragua frontier, the Court considers that they may be treated as public knowledge and thus sufficiently established.

4. The Court then examines the genesis, development and *activities of the contra* force, and the *role of the United States* in relation to it. According to Nicaragua, the United States "conceived, created and organized a mercenary army, the *contra* force." On the basis of the available information, the Court is not able to satisfy itself that the Respondent State "created" the *contra* force in Nicaragua, but holds it established that it largely financed, trained, equipped, armed and organized the FDN, one element of the force.

It is claimed by Nicaragua that the United States Government devised the strategy and directed the tactics of the *contra* force, and provided direct combat support for its military operations. In the light of the evidence and material available to it, the Court is not satisfied that all the operations launched by the *contra* force, at every stage of the conflict, reflected strategy and tactics solely devised by the United States. It therefore cannot uphold the contention of Nicaragua on this point. The Court however finds it clear that a number of operations were decided and planned, if not actually by United States advisers, then at least in close collaboration with them, and on the basis of the intelligence and logistic support which the United States was able to offer. It is also established in the Court's view that the support of the United States for the activities of the *contras* took various forms over the years, such as logistic support, the supply of information on the location and movements of the Sandinista troops, the use of sophisticated methods of communication, etc. The evidence does not however warrant a finding that the United States gave direct combat support, if that is taken to mean direct intervention by United States combat forces.

The Court has to determine whether the relationship of the *contras* to the United States Government was such that it would be right to equate the *contras*, for legal purposes, with an organ of the United States Government, or as acting on behalf of that Government. The Court considers that the evidence available to it is insufficient to demonstrate the total dependence of the *contras* on United States aid. A partial dependency, the exact extent of which the Court cannot establish, may be inferred from the fact that the leaders were selected by the United States, and from other factors such as the organization, training and equipping of the force, planning of operations, the choosing of targets and the operational support provided. There is no clear evidence that the United States actually exercised such a degree of control as to justify treating the *contras* as acting on its behalf.

5. Having reached the above conclusion, the Court takes the view that the *contras* remain responsible for their acts, in particular the alleged violations by them of humanitarian law. For the United States to be legally responsible, it would have to be proved that that State had effective control of the operations in the course of which the alleged violations were committed.

6. Nicaragua has complained of certain measures of an economic nature taken against it by the Government of the United States, which it regards as an indirect form of intervention in its internal affairs. Economic aid was suspended in January 1981; and terminated in April 1981, the United States acted to oppose or block loans to Nicaragua by international financial bodies; the sugar import quota from Nicaragua was reduced by 90 percent in September 1983; and a total trade embargo on Nicaragua was declared by an executive order of the President of the United States on 1 May 1985.

VIII. The Conduct of Nicaragua (paras. 126-171)

The Court has to ascertain, so far as possible, whether the activities of the United States complained of, claimed to have been the exercise of collective self-defence, may be justified by certain facts attributable to Nicaragua.

1. The United States has contended that Nicaragua was *actively supporting armed groups operating in certain of the neighbouring countries*, particularly in El Salvador, and specifically in the form of the *supply of arms*, an accusation which Nicaragua has repudiated. The Court first examines the activity of Nicaragua with regard to El Salvador.

Having examined various evidence, and taking account of a number of concordant indications, many of which were provided by Nicaragua itself, from which the Court can reasonably infer the provision of a certain amount of aid from Nicaraguan territory, the Court concludes that support for the armed opposition in El Salvador from Nicaraguan territory was a fact up to the early months of 1981. Subsequently, evidence of military aid from or through Nicaragua remains very weak, despite the deployment by the United States in the region of extensive technical monitoring resources. The Court cannot however conclude that no transport of or traffic in arms existed. It merely takes note that the allegations of arms traffic are not solidly established, and has not been able to satisfy itself that any continuing flow on a significant scale took place after the early months of 1981.

Even supposing it were established that military aid was reaching the armed opposition in El Salvador from the territory of Nicaragua, it still remains to be proved that such aid is imputable to the authorities of Nicaragua, which has not sought to conceal the possibility of weapons crossing its territory, but denies that this is the result of any deliberate official policy on its part. Having regard to the circumstances characterizing this part of Central America, the Court considers that it is scarcely possible for Nicaragua's responsibility for arms traffic on its territory to be automatically assumed. The Court considers it more consistent with the probabilities to recognize that an activity of that nature, if on a limited scale, may very well be pursued unknown to the territorial government. In any event the evidence is insufficient to satisfy the Court that the Government of Nicaragua was responsible for any flow of arms at either period.

2. The United States has also accused Nicaragua of being responsible for *cross-border military attacks* on Honduras and Costa Rica. While not as fully informed on the question as it would wish to be, the Court considers as established the fact that certain trans-border military incursions are imputable to the Government of Nicaragua.

3. The Judgment recalls certain events which occurred at the time of the fall of President Somoza, since reliance has been placed on them by the United States to contend that the present Government of Nicaragua is in violation of certain alleged *assurances* given by its immediate predecessor. The Judgment refers in particular to the "Plan to secure peace" sent on 12 July 1979 by the "Junta of the Government of National Reconstruction" of Nicaragua to the Secretary-General of the OAS, mentioning, *inter alia*, its "firm intention to establish full observance of human rights in our country" and "to call the first free elections our country has known in this century." The United States considers that it has a special responsibility regarding the implementation of these commitments.

* * *

JUDGMENT

194. With regard to the characteristics governing the right of self-defence, since the Parties consider the existence of this right to be established as a matter of customary international law, they have concentrated on the conditions governing its use. In view of the circumstances in which the dispute has arisen, reliance is placed by the Parties only on the right of self-defence in the case of an armed attack which has already occurred, and the issue of the lawfulness of a response to the imminent threat of armed attack has not been raised. Accordingly the Court expresses no view on that issue. The Parties also agree in holding that whether the response to the attack is lawful depends on observance of the criteria of the necessity and the proportionality of the measures taken in self-defence. Since the existence of the right of collective self-defence is established in customary international law, the Court must define the specific conditions which may have to be met for its exercise, in addition to the conditions of necessity and proportionality to which the Parties have referred.

195. In the case of individual self-defence, the exercise of this right is subject to the State concerned having been the victim of an armed attack. Reliance on collective self-defence of course does not remove the need for this. There appears now to be general agreement on the nature of the acts which can be treated as constituting armed attacks. In particular, it may be considered to be agreed that an armed attack must be understood as including not merely action by regular armed forces across an international border, but also "the sending by or on behalf of a State of armed bands, groups, irregulars or mercenaries, which carry out acts of armed force against another State of such

gravity as to amount to" (*inter alia*) an actual armed attack conducted by regular forces, "or its substantial involvement therein." This description, contained in Article 3, paragraph (g), of the Definition of Aggression annexed to General Assembly resolution 3314 (XXIX), may be taken to reflect customary international law. The Court sees no reason to deny that, in customary law, the prohibition of armed attacks may apply to the sending by a State of armed bands to the territory of another State, if such an operation, because of its scale and effects, would have been classified as an armed attack rather than as a mere frontier incident had it been carried out by regular armed forces. But the Court does not believe that the concept of "armed attack" includes not only acts by armed bands where such acts occur on a significant scale but also assistance to rebels in the form of the provision of weapons or logistical or other support. Such assistance may be regarded as a threat or use of force, or amount to intervention in the internal or external affairs of other States. It is also clear that it is the State which is the victim of an armed attack which must form and declare the view that it has been so attacked. There is no rule in customary international law permitting another State to exercise the right of collective self-defence on the basis of its own assessment of the situation. Where collective self-defence is invoked, it is to be expected that the State for whose benefit this right is used will have declared itself to be the victim of an armed attack.

196. The question remains whether the lawfulness of the use of collective self-defence by the third State for the benefit of the attacked State also depends on a request addressed by that State to the third State. A provision of the Charter of the Organization of American States is here in point: and while the Court has no jurisdiction to consider that instrument as applicable to the dispute, it may examine it to ascertain what light it throws on the content of customary international law. The Court notes that the OAS Charter includes, in Article 3(*f*), the principle that: "an act of aggression against one American State is an act of aggression against all the other American States" and a provision in Article 27 that:

> "Every act of aggression by a State against the territorial integrity or the inviolability of the territory or against the sovereignty or political independence of an American State shall be considered an act of aggression against the other American States."

* * *

199. At all events, the Court finds that in customary international law, whether of a general kind or that particular to the inter-American legal system, there is no rule permitting the exercise of collective self-defence in the absence of a request by the State which regards itself as the victim of an armed attack. The Court concludes that the requirement of a request by the State which is the victim of the alleged attack is additional to the requirement that such a State should have declared itself to have been attacked.

200. At this point, the Court may consider whether in customary international law there is any requirement corresponding to that found in the treaty law of the United Nations Charter, by which the State claiming to use the right of individual or collective self-defence must report to an international body, empowered to determine the conformity with international law of the measures which the State is seeking to justify on that basis. Thus Article 51 of the United Nations Charter requires that measures taken by States in exercise of this right of self-defence must be "immediately reported" to the Security Council. As the Court has observed above (paragraphs 178, 188), a principle enshrined in a treaty, if reflected in customary international law, may well be so unencumbered with the conditions and modalities surrounding it in the treaty. Whatever influence the Charter may have had on customary international law in these matters, it is clear that in customary international law it is not a condition of the lawfulness of the use of force in self-defence that a procedure so closely dependent on the content of a treaty commitment and of the institutions established by it, should have been followed. On the other hand, if self-defence is advanced as a justification for measures which would otherwise be in breach both of the principle of customary international law and of that contained in the Charter, it is to be expected that the conditions of the Charter should be respected. Thus for the purpose of enquiry into the customary law position, the absence of a report may be one of the factors indicating whether the State in question was itself convinced that it was acting in self-defence.

201. To justify certain activities involving the use of force, the United States has relied solely on the exercise of its right of collective self-defence. However the Court, having regard particularly to the non-participation of the United States in the merits phase, considers that it should enquire whether customary international law, applicable to the present dispute, may contain other rules which may exclude the unlawfulness of such activities. It does not, however, see any need to reopen the question of the conditions governing the exercise of the right of individual self-defence,

which have already been examined in connection with collective self-defence. On the other hand, the Court must enquire whether there is any justification for the activities in question, to be found not in the right of collective self-defence against an armed attack, but in the right to take counter-measures in response to conduct of Nicaragua which is not alleged to constitute an armed attack. It will examine this point in connection with an analysis of the principle of non-intervention in customary international law.

* * *

202. The principle of non-intervention involves the right of every sovereign State to conduct its affairs without outside interference; though examples of trespass against this principle are not infrequent, the Court considers that it is part and parcel of customary international law. As the Court has observed: "Between independent States, respect for territorial sovereignty is an essential foundation of international relations" (I.C.J. Reports 1949, p. 35), and international law requires political integrity also to be respected. Expressions of an *opinio juris* regarding the existence of the principle of non-intervention in customary international law are numerous and not difficult to find. Of course, statements whereby States avow their recognition of the principles of international law set forth in the United Nations Charter cannot strictly be interpreted as applying to the principle of nonintervention by States in the internal and external affairs of other States, since this principle is not, as such, spelt out in the Charter. But it was never intended that the Charter should embody written confirmation of every essential principle of international law in force. The existence in the *opinio juris* of States of the principle of non-intervention is backed by established and substantial practice. It has moreover been presented as a corollary of the principle of the sovereign equality of States. A particular instance of this is General Assembly resolution 2625 (XXV), the Declaration on the Principles of International Law concerning Friendly Relations and Co-operation among States. In the *Corfu Channel* case, when a State claimed a right of intervention in order to secure evidence in the territory of another State for submission to an international tribunal (I.C.J. Reports 1949, p. 34), the Court observed that:

"the alleged right of intervention as the manifestation of a policy of force, such as has, in the past, given rise to most serious abuses and such as cannot, whatever be the present defects in international organization, find a place in international law. Intervention is perhaps still less admissible in the particular form it would take here; for, from the nature of things, it would be reserved for the most powerful States, and might easily lead to perverting the administration of international justice itself." (I.C.J. Reports 1949, p. 35.)

* * *

209. The Court therefore finds that no such general right of intervention, in support of an opposition within another State, exists in contemporary international law. The Court concludes that acts constituting a breach of the customary principle of non-intervention will also, if they directly or indirectly involve the use of force, constitute a breach of the principle of non-use of force in international relations.

* * *

210. When dealing with the rule of the prohibition of the use of force, the Court considered the exception to it constituted by the exercise of the right of collective self-defence in the event of armed attack. Similarly, it must now consider the following question: if one State acts towards another State in breach of the principle of nonintervention, may a third State lawfully take such action by way of counter-measures against the first State as would otherwise constitute an intervention in its internal affairs? A right to act in this way in the case of intervention would be analogous to the right of collective self-defence in the case of an armed attack, but both the act which gives rise to the reaction, and that reaction itself, would in principle be less grave. Since the Court is here dealing with a dispute in which a wrongful use of force is alleged, it has primarily to consider whether a State has a right to respond to intervention with intervention going so far as to justify a use of force in reaction to measures which do not constitute an armed attack but may nevertheless involve a use of force. The question is itself undeniably relevant from the theoretical viewpoint. However, since the Court is bound to confine its decision to those points of law which are essential to the settlement of the dispute before it, it is not for the Court here to determine what direct reactions are lawfully open to a State which considers itself the victim of another State's acts of intervention, possibly involving the use of force. Hence it has not to determine whether, in the event of Nicaragua's having committed any such acts against El Salvador, the latter was lawfully entitled to take any particular counter-measure. It might however be suggested

that, in such a situation, the United States might have been permitted to intervene in Nicaragua in the exercise of some right analogous to the right of collective self-defence, one which might be resorted to in a case of intervention short of armed attack.

211. The Court has recalled above (paragraphs 193 to 195) that for one State to use force against another, on the ground that that State has committed a wrongful act of force against a third State, is regarded as lawful, by way of exception, only when the wrongful act provoking the response was an armed attack. Thus the lawfulness of the use of force by a State in response to a wrongful act of which it has not itself been the victim is not admitted when this wrongful act is not an armed attack. In the view of the Court, under international law in force today—whether customary international law or that of the United Nations system—States do not have a right of "collective" armed response to acts which do not constitute an "armed attack." Furthermore, the Court has to recall that the United States itself is relying on the "inherent right of self-defence" (paragraph 126 above), but apparently does not claim that any such right exists as would, in respect of intervention, operate in the same way as the right of collective self-defence in respect of an armed attack. In the discharge of its duty under Article 53 of the Statute, the Court has nevertheless had to consider whether such a right might exist; but in doing so it may take note of the absence of any such claim by the United States as an indication of *opinio juris*.

* * *

212. The Court should now mention the principle of respect for State sovereignty, which in international law is of course closely linked with the principles of the prohibition of the use of force and of nonintervention. The basic legal concept of State sovereignty in customary international law, expressed in, *inter alia* Article 2, paragraph 1, of the United Nations Charter, extends to the internal waters and territorial sea of every State and to the airspace above its territory. As to superjacent airspace, the 1944 Chicago Convention on Civil Aviation (Art. 1) reproduces the established principle of the complete and exclusive sovereignty of a State over the airspace above its territory. That convention, in conjunction with the 1958 Geneva Convention on the Territorial Sea, further specifies that the sovereignty of the coastal State extends to the territorial sea and to the airspace above it, as does the United Nations Convention on the Law of the Sea adopted on 10 December 1982. The Court has no doubt that these prescriptions of treaty-law merely respond to firmly established and longstanding tenets of customary international law.

213. The duty of every State to respect the territorial sovereignty of others is to be considered for the appraisal to be made of the facts relating to the mining which occurred along Nicaragua's coasts. The legal rules in the light of which these acts of mining should be judged depend upon where they took place. The laying of mines within the ports of another State is governed by the law relating to internal waters, which are subject to the sovereignty of the coastal State. The position is similar as regards mines placed in the territorial sea. It is therefore the sovereignty of the coastal State which is affected in such cases. It is also by virtue of its sovereignty that the coastal State may regulate access to its ports.

214. On the other hand, it is true that in order to enjoy access to ports, foreign vessels possess a customary right of innocent passage in territorial waters for the purposes of entering or leaving internal waters; Article 18, paragraph 1(b), of the United Nations Convention on the Law of the Sea of 10 December 1982, does no more than codify customary international law on this point. Since freedom of navigation is guaranteed, first in the exclusive economic zones which may exist beyond territorial waters (Article 58 of the Convention), and secondly, beyond territorial waters and on the high seas (Art. 87), it follows that any State which enjoys a right of access to ports for its ships also enjoys all the freedom necessary for maritime navigation. It may therefore be said that, if this right of access to the port is hindered by the laying of mines by another State, what is infringed is the freedom of communications and of maritime commerce. At all events, it is certain that interference with navigation in these areas prejudices both the sovereignty of the coastal State over its internal waters, and the right of free access enjoyed by foreign ships.

* * *

215. The Court has noted above (paragraph 77 *in fine*) that the United States did not issue any warning or notification of the presence of the mines which had been laid in or near the ports of Nicaragua. Yet even in time of war, the Convention relative to the laying of automatic submarine contact mines of 18 October 1907 (The Hague Convention No. VIII) provides that "every possible precaution must be taken for the security of peaceful shipping" and

belligerents are bound "to notify the danger zones as soon as military exigencies permit, by a notice addressed to ship owners, which must also be communicated to the Governments through the diplomatic channel" (Art. 3). Neutral Powers which lay mines off their own coasts must issue a similar notification, in advance (Art. 4). It has already been made clear above that in peacetime for one State to lay mines in the internal or territorial waters of another is an unlawful act; but in addition, if a State lays mines in any waters whatever in which the vessels of another State have rights of access or passage, and fails to give any warning or notification whatsoever, in disregard of the security of peaceful shipping, it commits a breach of the principles of humanitarian law underlying the specific provisions of Convention No. VIII of 1907. Those principles were expressed by the Court in the *Corfu Channel* case as follows:

> "certain general and well recognized principles, namely: elementary considerations of humanity, even more exacting in peace than in war" (I.C.J. Reports 1949, p. 22).

* * *

219. The conflict between the *contras'* forces and those of the Government of Nicaragua is an armed conflict which is "not of an international character." The acts of the *contras* towards the Nicaraguan Government are therefore governed by the law applicable to conflicts of that character; whereas the actions of the United States in and against Nicaragua fall under the legal rules relating to international conflicts. Because the minimum rules applicable to international and to non-international conflicts are identical, there is no need to address the question whether those actions must be looked at in the context of the rules which operate for the one or for the other category of conflict. The relevant principles are to be looked for in the provisions of Article 3 of each of the four Conventions of 12 August 1949, the text of which, identical in each Convention, expressly refers to conflicts not having an international character.

* * *

224. On the other hand, action taken in self-defence, individual or collective, might be considered as part of the wider category of measures qualified in Article XXI as "necessary to protect" the "essential security interests" of a party. In its Counter-Memorial on jurisdiction and admissibility, the United States contended that: "Any possible doubts as to the applicability of the FCN Treaty to Nicaragua's claims is dispelled by Article XXI of the Treaty . . ." After quoting paragraph 1(*d*)(set out in paragraph 221 above), the Counter-Memorial continues:

> "Article XXI has been described by the Senate Foreign Relations Committee as containing 'the usual exceptions relating . . . to traffic in arms, ammunition and implements of war and to measures for collective or individual self-defence.' "

It is difficult to deny that self-defence against an armed attack corresponds to measures necessary to protect essential security interests. But the concept of essential security interests certainly extends beyond the concept of an armed attack, and has been subject to very broad interpretations in the past. The Court has therefore to assess whether the risk run by these "essential security interests" is reasonable, and secondly, whether the measures presented as being designed to protect their interests are not merely useful but "necessary."

* * *

227. The Court will first appraise the facts in the light of the principle of the non-use of force, examined in paragraphs 187 to 200 above. What is unlawful, in accordance with that principle, is recourse to either the threat or the use of force against the territorial integrity or political independence of any State. For the most part, the complaints by Nicaragua are of the actual use of force against it by the United States. Of the acts which the Court has found imputable to the Government of the United States, the following are relevant in this respect:

— the laying of mines in Nicaraguan internal or territorial waters in early 1984 (paragraph 80 above);

— certain attacks on Nicaraguan ports, oil installations and a naval base (paragraphs 81 and 86 above).

These activities constitute infringements of the principle of the prohibition of the use of force, defined earlier, unless they are justified by circumstances which exclude their unlawfulness, a question now to be examined. The Court has also found (paragraph 92) the existence of military manoeuvres held by the United States near the Nicaraguan borders; and Nicaragua has made some suggestion that this constituted a "threat of force," which is equally forbidden by the principle of non-use of force. The Court is however not satisfied that the manoeuvres complained of, in the circumstances in which they were held, constituted on the part of the United States a breach, as against Nicaragua, of the principle forbidding recourse to the threat or use of force.

228. Nicaragua has also claimed that the United States has violated Article 2, paragraph 4, of the Charter, and has used force against Nicaragua in breach of its obligation under customary international law in as much as it has engaged in

"recruiting, training, arming, equipping, financing, supplying and otherwise encouraging, supporting, aiding, and directing military and paramilitary actions in and against Nicaragua" (Application, para. 26(*a*)and(*c*).

So far as the claim concerns breach of the Charter, it is excluded from the Court's jurisdiction by the multilateral treaty reservation. As to the claim that United States activities in relation to the *contras* constitute a breach of the customary international law principle of the non-use of force, the Court finds that, subject to the question whether the action of the United States might be justified as an exercise of the right of self-defence, the United States has committed a *prima facia* violation of that principle by its assistance to the *contras* in Nicaragua, by "organizing or encouraging the organization of irregular forces or armed bands . . . for incursion into the territory of another State," and "participating in acts of civil strife . . . in another State," in the terms of General Assembly resolution 2625(XXV). According to that resolution, participation of this kind is contrary to the principle of the prohibition of the use of force when the acts of civil strife referred to "involve a threat or use of force." In the view of the Court, while the arming and training of the *contras* can certainly be said to involve the threat or use of force against Nicaragua, this is not necessarily so in respect of all the assistance given by the United States Government. In particular, the Court considers that the mere supply of funds to the *contras*, while undoubtedly an act of intervention in the internal affairs of Nicaragua, as will be explained below, does not in itself amount to a use of force.

229. The Court must thus consider whether, as the Respondent claims, the acts in question of the United States are justified by the exercise of its right of collective self-defence against an armed attack. The Court must therefore establish whether the circumstances required for the exercise of this right of self-defence are present and, if so, whether the steps taken by the United States actually correspond to the requirements of international law. For the Court to conclude that the United States was lawfully exercising its right of collective self-defence, it must first find that Nicaragua engaged in an armed attack against El Salvador, Honduras or Costa Rica.

230. As regards El Salvador, the Court has found (paragraph 160 above) that it is satisfied that between July 1979 and the early months of 1981, an intermittent flow of arms was routed via the territory of Nicaragua to the armed opposition in that country. The Court was not however satisfied that assistance has reached the Salvadorian armed opposition, on a scale of any significance, since the early months of 1981, or that the Government of Nicaragua was responsible for any flow of arms at either period. Even assuming that the supply of arms to the opposition in El Salvador could be treated as imputable to the Government of Nicaragua, to justify invocation of the right of collective self-defence in customary international law, it would have to be equated with an armed attack by Nicaragua on El Salvador. As stated above, the Court is unable to consider that, in customary international law, the provision of arms to the opposition in another State constitutes an armed attack on that State. Even at a time when the arms flow was at its peak, and again assuming the participation of the Nicaraguan Government, that would not constitute such armed attack.

231. Turning to Honduras and Costa Rica, the Court has also stated (paragraph 164 above) that it should find established that certain trans-border incursions into the territory of those two States, in 1982, 1983 and 1984, were imputable to the Government of Nicaragua. Very little information is however available to the Court as to the circumstances of these incursions or their possible motivations, which renders it difficult to decide whether they may be treated for legal purposes as amounting, singly or collectively, to an "armed attack" by Nicaragua on either or both States. The Court notes that during the Security Council debate in March/April 1984, the representative of

Costa Rica made no accusation of an armed attack, emphasizing merely his country's neutrality and support for the Contadora process (S/PV.2529, pp. 13-23); the representative of Honduras however stated that "my country is the object of aggression made manifest through a number of incidents by Nicaragua against our territorial integrity and civilian population" (ibid., p. 37). There are however other considerations which justify the Court in finding that neither these incursions, nor the alleged supply of arms to the opposition in El Salvador, may be relied on as justifying the exercise of the right of collective self-defence.

232. The exercise of the right of collective self-defence presupposes that an armed attack has occurred; and it is evident that it is the victim State, being the most directly aware of that fact, which is likely to draw general attention to its plight. It is also evident that if the victim State wishes another State to come to its help in the exercise of the right of collective self-defence, it will normally make an express request to that effect. Thus in the present instance, the Court is entitled to take account, in judging the asserted justification of the exercise of collective self-defence by the United States, of the actual conduct of El Salvador, Honduras and Costa Rica at the relevant time, as indicative of a belief by the State in question that it was the victim of an armed attack by Nicaragua, and of the making of a request by the victim State to the United States for help in the exercise of collective self-defence.

233. The Court has seen no evidence that the conduct of those States was consistent with such a situation, either at the time when the United States first embarked on the activities which were allegedly justified by self-defence, or indeed for a long period subsequently. So far as El Salvador is concerned, it appears to the Court that while El Salvador did in fact officially declare itself the victim of an armed attack, and did ask for the United States to exercise its right of collective self-defence, this occurred only on a date much later than the commencement of the United States activities which were allegedly justified by this request. The Court notes that on 3 April 1984, the representative of El Salvador before the United Nations Security Council, while complaining of the "open foreign intervention practiced by Nicaragua in our internal affairs" (S/PV.2528, p. 58), refrained from stating that El Salvador had been subjected to armed attack, and made no mention of the right of collective self-defence which it had supposedly asked the United States to exercise. Nor was this mentioned when El Salvador addressed a letter to the Court in April 1984, in connection with Nicaragua's complaint against the United States. It was only in its Declaration of Intervention filed on 15 August 1984, that El Salvador referred to requests addressed at various dates to the United States for the latter to exercise its right of collective self-defence (para. XII), asserting on this occasion that it had been the victim of aggression from Nicaragua "since at least 1980." In that Declaration, El Salvador affirmed that initially it had "not wanted to present any accusation or allegation [against Nicaragua] to any of the jurisdictions to which we have a right to apply," since it sought "a solution of understanding and mutual respect" (para. III).

234. As to Honduras and Costa Rica, they also were prompted by the institution of proceedings in this case to address communications to the Court; in neither of these is there mention of armed attack or collective self-defence. As has already been noted (paragraph 231 above), Honduras in the Security Council in 1984 asserted that Nicaragua had engaged in aggression against it, but did not mention that a request had consequently been made to the United States for assistance by way of collective self-defence. On the contrary, the representative of Honduras emphasized that the matter before the Security Council "is a Central American problem, without exception, and it must be solved regionally" (S/PV.2529, p. 38), i.e., through the Contadora process. The representative of Costa Rica also made no reference to collective self-defence. Nor, it may be noted, did the representative of the United States assert during that debate that it had acted in response to requests for assistance in that context.

235. There is also an aspect of the conduct of the United States which the Court is entitled to take into account as indicative of the view of that State on the question of the existence of an armed attack. At no time, up to the present, has the United States Government addressed to the Security Council, in connection with the matters the subject of the present case, the report which is required by Article 51 of the United Nations Charter in respect of measures which a State believes itself bound to take when it exercises the right of individual or collective self-defence. The Court, whose decision has to be made on the basis of customary international law, has already observed that in context of that law, the reporting obligation enshrined in Article 51 of the Charter of the United Nations does not exist. It does not therefore treat the absence of a report on the part of the United States as the breach of an undertaking forming part of the customary international law applicable to the present dispute. But the Court is justified in observing that this conduct of the United States hardly conforms with the latter's avowed conviction that it was acting in the context of collective self-defence as consecrated by Article 51 of the Charter. This fact is all the more noteworthy because, in the Security Council, the United States has itself taken the view that failure to observe the

requirement to make a report contradicted a State's claim to be acting on the basis of collective self-defence (S/PV.2187).

236. Similarly, while no strict legal conclusion may be drawn from the date of El Salvador's announcement that it was the victim of an armed attack, and the date of its official request addressed to the United States concerning the exercise of collective self-defence, those dates have a significance as evidence of El Salvador's view of the situation. The declaration and the request of El Salvador, made publicly for the first time in August 1984, do not support the contention that in 1981 there was an armed attack capable of serving as a legal foundation for United States activities which began in the second half of that year. The States concerned did not behave as though there were an armed attack at the time when the activities attributed by the United States to Nicaragua, without actually constituting such an attack, were nevertheless the most accentuated; they did so behave only at a time when these facts fell furthest short of what would be required for the Court to take the view that an armed attack existed on the part of Nicaragua against El Salvador.

237. Since the Court has found that the condition *sine qua non* required for the exercise of the right of collective self-defence by the United States is not fulfilled in this case, the appraisal of the United States activities in relation to the criteria of necessity and proportionality takes on a different significance. As a result of this conclusion of the Court, even if the United States activities in question had been carried on in strict compliance with the canons of necessity and proportionality, they would not thereby become lawful. If however they were not, this may constitute an additional ground of wrongfulness. On the question of necessity, the Court observes that the United States measures taken in December 1981 (or, at the earliest, March of that year—paragraph 93 above) cannot be said to correspond to a "necessity" justifying the United States action against Nicaragua on the basis of assistance given by Nicaragua to the armed opposition in El Salvador. First, these measures were only taken, and began to produce their effects, several months after the major offensive of the armed opposition against the Government of El Salvador had been completely repulsed (January 1981), and the actions of the opposition considerably reduced in consequence. Thus it was possible to eliminate the main danger to the Salvadorian Government without the United States embarking on activities in and against Nicaragua. Accordingly, it cannot be held that these activities were undertaken in the light of necessity. Whether or not the assistance to the *contras* might meet the criterion of proportionality, the Court cannot regard the United States activities summarised in paragraphs 80, 81 and 86, i.e., those relating to the mining of the Nicaraguan ports and the attacks on ports, oil installations, etc., as satisfying that criterion. Whatever uncertainty may exist as to the exact scale of the aid received by the Salvadorian armed opposition from Nicaragua, it is clear that these latter United States activities in question could not have been proportionate to that aid. Finally on this point, the Court must also observe that the reaction of the United States in the context of what it regarded as self-defence was continued long after the period in which any presumed armed attack by Nicaragua could reasonably be contemplated.

238. Accordingly, the Court concludes that the plea of collective self-defence against an alleged armed attack on El Salvador, Honduras or Costa Rica, advanced by the United States to justify its conduct toward Nicaragua, cannot be upheld; and accordingly that the United States has violated the principle prohibiting recourse to the threat or use of force by the acts listed in paragraph 227 above, and by its assistance to the *contras* to the extent that this assistance "involve[s] a threat or use of force" (paragraph 228 above).

* * *

Discussion Questions

1. What is the difference between customary international law and a multilateral treaty?

2. How does the Court use the Friendly Relations Declaration of the General Assembly as support for its rulings in customary international law?

3. Do you agree or disagree with the Court in its ruling that the U.S. actions did not meet the requirements of necessity and proportionality that are required to sustain its actions in self-defense? Discuss.

4. Did the Court go too far in this decision to intervene in political questions that should have been handled by the Security Council?

Comment: A month after announcing the withdrawal of the United States from the Nicaragua case, Secretary of State Shultz suggested, and President Reagan later confirmed in a press conference, that the goal of U.S. policy was to overthrow the Sandinista Government of Nicaragua. What the President said was that, until the Sandinista Government says "uncle," the goal of U.S. policy was directly that of removing the "present structure" of that government (Presidential Press Conference, Feb. 22, 1985).

The United States refused to acknowledge the validity of the Court's decision, and the ICJ later decided the claim, awarding Nicaragua some $300 million in reparations. This situation persisted for five years without a settlement.

In 1984, Daniel Ortega signed a regional peace treaty drafted by the Contadora group, which was not accepted by the United States. The U.S. Congress voted in 1985 to cut off aid to the *contras*, which was not resumed until October of 1986. It was then discovered that the *contras* had benefited from funds diverted from payments made for secret arms sales to Iran by the United States while official military aid was suspended. The Iran-Contra Affair then brought to light the illegal activity that occurred in the Reagan administration.

In March 1988, at their first face-to-face peace talks, the *contras* and the Sandinistas agreed to a temporary truce. In an internationally monitored free election, Ortega was defeated by Violeta Barrios de Chamorro in national elections in 1990. The National Opposition Union (UNO), with Chamorro as its presidential candidate, won the presidency and a majority in the National Assembly. President Chamorro took office in April, and she launched a program of reconstruction that included demobilization of the contra rebels, a gradual reduction in government troop strength, and currency reform.

To shore up the ailing Nicaraguan economy, a substantial amount of U.S. foreign aid was successfully negotiated, which amounted to more than the Court award in the *Nicaragua* case. In 1991, the Nicaraguan government notified the Court that it had decided to "renounce all further right of action based on the case and did not wish to go on with the proceedings." Two weeks later, the legal adviser to the U.S. Department of State responded with a letter to the Court, "welcoming the discontinuance." The case was thus dropped from the ICJ's list of active cases.

The Role and Function of International Regimes

The natural tendency to focus on issues of war and peace in international relations may distort our understanding of the detailed methods used to maintain international peace and security as well as enforce international law. A famous nineteenth-century German military strategist, Karl von Clausewitz, in his classic book on military strategy (*On War*, 1833) maintained that "war is nothing but the continuation of diplomacy by other means." When peaceful means of settlement of disputes fails, military combat and force are used to settle disputes.

Prior to World War II, international security was defined almost exclusively in terms of military concerns of war, peace, and armed conflict. The U.N. Charter, however, embodied a broader definition of in-ternational security that is more related to the underlying causes of international conflict. These concerns involved economic and social well-being, respect for human rights, literacy, adequacy of food, and protection from diseases. In the postwar period, this expanded definition has been further broadened to include the security of a safe, nontoxic environment, the security of political and civil rights, and social and economic rights.

The proliferation of international IGOs, particularly since the 1960s, has played a prominent role in broadening the definition of security and has produced innovative and impressive efforts to address the multitude of persistent threats to that security. Field and Jordan (1988), using a rather sophisticated classification technique, were able to count some 378 IGOs operating in 1986 and estimated their growth pattern to indicate that by the year 2000 there will be some 450 such organizations. Over three-fourths of these organizations have been created since 1960.

This study indicates that the growth of international nongovernmental organizations (INGOs) is even more spectacular. They provide input and support for the intergovernmental efforts in many areas of nontraditional security interests. In 1986, 4,676 INGOs were listed by the Union of International Associations, and the union estimated a possible 10,815 by the year 2000 (Field & Jordan, 1988, p. 7).

These organizations are beginning to be identified as international regimes that have become prominent features of the international legal and political environment. They are not the traditional military alliances of the past, but function as integral parts of the networks of complex interdependence that have emerged in the twentieth century.

International organizations enlarge the possibilities and add to the constraints under which their member States develop and implement foreign policy. They provide common interests in enhancing predictability in inter-State interactions, information sharing, and problem solving. These common interests often work toward enhancing multilateral cooperation even among States whose specific interests may differ significantly (see Chapters 7 and 8 in this text and Karns & Mingst, 1990, for further elaboration).

These intergovernmental organizations are predominately economic, social, and cultural organizations stressing interests in economic development and human rights protection. States frequently join such organizations to use them as instruments of foreign policy. The institutions of these organizations then establish mechanisms for creating patterns of order and cooperation among States and other actors. Nongovernmental organizations have found that they can also work through these mechanisms to promote solutions to international problems.

As explained by Karns and Mingst (1991),

> They provide forums for legitimating viewpoints, principles, and norms, for coalition building, and for issue linkage. They establish regularized processes of information gathering, analysis, and surveillance. They institutionalize decision making and negotiating processes for rule creation and dispute settlement. They provide collective goods and support operational activities. (p. 267)

IGOs can be used for both good and evil, as is true of all bureaucratic institutions. They are susceptible to unnecessary growth, corruption, mismanagement, and dominance by special interests, but they promote cooperation and adherence to standards of behavior. They not only create opportunities for their member States as instruments of policy but also impose restraints on these States and influence process development. Policy outcomes must involve compromise and cooperation. They depend on the cooperation and resources of their member governments to implement decisions and recommendations.

The resulting **international regimes** constrain or affect member States by setting agendas, providing surveillance, generating decision-making and implementation procedures, and creating rules of behavior that States must adjust to if they wish to benefit from reciprocity.

> **International regimes:** The network of administrative legal constraints that results from the procedures of intergovernmental organizations.

Particularly, the effect of these organizations on the process of agenda setting in national political decision-making institutions is significant because this forces governments to make decisions. Their functional activities require information gathering and surveillance through information sharing. This makes available superior information for monitoring problems and encourages States to develop specialized decision-making and implementation procedures. Finally, they establish administrative legal procedures designating rules of behavior and compliance measures to ensure performance.

Economic, Environmental, and Human Rights Regimes

Several examples of international regimes have been discussed in this text. They include the new World Trade Organization (WTO) with its now-elaborate set of institutions that have evolved out of the General Agreement on Tariffs and Trade (GATT). This elaborate organization provides a clear example of the process of institutionalization of dispute settlement and enforcement techniques. The International Labor Organization (ILO) is one of the pioneering creators of an international regime in this functional area (see Chapter 7). The enormous proliferation of intergovernmental environmental organizations is now being linked through coordinating agencies and provides another example of a highly developed international regime (see Chapter 8).

The international human rights regime is becoming more coordinated through the creation of the new High Commissioner for Human Rights at the United Nations. However, this regime is a vast network of many private organizations, regional institutions, and global international efforts to bring more effective compliance procedures to bear on the enormous task of implementing human rights standards (see Chapter 4).

The international law of the sea regime represents enormous potential for the more effective development of compliance measures regarding the use of the international commons—the vast resources of the two-thirds of this planet covered by the world's oceans. Again, a very highly developed system of institutions has emerged, including the new Law of the Sea Tribunal and the Deep Seabed Authority. Integrating environmental regulations through the cooperation among the law of the sea regimes is a major new development (see Chapter 7).

The International Atomic Energy Agency (IAEA) provides an organizational core for the emerging international atomic energy regime that is developing. The Nuclear Non-Proliferation Treaty and regional treaties providing for nuclear-free zones in Latin America and the Pacific are part of the network that includes the European Atomic Energy Community (EURATOM) and other international disarmament agencies. These networks of scientific specialists are also cooperating across regimes with environmental groups and economic development groups (see Chapter 8).

Comprehensive regional organizations such as the Organization of American States (OAS), European Union (EU), and the Organization of African Unity (OAU) are also regimes of varied maturity and development. The EU is the most developed of these regional organizations with an intricate and successful program of economic integration, which is moving into an advanced stage of political integration. Here, and in the broader European community of the European Rights Convention, these regimes are clearly institutions with direct legal implementation machinery that acts through the national courts of member States. The

EU, as such, has recently ratified the 1982 International Law of the Sea Treaty, indicating the extent of the development of its international personality and acceptance of rights and duties under international law.

The OAS is a far less developed and integrated international regime that was initially organized with an emphasis on goals of peaceful settlement of disputes rather than on economic integration. However, elements of this regime are developing more effective institutions of human rights enforcement (see Chapter 4). The Andean Pact and the North American Free Trade Agreement (NAFTA) are more important examples of regimes of economic integration in the Western Hemisphere.

Regional Peacekeeping Actions

Regional international organizations are often evaluated on how effective they have been in taking military actions to enforce international law within their regional sphere of influence. This is probably an unfair criterion of evaluation, because they have no international legal authority to decide to use military force without the approval of the U.N. Security Council. Nonetheless, they have a responsibility to report to the Security Council any self-defense actions that have been taken.

In the recent Haitian Crisis, the OAS has taken its strongest countermeasures short of force, without the authority of the Security Council, in the form of what could be classified as a pacific blockade. This action was followed by U.N. Security Council action under Chapter VII of the U.N. Charter to eventually restore a democratically elected regime to power in Haiti (see Chapter 4).

The weakness of regional organizations as peacekeeping forces was displayed by the EU in the Yugoslav Crisis in which the eco-nomic strategy of this organization neglected important aspects of foreign policy and military integration. These latter areas were deliberately kept out of the process, to neutralize fears of loss of sovereignty and national control of foreign policy. Their inability to coordinate policy in the Bosnian situation resulted in the necessity of the United States to provide leadership through the North Atlantic Treaty Organization (NATO) with U.N. Security Council authority (see Chapter 13).

Nonetheless, individual national contingents of the OAS and Caribbean States have sent civilian observer forces as well as troops to assist in the Dominican Republic (1965), Nicaragua (1990), and Haiti (1993-1995); NATO and the Western European Union have cooperated in imposing a blockade around the former Yugoslavia and, later, in policing the Dayton Peace Accords; the sixteen-member West African Community sent a five-nation peacekeeping force into Liberia during its civil war; the OAU sent an Inter-African Force into Chad (1980-82) and, more recently, into Western Sahara where they are cooperating with the United Nations; the British Commonwealth sent troops into Southern Rhodesia (1979); and the six-nation Inter-Arab Deterrent Force was sent into Lebanon by the Arab league.

These actions were taken either with the approval of the nations where the intervention occurred or by approval of the U.N. Security Council. They have not involved integrated units when troops were sent in but, rather, individual State contingents. Regional organizations can only recommend actions, not mandate them. Some of these developments may be dangerous for the State having problems. In Lebanon, it took some eight years to get Syria to leave. States, even those organized into intergovernmental organizations, have been reluctant to allow their troops to be commanded by other States or even the United Nations. Military intervention is therefore not one of the strongest functional potentials for these organizations. They have been more successful in economic, social, and cultural integration and in the area of human rights.

However, they *have* provided alternative routes for **conflict management.** One recent example is that the Association of Southeast Asian Nations (ASEAN) has developed successful approaches in dealing with Vietnam and Cambodia.

> **Conflict management:** *Using the constraints of intergovernmental organizations to negotiate settlement of disputes.*

Here, the practice of bureaucratic and ministerial consultation for policy coordination on security issues has had some success. The OAU has been somewhat successful in resolving low-level disputes among African leaders. The OAS and EU have highly institutionalized mechanisms for dealing with such problems among their members.

Ernst B. Haas (1983) has attempted to quantify this dispute resolution function in a study of 282 disputes catalogued between 1945 and 1981. Of these, 44% were referred to the United Nations, 10% to the OAS, 9% to the OAU, 8% to the Arab League, and 2% to the Council of Europe.

Haas also assigned numerical values to the various categories of success, with a potential score of 100 if the organization made a major contribution on all applicable dimensions during the period. The OAS received the highest score of 34; the United Nations a score of 23; the OAU, 20; the Council of Europe, 18; and the Arab League, 15. Aggregating different levels of conflict management, the United Nations was neither the most successful nor the least successful IGO. He found that for virtually all organizations, there was a marked decline of success after 1970 in dealing with threats to the peace (Haas, 1983, p. 203).

This evaluation needs to be updated and could yield important new findings for the post-Cold War era.

Major Changes in the Political Climate

As a result of decolonization and the emergence of new States that have nearly quadrupled the number of independent nations, the agendas of international organizations have become much more heavily tilted toward issues of economic development and relations between developed countries of the industrial North and the less developed countries of the South. The coalition of developing countries (the so-called Group of 77, which is much larger now and consists of some 120 countries) commands a majority of votes in many NGOs where these countries have shown high cohesion across a broad range of issues (see Karns & Mingst, 1991, p. 276).

The North-South conflict dimension, proliferation of security issues, and declining U.S. dominance of IGOs are general features of the post-Cold War era. Separatist conflicts, nuclear proliferation, the issues of the international commons, and terrorism head a long list of important issues facing the world community.

The weakness of multilateral organizations that have become stalemated in various conflict situations has led to what Karns and Mingst (1991) have termed **ad hoc multilateral diplomacy,** which refers to efforts such as the Contadora Group's filling a vacuum created by Nicaragua's fear of U.S. influence in the

> **Ad hoc multilateral diplomacy:** *Use of smaller groups of nations to mediate and break impasses that deadlock official intergovernmental organizations.*

OAS and by U.S. concern about Nicaragua's popularity in the U.N. General Assembly.

The *contact group*, composed of the United States, the United Kingdom, Canada, the Federal Republic of Germany, and France, was eventually able to negotiate an agreement for Namibian independence, which materialized through the implementation of Security Council Resolution 435 (1978) in April of 1989. A similar contact group involving the United States, Russia, the United Kingdom, France, and Germany was ultimately successful in negotiating an interim settlement to the Bosnian crisis in the form of the Dayton Peace Accords (see Chapter 13).

The Role and Function of the U.N. Political Organs

The major political organs of the United Nations get the toughest, most difficult issues of international conflict; they are the real crème de la crème ("cream of the crop") of international disputes. Most of these disputes are irreconcilable. They are issues in which existing national institutions, diplomacy, countermeasures, organizational dispute settlement devices, and international tribunals have failed to produce a settlement. The U.N. Security Council has primary responsibility for maintenance of international peace and security in these disputes; however, the General Assembly maintains a secondary responsibility through the Uniting for Peace Resolution of the 1950s (see Chapter 2).

The difficulty of resolving these disputes is illustrated by the Arab-Israeli controversy, which has continued as a significant problem before the major political institutions of the United Nations since its establishment. The first session of the United Nations in 1947 resulted in a vote of thirty-three to thirteen to partition Palestine into Jewish and Arab States, with Jerusalem as an inter-

national zone under U.N. jurisdiction; the Jewish and Arab States would be joined in an economic union. Israel proclaimed itself a State after this partition vote in the General Assembly in 1948. Immediately, the Arab States of Jordan, Syria, Lebanon, and Iraq joined Palestinian and other Arab guerrillas in the first Arab-Israeli War.

The resulting Arab-Israeli conflict has produced a protracted situation that has gone on for fifty years with major military clashes in the second Arab-Israeli War of 1956, the Six-Day War of 1967, and the Yom Kippur War of 1973. Numerous peacekeeping efforts and resolutions of the U.N. Security Council have not solved the problem, which requires a comprehensive peace treaty among the warring parties.

Security Council Resolutions 242 (1967) and 338 (1973) set forth the principles for a comprehensive, just, and lasting peace and remain the basis for an overall settlement. Some of the Arab States are beginning to recognize the existence of Israel as a State, and Israel must recognize the existence of a Palestinian State, which is essential for the implementation of these plans. Above all, secure borders between Israel and its neighbors must be negotiated. But the violations of international law on both sides in this conflict account for many of the issues faced by the political organs of the United Nations since it began.

Two issues of similar intensity and protracted nature have been the issues related to a divided Korea and the remaining issues of the Taiwan-China conflict that were never resolved after the Chinese civil war. They will continue to occupy the agendas of the major political organs for some time to come. Attempting to resolve these issues by U.N.-backed military force would not maintain international peace and security but is likely to have the opposite effect.

Peacekeeping Missions

The U.N. Charter ensured that no collective security measures could be used against the permanent members of the Security Council. The debate at San Francisco seemed to indicate that if one of the permanent members was the direct party to a dispute, it would not be able to vote in the Security Council on that issue. The customary practice, however, has regarded the major-power veto as absolute. It must be exercised, however, to have this effect. The Uniting for Peace Resolution in 1950 has provided a backup responsibility of the General Assembly to exercise secondary responsibility when there is a stalemate in the Security Council (see Chapter 3).

The Security Council has primary responsibility for maintenance of international peace and security and is given the specific authority to determine when there has been a threat to the peace, act of aggression, or breach of the peace. When it can muster nine of fifteen votes and not be blocked by a permanent member's veto, it can mandate enforcement actions through sanctions that range from embargoes to direct military force. The ultimate use of all-out military force has been reserved as a last resort, not merely because of the veto provision but because the purpose of the Security Council is to preserve the peace. The veto power has been used by all the permanent members of the Security Council, including the United States, and it is now clear that it serves a useful purpose.

Nonetheless, the U.N. political organs have found ways to promote peace through actions by both the General Assembly and the Security Council. The Uniting for Peace Resolution, involving recommendations rather than mandates, has been used on four important occasions: (a) to continue the U.N. Security Council-authorized use of force in Korea in the 1950s, (b) to deal with the crises in Suez and Hungary in 1956, (c) to resolve the Middle East crisis of 1958, and (d) to deal with the situation in the Congo in 1960.

In all, nine emergency special sessions of the General Assembly have dealt with threats to international peace when the Security Council was deadlocked. Those in the Middle East and the Congo initiated the innovative procedure, never mentioned in the U.N. Charter, that has become known as U.N. peacekeeping. Peacekeeping has been defined as

> the prevention, containment, moderation, and termination of hostilities between or within states, through the medium of a peaceful third party intervention, organized and directed internationally, using multinational forces of soldiers, police, and civilians to restore and maintain peace. (Rikhye, Harbottle, & Egge 1974, quoted in Karns & Mingst, 1991, p. 270)

Since these initial actions, the Security Council has also authorized many peacekeeping missions. The advantages of the **peacekeeping** approach over **collective security** as envisioned in the U.N. Charter are numerous. Because peacekeeping requires the approval of the parties involved, there is at least a nominal commitment to cooperate with the mandate of the forces. Troops are volunteered by member countries, so the commitment by many members is relatively small. No aggressor need be identified, so no one

Peacekeeping: Involves actions to prevent, contain, moderate, or terminate hostilities with the approval of the parties involved.

Collective security: Involves actions to enforce compliance through the authority of the Security Council or recommendations of the General Assembly. These actions are often referred to as peace enforcement.

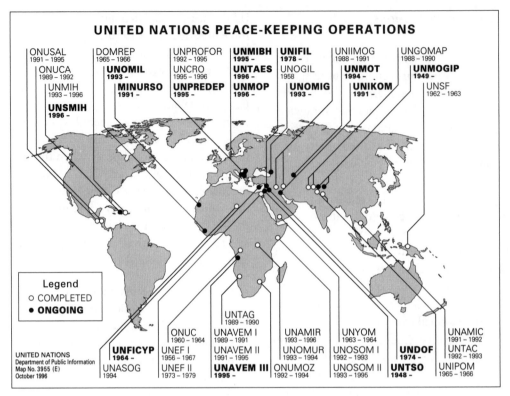

Figure 14.1. United Nations Peacekeeping Operations. Used with permission.

party to the conflict is singled out for blame.

These troops have been placed along cease-fire lines to monitor the cessation of hostilities and withdrawal of foreign troops and to facilitate negotiated settlement once tensions subside. They can contribute to nation building, as in Namibia, where U.N. peacekeepers organized elections, or as in Cambodia, where proposals call for the peacekeepers to provide a temporary administrative authority.

The demand for U.N. peacekeeping missions has increased dramatically since the end of the Cold War, with twenty-one new operations in the period from 1988 to 1994, compared with thirteen over the previous 40 years. In early 1995, about 69,000 U.N. troops, military observers, and civilian police, provided by seventy-seven countries,

were deployed in various areas of the world. More than 720,000 military personnel have served with the U.N. forces since 1948, and more than 1,100 peacekeepers have lost their lives in these efforts to maintain the peace (see Figure 14.1).

Evaluating the relative success of these peacekeeping operations is not an easy task. Each mission is unique in terms of what it can expect to accomplish and must be evaluated on the criteria of the mission. There have been many successful missions, and others that have failed. In the most protracted conflicts, several subsequent missions with redefined goals and objectives have been instituted.

If the criteria of success is the peaceful settlement of the conflict, then only a few missions have been successful. The U.N. Emergency Force (UNEF) II, which ended with the Camp David Accords between Egypt and Israel, and the U.N. Transition Assistance Group (UNTAG), which assisted Namibia to independence, would be two of these few. However, if success is defined in terms of ending armed hostilities and preventing their renewal, at least for a period of time, then all the operations except the U.N. Interim Force in Lebanon (UNIFIL) have been successful. UNIFIL attempted to maintain peace in the chaos in Lebanon after the Israeli invasion of that country. Ultimate success, measured in terms of stable peace, depends on the parties involved in the dispute as much as on the peacekeeping mission.

Peacekeeping is increasingly attractive because of its peace-building possibilities. That can include establishing an interim administrative authority (Cambodia), holding free elections (Nicaragua, Namibia, Cambodia), organizing humanitarian and reconstruction programs (Central America, Afghanistan, Cambodia), or preserving a country's independence and neutral status (Afghanistan, Cambodia) (see Karns & Mingst, 1991, p. 273).

Collective Security and Peacemaking Actions

The major change in international law instituted in the twentieth century is codified in the U.N. Charter and epitomized by Article 2(4), which defines a prohibition against transborder use of military force for purposes of territorial aggrandizement. By this definition, there have been only a few such flagrant violations since World War II. The North Korean invasion of South Korea in 1950, the India-Pakistan conflict over Kashmir, the Iran-Iraq War in the 1980s, and the Iraqi invasion of Kuwait in 1990 are the clearest of these violations. In none of these developments has the aggressor been allowed to keep the fruits of conquest. This

marks a significant change in the effective enforcement of international law.

Peace, in the form of absence of war and human suffering, has not resulted from these developments, but a new set of institutions and refined legal instruments are now available to assist in the process of building and maintaining peaceful relations. Justice and rule of law have been progressively developed through the efforts of the world community, and humanitarian interventions have assisted in reducing human suffering.

Most of the conflict situations that now proliferate and appear to overwhelm the resources of the international community are civil war situations, which threaten international peace and security because of the potential for foreign intervention and the escalation into broader conflicts. Isolating the violence to localized areas is one of the first objectives of the world community in these situations.

Particularly since the end of the Cold War, the U.N. Security Council has used its authority to authorize or impose sanctions on aggressor nations, as in the extensive number of sanctions imposed against Iraq after its invasion of Kuwait. These sanctions include the entire range of escalating methods outlined in the U.N. Charter and many innovative variations that are being used to ensure compliance. Chapter VII sanctions were used only fourteen times in the first forty-five years of the U.N.'s existence. However, in the last five years, such sanctions have become common occurrences with as many as twenty-five such actions a year.

The question of how just and effective these sanctions are is subject to a wide variation of praise and criticism. The important point is that actions are being taken in an attempt to pursue the worthy goals of the community of nations to preserve international peace and security with justice and respect for sovereign equality. These institutions need to be reconsidered in light of the fifty years of experience; this, too, is an ongoing process that is being given much attention at the present time. In the concluding chapter, this subject will be briefly explored.

■   ■   ■

Chapter Summary

1. Traditional international law makes a distinction between the law of peace and the law of war. Once war was declared, the laws of peace ceased to apply, except for those few rules that regulated the conduct of armed conflicts. War was accepted as a method of self-help in the absence of competent international governmental authority.

2. This text has emphasized the significant changes of the twentieth century that have been attempts to alter the traditional concepts of just and unjust wars and trial by combat that characterized traditional international law. The League of Nations Covenant, the Kellogg-Briand Pact, and the U.N. Charter were significant steps in this process, reflecting the practical effects of two world wars.

3. The most fundamental purpose of the United Nations Organization is to maintain international peace and security and to that end to create institutions for the effective prevention and removal of threats to the peace, acts of aggression, and breaches of the peace.

4. The U.N. Charter (Article 2[4]) prohibits "the threat or use of force against the territorial integrity or political independence of any State, or in any other manner inconsistent with the Purposes of the United Nations." And it declares that the organization shall ensure that States that are not members of the United Nations act in accordance with these principles.

5. The Security Council is given primary responsibility for determining threats to the peace, acts of aggression, or breaches of the peace, and the U.N. Charter gives it authority to take whatever actions are required to maintain the peace. Except for these enforcement measures, nothing in the Charter shall authorize the United Nations to intervene in matters that are essentially within the domestic jurisdiction of any State.

6. The U.N. Charter preserves the inherent right of individual or collective self-defense, if an armed attack occurs, until the Security Council has taken measures necessary to maintain international peace and security. Such actions must be reported to the Security Council as soon as possible.

7. All law is enforced by imposing deprivations of entitlements against those who violate the duties and responsibilities required by law. Individual States still retain some forms of self-help under the U.N. Charter, enabling them unilaterally to enforce the law. These legal forms of self-help include countermeasures and self-defense.

8. Countermeasures include actions short of use of force, such as diplomatic protests, breaking of diplomatic relations, deportation of nationals of the offending State, economic sanctions, and seizure of property belonging to the offending State. They

may also include the suspension of the benefits of any treaty provisions between the two States when there has been a material breach of the treaty obligations. But these actions must not involve military force or violations of international law, and they must be proportional to the offenses involved.

9. The doctrine of self-defense does not permit excessive response to even an armed attack. It must be necessary and proportional to the magnitude of the attack.

10. The Cuban Missile Crisis demonstrates an innovative form of self-help involving a quarantine on the high seas. It represents a controversial action in that its legality is uncertain. However, its use in this instance was supported by the international community, and the Security Council refused to condemn or condone this action.

11. Unilateral humanitarian intervention has been severely restricted by twentieth-century changes in customary international law. It may permit hostage rescue missions when they are limited by extreme necessity to save lives and take all reasonable precautions to keep the action proportional to these humanitarian interests.

12. Preemptive strikes and other forms of "anticipatory" self-defense are illegal forms of self-help under modern international law. However, when a nation's very existence is at stake and the situation is of such urgency that it "leaves no moment for deliberation," such action may be seen as politically necessary. This does not absolve that nation of liability for its action.

13. Reprisals involve the unilateral use of force in response to alleged violations of international law. This form of self-help is prohibited under modern international law.

14. The *Nicaragua* case illustrates the legal limits to the concept of individual and collective self-defense under modern customary international law. It allows self-defense only in response to an armed attack; a third State may assist a State in its self-defense when requested by that State, but the attack must be reported to the Security Council. Actions in self-defense must be necessary and proportional to the offense.

15. IGOs have produced legal regimes whose procedures constrain member States by setting national agendas, providing information for monitoring and surveillance, and providing decision-making and implementation procedures creating rules of behavior that must be followed to enjoy the benefits of reciprocity.

16. Economic, environmental, and human rights regimes with extensively developed systems of compliance include the WTO, ILO, the network of human rights and environmental regimes, the law of the sea regimes, the IAEA, the OAS, EU, OAU, and the U.N. special agencies, along with many others.

17. Regional institutions are not given mandatory peace enforcement authority under the U.N. Charter but may act in collective self-defense. They have contributed to U.N. peacekeeping and peacemaking decisions; however, they have acted not as collective units but as national contingents with the support of these organizations.

18. Regional organizations function as alternative systems of conflict management through their own dispute settlement devices. Studies of this function indicate that the United Nations gets the largest number of these disputes, but many are handled by regional organizations. The OAS appears to be especially active in conflict management.

19. Most of these regional regimes are more specialized in management of economic, environmental, and humanitarian disputes than in handling political disputes involving use of force.

20. Ad hoc multilateral diplomacy has contributed to the solution to problems that have deadlocked larger formal organizations in recent conflicts. These efforts are illustrated by the Contadora proposals and the contact groups formed in the Namibian situation and the Bosnian conflict.

21. The political organs of the United Nations get the toughest issues that have not been solved at lower levels. The primary responsibility for international peace and security is given to the Security Council, but when the veto blocks effective action, the General Assembly can assume responsibility through the Uniting for Peace Resolution. However, the General Assembly may only recommend actions to maintain international peace and security.

22. Peacekeeping actions involve the approval of the parties to an armed conflict or dispute to allow neutral U.N. organized forces to police the cease-fire agreements, oversee elections, administer necessary services, monitor actions such as withdrawal of troops, and facilitate negotiated settlement once tensions have subsided.

23. The number of peacekeeping missions has dramatically increased since 1988. Twenty-one new operations have been launched since the end of the Cold War compared with only thirteen over the previous forty years. Many have been successful in obtaining positive outcomes to their objectives, but others have failed.

24. Peace enforcement actions involve the use of the compulsory authority of the Security Council in the form of direct orders and use of military force. The objective of this political body is to maintain the peace and to stop transborder aggression. There have been few of these direct acts of territorial aggression since World War II; however, in none of them has the aggressor been allowed to keep possession of outright territorial conquests.

25. Most conflict situations since World War II have been civil war situations that threaten international peace and security because of the potential for foreign intervention and escalation into broader conflicts. The United Nations has been successful in isolating these conflicts and has dramatically increased its use of mandatory sanctions, ranging from cease and desist orders to organized military force to repel the invaders in cases of territorial aggression.

Key Terms

diplomatic protests
countermeasures
self-defense
pacific blockade
humanitarian
    intervention

preemptive strike
reprisals
international
    regimes
conflict
    management

ad hoc multilateral
    diplomacy
peacekeeping
collective security

Discussion Questions

1. How has the traditional international law of war been altered by twentieth-century legal developments?

2. Are there inherent aspects of wartime situations that make legal rules irrelevant? Discuss.

3. Has the United Nations fulfilled its obligations to the extent that self-help in the form of unilateral use of force is no longer necessary?

4. What forms of self-help are legally justified under modern international law?

5. Can "anticipatory" self-defense ever be justified under modern international law?

6. Under what conditions can unilateral humanitarian intervention be justified?

7. What are the dangers of allowing an exception to the self-defense doctrine for preemptive strikes?

8. How does the *Nicaragua* case illustrate the limits of the legal use of force in individual and collective self-defense?

9. What roles and functions do international regimes have in inducing compliance measures under international law?

10. What roles and functions do the U.N. political organs have in enforcing international law?

Suggested Readings

Council on Foreign Relations. (1991). *Right v. might: International law and the use of force* (2nd ed.). New York: Council on Foreign Relations Press. (Excellent discussion of the issues of use of force in the transition to a more effective collective security system; articles by Henkin, Hoffman, Kirkpatrick and Gerson, Rogers, and Scheffer.)

Damrosch, L. F. (Ed.). (1993). *Enforcing restraint: Collective intervention in internal conflicts*. New York: Council on Foreign Relations Press. (Excellent articles on Yugoslavia, Iraq, Haiti, Liberia, Somalia, Cambodia, and civilian impact on economic sanctions.)

Karns, M. P., & Mingst, K. A. (Eds.). (1990). *The United States and multilateral institutions: Patterns of changing instrumentality and influence*. Boston: Unwin Hyman.

Klare, M. T., & Thomas, D. C. (1991). *World security: Trends and challenges at century's end*. New York: St. Martin's Press. (Excellent articles on a wide range of security issues including theory, use of force issues, nuclear proliferation, arms trade, terrorism, international regimes, human rights, global debt, world hunger, and environmental issues.)

Wilson, H. A. (1988). *International law and the use of force by national liberation movements*. New York: Oxford University Press.

Internet Sources

Browse: Use U.N. Home Page (http://www.un.org/) to search for related material, including Security Council votes and General Assembly actions as well as peacekeeping operations. The map of peacekeeping operations is located within the Secretariat and will provide access to each mission (current and discontinued), giving access to historical and current developments.

15 *Toward the Future*

This introduction to international law and organization has attempted to provide readers with a broad understanding of the historical development of the concept of international law. That concept has been variously defined by emperors, kings, academic scholars, judges, practicing lawyers, political scientists, and binding legal documents. As noted in the beginning of this text, international law is not *world law*. It initially began to be conceptualized as *jus gentium*, or the law of tribes; and then in the era of the rise of the nation-state system, as the *law of nations;* toward the end of that era, it became known as *international law*, with a particularly restrictive definition that seemed to exclude the individual from its scope.

The modern era of international law is returning to the broader scope of international law expressed in Chapter 3 by Blackstone (1769/1969) and Jessup (1956) that encompasses "all law which regulates actions or events that transcend national frontiers," regulating the actions of both "independent states, and the individuals belonging

to each." This broader definition includes the individual, who has become increasingly involved in world affairs in a more highly interdependent world community of nations. Individuals are affected by international law; they can influence their government's actions in modern society, and today, they are increasingly entitled to certain rights and duties under modern international law. Although individuals have not seen themselves as actors in the process of international law development, citizens must come to view the community of nations as their community and not the responsibility of governments only.

For this reason, the framers of the U.N. Charter began the Preamble of that document with these words: "WE THE PEOPLES OF THE UNITED NATIONS." The assertion that it was the people who created the institutions of a world body dedicated to the preservation of peace and cooperation among nations is presumptuous indeed. However, it was also presumptuous of the framers of our own Constitution to proclaim the Constitution in the name of

"WE THE PEOPLE" in 1789. That document also created new relationships between the independent nation-states who called themselves the United States of America, and the states themselves had to ratify that document for it to become a reality.

The instruments of international law cannot change the Constitution of the United States without going through the amendment process described in Article Five of the U.S. Constitution, which requires ratification by three-fourths of the states of the union. However, the development of international law and the strength of the institutions that have been created by it depend on the support of the people organized into the nations that occupy this planet. For they, too, are the beneficiaries of the fruits of peace and prosperity.

The development of law is essential to any system of ordered liberty. The right of a people to exercise sovereignty over a particular territory is conditioned by the responsibility to exercise that sovereignty so as not to restrict the equally sovereign rights of other nations. This is the essential premise of international law. In modern times, this law has placed greater emphasis on human rights and the duty of States to protect the most fundamental rights of the individual.

The new humanitarian rights of evolving international law is a modern development that began with attempts to abolish piracy and slavery but in the twentieth century has expanded to include abolishment of war crimes, torture, and genocide. This expansion of international law is intended to protect the most basic rights of individuals. Its implementation still leaves much to be desired. This is a very different objective than merely promoting the concept of sovereign equality of nations. Traditional international law was expressed in nationalistic terms that seemed to care less what happened to the people within the individual nation-state. Any redress for personal grievances had to be exercised only through the executive authority of the nationality of the person who had been harmed. Modern international law is beginning to fashion areas of direct legal action that may be instituted by private parties to remedy wrongs that have been committed against them by their own governments and even by foreign governments.

Private international law is still severely restricted by the act of State doctrine; however, there has been considerable liberalization of the concept of sovereign immunity in domestic courts in areas of commercial activity in which governments act as private parties. This expanding access to national courts provides the individual with a greater stake in the system. However, the legal rights of the individual in international law are severely limited, not only by the act of State doctrine but also by the political question doctrine and the varied doctrines of standing requiring that treaties must be self-executing—that is, intended to confer such rights on individuals.

International law, nonetheless, differs considerably, and perhaps fundamentally, from domestic law in that it is a decentralized system of rights and duties of States rather than of individuals. States have accepted responsibilities to individuals under modern international law. However, the international legal system operates primarily on the international plane where disputes develop among nations and are regulated by the law of nations.

Although there is an increasingly significant development of overlapping jurisdiction in the area of criminal law, the basic character of international law is more analogous to private and administrative legal remedies than it is to criminal punishment. Criminal law is still most exclusively municipal in character, and sovereign States are most reluctant to surrender this area of law to regulation by the international community. They have not done so, but recent developments indicate that they are at least more willing to share this jurisdiction with international tribunals in cases involving universal crimes.

International law also differs from municipal law in that it has not developed clearly defined institutions of lawmaking, law interpretation, and law enforcement. Institutional specialization on the international plane is nonetheless beginning to be defined. States may create international law by engaging in practices that become recognized as legally binding. This customary development of law by the practice of States is the most fundamental method of law development. Modern international law is built on this concept.

However, the modern method of codification and alteration of law through lawmaking treaties has produced a progressive means of law development. Customary law development has proceeded not through majority rule but by consensus. The development of international law must take place by consensus (near unanimity) or by expressed consent in the form of treaty obligations that each individual State agrees to regard as legally binding. This method of law creation and alteration is slow and cumbersome, but unlike domestic law, it reflects a process of law development that is formed by consent and not imposed by any central authority.

The fundamental nature of international law has been the key to its generally successful implementation. It is observed by "almost all nations almost all the time" because it is so fundamental and its rules are so few. Since its rules have been derived by consent, to violate international law is self-contradictory. Those nations, today, that violate in-

ternational law do so surreptitiously, conducting their actions in a secret and clandestine manner. For example, no nation claims a right to torture its people. A State that asserts the legally binding obligation of other States must reciprocally accept that responsibility in its own behavior.

However, modern rules of international law may be sacrificing some of their inherent self-implementing character by attempting too much. International law is weak in its ability to promote moral values and desired behavior. Justice has not been the primary character of international law; peace has taken the priority role in this area of law development. The idea that some law is better than no law at all has been viewed as paramount. Peace with justice is still primarily viewed in terms of equality of States before the law rather than equality of individuals before the law.

Law interpretation on the international plane is also weak, in comparison with municipal law, in that there are relatively few international tribunals with compulsory jurisdiction to handle disputes that arise between nations. Most international tribunals have very limited jurisdiction that depends on prior consent by the parties to agree to adjudicate their disputes. Those that do have compulsory jurisdiction involve smaller groups of States or narrowly limited types of issues that have been given compulsory jurisdiction. Nonetheless, the international community is developing a body of international jurisprudence in these limited areas in which States have consented to settle their disputes through adjudication.

The World Court has significantly enhanced and clarified the principles of international law through the many decisions it has made in both its contentious and advisory jurisdictions. Greater knowledge and clarity of how the law will be applied in such tribunals builds trust and confidence in the

Court, if these decisions are considered fair and just. However, the Court is generally confined to accept only legal issues as the basis for dispute settlement. Political issues involve demands for a change in the law and assertions that the existing law is unfair or unjust.

The political institutions that have developed in the global international community also lack a clearly defined executive or administrative function. There are many such agencies, all with limited authority to administer the law. These agencies include individual States as well as intergovernmental organizations (IGOs). The United Nations is only one of these intergovernmental agencies, but its wide membership, including 185 States, makes it the most important global set of institutions. Even within the U.N. system, there is considerable confusion about who has authority to do what and whether or not States are willing to give these administrative agencies the authority needed to carry out the goals and objectives of the United Nations Organization.

The United Nations Organization has been considered the best hope for fulfilling the aspirations of the world community of nations, by strengthening international law and acting against threats to the peace, acts of aggression, and breaches of the peace. These objectives have not been fully met in the fifty years of its existence. The Security Council has only recently begun to function as it was intended, and even now, there is much criticism about the actions it has taken.

There is a general tendency even among the new nations that in large part owe their existence to the United Nations that the United Nations does not belong to them. This sense of ownership by the peoples of the United Nations, which the U.N. Charter proclaims to be the source of its authority,

has not really taken hold of the community in the sense that average citizens see it as "us" instead of "them." Most individuals, even in advanced societies, view the United Nations as essentially belonging to governments, and many see it as dominated by the most powerful governments. Governments themselves have viewed it only slightly differently. For many, if not most, governments, the United Nations is there to be used and, not infrequently, abused—to be an instrument of national interest where possible and to be bypassed where it cannot be made to serve their interests.

As was true of the League of Nations, the most important failure of the institutions of the world community can be attributed to the lack of will of the nations that make up the membership of the community. This lack of will and commitment has many explanations in the fears of uncertainty and lack of confidence in the institutions. Many of these fears are realistic and founded in reason and experience. However, the major point is that strengthening these institutions requires a broader willingness on the part of the average citizen, and the governments of nations around world, to regard themselves as belonging to the United Nations. The greatest failures of the United Nations have not been caused by structural problems but by collective failings of the member States. The United Nations is only as powerful as its member States are willing to make it.

Twenty-First Century Issues

The bipolar world of the Cold War era has given way to a much more decentralized world community of nations, each desirous of maintaining its cultural identity and unique values even while acknowledging its interdependence. The proliferation of new nation-states, due to decolonization and disintegration of oppressive imperialistic governments, has become the most significant development in the post Cold War era. This has led to separatist movements in many countries, even those once considered highly stable and nonoppressive. The modern emphasis on human rights has awakened a desire for protection of basic cultural identity among ethnic, racial, religious, and linguistic groups within established nation-states.

These cultural differences may be so great as to warrant development of new national identities; however, protection of these distinctions within the nation-state is being addressed by greater emphasis on national legislation to ensure protection of cultural differences and greater recognition of these rights by the international community. Economic integration of political communities, following the European model, appears to be a reverse tendency. However, the European model has accepted the idea that human rights must be protected by the rule of law. The key role of the protection of human rights against racial, religious, linguistic, national origin, and political discrimination is fundamental to the European model, which attempts to secure the benefits of economic integration while preserving cultural diversity.

The North-South cleavage orienting developed and developing States along economic lines is a division of fundamental interests of great importance to the stability of the international community. The vast differences in standards of living that characterize these two blocs have political ramifications and contribute to animosities. Greater communication and involvement of these vastly different societies working within intergovernmental organizations is producing greater awareness of the problems. However, solutions are difficult to come by. The end of the Cold War has reduced the tendency to view these conflicts in ideological terms, but it has also lessened the urgency and saliency of these issues among the great powers.

The United States no longer dominates the institutions of the international community as it once did during the tensions of the Cold War era. This development could have been predicted by the principles and democratic values of pluralistic decision making it has promoted. With 4.5% of the world's population and 26% of the world's wealth, the United States must accept the idea, as does the rest of the world, that it must cooperate with other nations in pursuing its international interests. This declining influence should not be viewed as failure but, rather, as an indication of success in the building of pluralistic international institutions.

The United States finds itself in a position of relative decline in economic and political resources and has become increasingly defensive. Its control over IGO agendas has slipped; its ability to mobilize votes has eroded; and, more frequently, it has found need to cast its veto in the Security Council and threaten the withholding of funds to influence IGO outcomes. These are defensive tactics, but they are now viewed as part of the politics of the post-Cold War era.

Nuclear nonproliferation has also assumed a leading place on the issue agenda of the post-Cold War era. The threat of nuclear weapons is now seen less as a threat of nuclear war and mutual assured destruction strategy than as the potential for nuclear terrorism and blackmail. There is not only a nuclear threat but also a similar threat involving other forms of dangerous weapons of mass destruction, such as those produced by chemical and biological technologies. This has led to a new proliferation of security issues.

Modern technology has contributed to problems not only of mass destruction but also to issues relating to the areas concerning *the global commons*—the air and water environment, Antarctica, the seas and sea-bed resources, and outer space. The problems of international criminal conspiracies related to corruption, illegal drug traffic, terrorism, and illegal immigration are also items high on the agenda of the world community in the twenty-first century.

We live in a highly interdependent world that has seen astounding changes in the ease of travel, communication, industrialization, and population density. These changes also create challenges that can be perceived as new problems or as opportunities for solving problems. Environmental pollution is a by-product of this development that threatens, in perhaps an even more sinister way, the preservation of life on the planet. These problems require a reassessment of the adequacy of the institutions that have been developed by the international community.

A Current Assessment of U.N. Structural Problems

U.N. agencies have been given bigger problems to solve than they have resources to devote to solving these problems. The proliferation of peacekeeping missions and the magnitude of the other problems that we expect the United Nations to deal with are such that failure is almost inevitable. Politics and government are all about the art of the possible, and when an agency is given an impossible mission, it is easy to predict failure.

The lack of coordination of the astounding number of intergovernmental organizations, both within the U.N. system and outside it, is one of the most important problems. U.N. agencies are notoriously un-coordinated and unable to adequately focus their efforts. This is due in part to the well-founded fear that abuses will result from the concentration of power and that there will be no way to retrieve this power once it is given up. Thus, nations have refused to provide the United Nations with an independent financing power or an independent military potential.

The financial crisis faced by the United Nations is now critical. The funding formula, which determines the assessment for each national member, is adopted by the General Assembly. The resulting national assessments are based on the proportion of the world's population, and ability to pay, derived from aggregate figures of gross national product. The assessment for the United States is some $315 million a year (or 25% of the regular budget expenses including funds for the international tribunals). Many in the U.S. Congress consider the annual U.N. budget assessment unfair; however, it may be the best buy in government services, costing the taxpayers only about $1.24 per U.S. citizen, or about $6 for every family of four in the United States annually. That is about as much as U.S. families spend for a subscription to *TV Guide* for a year.

Peacekeeping operations are funded separately because of their fluctuation from year to year and the special responsibility of the permanent members of the Security Council for peacekeeping actions. The U.S. Congress unilaterally decided to reduce the country's share of peacekeeping expenses to 25% when it had been assessed 31% of the yearly total, or about $1 billion a year.

Since the beginning of FY1996 (October 1, 1995), U.S. payment of its U.N. dues has been sporadic. A series of continuing appropriations has enabled the United States to pay only $140 million of the $315 million assessed for 1995 U.N. regular budget expenses and only $205 million of the nearly $1 billion for peacekeeping.

The specialized agencies' budgets are also separately assessed, since they have varying membership. The United States has paid only about $113 million of the $363 million in assessments for eleven organizations to which it belongs. The total operation expenses for the entire U.N. system—including the World Bank, the International Monetary Fund (IMF), and all the U.N. funds, programs, and specialized agencies—come to $18.2 billion a year.

As of March 1996, the United States owes $1.6 billion in unpaid assessments, which is more delinquent debt than that of any other member State of the United Nations. The use of withholding funds as a reform effort is now being questioned by many U.N. member States, including many European allies. But they have supported U.S.-led reforms that have been instituted since the mid-1980s.

These reforms include the adoption of consensus-based budgeting, the creation of a U.S.-style inspector general, and the 1995 approval of a biennial budget in which inflation and exchange rate fluctuations must be absorbed within existing resources. Under the supervision of Under-Secretary-General for Administration and Management Joseph E. Connor, a U.S. citizen, the U.N. Secretariat operates on a zero-growth basis. The $2.6 billion budget for the next two years ($1.3 billion a year) represents $250 million in savings, which Mr. Connor said will be achieved through efficiency gains and a new 10% staff cut in the U.N. Secretariat.

Article 17 of the U.N. Charter and a 1962 decision of the International Court of Justice (ICJ) interpreting the Charter on this point require members to pay the organization's expenses as a matter of law. The penalty is suspension from voting privileges as pro-

vided for in Article 19: "If the amount of its arrears equals or exceeds the amount of the contributions due from it for the preceding two full years," a member nation "shall have no vote in the General Assembly."

This crisis is undoubtedly one of the most important immediate problems facing the international community. The increase in peacekeeping operations requires more troops to administer the programs established by the major political organs. These missions have had to depend on voluntary commitments of individual nations that must be assembled on an ad hoc basis each time a mission is organized. This contributes to delay and failure of missions that depend on immediacy for their success. The failure of the permanent members of the Security Council to put into effect the provisions of Article 47, calling for a coordinated military command structure, is perhaps the most significant structural failure of the system envisioned by the drafters at San Francisco.

These ad hoc peacekeeping and peace enforcement missions are increasingly more dangerous for the U.N. personnel who undertake them. The rising costs in terms of lives lost by these peacekeepers is of major concern to the international community. Ways must be found to improve the security of the forces that are sent in harm's way to preserve peace or reverse aggression.

The composition of the U.N. Security Council is no longer a realistic reflection of the relative power positions of major nations in a world in which Japan and Germany have emerged as world economic powers with the commitment and will to assume a larger role in the functioning of that institution. The initial criticism of the Security Council's provision for the veto power of its permanent members, in contradiction of the fundamental concept of State equality, is still expressed by most of the new nations that have quadrupled the membership of the United Nations. They argue that the Security Council should be made more representative of the General Assembly. These issues present a major structural problem that is in need of a solution.

There are many other problems, including the thorny issues of how to use sanctions against an entire nation when its leaders refuse to comply with Security Council mandates. The available sanctions seem to punish the population rather than the leaders, creating a fundamental unfairness that is recognized by all concerned. Innovative strategies are being devised, but this set of issues is inherently problematic and difficult to overcome, given the nature of international law (see Damrosch, 1993a, for further discussion of this issue).

An Agenda for Peace

In 1992, the Security Council requested the secretary-general to prepare an "analysis and recommendations on ways of strengthening and making more efficient within the framework and provisions of the Charter the capacity of the United Nations for preventive diplomacy, for peacemaking and for peacekeeping." Secretary-General Boutros Boutros-Ghali responded with an analysis and set of recommendations that called on the world community to focus greater attention on the identification and prevention of conflict situations before they occur rather than waiting to deal with crucial issues after they have erupted into armed conflict. Greater emphasis on fact-finding procedures that improve the availability of timely and accurate information concerning explosive situations and their causes, an early warning system, and preventive deployment of resources were some of the secretary-general's major recommendations.

He recommended that all members accept the compulsory jurisdiction of the ICJ without reservation, greater use of the smaller chambers of the Court, and the establishment of a trust fund to assist nations unable to afford the cost involved in bringing actions before the court.

In regard to peacemaking actions, the secretary-general recommended greater attention to the problems of suffering imposed on the people of nations where extreme economic sanctions are being imposed. In Iraq and Haiti, there is evidence that such sanctions created more problems than they solved. He stressed that it is important that States confronted with such special economic problems "not only have the right to consult the Security Council regarding such problems, as Article 50 provides, but also have a realistic possibility of having their difficulties addressed."

Boutros Boutros-Ghali also recommended the development of a permanent U.N. military force as envisioned in Articles 42 and 43 of the U.N. Charter. Such a force would, in itself, serve as a means of deterring breaches of the peace because a potential aggressor would know in advance that the Security Council had at its disposal a means of response. This reserve force should be seen in the context of Chapter VII sanctions that involve use of military force and not that of planning or conducting peacekeeping operations. Many of these acts of aggression have been attempts to test the will and resolve of the international community.

An Agenda for Peace (Boutros-Ghali, 1992), outlined by the secretary-general, calls for greater cooperation with regional arrangements and organizations to relieve some of the pressure on the United Nations for peacekeeping operations. Greater emphasis on devising methods of employing sanctions and deterrence for the protection of U.N. personnel engaged in peacekeeping operations were also called for in this agenda, along with measures to deal with the financial crisis that threatens the effective functioning of the organization.

This *Agenda for Peace* recommends (a) immediate establishment of a revolving peacekeeping reserve fund of $50 million, (b) that the General Assembly appropriate one-third of the costs of each new peacekeeping operation established by the Security Council, and (c) increased efforts to improve the efficiency of the Secretariat.

Some of these recommendations have produced minor results, but they are not likely to be implemented without great effort, debate, and discussion, resulting in many compromises. The United States openly opposed another term for Boutros Boutros-Ghali in 1996, and exercised its veto in the Security Council to prevent his reelection. A candidate considered by the United States to be more dedicated to administrative reforms and greater efficiency within the United Nations, Kofi Annan, became the new secretary-general January 1, 1997. This dramatic exercise of influence on the part of the Clinton administration may be more calculated to satisfy congressional opponents who support refusal to pay the U.N. assessments than it is personal opposition to Boutros-Ghali or his proposals in *An Agenda for Peace*.

Our Global Neighborhood

A much broader set of recommendations is being considered by task forces, multilateral coalitions, and individual nations concerning U.N. reform to modernize its institutions to meet the challenges of the future. An excellent report by the Commission on Global Governance, titled *Our Global Neighborhood*, was published in 1995. This commission grew out of the efforts of for-

mer German Chancellor Willi Brandt and the 1991 Stockholm Initiative on Global Security and Governance. Some three dozen international public figures met in Stockholm, Sweden, to initiate the commission, whose task was to explore the opportunities created by the end of the Cold War to build a more effective system of world security and governance. The resulting report, produced by independent members from around the world acting without instructions from any government or organization, provides much insight into the problems facing the world community in the twenty-first century and beyond.

It urges measures to stimulate a greater sense of belonging and "ownership" of the United Nations by the people of the world and produces a set of specific recommendations that call for changes in the form of refinements in the institutions that have been described in this text. It does not propose world government but better management of the basic authority included in the U.N. Charter.

These proposals are divided into consideration of the economic issues facing the world community and those concerning international law and its enforcement. The major economic recommendations include the creation of an Economic Security Council within the U.N. system to provide political leadership and promote consensus on international economic issues and balanced sustainable development. Such a new institution should be more representative than the G-7[1] and could help to coordinate activities of the IMF, the World Bank, the World Trade Organization, and the Commission on Sustainable Development.

The commission recommends reform of the decision-making structure of the IMF to make it more democratic and enhance its capacity to provide balance-of-payments support and influence global economic stability. It urges governments to redouble their efforts to meet the target of 0.7% of gross domestic product for official development assistance to developing economies. The World Bank should be strengthened; more countries should adopt the U.N. convention on migrant workers; governments should cooperate in environmental policy adopting strong "polluter pays" legislation and support innovative concepts such as the European Union's proposal for a carbon tax.

The commission strongly encourages the exploration of potential international tax sources, such as an international tax on foreign currency transactions and charges for use of common global resources—for example, flight lanes, sea-lanes for ships, ocean fishing areas, and the electromagnetic spectrum—to provide money for global purposes. These are some of the many new ideas being generated by such progressive international groups in the economic and financial areas.

In the areas of international law and U.N. structural reform, the commission recom-

mends strengthening the World Court by giving it compulsory jurisdiction, enlarging the Security Council to make it more representative of the members of the United Nations, improving the financial soundness and accountability of the agencies of the United Nations, and revitalizing the General Assembly as a universal forum of the world's nations.

This list of reform proposals is not long and does not require revolutionary changes in world governance. Creating a "world government" is not part of these recommendations because this would mean destruction of the nation-state system that has been evolving for more than four hundred years. The growing community of nations is built on the legal principles of sovereign equality of nations. Law development is being built by consensus and institutionalized cooperation rather than by command and control concepts. It increasingly involves people-to-people cooperation and development that promises a deeper commitment than that of governments alone.

Note

1. The G-7, or Group of Seven, refers to the seven most economically powerful nations: the United States, the United Kingdom, France, Canada, Italy, Germany, and Japan. In 1994, the G-7 became the G-8 when Russia was admitted to this select group who hold periodic summit meetings to discuss trade and financial issues.

Appendix A

United Nations Charter

CHARTER OF THE UNITED NATIONS

[The Charter of the United Nations was established as a consequence of the U.N. Conference on International Organization held at San Francisco and was brought into force on October 24, 1945. Membership of the United Nations has reached a total of 185 States. The charter has been the subject of a good deal of interpretation in the half century of its existence. Judicial interpretation of the charter by the International Court of Justice has been illustrated in the *Reparation* case, and the *Namibia* case in this text. Other illustrations of judicial interpretation of the Charter include the *Admission of a State to the United Nations*, I.C.J. Reports, 1947-8, p. 57; *Competence of the General Assembly for the Admission of a State to the United Nations*, ibid., 1950, p. 4; *International Status of South-West Africa*, ibid., p. 128; *Voting Procedure* case, ibid., 1955, p. 67; *Admissibility of Hearing of Petitioners*, ibid., 1956, p. 23; *U.N. Administrative Tribunal* case, ibid., 1954, p. 47, ibid., 1971, p. 16.

Note: The amendments in force are italicized. The amendments were adopted by General Assembly Resol. 1991 (XVII) (1965). In 1971, the membership of the Economic and Social Council was increased from twenty-seven to fifty-four.]

TEXT

WE THE PEOPLES OF THE UNITED NATIONS DETERMINED

to save succeeding generations from the scourge of war, which twice in our lifetime has brought untold sorrow to mankind, and

to reaffirm faith in fundamental human rights, in the dignity and worth of the human person, in the equal rights of men and women and of nations large and small, and

to establish conditions under which justice and respect for the obligations arising from treaties and other sources of international law can be maintained, and

to promote social progress and better standards of life in larger freedom,

AND FOR THESE ENDS

to practice tolerance and live together in peace with one another as good neighbours, and

to unite our strength to maintain international peace and security, and

to ensure, by the acceptance of principles and the institution of methods, that armed forces shall not be used, save in the common interest, and

to employ international machinery for the promotion of the economic and social advancement of all peoples,

HAVE RESOLVED TO COMBINE OUR EFFORTS TO ACCOMPLISH THESE AIMS

Accordingly, our respective Governments, through representatives assembled in the City of San Francisco, who have exhibited their full powers found to be in good and due form, have agreed to the present Charter of the United Nations and do hereby establish an international organization to be known as the United Nations.

CHAPTER I. PURPOSES AND PRINCIPLES

Article 1

The Purposes of the United Nations are:

1. To maintain international peace and security, and to that end: to take effective collective measures for the prevention and removal of threats to the peace, and for the suppression of acts of aggression or other breaches of the peace, and to bring about by peaceful means, and in conformity with the principles of justice and international law, adjustment or settlement of international disputes or situations which might lead to a breach of the peace;

2. To develop friendly relations among nations based on respect for the principle of equal rights and self-determination of peoples, and to take other appropriate measures to strengthen universal peace;

3. To achieve international co-operation in solving international problems of an economic, social, cultural or humanitarian character, and in promoting and encouraging respect for human rights and for fundamental freedoms for all without distinction as to race, sex, language, or religion; and

4. To be a centre for harmonizing the actions of nations in the attainment of these common ends.

Article 2

The Organization and its Members, in pursuit of the Purposes stated in Article 1, shall act in accordance with the following Principles:

1. The Organization is based on the principle of the sovereign equality of all its Members.

2. All Members, in order to ensure to all of them the rights and benefits resulting from membership, shall fulfil in good faith the obligations assumed by them in accordance with the present Charter.

3. All Members shall settle their international disputes by peaceful means in such a manner that international peace and security, and justice, are not endangered.

4. All Members shall refrain in their international relations from the threat or use of force against the territorial integrity or political independence of any State, or in any other manner inconsistent with the Purposes of the United Nations.

5. All Members shall give the United Nations every assistance in any action it takes in accordance with the present Charter, and shall refrain from giving assistance to any State against which the United Nations is taking preventive or enforcement action.

6. The Organization shall ensure that States which are not Members of the United Nations act in accordance with these Principles so far as may be necessary for the maintenance of international peace and security.

7. Nothing contained in the present Charter shall authorize the United Nations to intervene in matters which are essentially within the domestic jurisdiction of any State or shall require the Members to submit such matters to settlement under the present Charter; but this principle shall not prejudice the application of enforcement measures under Chapter VII.

CHAPTER II. MEMBERSHIP

Article 3

The original Members of the United Nations shall be the States which, having participated in the United Nations Conference on International Organization at San Francisco, or having previously signed the Declaration by United Nations of January 1, 1942, sign the present Charter and ratify it in accordance with Article 110.

Article 4

1. Membership in the United Nations is open to all other peace loving States which accept the obligations contained in the present Charter and, in the judgment of the Organization, are able and willing to carry out these obligations.

2. The admission of any such State to membership in the United Nations will be effected by a decision of the General Assembly upon the recommendation of the Security Council.

Article 5

A member of the United Nations against which preventive or enforcement action has been taken by the Security Council may be suspended from the exercise of the rights and privileges of membership by the General Assembly upon the recommendation of the Security Council. The exercise of these rights and privileges may be restored by the Security Council.

Article 6

A Member of the United Nations which has persistently violated the Principles contained in the present Charter may be expelled from the Organization by the General Assembly upon the recommendation of the Security Council.

CHAPTER III. ORGANS

Article 7

1. There are established as the principal organs of the United Nations: a General Assembly, a Security Council, an Economic and Social Council, a Trusteeship Council, an International Court of Justice, and a Secretariat.

2. Such subsidiary organs as may be found necessary may be established in accordance with the present Charter.

Article 8

The United Nations shall place no restrictions on the eligibility of men and women to participate in any capacity and under conditions of equality in its principal and subsidiary organs.

CHAPTER IV. THE GENERAL ASSEMBLY

Composition

Article 9

1. The General Assembly shall consist of all the Members of the United Nations.

2. Each Member shall have not more than five representatives in the General Assembly.

Functions and Powers

Article 10

The General Assembly may discuss any questions or any matters within the scope of the present Charter or relating to the powers and functions of any organs provided for in the present Charter, and, except as provided in Article 12, may make recommendations to the Members of the United Nations or to the Security Council or to both on any such questions or matters.

Article 11

1. The General Assembly may consider the general principles of co-operation in the maintenance of international peace and security, including the principles governing disarmament and the regulation of armaments, and may make recommendations with regard to such principles to the Members or to the Security Council or to both.

2. The General Assembly may discuss any questions relating to the maintenance of international peace and security brought before it by any Member of the United Nations, or by the Security Council, or by a State which is not a Member of the United Nations in accordance with Article 35, paragraph 2, and, except as provided in Article 12, may make recommendations with regard to any such questions to the State or States concerned or to the Security Council or to both. Any such question, on which action is necessary, shall be referred to the Security Council by the General Assembly either before or after discussion.

3. The General Assembly may call the attention of the Security Council to situations which are likely to endanger international peace and security.

4. The powers of the General Assembly set forth in this Article shall not limit the general scope of Article 10.

Article 12

1. While the Security Council is exercising in respect of any dispute or situation the functions assigned to it in the present Charter, the General Assembly shall not make any recommendation with regard to that dispute or situation unless the Security Council so requests.

2. The Secretary-General, with the consent of the Security Council, shall notify the General Assembly at each session of any matters relative to the maintenance of international peace and security which are being dealt with by the Security Council and shall similarly notify the General Assembly, or the Members of the United Nations if the General Assembly is not in session, immediately the Security Council ceases to deal with such matters.

Article 13

1. The General Assembly shall initiate studies and make recommendations for the purpose of:
   (a) Promoting international co-operation in the political field and encouraging the progressive development of international law and its codification;
   (b) Promoting international co-operation in the economic, social, cultural, educational, and health fields, and assisting in the realization of human rights and fundamental freedoms for all without distinction as to race, sex, language, or religion.

2. The further responsibilities, functions, and powers of the General Assembly with respect to matters mentioned in paragraph 1 (b) above are set forth in Chapters IX and X.

Article 14

Subject to the provisions of Article 12, the General Assembly may recommend measures for the peaceful adjustment of any situation, regardless of origin, which it deems likely to impair the general welfare or friendly relations among nations, including situations resulting from a violation of the provisions of the present Charter setting forth the Purposes and Principles of the United Nations.

Article 15

1. The General Assembly shall receive and consider annual and special reports from the Security Council; these reports shall include an account of the measures that the Security Council has decided upon or taken to maintain international peace and security.

2. The General Assembly shall receive and consider reports from the other organs of the United Nations.

Article 16

The General Assembly shall perform such functions with respect to the international trusteeship system as are assigned to it under Chapters XII and XIII, including the approval of the trusteeship agreements for areas not designated as strategic.

Article 17

1. The General Assembly shall consider and approve the budget of the Organization.

2. The expenses of the Organization shall be borne by the Members as apportioned by the General Assembly.

3. The General Assembly shall consider and approve any financial and budgetary arrangements with specialized agencies referred to in Article 57 and shall examine the administrative budgets of such specialized agencies with a view to making recommendations to the agencies concerned.

Voting

Article 18

1. Each Member of the General Assembly shall have one vote.

2. Decisions of the General Assembly on important questions shall be made by a two-thirds majority of the Members present and voting. These questions shall include: recommendations with respect to the maintenance of international peace and security, the election of the non-permanent members of the Security Council, the election of the members of the Economic and Social Council, the election of members of the Trusteeship Council in accordance with paragraph 1 (c) of Article 86, the admission of new Members to the United Nations, the suspension of the rights and privileges of membership, the expulsion of Members, questions relating to the operation of the trusteeship system, and budgetary questions.

3. Decisions on other questions, including the determination of additional categories of questions to be decided by a two-thirds majority, shall be made by a majority of the Members present and voting.

Article 19

A Member of the United Nations which is in arrears in the payment of its financial contributions to the Organization shall have no vote in the General Assembly if the amount of its arrears equals or exceeds the amount of the contributions due from it for the preceding two full years. The General Assembly may, nevertheless, permit such a Member to vote if it is satisfied that the failure to pay is due to conditions beyond the control of the Member.

Procedure

Article 20

The General Assembly shall meet in regular annual sessions and in such special sessions as occasion may require. Special sessions shall be convoked by the Secretary-General at the request of the Security Council or of a majority of the Members of the United Nations.

Article 21

The General Assembly shall adopt its own rules of procedure. It shall elect its President for each session.

Article 22

The General Assembly may establish such subsidiary organs as it deems necessary for the performance of its functions.

CHAPTER V. THE SECURITY COUNCIL

Composition

Article 23

1. The Security Council shall consist of *fifteen* Members of the United Nations. The Republic of China, France, the Union of Soviet Socialist Republics [*Russian Federation*], the United Kingdom of Great Britain and Northern Ireland, and the United States of America shall be permanent members of the Security Council. The General Assembly shall elect *ten* other Members of the United Nations to be non-permanent members of the Security Council, due regard being specially paid, in the first instance, to the contribution of Members of the United Nations to the maintenance of international peace and security and to the other purposes of the Organization, and also to equitable geographical distribution.

2. The non-permanent members of the Security Council shall be elected for a term of two years. *In the first election of the non-permanent members after the increase of the membership of the Security Council from eleven to fifteen, two of the four additional members shall be chosen for a term of one year.*

3. Each member of the Security Council shall have one representative.

Functions and Powers

Article 24

1. In order to ensure prompt and effective action by the United Nations, its Members confer on the Security Council primary responsibility for the maintenance of international peace and security, and agree that in carrying out its duties under this responsibility the Security Council acts on their behalf.

2. In discharging these duties the Security Council shall act in accordance with the Purposes and Principles of the United Nations. The specific powers granted to the Security Council for the discharge of these duties are laid down in Chapters VI, VII, VIII, and XII.

3. The Security Council shall submit annual and, when necessary, special reports to the General Assembly for its consideration.

Article 25

The Members of the United Nations agree to accept and carry out the decisions of the Security Council in accordance with the present Charter.

Article 26

In order to promote the establishment and maintenance of international peace and security with the least diversion for armaments of the world's human and economic resources, the Security Council shall be responsible for formulating, with the assistance of the Military Staff Committee referred to in Article 47, plans to be submitted to the Members of the United Nations for the establishment of a system for the regulation of armaments.

Voting

Article 27

1. Each member of the Security Council shall have one vote.

2. Decisions of the Security Council on procedural matters shall be made by an affirmative vote of *nine* members.

3. Decisions of the Security Council on all other matters shall be made by an affirmative vote of *nine* members including the concurring votes of the permanent members; provided that, in decisions under Chapter VI, and under paragraph 3 of Article 52, a party to a dispute shall abstain from voting.

Procedure

Article 28

1. The Security Council shall be so organized as to be able to function continuously. Each member of the Security Council shall for this purpose be represented at all times at the seat of the Organization.

2. The Security Council shall hold periodic meetings at which each of its members may, if it so desires, be represented by a member of the government or by some other specially designated representative.

3. The Security Council may hold meetings at such places other than the seat of the Organization as in its judgment will best facilitate its work.

Article 29

The Security Council may establish such subsidiary organs as it deems necessary for the performance of its functions.

Article 30

The Security Council shall adopt its own rules of procedure, including the method of selecting its President.

Article 31

Any Member of the United Nations which is not a member of the Security Council may participate, without vote, in the discussion of any question brought before the Security Council whenever the latter considers that the interests of that Member are specially affected.

Article 32

Any Member of the United Nations which is not a member of the Security Council or any State which is not a Member of the United Nations, if it is a party to a dispute under consideration by the Security Council, shall be invited to participate, without vote, in the discussion relating to the dispute. The Security Council shall lay down such conditions as it deems just for the participation of a State which is not a Member of the United Nations.

CHAPTER VI. PACIFIC SETTLEMENT OF DISPUTES

Article 33

1. The parties to any dispute, the continuance of which is likely to endanger the maintenance of international peace and security, shall, first of all, seek a solution by negotiation, enquiry, mediation, conciliation, arbitration, judicial settlement, resort to regional agencies or arrangements, or other peaceful means of their own choice.

2. The Security Council shall, when it deems necessary, call upon the parties to settle their dispute by such means.

Article 34

The Security Council may investigate any dispute, or any situation which might lead to international friction or give rise to a dispute, in order to determine whether the continuance of the dispute or situation is likely to endanger the maintenance of international peace and security.

Article 35

1. Any Member of the United Nations may bring any dispute, or any situation of the nature referred to in Article 34, to the attention of the Security Council or of the General Assembly.

2. A State which is not a Member of the United Nations may bring to the attention of the Security Council or of the General Assembly any dispute to which it is a party if it accepts

in advance, for the purposes of the dispute, the obligations of pacific settlement provided in the present charter.

3. The proceedings of the General Assembly in respect of matters brought to its attention under this Article will be subject to the provisions of Articles 11 and 12.

Article 36

1. The Security Council may, at any stage of a dispute of the nature referred to in Article 33 or of a situation of like nature, recommend appropriate procedures or methods of adjustment.

2. The Security Council should take into consideration any procedures for the settlement of the dispute which have already been adopted by the parties.

3. In making recommendations under this Article the Security Council should also take into consideration that legal disputes should as a general rule be referred by the parties to the International Court of Justice in accordance with the provisions of the Statute of the Court.

Article 37

1. Should the parties to a dispute of the nature referred to in Article 33 fail to settle it by the means indicated in that Article, they shall refer it to the Security Council.

2. If the Security Council deems that the continuance of the dispute is in fact likely to endanger the maintenance of international peace and security, it shall decide whether to take action under Article 36 or to recommend such terms of settlement as it may consider appropriate.

Article 38

Without prejudice to the provisions of Articles 33 to 37, the Security Council may, if all the parties to any dispute so request, make recommendations to the parties with a view to a pacific settlement of the dispute.

CHAPTER VII. ACTION WITH RESPECT TO THREATS TO THE PEACE, BREACHES OF THE PEACE, AND ACTS OF AGGRESSION

Article 39

The Security Council shall determine the existence of any threat to the peace, breach of the peace, or act of aggression and shall make recommendations, or decide what measures shall be taken in accordance with Articles 41 and 42, to maintain or restore international peace and security.

Article 40

In order to prevent an aggravation of the situation, the Security Council may, before making the recommendations or deciding upon the measures provided for in Article 39, call upon the parties concerned to comply with such provisional measures as it deems necessary or desirable. Such provisional measures shall be without prejudice to the rights, claims or position of the parties concerned. The Security Council shall duly take account of failure to comply with such provisional measures.

Article 41

The Security Council may decide what measures not involving the use of armed force are to be employed to give effect to its decisions, and it may call upon the Members of the United Nations to apply such measures. These may include complete or partial interruption of economic relations and of rail, sea, air, postal, telegraphic, radio, and other means of communication, and the severance of diplomatic relations.

Article 42

Should the Security Council consider that measures provided for in Article 41 would be inadequate or have proved to be inadequate, it may take such action by air, sea, or land forces as may be necessary to maintain or restore international peace and security. Such action may include demonstrations, blockade, and other operations by air, sea, or land forces of Members of the United Nations.

Article 43

1. All Members of the United Nations, in order to contribute to the maintenance of international peace and security, undertake to make available to the Security Council, on its call and in accordance with a special agreement or agreements, armed forces, assistance, and facilities, including rights of passage, necessary for the purpose of maintaining peace and security.

2. Such agreement or agreements shall govern the numbers and types of forces, their degree of readiness and general location, and the nature of the facilities and assistance to be provided.

3. The agreement or agreements shall be negotiated as soon as possible on the initiative of the Security Council. They shall be concluded between the Security Council and Members or between the Security Council and groups of Members and shall be subject to ratification by the signatory States in accordance with their respective constitutional processes.

Article 44

When the Security Council has decided to use force it shall, before calling upon a Member not represented on it to provide armed forces in fulfilment of the obligations assumed under Article 43, invite that Member, if the Member so desires, to participate in the decisions of the Security Council concerning the employment of contingents of that Member's armed forces.

Article 45

In order to enable the United Nations to take urgent military measures, Members shall hold immediately available national air-force contingents for combined international enforcement action. The strength and degree of readiness of these contingents and plans for their combined action shall be determined, within the limits laid down in the special agreement or agreements referred to in Article 43, by the Security Council with the assistance of the Military Staff Committee.

Article 46

Plans for the application of armed force shall be made by the Security Council with the assistance of the Military Staff Committee.

Article 47

1. There shall be established a Military Staff Committee to advise and assist the Security Council on all questions relating to the Security Council's military requirements for the maintenance of international peace and security, the employment and command of forces placed at its disposal, the regulation of armaments, and possible disarmament.

2. The Military Staff Committee shall consist of the Chiefs of Staff of the permanent members of the Security Council or their representatives. Any Member of the United Nations not permanently represented on the Committee shall be invited by the Committee to be associated with it when the efficient discharge of the Committee's responsibilities requires the participation of that Member in its work.

3. The Military Staff Committee shall be responsible under the Security Council for the strategic direction of any armed forces placed at the disposal of the Security Council. Questions relating to the command of such forces shall be worked out subsequently.

4. The Military Staff Committee, with the authorization of the Security Council and after consultation with appropriate regional agencies, may establish regional sub-committees.

Article 48

1. The action required to carry out the decisions of the Security Council for the maintenance of international peace and security shall be taken by all the Members of the United Nations or by some of them, as the Security Council may determine.

2. Such decisions shall be carried out by the Members of the United Nations directly and through their action in the appropriate international agencies of which they are members.

Article 49

The Members of the United Nations shall join in affording mutual assistance in carrying out the measures decided upon by the Security Council.

Article 50

If preventive or enforcement measures against any State are taken by the Security Council, any other State, whether a Member of the United Nations or not, which finds itself confronted with special economic problems arising from the carrying out of those measures shall have the right to consult the Security Council with regard to a solution of those problems.

Article 51

Nothing in the present Charter shall impair the inherent right of individual or collective self-defence if an armed attack occurs against a Member of the United Nations, until the Security Council has taken measures necessary to maintain international peace and security. Measures taken by members in the exercise of this right of self-defence shall be immediately reported to the Security Council and shall not in any way affect the authority and responsibility of the Security Council under the present Charter to take at any time such action as it deems necessary in order to maintain or restore international peace and security.

CHAPTER VIII. REGIONAL ARRANGEMENTS

Article 52

1. Nothing in the present Charter precludes the existence of regional arrangements or agencies for dealing with such matters relating to the maintenance of international peace and security as are appropriate for regional action, provided that such arrangements or agencies and their activities are consistent with the Purposes and Principles of the United Nations.

2. The Members of the United Nations entering into such arrangements or constituting such agencies shall make every effort to achieve pacific settlement of local disputes through such regional arrangements or by such regional agencies before referring them to the Security Council.

3. The Security Council shall encourage the development of pacific settlement of local disputes through such regional arrangements or by such regional agencies either on the initiative of the States concerned or by reference from the Security Council.

4. The Article in no way impairs the application of Articles 34 and 35.

Article 53

1. The Security Council shall, where appropriate, utilize such regional arrangements or agencies for enforcement action under its authority. But no enforcement action shall be taken under regional arrangements or by regional agencies without the authorization of the

Security Council, with the exception of measures against any enemy State, as defined in paragraph 2 of this Article, provided for pursuant to Article 107 or in regional arrangements directed against renewal of aggressive policy on the part of any such State, until such time as the Organization may, on request of the Governments concerned, be charged with the responsibility for preventing further aggression by such a State.

2. The term 'enemy State' as used in paragraph 1 of this Article applies to any State which during the Second World War has been an enemy of any signatory of the present Charter.

Article 54

The Security Council shall at all times be kept fully informed of activities undertaken or in contemplation under regional arrangements or by regional agencies for the maintenance of international peace and security.

CHAPTER IX. INTERNATIONAL ECONOMIC AND SOCIAL CO-OPERATION

Article 55

With a view to the creation of conditions of stability and well being which are necessary for peaceful and friendly relations among nations based on respect for the principle of equal rights and self-determination of peoples, the United Nations shall promote:

(a) higher standards of living, full employment, and conditions of economic and social progress and development;

(b) solutions of international economic, social, health, and related problems; and international cultural and educational co-operation; and

(c) universal respect for, and observance of, human rights and fundamental freedoms for all without distinction as to race, sex, language, or religion.

Article 56

All Members pledge themselves to take joint and separate action in co-operation with the Organization for the achievement of the purposes set forth in Article 55.

Article 57

1. The various specialized agencies, established by inter-governmental agreement and having wide international responsibilities, as defined in their basic instruments, in economic, social, cultural, educational, health, and related fields, shall be brought into relationship with the United Nations in accordance with the provisions of Article 63.

2. Such agencies thus brought into relationship with the United Nations are hereinafter referred to as specialized agencies.

Article 58

The Organization shall make recommendations for the co-ordination of the policies and activities of the specialized agencies.

Article 59

The Organization shall, where appropriate, initiate negotiations among the States concerned for the creation of any new specialized agencies required for the accomplishment of the purposes set forth in Article 55.

Article 60

Responsibility for the discharge of the functions of the Organization set forth in this Chapter shall be vested in the General Assembly and, under the authority of the General Assembly, in the Economic and Social Council, which shall have for this purpose the powers set forth in Chapter X.

CHAPTER X. THE ECONOMIC AND SOCIAL COUNCIL

Composition

Article 61

1. The Economic and Social Council shall consist of fifty-four Members of the United Nations elected by the General Assembly.

2. Subject to the provisions of paragraph 3, nine members of the Economic and Social Council shall be elected each year for a term of three years. A retiring member shall be eligible for immediate re-election.

3. *At the first election after the increase in the membership of the Economic and Social Council from eighteen to twenty-seven members, in addition to the members elected in place of the six members whose term of office expires at the end of that year, nine additional members shall be elected. Of these nine additional members, the term of office of three members so elected shall expire at the end of one year, and of three other members at the end of two years, in accordance with arrangements made by the General Assembly.*

4. Each member of the Economic and Social Council shall have one representative.

Functions and Powers

Article 62

1. The Economic and Social Council may make or initiate studies and reports with respect to international economic, social, cultural, educational, health, and related matters and may

make recommendations with respect to any such matters to the General Assembly, to the Members of the United Nations, and to the specialized agencies concerned.

2. It may make recommendations for the purpose of promoting respect for, and observance of, human rights and fundamental freedoms for all.

3. It may prepare draft conventions for submission to the General Assembly, with respect to matters falling within its competence.

4. It may call, in accordance with the rules prescribed by the United Nations, international conferences on matters falling within its competence.

Article 63

1. The Economic and Social Council may enter into agreements with any of the agencies referred to in Article 57, defining the terms on which the agency concerned shall be brought into relationship with the United Nations. Such agreements shall be subject to approval by the General Assembly.

2. It may co-ordinate the activities of the specialized agencies through consultation with and recommendations to such agencies and through recommendations to the General Assembly and to the Members of the United Nations.

Article 64

1. The Economic and Social Council may take appropriate steps to obtain regular reports from the specialized agencies. It may make arrangements with the Members of the United Nations and with the specialized agencies to obtain reports on the steps taken to give effect to its own recommendations and to recommendations on matters falling within its competence made by the General Assembly.

2. It may communicate its observations on these reports to the General Assembly.

Article 65

The Economic and Social Council may furnish information to the Security Council and shall assist the Security Council upon its request.

Article 66

1. The Economic and Social Council shall perform such functions as fall within its competence in connexion with the carrying out of the recommendations of the General Assembly.

2. It may, with the approval of the General Assembly, perform services at the request of Members of the United Nations and at the request of specialized agencies.

3. It shall perform such other functions as are specified elsewhere in the present Charter or as may be assigned to it by the General Assembly.

Voting

Article 67

1. Each member of the Economic and Social Council shall have one vote.

2. Decisions of the Economic and Social Council shall be made by a majority of the members present and voting.

Procedure

Article 68

The Economic and Social Council shall set up commissions in economic and social fields and for the promotion of human rights, and such other commissions as may be required for the performance of its functions.

Article 69

The Economic and Social Council shall invite any Member of the United Nations to participate, without vote, in its deliberations on any matter of particular concern to that Member.

Article 70

The Economic and Social Council may make arrangements for representatives of the specialized agencies to participate, without vote, in its deliberations and in those of the commissions established by it and for its representatives to participate in the deliberations of the specialized agencies.

Article 71

The Economic and Social Council may make suitable arrangements for consultation with non-governmental organizations which are concerned with matters within its competence.

Such arrangements may be made with international organizations and, where appropriate, with national organizations after consultation with the Members of the United Nations concerned.

Article 72

1. The Economic and Social Council shall adopt its own rules of procedure, including the method of selecting its President.

2. The Economic and Social Council shall meet as required in accordance with its rules, which shall include provisions for the convening of meetings on the request of a majority of its members.

CHAPTER XI. DECLARATION REGARDING NON-SELF-GOVERNING TERRITORIES

Article 73

Members of the United Nations which have or assume responsibilities for the administration of territories whose peoples have not yet attained a full measure of self-government recognize the principle that the interests of the inhabitants of these territories are paramount, and accept as a sacred trust the obligation to promote to the utmost, within the system of international peace and security established by the present Charter, the well-being of the inhabitants of these territories, and to this end:

(a) to ensure, with due respect for the culture of the peoples concerned, their political, economic, social and educational advancement, their just treatment, and their protection against abuses;

(b) to develop self-government, to take due account of the political aspirations of the peoples, and to assist them in the progressive development of their free political institutions, according to the particular circumstances of each territory and its peoples and their varying stages of advancement;

(c) to further international peace and security;

(d) to promote constructive measures of development, to encourage research, and to co-operate with one another and, when and where appropriate, with specialized international bodies with a view to the practical achievement of the social, economic, and scientific purposes set forth in this Article; and

(e) to transmit regularly to the Secretary-General for information purposes, subject to such limitation as security and constitutional considerations may require, statistical and other information of a technical nature relating to economic, social, and educational conditions in the territories for which they are respectively responsible other than those territories to which Chapters XII and XIII apply.

Article 74

Members of the United Nations also agree that their policy in respect of the territories to which this Chapter applies, no less than in respect of their metropolitan areas, must be based on the general principle of good neighbourliness, due account being taken of the interests and well-being of the rest of the world, in social, economic, and commercial matters.

CHAPTER XII. INTERNATIONAL TRUSTEESHIP SYSTEM

Article 75

The United Nations shall establish under its authority an international trusteeship system for the administration and supervision of such territories as may be placed thereunder by subsequent individual agreements. These territories are hereinafter referred to as trust territories.

Article 76

The basic objectives of the trusteeship system, in accordance with the Purposes of the United Nations laid down in Article 1 of the present Charter, shall be:

(a) to further international peace and security;

(b) to promote the political, economic, social, and educational advancement of the inhabitants of the trust territories, and their progressive development towards self-government or independence as may be appropriate to the particular circumstances of each territory and its peoples and the freely expressed wishes of the people concerned, and as may be provided by the terms of each trusteeship agreement;

(c) to encourage respect for human rights and for fundamental freedoms for all without distinction as to race, sex, language, or religion, and to encourage recognition of the interdependence of the peoples of the world; and

(d) to ensure equal treatment in social, economic and commercial matters for all Members of the United Nations and their nationals, and also equal treatment for the latter in the administration of justice, without prejudice to the attainment of the foregoing objectives and subject to the provisions of Article 80.

Article 77

1. The trusteeship system shall apply to such territories in the following categories as may be placed thereunder by means of trusteeship agreements:

(a) territories now held under mandate;

(b) territories which may be detached from enemy States as a result of the Second World War; and

(c) territories voluntarily placed under the system by States responsible for their administration.

2. It will be a matter for subsequent agreement as to which territories in the foregoing categories will be brought under the trusteeship system and upon what terms.

Article 78

The trusteeship system shall not apply to territories which have become Members of the United Nations, relationship among which shall be based on respect for the principle of sovereign equality.

Article 79

The terms of trusteeship for each territory to be placed under the trusteeship system, including any alteration or amendment, shall be agreed upon by the States directly concerned, including the mandatory power in the case of territories held under mandate by a Member of the United Nations, and shall be approved as provided for in Articles 83 and 85.

Article 80

1. Except as may be agreed upon in individual trusteeship agreements, made under Articles 77, 79, and 81, placing each territory under the trusteeship system, and until such agreements have been concluded, nothing in this Chapter shall be construed in or of itself to alter in any manner the rights whatsoever of any States or any peoples or the terms of existing international instruments to which Members of the United Nations may respectively be parties.

2. Paragraph 1 of this Article shall not be interpreted as giving grounds for delay or postponement of the negotiation and conclusion of agreements for placing mandated and other territories under the trusteeship system as provided for in Article 77.

Article 81

The trusteeship agreement shall in each case include the terms under which the trust territory will be administered and designate the authority which will exercise the administration of the trust territory. Such authority, hereinafter called the administering authority, may be one or more States or the Organization itself.

Article 82

There may be designated, in any trusteeship agreement, a strategic area or areas which may include part or all of the trust territory to which the agreement applies, without prejudice to any special agreement or agreements made under Article 43.

Article 83

1. All functions of the United Nations relating to strategic areas, including the approval of the terms of the trusteeship agreements and of their alteration or amendment, shall be exercised by the Security Council.

2. The basic objectives set forth in Article 76 shall be applicable to the people of each strategic area.

3. The Security Council shall, subject to the provisions of the trusteeship agreements and without prejudice to security considerations, avail itself of the assistance of the Trusteeship Council to perform those functions of the United Nations under the trusteeship system relating to political, economic, social, and educational matters in the strategic areas.

Article 84

It shall be the duty of the administering authority to ensure that the trust territory shall play its part in the maintenance of international peace and security. To this end the administering authority may make use of volunteer forces, facilities, and assistance from the trust territory in carrying out the obligations towards the Security Council undertaken in this regard by the administering authority, as well as for local defence and the maintenance of law and order within the trust territory.

Article 85

1. The functions of the United Nations with regard to trusteeship agreements for all areas not designated as strategic, including the approval of the terms of the trusteeship agreements and of their alteration or amendment, shall be exercised by the General Assembly.

2. The Trusteeship Council, operating under the authority of the General Assembly, shall assist the General Assembly in carrying out these functions.

CHAPTER XIII. THE TRUSTEESHIP COUNCIL

Composition

Article 86

1. The Trusteeship Council shall consist of the following Members of the United Nations:
    (a) those Members administering trust territories;
    (b) such of those Members mentioned by name in Article 23 as are not administering trust territories; and
    (c) as many other Members elected for three-year terms by the General Assembly as may be necessary to ensure that the total number of members of the Trusteeship Council is equally divided between those Members of the United Nations which administer trust territories and those which do not.

2. Each member of the Trusteeship Council shall designate one specially qualified person to represent it therein.

Functions and Powers

Article 87

The General Assembly and, under its authority, the Trusteeship Council, in carrying out their functions, may:
    (a) consider reports submitted by the administering authority;
    (b) accept petitions and examine them in consultation with the administration authority;
    (c) provide for periodic visits to the respective trust territories at times agreed upon with the administering authority; and
    (d) take these and other actions in conformity with the terms of the trusteeship agreements.

Article 88

The Trusteeship Council shall formulate a questionnaire on the political, economic, social, and educational advancement of the inhabitants of each trust territory, and the administering authority for each trust territory within the competence of the General Assembly shall make an annual report to the General Assembly upon the basis of such questionnaire.

Voting

Article 89

1. Each member of the Trusteeship Council shall have one vote.

2. Decisions of the Trusteeship Council shall be made by a majority of the members present and voting.

Procedure

Article 90

1. The Trusteeship Council shall adopt its own rules of procedure, including the method of selecting its President.

2. The Trusteeship Council shall meet as required in accordance with its rules, which shall include provision for the convening of meetings on the request of a majority of its members.

Article 91

The Trusteeship Council shall, when appropriate, avail itself of the assistance of the Economic and Social Council and of the specialized agencies in regard to matters with which they are respectively concerned.

CHAPTER XIV. THE INTERNATIONAL COURT OF JUSTICE

Article 92

The International Court of Justice shall be the principal judicial organ of the United Nations. It shall function in accordance with the annexed Statute, which is based upon the Statute of the Permanent Court of International Justice and forms an integral part of the present Charter.

Article 93

1. All members of the United Nations are ipso facto parties to the Statute of the International Court of Justice.

2. A State which is not a Member of the United Nations may become a party to the Statute of the International Court of Justice on conditions to be determined in each case by the General Assembly upon the recommendation of the Security Council.

Article 94

1. Each Member of the United Nations undertakes to comply with the decision of the International Court of Justice in any case to which it is a party.

2. If any party to a case fails to perform the obligations incumbent upon it under a judgment rendered by the Court, the other party may have recourse to the Security Council, which may, if it deems necessary, make recommendations or decide upon measures to be taken to give effect to the judgment.

Article 95

Nothing in the present Charter shall prevent Members of the United Nations from entrusting the solution of their differences to other tribunals by virtue of agreements already in existence or which may be concluded in the future.

Article 96

1. The General Assembly or the Security Council may request the International Court of Justice to give an advisory opinion on any legal question.

2. Other organs of the United Nations and specialized agencies, which may at any time be so authorized by the General Assembly; may also request advisory opinions of the Court on legal questions arising within the scope of their activities.

CHAPTER XV. THE SECRETARIAT

Article 97

The Secretariat shall comprise a Secretary-General and such staff as the Organization may require. The Secretary-General shall be appointed by the General Assembly upon the recommendation of the Security Council. He shall be the chief administrative officer of the Organization.

Article 98

The Secretary-General shall act in that capacity in all meetings of the General Assembly, of the Security Council, of the Economic and Social Council, and of the Trusteeship Council, and shall perform such other functions as are entrusted to him by these organs. The Secretary-General shall make an annual report to the General Assembly on the work of the Organization.

Article 99

The Secretary-General may bring to the attention of the Security Council any matter which in his opinion may threaten the maintenance of international peace and security.

Article 100

1. In the performance of their duties the Secretary-General and the staff shall not seek or receive instructions from any Government or from any other authority external to the Organization. They shall refrain from any action which might reflect on their position as international officials responsible only to the Organization.

2. Each Member of the United Nations undertakes to respect the exclusively international character of the responsibilities of the Secretary-General and the staff and not to seek to influence them in the discharge of their responsibilities.

Article 101

1. The staff shall be appointed by the Secretary-General under regulations established by the General Assembly.

2. Appropriate staffs shall be permanently assigned to the Economic and Social Council, the Trusteeship Council, and, as required, to other organs of the United Nations. These staffs shall form a part of the Secretariat.

3. The paramount consideration in the employment of the staff and in the determination of the conditions of service shall be the necessity of securing the highest standard of efficiency, competence, and integrity. Due regard shall be paid to the importance of recruiting the staff on as wide a geographical basis as possible.

CHAPTER XVI. MISCELLANEOUS PROVISIONS

Article 102

1. Every treaty and every international agreement entered into by any Member of the United Nations after the present Charter comes into force shall as soon as possible be registered with the Secretariat and published by it.

2. No party to any such treaty or international agreement which has not been registered in accordance with the provisions of paragraph 1 of this Article may invoke that treaty or agreement before any organ of the United Nations.

Article 103

In the event of a conflict between the obligations of the Members of the United Nations under the present Charter and their obligations under any other international agreement, their obligations under the present Charter shall prevail.

Article 104

The Organization shall enjoy in the territory of each of its Members such legal capacity as may be necessary for the exercise of its functions and the fulfilment of its purposes.

Article 105

1. The Organization shall enjoy in the territory of each of its Members such privileges and immunities as are necessary for the fulfilment of its purposes.

2. Representatives of the Members of the United Nations and officials of the Organization shall similarly enjoy such privileges and immunities as are necessary for the independent exercise of their functions in connexion with the Organization.

3. The General Assembly may make recommendations with a view to determining the details of the application of paragraphs 1 and 2 of this Article or may propose conventions to the Members of the United Nations for this purpose.

CHAPTER XVII. TRANSITIONAL SECURITY ARRANGEMENTS

Article 106

Pending the coming into force of such special agreements referred to in Article 43 as in the opinion of the Security Council enable it to begin the exercise of its responsibilities under Article 42, the parties to the Four-Nation Declaration, signed at Moscow, October 30, 1943, and France shall, in accordance with the provisions of paragraph 5 of that Declaration, consult with one another and as occasion requires with other Members of the United Nations with a view to such joint action on behalf of the Organization as may be necessary for the purpose of maintaining international peace and security.

Article 107

Nothing in the present Charter shall invalidate or preclude action, in relation to any State which during the Second World War has been an enemy of any signatory to the present Charter, taken or authorized as a result of that war by the Governments having responsibility for such action.

CHAPTER XVIII. AMENDMENTS

Article 108

Amendments to the present Charter shall come into force for all Members of the United Nations when they have been adopted by a vote of two-thirds of the members of the General Assembly and ratified in accordance with their respective constitutional processes by two-thirds of the Members of the United Nations, including all the permanent members of the Security Council.

Article 109

1. A General Conference of the Members of the United Nations for the purpose of reviewing the present Charter may be held at a date and place to be fixed by a two-thirds vote of the members of the General Assembly and by a vote of any *nine* members of the Security Council. Each Member of the United Nations shall have one vote in the conference.

2. Any alteration of the present Charter recommended by a two-thirds vote of the conference shall take effect when ratified in accordance with their respective constitutional processes by two-thirds of the Members of the United Nations including all the permanent members of the Security Council.

3. If such a conference has not been held before the tenth annual session of the General Assembly following the coming into force of the present Charter, the proposal to call such a conference shall be placed on the agenda of that session of the General Assembly, and the conference shall be held if so decided by a majority vote of the members of the General Assembly and by a vote of any seven members of the Security Council.

CHAPTER XIX. RATIFICATION AND SIGNATURE

Article 110

1. The present Charter shall be ratified by the signatory States in accordance with their respective constitutional processes.

2. The ratifications shall be deposited with the Government of the United States of America, which shall notify all the signatory States of each deposit as well as the Secretary-General of the Organization when he has been appointed.

3. The present Charter shall come into force upon the deposit of ratifications by the Republic of China, France, the Union of Soviet Socialist Republics, the United Kingdom of Great Britain and Northern Ireland, and the United States of America, and by a majority of the other signatory States. A protocol of the ratifications deposited shall thereupon be drawn up by the Government of the United States of America which shall communicate copies thereof to all the signatory States.

4. The States signatory to the present Charter which ratify it after it has come into force will become original Members of the United Nations on the date of the deposit of their respective ratifications.

Article 111

The present Charter, of which the Chinese, French, Russian, English, and Spanish texts are equally authentic, shall remain deposited in the archives of the Government of the United States of America. Duly certified copies thereof shall be transmitted by that Government to the Governments of the other signatory States.

In faith whereof the representatives of the Governments of the United Nations have signed the present Charter.

Done at the City of San Francisco the twenty-sixth day of June, one thousand nine hundred and forty-five.

Appendix B

Treaty on European Union (Maastricht)

TREATY ON EUROPEAN UNION

[Signed at Maastricht on February 7, 1992, came into force on November 1, 1993. The official English text appears at Official Journal of the European Communities No. C 224/79, August 31, 1992. Title I established the European Union and is set forth below. Title II amended the Treaty of Rome and is omitted in the excerpts below. Titles III and IV amended the treaties establishing the European Coal and Steel Community and European Atomic Energy Community, respectively; they are omitted here. Titles V and VI are excerpted here. Title VII, Final Provisions, is omitted. Various supplementary provisions annexed to the treaty as it came into force are also omitted.]

TITLE I

Article A

By this Treaty, the High Contracting Parties establish among themselves a European Union, hereinafter called "the Union."

This Treaty marks a new stage in the process of creating an ever closer union among the peoples of Europe, in which decisions are taken as closely as possible to the citizen.

The Union shall be founded on the European Communities, supplemented by the policies and forms of cooperation established by this Treaty. Its task shall be to organize, in a manner demonstrating consistency and solidarity, relations between the Member States and between their peoples.

Article B

The Union shall set itself the following objectives:

— to promote economic and social progress which is balanced and sustainable, in particular through the creation of an area without internal frontiers, through the strengthening of economic and social cohesion and through the establishment of economic and monetary union, ultimately including a single currency in accordance with the provisions of this Treaty;

— to assert its identity on the international scene, in particular through the implementation of a common foreign and security policy including the eventual framing of a common defence policy, which might in time lead to a common defence;

— to strengthen the protection of the rights and interests of the nationals of its Member States through the introduction of a citizenship of the Union;

— to develop close cooperation on justice and home affairs;

— to maintain in full the "acquis communautaire" and build on it with a view to considering, through the procedure referred to in Article N(2), to what extent the policies and forms of cooperation introduced by this Treaty may need to be revised with the aim of ensuring the effectiveness of the mechanisms and the institutions of the Community.

The objectives of the Union shall be achieved as provided in this Treaty and in accordance with the conditions and the timetable set out therein while respecting the principle of subsidiarity as defined in Article 3b of the Treaty establishing the European Community.

Article C

The Union shall be served by a single institutional framework which shall ensure the consistency and the continuity of the activities carried out in order to attain its objectives while respecting and building upon the "acquis communautaire."

The Union shall in particular ensure the consistency of its external activities as a whole in the context of its external relations, security, economic and development policies. The Council and the Commission shall be responsible for ensuring such consistency. They shall ensure the implementation of these policies, each in accordance with its respective powers.

Article D

The European Council shall provide the Union with the necessary impetus for its development and shall define the general political guidelines thereof. . . .

Article E

The European Parliament, the Council, the Commission and the Court of Justice shall exercise their powers under the conditions and for the purposes provided for, on the one hand, by the provisions of the Treaties establishing the European Communities and of the subsequent Treaties and Acts modifying and supplementing them and, on the other hand, by the other provisions of this Treaty.

Article F

1. The Union shall respect the national identities of its Member States, whose systems of government are founded on the principles of democracy.

2. The Union shall respect fundamental rights, as guaranteed by the European Convention for the Protection of Human Rights and Fundamental Freedoms signed in Rome on 4 November 1950 and as they result from the constitutional traditions common to the Member States, as general principles of Community law.

3. The Union shall provide itself with the means necessary to attain its objectives and carry through its policies.

TITLE V

Provisions on a Common Foreign and Security Policy

Article J

A common foreign and security policy is hereby established which shall be governed by the following provisions.

Article J.1

1. The Union and its Member States shall define and implement a common foreign and security policy, governed by the provisions of this Title and covering all areas of foreign and security policy.

2. The objectives of the common foreign and security policy shall be:

— to safeguard the common values, fundamental interests and independence of the Union;
— to strengthen the security of the Union and its Member States in all ways;
— to preserve peace and strengthen international security, in accordance with the principles of the United Nations Charter as well as the principles of the Helsinki Final Act and the objectives of the Paris Charter;
— to promote international cooperation;
— to develop and consolidate democracy and the rule of law, and respect for human rights and fundamental freedoms.

3. The Union shall pursue these objectives:

— by establishing systematic cooperation between Member States in the conduct of policy, in accordance with Article 5.2;
— by gradually implementing, in accordance with Article 5.3, joint action in the areas in which the Member States have important interests in common.

4. The Member States shall support the Union's external and security policy actively and unreservedly in a spirit of loyalty and mutual solidarity. They shall refrain from any action which is contrary to the interests of the Union or likely to impair its effectiveness as a cohesive force in international relations. The Council shall ensure that these principles are complied with.

Article J.2

1. Member States shall inform and consult one another within the Council on any matter of foreign and security policy of general interest in order to ensure that their combined influence is exerted as effectively as possible by means of concerted and convergent action.

2. Whenever it deems it necessary, the Council shall define a common position.

Member States shall ensure that their national policies conform to the common positions.

3. Member States shall coordinate their action in international organizations and at international conferences. They shall uphold the common positions in such forums.

In international organizations and at international conferences where not all the Member States participate, those which do take part shall uphold the common positions.

Article J.3

The procedure for adopting joint action in matters covered by the foreign and security policy shall be the following:

1. The Council shall decide, on the basis of general guidelines from the European Council, that a matter should be the subject of joint action.

Whenever the Council decides on the principle of joint action, it shall lay down the specific scope, the Union's general and specific objectives in carrying out such action, if necessary its duration, and the means, procedures and conditions for its implementation.

2. The Council shall, when adopting the joint action and at any stage during its development, define those matters on which decisions are to be taken by a qualified majority.

Where the Council is required to act by a qualified majority pursuant to the preceding subparagraph, the votes of its members shall be weighted in accordance with Article 148(2) of the Treaty establishing the European Community, and for their adoption, acts of the Council shall require at least 54 votes in favour, cast by at least eight members.

* * *

4. Joint actions shall commit the Member States in the positions they adopt and in the conduct of their activity.

5. Whenever there is any plan to adopt a national position or take national action pursuant to a joint action, information shall be provided in time to allow, if necessary, for prior consultations within the Council. The obligation to provide prior information shall not apply to measures which are merely a national transposition of Council decisions.

6. In cases of imperative need arising from changes in the situation and failing a Council decision, Member States may take the necessary measures as a matter of urgency having regard to the general objectives of the joint action. The Member State concerned shall inform the Council immediately of any such measures.

7. Should there be any major difficulties in implementing a joint action, a member State shall refer them to the Council which shall discuss them and seek appropriate solutions. Such solutions shall not run counter to the objectives of the joint action or impair its effectiveness.

Article J.4

1. The common foreign and security policy shall include all questions related to the security of the Union, including the eventual framing of a common defence policy, which might in time lead to a common defence.

2. The Union requests the Western European Union (WEU), which is an integral part of the development of the Union, to elaborate and implement decisions and actions of the Union which have defence implications. The Council shall, in agreement with the institutions of the WEU, adopt the necessary practical arrangements.

3. Issues having defence implications dealt with under this Article shall not be subject to the procedures set out in Article 5.3.

4. The policy of the Union in accordance with this Article shall not prejudice the specific character of the security and defence policy of certain Member States and shall respect the obligations of certain Member States under the North Atlantic Treaty and be compatible with the common security and defence policy established within that framework.

5. The provisions of this Article shall not prevent the development of closer cooperation between two or more Member States on a bilateral level, in the framework of the WEU and the Atlantic Alliance, provided such cooperation does not run counter to or impede that provided for in this Title.

Article J.5

1. The Presidency shall represent the Union in matters coming within the common foreign and security policy.

2. The Presidency shall be responsible for the implementation of common measures; in that capacity it shall in principle express the position of the Union in international organizations and international conferences.

* * *

4. Without prejudice to Article 5.2(3) and Article 5.3(4), Member States represented in international organizations or international conferences where not all the Member States participate shall keep the latter informed of any matter of common interest.

Member States which are also members of the United Nations Security Council will concert and keep the other Member States fully informed. Member States which are permanent members of the Security Council will, in the execution of their functions, ensure the defence of the positions and the interests of the Union, without prejudice to their responsibilities under the provisions of the United Nations Charter.

Article J.6

The diplomatic and consular missions of the Member States and the Commission Delegations in third countries and international conferences, and their representations to international organizations, shall cooperate in ensuring that the common positions and common measures adopted by the Council are complied with and implemented.

They shall step up cooperation by exchanging information, carrying out joint assessments and contributing to the implementation of the provisions referred to in Article 8c of the Treaty establishing the European Community.

Article J.7

The Presidency shall consult the European Parliament on the main aspects and the basic choices of the common foreign and security policy and shall ensure that the views of the European Parliament are duly taken into consideration. The European Parliament shall be kept regularly informed by the Presidency and the Commission of the development of the Union's foreign and security policy.

The European Parliament may ask questions of the Council or make recommendations to it. It shall hold an annual debate on progress in implementing the common foreign and security policy.

Article J.8

1. The European Council shall define the principles of and general guidelines for the common foreign and security policy.

2. The Council shall take the decisions necessary for defining and implementing the common foreign and security policy on the basis of the general guidelines adopted by the European Council. It shall ensure the unity, consistency and effectiveness of action by the Union.

The Council shall act unanimously, except for procedural questions and in the case referred to in Article 5.3(2).

3. Any Member State or the Commission may refer to the Council any question relating to the common foreign and security policy and may submit proposals to the Council.

4. In cases requiring a rapid decision, the Presidency, of its own motion, or at the request of the Commission or a Member State, shall convene an extraordinary Council meeting within 48 hours or, in an emergency, within a shorter period.

TITLE VI
Provisions on Cooperation in the Fields of Justice and Home Affairs

Article K

Cooperation in the fields of justice and home affairs shall be governed by the following provisions.

Article K.1

For the purposes of achieving the objectives of the Union, in particular the movement of persons, and without prejudice to the powers of the European Community, Member States shall regard the following areas as matters of common interest:

1. asylum policy;

2. rules governing the crossing by persons of the external borders of the Member States and the exercise of controls thereon;

3. immigration policy and policy regarding nationals of third countries:

(a) conditions of entry and movement by nationals of third countries on the territory of Member States;

(b) conditions of residence by nationals of third countries on the territory of Member States, including family reunion and access to employment;

(c) combating unauthorized immigration, residence and work by nationals of third countries on the territory of Member States;

4. combating drug addiction in so far as this is not covered by (7) to (9);

5. combating fraud on an international scale in so far as this is not covered by (7) to (9);

6. judicial cooperation in civil matters;

7. judicial cooperation in criminal matters;

8. customs cooperation;

9. police cooperation for the purposes of preventing and combating terrorism, unlawful drug trafficking and other serious forms of international crime, including if necessary certain aspects of customs cooperation, in connection with the organization of a Union-wide system for exchanging information within a European Police Office (Europol).

Article K.2

1. The matters referred to in Article K.1 shall be dealt with in compliance with the European Convention for the Protection of Human Rights and Fundamental Freedoms of 4 November 1950 and the Convention relating to the Status of Refugees of 28 July 1951 and having regard to the protection afforded by Member States to persons persecuted on political grounds.

2. This Title shall not affect the exercise of the responsibilities incumbent upon Member States with regard to the maintenance of law and order and the safeguarding of internal security.

Article K.3

1. In the areas referred to in Article K.1, Member States shall inform and consult one another within the Council with a view to coordinating their action. To that end, they shall establish collaboration between the relevant departments of their administrations.

2. The Council may:

— on the initiative of any Member State or of the Commission, in the areas referred to in Article K.1(1) to (6);

— on the initiative of any Member State, in the areas referred to in Article K.1(7) to (9):

    (a) adopt joint positions and promote, using the appropriate form and procedures, any cooperation contributing to the pursuit of the objectives of the Union;

    (b) adopt joint action in so far as the objectives of the Union can be attained better by joint action than by the Member States acting individually on account of the scale or effects of the action envisaged; it may decide that measures implementing joint action are to be adopted by a qualified majority;

    (c) without prejudice to Article 220 of the Treaty establishing the European Community, draw up conventions which it shall recommend to the Member States for adoption in accordance with their respective constitutional requirements.

Unless otherwise provided by such conventions, measures implementing them shall be adopted within the Council by a majority of two-thirds of the High Contracting Parties.

Such conventions may stipulate that the Court of Justice shall have jurisdiction to interpret their provisions and to rule on any disputes regarding their application, in accordance with such arrangements as they may lay down.

Appendix C

Universal Declaration of Human Rights

UNIVERSAL DECLARATION OF HUMAN RIGHTS

G.A.Res. 217k U.N. Dec. A/810 (1948).

PREAMBLE

Whereas recognition of the inherent dignity and of the equal and inalienable rights of all members of the human family is the foundation of freedom, justice and peace in the world,

Whereas disregard and contempt for human rights have resulted in barbarous acts which have outraged the conscience of mankind, and the advent of a world in which human beings shall enjoy freedom of speech and belief and freedom from fear and want has been proclaimed as the highest aspiration of the common people,

Whereas it is essential, if man is not to be compelled to have recourse, as a last resort, to rebellion against tyranny and oppression, that human rights should be protected by the rule of law,

Whereas it is essential to promote the development of friendly relations between nations,

Whereas the peoples of the United Nations have in the Charter reaffirmed their faith in fundamental human rights, in the dignity and worth of the human person and in the equal rights of men and women and have determined to promote social progress and better standards of life in larger freedom,

Whereas Member States have pledged themselves to achieve, in co-operation with the United Nations, the promotion of universal respect for and observance of human rights and fundamental freedoms,

Whereas a common understanding of these rights and freedoms is of the greatest importance for the full realization of this pledge,

Now, therefore,

The General Assembly

Proclaims this Universal Declaration of Human Rights as a common standard of achievement for all peoples and all nations, to the end that every individual and every organ of society, keeping this Declaration constantly in mind, shall strive by teaching and education to promote respect for these rights and freedoms and by progressive measures, national and international, to secure their universal and effective recognition and observance, both among the peoples of Member States themselves and among the peoples of territories under their jurisdiction.

Article 1

ALL human beings are born free and equal in dignity and rights. They are endowed with reason and conscience and should act towards one another in a spirit of brotherhood.

Article 2

Everyone is entitled to all the rights and freedoms set forth in this Declaration, without distinction of any kind, such as race, colour, sex, language, religion, political or other opinion, national or social origin, property, birth or other status.

Furthermore, no distinction shall be made on the basis of the political, jurisdictional or international status of the country or territory to which a person belongs, whether it be independent, trust, non-self-governing or under any other limitation of sovereignty.

Article 3

Everyone has the right to life, liberty and security of person.

Article 4

No one shall be held in slavery or servitude; slavery and the slave trade shall be prohibited in all their forms.

Article 5

No one shall be subjected to torture or to cruel, inhuman or degrading treatment or punishment.

Article 6

Everyone has the right to recognition everywhere as a person before the law.

Article 7

All are equal before the law and are entitled without any discrimination to equal protection of the law. All are entitled to equal protection against any discrimination in violation of this Declaration and against any incitement to such discrimination.

Article 8

Everyone has the right to an effective remedy by the competent national tribunals for acts violating the fundamental rights granted him by the constitution or by law.

Article 9

No one shall be subjected to arbitrary arrest, detention or exile.

Article 10

Everyone is entitled in full equality to a fair and public hearing by an independent and impartial tribunal, in the determination of his rights and obligations and of any criminal charge against him.

Article 11

1. Everyone charged with a penal offence has the right to be presumed innocent until proved guilty according to law in a public trial at which he has had all the guarantees necessary for his defence.

2. No one shall be held guilty of any penal offence on account of any act or omission which did not constitute a penal offence, under national or international law, at the time when it was committed. Nor shall a heavier penalty be imposed than the one that was applicable at the time the penal offence was committed.

Article 12

No one shall be subjected to arbitrary interference with his privacy, family, home or correspondence, nor to attacks upon his honour and reputation. Everyone has the right to the protection of the law against such interference or attacks.

Article 13

1. Everyone has the right to freedom of movement and residence within the borders of each State.

2. Everyone has the right to leave any country, including his own, and to return to his country.

Article 14

1. Everyone has the right to seek and to enjoy in other countries asylum from persecution.

2. This right may not be invoked in the case of prosecutions genuinely arising from non-political crimes or from acts contrary to the purposes and principles of the United Nations.

Article 15

1. Everyone has the right to a nationality.

2. No one shall be arbitrarily deprived of his nationality nor denied the right to change his nationality.

Article 16

1. Men and women of full age, without any limitation due to race, nationality or religion, have the right to marry and to found a family. They are entitled to equal rights as to marriage, during marriage and at its dissolution.

2. Marriage shall be entered into only with the free and full consent of the intending spouses.

3. The family is the natural and fundamental group unit of society and is entitled to protection by society and the State.

Article 17

1. Everyone has the right to own property alone as well as in association with others.

2. No one shall be arbitrarily deprived of his property.

Article 18

Everyone has the right to freedom of thought, conscience and religion; this right includes freedom to change his religion or belief, and freedom, either alone or in community with others and in public or private, to manifest his religion or belief in teaching, practice, worship and observance.

Article 19

Everyone has the right to freedom of opinion and expression; this right includes freedom to hold opinions without interference and to seek, receive and impart information and ideas through any media and regardless of frontiers.

Article 20

1. Everyone has the right to freedom of peaceful assembly and association.

2. No one may be compelled to belong to an association.

Article 21

1. Everyone has the right to take part in the government of his country, directly or through freely chosen representatives.

2. Everyone has the right to equal access to public service in his country.

3. The will of the people shall be the basis of the authority of government; this will shall be expressed in periodic and genuine elections which shall be by universal and equal suffrage and shall be held by secret vote or by equivalent free voting procedures.

Article 22

Everyone, as a member of society, has the right to social security and is entitled to realization, through national effort and international co-operation and in accordance with the organization and resources of each State, of the economic, social and cultural rights indispensable for his dignity and the free development of his personality.

Article 23

1. Everyone has the right to work, to free choice of employment, to just and favourable conditions of work and to protection against unemployment.

2. Everyone, without any discrimination, has the right to equal pay for equal work.

3. Everyone who works has the right to just and favourable remuneration ensuring for himself and his family an existence worthy of human dignity, and supplemented, if necessary, by other means of social protection.

4. Everyone has the right to form and to join trade unions for the protection of his interests.

Article 24

Everyone has the right to rest and leisure, including reasonable limitation of working hours and periodic holidays with pay.

Article 25

1. Everyone has the right to a standard of living adequate for the health and well-being of himself and of his family, including food, clothing, housing and medical care and necessary social services, and the right to security in the event of unemployment, sickness, disability, widowhood, old age or other lack of livelihood in circumstances beyond his control.

2. Motherhood and childhood are entitled to special care and assistance. All children, whether born in or out of wedlock, shall enjoy the same social protection.

Article 26

1. Everyone has the right to education. Education shall be free, at least in the elementary and fundamental stages. Elementary education shall be compulsory. Technical and professional education shall he made generally available and higher education shall be equally accessible to all on the basis of merit.

2. Education shall be directed to the full development of the human personality and to the strengthening of respect for human rights and fundamental freedoms. It shall promote understanding, tolerance and friendship among all nations, racial or religious groups, and shall further the activities of the United Nations for the maintenance of peace.

3. Parents have a prior right to choose the kind of education that shall be given to their children.

Article 27

1. Everyone has the right freely to participate in the cultural life of the community, to enjoy the arts and to share in scientific advancement and its benefits.

2. Everyone has the right to the protection of the moral and material interests resulting from any scientific, literary or artistic production of which he is the author.

Article 28

Everyone is entitled to a social and international order in which the rights and freedoms set forth in this Declaration can be fully realized.

Article 29

1. Everyone has duties to the community in which alone the free and full development of his personality is possible.

2. In the exercise of his rights and freedoms, everyone shall be subject only to such limitations as are determined by law solely for the purpose of securing due recognition and respect for the rights and freedoms of others and of meeting the just requirements of morality, public order and the general welfare in a democratic society.

3. These rights and freedoms may in no case be exercised contrary to the purposes and principles of the United Nations.

Article 30

Nothing in this Declaration may be interpreted as implying for any State, group or person any right to engage in any activity or to perform any act aimed at the destruction of any of the rights and freedoms set forth herein.

Appendix D

International Covenant on Civil and Political Rights

INTERNATIONAL COVENANT ON CIVIL AND POLITICAL RIGHTS

999 U.N.T.S. 171, 302. Adopted Dec. 16, 1966, entered into force for United States, Sept. 8, 1992. For U.S. reservations and understandings see main text.

PREAMBLE

The States Parties to the present Covenant,

Considering that, in accordance with the principles proclaimed in the Charter of the United Nations, recognition of the inherent dignity and of the equal and inalienable rights of all members of the human family is the foundation of freedom, justice and peace in the world,

Recognizing that these rights derive from the inherent dignity of the human person,

Recognizing that, in accordance with the Universal Declaration of Human Rights, the ideal of free human beings enjoying civil and political freedom and freedom from fear and want can only be achieved if conditions are created whereby everyone may enjoy his civil and political rights, as well as his economic, social and cultural rights,

Considering the obligation of States under the Charter of the United Nations to promote universal respect for, and observance of, human rights and freedoms,

Realizing that the individual, having duties to other individuals and to the community to which he belongs, is under a responsibility to strive for the promotion and observance of the rights recognized in the present Covenant,

Agree upon the following articles:

PART I

Article 1

1. All peoples have the right of self-determination. By virtue of that right they freely determine their political status and freely pursue their economic, social and cultural development.

2. All peoples may, for their own ends, freely dispose of their natural wealth and resources without prejudice to any obligations arising out of international economic co-operation, based upon the principle of mutual benefit, and international law. In no case may a people be deprived of its own means of subsistence.

3. The States Parties to the present Covenant, including those having responsibility for the administration of Non-Self-Governing and Trust Territories, shall promote the realization of the right of self-determination, and shall respect that right, in conformity with the provisions of the Charter of the United Nations.

PART II

Article 2

1. Each State Party to the present Covenant undertakes to respect and to ensure to all individuals within its territory and subject to its jurisdiction the rights recognized in the present Covenant, without distinction of any kind, such as race, colour, sex, language, religion, political or other opinion, national or social origin, property, birth or other status.

2. Where not already provided for by existing legislative or other measures, each State Party to the present Covenant undertakes to take the necessary steps, in accordance with its constitutional processes and with the provisions of the present Covenant, to adopt such legislative or other measures as may be necessary to give effect to the rights recognized in the present Covenant.

3. Each State Party to the present Covenant undertakes:

(a) To ensure that any person whose rights or freedoms as herein recognized are violated shall have an effective remedy, notwithstanding that the violation has been committed by persons acting in an official capacity;

(b) To ensure that any person claiming such a remedy shall have his right thereto determined by competent judicial, administrative or legislative authorities, or by any other competent authority provided for by the legal system of the State, and to develop the possibilities of judicial remedy;

(c) To ensure that the competent authorities shall enforce such remedies when granted.

Article 3

The States Parties to the present Covenant undertake to ensure the equal right of men and women to the enjoyment of all civil and political rights set forth in the present Covenant.

Article 4

1. In time of public emergency which threatens the life of the nation and the existence of which is officially proclaimed, the States Parties to the present Covenant may take measures derogating from their obligations under the present Covenant to the extent strictly required by the exigencies of the situation, provided that such measures are not inconsistent with their other obligations under international law and do not involve discrimination solely on the ground of race, colour, sex, language, religion or social origin.

2. No derogation from articles 6, 7, 8 (paragraphs 1 and 2), 11, 15, 16 and 18 may be made under this provision.

3. Any State party to the present Covenant availing itself of the right of derogation shall immediately inform the other States Parties to the present Covenant, through the intermediary of the Secretary-General of the United Nations, of the provisions from which it has derogated and of the reasons by which it was actuated. A further communication shall be made, through the same intermediary, on the date on which it terminates such derogation.

Article 5

1. Nothing in the present Covenant may be interpreted as implying for any State, group or person any right to engage in any activity or perform any act aimed at the destruction of any of the rights and freedoms recognized herein or at their limitation to a greater extent than is provided for in the present Covenant.

2. There shall be no restriction upon or derogation from any fundamental human rights recognized or existing in any State Party to the present Covenant pursuant to law, conventions, regulations or custom pretext that the present Covenant does not recognize such rights or recognizes them to a lesser extent.

PART III

Article 6

1. Every human being has the inherent right to life. This right shall be protected by law. No one shall be arbitrarily deprived of his life.

2. In countries which have not abolished the death penalty, sentence of death may be imposed only for the most serious crimes in accordance with the law in force at the time of the commission of the crime and not contrary to the provisions of the present Covenant and to the Convention on the Prevention and Punishment of the Crime of Genocide. This penalty can only be carried out pursuant to a final judgment rendered by a competent court.

3. When deprivation of life constitutes the crime of genocide, it is understood that nothing in this article shall authorize any State Party to the present Covenant to derogate in any way from any obligation assumed under the provisions of the Convention on the Prevention and Punishment of the Crime of Genocide.

4. Anyone sentenced to death shall have the right to seek pardon or commutation of the sentence. Amnesty, pardon or commutation of the sentence of death may be granted in all cases.

5. Sentence of death shall not be imposed for crimes committed by persons below eighteen years of age and shall not be carried out on pregnant women.

6. Nothing in this article shall be invoked to delay or to prevent the abolition of capital punishment by any State Party to the present Covenant.

Article 7

No one shall be subjected to torture or to cruel, inhuman or degrading treatment or punishment. In particular, no one shall be subjected without his free consent to medical or scientific experimentation.

Article 8

1. No one shall be held in slavery; slavery and the slave-trade in all their forms shall be prohibited.

2. No one shall be held in servitude.

3. (a) No one shall be required to perform forced or compulsory labour;

   (b) Paragraph 3 (a) shall not be held to preclude, in countries where imprisonment with hard labour may be imposed as a punishment for a crime, the performance of hard labour in pursuance of a sentence to such punishment by a competent court;

   (c) For the purpose of this paragraph the term "forced or compulsory labour" shall not include:

      (i) Any work or service, not referred to in subparagraph (b), normally required of a person who is under detention in consequence of a lawful order of a court, or of a person during conditional release from such detention;

      (ii) Any service of a military character and, in countries where conscientious objection is recognized, any national service required by law of conscientious objectors;

      (iii) Any service exacted in cases of emergency or calamity threatening the life or well-being of the community;

      (iv) Any work or service which forms part of normal civil obligations.

Article 9

1. Everyone has the right to liberty and security of person. No one shall be subjected to arbitrary arrest or detention. No one shall be deprived of his liberty except on such grounds and in accordance with such procedures as are established by law.

2. Anyone who is arrested shall be informed, at the time of arrest, of the reasons for his arrest and shall be promptly informed of any charges against him.

3. Anyone arrested or detained on a criminal charge shall be brought promptly before a judge or other officer authorized by law to exercise judicial power and shall be entitled to trial within a reasonable time or to release. It shall not be the general rule that persons awaiting trial shall be detained in custody, but release may be subject to guarantees to appear for trial, at any other stage of the judicial proceedings, and, should occasion arise, for execution of the judgment.

4. Anyone who is deprived of his liberty by arrest or detention shall be entitled to take proceedings before a court, in order that that court may decide without delay on the lawfulness of his detention and order his release if the detention is not lawful.

5. Anyone who has been victim of unlawful arrest or detention shall have an enforceable right to compensation.

Article 10

1. All persons deprived of their liberty shall be treated with humanity and with respect for the inherent dignity of the human person.

2. (a) Accused persons shall, save in exceptional circumstances, be segregated from convicted persons and shall be subject to separate treatment appropriate to their status as unconvicted persons;

   (b) Accused juvenile persons shall be separated from adults and brought as speedily as possible for adjudication.

3. The penitentiary system shall comprise treatment of prisoners the essential aim of which shall be their reformation and social rehabilitation. Juvenile offenders shall be segregated from adults and be accorded treatment appropriate to their age and legal status.

Article 11

No one shall be imprisoned merely on the ground of inability to fulfill a contractual obligation.

Article 12

1. Everyone lawfully within the territory of a State shall, within that territory, have the right to liberty of movement and freedom to choose his residence.

2. Everyone shall be free to leave any country, including his own.

3. The above-mentioned rights shall not be subject to any restrictions except those which are provided by law, are necessary to protect national security, public order (*ordre public*), public health or morals or the rights and freedoms of others, and are consistent with the other rights recognized in the present Covenant.

4. No one shall be arbitrarily deprived of the right to enter his own country.

Article 13

An alien lawfully in the territory of a State Party to the present Covenant may be expelled therefrom only in pursuance of a decision reached in accordance with law and shall, except w ıere compelling reasons of national security otherwise require, be allowed to submit the reasons against his expulsion and to have his case reviewed by, and be represented for the purpose before the competent authority or a person or persons especially designated by the competent authority.

Article 14

1. All persons shall be equal before the courts and tribunals. In the determination of any criminal charge against him, or of his rights and obligations in a suit at law, everyone shall be entitled to a fair and public hearing by a competent, independent and impartial tribunal established by law. The Press and the public may be excluded from all or part of a trial for reasons of morals, public order (*ordre public*) or national security in a democratic society, or when the interest of the private lives of the parties so requires, or to the extent strictly necessary in the opinion of the court in special circumstances where publicity would prejudice the interests of justice; but any judgment rendered in a criminal case or in a suit at law shall be made public except where the interest of juvenile persons otherwise requires or the proceedings concern matrimonial disputes of the guardianship of children.

2. Everyone charged with a criminal offence shall have the right to be presumed innocent until proved guilty according to law.

3. In the determination of any criminal charge against him, everyone shall be entitled to the following minimum guarantees, in full equality:

    (a) To be informed promptly and in detail in a language which he understands of the nature and cause of the charge against him;
    (b) To have adequate time and facilities for the preparation of his defence and to communicate with counsel of his own choosing;
    (c) To be tried without undue delay;
    (d) To be tried in his presence, and to defend himself in person or through legal assistance of his own choosing; to be informed, if he does not have legal assistance, of this right; and to have legal assistance assigned to him, in any case where the interests of justice so require, and without payment by him in any such case if he does not have sufficient means to pay for it;
    (e) To examine, or have examined, the witnesses against him and to obtain the attendance and examination of witnesses on his behalf under the same conditions as witnesses against him;
    (f) To have the free assistance of an interpreter if he cannot understand or speak the language used in court;
    (g) Not to be compelled to testify against himself or to confess guilt.

4. In the case of juvenile persons, the procedure shall be such as will take account of their age and the desirability of promoting their rehabilitation.

5. Everyone convicted of a crime shall have the right to his conviction and sentence being reviewed by a higher tribunal according to law.

6. When a person has by a final decision been convicted of a criminal offence and when subsequently his conviction has been reversed or he has been pardoned on the ground that a new or newly discovered fact shows conclusively that there has been a miscarriage of justice, the person who has suffered punishment as a result of such conviction shall be compensated according to law, unless it is proved that the non-disclosure of the unknown fact in time is wholly or partly attributable to him.

7. No one shall be liable to be tried or punished again for an offence for which he has already been finally convicted or acquitted in accordance with the law and penal procedure of each country.

Article 15

1. No one shall be held guilty of any criminal offence on account of any act or omission which did not constitute a criminal offence, under national or international law, at the time when it was committed. Nor shall a heavier penalty be imposed than the one that was applicable at the time when the criminal offence was committed. If, subsequent to the commission of the offence, provision is made by law for the imposition of the lighter penalty, the offender shall benefit thereby.

2. Nothing in this article shall prejudice the trial and punishment of any person for any act or omission which, at the time when it was committed, was criminal according to the general principles of law recognized by the community of nations.

Article 16

Everyone shall have the right to recognition everywhere as a person before the law.

Article 17

1. No one shall be subjected to arbitrary or unlawful interference with his privacy, family, home or correspondence, nor to unlawful attacks on his honour and reputation.

2. Everyone has the right to the protection of the law against such interference or attacks.

Article 18

1. Everyone shall have the right to freedom of thought, conscience and religion. This right shall include freedom to have or to adopt a religion or belief of his choice, and freedom, either individually or in community with others and in public or private, to manifest his religion or belief in worship, observance, practice and teaching.

2. No one shall be subject to coercion which would impair his freedom to have or to adopt a religion or belief of his choice.

3. Freedom to manifest one's religion or beliefs may be subject only to such limitations as are prescribed by law and are necessary to protect public safety, order, health, or morals or the fundamental rights and freedoms of others.

4. The States Parties to the present Covenant undertake to have respect for the liberty of parents and, when applicable, legal guardians to ensure the religious and moral education of their children in conformity with their own convictions.

Article 19

1. Everyone shall have the right to hold opinions without interference.

2. Everyone shall have the right to freedom of expression; this right shall include freedom to seek, receive and impart information and ideas of all kinds, regardless of frontiers, either orally, in writing or in print, in the form of art, or through any other media of his choice.

3. The exercise of the rights provided for in paragraph 2 of this article carries with it special duties and responsibilities. It may therefore be subject to certain restrictions, but these shall only be such as are provided by law and are necessary:

    (a) For respect of the rights or reputations of others;

    (b) For the protection of national security or of public order (*ordre public*), or of public health or morals.

Article 20

1. Any propaganda for war shall be prohibited by law.

2. Any advocacy of national, racial or religious hatred that constitutes incitement to discrimination, hostility or violence shall be prohibited by law.

Article 21

The right of peaceful assembly shall be recognized. No restrictions may be placed on the exercise of this right other than those imposed in conformity with the law and which are necessary in a democratic society in the interests of national security or public safety, public order (*ordre public*), the protection of public health or morals or the protection of the rights and freedoms of others.

Article 22

1. Everyone shall have the right to freedom of association with others, including the right to form and join trade unions for the protection of his interests.

2. No restrictions may be placed on the exercise of this right other than those which are prescribed by law and which are necessary in a democratic society in the interests of national security or public safety, public order (*ordre public*), the protection of public health or morals or the protection of the rights and freedoms of others. This article shall not prevent the imposition of lawful restrictions on members of the armed forces and of the police in their exercise of this right.

3. Nothing in this article shall authorize States Parties to the International Labour Organization Convention of 1948 concerning Freedom of Association and Protection of the Right to Organize to take legislative measures which would prejudice, or to apply the law in such a manner as to prejudice the guarantees provided for in that Convention.

Article 23

1. The family is the natural and fundamental group unit of society and is entitled to protection by society and the State.

2. The right of men and women of marriageable age to marry and to found a family shall be recognized.

3. No marriage shall be entered into without the free and full consent of the intending spouses.

4. States Parties to the present Covenant shall take appropriate steps to ensure equality of rights and responsibilities of spouses as to marriage, during marriage and at its dissolution. In the case of dissolution, provision shall be made for the necessary protection of any children.

Article 24

1. Every child shall have, without any discrimination as to race, colour, sex, language, religion, national or social origin, property or birth, the right to such measures of protection as are required by his status as a minor, on the part of his family, society and the State.

2. Every child shall be registered immediately after birth and shall have a name.

3. Every child has the right to acquire a nationality.

Article 25

Every citizen shall have the right and the opportunity, without any of the distinctions mentioned in article 2 and without unreasonable restrictions:

(a) To take part in the conduct of public affairs, directly or through freely chosen representatives;

(b) To vote and to be elected at genuine periodic elections which shall be by universal and equal suffrage and shall be held by secret ballot, guaranteeing the free expression of the will of the electors;

(c) To have access, on general terms of equality, to public service in his country.

Article 26

All persons are equal before the law and are entitled without any discrimination to the equal protection of the law. In this respect, the law shall prohibit any discrimination and guarantee to all persons equal and effective protection against discrimination on any ground such as race, colour, sex, language, religion, political or other opinion, national or social origin, property, birth or other status.

Article 27

In those States in which ethnic, religious or linguistic minorities exist, persons belonging to such minorities shall not be denied the right, in community with the other members of their group, to enjoy their own culture, to profess and practice their own religion, or to use their own language.

PART IV

Article 28

1. There shall be established a Human Rights Committee (hereafter referred to in the present Covenant as the Committee). It shall consist of eighteen members and shall carry out the functions hereinafter provided.

2. The Committee shall be composed of nationals of the States Parties to the present Covenant who shall be persons of high moral character and recognized competence in the field of human rights, consideration being given to the usefulness of the participation of some persons having legal experience.

3. The members of the Committee shall be elected and shall serve in their personal capacity.

Article 29

1. The members of the Committee shall be elected by secret ballot from a list of persons possessing the qualifications prescribed in article 28 and nominated for the purpose by the States Parties to the present Covenant.

2. Each State Party to the present Covenant may nominate not more than two persons. These persons shall be nationals of the nominating State.

3. A person shall be eligible for renomination.

Article 30

4. Election of the members of the Committee shal be held at a meeting of the parties to the present Covenant . . .

Article 31

1. The Committee may not include more than one national of the same State.

2. In the election of the Committee, consideration shall be given to equitable geographical distribution of membership and to the representation of the different forms of civilization and of the principal legal systems.

* * *

Article 40

1. The States Parties to the present Covenant undertake to submit reports on the measures they have adopted which give effect to the rights recognized herein and on the progress made in the enjoyment of those rights:

   (a) Within one year of the entry into force of the present Covenant for the States Parties concerned;

   (b) Thereafter whenever the Committee so requests.

2. All reports shall be submitted to the Secretary-General of the United Nations, who shall transmit them to the Committee for consideration. Reports shall indicate the factors and difficulties, if any, affecting the implementation of the present Covenant.

3. The Secretary-General of the United Nations may, after consultation with the Committee, transmit to the specialized agencies concerned copies of such parts of the reports as may fall within their field of competence.

4. The Committee shall study the reports submitted by the States Parties to the present Covenant. It shall transmit its reports, and such general comments as it may consider appropriate, to the States Parties. The Committee may also transmit to the Economic and Social Council these comments along with the copies of the reports it has received from States Parties to the present Covenant.

5. The States Parties to the present Covenant may submit to the Committee observations on any comments that may be made in accordance with paragraph 4 of this article.

Article 41

1. A State Party to the present Covenant may at any time declare under this article that it recognizes the competence of the Committee to receive and consider communications to the effect that a State Party claims that another State Party is not fulfilling its obligations under the present Covenant. Communications under this article may be received and considered only if submitted by a State Party which has made a declaration recognizing in regard to itself the competence of the Committee. No communication shall be received by the Committee if it concerns a State Party which has not made such a declaration. Communications received under this article shall be dealt with in accordance with the following procedure:

   (a) If a State Party to the present Covenant considers that another State Party is not giving effect to the provisions of the present Covenant, it may, by written communication, bring the matter to the attention of that State Party. Within three months after the receipt of the communication the receiving State shall afford the State which sent the communication an explanation, or any other statement in writing clarifying the matter which should include, to the extent possible and pertinent, reference to domestic procedures and remedies taken, pending, or available in the matter.

   (b) If the matter is not adjusted to the satisfaction of both States Parties concerned within six months after the receipt by the receiving State of the initial communication, either State shall have the right to refer the matter to the Committee, by notice given to the Committee and to the other State.

(c) The Committee shall deal with a matter referred to it only after it has ascertained that all available domestic remedies have been invoked and exhausted in the matter, in conformity with the generally recognized principles of international law. This shall not be the rule where the application of the remedies is unreasonably prolonged.

(d) The Committee shall hold closed meetings when examining communications under this article.

(e) Subject to the provisions of sub-paragraph (c), the Committee shall make available its good offices to the States Parties concerned with a view to a friendly solution of the matter on the basis of respect for human rights and fundamental freedoms as recognized in the present Covenant.

(f) In any matter referred to it, the Committee may call upon the States Parties concerned, referred to in sub-paragraph (b), to supply any relevant information.

(g) The States Parties concerned, referred to in sub-paragraph (b), shall have the right to be represented when the matter is being considered in the Committee and to make submissions orally and/or in writing.

(h) The Committee shall, within twelve months after the date of receipt of notice under sub-paragraph (b), submit a report:

　(i) If a solution within the terms of sub-paragraph (e) is reached, the Committee shall confine its report to a brief statement of the facts and of the solution reached;

　(ii) If a solution within the terms of sub-paragraph (e) is not reached, the Committee shall confine its report to a brief statement of the facts; the written submissions and record of the oral submissions made by the States Parties concerned shall be attached to the report.

In every matter, the report shall be communicated to the States Parties concerned.

* * *

Article 42

1. (a) If a matter referred to the Committee in accordance with article 41 is not resolved to the satisfaction of the States Parties concerned, the Committee may, with the prior consent of the States Parties concerned, appoint an *ad hoc* Conciliation Commission (hereinafter referred to as the Commission). The good offices of the Commission shall be made available to the States Parties concerned with a view to an amicable solution of the matter on the basis of respect for the present Covenant;

(b) The Commission shall consist of five persons acceptable to the States Parties concerned. If the States Parties concerned fail to reach agreement within three months on all or part of the composition of the Commission, the members of the Commission concerning whom no agreement has been reached shall be elected by secret ballot by a two-thirds majority vote of the Committee from among its members.

2. The members of the Commission shall serve in their personal capacity. They shall not be nationals of the States Parties concerned, or of a State not party to the present Covenant, or of a State Party which has not made a declaration under article 41.

* * *

7. When the Commission has fully considered the matter, but in any event not later than twelve months after having been seized of the matter, it shall submit to the Chairman of the Committee a report for communication to the States Parties concerned:

(a) If the Commission is unable to complete its consideration of the matter within twelve months, it shall confine its report to a brief statement of the status of its consideration of the matter;

(b) If an amicable solution to the matter on the basis of respect for human rights as recognized in the present Covenant is reached, the Commission shall confine its report to a brief statement of the facts and of the solution reached;

(c) If a solution within the terms of sub-paragraph (b) is not reached, the Commission's report shall embody its findings on all questions of fact relevant to the issues between the States Parties concerned, and its views on the possibilities of an amicable solution of the matter. This report shall also contain the written submissions and a record of the oral submissions made by the States Parties concerned;

(d) If the Commission's report is submitted under sub-paragraph (c), the States Parties concerned shall, within three months of the receipt of the report, notify the Chairman of the Committee whether or not they accept the contents of the report of the Commission.

8. The provisions of this article are without prejudice to the responsibilities of the Committee under article 41.

* * *

Article 44

The provisions for the implementation of the present Covenant shall apply without prejudice to the procedures prescribed in the field of human rights by or under the constituent instruments and the conventions of the United Nations and of the specialized agencies and shall not prevent the States Parties to the present Covenant from having recourse to other procedures for settling a dispute in accordance with general or special international agreements in force between them.

Article 45

The Committee shall submit to the General Assembly of the United Nations, through the Economic and Social Council, an annual report on its activities.

PART V

* * *

Article 47

Nothing in the present Covenant shall be interpreted as impairing the inherent right of all peoples to enjoy and utilize fully and freely their natural wealth and resources.

PART VI

* * *

Article 50

The provisions of the present Covenant shall extend to all parts of federal States without any limitations or exceptions.

Article 51

1. Any State Party to the present Covenant may propose an amendment and file it with the Secretary-General of the United Nations. The Secretary-General of the United Nations shall thereupon communicate any proposed amendments to the States Parties to the present Covenant with a request that they notify him whether they favour a conference of States Parties for the purpose of considering and voting upon the proposals. In the event that at least one third of the States Parties favours such a conference, the Secretary-General shall convene the conference under the auspices of the United Nations. Any amendment adopted by a majority of the States Parties present and voting at the conference shall be submitted to the General Assembly of the United Nations for approval.

2. Amendments shall come into force when they have been approved by the General Assembly of the United Nations and accepted by a two-thirds majority of the States Parties to the present Covenant in accordance with their respective constitutional processes.

3. When amendments come into force, they shall be binding on those States Parties which have accepted them, other States Parties still being bound by the provisions of the present Covenant and any earlier amendment which they have accepted.

Appendix E

Establishment Treaty

CONVENTION OF ESTABLISHMENT
BETWEEN THE UNITED STATES AND FRANCE

[Entered into force December 21, 1960. Signed at Paris, November 25, 1959. 11 U.S.T. & O.I.A. 2398, T.I.A.S. No. 4625.]

The President of the United States of America and the President of the French Republic, President of the Community, desirous of strengthening the ties of peace and friendship traditionally existing between the two countries and of encouraging closer economic intercourse between their peoples, conscious of the contribution which may be made to these ends by arrangements that provide in each country reciprocal rights and privileges on behalf of nationals and companies of the other country, thus encouraging mutually advantageous investments and mutually beneficial commercial relations, have resolved to conclude a convention of establishment. . . .

ARTICLE I

Each High Contracting Party shall accord equitable treatment to nationals and companies of the other High Contracting Party, both as to their persons and as to their property, enterprises and other interests, and shall assure them within its territories full legal and judicial protection.

ARTICLE II

1. Nationals of either High Contracting Party shall, subject to the laws relating to the entry and sojourn of aliens, be permitted to enter the territories of the other High Contracting Party, to travel therein freely, and to reside therein at places of their choice. They shall in particular be permitted to enter the territories of the other High Contracting Party and to remain therein, for the purpose of:

(a) carrying on trade between the territories of the two High Contracting Parties and engaging in related commercial activities;

(b) developing and directing the operations of an enterprise in which they have invested, or in which they are actively in the process of investing, a substantial amount of capital.

2. Nationals of each High Contracting Party shall enjoy, within the territories of the other High Contracting Party, freedom of conscience, of worship, of information and of the press.

3. The provisions of the present Article shall be subject to the right of either High Contracting Party to take measures that are necessary for the maintenance of public order and for the protection of public health, morals, and safety.

ARTICLE III

1. Nationals and companies of either High Contracting Party shall be accorded national treatment with respect to access to the courts of justice as well as to administrative tribunals and agencies, within the territories of the other High Contracting Party, in all degrees of jurisdiction, both in pursuit and in defense of their rights. Companies of either High Contracting Party not engaged in activities within the territories of the other High Contracting Party shall enjoy such access therein without any requirement of registration. Nationals of either High Contracting Party shall be accorded the benefits of legal aid within the territories of the other High Contracting Party under the same conditions as its own nationals.

2. Contracts entered into between nationals and companies of either High Contracting Party and nationals and companies of the other High Contracting Party, that provide for the settlement by arbitration of controversies, shall not be deemed unenforceable within the territories of such other High Contracting Party merely on the grounds that the place designated for the arbitration proceedings is outside such territories or that the nationality of one or more of the arbitrators is not that of such other High Contracting Party. No award duly rendered pursuant to any such contract, and final and enforceable under the laws of the place where rendered, shall be deemed invalid or denied effective means of enforcement within the territories of either High Contracting Party merely on the grounds that the place where such award was rendered is outside such territories or that the nationality of one or more of the arbitrators is not that of such High Contracting Party.

ARTICLE IV

1. The lawfully acquired rights and interests of nationals and companies of either High Contracting Party shall not be subjected to impairment, within the territories of the other High Contracting Party, by any measure of a discriminatory character.

2. The dwellings, offices, warehouses, factories and other premises of nationals and companies of either High Contracting Party located within the territories of the other High Contracting Party shall be free from molestation and other unjustifiable measures. Official searches conducted on such premises, when necessary, shall be carried out in conformity with the law and with every consideration for the convenience of the occupants and the conduct of business.

3. Property of nationals and companies of either High Contracting Party shall not be expropriated within the territories of the other High Contracting Party except for a public purpose and with payment of a just compensation. Such compensation shall represent the equivalent of the property taken; it shall be accorded in an effectively realizable form and without needless delay. Adequate provision for the determination and payment of the said compensation must have been made no later than the time of the taking.

4. Nationals and companies of either High Contracting Party shall in no case be accorded, within the territories of the other High Contracting Party, less than national treatment with respect to the matters set forth in paragraphs 2 and 3 of the present Article.

ARTICLE V

1. Nationals and companies of either High Contracting Party shall be accorded national treatment with respect to engaging in all types of commercial, industrial, financial and other activities for gain within the territories of the other High Contracting Party, whether directly or through the intermediary of an agent or of any other natural or juridical person. Accordingly, such nationals and companies shall be permitted within such territories:

(a) to establish and to maintain branches, agencies, offices, factories and other establishments appropriate to the conduct of their business;

(b) to organize companies under the general company laws of such other High Contracting Party, and to acquire majority interests in companies of such other High Contracting Party;

(c) to control and manage the enterprises which they have established or acquired.

Moreover, the enterprises which they control, whether in the form of an individual proprietorship, of a company or otherwise, shall, in all that relates to the conduct of the activities thereof, be accorded treatment no less favorable than that accorded like enterprises controlled by nationals and companies of such other High Contracting Party.

2. Each High Contracting Party reserves the right to determine the extent to which aliens may, within its territories, create, control, manage or acquire interests in, enterprises engaged in communications, air or water transport, banking involving depository or fiduciary functions, exploitation of the soil or other natural resources, and the production of electricity.

3. Each High Contracting Party undertakes not to intensify, within its territories, existing limitations as regards enterprises belonging to or controlled by nationals and companies of the other High Contracting Party which are already engaged in the activities cited in the preceding paragraph. Moreover, each High Contracting Party shall permit, within its territories, transportation, communications and banking companies of the other High Contracting Party to maintain branches and agencies, in conformity with the laws in force, which are necessary to the operations of an essentially international character in which they are engaged.

ARTICLE VI

1. Nationals and companies of either High Contracting Party shall be permitted to engage, at their choice, within the territories of the other High Contracting Party, accountants and other technical experts, lawyers, and personnel who by reason of their special capacities are essential to the functioning of the enterprise. But these persons must fulfill the conditions necessary to the exercise of their calling under the applicable legislation.

2. In any event, such nationals and companies shall be permitted to engage accountants and other technical experts, who are not nationals of the other High Contracting Party, without regard to their having qualified to practice a profession within the territories of such other High Contracting Party, but exclusively for conducting studies and examinations for internal purposes on behalf of such nationals and companies.

ARTICLE VII

1. Nationals and companies of either High Contracting Party shall be accorded, within the territories of the other High Contracting Party, national treatment with respect to leasing, utilizing and occupying real property of all kinds appropriate to the exercise of the rights accorded them by the other Articles of the present Convention. They shall also be accorded therein, as regards the acquisition and possession of real property, all other rights to which aliens and alien companies are entitled under the legislation of such other High Contracting Party, each High Contracting Party reserving the right to invoke reciprocity in this respect.

2. Nationals and companies of either High Contracting Party shall be accorded, within the territories of the other High Contracting Party, national treatment with respect to leasing and acquiring, by purchase or otherwise, as well as with respect to possessing, personal property of every kind, whether tangible or intangible, with the exception of ships. However, either High Contracting Party may impose restrictions on alien ownership of materials dangerous from the viewpoint of public safety and alien ownership of interests in enterprises carrying on particular types of activity, but only to the extent compatible with the enjoyment of the rights and privileges defined in Article V or provided by other provisions of the present Convention.

3. Nationals and companies of either High Contracting Party shall be accorded within the territories of the other High Contracting Party national treatment with respect to the right to dispose of property of all kinds.

ARTICLE VIII

1. Nationals and companies of either High Contracting Party shall be accorded, within the territories of the other High Contracting Party, national treatment with respect to obtaining and maintaining patents or invention and with respect to rights appertaining to trademarks, trade names and certification marks, or which in any manner relate to industrial property.

2. The High Contracting Parties undertake to cooperate with a view to furthering the interchange and use of scientific and technical knowledge, particularly in the interest of increasing productivity and improving standards of living within their respective territories.

ARTICLE IX

1. The following categories:

(a) nationals of either High Contracting Party residing within the territories of the other High Contracting Party,

(b) nationals of either High Contracting Party not residing within the territories of the other High Contracting Party but engaged in trade or other gainful pursuit within such territories whether or not through a permanent establishment or a fixed place of business,

(c) companies of either High Contracting Party engaged in trade or other gainful pursuit within the territories of the other High Contracting Party, whether or not through a permanent establishment or a fixed place of business,

(d) associations of either High Contracting Party that are engaged in scientific, educational, religious or philanthropic activities within the territories of the other High Contracting Party, whether through a fixed place of business or otherwise, shall not be subject to any form of taxation or any obligation relating thereto, within the territories of such other High Contracting Party, which is more burdensome than that to which nationals, companies and associations of such other High Contracting Party in the same situation are or may be subject.

2. Nationals, companies and associations of either High Contracting Party, not falling within one of the categories specified in paragraph 1 above, shall not be subject, within the territories of the other High Contracting Party, to any form of taxation or any obligation relating thereto which is more burdensome than that to which nationals, companies and associations of any third country in the same situation are or may be subject.

3. Enterprises of either High Contracting Party, the capital of which is owned or controlled in whole or in part, directly or indirectly, by one or more nationals of the other High Contracting Party, shall not be subject in the first High Contracting Party to any form of taxation or any obligation relating thereto which is more burdensome than that to which other like enterprises of the first High Contracting Party are or may be subject.

4. The nationals, companies and associations of either High Contracting Party referred to in paragraph 1(b), (c), and (d) of the present Article shall not be subject, within the territories of the other High Contracting Party, to any form of taxation upon capital, income, profits, or any other basis, except by reason of the property which they possess within those territories, the income and profits derived from sources therein, the business in which they are there engaged, the transactions which they accomplish there, or any other bases of taxation directly related to their activities within those territories.

5. The term "form of taxation," as used in the present Article, includes all taxes of whatever nature or denomination.

6. Each High Contracting Party reserves the right to:

(a) extend to the nationals, companies and associations of third countries, specific tax advantages on the basis of reciprocity;

(b) accord special tax advantages by virtue of agreements with third countries for the avoidance of double taxation;

(c) apply special provisions in allowing, to non-residents, exemptions of a personal nature in connection with income and inheritance taxes;

(d) extend special advantages to its own nationals and residents in connection with joint returns by husband and wife.

7. The foregoing provisions shall not prevent the levying, in appropriate cases, of fees relating to the accomplishment of police and other formalities, if these fees are also levied on other foreigners. The rates for such fees shall not exceed those charged the nationals of any other country.

ARTICLE X

1. Nationals and companies of either High Contracting Party shall be accorded by the other High Contracting Party the same treatment as nationals and companies of such other High Contracting Party in like situations, with respect to payments, remittances and transfers of funds or financial instruments between the territories of the two High Contracting Parties as well as between the territories of such other High Contracting Party and any third country. This treatment shall be not less favorable than that accorded to nationals and companies of any third country in like situations.

2. Neither High Contracting Party shall impose exchange restrictions as defined in paragraph 5 of the present Article except to the extent necessary to prevent its monetary reserves from falling to a very low level or to effect a moderate increase in very low monetary reserves. The provisions of the present Article do not alter the obligations either High Contracting Party may have to the International Monetary Fund or preclude imposition of particular restrictions whenever the Fund specifically authorizes or requests a High Contracting Party to impose such restrictions.

3. The two High Contracting Parties, recognizing that the freedom of movement of investment capital and of the returns thereon would be conducive to the realization of the objectives of the present Convention, are agreed that such movements shall not be unnecessarily hampered. In this spirit, each High Contracting Party will make every effort to accord, in the greatest possible measure, to nationals and companies of the other High Contracting Party the opportunity to make investments and to repatriate the proceeds of the liquidation thereof. This principle shall apply also to the compensation referred to in Article IV, paragraph 3, of the present Convention. Each High Contracting Party shall make reasonable provision for the withdrawal of earnings from investments, whether in the form of salaries, dividends, interest, commissions, royalties, payments for technical services, or payments for other current transactions relative to investments. If more than one rate of exchange is in force, the rate applicable to such withdrawals shall be a rate which is specifically approved by the International Monetary Fund for such transactions or, in the absence of a rate so approved, a rate which, inclusive of any taxes or surcharges on exchange transfers, is just and reasonable.

4. Exchange restrictions shall not be imposed by either High Contracting Party in a manner unnecessarily detrimental or arbitrarily discriminatory to the claims, investments, transport, trade, and other interests of the nationals and companies of the other High Contracting Party, nor to the competitive position thereof.

5. The term "exchange restrictions" as used in the present Article includes all restrictions, charges and taxes, regulations, or other requirements imposed by either High Contracting Party which burden or interfere with payments, remittances, or transfers of funds or of financial instruments between the territories of the two High Contracting Parties.

ARTICLE XI

Each High Contracting Party will take the measures it deems appropriate with a view to preventing commercial practices or arrangements, whether effected by one or more private or public commercial enterprises, which restrain competition, limit access to markets or foster monopolistic control, whenever such practices or arrangements have or might have harmful effects on trade between the two countries.

ARTICLE XII

The provisions of the present Convention shall not preclude the application of measures:

(a) regulating the importation and exportation of gold and silver;

(b) regarding fissionable materials, the radio-active by-products of the utilization or manufacture of such materials, or raw materials which are the source of fissionable materials;

(c) regulating the manufacture of and traffic in arms, munitions and implements of war, as well as traffic in other materials carried on directly or indirectly for the purpose of supplying military establishments;

(d) necessary to fulfill the obligations of a High Contracting Party for the maintenance or restoration of international peace and security, or necessary to protect its essential security interests.

ARTICLE XIII

The High Contracting Parties may deny to any company, in the ownership or direction of which nationals of a third country or countries have directly or indirectly a controlling interest, the advantages of the present Convention, except with respect to recognition of juridical status and access to the courts.

ARTICLE XIV

1. The term "national treatment" means treatment accorded to nationals and companies of either High Contracting Party within the territories of the other High Contracting Party upon terms no less favorable than the treatment therein accorded, in like situations, to the nationals and companies, as the case may be, of such other High Contracting Party.

2. National treatment accorded under the provisions of the present Convention to French companies shall, in any State, territory or possession of the United States of America, be the treatment accorded therein to companies constituted in other States, territories and possessions of the United States of America.

3. As used in the present Convention, the term "nationals" ("ressortissants") means natural persons having the nationality of a High Contracting Party and not domiciled in a non-metropolitan territory thereof to which the present Convention does not extend.

4. As used in the present Convention, the term "companies" ("sociétés") means:

(a) as concerns the United States of America, corporations, partnerships, limited liability companies, and other entities having legal personality, whether or not with limited liability, but for pecuniary profit;

(b) as concerns France, "sociétés civiles," "sociétés en nom collectif," "associations en participation," "sociétés en commandite simple," "sociétés en commandite par actions," "sociétés anonymes," "sociétés à responsabilite limitée" and, in general, entities having legal personality for pecuniary profit.

5. Companies constituted under the applicable laws and regulations within the territories of either High Contracting Party shall be deemed companies thereof and shall have their juridical status recognized within the territories of the other High Contracting Party.

6. Non-profit associations lawfully constituted within the territories of either High Contracting Party shall have their juridical status recognized by the other High Contracting Party and shall, *inter alia*, be accorded within the territories thereof the rights provided in Article III, paragraph 1, of the present Convention.

ARTICLE XV

1. The present Convention shall apply:

(a) As concerns the United States of America, to all territories under the sovereignty or authority thereof, other than the Panama Canal Zone and the Trust Territory of the Pacific Islands;

(b) As concerns the French Republic, to the metropolitan departments, the Algerian departments, the departments of The Oasis and Saoura, the departments of Martinique, Guadaloupe, Guiana and Reunion.

2. The present Convention may be made applicable, by virtue of exchanges of notes between the Governments of the High Contracting Parties, to the Overseas Territories of the French Republic or to one or several such Territories, under the conditions fixed, in each case, in the said exchanges of notes.

3. The present Convention may be made applicable, in the same manner, to the member States of the Community or to one or several such States.

ARTICLE XVI

1. Each High Contracting Party shall accord sympathetic consideration to such representations as the other High Contracting Party may make with respect to any question affecting the application of the present Convention, and shall afford opportunity for an exchange of views relative thereto.

2. Any dispute between the High Contracting Parties as to the interpretation or application of the present Convention, not satisfactorily adjusted by diplomacy, shall be submitted to the International Court of Justice, unless the High Contracting Parties agree to settlement by some other pacific means.

ARTICLE XVII

The entry into force of the present Convention shall terminate the Trademark Convention signed at Washington April 16, 1869.

ARTICLE XVIII

1. The present Convention shall be ratified. It will enter into force one month after the exchange of the instruments of ratification, which will take place at Washington.

2. The present Convention shall have an initial term of ten years. It shall remain in force thereafter until either High Contracting Party terminates it by giving to the other High Contracting Party a written notice one year in advance.

IN WITNESS WHEREOF the respective Plenipotentiaries have signed the present Convention and have hereunto affixed their seals.

DONE in duplicate, in the English and French languages, both equally authentic, at Paris, this twenty-fifth day of November, one thousand nine hundred fifty-nine.

AMORY HOUGHTON
[seal]

M COUVE DE MURVILLE
[seal]

PROTOCOL

The undersigned Plenipotentiaries, duly authorized by their respective Governments, are further agreed on the following provisions, which shall form an integral part of the Convention of Establishment between the United States of America and France dated the twenty-fifth of November, one thousand nine hundred fifty-nine.

1. (a) The protection provided in Article I engages the competent authorities of each High Contracting Party to inform immediately the consuls of the other High Contracting Party of the arrest or detention of any of its nationals, if the latter so requests. The consul may then be authorized to visit such national, in conformity with the regulations of the institution of detention, and to confer with him. The competent authority will assure the transmission to the consul of all correspondence directed to him by such national.

   (b) Such national shall have the right to all guaranties provided in the laws of the High Contracting Party within the territories of which he is detained, and which assure accused persons of humane treatment, the right to be informed immediately of the accusations against them, to be defended by an attorney of their choice, and to be judged as rapidly as possible.

2. (a) Notwithstanding the provisions of the present Convention, the laws and regulations in force within the territories of either High Contracting Party which govern the access of aliens to the professions and occupations, as well as the exercise of such callings and other activities by them, remain applicable as concerns nationals and companies of the other High Contracting Party.

(b) However, the procedures provided for by the above-mentioned laws and regulations, as well as those provided for by the laws and regulations governing the entry and sojourn of aliens, must not have the effect of impairing the substance of the rights set forth in Article II, paragraph 1(a) and (b).

(c) The provisions of Article II, paragraph 1(b), shall be construed as extending to nationals of either High Contracting Party proceeding to the territories of the other High Contracting Party for the purpose of occupying a position of responsibility in an enterprise on behalf of nationals and companies of the first High Contracting Party that have invested a substantial amount of capital in such enterprise or that are in the process of making such an investment.

* * *

4. The provisions of the last sentence of Article III, paragraph 2, shall not affect the reservation concerning the place where the award is rendered, made by France in adhering to the Convention of New York of June 10, 1958 for the recognition and execution of foreign arbitral awards.

5. In Article IV, paragraph 3, the term "expropriated . . . for a public purpose" extends *inter alia* to nationalizations.

6. The provisions of Article IV paragraph 3, providing for the payment of compensation, shall extend to interests held directly or indirectly by nationals and companies of either High Contracting Party in property expropriated within the territories of the other High Contracting Party.

7. The provisions of Article V, paragraph 1, shall not impair the laws and regulations in force within the territories of either High Contracting Party which reserve the practice of certain professions to nationals.

* * *

10. The right to invoke reciprocity as provided in Article VII, paragraph 1, shall permit the French Government, taking into account the treatment accorded French nationals and companies in a State, territory or possession of the United States of America, to apply analogous treatment to nationals and companies of the United States of America, respectively domiciled in such State, territory or possession or constituted under its laws.

11. In the event that a French national or company, having acquired real property by testate or intestate succession, should be precluded by reason of alienage from enjoying

rights of ownership in such property in a State, territory or possession of the United States of America, such national or company will be allowed a period of at least five years in which to dispose of it.

* * *

13. The provisions of Article X, paragraph 1, shall not preclude differing treatment from being applied to different currencies, as may be required by the state of the balance of payments of either High Contracting Party.

14. Either High Contracting Party, with a view to protecting its currency or facilitating the servicing of the proceeds of investments and the repatriation of capital, may subject to authorization the making of investments by foreign nationals and companies.

15. The phrase, "in the greatest possible measure," employed in Article X, paragraph 3, shall be understood to refer to the conditions cited in Article X, paragraph 2.

16. Residence criteria may be applied for purposes of determining whether or not nationals and companies of either High Contracting Party are in "like situations" as that term is employed in paragraph 1 of Article XIV and in the other provisions of the present Convention.

JOINT DECLARATION

The two Governments deem it appropriate to clarify, at the moment of proceeding to the signing of the Convention of Establishment between the United States of America and France, the import of the reservations relating, on the one hand, to the enforcement of the laws governing the entry and sojourn of aliens and, on the other hand, to the enforcement of the laws regulating the access of aliens to the professions and occupations.

It is expressly stipulated in the Protocol to the Convention that those reservations shall not impair the substance of the rights granted to the nationals of either High Contracting Party who have invested a substantial amount of capital or are in the process of making such an investment within the territories of the other High Contracting Party, or who proceed thereto for the purpose of engaging in trade between the two High Contracting Parties.

However, the two Governments also have the intention of facilitating, to the greatest possible extent and on a basis of real and effective reciprocity, the establishment of nationals who are not within the above-cited categories and, in particular, of qualified personnel who are indispensable to the conduct of the enterprises created by nationals and companies of either High Contracting Party within the territories of the other High Contracting Party.

Consequently, and in conformity with the spirit which animated the negotiation of the present Convention, the two Governments consider that they should reciprocally exercise the greatest possible liberality consistent with their national laws both with respect to the entry and sojourn of aliens and with respect to their establishment, effective reciprocity being understood by them as pertaining globally to the whole of the two systems of regulation.

The present Declaration shall be annexed to the Convention of Establishment between the United States of America and France dated the twenty-fifth of November, one thousand nine hundred fifty-nine.

Appendix F

Economic, Social, and Cultural Rights

INTERNATIONAL COVENANT ON ECONOMIC, SOCIAL AND CULTURAL RIGHTS

993 U.N.T.S. 3, adopted December 16, 1966.

PREAMBLE

The States Parties to the present Covenant,

* * *

Recognizing that, in accordance with the Universal Declaration of Human Rights, the ideal of free human beings enjoying freedom from fear and want can only be achieved if conditions are created whereby everyone may enjoy his economic, social and cultural rights, as well as his civil and political rights,

* * *

Agree upon the following articles:

PART I

Article 1

1. All peoples have the right of self-determination. By virtue of that right they freely determine their political status and freely pursue their economic, social and cultural development.

2. All peoples may, for their own ends, freely dispose of their natural wealth and resources without prejudice to any obligations arising out of international economic co-operation, based upon the principle of mutual benefit, and international law. In no case may a people be deprived of its own means of subsistence.

3. The States Parties to the present Covenant, including those having responsibility for the administration of Non-Self-Governing and Trust Territories, shall promote the realization of the right of self-determination, and shall respect that right, in conformity with the provisions of the Charter of the United Nations.

PART II

Article 2

1. Each State Party to the present Covenant undertakes to take steps, individually and through international assistance and co-operation, especially economic and technical, to the

maximum of its available resources, with a view to achieving progressively the full realization of the rights recognized in the present Covenant by all appropriate means, including particularly the adoption of legislative measures.

2. The States Parties to the present Covenant undertake to guarantee that the rights enunciated in the present Covenant will be exercised without discrimination of any kind as to race, colour, sex, language, religion, political or other opinion, national or social origin, property, birth or other status.

3. Developing countries, with due regard to human rights and their national economy, may determine to what extent they would guarantee the economic rights recognized in the present Covenant to non-nationals.

Article 3

The States Parties to the present Covenant undertake to ensure the equal right of men and women to the enjoyment of all economic, social and cultural rights set forth in the present Covenant.

Article 4

The States Parties to the present Covenant recognize that, in the enjoyment of those rights provided by the State in conformity with the present Covenant, the State may subject such rights only to such limitations as are determined by law only in so far as this may be compatible with the nature of these rights and solely for the purpose of promoting the general welfare in a democratic society.

* * *

PART III

Article 6

1. The States Parties to the present Covenant recognize the right to work, which includes the right of everyone to the opportunity to gain his living by work which he freely chooses or accepts, and will take appropriate steps to safeguard this right.

2. The steps to be taken by a State Party to the present Covenant to achieve the full realization of this right shall include technical and vocational guidance and training programmes, policies and techniques to achieve steady economic, social and cultural development and full and productive employment under conditions safeguarding fundamental political and economic freedoms to the individual.

Article 7

The States Parties to the present Covenant recognize the right of everyone to the enjoyment of just and favourable conditions of work which ensure, in particular:

(a) Remuneration which provides all workers, as a minimum, with:
  (i) Fair wages and equal remuneration for work of equal value without distinction of any kind, in particular women being guaranteed conditions of work not inferior to those enjoyed by men, with equal pay for equal work;
  (ii) A decent living for themselves and their families in accordance with the provisions of the present Covenant;
(b) Safe and healthy working conditions;
(c) Equal opportunity for everyone to be promoted in his employment to an appropriate higher level, subject to no considerations other than those of seniority and competence;
(d) Rest, leisure and reasonable limitation of working hours and periodic holidays with pay, as well as remuneration for public holidays.

Article 8

1. The States Parties to the present Covenant undertake to ensure:

(a) The right of everyone to form trade unions and join the trade union of his choice, subject only to the rules of the organization concerned, for the promotion and protection of his economic and social interests. No restrictions may be placed on the exercise of this right other than those prescribed by law and which are necessary in a democratic society in the interests of national security or public order or for the protection of the rights and freedoms of others;
(b) The right of trade unions to establish national federations or confederations and the right of the latter to form or join international trade-union organizations;
(c) The right of trade unions to function freely subject to no limitations other than those prescribed by law and which are necessary in a democratic society in the interests of national security or public order or for the protection of the rights and freedoms of others;
(d) The right to strike, provided that it is exercised in conformity with the laws of the particular country,

2. This article shall not prevent the imposition of lawful restrictions on the exercise of these rights by members of the armed forces or of the police or of the administration of the State.

* * *

Article 9

The States Parties to the present Covenant recognize the right of everyone to social security, including social insurance.

Article 10

The States Parties to the present Covenant recognize that:

1. The widest possible protection and assistance should be accorded to the family, which is the natural and fundamental group unit of society, particularly for its establishment and while it is responsible for the care and education of dependent children. Marriage must be entered into with the free consent of the intending spouses.

2. Special protection should be accorded to mothers during a reasonable period before and after childbirth. During such period working mothers should be accorded paid leave or leave with adequate social security benefits.

3. Special measures of protection and assistance should be taken on behalf of all children and young persons without any discrimination for reasons of parentage or other conditions. Children and young persons should be protected from economic and social exploitation. Their employment in work harmful to their morals or health or dangerous to life or likely to hamper their normal development should be punishable by law. States should also set age limits below which the paid employment of child labour should be prohibited and punishable by law.

Article 11

1. The States Parties to the present Covenant recognize the right of everyone to an adequate standard of living for himself and his family, including adequate food, clothing and housing, and to the continuous improvement of living conditions. The States Parties will take appropriate steps to ensure the realization of this right, recognizing to this effect the essential importance of international co-operation based on free consent.

2. The States Parties to the present Covenant, recognizing the fundamental right of everyone to be free from hunger, shall take, individually and through international co-operation, the measures, including specific programmes, which are needed.

(a) To improve methods of production, conservation and distribution of food by making full use of technical and scientific knowledge, by disseminating knowledge of the principles of nutrition and by developing or reforming agrarian systems in such a way as to achieve the most efficient development and utilization of natural resources;

(b) Taking into account the problems of both food-importing and food exporting countries, to ensure an equitable distribution of world food supplies in relation to need.

Article 12

1. The States Parties to the present Covenant recognize the right of everyone to the enjoyment of the highest attainable standard of physical and mental health.

2. The steps to be taken by the States Parties to the present Covenant to achieve the full realization of this right shall include those necessary for:

(a) The provision for the reduction of the stillbirth-rate and of infant mortality and for the healthy development of the child;

(b) The improvement of all aspects of environmental and industrial hygiene;

(c) The prevention, treatment and control of epidemic, endemic, occupational and other diseases;

(d) The creation of conditions which would assure to all medical service and medical attention in the event of sickness.

Article 13

1. The States Parties to the present Covenant recognize the right of everyone to education. They agree that education shall be directed to the full development of the human personality and the sense of its dignity, and shall strengthen the respect for human rights and fundamental freedoms. They further agree that education shall enable all persons to participate effectively in a free society, promote understanding, tolerance and friendship among all nations and all racial, ethnic or religious groups, and further the activities of the United Nations for the maintenance of peace.

2. The States Parties to the present Covenant recognize that, with a view to achieving the full realization of this right:

(a) Primary education shall be compulsory and available free to all;

(b) Secondary education in its different forms, including technical and vocational secondary education, shall be made generally available and accessible to all by every appropriate means, and in particular by the progressive introduction of free education;

(c) Higher education shall be made equally accessible to all, on the basis of capacity, by every appropriate means, and in particular by the progressive introduction of free education;

(d) Fundamental education shall be encouraged or intensified as far as possible for those persons who have not received or completed the whole period of their primary education;

(e) The development of a system of schools at all levels shall be actively pursued, an adequate fellowship system shall be established, and the material conditions of teaching staff shall be continuously improved.

3. The States Parties to the present Covenant undertake to have respect for the liberty of parents and, when applicable, legal guardians to choose for their children schools, other than those established by the public authorities, which conform to such minimum educational standards as may be laid down or approved by the State and to ensure the religious and moral education of their children in conformity with their own convictions.

4. No part of this article shall be construed so as to interfere with the liberty of individuals and bodies to establish and direct educational institutions, subject always to the observance of the principles set forth in paragraph 1 of this article and to the requirement that the education given in such institutions shall conform to such minimum standards as may be laid down by the State.

Article 14

Each State Party to the present Covenant which, at the time of becoming a Party, has not been able to secure in its metropolitan territory or other territories under its jurisdiction compulsory primary education, free of charge, undertakes, within two years, to work out and adopt a detailed plan of action for the progressive implementation, within a reasonable number of years, to be fixed in the plan, of the principle of compulsory education free of charge for all.

Article 15

1. The States Parties to the present Covenant recognize the right of everyone:

   (a) To take part in cultural life;

   (b) To enjoy the benefits of scientific progress and its applications;

   (c) To benefit from the protection of the moral and material interests resulting from any scientific, literary or artistic production of which he is the author.

2. The steps to be taken by the States Parties to the present Covenant to achieve the full realization of this right shall include those necessary for the conservation, the development and the diffusion of science and culture.

3. The States Parties to the present Covenant undertake to respect the freedom indispensable for scientific research and creative activity.

4. The States Parties to the present Covenant recognize the benefits to be derived from the encouragement and development of international contacts and co-operation in the scientific and cultural fields.

PART IV

Article 16

1. The States Parties to the present Covenant undertake to submit in conformity with this part of the Covenant reports on the measures which they have adopted and the progress made in achieving the observance of the rights recognized herein.

2. (a) All reports shall be submitted to the Secretary-General of the United Nations, who shall transmit copies to the Economic and Social Council for consideration in accordance with the provisions of the present Covenant;

   (b) The Secretary-General of the United Nations shall also transmit to the specialized agencies copies of the reports, or any relevant parts therefrom, from States Parties to the present Covenant which are also members of these specialized agencies in so far as these reports, or parts therefrom, relate to any matters which fall within the responsibilities of the said agencies in accordance with their constitutional instruments.

* * *

Article 18

Pursuant to its responsibilities under the Charter of the United Nations in the field of human rights and fundamental freedoms, the Economic and Social Council may make arrangements with the specialized agencies in respect of their reporting to it on the progress made in achieving the observance of the provisions of the present Covenant falling within the scope of their activities. These reports may include particulars of decisions and recommendations on such implementation adopted by their competent organs.

* * *

Article 21

The Economic and Social Council may submit from time to time to the General Assembly reports with recommendations of a general nature and a summary of the information received from the States Parties to the present Covenant and the specialized agencies on the measures taken and the progress made in achieving general observance of the rights recognized in the present Covenant.

Article 22

The Economic and Social Council may bring to the attention of other organs of the United Nations, their subsidiary organs and specialized agencies concerned with furnishing technical assistance any matters arising out of the reports referred to in this part of the present Covenant which may assist such bodies in deciding, each within its field of competence, on the advisability of international measures likely to contribute to the effective progressive implementation of the present Covenant.

Appendix G

Settlement of Investment Disputes

CONVENTION ON THE SETTLEMENT OF INVESTMENT DISPUTES BETWEEN STATES AND NATIONALS OF OTHER STATES

Published by the International Bank for Reconstruction and Development, March 18, 1965. 17 U.S.T. & O.I.A. 1270. T.I.A.S. No. 6090, 575 U.N.T.S. 159.

PREAMBLE

The Contracting States

Considering the need for international cooperation for economic development, and the role of private international investment therein;

Bearing in mind the possibility that from time to time disputes may arise in connection with such investment between Contracting States and nationals of other Contracting States;

Recognizing that while such disputes would usually be subject to national legal processes, international methods of settlement may be appropriate in certain cases;

Attaching particular importance to the availability of facilities for international conciliation or arbitration to which Contracting States and nationals of other Contracting States may submit such disputes if they so desire;

Desiring to establish such facilities under the auspices of the International Bank for Reconstruction and Development;

Recognizing that mutual consent by the parties to submit such disputes to conciliation or to arbitration through such facilities constitutes a binding agreement which requires in particular that due consideration be given to any recommendation of conciliators, and that any arbitral award be complied with; and

Declaring that no Contracting State shall by the mere fact of its ratification, acceptance or approval of this Convention and without its consent be deemed to be under any obligation to submit any particular dispute to conciliation or arbitration,

Have agreed as follows:

Article 1

(1) There is hereby established the International Centre for Settlement of Investment Disputes (hereinafter called the Centre).

(2) The purpose of the Centre shall be to provide facilities for conciliation and arbitration of investment disputes between Contracting States and nationals of other Contracting States in accordance with the provisions of this Convention.

Article 2

The seat of the Centre shall be at the principal office of the International Bank for Reconstruction and Development (hereinafter called the Bank). The seat may be moved to another place by decision of the Administrative Council adopted by a majority of two-thirds of its members.

Article 3

The Centre shall have an Administrative Council and a Secretariat and shall maintain a Panel of Conciliators and a Panel of Arbitrators.

* * *

Article 12

The Panel of Conciliators and the Panel of Arbitrators shall each consist of qualified persons, designated as hereinafter provided, who are willing to serve thereon.

Article 13

(1) Each Contracting State may designate to each Panel four persons who may but need not be its nationals.

(2) The Chairman may designate ten persons to each Panel. The persons so designated to a Panel shall each have a different nationality.

Article 14

(1) Persons designated to serve on the Panels shall be persons of high moral character and recognized competence in the fields of law, commerce, industry or finance, who may be relied upon to exercise independent judgment. Competence in the field of law shall be of particular importance in the case of persons on the Panel of Arbitrators.

(2) The Chairman, in designating persons to serve on the Panels, shall in addition pay due regard to the importance of assuring representation on the Panels of the principal legal systems of the world and of the main forms of economic activity.

* * *

Article 25

(1) The jurisdiction of the Centre shall extend to any legal dispute arising directly out of an investment, between a Contracting State (or any constituent subdivision or agency of a Contracting State designated to the Centre by that State) and a national of another Contracting State, which the parties to the dispute consent in writing to submit to the Centre. When the parties have given their consent, no party may withdraw its consent unilaterally.

(2) "National of another Contracting State" means:

(a) any natural person who had the nationality of a Contracting State other than the State party to the dispute on the date on which the parties consented to submit such dispute to conciliation or arbitration as well as on the date on which the request was registered pursuant to paragraph (3) of Article 28 or paragraph (3) of Article 36, but does not include any person who on either date also had the nationality of the Contracting State party to the dispute; and

(b) any juridical person which had the nationality of a Contracting State other than the State party to the dispute on the date on which the parties consented to submit such dispute to conciliation or arbitration and any juridical person which had the nationality of the Contracting State party to the dispute on that date and which, because of foreign control, the parties have agreed should be treated as a national of another Contracting State for the purposes of this Convention.

(3) Consent by a constituent subdivision or agency of a Contracting State shall require the approval of that State unless that State notifies the Centre that no such approval is required.

(4) Any Contracting State may, at the time of ratification, acceptance or approval of this Convention or at any time thereafter, notify the Centre of the class or classes of disputes which it would or would not consider submitting to the jurisdiction of the Centre. The Secretary-General shall forthwith transmit such notification to all Contracting States. Such notification shall not constitute the consent required by paragraph (1).

Article 26

Consent of the parties to arbitration under this Convention shall, unless otherwise stated, be deemed consent to such arbitration to the exclusion of any other remedy. A Contracting State may require the exhaustion of local administrative or judicial remedies as a condition of its consent to arbitration under this Convention.

Article 27

(1) No Contracting State shall give diplomatic protection, or bring an international claim, in respect of a dispute which one of its nationals and another Contracting State shall have consented to submit or shall have submitted to arbitration under this Convention, unless such other Contracting State shall have failed to abide by and comply with the award rendered in such dispute.

(2) Diplomatic protection, for the purposes of paragraph (1), shall not include informal diplomatic exchanges for the sole purpose of facilitating a settlement of the dispute.

* * *

Article 36

(1) Any Contracting State or any national of a Contracting State wishing to institute arbitration proceedings shall address a request to that effect in writing to the Secretary-General who shall send a copy of the request to the other party.

(2) The request shall contain information concerning the issues in dispute, the identity of the parties and their consent to arbitration in accordance with the rules of procedure for the institution of conciliation and arbitration proceedings.

(3) The Secretary-General shall register the request unless he finds, on the basis of the information contained in the request, that the dispute is manifestly outside the jurisdiction of the Centre. He shall forthwith notify the parties of registration or refusal to register.

Article 37

(1) The Arbitral Tribunal (hereinafter called the Tribunal) shall be constituted as soon as possible after registration of a request pursuant to Article 36.

(2)(a) The Tribunal shall consist of a sole arbitrator or any uneven number of arbitrators appointed as the parties shall agree.

(b) Where the parties do not agree upon the number of arbitrators and the method of their appointment, the Tribunal shall consist of three arbitrators, one arbitrator appointed by each party and the third, who shall be the president of the Tribunal, appointed by agreement of the parties.

Article 38

If the Tribunal shall not have been constituted within 90 days after notice of registration of the request has been dispatched by the Secretary-General in accordance with paragraph (3) of Article 36, or such other period as the parties may agree, the Chairman shall, at the request of either party and after consulting both parties as far as possible, appoint the arbitrator or arbitrators not yet appointed. Arbitrators appointed by the Chairman pursuant to this Article shall not be nationals of the Contracting State party to the dispute or of the Contracting State whose national is a party to the dispute.

Article 39

The majority of the arbitrators shall be nationals of States other than the Contracting State party to the dispute and the Contracting State whose national is a party to the dispute; provided, however, that the foregoing provisions of this Article shall not apply if the sole arbitrator or each individual member of the Tribunal has been appointed by agreement of the parties.

Article 40

(1) Arbitrators may be appointed from outside the Panel of Arbitrators, except in the case of appointments by the Chairman pursuant to Article 38.

(2) Arbitrators appointed from outside the Panel of Arbitrators shall possess the qualities stated in paragraph (1) of Article 14.

Article 41

(1) The Tribunal shall be the judge of its own competence.

(2) Any objection by a party to the dispute that that dispute is not within the jurisdiction of the Centre, or for other reasons is not within the competence of the Tribunal, shall be considered by the Tribunal which shall determine whether to deal with it as a preliminary question or to join it to the merits of the dispute.

Article 42

(1) The Tribunal shall decide a dispute in accordance with such rules of law as may be agreed by the parties. In the absence of such agreement, the Tribunal shall apply the law of the Contracting State party to the dispute (including its rules on the conflict of laws) and such rules of international law as may be applicable.

(2) The Tribunal may not bring in a finding of non liquet on the ground of silence or obscurity of the law.

(3) The provisions of paragraphs (1) and (2) shall not prejudice the power of the Tribunal to decide a dispute *ex aequo et bone* if the parties so agree.

* * *

Article 45

(1) Failure of a party to appear or to present his case shall not be deemed an admission of the other party's assertions.

(2) If a party fails to appear or to present his case at any stage of the proceedings the other party may request the Tribunal to deal with the questions submitted to it and to render an award. Before rendering an award, the Tribunal shall notify, and grant a period of grace to, the party failing to appear or to present its case, unless it is satisfied that that party does not intend to do so.

* * *

Article 47

Except as the parties otherwise agree, the Tribunal may, if it considers that the circumstances so require, recommend any provisional measures which should be taken to preserve the respective rights of either party.

Article 48

(1) The Tribunal shall decide questions by a majority of the votes of all its members.

(2) The award of the Tribunal shall be in writing and shall be signed by the members of the Tribunal who voted for it.

(3) The award shall deal with every question submitted to the Tribunal, and shall state the reasons upon which it is based.

(4) Any member of the Tribunal may attach his individual opinion to the award, whether he dissents from the majority or not, or a statement of his dissent.

(5) The Centre shall not publish the award without the consent of the parties.

* * *

Article 52

(1) Either party may request annulment of the award by an application in writing addressed to the Secretary-General on one or more of the following grounds:

(a) that the Tribunal was not properly constituted;

(b) that the Tribunal has manifestly exceeded its powers;

(c) that there was corruption on the part of a member of the Tribunal;

(d) that there has been a serious departure from a fundamental rule of procedure; or

(e) that the award has failed to state the reasons on which it is based.

(2) The application shall be made within 120 days after the date on which the award was rendered except that when annulment is requested on the ground of corruption such application shall be made within 120 days after discovery of the corruption and in any event within three years after the date on which the award was rendered.

(3) On receipt of the request the Chairman shall forthwith appoint from the Panel of Arbitrators an *ad hoc* Committee of three persons. None of the members of the Committee shall have been a member of the Tribunal which rendered the award, shall be of the same nationality as any such member, shall be a national of the State party to the dispute or of the State whose national is a party to the dispute, shall have been designated to the Panel of Arbitrators by either of those States, or shall have acted as a conciliator in the same dispute. The Committee shall have the authority to annul the award or any part thereof on any of the grounds set forth in paragraph (1).

(4) The provisions of Articles 41-45, 48, 49, 53 and 54, and of Chapters VI and VII shall apply *mutatis mutandis* to proceedings before the Committee.

(5) The Committee may, if it considers that the circumstances so require, stay enforcement of the award pending its decision. If the applicant requests a stay of enforcement of the award in his application, enforcement shall be stayed provisionally until the Committee rules on such request.

(6) If the award is annulled the dispute shall, at the request of either party, be submitted to a new Tribunal constituted in accordance with Section 2 of this Chapter.

Article 53

(1) The award shall be binding on the parties and shall not be subject to any appeal or to any other remedy except those provided for in this Convention. Each party shall abide by and comply with the terms of the award except to the extent that enforcement shall have been stayed pursuant to the relevant provisions of this Convention.

(2) For the purposes of this Section, "award" shall include any decision interpreting, revising or annulling such award pursuant to Articles 50, 51 or 52.

Article 54

(1) Each Contracting State shall recognize an award rendered pursuant to this Convention as binding and enforce the pecuniary obligations imposed by that award within its territories as if it were a final judgment of a court in that State. A Contracting State with a federal constitution may enforce such an award in or through its federal courts and may provide that such courts shall treat the award as if it were a final judgment of the courts of a constituent state.

(2) A party seeking recognition or enforcement in the territories of a Contracting State shall furnish to a competent court or other authority which such State shall have designated for this purpose a copy of the award certified by the Secretary-General. Each Contracting State shall notify the Secretary-General of the designation of the competent court or other authority for this purpose and of any subsequent change in such designation.

(3) Execution of the award shall be governed by the laws concerning the execution of judgments in force in the State in whose territories such execution is sought.

Article 55

Nothing in Article 54 shall be construed as derogating from the law in force in any Contracting State relating to immunity of that State or of any foreign State from execution.

* * *

Article 64

Any dispute arising between Contracting States concerning the interpretation or application of this Convention which is not settled by negotiation shall be referred to the International Court of Justice by the application of any party to such dispute, unless the States concerned agree to another method of settlement.

* * *

Article 69

Each Contracting State shall take such legislative or other measures as may be necessary for making the provisions of this Convention effective in its territories.

Appendix H

Genocide Convention

CONVENTION ON THE PREVENTION AND PUNISHMENT OF THE CRIME OF GENOCIDE

[Done at New York, December 9, 1948. Entered into force, January 12, 1951; for the United States, February 23, 1989., 78 U.N.T.S. 277.]

Article I. The Contracting Parties confirm that genocide, whether committed in time of peace or in time of war, is a crime under international law which they undertake to prevent and to punish.

Article II. In the present Convention, genocide means any of the following acts committed with intent to destroy, in whole or in part, a national, ethnical, racial or religious group, as such:

(a) Killing members of the group;
(b) Causing serious bodily or mental harm to members of the group;
(c) Deliberately inflicting on the group conditions of life calculated to bring about its physical destruction in whole or in part;
(d) Imposing measures intended to prevent births within the group;
(e) Forcibly transferring children of the group to another group.

Article III. The following acts shall be punishable:

(a) Genocide;
(b) Conspiracy to commit genocide;
(c) Direct and public incitement to commit genocide;
(d) Attempt to commit genocide;
(e) Complicity in genocide.

Article IV. Persons committing genocide or any of the other acts enumerated in Article III shall be punished, whether they are constitutionally responsible rulers, public officials or private individuals.

Article V. The Contracting Parties undertake to enact, in accordance with their respective Constitutions, the necessary legislation to give effect to the provisions of the present Convention and, in particular, to provide effective penalties for persons guilty of genocide or of any of the other acts enumerated in Article III.

Article VI. Persons charged with genocide or any of the other acts enumerated in Article III shall be tried by a competent tribunal of the State in the territory of which the act was committed, or by such international penal tribunal as may have jurisdiction with respect to those Contracting Parties which shall have accepted its jurisdiction.

Article VII. Genocide and the other acts enumerated in Article III shall not be considered as political crimes for the purpose of extradition.

The Contracting Parties pledge themselves in such cases to grant extradition in accordance with their laws and treaties in force.

Article VIII. Any Contracting Party may call upon the competent organs of the United Nations to take such action under the Charter of the United Nations as they consider appropriate for the prevention and suppression of acts of genocide or any of the other acts enumerated in Article III.

Article IX. Disputes between the Contracting Parties relating to the interpretation, application or fulfilment of the present Convention, including those relating to the responsibility of a State for genocide or for any of the other acts enumerated in Article III, shall be submitted to the International Court of Justice at the request of any of the parties to the dispute.

Appendix I

Apartheid Convention

INTERNATIONAL CONVENTION ON THE SUPPRESSION AND PUNISHMENT OF THE CRIME OF "APARTHEID"

[Done at New York, November 30, 1973. Entered into force, July 18, 1976. U.N.G.A. Res. 3068 (XXVIII), 28 U.N. GAOR, Supp. (No. 30) 75, U.N. December A/9030 (1974), reprinted in 13 I.L.M. 50 (1974).]

Article I. (1) The States Parties to the present Convention declare that apartheid is a crime against humanity and that inhuman acts resulting from the policies and practices of apartheid and similar policies and practices of racial segregation and discrimination, as defined in article II of the Convention, are crimes violating the principles of international law, in particular the purposes and principles of the Charter of the United Nations, and constituting a serious threat to international peace and security.

(2) The States Parties to the present Convention declare criminal those organizations, institutions and individuals committing the crime of apartheid.

Article II. For the purpose of the present Convention, the term "the crime of apartheid" which shall include similar policies and practices of racial segregation and discrimination as practiced in southern Africa, shall apply to the following inhuman acts committed for the purpose of establishing and maintaining domination by one racial group of persons over any other racial group of persons and systematically oppressing them:

(a) Denial to a member or members of a racial group or groups of the right to life and liberty of person:
   (i) By murder of members of a racial group or groups;
   (ii) By the infliction upon the members of a racial group or groups of serious bodily or mental harm by the infringement of their freedom or dignity, or by subjecting them to torture or to cruel, inhuman or degrading treatment or punishment;
   (iii) By arbitrary arrest and illegal imprisonment of the members of a racial group or groups;
(b) Deliberate imposition on a racial group or groups of living conditions calculated to cause its or their physical destruction in whole or in part;
(c) Any legislative measures and other measures calculated to prevent a racial group or groups from participation in the political, social, economic and cultural life of the country and the deliberate creation of conditions preventing the full development of such a group or groups, in particular by denying to members of a racial group or groups basic human rights and freedoms, including the right to work, the right to form recognized trade unions, the right to education, the right to leave and to return to their country, the right to freedom of opinion and expression, and the right to freedom of peaceful assembly and association;

(d) Any measures, including legislative measures, designed to divide the population along racial lines by the creation of separate reserves and ghettos for the members of a racial group or groups, the prohibition of mixed marriages among members of various racial groups, the expropriation of landed property belonging to a racial group or groups or to members thereof;

(e) Exploitation of the labour of the members of a racial group or groups, in particular by submitting them to forced labour;

(f) Persecution of organizations and persons, by depriving them of fundamental rights and freedoms, because they oppose apartheid.

Article III. International criminal responsibility shall apply, irrespective of the motive involved, to individuals, members of organizations and institutions and representatives of the State, whether residing in the territory of the State in which the acts are perpetrated or in some other State, whenever they:

(a) Commit, participate in, directly incite or conspire in the commission of the acts mentioned in article II of the present Convention;

(b) Directly abet, encourage or co-operate in the commission of the crime of apartheid.

Article IV. The States Parties to the present Convention undertake:

(a) To adopt any legislative or other measure necessary to suppress as well as to prevent any encouragement of the crime of apartheid and similar segregationist policies or their manifestations and to punish persons guilty of that crime;

(b) To adopt legislative, judicial and administrative measures to prosecute, bring to trial and punish in accordance with their jurisdiction; persons responsible for, or accused of, the acts defined in article II of the present Convention, whether or not such persons reside in the territory of the State in which the acts are committed or are nationals of that State or of some other State or are stateless persons.

Article V. Persons charged with the acts enumerated in article II of the present Convention may be tried by a competent tribunal of any State Party to the Convention which may acquire jurisdiction with respect to those State Parties which shall have accepted its jurisdiction.

Article VI. The States Parties to the present Convention undertake to accept and carry out in accordance with the Charter of the United Nations the decisions taken by the Security Council aimed at the prevention, suppression and punishment of the crime of apartheid, and to cooperate in the implementation of decisions adopted by other competent organs of the United Nations with a view to achieving the purposes of the Convention.

Article VII. (1) The States Parties to the present Convention undertake to submit periodic reports to the group established under article IX on the legislative, judicial, administrative or other measures that they have adopted and that give effect to the provisions of the Convention.

(2) Copies of the reports shall be transmitted through the Secretary-General of the United Nations to the Special Committee on Apartheid.

Article VIII. Any State Party to the present Convention may call upon any competent organ of the United Nations to take such action under the Charter of the United Nations as it considers appropriate for the prevention and suppression of the crime of apartheid.

Article IX. (1) The Chairman of the Commission on Human Rights shall appoint a group consisting of three members of the Commission on Human Rights, who are also representatives of States Parties to the present Convention, to consider reports submitted by States Parties in accordance with article VII.

(2) If, among the members of the Commission on Human Rights, there are no representatives of States Parties to the present Convention or if there are fewer than three such representatives, the Secretary-General of the United Nations shall, after consulting all States Parties to the Convention, designate a representative of the State Party or representatives of the States Parties which are not members of the Commission on Human Rights to take part in the work of the group established in accordance with paragraph 1 of this article, until such time as representatives of the States Parties to the Convention are elected to the Commission on Human Rights.

(3) The group may meet for a period of not more than five days, either before the opening or after the closing of the session of the Commission on Human Rights, to consider the reports submitted in accordance with article VII.

Article X. (1) The States Parties to the present Convention empower the Commission on Human Rights:

(a) To request United Nations organs, when transmitting copies of petitions under article 15 of the International Convention on the Elimination of All Forms of Racial Discrimination, to draw its attention to complaints concerning acts which are enumerated in article II of the present Convention;

(b) To prepare, on the basis of reports from competent organs of the United Nations and periodic reports from States Parties to the present Convention, a list of individuals, organizations, institutions and representatives of States which are alleged to be responsible for the crimes enumerated in article II of the Convention, as well as those against whom legal proceedings have been undertaken by States Parties to the Convention;

(c) To request information from the competent United Nations organs concerning measures taken by the authorities responsible for the administration of Trust and Non-Self-Governing Territories, and all other Territories to which General Assembly resolution 1514(XV) of 14 December 1960 applies, with regard to such individuals alleged to be responsible for crimes under article II of the Convention who are believed to be under their territorial and administrative jurisdiction.

(2) Pending the achievement of the objectives of the Declaration on the Granting of Independence to Colonial Countries and Peoples, contained in General Assembly resolution 1514(XV), the provisions of the present Convention shall in no way limit the right of petition granted to those peoples by other international instruments or by the United Nations and its specialized agencies.

Article XI. (1) Acts enumerated in article II of the present Convention shall not be considered political crimes for the purpose of extradition.

(2) The States Parties to the present Convention undertake in such cases to grant extradition with their legislation and with the treaties in force.

* * *

Appendix J

Foreign Sovereign Immunities Act

FOREIGN SOVEREIGN IMMUNITIES ACT OF 1976

28 U.S.C.A. §§ 1602-1611 (Supp.1989)

§ 1602. Findings and declaration of purpose

The Congress finds that the determination by United States courts of the claims of foreign states to immunity from the jurisdiction of such courts would serve the interests of justice and would protect the rights of both foreign states and litigants in United States courts. Under international law, states are not immune from the jurisdiction of foreign courts insofar as their commercial activities are concerned, and their commercial property may be levied upon for the satisfaction of judgments rendered against them in connection with their commercial activities. Claims of foreign states to immunity should henceforth be decided by courts of the United States and of the States in conformity with the principles set forth in this chapter.

§ 1603. Definitions

For purposes of this chapter—

(a) A "foreign state," except as used in section 1608 of this title, includes a political subdivision of a foreign state or an agency or instrumentality of a foreign state as defined in subsection (b).

(b) An "agency or instrumentality of a foreign state" means any entity—
   (1) which is a separate legal person, corporate or otherwise, and
   (2) which is an organ of a foreign state or political subdivision thereof, or a majority of whose shares or other ownership interest is owned by a foreign state or political subdivision thereof, and
   (3) which is neither a citizen of a State of the United States as defined in section 1332(c) and (d) of this title, nor created under the laws of any third country.

(c) The "United States" includes all territory and waters, continental or insular, subject to the jurisdiction of the United States.

(d) A "commercial activity" means either a regular course of commercial conduct or a particular commercial transaction or act. The commercial character of an activity shall be determined by reference to the nature of the course of conduct or particular transaction or act, rather than by reference to its purpose.

(e) A "commercial activity carried on in the United States by a foreign state" means commercial activity carried on by such state and having substantial contact with the United States.

§ 1604. Immunity of a foreign state from jurisdiction

Subject to existing international agreements to which the United States is a party at the time of enactment of this Act a foreign state shall be immune from the jurisdiction of the courts of the United States and of the States except as provided in sections 1605 to 1607 of this chapter.

§ 1605. General exceptions to the jurisdictional immunity of a foreign state

(a) A foreign state shall not be immune from the jurisdiction of courts of the United States or of the States in any case—

(1) in which the foreign state has waived its immunity either explicitly or by implication, notwithstanding any withdrawal of the waiver which the foreign state may purport to effect except in accordance with the terms of the waiver;

(2) in which the action is based upon a commercial activity carried on in the United States by the foreign state; or upon an act performed in the United States in connection with a commercial activity of the foreign state elsewhere; or upon an act outside the territory of the United States in connection with a commercial activity of the foreign state elsewhere and that act causes a direct effect in the United States;

(3) in which rights in property taken in violation of international law are in issue and that property or any property exchanged for such property is present in the United States in connection with a commercial activity carried on in the United States by the foreign state; or that property or any property exchanged for such property is owned or operated by an agency or instrumentality of the foreign state and that agency or instrumentality is engaged in a commercial activity in the United States;

(4) in which rights in property in the United States acquired by succession or gift or rights in immovable property situated in the United States are in issue;

(5) not otherwise encompassed in paragraph (2) above, in which money damages are sought against a foreign state for personal injury or death, or damage to or loss of property, occurring in the United States and caused by the tortious act or omission of that foreign state or of any official or employee of that foreign state while acting within the scope of his office or employment; except this paragraph shall not apply to—

(A) any claim based upon the exercise or performance or the failure to exercise or perform a discretionary function regardless of whether the discretion be abused, or

(B) any claim arising out of malicious prosecution, abuse of process, libel, slander, misrepresentation, deceit, or interference with contract rights; or

(6) in which the action is brought, either to enforce an agreement made by the foreign State with or for the benefit of a private party to submit to arbitration all or any differences which have arisen or which may arise between the parties with respect to a defined legal relationship, whether contractual or not, concerning a subject matter capable of settlement by arbitration under the laws of the United States, or to confirm an award made pursuant to such an agreement to arbitrate, if (A) the arbitration takes place or is intended to take place in the United States, (B) the agreement or award is or may be governed by a treaty or other international

agreement in force for the United States calling for the recognition and enforcement of arbitral awards, (C) the underlying claim, save for the agreement to arbitrate, could have been brought in a United States court under this section or section 1607, or (D) paragraph (1) of this subsection is otherwise applicable.

(b) A foreign state shall not be immune from the jurisdiction of the courts of the United States in any case in which a suit in admiralty is brought to enforce a maritime lien against a vessel or cargo of the foreign state, which maritime lien is based upon a commercial activity of the foreign state: *Provided*, That—

(1) notice of the suit is given by delivery of a copy of the summons and of the complaint to the person, or his agent, having possession of the vessel or cargo against which the maritime lien is asserted; and if the vessel or cargo is arrested pursuant to process obtained on behalf of the party bringing the suit, the service of process of arrest shall be deemed to constitute valid delivery of such notice, but the party bringing the suit shall be liable for any damages sustained by the foreign state as a result of the arrest if the party bringing the suit had actual or constructive knowledge that the vessel or cargo of a foreign state was involved; and

(2) notice to the foreign state of the commencement of suit as provided in section 1608 of this title is initiated within ten days either of the delivery of notice as provided in paragraph (1) of this subsection or, in the case of a party who was unaware that the vessel or cargo of a foreign state was involved, of the date such party determined the existence of the foreign state's interest.

(c) Whenever notice is delivered under subsection (b)(1), the suit to enforce a maritime lien shall thereafter proceed and shall be heard and determined according to the principles of law and rules of practice of suits in *rem* whenever it appears that, had the vessel been privately owned and possessed, a suit in *rem* might have been maintained. A decree against the foreign state may include costs of the suit and, if the decree is for a money judgment, interest as ordered by the court, except that the court may not award judgment against the foreign state in an amount greater than the value of the vessel or cargo upon which the maritime lien arose. Such value shall be determined as of the time notice is served under subsection (b)(1). Decrees shall be subject to appeal and revision as provided in other cases of admiralty and maritime jurisdiction. Nothing shall preclude the plaintiff in any proper case from seeking relief in *personam* in the same action brought to enforce a maritime lien as provided in this section.

(d) A foreign state shall not be immune from the jurisdiction of the courts of the United States in any action brought to foreclose a preferred mortgage, as defined in the Ship Mortgage Act, 1920 (46 U.S.C. 911 and following). Such action shall be brought, heard, and determined in accordance with the provisions of that Act and in accordance with the principles of law and rules of practice of suits in *rem*, whenever it appears that had the vessel been privately owned and possessed a suit in *rem* might have been maintained.

§ 1606. Extent of liability

As to any claim for relief with respect to which a foreign state is not entitled to immunity under section 1605 or 1607 of this chapter, the foreign state shall be liable in the same manner and to the same extent as a private individual under like circumstances; but a foreign state except for an agency or instrumentality thereof shall not be liable for punitive damages; if, however, in any case wherein death was caused, the law of the place where the action or omission occurred provides, or has been construed to provide, for damages only punitive in nature, the foreign state shall be liable for actual or compensatory damages measured by the pecuniary injuries resulting from such death which were incurred by the persons for whose benefit the action was brought.

§ 1607. Counterclaims

In any action brought by a foreign state, or in which a foreign state intervenes, in a court of the United States or of a State, the foreign state shall not be accorded immunity with respect to any counterclaim—

(a) for which a foreign state would not be entitled to immunity under section 1605 of this chapter had such claim been brought in a separate action against the foreign state; or

(b) arising out of the transaction or occurrence that is the subject matter of the claim of the foreign state;

(c) to the extent that the counterclaim does not seek relief exceeding in amount or differing in kind from that sought by the foreign state.

§ 1608. Service; time to answer; default

(a) Service in the courts of the United States and of the States shall be made upon a foreign state or political subdivision of a foreign state:

(1) by delivery of a copy of the summons and complaint in accordance with any special arrangement for service between the plaintiff and the foreign state or political subdivision; or

(2) if no special arrangement exists, by delivery of a copy of the summons and complaint in accordance with an applicable international convention on service of judicial documents; or

(3) if service cannot be made under paragraphs (1) or (2), by sending a copy of the summons and complaint and a notice of suit, together with a translation of each into the official language of the foreign state, by any form of mail requiring a signed receipt, to be addressed and dispatched by the clerk of the court to the head of the ministry of foreign affairs of the foreign state concerned, or

(4) if service cannot be made within 30 days under paragraph (3), by sending two copies of the summons and complaint and a notice of suit, together with a translation of each into the official language of the foreign state, by any form of mail requiring a signed receipt, to be addressed and dispatched by the clerk of the court to the Secretary of State in Washington, District of Columbia, to the attention of the Director of Special Consular Services—and the Secretary shall transmit one copy of the papers through diplomatic channels to the foreign state and shall send to the clerk of the court a certified copy of the diplomatic note indicating when the papers were transmitted.

As used in this subsection, a "notice of suit" shall mean a notice addressed to a foreign state and in a form prescribed by the Secretary of State by regulation.

(b) Service in the courts of the United States and of the States shall be made upon an agency or instrumentality of a foreign state:

    (1) by delivery of a copy of the summons and complaint in accordance with any special arrangement for service between the plaintiff and the agency or instrumentality; or

    (2) if no special arrangement exists, by delivery of a copy of the summons and complaint either to an officer, a managing or general agent, or to any other agent authorized by appointment or by law to receive service of process in the United States; or in accordance with an applicable international convention on service of judicial documents; or

    (3) if service cannot be made under paragraphs (1) or (2), and if reasonably calculated to give actual notice, by delivery of a copy of the summons and complaint, together with a translation of each into the official language of the foreign state—

        (A) as directed by an authority of the foreign state or political subdivision in response to a letter rogatory or request or

        (B) by any form of mail requiring a signed receipt, to be addressed and dispatched by the clerk of the court to the agency or instrumentality to be served, or

        (C) as directed by order of the court consistent with the law of the place where service is to be made.

(c) Service shall be deemed to have been made—

    (1) in the case of service under subsection (a)(4), as of the date of transmittal indicated in the certified copy of the diplomatic note; and

    (2) in any other case under this section, as of the date of receipt indicated in the certification, signed and returned postal receipt, or other proof of service applicable to the method of service employed.

(d) In any action brought in a court of the United States or of a State, a foreign state, a political subdivision thereof, or an agency or instrumentality of a foreign state shall serve an answer or other responsive pleading to the complaint within sixty days after service has been made under this section.

(e) No judgment by default shall be entered by a court of the United States or of a State against a foreign state, a political subdivision thereof, or an agency or instrumentality of a foreign state, unless the claimant establishes his claim or right to relief by evidence satisfactory to the court. A copy of any such default judgment shall be sent to the foreign state or political subdivision in the manner prescribed for service in this section.

§ 1609. Immunity from attachment and execution or property of a foreign state

Subject to existing international agreements to which the United States is a party at the time of enactment of this Act the property in the United States of a foreign state shall be immune from attachment arrest and execution except as provided in sections 1610 and 1611 of this chapter.

§ 1610. Exceptions to the immunity from attachment or execution

(a) The property in the United States of a foreign state, as defined in section 1603(a) of this chapter, used for a commercial activity in the United States, shall not be immune from attachment in aid of execution, or from execution, upon a judgment entered by a court of the United States or of a State after the effective date of this Act, if—

   (1) the foreign state has waived its immunity from attachment in aid of execution or from execution either explicitly or by implication, notwithstanding any withdrawal of the waiver the foreign state may purport to effect except in accordance with the terms of the waiver, or

   (2) the property is or was used for the commercial activity upon which the claim is based, or

   (3) the execution relates to a judgment establishing rights in property which has been taken in violation of international law or which has been exchanged for property taken in violation of international law, or

   (4) the execution relates to a judgment establishing rights in property—

      (A) which is acquired by succession or gift, or

      (B) which is immovable and situated in the United States: *Provided*, that such property is not used for purposes of maintaining a diplomatic or consular mission or the residence of the Chief of such mission, or

   (5) the property consists of any contractual obligation or any proceeds from such a contractual obligation to indemnify or hold harmless the foreign state or its employees under a policy of automobile or other liability or casualty insurance covering the claim which merged into the judgment, or

   (6) the judgment is based on an order confirming an arbitral award rendered against the foreign State, provided that attachment in aid of execution, or execution, would not be inconsistent with any provision in the arbitral agreement.

(b) In addition to subsection (a), any property in the United States of an agency or instrumentality of a foreign state engaged in commercial activity in the United States shall not be immune from attachment in aid of execution, or from execution, upon a judgment entered by a court of the United States or of a State after the effective date of this Act if—

   (1) the agency or instrumentality has waived its immunity from attachment in aid of execution or from execution either explicitly or implicitly, notwithstanding any withdrawal of the waiver the agency or instrumentality may purport to effect except in accordance with the terms of the waiver, or

   (2) the judgment relates to a claim for which the agency or instrumentality is not immune by virtue of section 1605(a)(2), (3), or (5), or 1605(b) of this chapter, regardless of whether the property is or was used for the activity upon which the claim is based.

(c) No attachment or execution referred to in subsection (a) and (b) of this section shall be permitted until the court has ordered such attachment and execution after having determined that a reasonable period of time has elapsed following the entry of judgment and the giving of any notice required under section 1608(e) of this chapter.

(d) The property of a foreign state, as defined in section 1693(a) of this chapter, used for a commercial activity in the United States, shall not be immune from attachment prior to the entry of judgment in any action brought in a court of the United States or of a State, or prior to the elapse of the period of time provided in subsection (c) of this section, if—

(1) the foreign state has explicitly waived its immunity from attachment prior to judgment, notwithstanding any withdrawal of the waiver the foreign state may purport to effect except in accordance with the terms of the waiver, and

(2) the purpose of the attachment is to secure satisfaction of a judgment that has been or may ultimately be entered against the foreign state, and not to obtain jurisdiction.

(e) The vessels of a foreign State shall not be immune from arrest in *rem*, interlocutory sale, and execution in actions brought to foreclose a preferred mortgage as provided in section 1605(d).

§ 1611. Certain types of property immune from execution

(a) Notwithstanding the provisions of section 1610 of this chapter, the property of those organizations designated by the President as being entitled to enjoy the privileges, exemptions, and immunities provided by the International Organizations Immunities Act shall not be subject to attachment or any other judicial process impeding the disbursement of funds to, or on the order of, a foreign state as the result of an action brought in the courts of the United States or of the States.

(b) Notwithstanding the provisions of section 1610 of this chapter, the property of a foreign state shall be immune from attachment and from execution, if—

(1) the property is that of a foreign central bank or monetary authority held for its own account, unless such bank or authority, or its parent foreign government, has explicitly waived its immunity from attachment in aid of execution, or from execution, notwithstanding any withdrawal of the waiver which the bank, authority or government may purport to effect except in accordance with the terms of the waiver; or

(2) the property is, or is intended to be, used in connection with a military activity and

   (A) is of a military character, or

   (B) is under the control of a military authority or defense agency.

Appendix K

"Friendly Relations" Declaration

DECLARATION ON PRINCIPLES OF INTERNATIONAL LAW CONCERNING FRIENDLY RELATIONS AND CO-OPERATION AMONG STATES IN ACCORDANCE WITH THE CHARTER OF THE UNITED NATIONS

[The Declaration set out below is contained in the Annex to Resolution 2625 (XXV) of the U.N. General Assembly, adopted without vote, October 24, 1970. The legal significance of the declaration lies in the fact that it provides evidence of the consensus among member States of the United Nations on the meaning and elaboration of the principles of the U.N. Charter.]

The General Assembly

Reaffirming in the terms of the Charter that the maintenance of international peace and security and the development of friendly relations and co-operation between nations are among the fundamental purposes of the United Nations,

Recalling that the peoples of the United Nations are determined to practice tolerance and live together in peace with one another as good neighbours,

Bearing in mind the importance of maintaining and strengthening international peace founded upon freedom, equality, justice and respect for fundamental human rights and of developing friendly relations among nations irrespective of their political, economic and social systems or the levels of their development,

Bearing in mind also the paramount importance of the Charter of the United Nations in the promotion of the rule of law among nations,

Considering that the faithful observance of the principles of international law concerning friendly relations and co-operation among States and the fulfillment in good faith of the obligations assumed by States, in accordance with the Charter, is of the greatest importance for the maintenance of international peace and security and for the implementation of the other purposes of the United Nations,

Noting that the great political, economic and social changes and scientific progress which have taken place in the world since the adoption of the Charter of the United Nations give increased importance to these principles and to the need for their more effective application in the conduct of States wherever carried on,

Recalling the established principle that outer space, including the moon and other celestial bodies, is not subject to national appropriation by claim of sovereignty, by means of use or occupation, or by any other means, and mindful of the fact that consideration is being given in the United Nations to the question of establishing other appropriate provisions similarly inspired,

Convinced that the strict observance by States of the obligation not to intervene in the affairs of any other State is an essential condition to ensure that nations live together in peace with one another, since the practice of any form of intervention not only violates the spirit and letter of the Charter, but also leads to the creation of situations which threaten international peace and security,

Recalling the duty of States to refrain in their international relations from military, political, economic or any other form of coercion aimed against the political independence or territorial integrity of any State,

Considering it essential that all States shall refrain in their international relations from the threat or use of force against the territorial integrity or political independence of any State, or in any other manner inconsistent with the purposes of the United Nations,

Considering it equally essential that all States shall settle their international disputes by peaceful means in accordance with the Charter,

Reaffirming, in accordance with the Charter, the basic importance of sovereign equality and stressing that the purposes of the United Nations can be implemented only if States enjoy sovereign equality and comply fully with the requirements of this principle in their international relations,

Convinced that the subjection of peoples to alien subjugation, domination and exploitation constitutes a major obstacle to the promotion of international peace and security,

Convinced that the principle of equal rights and self-determination of peoples constitutes a significant contribution to contemporary international law, and that its effective application is of paramount importance for the promotion of friendly relations among States, based on respect for the principle of sovereign equality,

Convinced in consequence that any attempt aimed at the partial or total disruption of the national unity and territorial integrity of a State or country or at its political independence is incompatible with the purposes and principles of the Charter,

Considering the provisions of the Charter as a whole and taking into account the role of relevant resolutions adopted by the competent organs of the United Nations relating to the content of the principles,

Considering that the progressive development and codification of the following principles:

(a) The principle that States shall refrain in their international relations from the threat or use of force against the territorial integrity or political independence of any State, or in any other manner inconsistent with the purposes of the United Nations;

(b) The principle that States shall settle their international disputes by peaceful means in such a manner that international peace and security and justice are not endangered;

(c) The duty not to intervene in matters within the domestic jurisdiction of any State, in accordance with the Charter;

(d) The duty of States to co-operate with one another in accordance with the Charter;

(e) The principle of equal rights and self-determination of peoples;
(f) The principle of sovereign equality of States;
(g) The principle that States shall fulfill in good faith the obligations assumed by them in accordance with the Charter;

So as to secure their more effective application within the international community would promote the realization of the purposes of the United Nations;

Having considered the Principles of international law relating to friendly relations and co-operation among States,

1. Solemnly Proclaims the following principles:

The principle that States shall refrain in their international relations from threat or use of force against the territorial integrity or political independence of any State, or in any other manner inconsistent with the purposes of the United Nations

Every State has the duty to refrain in its international relations from the threat or use of force against the territorial integrity or political independence of any State, or in any other manner inconsistent with the purposes of the United Nations. Such a threat or use of force constitutes a violation of international law and the Charter of the United Nations and shall never be employed as a means of settling international issues.

A war of aggression constitutes a crime against the peace, for which there is responsibility under international law.

In accordance with the Purposes and Principles of the United Nations, States have the duty to refrain from propaganda for wars of aggression.

Every State has the duty to refrain from the threat or use of force to violate the existing international boundaries of any State or as a means of solving international disputes, including territorial disputes and problems concerning frontiers of States.

Every State likewise has the duty to refrain from the threat or use of force to violate international lines of demarcation, such as armistice lines, established by or pursuant to an international agreement to which it is a party or which it is otherwise bound to respect. Nothing in the foregoing shall be construed as prejudicing the positions of the parties concerned with regard to the status and effects of such lines under their special regimes or as affecting their temporary character.

States have a duty to refrain from acts of reprisal involving the use of force.

Every State has the duty to refrain from any forcible action which deprives peoples referred to in the elaboration of the principle of equal rights and self-determination of their right to self-determination and freedom and independence.

Every State has the duty to refrain from organizing or encouraging the organization of irregular forces or armed bands, including mercenaries, for incursion into the territory of another State.

Every State has the duty to refrain from organizing, instigating, assisting or participating in acts of civil strife or terrorist acts in another State or acquiescing in organized activities within its territory directed towards the commission of such acts, when the acts referred to in the present paragraph involve a threat or use of force.

The territory of a State shall not be the object of military occupation resulting from the use of force in contravention of the provisions of the Charter. The territory of a State shall not be the object of acquisition by another State resulting from the threat or use of force. No territorial acquisition resulting from the threat or use of force shall be recognized as legal. Nothing in the foregoing shall be construed as affecting:

(a) provisions of the Charter or any international agreement prior to the Charter regime and valid under international law; or

(b) the powers of the Security Council under the Charter.

All States shall pursue in good faith negotiations for the early conclusion of a universal treaty on general and complete disarmament under effective international control and strive to adopt appropriate measures to reduce international tensions and strengthen confidence among States.

All States shall comply in good faith with their obligations under the generally recognized principles and rules of international law with respect to the maintenance of international peace and security, and shall endeavour to make the United Nations security system based on the Charter more effective.

Nothing in the foregoing paragraphs shall be construed as enlarging or diminishing in any way the scope of the provisions of the Charter concerning cases in which the use of force is lawful.

The principle that States shall settle their international disputes by peaceful means in such a manner that international Peace and security and justice are not endangered

Every State shall settle its international disputes with other States by peaceful means, in such a manner that international peace and security and justice are not endangered.

States shall accordingly seek early and just settlement of their international disputes by negotiation, inquiry, mediation, conciliation, arbitration, judicial settlement, resort to regional agencies or arrangements or other peaceful means of their choice. In seeking such a settlement the parties shall agree upon such peaceful means as may be appropriate to the circumstances and nature of the dispute.

The parties to a dispute have the duty, in the event of failure to reach a solution by any one of the above peaceful means, to continue to seek a settlement of the dispute by other peaceful means agreed upon by them.

States parties to an international dispute, as well as other States, shall refrain from any action which may aggravate the situation so as to endanger the maintenance of international peace and security, and shall act in accordance with the purposes and principles of the United Nations.

International disputes shall be settled on the basis of the sovereign equality of States and in accordance with the principle of free choice of means. Recourse to, or acceptance of, a settlement procedure freely agreed to by States with regard to existing or future disputes to which they are parties shall not be regarded as incompatible with sovereign equality.

Nothing in the foregoing paragraphs prejudices or derogates from the applicable provisions of the Charter, in particular those relating to the pacific settlement of international disputes.

The principle concerning the duty not to intervene in matters within the domestic jurisdiction of any state, in accordance with the Charter

No State or group of States has the right to intervene, directly or indirectly, for any reason whatever, in the internal or external affairs of any other State. Consequently, armed intervention and all other forms of interference or attempted threats against the personality of the State or against its political, economic and cultural elements, are in violation of international law.

No State may use or encourage the use of economic, political or any other type of measures to coerce another State in order to obtain from it the subordination of the exercise of its sovereign rights and to secure from it advantages of any kind. Also, no State shall organize, assist, foment, finance, incite or tolerate subversive, terrorist or armed activities directed towards the violent overthrow of the regime of another State, or interfere in civil strife in another State.

The use of force to deprive peoples of their national identity constitutes a violation of their inalienable rights and of the principle of non-intervention.

Every State has an inalienable right to choose its political, economic, social and cultural systems, without interference in any form by another State.

Nothing in the foregoing paragraphs shall be construed as affecting the relevant provisions of the Charter relating to the maintenance of international peace and security.

The duty of states to co-operate with one another in accordance with the Charter

States have the duty to co-operate with one another, irrespective of the differences in their political, economic and social systems, in the various spheres of international relations, in order to maintain international peace and security and to promote international economic stability and progress, the general welfare of nations and international co-operation free from discrimination based on such differences.

To this end:

(a) States shall co-operate with other States in the maintenance of international peace and security;

(b) States shall co-operate in the promotion of universal respect for and observance of human rights and fundamental freedoms for all, and in the elimination of all forms of racial discrimination and all forms of religious intolerance;

(c) States shall conduct their international relations in the economic, social, cultural, technical and trade fields in accordance with the principles of sovereign equality and non-intervention;

(d) States Members of the United Nations have the duty to take joint and separate action in co-operation with the United Nations in accordance with the relevant provisions of the Charter.

States should co-operate in the economic, social and cultural fields as well as in the field of science and technology and for the promotion of international cultural and educational progress. States should co-operate in the promotion of economic growth throughout the world, especially that of the developing countries.

The principle of equal rights and self-determination of peoples

By virtue of the principle of equal rights and self-determination of peoples enshrined in the Charter of the United Nations, all peoples have the right freely to determine, without external interference, their political status and to pursue their economic, social and cultural development, and every State has the duty to respect this right in accordance with the provisions of the Charter.

Every State has the duty to promote, through joint and separate action, realization of the principle of equal rights and self-determination of peoples, in accordance with the provisions of the Charter, and to render assistance to the United Nations in carrying out the responsibilities entrusted to it by the Charter regarding the implementation of the principle, in order:

(a) to promote friendly relations and co-operation among States; and

(b) to bring a speedy end to colonialism, having due regard to the freely expressed will of the peoples concerned;

and bearing in mind that subjection of peoples to alien subjugation, domination and exploitation constitutes a violation of the principle, as well as a denial of fundamental human rights, and is contrary to the Charter.

Every State has the duty to promote through joint and separate action universal respect for and observance of human rights and fundamental freedoms in accordance with the Charter.

The establishment of a sovereign and independent State, the free association or integration with an independent State or the emergence into any other political status freely determined by a people constitute modes of implementing the right of self-determination by that people.

Every State has the duty to refrain from any forcible action which deprives peoples referred to above in the elaboration of the present principle of their right to self-determination and freedom and independence. In their actions against, and resistance to, such forcible action in pursuit of the exercise of their right to self-determination, such peoples are entitled to seek and to receive support in accordance with the purposes and principles of the Charter.

The territory of a colony or other non-self-governing territory has, under the Charter, a status separate and distinct from the territory of the State administering it; and such separate and distinct status under the Charter shall exist until the people of the colony or non-self-governing territory have exercised their right of self-determination in accordance with the Charter, and particularly its purposes and principles.

Nothing in the foregoing paragraphs shall be construed as authorizing or encouraging any action which would dismember or impair, totally or in part, the territorial integrity or political unity of sovereign and independent States conducting themselves in compliance with the principle of equal rights and self-determination of peoples as described above and thus possessed of a government representing the whole people belonging to the territory without distinction as to race, creed or colour.

Every State shall refrain from any action aimed at the partial or total disruption of the national unity and territorial integrity of any other State or country.

The principle of sovereign equality of states

All States enjoy sovereign equality. They have equal rights and duties and are equal members of the international community, notwithstanding differences of an economic, social, political or other nature.

In particular, sovereign equality includes the following elements:

(a) States are juridically equal;
(b) Each State enjoys the rights inherent in full sovereignty;
(c) Each State has the duty to respect the personality of other States;
(d) The territorial integrity and political independence of the State are inviolable;
(e) Each State has the right freely to choose and develop its political, social, economic and cultural systems;
(f) Each State has the duty to comply fully and in good faith with its international obligations and to live in peace with other States.

The principle that States shall fulfill in good faith the obligations assumed by them in accordance with the Charter

Every State has the duty to fulfill in good faith the obligations assumed by it in accordance with the Charter of the United Nations.

Every State has the duty to fulfill in good faith its obligations under the generally recognized principles and rules of international law.

Every State has the duty to fulfill in good faith its obligations under international agreements valid under the generally recognized principles and rules of international law.

Where obligations arising under international agreements are in conflict with the obligations of Members of the United Nations under the Charter of the United Nations, the obligations under the Charter shall prevail.

General Part

2. Declares that:

In their interpretation and application the above principles are interrelated and each principle should be construed in the context of the other principles.

Nothing in this Declaration shall be construed as prejudicing in any manner the provisions of the Charter or the rights and duties of Member States under the Charter or the rights of peoples under the Charter, taking into account the elaboration of these rights in this Declaration,

3. *Declares further that:*

The principles of the Charter which are embodied in this Declaration constitute basic principles of international law, and consequently appeals to all States to be guided by these principles in their international conduct and to develop their mutual relations on the basis of the strict observance of these principles.

Appendix L

Statute of the International Court of Justice

STATUTE OF THE INTERNATIONAL COURT OF JUSTICE

[The statute, annexed to the Charter of the United Nations, is set forth in 59 Stat. 1055 (1945), T.S. No. 993 (at p. 25). The statute entered into force on October 24, 1945. All member States of the United Nations, plus Switzerland, San Marino, Liechtenstein, and Nauru are parties to the statute. As of December 1996, sixty-two states have accepted compulsory jurisdiction under Article 36(2).]

ARTICLE 1. THE INTERNATIONAL COURT OF JUSTICE established by the Charter of the United Nations as the principle judicial organ of the United Nations shall be constituted and shall function in accordance with the provisions of the present Statute.

CHAPTER I. ORGANIZATION OF THE COURT

ARTICLE 2. The Court shall be composed of a body of independent judges, elected regardless of their nationality from among persons of high moral character, who possess the qualifications required in their respective countries for appointment to the highest judicial offices, or are jurisconsults of recognized competence in international law.

ARTICLE 3.—1. The Court shall consist of fifteen members, no two of whom may be nationals of the same state.

2. A person who for the purposes of membership in the Court could be regarded as a national of more than one state shall be deemed to be a national of the one in which he ordinarily exercises civil and political rights.

* * *

ARTICLE 5.—1. At least three months before the date of the election, the Secretary-General of the United Nations shall address a written request to the members of the Permanent Court of Arbitration belonging to the states which are parties to the present Statute, and to the members of the national groups appointed under Article 4, paragraph 2, inviting them to undertake, within a given time, by national groups, the nomination of persons in a position to accept the duties of a member of the Court.

2. No group may nominate more than four persons, not more than any two of whom shall be of their own nationality. In no case may the number of candidates nominated by a group be more than double the number of seats to be filled.

ARTICLE 6. Before making these nominations, each national group is recommended to consult its highest court of justice, its legal faculties and schools of law, and its national academies and national sections of international academies devoted to the study of law.

ARTICLE 7.—1. The Secretary-General shall prepare a list in alphabetical order of all the persons thus nominated. Save as provided in Article 12, paragraph 2, these shall be the only persons eligible.

2. The Secretary-General shall submit this list to the General Assembly and to the Security Council.

ARTICLE 8. The General Assembly and the Security Council shall proceed independently of one another to elect the members of the Court.

ARTICLE 9. At every election, the electors shall bear in mind not only that the persons to be elected should individually possess the qualifications required, but also that in the body as a whole the representation of the main forms of civilization and of the principal legal systems of the world should be assured.

ARTICLE 10.—1. Those candidates who obtain an absolute majority of votes in the General Assembly and in the Security Council shall be considered as elected.

2. Any vote of the Security Council, whether for the election of judges or for the appointment of members of the conference envisaged in Article 12, shall be taken without any distinction between permanent and non-permanent members of the Security Council.

3. In the event of more than one national of the same state obtaining an absolute majority of the votes both of the General Assembly and of the Security Council, the eldest of these only shall be considered elected.

* * *

ARTICLE 13.—1. The members of the Court shall be elected for nine years and may be re-elected; provided, however, that of the judges elected at the first election, the terms of five judges shall expire at the end of three years and the terms of five more judges shall expire at the end of six years.

* * *

ARTICLE 31.—1. Judges of the nationality of each of the parties shall retain their right to sit in the case before the Court.

2. If the Court includes upon the Bench, a judge of the nationality of one of the parties, any other party may choose a person to sit as judge. Such person shall be chosen preferably from among those persons who have been nominated as candidates as provided in Articles 4 and 5.

3. If the Court includes upon the Bench no judge of the nationality of the parties, each of these parties may proceed to choose a judge as provided in paragraph 2 of this Article.

* * *

CHAPTER II. COMPETENCE OF THE COURT

ARTICLE 34.—1. Only states may be parties in cases before the Court.

* * *

ARTICLE 35.—1. The Court shall be open to the states parties to the present Statute.

2. The conditions under which the Court shall be open to other states shall, subject to the special provisions contained in treaties in force, be laid down by the Security Council, but in no case shall such conditions place the parties in a position of inequality before the Court.

* * *

ARTICLE 36.—1. The jurisdiction of the Court comprises all cases which the parties refer to it and all matters specially provided for in the Charter of the United Nations or in treaties and conventions in force.

2. The states parties to the present Statute may at any time declare that they recognize as compulsory *ipso facto* and without special agreement, in relation to any other state accepting the same obligation, the jurisdiction of the Court in all legal disputes concerning:

a. the interpretation of a treaty;
b. any question of international law;
c. the existence of any fact which, if established, would constitute a breach of an international obligation;
d. the nature or extent of the reparation to be made for the breach of an international obligation.

3. The declarations referred to above may be made unconditionally or on condition of reciprocity on the part of several or certain states, or for a certain time.

4. Such declarations shall be deposited with the Secretary-General of the United Nations, who shall transmit copies thereof to the parties to the Statute and to the Registrar of the Court.

5. Declarations made under Article 36 of the Statute of the Permanent Court of International Justice and which are still in force shall be deemed, as between the parties to the present Statute, to be acceptances of the compulsory jurisdiction of the International Court of Justice for the period which they still have to run and in accordance with their terms.

6. In the event of a dispute as to whether the Court has jurisdiction, the matter shall be settled by the decision of the Court.

ARTICLE 37. Whenever a treaty or convention in force provides for reference of a matter to a tribunal to have been instituted by the League of Nations, or to the Permanent Court of International Justice, the matter shall, as between the parties to the present Statute, be referred to the International Court of Justice.

ARTICLE 38.—1. The Court, whose function is to decide in accordance with international law such disputes as are submitted to it, shall apply:

a. international conventions, whether general or particular, establishing rules expressly recognized by the contesting states;

b. international custom, as evidence of a general practice accepted as law;

c. the general principles of law recognized by civilized nations;

d. subject to the provisions of Article 59, judicial decisions and the teachings of the most highly qualified publicists of the various nations, as subsidiary means for the determination of rules of law.

2. This provision shall not prejudice the power of the Court to decide a case *ex aequo et bono*, if the parties agree thereto.

* * *

CHAPTER III. PROCEDURE

ARTICLE 55.—1. All questions shall be decided by a majority of the judges present.

2. In the event of an equality of votes, the President or the judge who acts in his place shall have a casting vote.

ARTICLE 56.—1. The judgment shall state the reasons on which it is based.

2. It shall contain the names of the judges who have taken part in the decision.

ARTICLE 57. If the judgment does not represent in whole or in part the unanimous opinion of the judges, any judge shall be entitled to deliver a separate opinion.

* * *

ARTICLE 59. The decision of the Court has no binding force except between the parties and in respect of that particular case.

ARTICLE 60. The judgment is final and without appeal. In the event of dispute as to the meaning or scope of the judgment, the Court shall construe it upon the request of any party.

* * *

ARTICLE 62.—1. Should a state consider that it has an interest of a legal nature which may be affected by the decision in the case, it may submit a request to the Court to be permitted to intervene.

2. It shall be for the Court to decide upon this request.

ARTICLE 63.—1. Whenever the construction of a convention to which states other than those concerned in the case are parties is in question, the Registrar shall notify all such states forthwith.

2. Every state so notified has the right to intervene in the proceedings; but if it uses this right, the construction given by the judgment will be equally binding upon it.

ARTICLE 64. Unless otherwise decided by the Court, each party shall bear its own costs.

CHAPTER IV. ADVISORY OPINIONS

ARTICLE 65.—1. The Court may give an advisory opinion on any legal question at the request of whatever body may be authorized by or in accordance with the Charter of the United Nations to make such a request.

2. Questions upon which the advisory opinion of the Court is asked shall be laid before the Court by means of a written request containing an exact statement of the question upon which an opinion is required, and accompanied by all documents likely to throw light upon the question.

* * *

References

Acevedo, D. E. (1993). The Haitian crisis and the OAS response: A test of effectiveness in protecting democracy. In L. F. Damrosch (Ed.), *Enforcing restraint* (pp. 119-155). New York: Council on Foreign Relations Press.

Address to joint session of Congress. (1991). *Dispatch, 7*(2), 162.

American Law Institute. (1987). *Restatement (third) of the foreign relations law of the United States.* St. Paul, MN: Author.

August, R. (1993). *International business law.* Englewood Cliffs, NJ: Prentice Hall.

Bekker, P. H. F. (1996). The 1995 judicial activity of the International Court of Justice. *American Journal of International Law, 90*(2), 328-330.

Bennett, A. L. (1988). *International organizations* (4th ed.). Englewood Cliffs, NJ: Prentice Hall.

Bennett, A. L. (1995). *International organizations* (6th ed.). Englewood Cliffs, NJ: Prentice Hall.

Birnie, P. W., & Boyle, A. E. (1992). *International law and the environment.* New York: Oxford University Press.

Blackstone, W. (1969). *Commentaries on the laws of England* (Vol. 4). South Hackensack, NJ: Rothman Reprints. (Original work published 1765-1769)

Bledsoe, R. L., & Boczek, B. A. (1987). *The international law dictionary.* Santa Barbara, CA: ABC-Clio.

Boutros-Ghali, B. (1992). *An agenda for peace.* New York: United Nations.

Brierly, J. L. (1963). *The law of nations* (6th ed., H. Waldock, Ed.). New York: Oxford University Press.

Brownlie, I. (1963). *International law and the use of force by states.* Oxford, UK: Clarendon.

Brownlie, I. (1979). *Principles of public international law* (3rd ed.). London: Oxford University Press.

Brownlie, I. (1990). *Principles of public international law* (4th ed.). New York: Oxford University Press.

Cassese, A. (1995). *Self-determination of peoples: A legal reappraisal.* New York: Cambridge University Press.

Charney, J. I. (1993). Universal International law. *American Journal of International Law, 87, 529-551.*

Chayes, A. (1963). Law and the quarantine of Cuba. *Foreign Affairs, 41, 550-557.*

Claude, I. L. (1984). *Swords into plowshares* (4th ed.). New York: Random House.

Coplin, W. D. (1966). *The functions of international law.* Chicago: Rand McNally.

D'Amato, A. (1995). *International law: Process and prospect* (2nd ed.). Irvington, NY: Transnational.

Damrosch, L. F. (1993a). The civilian impact of economic sanctions. In L. F. Damrosch (Ed.), *Enforcing restraint: Collective intervention in internal conflicts* (pp. 274-315). New York: Council on Foreign Relations Press.

Damrosch, L. F. (Ed.). (1993b). *Enforcing restraint: Collective intervention in internal conflicts.* New York: Council on Foreign Relations Press.

Delaume, G. R. (1994). The Foreign Sovereign Immunities Act and Public Debt Litigation: Some fifteen years later. *American Journal of International Law, 88(2), 257-279.*

Excerpts from report of ICAO fact-finding investigation pursuant to decisions of ICAO Council of July 14, 1988. (1989). *American Journal of International Law, 83, 332-335.*

Field, W. J., & Jordan, R. S. (1988). *International organizations: A comparative approach* (2nd ed.). New York: Praeger.

Folsom, R. H. (1995). *European union law in a nutshell* (2nd ed.). St. Paul, MN: West.

Folsom, R. H., Gordon, M. W., & Spanogle, J. A. (1992). *International business transactions* (4th ed.). St. Paul, MN: West.

Franck, T. (1970). Who killed Article 2(4)? or: Changing norms governing the use of force by states. *American Journal of International Law, 64, 809-907.*

Franck, T. M. (1976). The stealing of the Sahara. *American Journal of International Law, 70, 694-721.*

Franck, T. M. (1991). Fact-finding by the International Court of Justice. In R. B. Lillich (Ed.), *Fact-finding before international tribunals* (pp. 21-32). Ardsley-on-Hudson, NY: Transnational.

Franck, T. M. (1992). The emerging right to democratic governance. *American Journal of International Law, 86 46-91.*

Friedman, W. (1964). *The changing structure of international law.* New York: Columbia University Press.

Gamble, J. (1980). Reservations to multilateral treaties: A macroscopic view of state practice. *American Journal of International Law, 74, 372-389.*

Haas, E. B. (1983). Regime decay: Conflict management and international organizations, 1945-1981. *International Organization, 37(2), 189-256.*

Henkin, L. (1971). The reports of the death of Article 2(4) are greatly exaggerated. *American Journal of International Law, 65, 544-548.*

Henkin, L. (1979). *How nations behave: Law and foreign policy* (2nd ed.). New York: Columbia University Press.

Henkin, L., Pugh, R. C., Schachter, O., & Smit, H. (1987). *International law: Cases and materials* (2nd ed.). St. Paul, MN: West.

Higgins, R. (1994). *Problems and process: International law and how we use it.* New York: Oxford University Press.

Hoellering, M. F. (1994). Managing international commercial arbitration: The institution's role. In J. C. Green (Ed.), *Doing business worldwide: Executing the international transaction.* Chicago: American Bar Association and American Society of International Law.

International Law Commission Report. (1966). In *Yearbook of the International Law Commission.* New York: United Nations.

Janis, M. W. (1993). *An introduction to international law* (2nd ed.). Boston: Little, Brown.

Jessup, P. C. (1956). *Transnational law.* New Haven, CT: Yale University Press.

Karns, M. P., & Mingst, K. A. (Eds.). (1990). *The United States and multilateral institutions: Patterns of changing instrumentality and influence.* Boston: Unwin Hyman.

Karns, M. P., & Mingst, K. A. (1991). Multilateral institutions and international security. In M. T. Klare & D. C. Thomas (Eds.), *World security: Trends and challenges at century's end.* New York: St. Martin's.

Kelly, A. H., Harbison, W. A., & Belz, H. (1983). *The American Constitution: Its origins and development* (6th ed.). New York: Norton.

Kelsen, H. (1967). *Principles of international law* (2nd ed., R. W. Tucker, Ed.). New York: Holt, Rinehart & Winston.

Kritz, N. J. (1996). War crimes on trial. *Issues of Democracy* [On-line USIA Electronic Journals], *1*(3). Available: Internet access through the U.S. Information Agency (USIA).

La Piana, G. (1969). Reformation. In *Collier's encyclopedia* (Vol. 19). Old Tappan, NJ: Crowell-Collier.

Lauterpacht, H. (1946). The Grotian Tradition in international law. In *British yearbook of international law.* London: Oxford University Press. (Reprinted in Falk, R. A., Kratochwil, F. V., & Mendlowitz, S. H. (Eds.). (1985). *International law: A contemporary perspective.* Boulder, CO: Westview)

Lillich, R. B. (Ed.). (1991). *Fact-finding before international tribunals.* Ardsley-on-Hudson, NY: Transnational.

Mann, F. A. (1979). Contempt of court in the House of Lords and the European Court of Human Rights. *Law Quarterly Review, 95,* 348-349.

Martin, D. (1982). Large scale migrations of asylum seekers. *American Journal of International Law, 76,* 598-609.

Moy, L. L. (1988). The U.S. legal role in international labor organization conventions and recommendations. *International Lawyer, 22,* 768-769.

Moynihan, D. P. (1993). *Pandaemonium: Ethnicity in international politics.* New York: Oxford University Press.

Nadelmann, E. A. (1985). Negotiations in criminal law assistance treaties. *American Journal of Comparative Law, 33,* 467-504.

Nash, M. (1994). Open Skies Treaty [report]. *American Journal of International Law, 88*(1), 96-103.

National Center for State Courts. (1991). *State court caseload statistics: Annual report, 1991.* Williamsburg, VA: Author.

News almanac. (1995a, September). *UN Chronicle,* p. 78.

News almanac. (1995b, December). *UN Chronicle,* p. 79.

O'Brien, D. M. (1995). *Constitutional law and politics: Vol 1. Struggles for power and governmental accountability* (2nd ed.). New York: Norton.

Official documents—United Nations reports of the International Law Commission [Commentaries]. (1967). *American Journal of International Law, 61,* 248-473.

Official documents. (1992). *American Journal of International Law, 86*(3), 638-669.

Oliver, C. T., Firmage, E. B., Blankesley, C. L., Scott, R. F., & Williams, S. A. (1995). *The international legal system* (4th ed.). Westbury, NY: Foundation Press.

Oppenheim, L. (1955). *International law* (8th ed., H. Lauterpacht, Ed.). London: Longmans, Green.

Organization for Economic Cooperation and Development. (1994). *Regulatory co-operation for an interdependent world.* Washington, DC: Author.

Oxman, B. H. (1994). Law of the Sea Forum: The 1994 Agreement on Implementation of the Seabed Provisions of the Convention on the Law of the Sea: The 1994 agreement and the convention. *American Journal of International Law, 88,* 687-696.

Payne, R. (1973). *The life and death of Adolf Hitler.* New York: Praeger.

Rosecrance, R. (1986). *The rise of the trading state.* New York: Basic Books.

Schachter, O. (1979). The obligation of the parties to give effect to the Covenant on Civil and Political Rights. *American Journal of International Law, 73,* 462-465.

Schachter, O. (1994). United Nations law. *American Journal of International Law, 88,* 1-23.

Schwebel, S. M. (1991). Three cases of fact-finding by the International Court of Justice. In R. B. Lillich (Ed.), *Fact-finding before international tribunals.* Ardsley-on-Hudson, NY: Transnational.

Slomanson, W. R. (1995). *Fundamental perspectives on international law* (2nd ed.). St. Paul, MN: West.

Spinedi, M., & Sunma, B. (Eds.). (1987). *United Nations codification of state responsibility.* New York: Oceana.

Steiner, H. J., Vagts, D. F., & Koh, H. H. (1994). *Transnational legal problems* (4th ed.). New York: Foundation Press.

Stephens, B., & Ratner, M. (1996). *International human rights litigation in U.S. courts.* Irvington-on-Hudson, NY: Transnational.

Stoessinger, J. G. (1974). *Why nations go to war.* New York: St. Martin's.

Tuchman, B. (1962). *The guns of August.* New York: Macmillan.

Vienna declaration and programme of action. (1994, March). *UN Chronicle,* p. 84.

von Glahn, G. (1992). *Law among nations: An introduction to public international law* (6th ed.). New York: Macmillan.

von Glahn, G. (1996). *Law among nations: An introduction to public international law* (7th ed.). Boston: Allyn & Bacon.

Young, O. R. (1980). International regimes: Problem of concept formations. *World Politics, 32,* 331-356.